Yale Historical Publications

Concepts

of

Free Labor

in

Antebellum

America

Jonathan A. Glickstein

Yale University Press

New Haven and London

Set in Galliard type by Keystone Typesetting, Inc.
Printed in the United States of America by
BookCrafters, Inc., Chelsea, Michigan.

Library of Congress Cataloging-in-Publication Data

Glickstein, Jonathan A., 1948–
Concepts of free labor in Antebellum America /
Jonathan A. Glickstein.
    p. cm. — (Yale historical publications)
Includes bibliographical references and index.
ISBN 0-300-04789-4
1. Manual work—United States—History—19th
century—Public opinion. 2. Public opinion—United
States—History—19th century. 3. Manual work—
Great Britain—History—19th century—Public
opinion. 4. Public opinion—Great Britain—
History—19th century.
I. Title. II. Series.
HD8070.G58 1991
331.11′72′09034—dc20   91-12224 CIP

The paper in this book meets the guidelines for
permanence and durability of the Committee on
Production Guidelines for Book Longevity of the
Council on Library Resources.

10 9 8 7 6 5 4 3 2 1

For my mother and father

Contents

Acknowledgments

I would like to single out the following individuals for their advice and comments on earlier versions of this study: Jon Butler; Jean-Christophe Agnew; and most particularly of all, my dissertation advisor, David Brion Davis. I also wish to thank Charles Grench of Yale University Press as well as the anonymous outside reader for the press. I owe a special debt of gratitude to my manuscript editor, Jane T. Hedges.

Thanks are also due to John J. Guerra for computer assistance and to the National Endowment for the Humanities, which provided funding to support this study. During the course of my research, the staffs of three libraries provided particularly valuable assistance: Columbia University Libraries, Barnard College Library, and the Library of Congress. I would also like to acknowledge the assistance of the staffs of the following libraries and institutions: Union Theological Seminary Library, Teachers College Library (Columbia University), New York University Libraries, New York Public Library, New York Historical Society, the library of Cooper Union for the Advancement of Science and Art, Syracuse University Libraries, University of Rochester Libraries, New York State Library, Yale University Libraries, Harvard University Libraries, Boston Public Library, Massachusetts Historical Society, Massachusetts Antiquarian Society, Amherst College Library, Forbes Public Library (Northampton, Mass.), Lowell Public Library, Fall River (Mass.) Public Library, Lynn (Mass.) Historical Society, Rhode Island Historical Society, New Hampshire Historical Society, Historical Society of Pennsylvania, Georgetown University Libraries, and the University of Notre Dame Archives. I am also grateful to the many additional libraries that assisted my research through their cooperation with the Columbia University Interlibrary Loan Office.

On a more personal note, I wish to thank my sons, Ethan and Samuel. I owe the greatest debt of all to my wife, Eileen Agard.

Concepts of Free Labor in Antebellum America

1

Introduction

There are two points on which you can easily test the real extent of a man's sympathies with labor—his sense of justice with regard to the wages of labor, and his sentiments with regard to the intrinsic dignity of labor itself.
—*The abolitionist newspaper,*
The Emancipator
(New York), 1844

How did Americans view the intrinsic character of manual labor during the three decades before the Civil War? What were the traditions of thought that helped shape these views? How did perceptions of the inherent rewards and pains of various forms of handwork figure in responses to key social and political developments of the period? And how did such perceptions contribute to mid-nineteenth-century agreement and disagreement over the nature of dignified, *truly free* labor?[1] This work examines all these questions.

    Labor and *work* are terms laden with multiple meanings, ambiguities, and historical ironies.[2] And "free labor" itself is an elusive idea. Recent scholarship has shown that even the minimal, objective criterion of nineteenth-century free labor—the worker's legal self-ownership—was hardly clear-cut; modern Western societies have afforded a variety of conditions and statuses, apart from legalized chattel bondage, where juridical self-ownership was obscured or qualified and where the individual's right to sell or alienate his or her labor power in the marketplace was therefore limited.[3] In the realm of shifting perspectives, values, and attitudes, the question of what "free labor" is becomes even more moot. To many of the antebellum proponents of American exceptionalism, the United States was a veritable "workingman's paradise," an open and egalitarian society where manual labor, at least in the Northern free states, was honored and rewarded as nowhere else.[4] Yet whatever their actual advantages, antebellum workers were by modern standards and values unfree, because they lacked the basic rights and guarantees—collective bargaining, the closed shop, disability benefits, and the like—that were subsequently won and enjoyed by organized labor. The noted journalist and reformer Horace Greeley observed in the 1850s that Northern free labor at this time may have enjoyed a more elevated and progressive character than Southern slave labor or, for that matter, manual labor anywhere else; but it, too, would assuredly evolve into something quite different from its present form. "The world has as yet," Greeley claimed, "hardly known what Free Labor is—it has had few or no full and fair specimens of it."[5]

Greeley and other mid-nineteenth-century Americans employed a variety of criteria in setting forth their concepts of truly free manual labor. Those criteria included levels of compensation, working conditions, opportunities for advancement and economic independence, worker job security and degree of control over the work process.[6] Debate and disagreement frequently reflected the varying emphasis which Americans of different social groups and interests attached to these different criteria, interrelated as some of them were. Inextricably tied up with all of these other criteria, too, was free labor's ability to resist infiltration and debasement from various forms of "unfree" labor. Even a limited exposure to the political speeches and other literature of this period in American history acquaints the student with the specters of the degraded black bondsmen of the South and the industrial "wage slaves" and subsistent "pauper laborers" of the Old World, particularly Great Britain. Influenced by these images, as well as by perceptions of the course of industrialization within the United States itself, antebellum Americans engaged in a continuous process of defining and redefining truly free manual labor and of predicting its prospects for survival. In what respects and for what reasons, mid-nineteenth-century Americans asked, could dignified, truly free labor, such as already existed in their nation, experience so serious a decline in material well-being and respectability as to become another form of "unfree" labor, in actual fact if not in the strict legal or formal sense?[7] Where did the greatest threats to truly free labor in American reside—in its own submission to industrial proletarianization and work regimentation, or in the erosion of its position through economic competition with one or more of the forms of "cheap," servile labor?[8] And how far, Americans inquired and argued, had the degeneration of free labor, whatever its cause, already proceeded in the three decades before the Civil War? Incipient industrialization and the indigenous, intensifying sectional conflict over black slave labor, together with the massive influx of impoverished, unskilled immigrants from Ireland, loomed as the central mid-nineteenth-century developments that gave pronounced shaped and edge to American beliefs and concerns regarding legally free manual labor and its meaning in this period.

There already exist many fine studies of these developments. We have, for example, social histories of the American industrial capitalist processes that both utilized unskilled immigrant labor and reduced the economic autonomy of native-born craft labor. And we have political histories that chronicle the emergence of a Northern sectional movement bent on preventing the expansion of black chattel slavery into the federal territories. Relatively neglected is the matter of how perceptions of the specifically intrinsic rewards and pains of manual labor conditioned responses to mid-nineteenth-century developments and helped define the positions that individuals staked out in the controversies over industrialization, immigration, and Southern slavery. American beliefs about manual labor's intrinsic character were not, to be sure, frozen; nor did they exist in a vacuum. In some ways they themselves were an ongoing reaction to the contemporary controversies. There was, nevertheless, another, older phenomenon that was of critical importance in shaping antebellum perceptions of manual labor's inherent nature, and in contributing thereby to the antebellum conceptualizations of truly free labor. This phenomenon served as a primary prism through which mid-nineteenth-century Americans viewed and evaluated the events unfolding around them. That phenomenon was the centuries-old division between mental and manual labor and the differential rewards and esteem that attended this division.[9]

MENTAL VERSUS MANUAL LABOR

Of this division Lawrence Stone has written with respect to sixteenth-century English society, that, despite that society's manifold social gradations, "the most fundamental dichotomy . . . was between the gentleman and the non-gentleman, a division that was based essentially upon the distinction between those who did, and those who did not, have to work with their hands."[10] And James Henretta has suggested that this dichotomy retained much of its force in eighteenth-century, preindustrial America: "Farmers who worked for themselves," he noted, "could derive a good deal of pleasure from their achievements." But "high status in society had always been the prerogative of those whose wealth or occupation enabled them to escape from the rigors of hard manual labor."[11]

Mid-nineteenth-century Americans brought special perspectives and emphases to the mental-manual labor division. For example, a common observation of those who promoted land and other labor reforms in this period was that "No one ever became wealthy by the fair reward of his own [manual] labour."[12] Now whatever the truth of this observation, it is suggestive of a number of things. It is indicative, first, of the emergence of a consciousness of labor *exploitation* that distinguishes so much of the history of the first part of the nineteenth century.[13] It can also be read as a measure of the influence wielded by "liberal capitalist," acquisitive values, and their general ascendancy over more traditional "republican" ones by this point in time.[14] For although there is little reason to suppose that it was any easier for manual laborers in eighteenth-century America to "become wealthy," there existed, compared to the mid-nineteenth century, little impetus to regard this difficulty as signifying a particular social injustice.[15] Why should manual laborers aspire to wealth when so much of the discourse of the eighteenth century was weighted against both economic extremes, wealth hardly less than poverty, and toward instead that healthy and virtuous "middle" state of comfortable economic independence?[16]

But the observation quoted above reveals something else as well, a social fact of such fundamental significance that it was taken for granted more often than it was articulated: if in some civilized societies, past and present, the greatest wealth and privilege resided in leisured elements that disdained the pursuit of any "active" occupation at all, it was even more axiomatic of civilized societies that the wealthy and privileged were not members of the laboring population. To the labor reform remark quoted above we can add its unstated corollary: that manual laborers who did manage to become wealthy would not continue in manual labor employments, that the wealthy members of society might be and often were merchants, or manufacturing capitalists, or lawyers, but they would never be, or remain, manual workers.[17] If perceptions of Southern black bondsmen and British industrial wage laborers figured prominently, and for the most part negatively, in antebellum American definitions of free manual labor, those definitions were no less profoundly shaped by a different set of perceptions, those centering on the exclusively "mental labor" engaged in by capitalists and professional men.

I have no wish to oversimplify antebellum patterns of social stratification. Some skilled craft labor continued to enjoy relatively high status into the period of industrialization, whereas expanding white-collar, dead-end clerical positions laid claim to only limited esteem. Even members of the learned professions varied considerably in their prestige, on the basis of such criteria as the wealth and status of their clientele.[18] Moreover, lawyers, like urban merchants, labored under their own particular long-standing stigmas, those that associated their calling with greed, unscrupulousness, and economic parasitism. And in a period when America's modern occupational hierarchy was still in the formative stages, when the legal and medical professions had yet to develop the credentials and formal educational requirements that would institutionalize and consolidate their place in that hierarchy, labor reform and populist antagonisms insured that the claims to high status and exclusive expertise and privileges made by the professions were frequently contested.[19] The mid-nineteenth century was a period of American history when a virtually universal resignation to an occupational hierarchy dominated by professional and capitalist mental labor, a resignation seemingly shared in modern times by most "blue-collar" workers, was still a development of the future.

Yet despite all of the circumstances that muddied it, the division between mental and manual labor retained great force even in antebellum America, and the venerable nature of that division raises basic, even timeless, questions that are as much the subject of debate among philosophers and sociologists as among historians.[20] The first of these questions tended to remain in the background of nineteenth-century American discussions regarding manual labor's intrinsic nature. What relation does an individual's employment, and therefore his position in the class structure, bear to his native endowment, particularly in those more "openly stratified" societies where prescribed positions and institutionalized impediments to occupational mobility have been largely removed?[21] American thinkers of the Revolutionary generation never appeared to doubt the existence of innate differences in talent, and the late antebellum period seems clearly to have been marked by the emergence of hereditarian ideas that posited the existence of large and fixed differences in aptitude among individuals.[22] For the years in between these periods, social beliefs regarding the size and significance of differences in native capacity, at least for white males, appear to have been more ambiguous, although one historian has made a good case for the position that leaders in the mainstream and radical portions of one of the two major parties, the Jacksonian Democrats, tended discernibly more than most Whig spokesmen to minimize the innate variations in talent and aptitude among white men.[23]

Were individuals who began and remained manual laborers in antebellum America commonly adjudged to be inferior in intellectual aptitude and other valued native talents to those who pursued more lucrative, mental labor employments, notably business or one of the "learned" professions? The question was not explicitly raised very often, perhaps because a culture of egalitarian uplift was intent on placing far more emphasis upon enterprise, virtue, and all those qualities, including raw intellect, that could be developed and stretched by anyone through discipline and training. Yet egalitarian values did not by any means remove the age-old prejudice against manual labor. James T. Brady, the New York gubernatorial candidate on the 1860 Breckinridge presidential ticket, reminded his Republican opponents, leaders of the party that exalted the dignity of Northern "free labor," that their candidate for president that year was not, after all, an educated rail-splitter but a former rail-splitter turned lawyer, an individual who had used his education to leave his laboring status behind him. And there was nothing at all wrong with this circumstance, Brady suggested, as attested to by the fact that manual laborers in the free states revealed an ambivalence toward their own callings every time they threw their political support to a professional man like Lincoln rather than to an individual within their own ranks. "The humblest toiler in our land," Brady insisted, "looked with reverence on intellectual superiority or culture," and he labored and sacrificed in order "to place some favorite son or relative in a higher social position than he himself occupied"—to qualify him through education for those professional occupations and high political offices to which "mental discipline" was alike "indispensable."[24]

Whether or not Brady was correct about the sentiments of Northern laboring men, his observations lead to a second question: even supposing that professional and other nonmanual occupations do generally require more in the way of mental talent and "discipline," either innate or developed through training, why does it follow that these occupations seem invariably, in every civilized society, to enjoy greater material rewards and social esteem than manual labor employments? Sociologists have long pondered why occupational differentiation has in nearly every known society, "market-oriented" or otherwise, complex or not, been attended by some degree of social stratification, whereby different amounts of power, prestige, and material rewards attach to different social and occupational positions.[25] The so-called functionalist school, whose contribution in this area was particularly prominent, argued in explanation—or, some would say, justification—of what it insisted was the "empirical ubiquity" of social stratification that societies must provide rewards to induce individuals to fill the positions required by the society.[26] Rewards are of necessity distributed unequally to the various positions because those positions are neither equally pleasant nor equally demanding in the training required. The social rank of different occupations is determined by two essential criteria: their functional importance for society and the ability, trained or innate, needed to fill them. Some positions demand such extensive innate talents that the individuals who occupy them are invariably rare. In many other cases, the innate capacity required to fill the position may be fairly common in the population but because the capital investment is substantial or the training process costly or long, most of this population, which must meet immediate economic needs, are excluded from qualifying. In these cases, the greater prestige and material rewards of a position reflect both the "sacrificial" commitment that individuals have made by way of time and money to the qualifying process and the fact that those same constraints of time and money restrict the number of qualified individuals and thus limit the possibility that they will ultimately bring down the rank of their employments by becoming, like many unskilled laborers, a glut on the market.[27]

The issues raised by the functionalist explanation of social stratification recur explicitly and repeatedly in antebellum discussions regarding the division between mental and manual labor. Brady's reference to the superior education and "mental discipline" required by the practice of law is simply an abbreviated statement of the second criterion of social rank invoked by the functionalists. The radical versions of the "labor theory of value" articulated by Anglo-American labor reformers and trade union movements, together with their general insistence that the rewards and status of "productive" manual labor be upgraded to reflect its social importance, signified the almost exclusive emphasis they placed on the first criterion of that school. Vital to this emphasis was the presumption that nonmanual labor employments were of lesser functional importance, if not necessarily useless and altogether fraudulent in their claims to being true "work."[28] Definitions of work are themselves matters of long-standing, interdisciplinary debate. Defending the superior rewards of mental labor on the basis of its functional importance rather than, as Brady did, on the grounds of training and intellectual requirements, one philosopher, Kenneth R. Minogue, has thus complained about the misguided domination of the idea of labor "by the metaphor of sweat on the brow." Owing in large part to the influence of socialist doctrine, protests Minogue, "the least imaginative work counts most securely as labor. The squires and merchants of the seventeenth century were far from idle men, but administration and entrepreneurship do not so obviously qualify for the title of labor as the felling of trees and the planting of corn."[29]

Antebellum discussions of the intrinsic nature of manual labor and its division from mental labor raise further issues of social stratification that are of continuing and possibly timeless relevance. One of the major sociological critics of the "functionalist" approach, Melvin M. Tumin, has suggested that even if unequal distribution of power and property must attend occupational differentiation, this in itself is no reason why differential prestige must also be the consequence.[30] "Historically," Tumin writes, "no systematic effort has ever been made, under propitious circumstances, to develop the tradition that each man is as socially worthy as all other men so long as he performs his appropriate tasks conscientiously. While such a tradition seems utterly utopian, no known facts in psychological or social science have yet demonstrated its impossibility or its dysfunctionality for the continuity of a society."[31] Although it can be argued that the Fourierist movements of the mid-nineteenth century hardly operated under "propitious circumstances," theirs was indeed an attempt to retain for capital its rights to property while at the same time removing the status liabilities suffered by individuals who "conscientiously" performed the manual labor of a community. And as Tumin himself has done in his criticisms of the functionalist approach, Fourierists, along with some of the earlier Brook Farmers and other labor reformers, explicitly repudiated the notion that the superior rewards enjoyed by mental labor employments could be justified by claims that those employments involved onerous or "sacrificial" demands.[32] To the contrary, as we shall see, Elizabeth Palmer Peabody, Fourierists, and other labor reformers claimed that mental labor merited fewer extrinsic rewards than physical labor did in large part because mental labor was of a more pleasurable and fulfilling nature; it was those individuals who took on the manual labor of society, particularly its most "repugnant" yet socially necessary kinds, who should be compensated for their efforts with greater material rewards.[33]

Nineteenth-century utopian "social justice" arguments, like their more modern versions, have been rejected on a number of grounds, most insistently by those whose commitment to the distribution of material rewards by free market forces leads them to defend existing patterns of social stratification.[34] We need not consider the modern objections here because whatever their true validity, they do in fact achieve a level of sophistication and refinement that leaves them with no real counterpart in the antebellum American defenses of mental labor's superior rewards.[35] There is, in this connection, a good deal to be said for David Riesman's claim that "the America of the last century, . . . made room for a limited amount of utopian thought and experiment because, among many other factors, the capitalism of that period was singularly unconcerned about propagandizing itself as an ideological system. Perhaps this is because it was so much taken for granted that it did not need verbal defense. . . . The system was written into the landscape, so to speak; it did not need to be written into books."[36]

Riesman does exaggerate: antebellum America did have its Daniel Websters, Nathan Appletons, and scores of other, lesser-known ideologists for capitalism. Indeed, one of the signal conclusions that may be drawn from mid-nineteenth-century discussions of free labor, in England as well as America, is how so many quite different arguments were in fundamental agreement concerning the sanctity of private property and the rights of capitalists and other mental laborers to their superior rewards. One specimen of this consensus might be noted here. For centuries a central, possibly the prevailing sentiment among more privileged members of Western societies had been that the divorce of education from manual labor was desirable to keep the laboring population's nose to the grindstone. Presenting one of the classic statements of this position, Bernard Mandeville thus objected even to the very limited education offered the English laboring poor by the early eighteenth-century charity schools: "No Creatures submit contentedly to their Equals, and should a Horse know as much as a Man, I should not desire to be his Rider."[37] The continued growth of educational opportunities for the working classes sponsored by the middle and upper classes represented a clear refutation of Mandeville's perspective. But even the more liberal and expansive of these movements, such as Horace Mann's promotion of the American common school in the mid-nineteenth century, did not, unlike some of the radical utopian educational schemes, depart from Mandeville's underlying objective: if education and increased literacy facilitated the ability of some manual laborers or their sons to rise out of the working classes, its overriding effect would nonetheless still be to solidify rather than to erode manual laborers' allegiance to social arrangements that legitimated and secured private property and the existing hierarchy of employments. The sentiment which to an increasing degree supplanted Mandeville's was that it was as dangerous and dysfunctional for society as it was socially unjust to keep members of the laboring population uninstructed.[38]

The existence of extensive agreement, in both nineteenth-century America and Britain, regarding the legitimacy of capitalist social division of labor and the scale of incentives attaching to different employments, is an underlying theme of this study.[39] And although members of the American Fourierist movement were among those who departed conspicuously and significantly from this agreement, even they acknowledged the force of the social assumption, embedded in the fabric of Western culture, of a natural and deep association between working with one's hands and the absence of wealth, privilege, and substantive mental activity. That assumption reflected not only the weight of venerable traditions of thought, but also centuries of social reality. The distribution of manual labor, particularly its most onerous and disagreeable kinds, among a society's most impoverished, uneducated, powerless, and stigmatized elements would seem to have been, just as it continues to be, a fundamental historical circumstance, one that antedates and transcends more modern market-oriented, "acquisitive" cultures.[40] It is a basic, but probably unanswerable, question whether the historically minimal prestige attaching to much manual labor is attributable to the intrinsic nature of the work, or to the poverty and other low-status characteristics of the individuals who have traditionally performed it. But it would seem more certain in any case that pervasive nineteenth-century American attitudes toward the intrinsic nature of manual labor reflected these deep and negative associations, and to the extent that they did so, American "free labor" concepts were very unexceptional compared to those in other Western, as well as Eastern, cultures. More succinctly even than James T. Brady a few years before him, the labor reformer Ira Steward captured the ambivalence for manual labor callings with his well-known rhetorical question: "Are Abraham Lincoln, Andrew Johnson, and N. P. Banks honored because they once toiled with their hands, or because they were fortunate enough to lift themselves into a position where it was no longer necessary?"[41] The dignity of "free" manual labor, Steward was suggesting, resided for an indeterminate number of Americans in its instrumental value, in its escapability into something "better."

One might object that the American ambivalence to which Steward was referring was directed not at manual labor per se, but at the condition of manual *wage labor*. I do not wish to discount the persisting influence of republican values extolling self-employed, economically independent, manual labor in America; nor do I wish to understate the corresponding degree to which the ambivalence described by Steward was a product of the tensions created by new social processes—of the public discomfort created by the manifest tendency of mid-nineteenth-century industrialization to produce increasing numbers of manual laborers who would never be anything other than wage-earning manual laborers.[42] But I would nonetheless maintain that the proletarianization and economic dependence fostered by mid-nineteenth-century industrialization confirmed and reinforced the long-standing stigmas attaching to manual labor generally, stigmas that had always coexisted with American republican values. With its twin underpinnings in skill and capitalized economic independence, preindustrial master craftsmanship had enjoyed, along with freehold farming, undeniable claims to middle-class status, even as the physical labor component detracted from such status claims. Labor processes in the mid-nineteenth century may have done less to destroy the prestige of skilled craft work which remained intact than to render that work an increasing rarity, undermining in this way what preindustrial links had existed between manual labor and middle-class status.[43] The rise of "semiskilled" factory work, and of the subdivision of labor and "deskilling" in the urban crafts, dramatized the historically perceived separation of significant mental activity from manual labor. That hand labor might seem increasingly incompatible not only with mental labor but with the possession of capital received reinforcement from yet another development: the tendency of the most successful master craftsmen to divorce themselves from the production processes they were helping to routinize and to convert themselves into full-time businessmen.[44]

Another social development that underscored the material and status limitations of a livelihood involving physical labor and reflected the ascendancy of liberalist capitalist success values in the antebellum period was the declining economic and social appeal of New England agricultural life and the attempts by the ambitious sons of farmers to escape the "dignified toil" of their fathers and seek alternative employment in the cities.[45] That the work that most attracted these "country boys," in addition to other young men, did not involve manual labor was a fact that occasioned no little bitterness, and some frustration and defensiveness as well, among workingmen and their spokesmen in various labor reform movements, as well as among members of the agricultural press.[46] It also produced considerable concern among middle-class moralists like Freeman Hunt, individuals who generally defended the expanding avenues of commerce and enterprise, that rural-urban migration and the "excessive" valuation of wealth it signalled were leading to a labor imbalance and to the overcrowding of the favored business and professional occupations. Reactions such as these to emergent occupational preferences serve as reminders that liberal capitalist success values, values which in their own fashion disesteemed manual labor employments, were, together with key social changes, still generating substantial resistance, tension, and anxiety in this period.[47]

A notable, alternative interpretation of antebellum American work values, one advanced most prominently by Alexis de Tocqueville and reaffirmed by some recent historians, holds that a broad cross section of mid-nineteenth-century Americans had "a common enemy" in the "age-old aristocratic contempt" for working for a profit, and that their shared rejection of this contempt led them to "fervently" exalt the dignity of working for a living, seemingly regardless of the nature of that work.[48] My study suggests that this interpretation requires substantial qualification, that the heightened emphasis on competitive individualism and private material accumulation reinforced in essential ways the centuries-old stigmas that reflected physical labor's traditional association with poverty, brutishness, and lack of mental content. The stigmas attaching to physical labor, particularly its most unskilled kinds, fueled a pervasive ambivalence about manual labor and encouraged many mid-nineteenth-century Americans, as Ira Steward suggested, to chiefly value manual labor for those escape routes that appeared to be exceptionally unclogged in the United States.[49] This work attempts to capture the American ambivalence about manual labor employments; it also explores the varying reasons which prompted some commentators, both within and outside the laboring population, to clearly insist upon the specifically inherent worth and dignity of manual labor, however deeply some of these individuals may have in fact shared the pervasive ambivalence about it.

FREE LABOR IDEOLOGY

This study bears a problematic relationship to existing discussions of antebellum free labor "ideology." The fullest and still the most influential treatment of that ideology characterized it as pronouncedly, almost invariably anti-Southern and antislavery extensionist, the world view of Republican party politicians and their following in the Northern states and territories.[50] More recent studies have maintained or implied that this interpretation understates the appeal that free labor ideology, or at least such crucial free labor "values" as the spirit of enterprise and the commitment to an economically dynamic society, in fact enjoyed in antebellum America. These studies have concluded that free labor values were also upheld, but without a dominant "antislavery" intent or agenda, by a variety of broad and sometimes overlapping social and political groups: anti-

Catholic Know-Nothings; Northern capitalists and some of the workers in
their employ; Northern and even Southern Democratic politicians and
voters, including slaveholders.[51]

These more recent discussions have performed the valuable service of
raising the possibility that free labor "ideology," as an exclusively and
pronouncedly antislavery ideology, may be a distortion of reality, something of an intellectual construct of historians. And what such discussions
suggest about free labor ideology I argue below was in fact true of a number
of free labor "concepts": that they could be strongly tolerant and protective
of chattel slavery, rather than antagonistic to it. Yet from a semantic standpoint alone, there would still seem to be something confusing and misleading about speaking of versions of free labor ideology that were avowedly
indifferent and even favorably disposed to the expansion of slavery.[52] More
than this, there remains good reason for adhering to the position that free
labor ideology did historically develop with strong roots in antagonism to
slavery.

Discernible in antebellum free labor ideology, to begin with, were
the influences of centuries-old religious and secular intellectual traditions,
prominent among these being bourgeois liberal notions of "possessive
individualism" which, as an accompaniment to seventeenth- and eighteenth-century English mercantile capitalism, legitimated in a general way
the condition of legally free manual laborers who possessed no capital and
had only their labor to sell in a market economy.[53] Late eighteenth- and
early nineteenth-century British antislavery thought linked these possessive
individualist notions with a far more explicit and powerful animus toward
black chattel slavery; and British abolitionism provided the most immediate, and perhaps the most prominent, influence upon the central tenet of
American antebellum free labor ideology: that the dignity of labor, irrespective of the laborer's race, required as a minimal condition the laborer's
legal self-ownership and autonomy.[54] But although American free labor
ideology emerged in antagonism to the condition of chattel servitude, it
simultaneously took shape as a mid-nineteenth-century variation of American exceptionalism dating back to the colonial settlements.[55] It was an
affirmation of the unsurpassed economic opportunity and advancement
available to legally free, *male* laborers residing in the Northern states.[56]
Some American abolitionists, in certain contexts at least, attached overwhelming emphasis to free labor ideology's first tenet and insisted that
"Poverty is not Slavery," that "even the name of Liberty"—bare legal
freedom—"is much."[57] But it was more characteristic of politicians, capitalists, and other antebellum middle-class proponents of free labor ideology to draw more fully on American exceptionalist themes, to stress the
uniquely favorable outcomes that the formal right to sell one's labor
brought in the open, "dynamic" society of the North. Only here, indeed,

did self-ownership attain its true meaning for laborers. Republican party leaders repeatedly represented legally autonomous white workers in the Old World as economically subjugated and depressed, scarcely less degraded than chattel slaves; they extended a similar characterization to the politically enfranchised white laboring population of the antebellum South.[58]

To the great extent that it celebrated economic opportunity and social fluidity in the free states, free labor ideology reflected that ambiguity which may have been a major basis of its appeal—its identity as an amalgam of "small producer," republican values that exalted virtuous, comfortable economic independence and of those more resolutely liberal capitalist values which, in drawing on the mythology of America as a "country of self-made men," exalted the ability of the talented and enterprising to rise to something beyond such economic independence.[59] The American exceptionalist themes upon which free labor ideology drew, far from being restricted to abolitionist and Republican party antislavery circles, continued to exert an appeal considerably wider than that of free labor ideology itself. Those themes appealed to masses of white Democratic voters in the Northern and Southern states who, although they naturally saw legal freedom as important for themselves, deviated in essential respects from central antislavery perspectives. They did not regard the enslavement of blacks as significantly compounding the degradation of a race they deemed inferior to their own.[60] Nor did they regard black slave labor or its territorial expansion as fundamentally inimical either to the national well-being or their own access to American opportunity.[61] And in its emphasis upon the relatively benign nature of the competitive process in the North, upon the capacity of that process to reward all who were truly industrious and deserving, free labor ideology itself certainly counted among its functions and effects those unrelated to checking slavery's territorial expansion and discrediting the Southern social order. By affirming, for example, both the "mutuality of interests" and the equality of economic power between capitalist and laborer in the face of industrial changes that suggested otherwise, free labor ideology aimed, in some cases successfully, at forestalling in a number of antebellum Northern communities the development of an alternative working-class consciousness.[62] This last phenomenon points to the two distinct sets of questions that invariably confront treatments of free labor ideology: the largely quantitative issues of when, how, and to what extent social change came to render obsolete the favorable picture of Northern economic opportunity and upward social mobility painted by free labor ideology, and the hardly less difficult questions involving intentions and consequences—the degree, for example, to which free labor ideology's "isolation" of chattel slavery as an iniquitous institution may have derived from a desire, conscious or otherwise, on the part of various of its proponents to blind themselves to developing inequities and inequalities in the Northern capitalist social order.[63]

Rather than attempting to resolve these issues, this book places free labor ideology in a heretofore neglected perspective. The long-standing Western stigmas attaching to physical labor partially explained why Northern proponents of free labor ideology should have emphasized in their definitions of dignified labor various extrinsic criteria, the opportunities truly free manual labor afforded for material gain, advancement, economic independence, and even an eventual "rising" into exclusively mental labor employments. Particularly in its more pragmatic political antislavery manifestations, free labor ideology would have been unlikely to dwell on the intrinsic characteristics of manual labor in the free states, for these were hardly the characteristics that most conspicuously distinguished much of this labor. Canal digging, street sweeping, even a good deal of manufacturing and agricultural labor in the North did not have the appearance of being substantially more inherently stimulating or rewarding than the activities performed by slaves on Southern plantations. An ideology committed to affirming the exceptionally elevated nature of Northern free labor, and to accentuating how that labor would be economically damaged and "degraded" by slavery's future geographic expansion, would in considerable measure be understandably drawn to underscoring those features of Northern free labor that lay outside its intrinsic nature altogether.[64] As a consequence of the exigencies of late antebellum Northern nationalism, concepts of dignified labor that emphasized the instrumental value of Northern manual labor likely attracted increasingly great appeal even as such instrumental value was in significant ways being objectively diminished by industrial and other social changes.[65]

My study also casts a different light on free labor ideology by underscoring the degree to which that ideology was a selective drawing out from a very large pool of ideas about dignified labor. My emphasis thus far has been upon the negative associations attaching to physical labor in Western societies, associations embodied in the historic mental-manual labor division. But as I have also indicated, numerous individuals in the mid-nineteenth century did exalt for a variety of reasons the strictly intrinsic nature of manual labor; all such exercises, as efforts to confront manual labor's traditional negative associations, to deny that these were truly inevitable or "natural," themselves reflected the influence of those negative associations. But the special point I would make here is that although some prominent antislavery proponents were among these individuals, concepts of free labor that stressed manual labor's intrinsic rewards sometimes worked at sharp ideological cross-purposes with Northern antislavery free labor "ideology." Such concepts tended to dismiss as meaningful the basic, legal dividing line between free and slave labor. Thomas Carlyle made the paradoxical argument that the black man could realize what potential he had for truly free, dignified labor only in a condition of legalized compulsory servitude. All hard physical toil, Carlyle insisted, carried great intrinsic moral worth and dignity, but because of his innate inferiority, the black man would fail to apply himself, to experience hard work's intrinsic rewards, so long as he remained in what was for him a meaningless legal freedom.

Carlyle's concept of "free" labor, as applied to the black man, was among those ideas that was understandably passed over by antislavery free labor ideology, with its insistence that the dignity of labor required as a minimal condition the laborer's legal self-ownership and autonomy. Yet Carlyle's argument was characteristic not only of mid-nineteenth-century proslavery thought, but possibly of nineteenth-century Anglo-American thought in general in its suggestion that the propriety and dignity of work could not be considered apart from the capacities and propensities of the particular social groups that performed it. Later I discuss in detail this stereotyping of work, whereby employment commonly considered fit work for, say, blacks or females, was rejected as inappropriate and contemptible work for white males. Antislavery free labor ideology itself showed some evidence of this stereotyping. To the extent that some of the proponents of that ideology acknowledged the failure of free blacks or Irish immigrants to advance out of Northern drudge labor, they not uncommonly indicated that the very qualities which explained the failure of these groups to advance explained why they were suited for such work in the first place.[66]

A number of other observations can be made about the nineteenth-century proclivity for judging the propriety of labor in terms of the presumed attributes of the individuals performing it. That the dignity of a task, first of all, might depend upon who performed it provides added confirmation that the idea of free labor is singularly relativistic and variable.[67] Second, although the proclivity to identify a match between labor and social group usually reflected the desire to legitimate rather than discredit existing labor exploitation, this was not invariably the case.[68] Finally, the social stereotyping of work was capable of accommodating two theoretically distinct attitudes toward manual labor: what was regarded as appropriate work for a particular social group might be perceived and represented as useful, dignified labor, but it might also be regarded and accepted as useful, contemptible labor. In practice these two attitudes frequently merged in nineteenth-century discourse. Exalt though he did the propriety and the intrinsic moral worth of hard, enforced agricultural labor for blacks, Carlyle hardly considered that labor equal in dignity to that of the disciplined work performed by members of his own, allegedly superior race.

Mid-nineteenth-century American and British perceptions of manual labor bore the imprint of two essential facts: the social indispensability of that labor and the age-old supremacy of mental labor. Working within this framework of common awareness, individuals brought different perspectives and objectives to their discussions of what "free" manual labor was, or could be. The consequence was a dense and complex crosscutting of positions, one reflecting the varying emphases individuals attached to the different criteria of free labor. When these emphases varied sufficiently, as they so often did, they added up to different concepts of free labor altogether. We have already seen an example of this tendency, in Carlyle's fixation upon the intrinsic moral worth of hard work to challenge antislavery thought. The chapters below provide many more examples.

Although I have put off to a second volume sustained analysis of those free labor concepts that relied particularly on nonintrinsic criteria, within a given document some definitions of free labor, including some notable antislavery formulations, were significantly and intricately multidimensional; they relied in important ways upon both intrinsic and nonintrinsic criteria. Some of my commentators on free labor, moreover, wrote extensively or over long periods on the subject, and either different immediate objectives or changes in their point of view led them to attach, in their varied writings, very different emphases to the different criteria of free labor. My sense is that we can attribute to such individuals more than one concept of free labor, while bearing in mind the *possibility* that each of these concepts was part of a broader, if not necessarily entirely coherent or consistent, vision. The overall point I would wish to stress here with regard to my commentators is that I have tried to remain sensitive to the complexity and interconnectedness of antebellum social perceptions, to the ways in which beliefs about free labor's inherent rewards may have connected in people's minds, say, with beliefs about manual labor's proper instrumental value. I have attempted, that is, notwithstanding the focus of this book, to avoid unduly isolating strands of an argument that were really indissoluble. It is very largely because of this attempt that I believe this first of two volumes can be properly characterized as self-contained; it does not, for the most part at least, treat fragments of free labor concepts whose complete and accurate representation must await the second volume. I have, at the same time, had to make some hard, admittedly arbitrary decisions about what to include and not to include for discussion in this first volume. Although, for example, many scholars have noted the impact which the degree and nature of supervision have upon the "job satisfaction" experienced by factory operatives and other workers, this inquiry gives relatively little consideration to the question of surveillance, regarding it as an issue pertaining more to work autonomy and working conditions than to the intrinsic nature of labor.

THE SOURCES FOR THIS STUDY: ANTEBELLUM COMMENTATORS

This study explores the perceptions, beliefs, and attitudes that define intellectual history in its less rarefied form.[69] Relevant "formal systems of thought," such as the technical subject matter of classical political economy, are of less concern in themselves than the extent to which their complex and, in some instances, deeply ambiguous doctrines entered the "public domain" of ideas and were variously interpreted, transformed, and utilized there.[70] The focus is upon the large and varied body of mid-nineteenth-century literature in which politicians, government officials, journalists, clergymen, reformers, intellectuals, and capitalists discussed labor in generally more mundane and accessible terms than those used by trained economists.[71] The greatest emphasis falls upon literature relating to the northeastern states, where the relatively advanced and rapid industrialization and urban development generated the most extensive examinations into the condition of legally free manual labor.

With some notable exceptions, the politicians, writers, and others who created this literature were white, male, Protestant, and middle or upper-middle class; some of them, too, are rather well-worn subjects of historical analysis. I make no claims that these commentators articulated ideas that were widely or enthusiastically shared by members of less powerful and privileged social groups. Nevertheless, some of the venerable Western values embraced by the educated classes, together with the spectacle of capitalist and professional success, do seem to have contributed to a certain defensiveness among American manual laborers regarding the intellectual and economic limitations of their callings. Thanks to the recent efforts of historians, it is becoming increasingly evident that manual laborers generally, and not merely the most highly skilled ones, have frequently invested their own complex and varied meanings in their employments, that although wages and other pressing matters have consumed much of their attention, their concerns have also encompassed in one sense or another the more intrinsic intellectual and moral dimensions of their tasks.[72] It seems possible to recognize this fact and yet still maintain that in the nineteenth century the inherent content and value of work, above all work as an existing or potential end in itself, was preeminently the theme of middle-class intellectuals and reformers—Thomas Carlyle, William Ellery Channing, or Karl Marx, for example—individuals who had greater luxury to sit back, contemplate, and record their thoughts on such subjects. There is at least one central irony, or paradox, involved here, one that has hardly escaped the attention of scholars: that the bourgeois "celebration, the idolization almost, of work . . . as the essential basis of all truly human activity . . . proceeds against a background of its imminent redundancy" and declining creativity at the hands of industrial routinization and mechanization.[73] Rather than further consider this paradox here, I underscore that my focus remains on middle-class commentary, although the views of manual laborers and labor organizations do receive some attention throughout the chapters below.

Something more should be said about my frequent references to the "middle-class." Several historians have recently made some interesting attempts either to bring some precision to the concept of "middle class" or to specifically distinguish the values of nineteenth-century middle-class professional men and intellectuals from those held by "capitalist" members of the middle class, individuals who occupied a more direct or "active" relationship to the means of production.[74] This study gives little attention to these definitional matters, both because it can hardly improve upon the scholarly efforts that have already been made in this area, and because an individual's particular occupation or position in the class structure, whether a factory entrepreneur, clergyman, journalist, or whatever, provides an inadequate guide to his beliefs about labor. There existed an overriding agreement legitimating private property, the social division of labor, and the existing structure—if not necessarily the precise distribution—of the differential rewards attaching to mental and manual labor. But within this agreement was a wide spectrum of views, with members of the same occupational groups frequently lining up on different ends of the spectrum. Horace Greeley and James Watson Webb were both middle-class New York journalists but their beliefs on most issues of the day hardly coincided.[75] Ideology is, among other things, an expression of the need to make the pursuit of one's self-interest palatable to oneself, if not to others as well, but individuals respond quite differently to this need. Even members of the middle classes whose livelihood was most directly dependent on the profits extractable from labor's toil might accordingly perceive their primary self-interest in quite different and broader terms than others who were similarly dependent. They might acknowledge in practice as well as theory, for example, that a reduction in working hours to accommodate the intellectual and moral "elevation" of labor met their own perceived needs, not only for the reason that reduced hours made for more contented, "productive" workers, but because they promoted the long-term stability of the social structure. For the reason that people belonging to the same occupation or some other social group were indeed capable of defining both their own interest and that of the public quite differently, even as most of these differences remained within the consensual framework referred to, this study does not make any strong arguments for the "representativeness" of the particular ideas and beliefs analyzed below. Those ideas and beliefs receive attention because what they indicate about "free labor" is both interesting and revealing of American social values. But to conclude this much is not equivalent to making the stronger and more tenuous claim that these ideas were necessarily "typical" of the class, occupation, or some other social configuration to which the individual who expressed them belonged.

Something, too, must be said here about the "sincerity" of my commentators on manual labor, for the body of argument, of rhetoric, which they produced invariably raises questions of opportunism and hypocrisy.[76] Of a particular group within their number, one antebellum writer, Peter Walker, sarcastically remarked: "The men who talk of 'the dignity of labor,' and of its being 'the God with us in the flesh,' are those who, unless the click-clack of the tongue can be accounted labor, willingly for themselves forego all its dignities and divine incarnations."[77] Walker was hardly alone in characterizing the mid-nineteenth-century as an age of "cant" about manual labor, one in which clergymen, political economists, politicians, and other propertied middle-class commentators indulged in pieties about the dignity and nobility of employments with which they themselves had no practical acquaintance.[78] These pieties could prove equally serviceable in the defense of both chattel slavery and systems of "free labor," but of greater relevance here is that the predominantly middle-class commentary discussed below would seem to offer the possibility of two levels of hypocrisy. Commentators may indeed have been deliberately issuing "homilies" and advancing other arguments about manual labor that they did not believe. One cannot, certainly, altogether discount the element of calculated and devious hypocrisy and opportunism, of cynical posturing and propagandizing, that entered into discussions of manual labor. That a given argument contained an element of calculated hypocrisy does not, at the same time, necessarily diminish that argument's import as an index of social attitudes; the words and platitudes of even the most insincere and cynically opportunistic commentators are worthy of analysis precisely because such commentators, in telling their constituency, audience, or readership what they believed it wished to hear did not think in a vacuum but drew from the public domain of ideas.[79]

My sense, however, is that we are more typically confronted with hypocrisy in the looser sense of the word, that middle-class commentators on manual labor, including many of those to whom Walker was referring, were more often and in greater measure indulging in a less calculated form of sanctimoniousness than that they were guilty of outright insincerity and intentional deception. In suggesting that the preponderance of positions they staked out reflected more or less genuinely held beliefs, perceptions, and attitudes, I in no way intend to slight the role of rationalization and opportunism, the frequency with which commentators convinced themselves of the truth of arguments that were in some respect self-serving.[80] That sincerity was often built upon a process of rationalization seems particularly evident in certain situations—when, for example, commentators acted to stretch, adjust, distort, or otherwise utilize a popular idea about work in order to legitimate economic self-interest or to justify new kinds of economic enterprise.[81]

To measure hypocrisy or to single out those free labor concepts that reflected truly insincere argumentation from positions that, although often self-serving and even sanctimonious, were nonetheless more genuinely embraced would require an intimacy with antebellum commentators that is almost always precluded by the available evidence. It is worth adding here a related point, one that is underscored by all of the recent work on ideology formation, the complex process by which individuals and groups develop their world views by screening or filtering out unpalatable social truths: some of those proslavery and other arguments regarding manual labor that seem most outrageous to us today may have been among those that, at the time, were least reflective of hypocrisy in its more blatant or calculated forms.[82]

Although assessing the sincerity of a commentator's argument is highly problematic, many of the commentator's primary intentions and objectives, including some unstated ones, often reveal themselves in his argument; in fact, they often form an integral part of that argument. This would seem to be at least as true of the polemical newspaper editorial or congressional speech, pushing to legitimate or discredit a form of labor or set of working conditions, as it is of the longer historical tract. In considering these intentions and objectives central to my analysis, I am far from making the claim that all of the motives and purposes, least of all the unconscious ones, which lie behind a position are understandable or discoverable.[83] I find suggestive and interesting in this connection some of the recent contributions in philosophy and literary criticism regarding the interpretation of historical texts. Many of these contributions minimize the possibility, even the value, of recovering past "authorial intention" and meaning. Either they invoke the diverse meanings that are invariably generated by readers of the text, who bring to it their own preconceptions; or they stress, indeed exalt, the ambiguities that reside in the text itself, in the instability and indeterminacy of its linguistic meanings; or they argue that our knowledge of authorial intention and meaning is dependent upon an impossible identification and reconstruction of all the relevant discourse of which the author's text formed a part.[84] All of these contributions serve as useful reminders of the historian's limited reach into the minds of his subjects. Yet I nonetheless find them of uncertain merit with regard to my own particular inquiry. It still seems to me that the concerns and objectives which prompted antebellum debates over "free labor" are largely discernible and that this circumstance is in no small measure due to the very timelessness of the overriding issue which generated those concerns and objectives: how can the employments of a society, particularly its most disagreeable ones, be distributed and rewarded in a manner most consistent with national prosperity, social order, and social justice? At the same time, I do find some relevance and validity in poststructuralist claims that reducing the meaning of a text to the author's intentions is both unnecessary and misguided, even supposing such an exercise were possible. Some of the ways in which the contributions of my commentators illumine antebellum attitudes toward manual labor did not emanate at all from the actual conscious objectives of the commentators.[85]

I attempt to provide enough description of mid-nineteenth-century social conditions to make my treatment of ideas intelligible and meaningful, but no two historians will completely agree on the best balance between intellectual and social history for which a study such as mine calls.[86] In pursuing certain themes, my approach is to move back and forth from one geographic area or occupational group to another, often over many decades, and sometimes quite abruptly. To the extent that this approach detaches ideas from their specific social contexts, it carries an inevitable risk of flattening out and reifying those ideas and of obscuring one's sense of historical development. Although I try to reduce this risk by discussing the specific situations and objectives of some of my most important commentators, I also believe that it is the very persistence of certain basic ideas over long periods of time which validates my approach overall.[87] I would reiterate again that many of the objectives of the individuals who discussed free labor, when we move outside the most utopian and radical Anglo-American circles particularly, were quite uniform: to lend legitimacy to private property, the capitalist social division of labor, and the scale of incentives attaching to mental and manual labor. Individuals divided by space, time, occupational group, and even immediate economic interest were more often than not voicing only variations on a theme, and although these variations are of interest and significance, the fact that they were merely variations justifies the shifting back and forth in which this study frequently engages.

Something more should be said about the spatial and temporal dimensions of this inquiry. That mid-nineteenth-century America shared with England an absorbing interest in a variety of issues related to "free labor" suggested the value of including a comparative dimension in this study. In many instances British and American attitudes were parallel and interacting; in other instances ideas and attitudes on one side of the Atlantic— usually the British side—more clearly preceded and shaped those on the other side. I underscore this distinction where it seems to have been particularly striking or important.[88] Although its principal temporal focus is upon perceptions of manual labor's intrinsic character in the mid-nineteenth century, this study ranges far back in time to explore those intellectual traditions that prominently influenced antebellum perceptions, and it occasionally ventures into the post-1860 period. Some readers may feel that an examination of free labor concepts should concern itself not only with the antebellum ideological conflict over slave labor but with the ideological implications attaching to slavery's destruction. Clearly, emancipation and postemancipation developments must have significantly affected Americans' perceptions of free labor. At the same time, the limitations of preexisting Northern Republican "free labor ideology"—together with such other factors as the weight of Southern white political and economic interests— helped determine some of these postemancipation developments, notably the failure of most freedmen to acquire the economic resources needed to underpin their newly won civil and political equality. So basic, indeed, are all these questions relating to post-1860 free labor concepts that they require treatment in a separate book from this one, although some of them, too, have already been incisively addressed in a number of recent studies.[89]

I would like to offer a few concluding comments primarily in explanation of this book's many long content notes. My overriding purpose in using such notes is to maintain a smooth and coherent flow in the essentially intellectual history of the main text. Tracing the diversity of free labor concepts, and the multiciplicity of social issues on which those concepts turned, is something like following the divergent paths taken by the fragments of an exploding object. The notes seem to be the appropriate place to treat all those disparate historiographic controversies; all those examples, amplifications, and qualifications of arguments; all those additional complexities which, interesting and significant though they are, would unavoidably disrupt the flow of the main text were they incorporated into it. Many of the content notes are, for related reasons, of a rather different order from the main text: they tend to be more exclusively concerned with providing some of the important social history and social context that provides a background for this study's history of ideas and perceptions. I have limited the citations in the notes to those primary and secondary materials of particular importance or relevance to the point at hand. Readers who are curious about additional sources should consult the footnotes in my dissertation.[90]

2

Mental Content in
Manual Labor

In this work, my focus will be upon manual labor
performed for a recompense and as a means of
securing a livelihood. Even the most onerous and
unappealing physical chores performed by individuals during their free time exist on another
level altogether from manual labor employments; they are not obligatory in the fundamental sense that paid work is.[1] And *manual* labor
employments, most of all, have been perceived as
involuntary; perceptions of handwork especially
have been intimately bound up with the condition of economic necessity and absence of choice
that have historically impelled them. The classical
Greek, above all Aristotelian, contempt for manual labor was not a commentary on physical activity that might be freely undertaken for its own
sake; that disdain reflected the doctrine that activity which was so closely tied to the provision
of economic needs was involuntary and for this
reason base. Manual labor could hardly be a good
or an end in itself, but possessed only inferior use
or instrumental value; it was, accordingly, the
natural activity of slaves, from whom it was exacted as a means toward the higher end of freeing
citizens of the polis to meet responsibilities and
indulge interests that were virtuous or good in
themselves.[2] Operating from a perspective far

different from that of the various classical thinkers, nineteenth-century Americans like Horace Greeley and William Ellery Channing insisted, to the contrary, that manual labor had intrinsic value; and they deplored the sensuality, even the "slavery," of "free" laborers who could find no meaning in their work apart from its instrumental value, those who performed manual labor solely for its material or extrinsic rewards.[3] Universally recognized as was the connection between handwork and economic necessity, different cultures have varied significantly in the meanings with which they have invested the connection.[4] It was just such efforts as Greeley's and Channing's to cling to a work ethic in nineteenth-century America, to make a virtue out of what was economic necessity for most, that form part of the subject of this study.

Manual labor, even when considered only as an activity engaged in for securing a livelihood, remains, however, ambiguous, insofar as it can never be wholly distinct from nonmanual labor, "white-collar" work of a salaried or professional nature.[5] The simplest, most repetitive and menial manual labor makes some mental demands on the performer, perhaps as much as some forms of clerical work, whereas the most intellectually exacting and creative professions, those drawing upon a large fund of technical knowledge or artistic inspiration such as that of a surgeon or a ballet dancer, may require great manual or bodily dexterity as well.[6] The relative importance played by handwork and headwork within most occupations may be evident enough to permit their easy classification into the manual and nonmanual categories; but in some instances, such as the highly skilled preindustrial artisanal crafts, the mix of faculties and talents required suggests that terminological convenience obscured a more complex reality.[7]

In early nineteenth-century America, too, the important units of production reinforced the interplay between handwork and headwork acting to blur the line between manual and nonmanual labor. Within the preindustrial workshop, master craftsmen were, like working farm proprietors, both capitalist and laborer: they owned the means of production and employed and trained journeymen and apprentices, but they also contributed to the shop's output.[8] As mercantile capitalism and industrialism eroded the craft structure during the first part of the century, class consciousness among journeymen who suffered the brunt of the changes developed and yet was also impeded by the lingering belief that master craftsmen remained productive, fellow laborers as well as employers.[9] During this period, too, the emerging industrial capitalism was accompanied by legitimating concepts that challenged standard preindustrial ones; these alternative concepts questioned whether desirable manual labor employments need be limited to those which embodied capital as well as labor, and they also denied that the most attractive manual labor employments were necessarily restricted to those same traditional preindustrial skilled callings that naturally incorporated significant headwork as well as manual activity.[10]

We examine elsewhere some of these newer arguments that emerged in the defense of developing industrial labor, including the argument that factory workers were encouraged precisely by the mentally undemanding nature of their tasks to find more than adequate intellectual stimulation in their larger work environment. Here, however, we begin our exploration of attitudes toward the intrinsic character of manual labor by making two other observations. First, although such profactory arguments may have been the particular property of a relatively small circle of polemicists, they nonetheless ratified older and more widespread assumptions concerning the limited intrinsic mental content of manual labor employments, particularly the mental content of "common labor" employments that in social rank and remuneration had traditionally fallen below the level of preindustrial skilled artisanal trades. Second, and no less important, some of the proindustrial arguments that tried to turn the mentally unstimulating character of factory work to their advantage were innovative precisely because the more widespread assumptions regarding handwork's limited mental content upon which they drew had, to the contrary, long contributed to the powerful stigmas attaching to physical labor. Consider the following remarks by the intellectual, educator, and social reformer Elizabeth Palmer Peabody. Writing for the major organ of American Transcendentalism, the *Dial* in 1842, Peabody described with approbation the plan of the early Brook Farm Community: "All labor, whether bodily or intellectual, is to be paid at the same rate of wages; on the principle that as the labor becomes merely bodily, it is a greater sacrifice to the individual laborer, to give his time to it; because time is desirable for the cultivation of the intellect, in exact proportion to ignorance. Besides, intellectual labor involves in itself higher pleasures, and is more its own reward, than bodily labor."[11] Peabody's first justification for equal remuneration of physical and intellectual labor did not itself assert that handwork was less rewarding or less self-justifying than headwork. It suggested rather that individuals engaged in manual labor might be at greater risk than others in failing to employ and "cultivate" their mental faculties. It was perfectly consistent with the theme, to be taken up in chapter 3, that members of a republican society must maintain a healthy balance between physical and mental activity, that the two kinds of activity are both essential as well as mutually reinforcing. Our immediate concern is instead with the implications of Peabody's further observation that manual labor deserved compensatory wages because it indeed lacked the intrinsic rewards, the "higher pleasures," of "intellectual labor." That observation represented more than the conceit of a middle-class intellectual. Strikingly absent from most discussions of work in mid-nineteenth-century America was the notion that bodily labor might justify itself through the sheer physical satisfactions and euphoria it provided, that these might constitute rewards no less fulfilling and meaningful than the intellectual satisfactions offered by nonmanual labor. There was, to put the matter differently, no comparable emphasis on the idea that occupations relying primarily on intellectual labor, such as business and the "learned professions," or literary and scholarly pursuits, were any the less meaningful and elevating because they failed to incorporate the *pleasures* and *satisfactions* of physical activity.

Let us define still further the sense in which Peabody's remarks were representative of large segments of American culture. Among William Ellery Channing and certain other mainstream middle-class moralists, emphasis upon the pleasures of physical labor would have run quite contrary to one of their principal themes that such labor held moral value precisely because its difficulty and painfulness developed discipline and character.[12] Nor, with the possible exception of Fourierism, was the emphasis on the purely physical pleasures possible in manual labor characteristic of the various expressions of labor reform and labor radicalism, be those expressions middle-class or working-class in origin.[13] In pressing for new social arrangements that more fully rewarded manual labor, labor reformers defended its value on quite different grounds: its contribution to social wealth, its capacity, when not performed in excess, to assist in developing the individual's intellectual and moral faculties—the individual's so-called higher nature. Indeed, labor reform movements and working-class radicalism owed much to both Enlightenment and evangelical influences in the degree to which they shared the more conventional middle-class regard for man's "higher nature." And it was in considerable measure because they shared this regard, and because they also believed that excessive manual labor was reducing workers to mere "beasts of burden," depriving them of their equal and deserved right to develop their higher nature, that labor reformers placed so small a premium upon the strictly physical pleasures afforded by manual labor employments. Overwork, it is true, may in fact have been a no more typical experience, and a no more frequent subject of complaint, among many kinds of laborers in the nineteenth century than was insufficiency and irregularity of work—conditions of unemployment and underemployment.[14] And it is also quite possible that members of the antebellum working classes did derive intense physical pleasure from the labor they did perform—it would be arrogant to insist otherwise. But exaltation of the euphoric effects of manual labor remains in general less characteristic of workers themselves than of individuals who are in a position to take it or leave it, who can approach manual labor as "physical exercise" taken in respite from their other activities. Nowhere in the antebellum labor reform literature, which grew out of the contrary sense that manual labor was frequently all too-consuming for the bulk of those engaged in it, was there a counterpart to the exaltation of the "blissful," almost sexual experience of hard physical work that was made by the aristocrat Levin in *Anna Karenina*.[15]

On those occasions when Peabody was directly contradicted by her contemporaries, when reference was made to the possibility that the pleasures of manual labor in fact equalled or surpassed those of "intellectual labor," such references generally emanated from a perspective quite contrary to Peabody's labor reform sympathies. In his defense of existing social arrangements and the process of occupational division of labor, Alonzo Potter, the Episcopalian clergyman and professor of moral philosophy at Union College, insisted that it was not "much to be regretted that some modes of employment are less agreeable or more irksome than others," in part because the "original tastes" of some individuals, together with the power of "habit," led them to actually prefer these disagreeable employments. More than this even, Potter claimed, in a slight revision of the wording of George Poulett Scrope, a British M.P.: "Even severe manual labour is not necessarily a sacrifice. There is an animal pleasure in toil. It is questionable whether the mental or bodily exertion to which the highest and wealthiest classes are driven as a resource against ennui, communicates, in general, so pleasurable an excitement as the muscular exertions of the common labourer when not overworked."[16] In touting the self-justifying physical pleasures of manual labor as a means of defending the status quo, Potter, to be sure, acknowledged the pressures of labor reform agitation by conceding that such pleasures might be diluted through overwork. But the thrust of his position pitted him against an array of groups that criticized existing working conditions because they appeared inhospitable to the worker's development of his finer faculties. Potter's position, in turn, was related to other lines of argument, also protective of the status quo, which insisted that modes of livelihood dependent on intellectual labor were no less enslaving than manual labor employments. The conservative Southern writer George Frederick Holmes inquired of Horace Greeley and other proponents of Associationist utopian socialism how they proposed to "emancipate" the working classes from the necessities of hard toil when "the lawyer or physician frequently labours more assiduously than any mechanic or day labourer. The work of the intellect is not lighter, less difficult, less exacting, harassing, or exhausting than the work of the hands, but more so."[17]

The mental drudgery of the professions, Holmes suggested, confirmed the inexorable, sweeping character of the Creator's conception of labor as a curse (even if it was also "the parent of many blessings"); man's punishment for Original Sin, to forever earn his bread "by the sweat of [his] brow," was not to be construed too literally, but represented the scriptural sentence on all forms of labor, intellectual as well as physical. The targets of Holmes's criticism, the Associationists or American Fourierists, did not disagree with him in one sense: their writings also characterized nonmanual employments, hardly less than ditch digging, as forms of "repugnant labor" under most existing social arrangements. But the cause of the condition was for them not man's fallen state or divine decree, but a "false," pernicious, and—above all—preventible, process of specialization that pushed individuals into work that suppressed and thwarted their natural inclinations and talents.

Holmes's purpose was to expose as "chimerical" the various Associationist proposals to make physical labor "attractive." In many such efforts to represent all employments, both intellectual and manual, as the common expression of a universal economic necessity, there ran a similar objective of blunting the egalitarian claims of social reform. A contributor to the *The Plough, the Loom, and the Anvil* in 1854 noted that "to make the punishment [of earning his bread] greater, he [man] inherited a disposition preferring rest to labor [*sic*]. Man labors not from choice, but necessity." The author sought to demonstrate that, contrary to antislavery doctrine, the enforced labor of black slaves was no more degrading or onerous than any other form of labor.[18] In their writings in political economy, Jeremy Bentham, Thomas Malthus, Nassau Senior, and John Stuart Mill, followed by their American disciples, similarly argued that man's "natural indolence" and "love of ease" made labor painful and unappealing. As Bentham wrote, "desire of labour *for the sake of labour,*—of labour considered in the character of an end, without any view to any thing else, is a sort of desire that seems scarcely to have place in the human breast; . . . *Aversion*—not *desire*—is the emotion—the only emotion—which *labour,* taken by itself, is qualified to produce: . . . *love of labor* is a contradiction in terms."[19] Unlike much of the dependent and laboring poor, members of the middle classes had developed the foresight and self-restraint needed to rise above their natural indolence, forgo immediate pleasures, and deal responsibly with the painful necessity of labor in the pursuit of economic success. Thus in the classical economic writings the objects of attack were commonly systems of poor relief or socialist doctrines that sought to give the laboring and dependent classes more than their due and that would thereby deny the just operation of a competitive market economy.

The notion that intellectual labor was indeed onerous, and possibly no less contrary to man's indolent nature, than manual labor, a notion that British classical economists played a significant role in disseminating, was by the middle of the nineteenth century recurring repeatedly in Anglo-American discussions of work. And as the Fourierists, both European and American, demonstrated, reference to the travails of professionals and businessmen was not necessarily a form of apologetics for the sufferings of the laboring population. Pressures for career advancement and recognition, and for economic success far beyond what was necessary to meet basic material needs, undeniably generated its own kind of "slavery" among the middle classes in capitalist societies. A writer in the *North British Review* for 1854 shared John Stuart Mill's criticism of the "progressive state" of society in Britain and America, whereby a reflexive drive to strive, compete, and accumulate, eventuated in an habitual, almost mindless tendency toward overwork among professional men:

> The successful barrister at the summit of his profession and the height of his fame, is so overwhelmed with business that he has time neither for sleep, nor society, nor recreation, nor literature; his strength is overtasked, his life is slipping away, . . . he is amassing thousands which he does not want and cannot spend. . . . In these and similar cases, indeed, it often happens that it is not the desire of acquisition, nor yet the love of their profession, which retains these men in their unresting harness, but the conviction that they could enjoy no other life; they remain "slaves of the oar" because they could not be happy in their freedom. They have lived so long and so exclusively in their work that they have lost all relish for the simpler and quieter enjoyments of existence.[20]

While thus underscoring the oppressively narrow, driven, and "undignified" lives of nineteenth-century professionals and businessmen, the author of this essay nonetheless acknowledged along with Mill that the burdens and anxieties these men experienced were still of a different, less critical order from the travails faced by the bulk of the British laboring population. The American writers and clerics who took up the theme of upper-middle-class overwork and career anxiety were generally less inclined to make such an acknowledgment, at least with respect to the sufferings of their own country's working classes. In their overall exaltation of middle-class industriousness and other character virtues, such American commentators were expressing standard classical economic themes. But in their tendency to play down the contrasting nature of the travails of American laborers specifically, they probably drew more from Tocqueville; the French observer was instrumental in popularizing the notion that social values and consumption patterns in an egalitarian America were generating tremendous stress and anxiety throughout all levels of society by continuously raising the definition of what constituted an acceptable "competence."[21] An essay by the prominent Unitarian clergyman Henry W. Bellows offers in this connection an interesting comparison with the *North British Review* article quoted above. In his piece Bellows lamented the pressures upon his own country's professional men in very much the same terms as those of the British essay. But Bellows's lament also followed Tocqueville and bore the special imprint of the mythology of American exceptionalism. Writing in 1845 before the massive influx of impoverished Irish immigrants that might have given him pause to reconsider, Bellows observed how well-off the bulk of the American laboring population was. Noting "the widespread comfort, the facilities for livelihood, the spontaneous and cheap lands, the high price of labor," Bellows maintained that fully "nine-tenths of our population," and not merely America's professional and commercial men, were in the position to overwork from the impulses which he deplored: "To get, and to have the reputation of possessing, is the ruling passion. . . . We are ashamed of any thing but affluence."[22] The author of the *North British Review* essay, as suggested, could in contrast entertain no such illusion about his own nation's laboring population. "Thousands and thousands" in England, he observed, toiled not from a love of gain and success but merely to subsist.[23]

The exceptionalist theme that tended to homogenize the incentives, anxieties, and pressures experienced by different elements in American society could easily converge with and reinforce the more explicit claim, made by Potter and others, that manual labor employments were no more onerous in nature than mental ones. But the two were not identical, and it might be argued that Bellows's exceptionalist position was in fact more congruent with the argument, equally prominent in many exceptionalist formulations, that in America to a greater degree than anywhere else the dichotomy between mental and manual labor employments was actually fictitious, that here an extraordinarily high proportion of occupations were preindustrial ones in which manual labor called upon and incorporated significant mental activity.[24] As Potter's example indicates, the more deliberate efforts to deny or downplay the uniquely onerous nature of physical labor were not addressing such "mixed" employments at all, but were more exclusively directed at justifying the condition of strictly unskilled work, both European and American.

Even these latter efforts, quite apart from the radical Fourierist versions, hardly reflected a uniformity of perspective. George Frederick Holmes shared with the classical economists and Potter a belief in the legitimacy of the prevailing division of labor and its reward structure as a requisite of civilized societies. This belief was reflected in the emphasis he placed upon the travails experienced by business and professional men in their acquisition of social status and material success. Yet his anti-utopianism notwithstanding, Holmes also shared the utopian distaste for free market competitive individualism and the classical economists who, erroneously in his view, particularized the best possible civilized society as free market individualist in nature.[25] Nor was Holmes in close accord with a conventional proponent of Northern free labor ideology like Potter who, particularizing the good society still further, maintained that the exceptionally dynamic and open capitalist social order of the Northern states was the ideal setting for the implementation of classical free market competitive principles.[26]

Whatever the multiplicity of perspectives from which they emanated, the arguments that characterized manual labor as no more oppressive than mental labor did possess a certain timeless relevance. They accepted unskilled common labor, labor that was intrinsically deficient in intellectual "pleasures," on its own terms. In justifying the existence of this work and the division of labor in civilized societies in general, such arguments did not require American exceptionalist notions that exalted frequent mobility out of common labor; nor did they depend on equally standard exceptionalist notions which presumed that common labor remained less distinctive of the American occupational structure than other work that more clearly combined manual and mental activity.[27] One might even speculate that in accepting common labor on its own terms, commentators like Holmes and Potter were, whatever their differences, exhibiting a measure of resignation or fatalism, deliberately intended or not, toward industrial "deskilling," proletarianization, immigration, and other social changes that were during this period rendering various forms of "common labor" an increasingly important part of the American economic landscape.

The arguments that underscored either the redeeming satisfactions of purely unskilled labor or the burdens of mental labor, or those that claimed both groups were somehow "in the same boat," may not, then, have been, in contrast to some prominent exceptionalist themes, dependent on occupational fluidity or the maintenance of America's preindustrial occupational structure. But to suggest that such arguments could not be overthrown by key social changes is not to insist that they carried any great credibility. It is questionable, indeed, whether they ever possessed any more widespread currency than the variant which only a few individuals like Henry David Thoreau then appeared to develop from them and which has in fact become more popular in our own culture: that man's true sphere of freedom necessarily lies outside of *all* forms of work altogether, and that only in play and leisure activity can he truly realize himself.[28] For if members of the propertied business and professional classes often "toiled" longer hours than much of the laboring population, and if indeed, the necessity of meeting the most basic economic needs was at some level the rationale for their occupations as well, it was nonetheless readily apparent to most if not all that economic necessity had historically always operated on a far more *immediate* and brutal level for the mass of the working classes. The body of his writing indicates that Holmes himself acknowledged different kinds of pressures and burdens; his response to the utopians that the actual practice of mental labor imposed more "exacting" demands than did engagement in manual labor did not preclude his recognition elsewhere that the economic pressures driving legally free manual laborers were nonetheless more oppressive in the sense of being more immediate. But Holmes's recognition of these oppressive economic pressures always retained greater plausibility and more widespread credibility because it was more clearly supported by the weight of historical circumstance than his specifically anti-utopian argument asserting the travails of business and professional men. To an overwhelming degree, the issue in antebellum America remained not the freedom and dignity of mental and manual labor, but of manual labor specifically. Elizabeth Palmer Peabody's downplaying of the intrinsic rewards of "bodily labor" should be considered, then, in the context of the long-standing, universally recognized stigmatization of manual labor by a range of complex and interrelated associations.

THE STIGMATIZATION OF MANUAL LABOR

A good part of manual labor, commonly the most socially necessary kind, has always been back-breaking, injurious, tedious, or in some other sense intrinsically repugnant or undesirable. Egalitarian theorists have suggested that such inherent stigmas might diminish were this work more evenly distributed and shared.[29] But societies have instead, either through free market processes or through more blatantly coercive means, traditionally relegated their menial and "dirty" work to their most powerless and desperate elements: slaves, despised minorities, women and children, the enfeebled.[30] Low-status groups further stigmatized such physical labor by virtue of their association with it. In the mid-nineteenth century, to cite one prominent example, the term *nigger work* carried a common transatlantic meaning: labor of an onerous or otherwise menial and repellant nature frequently performed by Negro slaves and free blacks but sometimes undertaken by elements of the white population, elements often referred to as "white negroes."[31]

As much as any other factor, poverty defined the profoundly symbiotic relationship between undesirable work and low status or powerless groups.[32] There have always been instances of occupations whose unusually repugnant or hazardous character has been "sweetened" by their extrinsic rewards: the comparatively high wages paid mid-Victorian British coal miners were, as Raphael Samuel has noted, "a species of death money."[33] But generally speaking, as John Stuart Mill observed, "the really exhausting and the really repulsive labours, instead of being better paid than others, are almost invariably paid the worst of all."[34] Because they demanded minimal training and expertise, such occupations of "last resort" invariably attracted a surplus of the poor and desperate, those with the least economic choice and the fewest marketable skills, so long, at least, as such a supply of labor was physically extant. As the Philadelphia lawyer Sidney George Fisher noted, the "mere muscle market is always liable to be overstocked."[35] The poverty of individuals who were impelled under competitive market conditions to perform the most poorly recompensed labor became inextricably intertwined and associated with the inherently disagreeable features of that labor.

Venerable intellectual themes, ideas that contributed significantly to the nineteenth-century discussions of labor, served to confirm, even legitimate, manual labor's historical and seemingly natural connection with pain and poverty. The meaning of work in the book of Genesis has, to be sure, many nuances and ambiguities. That labor for securing a livelihood became man's punishment for Original Sin did not, first and foremost perhaps, necessarily make labor an "affliction" or "curse"; and nineteenth-century American moralists who insisted on the "blessings" of work expended a good deal of effort denying so negative an equation, arguing, for example, that Adam had "worked" in the Garden of Eden prior to his fall from grace, that work had from the beginning been God's purpose for mankind.[36] Yet most significantly, what the American moralists were struggling to uphold was the dignity of manual labor specifically. Notwithstanding George Frederick Holmes's interpretation, the language in the book of Genesis, wherein God condemned Adam to earn a subsistence "by the sweat of thy brow," had the effect for many of earmarking hard *bodily* labor as fallen man's penalty.[37] The Louisiana lawyer George L. Sawyer made the typical connection in a well-known proslavery work: "But what there is in physical labor itself calculated to purify the morals, promote the intelligence, and refine the sensibilities of a community, no one has yet been able to discover. According to Scripture it was a degrading curse inflicted upon the human race as a punishment for the first transgression."[38]

That man was obliged to work in order to secure needs that were physical in nature tended to further strengthen the association between the biblical penalty and manual labor employments particularly. Writing from a reform perspective wholly distinct from the proslavery defense of social stratification, Virginia Penny nonetheless concurred with Sawyer's interpretation of Scripture: "Instead of the activity of the great mass of people being of an intellectual kind, sin has made it to consist in activity of body, with the object mainly in view, of contributing to the necessities of the physical nature."[39] Society of course offered many examples of intellectual employments that individuals followed in order to meet their physical needs. Yet to Penny and other writers, intellectual activity still generally appeared to express the degree to which mankind had been able to loosen the binds of the scriptural punishment imposed for Original Sin.[40]

It would be inaccurate to claim that the Judeo-Christian legacy went significantly beyond the book of Genesis in seeming to throw manual labor into disrepute; in fact, there were pronounced countertendencies. Medieval Christianity's sanctification of the condition of poverty blended at times into appreciation of manual labor; Christ was a shepherd and the son of a carpenter, and he washed the feet of his disciples. As the expression of fallen man's humility and submission to God, labor was a means of salvation as well as a penalty. Jacques Le Goff has observed that the penitential physical labor done by the monk, who represented "the highest type of Christian perfection, . . . impressed his contemporaries in its favor. The monk's self-humiliation in labor raised labor in general esteem."[41] Lynn White, Jr., was even more emphatic: in part because the Benedictine monk became "the first intellectual to get dirt under his fingernails," the founder of the Benedictine order deserves the title of "the pivotal figure in the history of labor."[42]

Through his challenge to older traditions that disdained physical work, St. Benedict, White adds, anticipated the Protestant Reformation. By affirming the equal spiritual dignity of all callings performed by men in obedience to God, the teachings of Luther and Calvin indeed went somewhat further than early monasticism in blunting the stigmatization of manual labor.[43] In Calvinism especially, men's duty to labor and the sin of idleness assumed an importance that far overshadowed any possible theological distinctions between varieties of labor. In more secularized, accessible form, the same emphasis came to distinguish the nineteenth-century moralists' expressions of the "work ethic."[44]

Yet one can also overstate the degree to which the Protestant Reformation, along with the various versions of the "calling" it bequeathed Western civilization, eroded the comparative disdain for physical labor. Protestantism and the Protestant ethic, perhaps above all in seventeenth-century England and colonial New England, anticipated such nineteenth-century intellectual developments as philosophic radicalism and classical economy by casting a certain disrepute upon the frivolity, leisure, and "idleness" of titled, landed aristocrats, upon their "ostentatious consumption of inherited resources."[45] At the same time, albeit again in a vaguer way than these nineteenth-century developments, Protestantism and Puritanism solidified the prestige of productive, industrious, exclusively mental labor, and they accorded some recognition to the notion that the diligent middle-class elements that monopolized these employments deserved recognition as society's true "gentlemen," the bedrock of civilized society situated between the decadent "idle" rich and the undeserving "idle" vagrant poor. But in thereby bestowing a new legitimacy upon middle-class enterprise and mental labor, and upon the "bourgeois virtues" generally, the Protestant Reformation did nothing to challenge or weaken, and even provided some implicit ideological entrenchment for, the position of relative social subordination long occupied by pursuits more strictly dependent upon manual labor.[46]

Considerably more unequivocal and pronounced in the distinction it drew between debased manual labor and elevated intellectual activity was the body of classical philosophy directed toward justifying ancient slavery. Scholars continue to disagree over a range of issues regarding the nature and pervasiveness of the "Greek disdain" for physical work. They disagree, for example, over the extent to which such disdain reflected a more generalized contempt for any nonvoluntary activity: activity performed not for its own sake, but to meet the needs of another. But according to at least one school of ancient Greek thought, the degrading nature of manual labor specifically was confirmed by its close association with "natural" slaves and others who were marked as inferior beings precisely because they were judged incapable of acting from a motive more elevated than that of economic necessity. Classical philosophers, most notably Aristotle, disassociated intellectual activity from physical labor and situated it in the realm of leisure, free from economic necessity, where citizens might pursue the self-justifying, absolute goods of culture and virtue.[47]

The classical writings' stigmatization of manual labor found particular appeal among antebellum Southerners who were also seeking vindication of a slave-based, hierarchical society reflecting natural differences in talents among men. One of the most provocative of these justifications, however, an 1855 essay by George Frederick Holmes, insisted that modern civilization in general, and not simply the slave South, followed ancient Greece and Rome in disdaining physical labor. Although Holmes's anti-utopianism elsewhere prompted his claim that mental labor employments were more "harassing" than manual labor ones, in this essay he argued that mental labor callings were nonetheless universally preferred. Slavery, ancient or modern, was not responsible for the general aversion to physical labor; that aversion, Holmes suggested, was virtually primordial. Ancient civilizations were simply more candid than modern ones in acknowledging this fact:

> That, ordinarily, men who had the means of living comfortably without bodily labor preferred to depend upon their revenues or the superintendence of the labor of others, was true then: but is it less true now? If there has been any great change in this respect, how does it happen that the learned professions, government appointments, political avocations, trade, manufactures, speculation, and what are curiously termed intellectual and liberal occupations, are so constantly pursued by young and old, rather than the actual culture of the soil and handicrafts? And how does it happen that pursuits of the former class are so much more highly estimated than the latter by public sentiment and social remuneration? There is very little difference between ancient and modern feelings in this respect. . . .
> . . . Both display the same contempt of labor, and the same

repugnance to work; and both seek, as far as possible, to escape from the dire necessity. The esteem, or disesteem, has been nearly equal in both periods; but it was honest and avowed in antiquity, and is pretended or disguised at present.[48]

Holmes attributed the hypocritical pieties trumpeting the "dignity" of manual labor to the "treacherous" free labor tendencies of modern civilization. Those pieties disguised the fact that "young and old" alike everywhere avoided manual labor whenever possible; and in the mouths of the vested interests and other "apostles" of competitive labor market principles, they also masked the exploitation of legally free members of the working classes, a process of subjugation and degradation achieved through the introduction of "labor-saving" technology and other means.[49] Holmes's last indictment was penetrating but also overdrawn and itself self-serving; it passed over the extent to which some prominent defenders of black chattel servitude denied and obscured the realities of slave labor exploitation by using the same "homilies" extolling the divinity and nobility of manual labor.

Yet Holmes's related theme, which he advanced to rebut antislavery claims—that the societal aversion and relative disdain for physical work was enduring and not the special consequence of chattel slavery—retained particular merit. Throughout this inquiry we are concerned, among other things, with the various deviations from Holmes' perspective—those individuals, for example, who denied the truth of his accusation that manual labor was disesteemed and stigmatized in America, and those who agreed with him yet to a much greater extent than he deplored this disesteem, insisting instead upon the intrinsic dignity of manual labor employments in the face of the social, economic, and intellectual stigmas with which these employments had been historically burdened. The special contribution of the classical heritage which Holmes invoked was to systematize the disjunction between physical labor and intellectual activity: handwork was essentially unreflective, as tied to ignorance as it was to economic necessity; thinking was the essence of man's finer nature, the engine of civilization and what distinguished him from barbarians. It was entirely possible to accept the validity of these connections without tying them in, as prominent classical and antebellum Southern writers did, to an elitist defense of human slavery. In the 1831 volume of the *North American Review*, a young Harvard-trained lawyer, Timothy Walker, made the following argument in support of unlimited technological progress and in response to Thomas Carlyle's attack on "mechanical philosophy":

> So long as our souls are doomed to inhabit bodies, these bodies, however gross and unworthy they may be deemed, must be taken care of. Men have animal wants, which must and will be gratified

at all events. . . . But at the same time, as we have a higher and nobler nature, which must also be cared for, the necessary labor spent upon our bodies should be as much abridged as possible, in order to give us leisure for the concerns of this better nature . . . if machines could be so improved and multiplied, that all our corporeal necessities could be entirely gratified, without the intervention of human labor, there would be nothing to hinder all mankind from becoming philosophers, poets, and votaries of art. . . .

. . . There has never been a period, when so large a number of minds, in proportion to the whole, were left free to pursue the cultivation of the intellect . . . the advantage resulting from a release of so large a proportion of mankind from the thraldom of physical labor, will be as lasting as the mind.[50]

In an essay on "Popular Education" a few years earlier, Walker had hardly made so strong a connection between "thraldom" and "physical labor." He had suggested, rather, that the infusion of "useful knowledge" into the "lower classes" would make them "ambitious and aspiring" but in a way that would elevate and dignify their employments rather than make them wish to abandon their callings: "The whole mass of society will make a positive advancement; there will be the same gradations of condition, because each class will be elevated in the same proportion." The intellectual elevation of the working classes was rendered all the more compelling by the requirements of "our great political experiment" of republican government, for the foundation of republicanism was "knowledge and virtue in the mass of the people" and "the mind recoils with horror from the idea of submitting the most precious interests of society to the suffrages of an ignorant majority."[51]

"Compared with the mass of any other nation now existing," Walker concluded in this earlier essay, the "majority of our population . . . must be pronounced enlightened. But knowledge and ignorance are relative terms; and speaking with reference to that state to which well-directed efforts might speedily advance them, they are comparatively ignorant."[52] In contrast to his claims here that significant, if not unlimited, intellectual elevation, was compatible with the condition of manual labor, Walker seemed to disavow such a possibility in his later response to Carlyle. Perhaps it was not so much Walker's actual opinion which changed, but rather the purpose of his writing: from a defense in the earlier essay of the distribution of political power among manual laborers, Walker moved, as Leo Marx has noted, to a reminder in the face of Carlyle's antimechanistic doctrines that technology would hardly seem an evil to those upon whom society bestowed so "little dignity of soul (or status) in the first place."[53] The earlier purpose occasioned Walker's emphasis upon the necessity of educating enfranchised manual laborers; the later purpose generated a quite different emphasis.

Labor-saving machinery, Walker argued, would free modern civilization to reach intellectual and cultural summits comparable to those that the injustices of military aggression and slavery had made possible for the Greeks. Indeed, it was the more explicit expectation of another proponent of sweeping technological change, John A. Etzler, that the future's utopias of "superabundance" would have no more use for chattel slavery than for the legally free forms of "monotonous drudgery" that plagued existing societies.[54] But in Walker's case particularly, the characterization of physical labor as a servile provision for man's "animal wants" seemed clearly to reflect the wish that technological change would ultimately supersede all manual labor, and not merely its more menial and poorly recompensed grades. Walker's is the case par excellence of an enthusiasm for technological and economic development mingling expressed respect for the unfulfilled capacities of laboring people with pronounced contempt for the work they currently performed.[55] Certainly his particular example supports the view that men of Whiggish sentiment and affiliation were more disposed than Jacksonian Democratic leaders to underscore the intrinsic limitations of manual labor employments, to move from this on occasion to actually conceptualizing all manual labor as "'corporeal drudgery' which degraded man."[56] In this later essay Walker was insisting that intellectual exercise and fulfillment constituted the essence of an activity's virtue and dignity and that manual labor necessarily precluded such exercise and fulfillment. His represented a more full-blown, extreme expression of the notion that Elizabeth Palmer Peabody touched on: that "intellectual labor involves in itself higher pleasures, and is more its own reward, than bodily labor." Other writers, including Carlyle, we will later find, took exception to Walker's position and contended that manual labor need not possess significant mental content and satisfactions to be virtuous and dignified, that all forms of "honest" work contained important intrinsic moral rewards independent of any intellectual ones.[57] Before considering this argument, however, we will examine more closely a number of others, all of which departed from Walker's in other important respects; the first of these suggested that dignified free labor should indeed embody substantial mental content, but that much manual labor in mid-nineteenth-century America already met this requirement.

THE MYTHOLOGY OF AMERICAN EXCEPTIONALISM

When mid-nineteenth-century American politicians, social reformers, and intellectuals advanced ideas and arguments about work, they did so within the context of one general, intensely divisive, question: to what

extent would the American environment, encompassing a unique configuration of abundant natural resources, republican political institutions, and
comparatively great demand for labor in relation to available supply, continue to offer opportunities that made it "the best poor man's country in the
world"?[58] How long, in other words, would that environment effectively
sustain the working classes above the impoverished and degraded level that
Americans believed generally prevailed in the Old World? In 1830 one of the
foremost articulators of the mythology of American exceptionalism, Edward Everett, thus congratulated the new manufacturing city of Lowell,
Massachusetts: "You have rolled off from the sacred cause of labor the
mountain reproach of ignorance, vice, and suffering under which it lay
crushed."[59] Although Everett was speaking here specifically of the material
well-being and high intellectual and moral character of Lowell's factory
population, and of the glorious future that lay ahead for the city, he might
well have been stating his opinion of the achievement of his country
generally in removing the stigmas that had historically burdened manual
labor.

Set against Everett's opinion even as he expressed it was the perspective of a range of social reformers and spokesmen for labor movements
which insisted that America had already, all too clearly, adopted European
social values and patterns, notwithstanding the conditions—indeed, the
"accidental" advantages—that appeared to make America uniquely hospitable to manual laborers.[60] Anticipating and reinforcing George Frederick
Holmes's remark that modern civilization everywhere held manual labor
employments in general "disesteem," the critical labor reform perspective
was well expressed by Horace Greeley in both his defense of Association in
1846 and in some of his later writings, even after he had moved away from
that utopian cause: "The Condition of the Worker—even in this favored
region—is a rugged and hard one"; here, just as in Europe, "nearly all at
heart believe downright Manual Labor degrading; they would avoid it if
possible: or, if not, they would gladly leave their children in a condition to
avoid it. The hod carrier and the washerwoman share this feeling equally,
with the banker and the fine lady."[61] As Greeley's own case well illustrates,
much of the labor reform energies of the 1830s and the 1840s were submerged in the rising tide of Northern anti-Southern nationalism of the
1850s. The intensifying sectional conflict over Southern black slave labor did
not so much eclipse concern with the Old World stigmas on physical labor.
Rather, it somewhat altered the terms in which Americans, including
former activists in Northern labor reform movements, raised that concern.
Increasingly, Southern slavery and the "Slave Power" came to be conceptualized as the indigenous, possibly most formidable expression yet, of the
"aristocratic" contempt for labor and love of idleness and rank that had
always threatened to infiltrate and degrade New World institutions.[62]

Pervasive as they were, the twin themes of American exceptionalism and the feared "Europeanization" of American labor had only limited bearing on perceptions of the intellectual and other intrinsic rewards of manual labor. It was hardly possible, for example, to contend that street sweeping and canal digging would undergo a radical transformation and become inherently stimulating or elevating activities when moved from the Old World to the New. Nor, for that matter, could one easily argue that much of the menial labor required in New York City was of a more intellectually rewarding character than that performed by slaves on Southern plantations. As suggested in the earlier discussion of Northern free labor ideology, Americans who confronted the issue of drudge work at all, and who sought to reconcile its existence in the Northern free states with a belief in the unsurpassed dignity of labor there, might suggest that the redeeming quality of such work lay outside of its intrinsic character altogether, perhaps in the certainty of a decent recompense, or in the promise of escape through geographic or upward mobility. Unskilled, often hard physical labor, like the poverty with which it was closely linked, generated profoundly ambivalent attitudes among middle-class Americans. This was a period in which the sons of the rich were routinely, almost universally, disdained and even pitied for their "effeminacy," a quality bred of their underexposure to hard work. Not having earned their wealth through such work, these youth, so the mythology ran, invariably failed to develop the virtues important to keeping that wealth.[63] As a form of adversity, then, even hard and tedious physical labor might be excused, even extolled, as a developer of character in the individual who was obliged to perform it early in life. But the benefits of this labor went beyond its supposed capacity to equip young men with the character virtues needed for material success. Horace Greeley informed aspiring professionals and scholars that learning to "live by the labor of your hands, the sweat of your face," was indeed necessary preparation for their careers. By instilling in them the discipline of living on a pittance, such experience would provide them with an invaluable integrity and fortitude, a resistance to the temptation to "sell" themselves to ambition once they entered their chosen professions.[64] Drawing upon and idealizing his own experiences as a farm youth, Greeley repeatedly argued that early training in manual labor would also provide young professionals with the "back-up" skill they would need if they failed to secure a livelihood in their highly competitive fields; only a small percentage of those seeking a living through intellectual labor could make one, he claimed.[65] Other writers, intent on extolling the Northern social order for antislavery or other purposes, went somewhat further than Greeley usually did and embraced like theme as actual empirical description rather than mere ideal. In contrast to the pitiable indolence that marked childhood and adolescence within the Southern planter class, there was in New

England, Harriet Martineau trumpeted, "scarcely a clergyman, lawyer, or physician, who, if deprived of his profession, could not," because of his upbringing, "support himself by manual labour."[66]

The demanding, not to say disagreeable, character of some forms of handwork has always recommended them to writers like Greeley as an antidote to elitist or undemocratic values.[67] Such activities served as a valuable temporary form of "education" for students and other advantaged middle-class youth, a humbling experience upon which they could build a lifelong bond of empathy with members of society who genuinely lacked the economic resources to avoid physical labor.

Yet whatever its character-forming and other salutary effects during early manhood, manual labor, above all its most unintellectual types, was far more likely to be disdained by middle-class writers as proof of defective character if still performed in middle life. The conviction that in the Northern states more clearly than anywhere else enterprising individuals could in time "rise" above their drudgery and poverty presupposed that the same kind of labor might well be evaluated in different terms depending on the age of the individual engaged in it. Greeley himself gave expression to this very idea:

> Though it be true that no man should be ashamed of a humble position, I qualify the statement by the proviso that he has had no opportunity to rise above it. A true man will much prefer to shoulder a hod or sweep streets rather than eat the bread of idleness and dependence; but, either our political institutions are mistakes, or a hale, two-handed person, who has not been pulled down by unavoidable misfortune, should be ashamed that, having had twenty years' control of his own time and faculties, he still finds hod-carrying or sweep-sweeping the best thing he is asked or enabled to do. If I had had a fair chance to do for myself for even twenty years, and could now find no better employment than the rudest and coarsest day labor, I should accept the situation, but not be inclined to brag of it.[68]

Egalitarian expectations, drawing on a belief in the existence of some considerable open opportunity, contributed to the middle-class disdain for those individuals who failed to rise above the "rudest" hireling work especially. In Greeley's particular case, egalitarian moralism derived more from a traditional agrarian republican ethic that disdained permanent wage-earning drudge laborers because they were economically dependent than from a liberal capitalist acquisitive ethic that scorned them because they were poor.[69] But liberal capitalist values nonetheless played an increasingly important part of exceptionalist mythology during the mid-nineteenth century, and they contributed in commensurately increased degree to the contempt for individuals who failed to improve upon the hard physical employments of their youth, who failed to show the tangible evidence of "talent, ingenuity, perseverance, or enterprise." Thus the German writer Francis J. Grund remarked with some discernible ambivalence toward what he was observing:

> But if the acquisition and accumulation of property in the United States is made comparatively easy, and credit given to those who succeed in it, a proportionally larger discredit must attach itself to those who are unfortunate and poor; and this is really carried to a melancholy extent, although from the unexampled prosperity of the country, there are few to whom it will apply. A man, in America, is not despised for being poor in the outset . . . but every year which passes, without adding to his prosperity, is a reproach to his understanding or industry.[70]

There was, to be sure, that one dimension of abolitionist thought and free labor ideology that tended to dismiss economic opportunity and other exceptionalist conditions in the North as superadded, irrelevant confirmation of the superiority of free labor over slave labor systems. This dimension encouraged the quite different notion that the redeeming quality of drudge work in the free states lay not so much even in the drudge laborer's possibilities for upward mobility as it did in the worker's mere possession of his legal freedom. An observer of the laboring poor and underclass of Philadelphia wrote: "The most miserable of bone-gatherers—the most oppressed of weavers, thank their God that they are not *slaves*. The one can gather bones, when he pleases, and go where he pleases to do it. The other can *strike,* and at least remind the despot that he is a *man*—and neither can be slaughtered with rifles nor torn to pieces by bloodhounds."[71]

Notwithstanding such invocations of bare legal freedom to confirm the dignity of Northern bone gatherers relative to that of Southern slaves, the arguments waged between those antebellum Americans who upheld and those who denied the strength of American exceptionalism, remained, to a very large extent, arguments over the living standards and remuneration enjoyed by manual labor in the Northern states. Or if not these precisely, they were closely related arguments regarding the ability of the free worker in the North, compared to the chattel slave, to improve himself, his working, or his living conditions by virtue of the particular status he occupied within the work process—that of free but economically dependent wage laborer or that of self-employed, economically independent farmer or craftsman. To a considerable degree, the upholders of American exceptionalism lodged the dignity not only of drudge work but of wage labor manual employments generally, in the capacity of those employments to offer industrious workers escape into something "better." And those who denied the strength of American exceptionalism—Northern labor reformers and radicals in the 1830s and 1840s and, more predominantly thereafter, proslavery Southerners—made their case, for the most part, on the basis of criteria that were similarly extrinsic to the nature of the work itself. The "wage slavery" that entrapped and destroyed the dignity of legally free workers was explicitly conceptualized not so much as a deficiency in the content of their labor. Rather, it was expressed as the absence of economic autonomy and power and as the consequent inability on the part of deserving wage workers to secure a just and decent recompense and to exercise due control over their working conditions.[72]

There was, however, one sense, a largely indirect or implicit one, in which the belief in American exceptionalism did come to specifically bear upon perceptions of intrinsic mental rewards in manual labor employments. A primary underpinning of that belief was a vision of America—or, specifically, of the Northern free states—as still predominantly a competitively open society of small producers, consisting of economically independent farmers and craftsmen. Although industrialization, urbanization, and immigration were by 1860 rendering a good part of that vision increasingly untenable, if not yet a fiction, it retained its force and even acquired new momentum as one of the exigencies of Northern anti-Southern nationalism.[73] It was not, however, the antislavery Republicans, but Daniel Webster who, in an 1840 speech in defense of Whig economic policies, provided perhaps the classic formulation of the small-producer vision of American society:

> What is *American labor*? It is best described by saying, *it is not* European labor. Nine tenths of the whole labor of this country is performed by those who cultivate the land they or their fathers own, or who, in their workshops, employ some little capital of their own, and mix it up with their manual toil. No such thing exists in other countries. Look at the different departments of industry, whether agricultural, manufacturing, or mechanical, and you will find that, in almost all, the laborers mix up some little capital with the work of their hands. The laborer of the United States is the United States. Strike out the laborers of the United States, including therein all who in some way or other belong to the industrious and working classes, and you reduce the population of the United States from sixteen millions to one million.[74]

The mythology of American exceptionalism not only stressed the ease and frequency of movement from the laboring into the middle classes. In the more extreme, Whig-Republican version favored by party leaders like Webster, it denied the very existence of such a class distinction. Apart from the relatively small wage-laboring segment, the American "working" class merged into and became one with the broad middle class of capitalists.[75] A vision which held that the individuals who performed the manual labor were, to an extraordinary degree, the capitalists as well, carried the implication that as capitalists, such individuals necessarily exercised their mental faculties as well as their muscles. In their capacity as independent proprietors, the working farmers and craftsmen to whom Webster was referring assumed the responsibilities and risks characteristic of any capitalistic investment in and operation of an enterprise. These responsibilities included the hiring, training, and supervision of help as well as the basic function of calculating "the extent of the market" for the firm's products. There was, to be sure, a basic stream of political economic thought which denied that the functions performed by capitalists justified their profits, or that their "head labor" was truly productive, if in fact labor at all.[76] But little of such radical criticism took issue with the notion that the capitalist's role was essentially an intellectual one, requiring the use of calculation and judgment.

To the extent that mid-nineteenth-century American farming and craftsmanship did in fact entail such small capitalist functions, this circumstance by no means alone accounted for their common representation as the manual labor employments most likely to offer significant mental rewards. The very nature of the physical activity that distinguished these employments was held to stimulate or to be conducive to the development of the intellectual faculties. Ironically, this line of argument, although issued like Webster's in praise of farming and craftsmanship, originated for the most part from the opposite corner. It was advanced primarily by groups or individuals who questioned the strength of American exceptionalism and who found much cause for apprehension in the social and economic changes American society was undergoing. In an extended testimony to farming's many virtues, one "Agricola" noted that unlike agricultural labor,

> many kinds of mechanical and other employments are rendered unhealthy by the constrained position in which they must be performed, and the close confinement which is necessary in carrying them on. It is obvious that mind and body must be exercised together in order to promote a regular and healthy growth in both . . . farming . . . is the most pleasant and agreeable business in which an intelligent man can be employed. The great diversity of exercise which it affords is equivalent to rest. . . . Its tendency is to enlarge the mind.[77]

Similarly, an 1836 report to the Massachusetts House of Representatives commented on the natural intellectual benefits of farming in considering why the children employed in factories were in special need of some formal education:

A change in occupation, from those diversified employments which characterize a sparse and agricultural population, to the simple operations consequent upon that minute subdivision of labor, upon which the success of manufacturing industry depends, is not a circumstance favorable to intellectual development. By the former, the ingenuity and inventive powers are called into action, in the combination and adaptation of means to ends, and thereby they are developed and strengthened. By the latter employment, the invention having been made by some master spirit, the operative is reduced, in some degree, to the humble sphere of a part of the machinery.[78]

Manual labor employments in industry, however, were not the only employments unfavorably compared to farming as a natural source of intellectual rewards. Horace Greeley suggested that the relentless pressures of career ambition and "money-getting" on urban business and professional men made them far less ideally inclined than the "country boy" to devote time to "true," reflective thought. After completing a day of manual labor, the farmer could bring to his books at night a freshness that the lawyer or doctor who had been engaged in mental exercise all day lacked. "If the farmer's mind remains undeveloped," Greeley observed, "the fault must be his own. His labor does not usually tax his brain a feather's weight in comparison with the incessant anxieties of the professional or mercantile man."[79]

In the same essay in which she noted the intention of Brook Farm to compensate "bodily labor" for its lesser intrinsic rewards, Elizabeth Palmer Peabody commented that the community also sought to make physical work more attractive by combining it with study. Agricultural labor was a particularly important and promising target to begin such efforts, Peabody remarked, because if Brook Farm

succeeds in uniting successful labor with improvement in mind and manners, it will teach a noble lesson to the agricultural population, and do something to check that rush from the country to the city, which is now stimulated by ambition, and by something better, even a desire for learning. Many a young man leaves the farmer's life, because only by so doing can he have intellectual companionship and opportunity; and yet, did he but know it, professional life is ordinarily more unfavorable to the perfection of mind, than the farmer's life; if the latter is lived with wisdom and moderation, and the labor mingled as it might be with study.[80]

Peabody's remarks are a reminder that although she identified intellectual activity with man's "higher nature" and consequently placed it on a higher plane than physical labor, she was hardly less critical than other writers of the narrow character and strictly calculative uses that "mental labor" so often assumed among professional and business men.[81] One of the fundamental ambiguities in American discussions of work involves the degree to which the conviction that nonmanual labor occupations more completely stimulated the mind than did most manual labor employments was tempered by recognition of the "money-making" pressures and career ambitions that to some degree reduced this advantage.[82] Greeley's suggestion that the intellectual strength of farming lay in its not unduly straining the mental faculties might be equally applied to any manual labor employment in the abstract; by only a slight extension of this logic, the very mindlessness of factory labor was touted by some for leaving the factory worker's brain untaxed and uncluttered, free to ponder weighty matters. A considerable part of the particular appeal freehold farming held for Greeley, as for Peabody and others, lay in the uniquely advantageous position this occupation could readily assume relative both to the bulk of manual labor employments and to many professional occupations. More naturally and completely than most forms of physical labor, conditions of freehold farming—or at least knowledgeable, "scientific" farming—held out the promise of intrinsic intellectual rewards as well as the opportunity for quiet repose for study.[83] In comparison to business and professional men, on the other hand, freehold farmers might maintain some healthy isolation and immunity from those market and career pressures that tended to tax, narrow, and distort intellectual activity.[84]

The particular arguments advanced in support of the natural intellectual stimulus of farming—its diversity of exercise and its greater opportunities for contemplation in an environment of more natural, less pressured work rhythms—were, in large measure, a reflexive response to industrial growth, population movement, and the specific kinds of employments into which the northeastern farm population was then draining. In underscoring the intrinsic dignity of farming in contrast to both the degrading and constricting nature of factory work and the "genteel" yet frenzied character of urban professional and business occupations, the entire body of antebellum agricultural rhetoric, of course, went beyond citing the strictly intellectual rewards of farming. "Agricola's" catalog of the benefits of farm life invoked as well virtually the entire legacy of pastoral, antiurban, and Jeffersonian themes attesting to the superior morality of living off the land under one's own "vine and fig tree." In suggesting that the freehold farmer's intellectual activity could assume, if it did not already, a more pristine and satisfying character than that which characterized most urban and nonmanual labor employments, "Agricola," Greeley, and Peabody were essentially articulating a specifically intellectual dimension of the long-standing tradition of republican yeoman and pastoral thought.[85] That writers could even make such arguments confirms the view of one scholar that this was still a period of time when "there remained space to fantasize an agrarian social order that might contain all."[86]

The arguments that focused upon the superior intellectual stimulation and rewards of *existing* farm labor, as distinct from what farm labor might conceivably become under the most optimum conditions, remained particularly strained and vulnerable to attack, no less so than the other themes that insisted upon the superiority of agricultural life. The tradition of freehold farming and the heritage of Jeffersonian values in America meant, it was true, that defenders of agricultural life need not labor under quite the same burden which confronted defenders of the incipient American factory system: that of denying and combating identification with a notorious Old World, particularly British, counterpart. The predominance of farm tenancy and wage labor in England, its history of agricultural labor insurrection, the special forms taken by female and child agricultural exploitation there, and the alleged "dumb beast lives" of England's impoverished farm laboring population, were too well publicized and presented too clearly a dissimilar a tradition from that of agriculture in the Northern free states to permit easy or frequent association between the two.[87]

Yet if, as Richard H. Abbott has claimed, the profarming "myth" disseminated by "Agricola" and writers in antebellum agricultural journals in fact convinced few of the farmers and others to whom it was directed, one reason was that northeastern farm labor could not escape the general suspicion that what was being extolled as honest, hard work did in fact share something of the "mindless drudgery," monotony, and plodding inefficiency common to the field labor of European "peasantry."[88] That the self-employed farmer or hired hand could, unlike the factory laborer, work according to seasonal rhythms at a variety of tasks was less of an advantage if most or all of these tasks appeared equally deadening. As *Harper's New Monthly Magazine* summarized its explanation for the common resistance to farming's appeal, "milking a brindle cow is not the height of happiness"; and as a writer in another popular magazine put the issue with similar bluntness: "The farmer's life is no better than the life of a street-sweeper, if it rise no higher than the farmer's work."[89] Greeley acknowledged the considerable gap between the ideal and the common actuality of agricultural labor when he lamented, partially on the basis of his own experience as the son of a poor New Hampshire farmer, that *"our farmers' sons escape from their fathers' calling whenever they can, because it is made a mindless, monotonous drudgery, instead of an ennobling, liberalizing, intellectual pursuit."*[90] Elsewhere he added that "our youth of largest promise too generally escape from the drudgery of their paternal acres to court the equally repulsive slavery of the office or the counter—not because it is preferable in itself, but because it gives scope to larger hopes, suggests larger possibilities, and at all events is supposed to afford larger opportunities for observation, for intellectual development, and choice of companions."[91]

And another of the leading participants in labor and land reform movements, William West, repudiated the agricultural, anti-industrial bias of a fellow reformer in explaining why "the general law of Human Progress" dictated that the United States, no more than France, England, and Scotland, would or should remain "three-fourths agricultural": "Here, as elsewhere, agricultural labor is the most tedious, monotonous, and the poorest paid. From the nature of their occupation, the distance which separates them from one another, and the difficulty of acquiring and diffusing knowledge among them, agricultural laborers are the most ignorant, superstitious, and intensely selfish. . . . As man becomes intelligent he flees the country, becomes peddler, trader, manufacturer, merchant, priest, lawyer, and legislator."[92]

As West's remarks suggest, the "shunning" of northeastern agricultural labor and the departure of "country boys"—and girls—for the cities and factories reflected a good deal more than disenchantment with the specific intellectual characteristics of farm work. Involved as well were a variety of related but distinct circumstances, including the physically laborious and relatively unlucrative nature of that work, the inability of small homesteads to provide sufficient employment opportunities for family members coming of age, and the isolation and routine of country life.[93] To his criticism of the "mindless" drudgery of existing agricultural labor, Greeley added that "at present, our youth escape from rural drudgery when they can,—not that they really hate work, but that they find their leisure hours even duller and less endurable than those they give to rugged toil."[94] George Fitzhugh observed that slaves were called upon to do much of the world's agricultural labor precisely because it "is the most arduous, least respectable, and worst paid of all labor. Nature and philosophy teach all who can to avoid and escape from it."[95] There was enough truth in Fitzhugh's remark to suggest that even had northeastern farm labor been somehow able to offer more intellectual rewards, the remaining drawbacks of agricultural life and work would likely have continued to generate the "factory fever" and an urge for the "soft" and seductive life of the cities that so exasperated writers like "Agricola."

We should keep this phenomenon of rural out-migration, and the "agrarian myth" that deplored it, in proper perspective. "Opportunities to remain on the land," as one historian has noted, "were more constricted than ever in the middle of the century."[96] But that untold numbers of the most "intelligent" and "enterprising" young men and women chose because of this and other circumstances to migrate to eastern cities and factories, as well as to western farmlands, during the antebellum period does not itself contravene the economic viability and appeal that northeastern farming retained for many of "those who stayed behind."[97] Competent overviews of the antebellum "northern rural economy" can be written in which the social and attitudinal strains we have been focusing upon here hardly figure at all.[98]

The "agrarian myth" perpetuated in the agricultural press may have been among the clearer cases where invoking the nobility of hard physical labor represented something other than cynical "cant"; it seems to have been in considerable measure a genuine "defensive reaction" by commentators to the growing disbelief in the myth among segments of the antebellum farm population itself, as particularly evidenced by the out-migration of northeastern farm youth.[99] Yet this commentary raises the same question as much of the other antebellum rhetoric extolling the dignity of physical labor. What were the possible implications arising from the fact that many of the individuals who engaged in this rhetoric—in this case members of the "agricultural press"—no longer continued to perform manual labor themselves, or indeed, had never experienced any prolonged and strong dependence on it for their livelihoods?[100] In the northeast as elsewhere, for example, an important part of this press consisted of amateur, or "gentleman farmers," individuals who were either independently wealthy or derived their income from some form of nonagricultural enterprise. At the very least, perhaps, the social situation of these individuals embodied a general, if not necessarily inevitable, orientation that distinguished them from genuine "operating farmers"—an orientation one scholar described as the philosophy of those "who thought more about farming as a way of life than as a way of making a living."[101] A recent study of a particularly prominent group of these gentlemen farmers, members of Boston's business and professional elite, has moved beyond this generalization to probe the changing class functions served by that elite's praise of, and amateur engagement in, farming, over the first six decades of the nineteenth century.[102] To draw attention to such class functions remains, again, perfectly compatible with the recognition that these and other gentlemen farmers, along with the great majority of the agricultural press, were "sincere" in perpetuating the "agrarian myth"—that many of them sought through their rhetoric to reverse a growing disesteem for agricultural labor that they genuinely believed to be invalid and socially unhealthy. And although it amounts to a tautology to note that the "agrarian myth" coincided not at all with the occupational opportunities pursued by growing numbers of rural youth, it remains possible that the social values of these youth mirrored the same tensions and contradictions within an economically maturing American society as those besetting the agricultural press. Regardless of their behavior, out-migrating farm youth may have continued to be torn by a certain ambivalence, a conflict in values arising from the clash between their aversion to unlucrative, hard physical, mentally tedious labor, on the one hand, and some lingering commitment to a myth which idealized and romanticized that labor, on the other.[103]

Substantial intellectual or creative satisfactions more unquestionably distinguished many of the jobs in the preindustrial "mechanic arts"—those trades possessing firm craft antecedents based in the major maritime cities. One should not exaggerate the quantitative significance of the skilled handicraft trades of the late eighteenth and early nineteenth centuries, either in terms of numbers employed or total manufacturing output. The economic role of these trades, particularly those producing goods for the so-called luxury market, was limited and should be seen in the perspective of the "vast scene of household manufacturing" that simultaneously flourished in the countryside as an adjunct to farming and that demanded substantially less expertise than did the urban crafts.[104] Perhaps even more important, recent findings increasingly underscore the folly of idealizing conditions or overlooking tensions in the preindustrial artisanal workshops themselves. Those findings are accentuating, and uncovering new instances of, unrest among skilled journeymen in the late eighteenth century, and they are also placing this unrest in the context of the swelling labor pools, mercantile capitalist innovations, and other disruptive social developments that were to accelerate and become far more pronounced over the course of time, and upon which nineteenth century industrialization was to build.[105]

But with these cautionary provisos firmly in mind, one can still conclude that many of the American artisanal workshops of the late eighteenth and early nineteenth centuries did produce highly skilled, custom work, reflecting the collaborative effort of master craftsmen, journeymen, and apprentices working with hand tools.[106] To a considerable extent, such workshops continued to exemplify the centuries-old informal educational process of "learning by doing," wherein the master craftsmen's function as teacher frequently obscured his other identity as owner of the means of production. As Karl Marx described this traditional role of the master craftsmen: "Within the process of production he appears as an artisan, like his journeymen, and it is he who initiates his apprentices into the mysteries of the craft. He has precisely the same relationship to his apprentices as a professor to his students."[107]

To the extent that any segment of manual labor employments was free of the stigmas attached to physical work, it was the skilled artisanal trades.[108] In this particular instance, labor in America was in fact less exceptional than that in Britain, where the legacy of the medieval guilds and corporate crafts, with their body of regulations and qualifications restricting entry into the trades, helped create a more assertive and entrenched "labor aristocracy" than existed anytime in America.[109] But the handicraft products of American workshops, scarcely less than those of Britain, reflected a pride in craftsmanship and exhibited at their best a trained and experienced mastery of physical movements that drew considerably upon the creative and mental resources of the craftsmen. With regard to these skilled artisanal trades particularly, the *Fall River News* had cause to assert that "there are many branches of manufacture and other kinds of labor, that require quite as much brain-power as some of the professions; and why should they not be equally honored?"[110]

American urban industrialization left a portion of these skilled trades relatively intact, and in fact created some new ones; but the general deterioration of the craft structure, beginning in the latter part of the eighteenth century, was marked by a "skill dilution" in the production process that implied a marked loss in the intellectual component of that process.[111] Northeastern agricultural labor lacked mental content because it had not sufficiently changed from what farming had traditionally been. Urban manufacturing labor in the large northeastern cities was largely deprived of its intellectual and creative dimension by a complex series of changes, occurring at different rates in different trades, that have been well described by a number of scholars. Foremost among these changes was the great expansion in the market for manufacturing goods and the actions taken by merchant capitalist entrepreneurs and master craftsmen to meet and capitalize on the increased demand by introducing a variety of new production techniques in their trades, all of which contributed to the minute division and deskilling of labor. The cumulative impact of these changes on work content was such that by 1860, occupations designated in the census and elsewhere as "journeyman cordwainer" or "master printer" bore little similarity to the jobs that carried the same terminology in 1820.[112]

With their skills devalued and their role in the manufacturing process increasingly restricted over time, journeymen were among the most obvious victims of the new techniques; disappearing was a work structure that had once provided them with the satisfactions of extensive training and participation in the creation of an entire product and the freedom to largely set their own work pace. Contrary to the general, more unambiguous deskilling tendency, there must have remained artisanal workshops where the division of labor actually operated to increase skill within restricted spheres of activity.[113] But the workers in such shops and factories were frequently not seasoned journeymen with entrenched skills but rather less experienced workers, often children, whom industrial entrepreneurs considered more receptive both to acquiring the newer, more specialized expertise and to conforming to pronounced surveillance and industrial work discipline. For journeymen, deskilling meant reduced autonomy in the work process, an autonomy which had itself provided intellectual satisfaction; but because deskilling in a trade also meant diminishing opportunity to participate in creating a whole product, journeymen's loss of intellectual involvement in the work process was compounded.[114]

Skilled journeymen indirectly acknowledged the loss of the intellectual content or "meaning" in their work when they spoke of declining work standards in their trades or participated in labor organizations that pushed for "equal rights" to education, although the precise economic value, if any, that journeymen attached to education remains somewhat unclear.[115] Yet as noted earlier with reference to wage-earning labor in general, journeymen did not explicitly conceptualize the erosion in their position as above all a loss of creative or intellectual satisfactions. In part this may be attributable to the incremental and gradual nature of the skill dilution process and to the possibility that many journeymen did not persist in their jobs long enough to experience its total effect over time.[116] More decisive, in all likelihood, were the immediate pressures to earn a living, together with the journeymen's diminishing prospect of becoming independent, self-employed craftsmen in an "honorable" trade; both circumstances may have simply eclipsed or obscured their concern with the intrinsic "meaning" of their work.[117] In any case, disgruntled journeymen expressed their loss as preeminently a decline in living standards, in economic power, and in general societal esteem for their labor; and they directed their criticism against three discrete parties whom they held primarily responsible for their eroding position: (1) the merchants and bankers who created systems of "unequal exchange" and who frequently used these to finance the new production processes in the trades; (2) the master craftsmen who in yielding to, when they were not themselves primarily responsible for, the introduction of these new processes forsook the roles of both coworker and good employer to the journeymen; and (3) the unskilled labor pool of women, children, and immigrants, whose entry into the trades as "slop workers" and "outworkers" had been made possible by the new processes and who exerted a relentless downward pull on the wages of the skilled journeymen.[118]

3

Division of Labor and Mechanization in Factories Pressures to Redefine Intelligent Manual Labor

As with antebellum protestations of the nobility of farming, the contemporary sense of the dignity of preindustrial craftsmanship, including its mental and creative content, was stimulated by an awareness of the changes assaulting it; the disintegration of the craft structure is one of the great themes of nineteenth-century intellectuals like John Ruskin.[1] A less well known case in point was a lecture by the Louisiana politician, novelist, and historian Charles Gayarré, delivered before the Mechanics' Institute of New Orleans and subsequently published in the 1854 volume of *De Bow's Review.* In contrast to writers like Timothy Walker who damned manual labor because they regarded it as mindless, Gayarré insisted that down through the ages the least skilled of the mechanic arts, even the rudest and most repetitive physical work, had allowed for the development of the laborer's mental faculties, and that this circumstance was actually the mainspring of technological progress and invention:

> How do we know that the individual who is heaving up the hammer, or driving the plane on a common board, and pursuing an occupation so humble that it is apparently unconnected with any

exercise of the mind, is not theorizing about it, without perhaps being aware himself of the mental process he applies to his manual labor, and by which he may suddenly strike out some wonderful improvement, by chance, as it is commonly said, or seemingly, by a flash of inspiration? How do we know, when we only see bodily fatigue pearling out into drops on his bent brow, and exhaustion thickening his panting breath, that, whilst his arms work, he is not weaving comparisons, pursuing a train of deductions and inductions, discovering connections between particular operations, and lifting up his foot to step beyond the line of mere habit?[2]

That Gayarré romanticized and idealized physical labor is not at issue; of greater relevance was his subsequent argument that the intellectual stimulus provided by the traditional mechanic arts could be truly appreciated by invoking comparison with that recent development in civilization, the ominous and spreading division of labor in manufactures. In "countries thinly peopled," Gayarré observed, "it is not uncommon to see the same man engaged in various arts or operations." There

the Mechanic Arts are a blessing, for they sharpen the intellect, and the labor which they impose on man is sufficiently remunerated to enable him to satisfy his wants. But, in populous countries, where the simplest art is split into parts—where, for instance, an incredible number of hands are employed in the single operation of making a needle—it is evident that this distribution of labor secures the rapidity, the cheapness, and the perfection of the production, but the wages of each operative are barely sufficient to enable him to keep up the breath of life in an emaciated and sickly body frame; and the mind, confining its attention to a single object, shrinks gradually into so contracted a space as to leave no room for thought or invention; and we may easily understand how a man of the most splendid intellect, who, for the sake of procuring scanty morsels of bread for himself and family, should consent for years to do nothing else than roll a pack of thread round his index, would turn out to be an idiot at the end of his probation.[3]

Of concern here is not the overpopulation and impoverishment to which Gayarré attributed the growing division of labor in manufactures, but rather his understanding of the repetitive and constricting character of the process and the unprecedented intellectual damage it inflicted on the laboring population. It was not merely a case of manual labor bereft of significant mental content; the laboring process itself, in Gayarré's view, systematically attacked and destroyed the native intellectual capacity of the "operative."

THE DELETERIOUS EFFECTS OF
DIVISION OF LABOR

It was hardly coincidental that Gayarré's description of the intellectually deleterious effects of manufacturing division of labor corresponded to the one appearing in a 1836 Massachusetts House report, quoted in chapter 2 in the discussion of farming. Since the time of Adam Ferguson's and Adam Smith's writing, perhaps no economic idea with a direct bearing on the laboring population, with the exception of Malthus's doctrine of overpopulation, came to surpass in influence the theme of the narrowing and deadening impact of division of labor on the manufacturing worker's mind. Smith's contribution was particularly well known.[4] In Book One of *The Wealth of Nations,* published in 1776, Smith illustrated through his example of an unmechanized pin-making manufactory the effect of the division of labor in increasing the dexterity and efficiency of workers and thereby contributing to the economic growth of society.[5] But in Book Five of his treatise, in what some scholars have regarded as virtually an afterthought, Smith made his oft-quoted statement of the additional, more insidious impact of the division of labor on the intellectual or cognitive faculties of manufacturing workers:

> In the progress of the division of labour, the employment of the far greater part of those who love by labour, that is, of the great body of the people, comes to be confined to a very few simple operations, frequently to one or two. But the understandings of the greater part of men are necessarily formed by their ordinary employments. The man whose whole life is spent in performing a few simple operations, . . . has no occasion to exert his understanding, . . . He . . . generally becomes as stupid and ignorant as it is possible for a human creature to become.[6]

Smith may have done little more than articulate a theme that was already present in economic works of the eighteenth century; and the Scottish economist himself was writing in response to a division of labor and a "trivialization of work" that had been occurring over the course of three centuries, long before the appearance of any factories. As Melvin Dubofsky has reminded us, "The commercial revolution of the fifteenth and sixteenth centuries, with its widening of markets and the impetus given to capitalist forms of production, led employers to combine laborers in workshop settings, to subdivide tasks, and undermine the skill of artisans."[7]

But *The Wealth of Nations* nonetheless decisively popularized a theme that became part of the intellectual baggage of the educated classes of the mid-nineteenth century.[8] In one of his series of lectures before an audience of mechanics' apprentices, William Ellery Channing warned that "the division of labour, which distinguishes civilized from savage life, and to which we owe chiefly the perfection of the arts, tends to dwarf the intellectual powers, by confining the activity of the individual to a narrow range, to a few details, perhaps to the heading of pins, the pointing of nails, or the tying together of broken strings; so that while the savage has his faculties sharpened by various occupations . . . the civilized man treads a monotonous, stupefying round of unthinking toil."[9] And in France's Chamber of Peers, Baron Joseph-Marie de Gérando alike referred to Smith's pin-making example and went on to claim an important distinction between "an apprenticed child and an "operative [factory] child": the former

> is in a course of instruction; . . . his faculties are exercised in a variety of ways; he learns the elements of a process, and by and by he becomes more skilful [*sic*]: in short, he learns a trade. With the operative child it is very different. . . . A child, that has passed ten years of his life as a piercer [*sic*] in a spinning-mill, will have learned nothing; he will only have acquired the power of doing that which might be performed by a brute, for a tolerably docile ape might be taught to do as much.[10]

It carried great significance that it was an instance of mechanized factory labor which prompted Gérando's affirmation of Smith's theme—his distinction between cultivation of the mental faculties and the acquisition of a narrow, virtually mindless dexterity in one task alone. Gayarré's discussion of the division of labor was, like Gérando's, inspired specifically by "the operatives in manufacturing districts which are celebrated all over the world."[11] The onset of water- and steam-powered mechanization of factories since the time that *The Wealth of Nations* made its appearance served to dramatize and reinforce for these particular writers the relevance of Smith's theme of the intellectually deleterious effects of the division of labor. Overall, however, mechanized factory labor, and especially its occurrence within the context of a capitalist "factory system," had the effect of greatly complicating contemporary perceptions of Smith's theme. We need to carefully sort out these perceptions because they were of critical importance to the ongoing attempts to include significant intellectual activity as a basic criterion of dignified free manual labor. The intellectual, as well as the moral and physical, condition of adult and child factory workers captured American and British public interest and fueled the general apprehension, to a degree that the plight of outworkers, slop workers, and skilled journey-men in the debased artisanal trades never did.[12] As the cutting edge and symbol of technological change, the cotton textile industry especially played a role in contemporary discussions that was out of all proportion to its economic representativeness; Manchester, England, and Lowell, Massachusetts, became the "shock cities" of their respective nation's early industrial development.[13] Some of the definitions of intelligent free labor came to terms with and even celebrated mechanized factory work, just as others resisted and rejected accommodation with it; but most nonetheless took it into account in one fashion or another. As at least all of these definitions suggested, arguments concerning the prevalence of intelligent, dignified free manual labor in the northeastern states could not easily be waged solely with reference to work in farming and the skilled crafts; factory labor and the factory system constituted too conspicuous and troubling a presence to be generally ignored.

Before exploring attempts to defend or reject mechanized factory work on intellectual grounds, we might provide some context to these discussions by situating them in relation to those other arguments emphasizing either the physical or the "moral" evils of the factory system.[14] Between these two other categories of arguments, the claims which drew on Smith's insight would seem to occupy a middle ground of hazy, indeterminate plausibility.[15] The physical hazards confronting factory hands, particularly in England but also in America—hazards which included bodily deformities and injuries arising from repetitive motions and constrained positions maintained for long periods, injuries and deaths inflicted by unfenced machinery, disease and sheer exhaustion resulting from many hours of work in poorly ventilated, confined spaces—are without question verifiable.[16] This would appear to be true even if the precise magnitude of the physical toll remains controversial because it varied from mill to mill and waxed and waned from one decade to another. Nor is the existence of the factory system's physical hazards rendered more doubtful by the possibility that they may have actually been no "worse" either than the less conspicuous "silent suffering" endured by contemporaneous agricultural laborers and outworkers in the sweated trades, or the physical hardships experienced by earlier generations of workers in the so-called Golden Age of domestic manufactures.[17]

Allegations regarding the moral evils of the factory system, by contrast, provoke greater skepticism; and some of these claims, such as those attesting to the sexual precocity and promiscuity stimulated in child operatives by high mill temperatures, now seem frankly preposterous.[18] Whatever their empirical validity, other themes in this category of evils, including the "mixing" of the sexes in the mill rooms and the undermining of feminine domestic skills by female employment in factories, no longer strike us as particular evils at all, but rather an expression of distinctly, if not exclusively, Victorian middle-class social values.[19] They may, in addition, have been a manifestation of the fears of adult male laborers that both their authority within the working-class family and their economic supremacy within the labor market were being threatened by a system that gave independent employment to heretofore subordinate family members.[20]

That mechanized factory work was mentally pernicious, acting to deaden the minds of operatives, as Gayarré and others claimed, appears, on the other hand, far more difficult to either confirm or dismiss; and there is some suggestive evidence on either side of this question. Both contemporaries and scholars have noted, with regard to the first generation of native New England mill girls, that economic conditions minimized the possibility that they would be locked into the "continuous monotony" of factory labor. Mill girls frequently alternated employment in the factories with teaching and other work over the course of a year.[21] More significantly, they were distinguished, indeed world renowned, among all factory populations for the short length of their total tenure in the mills. Observers marvelled how these young women, far from being a class permanently entrapped in factory labor, instead passed through the mills as a prelude to marriage and other life experiences.[22] Factory proprietors and managers themselves welcomed and endorsed such favorable assessment of their enterprises; the decision to make young single women the core of the labor force had indeed been partially dictated by the determination of the Boston Associates to avoid the problems of a "permanent" factory population that had scandalized the British system. Yet proprietors and managers also complained chronically of the problems created by the constant labor turnover; they were forever being obliged to replace and train a new "succession of learners."[23]

Quite aside from the special facility enjoyed by New England mill girls to leave factory work altogether, mechanized factory jobs in the early factory system encompassed a fairly wide range of skill requirements and mental demands. Notwithstanding a common tendency of observers, both past and present, to merge or homogenize all factory jobs into a vague image of "mechanized, routinized factory work," only some of these jobs may have constituted mechanized drudgery. The term *semiskilled labor,* introduced by scholars to categorize factory work and locate it on the blue-collar skill spectrum between skilled artisanal labor and unskilled casual and drudge work, would therefore seem misleadingly all-inclusive.[24] The parish apprentice children who operated the primitive frames in the early British water-powered mills, to take a dramatic example, clearly experienced factory labor in a different sense than did highly skilled adult male mule spinners two decades later. On a more general level, the operatives employed in mills devoted to the production of coarse cotton fabric experienced different conditions than those who tended machinery in fine cotton cloth mills, and these in turn were faced with different work challenges than those confronting factory hands in woolen or carpet weaving factories.[25]

Within a single New England mill of the so-called Waltham system type, to push the point still further, the various departments through which the cotton passed—spinning, weaving, drawing, and so on—all required somewhat different levels of training and experience; a job hierarchy was established by which those women who did remain in the mills long enough might, within certain limitations of sex discrimination, gradually move up the job ladder, from one department to another.[26] The mill structure itself, in other words, reflected to a certain point the traditional fluidity of American employment patterns, by which, in the opinion of many observers, American workers could engage in "free occupations" and avoid being confined "to the head of a pin" for life.[27]

The story of the early factory system, in Britain as in America, was largely one of the continuous introduction of new technology that just as continuously altered the skill requirements and intellectual demands of particular processes. Each innovation shifted the relative advantages held by children, unskilled women, and skilled and unskilled men as contributing segments of the labor force. The effect of particular factory machinery in placing segments of the laboring population in comparative disadvantage with one other is beyond the province of this study, as are the complex of factors that prompted factory proprietors to introduce the new technology—factors that included the incentive to minimize labor costs, the pressure to conform to regulatory factory legislation, and the urge to reduce dependence on elements of the labor force particularly resistant to factory authority and the work regimen. Of greater relevance here is that the state of flux created by the stream of technological innovation meant that a particular component of the labor force might not be locked into the same kind of mechanized drudgery indefinitely. This may have represented a slightly redeeming feature of technological unemployment and its attendant economic distress, especially for those *unskilled* machine tenders who were displaced and forced to reenter the job market with no marketable skills. By the time Mrs. Trollope published her story of the suffering of Michael Armstrong, "the factory boy," in 1840, the English system of parish apprentice factory labor, which had been the most consummate expression of the exploitation of child operatives, had virtually disappeared, a circumstance that had as much to do with the system's technological obsolescence as with hostile factory legislation.[28] What occupational fluidity and opportunities for social mobility facilitated in America especially, technological change tended to encourage in the transatlantic textile industry generally: a limitation upon prolonged entrapment in any one kind of intellectually stultifying factory task.

However, some evidence also suggests that the mechanization of factory labor may have rendered Smith's thesis more than a groundless abstraction. Training in the preindustrial skilled handicrafts might not have necessarily stimulated the development of a broad intelligence; but the mastery of specialized tasks by unskilled laborers in the early stages of industrialization especially, did appear to promote a narrow intelligence. When Samuel Colt related to a committee of the House of Commons his experience in employing workers at his London arms factory, he observed that "the more ignorant a man was, the more brains he had for my purpose." Colt maintained that he got better productivity from "raw material"—from workers who at the time of their employment had little or no previous knowledge of arms manufacturing processes.[29] Granted, Colt's remarks display a certain ambiguity. His objective may well have been not to point up the mentally undemanding character of factory labor per se but rather to underscore the point that factory labor merely favored those workers who had the fewest old skills to unlearn. Yet it also seems clear that Colt, in common with other factory proprietors, looked only to develop a narrow, if well-defined, dexterity in his operatives, and that he believed, furthermore, that there was a natural association between this narrow dexterity and a welcome disinclination on the part of the worker to think and act independently. Factory proprietors like Colt demanded efficiency and docility in their operatives, but hardly a broader experience and intelligence that might encourage a spirit of independence and resistance to the industrial work discipline they sought. Herein lay the appeal of younger children as factory hands; despite limitations in their attention span, they represented the ideal "empty vessel" sought by Colt and other factory proprietors. Aside from the ease with which they might acquire their narrow expertise, they were far more unlikely than skilled craftsmen either to drink or "loaf" on the job, or to strike out in more "troublesome" and "radical" ways against working conditions.[30] When to all of these considerations is added the fact that child operatives could be paid lower wages than adult workers, one should perhaps find unsurprising Michael Sanderson's discovery that early industrialization in Britain stimulated the demand for an uneducated, largely child labor force and had a negative impact upon literacy rates is hardly surprising. Both these circumstances in turn reflected the minimal mental content of the new employments: "Many of the new occupations were sub-literate and certainly less literate than most preexisting craft occupations. . . . The very process of industrialization was creating a vast number and wide range of jobs that could be performed by sub-literate labour; indeed, in the specific case of weaving, it actually substituted, by machinery, lower levels of literacy than those required and possessed by hand workers."[31]

Lecturing before the Young Men's Association of Albany in 1841, the Reverend E. D. Allen took issue with those labor reform platforms that bemoaned the inferior opportunities for intellectual improvement available to workingmen. Like others of his persuasion, Allen invoked the well-known scholarly proclivities and achievements of Elihu Burritt, the "learned blacksmith," to demonstrate that other mechanics could have no excuse for their "mental indolence"; the avenue to "mental improvement" was not closed to them, even though they might experience obstacles not faced by members of the professional and business classes. The *New York State Mechanic* agreed with Allen, noting that "a thousand examples" suggest "that the most mechanical occupations are favorable to the development of the mind and its godlike powers; habits of close thinking are acquired."[32]

One measure of the influence of factory labor and the factory system on the public consciousness was that those who sought to defend them without abandoning the notion of an intelligent and educated working class frequently felt impelled to argue, in complete contrast to the *New York State Mechanic,* that the very mindlessness of manual work might constitute a source of intellectual stimulus. The British classical economist John Ramsay McCulloch took issue with the dour conclusion Adam Smith had drawn from the monotony characterizing subdivided manufacturing tasks. Far from being made "stupid" by the monotony, McCulloch claimed, manufacturing operatives

> are thus driven to seek for recreation in mental excitement; and the circumstances under which they are placed afford them every possible facility for gratifying themselves in this manner. By working together in considerable numbers, they have constant opportunities of discussing every topic of interest or importance. They are thus gradually trained to habits of thinking and reflection: their intellects are sharpened by the collision of conflicting opinions. . . . The intelligence of the workmen employed in manufactures and commerce has increased according as their numbers have increased, and as their employments have been more and more subdivided.[33]

McCulloch's revision of Smith was cited and affirmed on the floors of Congress by a number of Whig legislators who frequently benefited from strong political ties with state manufacturing interests but who were in any case ideologically committed to defending the protective tariff and factory enterprises from Democratic assault. In a virtual echo of McCulloch, Rufus

Choate, the Massachusetts Senator, argued that factory workers and other urban manufacturing workers were "driven by the craving for stimulus which the monotony of their employments, their own mental activity, and all the influences about them, are so well calculated to produce; driven to the search of some external objects of interest, they find these in conversation, in discussion, in reading newspapers and books, in all the topics which agitate the crowded community of which they are part; and thus they become curious, flexible, quick, progressive."[34]

One might be tempted to dismiss such defenses of factory labor as the strained rationalizations of intellectuals who had never set a foot inside a mill. Yet we should also note that operatives themselves, at least some of those intent on refuting claims that their employment was degrading, made recourse to the same argument. One of the articles in the *Lowell Offering*, which was "Written, Edited, and Published by Female Operatives Employed in the Mills," conceded that "too large a portion of our time is confined to labor," but it then went on to say that "a factory girl's work is neither hard or [*sic*] complicated; she may go on with perfect regularity in her duties, while her mind may be actively employed on any other subject. There can be no better place for reflection, when there must be toil, than the factory."[35] Surveys of twentieth-century factory workers, it might be added, have indicated that some workers in fact value peer relationships more than intellectual challenge in their work, and that they accordingly prefer mentally undemanding labor in order to more easily engage in meaningful interpersonal relationships on the job.[36]

McCulloch, Choate, and others who made an intellectual virtue out of the monotony of factory labor were actually defending new processes of labor by invoking a very old argument; medieval monks had partially justified their menial labor by suggesting that its very want of mental demands permitted them the luxury of contemplation.[37] Proponents of the factory system, however, also developed an argument with a more modern twist, one which made important use of the factor of machinery itself. Smith may well have been correct about the intellectually deadening effects of repetitive and monotonous unmechanized manufacturing division of labor; in industries not aided by machinery, as one such British factory proponent, William Cooke Taylor claimed, tasks were relentless "for in them the man becomes the machine."[38] But "the progressive degradation of the operative" had been halted, and Smith's warnings rendered outdated, by the entrance of machinery into modern industry.[39] The key figure in developing this theme was Andrew Ure, a professor of chemistry at the University of Glasgow before he moved to London in 1830. Impressed with the "self-acting" machines then coming into prominence in the cotton textile mills of Lancashire, Ure concluded that the modern operative

may find many leisure moments for either amusement or medita-
tion, without detriment to his master's interests or his own. As his
business consists in tending the work of a well-regulated mechanism, he can learn it in a short period; and when he transfers his
services from one machine to another, he varies his task, and
enlarges his views, by thinking on those general combinations
which result from his and his companions' labours. Thus, that
cramping of the faculties, that narrowing of the mind, that stunting of the frame, which were ascribed, and not unjustly, by moral
writers, to the division of labour, cannot, in common circumstances, occur under the equable distribution of industry.[40]

Ure invested factory machinery with a positive cognitive or educational function, while also suggesting that it freed operatives to indulge in
"amusement." In both respects, machinery was the antidote to, the vehicle
of escape from, the monotony imposed by manufacturing division of labor.
Use of the notion that manufacturing workers required such a vehicle to
achieve escape from monotony constituted the sense in which Ure's defense
of the factory system went beyond that of McCulloch and others. His
emphasis upon the undemanding, almost recreational side of machine-
tending achieved greater fame, or notoriety, than his inclusion of an educational role; mechanized mills, he contended, would be increasingly dependent on the low-cost labor of "lively elves"—children—who playfully
moved from one machine to another.[41] The suitability of children for such
work, William Cooke Taylor added, doomed trade union efforts to create
demand for more expensive adult male operatives by abolishing child
factory labor through Parliamentary legislation; factory proprietors would
simply not pay for "skill, strength and intelligence to perform tasks in which
these qualities are not necessary."[42]

Other proponents of the factory system embraced the ideas of Ure and
Taylor but more sharply emphasized the serious educational side of machinery for operatives. The Whig representative from Vermont, George
Perkins Marsh, in fact turned the common anti-industrial imagery on its
head, maintaining that the standard criticisms of factory labor had greater
applicability for traditional preindustrial work:

A man trained to a simple handicraft, or even to the routine of
agriculture, which, as too often practised, is but a series of operations repeated unwaveringly from generation to generation, until
the reasons of them have been forgotten, sometimes degenerates
to a mere machine; but the complicated engines which fill our
factories can neither be constructed nor operated without some
knowledge of their principles. The laborers in these establish-

ments are, therefore, to some extent, obliged to be acquainted with scientific truth. . . . The very children in a factory often show a readiness in comprehending mechanical combinations, that might put to shame many a scientific lecturer.[43]

Marsh would appear to be a case where a polemical defense of factory work and the factory system derived from a genuinely personal and intense interest in all things scientific and mechanical.[44] But regardless of whether or not similar defenses were more typically an expression of relatively disinterested ideological commitment than they were of more blatant political or economic opportunism, they could nonetheless take rather extreme forms.[45] Admirers of the factory system even made use of one of its more ominous features, its physical hazards, in promoting the positive cognitive function of machinery. Hepworth Dixon described with wonder the education provided the "raw" farm lad who came to Manchester to work the looms. In a short time, Dixon observed, "his dull perceptions will have been quickened; his stolid face will be informed with thought. . . . The reasons for the change are obvious. The loom is dangerous. Without perpetual care and attention—without *constant presence of mind,* the attendant may be struck—the infliction may even be serious. The man is forced to become watchful, in self-defence. The mental tension, so required, is at first painful, but soon grows habitual."[46]

What all the foregoing defenses of the factory system shared was the argument that craft skill in the traditional sense of extensive training and experience had found a legitimate intellectual counterpart in the mills. Somewhere and somehow factories provided a mechanism by which workers could engage their minds; where the defenses differed was in the nature of the mechanism. The arguments of McCulloch and Choate, while aiming to discredit Smith's warnings about the intellectually narrowing effects of manufacturing division of labor, had another target as well. They sought to discredit a dominant criticism of machine-tending that work of a physically "unlaborious" nature by the standards of many traditional unskilled employments was paradoxically capable of generating so much fatigue in its performers. Opponents of the factory system commonly invoked by way of partial explanation for the paradox the physical "delicacy" of the children and females who were "harnessed" to machinery for long hours in the mills.[47] But a basic aspect of the criticism as well was the theme that factory labor, although requiring nothing in the way of meaningful thought, did in fact demand "close and steady attention" and was thus enormously tedious and fatiguing. The peculiar quality of factory labor was that it was sufficiently repetitive and undemanding to be boring, but not so undemanding that the operative could block it out. The *Fall River Mechanic* initiated an attack on New England factory conditions by observing that "A system of labor that demands the constant and undivided attention of those engaged in it—that destroys every intelligent inclination" is "the propagator of ignorance."[48] Disenchantment with factory labor and with, specifically, its modern incarnation, the assembly line, has persisted along the same lines into the twentieth century, voiced by intellectuals if not necessarily shared by factory hands themselves. Robert Blauner has observed that "the most unsatisfactory situation seems to be the job which is not intrinsically interesting and yet requires rather constant attention"; and her own limited personal experience working in factories outside of Paris in the 1930s led the writer Simone Weil to conclude that the most signal characteristic of factory work was the "exhausting passivity" it demanded from operatives.[49]

In refuting this line of criticism, McCulloch and Choate downplayed the degree of attentiveness required by operatives; factory hands were free to ponder weighty matters because their work was mentally untaxing. But in this respect they differed implicitly from proponents like Marsh and Dixon, who in addressing the same kind of factory tasks at Manchester and elsewhere placed much more stress on the operative's need for alertness and concentration on his work. In regarding machine tending itself as a source of intellectual stimulation and mental discipline, rather than as an activity of exhausting tedium, Marsh and others, of course, differed even more significantly from the critics of the factory system than they did from writers like McCulloch who followed their own somewhat different line in defense of factory labor. Some writers intent on disproving the argument that "the degradation of the operative must be the inevitable result of modern industry" were not above using both kinds of profactory arguments, however contradictory they might seem to be.[50]

The intellectual dimension of the factory labor issue—the mental qualities machine tending called for and the mental effects it had upon the operative—would appear to involve a morass of contradictions. Perhaps one of the primary reasons lay, again, in the varied and changing nature of factory technology itself. David Jeremy has suggested that the introduction of equipment with maximum automaticity and stop-motion devices into the Waltham-type cotton mills "lowered the levels of skill, mental alertness, and physical hazard involved in machine minding. . . . Only in dresser tending did the work remain onerous, because it required prolonged and concentrated attention to the sized warp yarns to check that none broke."[51] Additions to factory technology at Lowell appear by the 1860s to have so reduced the complexity and skill requirements of machine tending as to permit child laborers to assume a role there of comparable importance to their traditional role in the alternative "family system" mills.[52]

Different technology, which varied the skill requirements and intellectual characteristics of factory work, could prove fertile ground for confusion and controversy regarding those requirements and characteristics. But even more significantly, conflicting perceptions were perhaps rendered inevitable by the fact that the technology never operated in a vacuum but within a total system where important variables such as the level of work intensity could fluctuate independently of the particular technology in a mill. The whole point of technological innovation and the increased automaticity to which it was directed was, from the point of view of the textile factory proprietors, to increase the operators' productive capabilities. Any diminution in the mentally draining and relentless character of machine tending that Lowell girls might have experienced from increased automaticity was obviated in the 1840s by the pressures of a general "speed-up" and increased work load that were made possible by the same automaticity.[53]

The severest critics of the factory system, to whom its physical evils seemed so glaring, tended in particular to view the intellectual characteristics of machine tending in the context of the total system. Those characteristics—factory labor's mental content—were part and parcel of the oppressive working conditions, including the surveillance and regimen of "clock time," which capitalist authority imposed on a population of economically vulnerable "hireling" laborers.[54] The proceedings of the National Trades' Union Convention, held in New York in 1834, recorded the following remarks of Pennsylvania delegate John Ferral regarding "the condition of females in manufacturing establishments":

> Mr. F. regarded the factory system which had been introduced as subversive of liberty—as calculated to change the character of a people from that of a bold and free, to one enervated, dependent, and slavish. Any one familiar with our factories must regard them as contagious gaols, where the dependent inmates are confined in a state of servile slavery, and in impure air; where their physical powers necessarily become enfeebled, and their mental energies wasted and enervated. Even were health maintained, how is it possible for the mind to expand and improve, which is engaged from 14 to 16 hours a per day in watching a few threads, or the moving of a shuttle? All their waking hours are thus occupied; and what if they spend eight, ten or fifteen years in this way? The longer they exist, the more contracted must their minds become.[55]

We should recognize a basic distinction between anti-industrial and anticapitalist blueprints for reform—between those which viewed machine-based industry and factory labor as intrinsically injurious and degrading, and those which held that worker ownership or control of machinery would usher in radically new working conditions under which mechanized factory labor might be redeemed and "labor-saving" technology freed to realize its true value of benefiting the masses.[56] Our concern here, however, is not with detailing any of these alternative social arrangements, but with further delineating the impact that existing factory labor had upon attempts to define an intellectual criterion for dignified manual labor. As has already been suggested, a circle of proindustrial polemicists found mechanized factory labor quite comparable to the traditional skilled mechanic arts in the magnitude of the intellectual stimulus it offered workers. Such a viewpoint found little support among other writers and intellectuals to whom mechanization appeared to extend and exacerbate the assault on the factory worker's mental faculties that had been initiated by manufacturing division of labor. This continuity of intellectual degradation was summarized in an essay in the *North American Review* for 1852 entitled "The Future of Labor," written by Andrew Preston Peabody, the Unitarian clergyman and author from Massachusetts: "The minute subdivision of labor has a direct tendency to dwarf the intellect. A man is less of a man in intelligence, skill, range of ideas, and scope of activity, when he makes a twentieth part of a pin, than if he made the whole pin,—when he merely watches a spindle or mends a web, than if he took the wool or cotton home, and brought the finished cloth to market. Improvements in machinery tend to make the operative less and less an intelligent agent, and more and more a machine."[57]

It is impossible to know whether American commentators like Peabody simply drew on Adam Smith to support independently drawn observations of factory work or whether the views of the Scottish economist and of like-minded influential thinkers served more basically as a prism through which these commentators looked and upon which they were actually dependent in forming their perceptions of factory labor. In any case Smith's theme, together with the idea of the deadening monotony of machine labor, achieved something of the status of a cliché. Quite possibly many writers who felt no intense vested interest in the matter were simply following the course of least resistance by paying homage to it; mere verbal advocacy of Smith's warning may have defined for such writers the extent of their commitment to elevating the condition of the growing population of manufacturing laborers.[58] But for middle-class intellectuals who played a more active role in American labor reform movements, mechanized division of labor in factories dramatically epitomized manual labor's loss of significant mental content. The division between manual and intellectual labor, which found its most systematic description in the early writings of Marx in his analysis of the factory proletarian's "self-estrangement," was observed and criticized as well by a range of Americans intent on social reorganization of one form or another.[59] Orestes Brownson wrote that "the only division of labor to which I object, is that which assigns the head-work to one part of the community, and the hand-work to another. Since man is both soul and body, I would have no division of body-work and soul-work."[60] To remove this division was, as George Ripley noted, one of the primary goals of the Brook Farm community he was instrumental in establishing: "Our objects," he wrote to Ralph Waldo Emerson, "are to ensure a more natural union between intellectual and manual labor than now exists; to combine the thinker and the worker, as far as possible, in the same individual."[61]

British and American Owenite socialists also envisioned their cooperative communities as "combining in the same individual the producer, and the possessor of wealth, the communicator and the recipient of knowledge, the governor and the governed, to destroy the invidious distinctions that have split up the one great family of man into sections and classes."[62] Giving expression, albeit in more indirect form, to the same goal were perhaps the antebellum period's best exemplifiers of the "small producer" ideology: the workingmen's parties of the late 1820s and 1830s and the Land Reform movement of the 1840s. The union of capital and labor in the same person, on the order of master craftsmen and freehold farmers, subsumed the allied ideal of integrating manual and mental activity in the same employment. The condition of permanent wage-earning status represented the negation of both kinds of union; and this condition was abhorred by the small producer ideology in large part because the hireling's prolonged reliance on employment by others generated a lack of control over the quality and content of his labor.[63]

A number of historians have observed that the "utopian" and "arcadian" character of various antebellum labor reform movements reflected an assumption that industrial changes were still reversible at this point in time. They regarded the United States, in part because of the extent of its unsettled territory, as a relative tabula rasa, where undesirable institutions had not yet so entrenched themselves that they could not be replaced with radically different social arrangements.[64] When middle-class labor reformers spoke of the division between physical and mental labor, and the intellectual declension from the skilled mechanic arts that this division entailed, they were, in any case, addressing themselves to the totality of these industrial changes; they were responding not only to the notorious intellectual hazards posed by mechanized labor within the factory system, but to deterioration in the skilled craft structure. Labor reformers in fact often regarded the two developments as related. A writer in the *Chronotype*, one of the leading promoters of the principles of American Fourierism, observed of the mills at Lowell:

> Is that just, a Christian organization of labor in which thousands
> of young women, remote from their friends and all domestic
> influences, are compelled to work for some thirteen hours a day at
> a monotonous employment, standing on their feet till their ankles

become swollen, with the ceaseless jar of machinery deafening their ears, in an atmosphere made unwholesome by heat and the filaments of cotton. . . . And let it be borne in mind that this organization of labor by capitalists, for their own benefit alone, is rapidly extending to all branches of manufactures and must soon absorb them all, driving entirely out of employment the small workmen who labor on their own account, for the reason that, these great cos. can produce so much cheaper.[65]

Not the least because it appeared to drain manual labor employments of their mental content, industrial change threatened, from the radical labor reform perspective, to solidify the centuries-old division within societies between the class that did the thinking and governing and the class that did the working. From this perspective, the artisans in the deteriorating crafts whose skills were suffering erosion were no less exposed to debasement and subjugation than the young farm women or children who, without any significant expertise, had entered the labor market for the first time as factory operatives. The members of society to whom preindustrial casual labor and drudge work had traditionally fallen—society's erstwhile "hewers of wood and drawers of water"—had always borne an association with ignorance, even mindlessness, as well as the stigmas of their hard labor's pain and poverty.[66] What Catharine E. Beecher observed about housework might have been said of "menial" and "rude" labor as a whole: "It is because such work has generally been done by vulgar people, in a vulgar way, that we have such [degrading] associations."[67] Horace Greeley noted: "We believe that one great cause of the evils of society has been the contempt for manual labor; that it is not owing to the native repulsiveness of such labor that it has not been esteemed, but to the crude and inferior mode of conducting it, and the want of education among laborers."[68] And S. Flint, Jr. argued in the abolitionist and labor reform paper, the *Herald of Freedom,* that "the false notions of labor," which regarded handwork as incompatible with intellectual activity, explained as much as anything else why "labor has been despised in this country; at the North as well as South. . . . These [the working] classes have the power to rule the country, but have submitted to the iron rod of the thinking classes. A day laborer can think as well as anybody. He can work and think both. But the idle classes have made him believe, that he is not qualified to make his own laws, or do his own preaching, or plead his own case, but that he must employ some one of them to do these things for him."[69]

Mechanized factory labor within the context of the factory system appeared to strengthen the division between the thinking and the working classes. The range of antebellum radical creeds seeking to apply "the republican principle to labor"—Owenite and Associationist socialism, Land

Reform, labor cooperatives—shared the conviction that the removal of this division between thinkers and workers required, among other things, the radical transformation if not the wholesale eradication of the factory system; at the very least, that system needed to be shorn of the unequal power relations in which it was presently anchored.[70] But what of other middle-class intellectuals who rejected extreme measures yet were swayed by the power of Smith's abstraction and who believed, furthermore, that this abstraction was given alarming concrete support by the neglect of the mental development of child operatives in British and even American mills? Certainly many such intellectuals agreed that repetitive factory work, labor that to an unprecedented degree removed variety and personal idiosyncrasy from the productive process and was oppressive for this reason, exacerbated, or brought a new dimension to, the age-old divorce between significant mental activity and unskilled physical work. One writer in the *North British Review* went so far as to claim that "the slavery of the man who spends his life in making perfectly round holes in needles, perfect points to pins, or perfectly smooth stones, is more real than that of the negro who submits to the lash. It is the slavery of the mind, from which it is the boast of the other that he is exempt."[71]

As inexorably as they bemoaned the deleterious effects of factory division of labor upon the mental faculties of workers, writers like Gayarré, Channing, and Andrew Preston Peabody proceeded to embrace Adam Smith's own proposal, mass education, as the antidote to the deadening process, often in conjunction with support for limiting the hours of factory labor.[72] In his "The Future of Labor" essay, Peabody noted of the children who followed their parents into the mills:

> If driven in the incessant round of labor, from day-dawn till nightfall, they must rapidly degenerate in intelligence, taste, and character, and must become a race of mere drudges and serfs. To obviate this tendency, the schoolmaster's certificate ought to be an indispensable credential for the admission of the juvenile operative. There should be an age, beneath which no child should be furnished with employment. There should be libraries, public lectures, and evening schools, freely open to the operatives. . . . Philanthropy should devise and employ every possible means of stimulating minds wearied and jaded by the monotony of the noisy routine within the factory walls.[73]

REDEFINING DIGNIFIED MANUAL LABOR

For many middle-class intellectuals, recognition of the troubling character of existing factory labor clashed with an implicit acceptance of its economic importance and with a corresponding desire to find some accommodation with it. One outcome of this tension was the impetus given to a new definition of dignified manual labor, one in which the intrinsic mental characteristics of the labor were bypassed completely as a significant source of labor's dignity. Such a definition found the primary source of manual labor's dignity instead in the intellectual development and refinement the laborer achieved outside of his work and brought to it. This definition could itself embrace quite disparate viewpoints. Andrew Preston Peabody placed much of the responsibility for the worker's intellectual improvement upon philanthropy and state action, including legislative curtailment of the working day, and he was highly critical of the factory system. His position diverged significantly from one which insisted that the worker was already fully capable of achieving his intellectual improvement though his own efforts, without the need of any mandated changes in the factory system. Alonzo Potter acknowledged the arguments for an intellectual antidote to the effects of division of labor in a way that hardly fell short of the more uncompromising defenses of the factory system and factory work: "It is often objected to such division [of labor] that, by simplifying labor, and superseding, in consequence, much of the thought and care formerly necessary, it tends to degrade the artisan into a mere machine. And so it does, if the artisan chooses to be degraded; chooses to spend the leisure, thus given him, in a state of mere mental vacancy."[74]

Whether they placed the responsibility for the worker's intellectual improvement fully upon his own shoulders or that of the state, the writers considered here shared a definition of dignified manual labor in which educated laborers rather than mentally stimulating labor became the cornerstone of dignity. This definition by no means represented a complete break from the past. A special premium had been placed for decades on the intellectual enlightenment of apprentices and other members of the artisanal trades. However high the skill level and the mental content of some of the preindustrial crafts, mechanics were nonetheless generally held to be intellectually and educationally deficient compared to members of more prestigious vocations. Although they were organized for a variety of reasons, Mechanics' Institutes and other similar institutions aimed in part to reduce the handicap in status confronting manual laborers, a handicap summarized by the conservative Democrat Theodore Sedgwick: "The more a man labors with his mind, which is mental labor, and the less with his hands, which is bodily labor, the higher he is in the scale of laborers."[75]

Nor can it be said that disenchantment with factory labor and with skill dilution in the craft structure accounted by themselves for the increased emphasis on the laborer's need to find mental stimulus outside of the workplace. That emphasis was natural in an age permeated by the theme of uplift and self-improvement, one in which many institutions and practices were targeted for reform. Concern with the ravages of alcohol prompted the author of an article in a Dublin, Ireland, newspaper to note the "distasteful and degrading" association with which intemperance had unnecessarily burdened manual labor in the past. The author concluded that "all labor then may become high and dignified, provided that those who engage in it mix with it a large portion of intelligence, and bring to their manual occupations refined and cultivated minds."[76] And when William Ellery Channing claimed that "it is the man who determines the dignity of the occupation, not the occupation which measures the dignity of the man," it was the ignorance and consequent low status of all those who performed the "commonest labors . . . ploughing, digging, and trades," which on this occasion prompted his call for an uplifting "self-culture," not the intellectual needs of factory laborers specifically.[77]

We should stress, however, that many of these appeals for worker education carried the belief that "common" unskilled laborers, not to speak of skilled mechanics, could use outside mental development to increase the skill and intellectual stimulus of their tasks. Such appeals, in other words, generated definitions of dignified manual labor that continued to make some positive use of the tasks themselves. For Channing and many other critics, factory labor tended to fall outside such definitions precisely because it seemed so actively antagonistic to intellectual activity, so singularly unreceptive to injections of mental content. In suggesting the need for an antidote to its effects, mechanized factory labor, at least as it existed within the context of the capitalist factory system, constituted a specter that provided its own special impetus for the cause of worker education and intellectual development outside the workplace. The small segment of the well-bred New England mills girls who organized "Improvement Circles" and contributed to the *Lowell Offering* gained an international reputation and a large scholarly literature through their efforts to combat the stigma of factory work and demonstrate that there could indeed survive "mind amongst the spindles."[78] It was historical irony that the very form of employment that first gave the labor of American women significant monetary value and economic independence outside the home—and that the mill girls so highly prized for this reason—also embodied a set of associations that stigmatized it, above all, as generative of intellectual and economic slavery.[79]

When this population of native New England girls, moreover, began leaving the mills in large numbers beginning in the mid-1840s, having determined that the economic rewards of their work were being seriously undermined by deteriorating working conditions, long hours of factory labor appeared to some to assume implications that were all the more ominous. A report of a Massachusetts House Committee in 1850 noted that the moral and intellectual attainments of the state's factory population had never been the result of factory life, contrary to some of its defenders, but had instead been attributable to the New England common schools. The immigrant operatives who were replacing the native-born girls lacked their predecessors' strong moral and intellectual background and would be correspondingly more vulnerable to intemperance and the other degrading effects of factory labor. These new operatives, the report warned, were destined, furthermore, to be "a strictly manufacturing population, permanently bound by circumstances, to factory employments," with no kin in country towns among whom they might retire and recuperate.[80]

The impetus for factory worker education, together with proposals to limit the hours of factory labor, was generally reinforced by this sense that operatives enjoyed diminishing prospects for escape from factory labor through upward social mobility. One of the original Lowell mill girls, Lucy Larcom, noted years later that the shortness of her generation's tenure in the factories helped to alleviate the effects of work that was not "intrinsically elevating," work that was "too mechanical to be enjoyed by an intelligent person." But the immigrants who tended the machines in the late nineteenth century, Larcom argued, had indeed become a more permanent factory population. There was all the more compelling need in their case for compensatory education—"the [factory] toiler's only hope of elevation is in keeping his mind above his work."[81]

In the mid-nineteenth century, the sense of rigid class stratification, of the possibility of very limited upward mobility for the operative population out of the working class, remained considerably more acute in Britain than in America. Support for factory worker education on at least a limited scale became a signature of "enlightened" British factory proprietors; by extending their cooperation in this cause, such proprietors sought if nothing else to make their enterprises more palatable to Parliamentary and other elements distressed with the "unnatural toil" that engaged a seemingly permanent factory population. More than this, these proprietors, although representatives of a new form of wealth who in some instances had themselves risen from relatively modest origins, nonetheless accepted fixed class lines as inevitable and even desirable. They, along with certain British writers whom we will consider in chapter 7, correspondingly saw in factory worker education a means of reconciling the mass of operatives to their class position.[82] From the proper education would emerge a more self-respecting, contented and compliant, altogether better operative. In 1838 one English factory master, Samuel Greg, Jr., described how a factory enterprise such as his own should be managed,

> if the Proprietor wishes to make it really conducive to the welfare of his dependents, as well as pleasant and profitable to himself. . . . In all plans for the education of the labouring classes my object would be, *not to raise any individuals among them above their*

condition, but to elevate the condition itself. For I am not one of those who think that the highest ambition of a working man should be to rise above the station in which Providence has placed him.

. . . I would by no means be thought to discourage the development of superior talent, or refuse to afford it a field where it might find full scope for its activity. But I would not set this object before the mass of the people; it should be the exception, not the rule.

. . . I wish to make them ["manufacturing operatives"] feel that they have within their reach all the elements of earthly happiness, as abundantly as those to whose station their ambition sometimes leads them to aspire. That domestic happiness—real wealth—social pleasures—means of intellectual improvement—endless sources of rational amusement—all the freedom and independence possessed by *any class* of men,—are all before them. . . . My object . . . is . . . to show to my people and to others, that there is nothing in the nature of their employment, or in the condition of their humble lot, that condemns them to be rough, vulgar, miserable, or poor.[83]

A concept of dignified manual labor that relied so heavily on the refinement and education of factory workers was denounced as hopelessly untenable by labor radicals who were uncompromising in their antagonism to the factory system and to the structure of class power it embodied. Educating factory hands, Orestes Brownson suggested, would only add to their suffering by enlightening them to the pitifulness of their hireling condition, which for the great majority must remain unchanged without some radical social reorganization: "Suppose all your operatives in Birmingham, Leeds, Manchester, and Lowell, should become as knowing as Locke or Newton, the factory system remaining all the time unchanged, and they continuing to be operatives still, how much would their material condition be improved? Their sufferings would be increased a hundredfold. The nearer the condition of brutes you can keep men and women, *if they are to be treated as brutes,* the greater the service you do them".[84]

Brownson was criticizing middle-class writers like William Ellery Channing for insufficient boldness in their criticisms of capitalist industrial changes. But in perceiving, in contrast to Brownson, the economic gains those changes brought poor or underemployed workers, and in failing to demand radical alterations in the factory system, such writers may have been closer in viewpoint than Brownson himself was to the greater part of the factory labor force.[85] A more fruitful question, perhaps, than why leading intellectuals did not go further in their criticisms of the factory system, is why they went as far as they did. For embracing education as a means of compensating operatives for their work's lack of intellectual stimulus, and perhaps as well for their inability to rise from their laboring status, was by no means an inevitable response. As Marx noted, recognition of the division between "hand labor and head labor" within employments—specifically of manual labor's loss of mental content—could lead to the elitist conviction that the parallel division in society between "the Thinking and the Working" classes was a natural and even desirable development, one that should not be impeded by misguided government efforts to educate and intellectually elevate the working classes.[86]

We cannot explore all the reasons why many antebellum intellectuals rejected a hierarchical vision of society that regarded meaningful intellectual activity as beyond the province of those who performed industrial as well as more traditional forms of manual labor. There is an extensive and continuously growing literature on republican and democratic values in late eighteenth- and early nineteenth-century America; suffice it to say that by the age of Jackson—the era of the "common man"—such values were so entrenched in American culture that only in very qualified instances could that culture give credence to the once prevalent assumption that "the members of the labouring class . . . cannot live a fully rational life."[87]

The influence of republican and democratic values may help explain why American culture supported, at least as an ideal, the inclusion of manual laborers—above all native-born white male laborers—in intellectual activity.[88] In chapter 7 I explore how this inclusion, as Samuel Greg's observations illustrate, dovetailed with more sophisticated Anglo-American notions of "social control" that were developing among the middle classes, although these notions typically placed an even higher premium upon developing the laboring population's moral faculties than upon cultivating its strictly intellectual ones. Neither the influence of republican or democratic values nor the social control impulse among the middle classes, however, completely explains why American culture placed so high a premium on intellectual improvement and the exercise of the rational faculties in the first place. In regard to this question it has already been observed, in connection with the remarks of such writers as Elizabeth Palmer Peabody and Timothy Walker, that there was a significant tendency within American culture to extol the life of the mind and its "pleasures," together with man's moral consciousness, as the essence of elevated and civilized man, and that this virtual idealization of intellectual activity reflected in part the legacy of the classical Greek and Judeo-Christian stigmas on physical labor that treated the latter as an expression of man's coarser, animalistic needs. This is not to claim that formal schooling, as distinct, perhaps, from a more elemental kind of "brain work," enjoyed any real acclaim from middle-class moralists as a requisite of great success in commercial and other business pursuits; industriousness, frugality, and the other standard character virtues were here credited with a much larger role.[89] Nor can one deny that, regardless of the tributes accorded man's capacity for rational and intellectual development, much of the "purer" intellectual activity or "higher learning" in nineteenth-century America, particularly in the domain of scientific inquiry, was in fact of a rather "flabby" character by both contemporary European and modern standards.[90] Finally, one cannot overlook the frequent criticisms that intellectual activity within the "learned professions" was excessively narrow in character and materialistic in goal, as well as needlessly esoteric.[91] In this last regard, particularly, the interest various segments of the laboring community expressed in their own intellectual, as well as economic, uplift shared the stage and no doubt mixed at times with an American populist "anti-intellectualism" that resented and disdained legal, scientific, and other modes of mental activity whose specialized, demanding nature placed them out of reach of "the common man" and whose very existence was taken as unwelcome evidence of aristocratic and corrupting elitist privilege.[92]

Notwithstanding these truths, the exaltation of intellectual activity in American culture was sufficiently pervasive to help shape and render comprehensible one of the central themes of the early organized labor movements of the late 1820s and early to mid 1830s, the theme that workers, or at least native-born white male workers, were full citizens of the republic who were entitled to equal access to the fruits of culture and education, and that intellectual enlightenment offered a necessary if not necessarily sufficient means by which they might "level up" to more advantaged elements of society. Exercise of the rational faculties was valued by at least some segments of the laboring population during this period as both a good in itself—as something that distinguished man from beast—and as a means of securing labor's emancipation from subservience to capitalists, professional men, and other privileged members of society who had supposedly monopolized knowledge to secure and consolidate their positions of advantage.[93] The idealization of the mental faculties was, similarly, a guiding principle of the movement a decade later to enact a ten-hour working day in New England factories. As the *Mechanics' Monthly Review* explained:

> To force men and women to work more than ten hours a day is *wrong*, because you thereby deprive them of the time which their Maker designed should be improving their *higher nature* [*sic*]. By their *higher nature*, we mean that portion of it which our religion teaches us, and most solemnly too, is to survive our animal being, and be rendered immortal. . . .
>
> A man's first duty, no matter what his station in life may be, is to improve himself religiously and intellectually; no mere physical

consideration should be allowed to interfere with this paramount duty. Take away his religious and mental nature and what *is* man? A beast, nothing more. And what does it avail if he have the faculties of reason and religion, if they not be unfolded and educated.[94]

The idealization of man's rational and intellectual capabilities, the identification of these with man's "higher nature," intertwined with a republican and democratic ethos to suggest that manual laborers, no less than other elements of the population, must partake in intellectual activity if they were to realize their distinctive potential as members of the human race, and that this was above all necessary in a republican society. That the scholarly achievements of Elihu Burritt, "the learned blacksmith," possibly eclipsed in genuine interest and admiration the economic ones of another kind of "self-made man," John Jacob Astor, reveals something of the values and anxieties of the period; although it must also be said that Burritt, as in the case of the mill girls who wrote for the *Lowell Offering,* may have owed some of his prominence to writers who sought to manipulate his example to defend existing social arrangements, to demonstrate that manual laborers suffered no insuperable disadvantages under these arrangements.[95]

Hardly less significant than the exaltation of intellectual activity by both labor reformers and more mainstream middle-class intellectuals was the fact that it was not necessarily or generally accompanied by the downgrading of manual labor itself, at least on a rhetorical level. In this respect, in his explicit pronounced disdain for manual labor, Timothy Walker was exceptional among Northern middle-class writers; although as George Frederick Holmes also suggested, a view such as Walker's was to be commended for its refreshing candor, since the general "cant" about "the dignity of labor" in the free states concealed an equally general desire to avoid it in practice.[96] Cant or not, the rhetorical regard paid manual labor was such that Theodore Parker and a host of other middle-class thinkers who supported restrictions on the length of the working day took great pains to point out that it was not physical labor itself which they considered a "curse," but its "excess"; for it was not physical labor but "bodily exhaustion [that] kills all desire for mental labor."[97] In fact, in the opinion of one writer, the "terrible punishment" of excessive labor created the erroneous but "prevailing sentiment that labor in itself is disgraceful and a curse."[98] Were it confined to its proper limits, manual labor, as a productive form of physical exercise, would prove itself beyond question as hardly less necessary than cultivation of the mental faculties to both the development of virtuous human beings and the preservation of vigorous republican institutions. We need to take a closer look at this principle of balanced and harmonious faculties because it helped to explain why the middle-class intellectuals who subscribed to it maintained that factory hands and other manual laborers in American society should be given the intellectual stimulus their work could not provide.

MANUAL LABOR SCHOOL MOVEMENT

Although the notion of "a sound mind in a sound body" extends at least as far back as classical Greece, a debt acknowledged by Horace Greeley and other mid-nineteenth-century proponents of the idea, this principle received its first significant expression in America through the manual labor school movement of the late 1820s and early 1830s.[99] The manual labor schools established in this period had the immediate pecuniary purpose of enabling evangelical Protestant seminary students to meet their expenses through agricultural and handicraft work.[100] But in their principle of a natural physiological balance in healthy individuals between mind and body, Theodore Dwight Weld and other members of the Society of Promoting Manual Labor, etc. developed a full philosophic rationale for the addition of physical labor programs to the traditional curricula of theological seminaries. The physical degeneracy of sedentary students became an issue of much greater moment than their paucity of income. Continued education without manual labor, Weld claimed, would "sunder what God [had] joined together, and impeach the wisdom which pronounced that union good." It would destroy the "symmetry of human proportion and make man a monster."[101] Another leading proponent of the manual labor school movement, John Frost, noted of the symbiotic relationship between the physical and the mental faculties:

> The fact that the body and mind have a powerful influence upon each other, is well known. How often do we see the most vigorous mind rendered incapable of effort, when the body has become enfeebled by disease? And when the mind is borne down under disappointment and suffering, how often does the body become pale and emaciated, till at length it sinks under the oppressive load?
> . . . As God designed man for great mental as well as bodily effort, it would be a reflection on his wisdom to suppose, that properly regulated, these efforts are injurious to health. . . . The time will come, when the most cultivated and vigorous minds will be found connected with the most energetic bodies.[102]

The manual labor school movement's principle of balanced and harmonious faculties represented a peculiar compound of influences; the contributions of Christian millenialism, Enlightenment physiology, "folk wisdom," and "common-sense psychology" have all been noted by various scholars.[103] And in a movement whose specific concern was the under-developed physical faculties of students, the penchant that Sophocles and other ancient thinkers displayed for physical exercise became an important model of behavior.[104] At the same time, the commitment of Weld and others to the biblical decree of universal manual labor imposed limitations on their acceptance of the classical Greek ideal of balance.[105] The Greeks viewed physical development, such as that reflected in athletic contests, as they viewed politics, philosophy, or art: as part of the free man's cultivation of the virtuous self. But as already noted, a good part of classical Greek philosophy also disdained manual labor as an instrumental activity beneath the dignity of free men. Weld, in contrast, preferred manual labor to gymnastic and other mere physical exercises as the mode by which seminary students would develop and use their physical faculties; and he justified this preference on a number of philosophical grounds that would have appeared foreign to the ancient Greeks. Manual labor held, among other advantages, the virtue of being free of the frivolous overtones of physical exercise; it would furnish students with a practical knowledge of agriculture, gardening, and the mechanic arts, while at the same time promoting their habits of industry.[106] Perhaps even more important, manual labor would, unlike exercise, create bonds of sympathy and understanding between the "learned and the laboring classes," bonds necessary to the well-being of republican society. Weld suggested that workingmen would appreciate the effort of the manual labor movement to reverse the divorce of learning from labor that helped make labor disreputable. The students who engaged in such manual labor would, for their part, be enlightened and disabused of "those absurd distinctions in society that make the occupation of an individual the standard of his worth."[107]

One of the early students of the manual labor school movement, L. F. Anderson, has minimized the philosophical affinity between that movement and such later concerted efforts at social reorganization as Brook Farm. The former's "reports and announcements," Anderson claimed, "have little or nothing to say" regarding George Ripley's stated goal of "bringing about a more natural union than now exists between intellectual and manual labor" and combining "the thinker and the worker in the same individual."[108] Yet if Weld, Frost, and other proponents of the manual labor schools system were far from advocating an outright abolition of the division of labor between the thinking and the working classes, between, indeed, capitalists and laborers, their principle of a physiological symbiosis between the mental and the physical faculties nonetheless had deliberate republican and anti-elitist implications. Such participants in the early organized labor movement as Seth Luther, individuals who were far more direct and biting than Weld in their attacks on industrial capitalism and the system of class relations generally, welcomed manual labor schools as a kindred cause to their own efforts to direct public consciousness to the primacy and value of manual labor.[109] One of Britain's prominent formulators of the labor theory of value, the radical Thomas Hodgskin, noted how "the mind is rather invigorated than enfeebled by the labour of the hands," a tendency that added to productive manual labor's catalog of contributions to society.[110] Hodgskin's means of raising the condition of manual laborers in society went of course a good deal further than those of many others who also articulated his belief in the healthful and stimulating benefits of physical labor. But his example, as well as that of many other European labor and educational reformers, suggests the degree to which the various hopes invested in manual labor education reflected a felt need to confront class differences that was truly international in character; those hopes, that is to say, transcended the peculiarities of any one nation's social structure and extended beyond Weld's specific commitment to indigenous American republican institutions.[111]

Although America's manual labor schools themselves proved financially unviable, the principle of symbiotic faculties that they helped promote continued for two more decades to be linked by Horace Greeley and others with Weld's own hope that labor might be rendered more honorable, and the laboring classes more respected.[112] The *Chronotype* employed the principle to denounce, much like Britain's Ricardian socialists, the exploitation practiced by "idle" capitalists:

> Idleness is itself a vice. And here we do not excuse those who "work with the head." Mental labor cannot be divided from physical. No man has a right to let his physical frame be idle, on the plea of exercising his intellectual powers. This is idleness, and shall be punished as such. It is just as abominable in the sight of our adorable Maker for a man, with a glorious machinery of bones and muscles and nerves, to let them rust for want of occupation while his mind is slaving it, as it is to let the mind grow up to a bramble-field while his limbs are waiting on a steam-engine or swinging a pix-axe fourteen hours a day. . . .
>   . . . The disgrace of labor on the part of capitalists is now the great screw which gripes the poor.[113]

A burden and indeed a "curse" when its full weight fell upon the "working classes," manual labor demanded more equitable if not universal distribution, in the view of Associationists and other labor radicals, if the false but "prevailing sentiment that labor in itself is disgraceful" was to be corrected.[114] Only with its more just distribution, moreover, could manual labor realize the full potential of its contribution to society. Relieved of excessive physical labor, individuals currently engaged in manual labor employments would be free to develop their mental faculties and possibly, in the manner of Elihu Burritt, record important achievements in the intellectual arena. The capitalists and other members of the "thinking class" who undertook their fair share of physical labor would, for their part, discover their own mental faculties rested and replenished by their new alternative activity, as well as discarding their traditional disdain for manual labor.[115] Such were the most egalitarian and utopian implications of the notion that the healthy mind and body bore a symbiotic relation to each other. Ineffective and even comical as it often proved, the distribution of some of the most menial labor among middle-class intellectuals and scholars at Brook Farm and elsewhere reflected the sincerity of purpose behind efforts to observe the balance between mental and physical activity.[116] Such efforts expressed at once the idea of the healthy, fully developed individual and a sense of social justice; for under prevailing social arrangements, of course, it was not mental activity that individuals sought above all to escape. As George William Curtis indicated in his reminiscence of the early Brook Farm community many years later: "Man is made body and soul. The health of each requires reasonable exercise. If every man did his share of the muscular work of the world no other man would be overwhelmed by it. The man who does not work imposes the necessity of harder toil upon him who does. Thereby the first steals from the last the opportunity of mental culture—and at last we reach a world of pariahs and patricians, with all the inconceivable sorrow and suffering that surround us."[117] Curtis evidently had no fear that reduced hours for workingmen would deprive them of needed income. He may well have believed that any social reorganization capable of ridding the world of "patricians and pariahs" and resulting in a more even distribution of physical labor and opportunities for intellectual improvement would have no difficulty in providing a comfortable subsistence for all. Such was, in fact, a guiding conviction of the Fourierist, Owenite socialist, and other utopian reform movements.

It could hardly be said that most middle-class writers and intellectuals who wished to reduce class differences in "mental culture," and who asked that factory workers and other manual labors be given the opportunity to cultivate their mental faculties, gave their support as well to such radical ideas as the universalization of manual labor and the breakdown of the division of labor between employments. Yet individuals outside the radical labor reform movements were not averse to drawing on these utopian ideas, if the situation warranted. When South Carolina Senator James Henry Hammond proclaimed in 1858 quite the opposite doctrine, the inevitability of a hierarchical division of labor in all civilized societies whereby the very worst work was consigned to a class of "mud-sills," the antislavery Senator from Ohio, Benjamin F. Wade responded:

Sir, [manual] labor should never be done by a class. If you obeyed the mandate of the Almighty, and labor were distributed among all the able-bodied men, it would cease to be a task; it would become a mere amusement, and it would tax no man's physical powers above what would consist with his health and his welfare. It was designed—for God is just—that this drudgery of which the Senator speaks should be distributed among all the able-bodied men so as to make it light. . . . A class has been assigned [in both the Old World and the slave South] to do the drudgery, to do all that is valuable, to produce everything that is beneficial; and the system leaves aristocratic drones, useless, vicious idlers whom any community can well dispense with.[118]

Wade could scarcely have claimed that the free labor North whose superiority he extolled distributed manual labor so evenly and equitably that such work had become a "mere amusement" for all its members. But it suited Wade's antislavery purposes to articulate a radical, utopian social vision, one against which even the North fell short, when doing so put opponents like Hammond at an even greater disadvantage.

One historian, John L. Thomas, has noted that in the early 1830s the notion of "a natural balance between mind and body" was "an axiom which quickly formed the ethical base for a national middle-class culture."[119] That axiom indeed proved sufficiently pervasive and malleable to be embraced not only by the radical critics of exploitative class relations, the factory system, and long hours of manual toil—by those individuals who genuinely sought to break down the division between mental and manual labor. The axiom of balanced faculties could also be utilized by more conservative writers who supported mass education but within the context of a wholehearted defense of the capitalist's "mental labor" and of industrial capitalist change, including mechanized factory labor. Alonzo Potter upheld the right of all poor children under a "system purely republican" to common school instruction by arguing that labor necessarily invigorates and does not deaden or debase the intellect; to claim otherwise is "to impeach the wisdom and goodness of that Being who has made labour our great duty."[120] Potter explicitly targeted those proslavery Southern writers who, invoking traditional elitist notions, warned that education might render not only black slaves, but free white laborers as well, unhappy and restive in the employments assigned them by civilized society. If not necessarily subversive of the legitimate division of labor in society, such educational efforts, these writers argued, were in any case largely wasted on laborers who would be confined to their positions for life. But the principle of symbiotic faculties afforded Potter a means of refuting not only these arguments, but also the idea that any physical labor, including factory work, could be intellectually injurious. Potter did not value education as an antidote to the effects of factory division of labor, because in his view none was really needed.[121] Knowledge would, instead, perform the valuable function of assisting operatives to perform their labor "cheerfully" and diligently; educated factory workers, those who were taught an appreciation of the natural harmony of interests between labor and capital, were the most contented, "reasonable" and orderly operatives, the ones most resistant to misguided and disruptive labor agitation. Education of the general laboring population would also reduce crime, vice, and other forms of antisocial behavior.[122]

Potter was clearly less extreme than those elitists and conservatives who insisted on the incompatibility between thinking and physical labor and who denied, on that basis, the value of mass education.[123] Yet his own application of the principle of balanced faculties was toward a view of popular education as an intellectual sedative; that view was firmly within the tradition of popular nineteenth-century moral economists like Thomas Chalmers who proposed that working-class discontent over wages or poor laws might be defused through the laborer's absorption of the proper lessons of political economy.[124] Recent scholars have, indeed, tended to focus upon those American and British middle-class advocates of mass education who, far from wishing to promote the intellectual independence of the laboring population, sought like Potter and Chalmers to instill in them through moral training the work habits and attitudes that would render them more amenable to a spreading industrial capitalist work regimen.[125] In Britain especially, lingering, long-standing conservative suspicion of all efforts to educate and enlighten the laboring poor as potentially incendiary imposed limits on the objectives of the popular education movement; the education called for was, in many instances, less intellectual than moral and religious in nature, a circumstance that is treated at greater length in chapter 7.[126]

There was, undeniably, a significant dimension of the Anglo-American popular education movement—one that was especially pronounced in the reports issued by various correctional institutions—that was less interested in the intellectual uplift and independence of the laboring poor than in using school exercises to insure work discipline and social order in a period of disruptive economic change.[127] This emphasis was consistent with the acknowledged preferences of many factory proprietors and other capitalists for a tractable, not to say docile, labor force.[128] This emphasis is also consistent with the findings of some historians that much of the early industrial labor demanded minimal literacy and intellectual requirements. To some participants in the popular education movement, those who emphasized moral and religious training exclusively, it may have continued to seem dangerous as well as economically wasteful to provide laborers with the intellectual cultivation and enlightenment that their work did not demand.[129]

But it would also appear that a significant part of the impetus for popular education, above all that part contributed by organized labor and radical labor reform movements, did aim to develop a thinking, intellectually independent laboring class and that this objective drew a good deal of its inspiration from the principle of balanced faculties. That principle, moreover, could have a liberalizing influence even among those writers who were far from recognizing such radically egalitarian implications as a salutary, wholesale redistribution of manual labor among all social classes. Criticism of the effects of the social division of labor, that is to say, was in both America and England far more pervasive than was support for the antidote to those effects to which various radical writers and movements were committed: sweeping new social arrangements of one kind or another that would combine capital and labor in the same individual. As one writer in the *North British Review* expressed the general malaise, drawing upon a well-known remark by John Ruskin in *The Stones of Venice:* "We are perpetually trying to separate the workman and the work. We like one man to think and another to do; but the two will never really flourish apart; thought must govern action, and action must stimulate thought, or the mass of society will always be, as it is now, composed of 'morbid thinkers, and miserable workers.' It is only by labour that thought can be made healthy, and only by thought that labour can be made happy."[130]

A good deal more, however, than the influence of the principle of physiological balance explains why American middle-class writers should have associated the elevation of factory operatives and other workers with the awakening and cultivation of these workers' intellectual faculties. Playing a key role in this association as well were perceptions of black slave labor in the Southern states. Those writers who were simultaneously antislavery and sensitive to the notion that emerging kinds of "free" labor were mentally deadening may have felt a special need to affirm the free laborer's dignity by associating it with his opportunity for intellectual development outside the workplace. Antislavery writers who were more resistant to criticisms of the nature of industrial labor, who may have even joined in celebrating the factory system, understandably tended, in contrast, to adhere to a definition of dignified manual labor that emphasized that labor's intrinsic mental rewards. But even members of this second category of antislavery writers could be pushed by prevailing prejudices against slavery toward a definition of dignified manual labor that stressed the outside, educational opportunities workers must have to make their labor truly "intelligent."

We might begin by noting the basic theme in nineteenth-century antislavery literature that Southern agricultural slaves were "mechanical" or "machine-like" in the performance of their tasks yet flagrantly incapable of successfully expanding into manufacturing and industrial enterprises as tenders of machines. Antislavery writers were here using the terms *mechanical* and *machine-like* as synonyms of mindlessness; to this extent, they were in fact borrowing the positive imagery of industrialization which characterized machinery as a mindless instrument that promised to obviate the need of much human drudge labor. John Greenleaf Whittier noted the singular degree to which slave labor failed to develop and utilize the worker's mental faculties: "Slave labor is the labor of mere machines; a mechanical impulse of body and limb, with which the mind of the laborer has no sympathy, and from which it constantly and loathingly revolts."[131] In one of the best-known antislavery statements of the mechanical, or mindless, character of Southern slave labor, Frederick Law Olmsted wrote, with particular reference to the southwestern hoe-gangs: "The stupid, plodding, machine-like manner in which they labor, is painful to witness."[132]

By arguing that machine-like slave labor must lose whatever security and economic viability it had for slaveholders when they attempted to expand it beyond agricultural tasks into machine-tending industrial employments, many antislavery writers clearly rejected the negative imagery of industrialization which held that such machine-tending was itself mindless, if not intellectually injurious. One of the prominent Republican party newspapers, the *Springfield Republican,* either oblivious or dismissive of the successful use of slaves in sugar refining and other industries, to say nothing of certain skilled crafts, discounted the threats of proslavery Southerners to enter into serious, slave-based competition with Northern cotton manufactures: "It is perilous to the peculiar institution to set negroes about any business which requires so much intelligence, and is so mentally stimulating, as the process of manufacturing. The negroes who can manage the machinery of a cotton factory will not remain contented as slaves. . . . If anything is settled in regard to the peculiar institution, it is that the negroes must be employed only in the roughest labors, where the least amount of intelligence and skill are required."[133] Similarly, the abolitionist *National Anti-Slavery Standard* observed:

> A manufacturing people must be intelligent, and an intelligent people cannot long be slaves. . . . The introduction of manufactures is the introduction of an essential element of free labour; . . . A slave population may be forbidden by law to read and write; . . . and every effort resorted to keep them in ignorance and degradation. But so soon as a system of labour is introduced approaching to the system of free labour, free labourers will shake off the chains that bind them, and assert their right to the wages of their toil. . . . If there were no other differences in the conditions of the

poor freeman of Manchester and the poor bondsmen of the
Carolinas, than that which the discipline of machinery creates,
that alone is a difference as wide as the gulf between Slavery and
Freedom.

In support of its position, the *Standard* excerpted Hepworth Dixon's article
from the London *People's Journal,* quoted earlier, which extolled the dangerous character of factory machinery in Manchester's cotton mills for
requiring the operatives to develop their powers of alertness and mental
discipline. There could hardly have been a more dramatic convergence of
uncompromising hostility to chattel slavery with unabashed enthusiasm for
the coming of industrialization.[134]

A certain segment of antislavery opinion clearly regarded mechanized
factory labor, and not merely the traditional and highly skilled mechanic
arts, as demanding a level of intelligence and skill beyond that required in
agricultural slave labor. The common beliefs that slave labor was unintelligent labor and that it had retarded industrialization in the South may
have encouraged antislavery concurrence with the proindustrial argument
that factory labor required intelligence, just as the same beliefs appear to
have encouraged the view that continued efforts to industrialize slave labor
would stimulate the intelligence of slaves and thereby subvert slavery. What
requires some explanation, however, is the assumption of at least this
segment of antislavery opinion that the agricultural labor to which Southern slaves were primarily confined demanded less in the way of intelligence
and skill than industrial labor. Even more important, one is led to ask why
antislavery opinion should in general have concluded that slave labor was
necessarily unintelligent, mindless labor.

THE STIGMA OF AGRICULTURAL
FIELD LABOR

Despite the traditional importance attached to freehold farming in
America as a basis of republican morality, agricultural field labor bore its
own set of popular stigmas. Large-scale manufacturing enterprise had,
since at least the time of Benjamin Franklin, been commonly viewed as a
function of the population density and poverty of Old World societies; and
defenders of the factory system in particular not only had to contend with
the notoriety of Manchester's mills, but the factory's general association
with the confinement and regimentation of prisons, workhouses, and other
correctional institutions.[135] Agricultural field labor, on the other hand,
notwithstanding the rise of "scientific agriculture" in parts of Britain and
elsewhere, was commonly linked with the poverty, superstition, and ignorance of underdeveloped, scattered populations, an association that both

British and American proponents of manufacturing enterprise and economic diversity sought to emphasize and exploit. One of these leading
proponents, Henry Carey, argued that "Where . . . there is no pursuit but
agriculture, there is no power of association, little ability to maintain
schools, and little reason for effort to increase the intellectual power,
because men of every grade of intellect are forced to find employment in the
rude labor of the field. More than a century since Montesquieu told his
countrymen that 'a nation of agriculturists must be a nation either of slaves
or beggars,' and all experience proves that he was right" [*sic*].136

Slave labor, the antislavery argument ran, was more or less viable in an
underdeveloped, agricultural stage of civilization, but the higher stage of
manufacturing development made intellectual demands on the laboring
population that were incompatible with the condition of ignorance that
sustained slavery. Noting the remark made by James Henry Hammond,
that "Whenever a slave is made a mechanic, he is more than half freed," the
antislavery economist John C. Cairnes elaborated:

> The commodities which minister to comfort and luxury cannot
> be produced without skilled labour, and skilled labour implies a
> certain degree of mental cultivation, and a certain progress in
> social respect. To attain success in the more difficult industrial
> arts, the workman must respect his vocation, must take an interest
> in his task; habits of care, deliberation, forethought must be
> acquired; in short, there must be such a general awakening of the
> faculties, intellectual and moral, as, by leading men to a knowl-
> edge of their rights and of the means of enforcing them, inevitably
> disqualifies them for the servile condition.137

At the same time, one can hardly ignore one of the central arguments
made by Olmsted and other antislavery writers: that the capable and efficient performance of agricultural tasks demanded a level of skill and intelligence of which Southern slave labor was blatantly incapable.138 Horace
Mann, in this connection, expressed some reservations about "the common
idea . . . that intelligence in workmen is relatively less important in agricultural labors than in the mechanic and manufacturing arts," an idea Mann
attributed to the fact that "the great agricultural staples of the country—
corn, cotton, sugar, rice, and so forth—have been stigmatized, or at least
characterized, as 'coarser' products, and therefore, requiring less skill and
science for their culture and improvement than the fabrics of the loom and
the workshop."139

Yet it remains true that the general tendency of antislavery writing was
to argue that unintelligent slave labor was viable in agricultural field labor
to a degree that it could never be in the "higher" stage of manufacturing
development. But why did antislavery opinion insist that slave labor need

be unintelligent labor? A letter to the *New York Times* commending Olm-sted's series of articles on the South published in that paper provides two answers to this question: "The grand secret of the difference between Free and Slave labor is, that the latter is without *intelligence* and without *motive*." Slave labor is unproductive because it is "little more than brute force."[140] Slaves, first of all, supposedly had nothing to gain by making their labor more intelligent—that is to say, purposeful, efficient, and productive. Sec-ond, slaveholders could not assume the risk of developing the mental dimension of this "brute force." Invoking the principle of balanced and symbiotic faculties, Horace Mann argued that "there is scarcely any kind of labor, however simple or automatic, which can be so well performed without knowledge in the workman as with it."[141] But the knowledge and education that ostensibly made free labor more productive and profitable to its employers would prove the undoing of slave labor by sensitizing slaves to the intolerable character of their condition.[142] Educated slave labor, like manufacturing slave labor, was in antislavery opinion a contradiction in terms.

The antislavery argument that education and the condition of slavery were incompatible was itself, however, open to possible contradiction from the antislavery theme insisting on the compatibility between education and free labor. William Ellery Channing suggested that the intellectual develop-ment of the free laborer would enable him to discover new interest and challenges in his work, that the mental content of even "the commonest labors—ploughing, digging, and trades"—was in fact protean and expand-able:

> But it is said, that any considerable education lifts men above their work, makes them look with disgust on their trades as mean and low, makes drudgery intolerable. I reply, that a man becomes interested in labor just in proportion as the mind works with the hands. An enlightened farmer, who understands agricultural chemistry . . . who looks intelligently on his work, and brings knowledge to bear on exigencies, is a much more cheerful, as well as more dignified laborer, than the peasant whose mind is akin to the clod on which he treads, and whose whole life is the same dull, unthinking, unimproving toil.[143]

But if education could reduce rather than exacerbate the routine and tedious character of much free labor, might it not, conceivably, strengthen slavery by similarly making the slave's tasks more palatable to him? In implicitly rejecting this possibility and arguing that slave education, even if it was of a limited technical nature, would lead the bondsman to throw off his condition rather than find compensatory interest in his work, abolition-ist writers could only deal in abstractions; for the racist and elitist character of slaveholding practice and ideology would never permit the antislavery arguments regarding slave education to be put to a general test.[144]

Channing was somewhat exceptional among antislavery individuals in the pains he took to point out the value of education in making "free" manual labor, including many forms of "common labor," an intellectual end or good in itself. If more pragmatic antislavery politicians and journalists tacitly accepted Channing's claim that the mental content of free labor was expandable, their general emphasis was nonetheless on the purely instrumental value of education—on its capacity to increase, not the intrinsic intellectual rewards of manual labor, but its extrinsic rewards. By effecting an increase in the laborer's productivity, education would secure commensurate economic and social mobility gains for the worker, if not in the Old World then at least in the Northern free states where an open competitive structure generally rewarded hard and efficient labor. As the correspondent to the *Times* indicated, motive was intimately linked with intelligence because it was the free laborer's prospect of material gain which, more than anything else, induced him to make his labor intelligent and correspondingly productive. Even so incongruous a phenomenon as an educated slave, antislavery speculation occasionally ran, would remain relatively unproductive because he lacked the basic incentive—the free laborer's chance of significant social improvement—to apply his education to his labor.[145]

The antislavery movement's desire that political economy correspond with its sense of morality led it to ignore or screen out those objective developments that undercut this correspondence: above all, perhaps, the evidence of slave labor's actual viability in manufacturing, not to speak of agricultural, enterprise.[146] The disjunction between economic realities and antislavery morality in turn signalled some of the inconsistencies or weaknesses in antislavery logic. Antislavery writers characteristically embraced Adam Smith's well-known views on both the slave laborer's lack of incentive to be productive and on the manifold benefits of economic diversity and the division of labor.[147] But the same writers were, unlike a number of proslavery thinkers, unwilling to draw the most plausible conclusions from the negative side of Smith's division of labor theme and acknowledge on this basis alone, without reference even to the available empirical evidence, that factory labor might prove a congenial employment for "unintelligent" slave labor. A few antislavery voices did seem to recognize this possibility to the extent that they condemned the factory system in the North, no less than chattel slavery in the South, as exploiting the worker through the neglect of his "higher nature." "Slavery, in whatever form we find it," the *Herald of Freedom* wrote, "darkens and degrades the intellect."[148] Participants in the movement to reduce the hours in Northern factories sometimes borrowed the vocabulary of abolitionism to underscore what they perceived to be the same kind of abuse. The *Voice of Industry* observed that "In this 'wilderness of sin,' the holy and divine laws of God are disregarded and trampled upon with impunity, and his children compelled to toil the live-long day, and part of the night, to the neglect of their immortal minds, for a mere pittance, to quiet their physical demands."[149]

Some antislavery writers who did not exhibit quite this degree of antagonism to the factory system nonetheless acknowledged the intellectual tradition that characterized factory labor as mindless while also adhering to the prevailing, quite contradictory antislavery theme that factory work was too mentally demanding to provide new life for slavery. In summoning forth reasons for educating and enlightening the laboring population, William Ellery Channing remarked that the employment of a child who enters a "manufactory . . . is made up of a constant repetition of movements which require little thought, and are very poorly adapted to unfold his faculties . . . the manufacturing business" generally "is not congenial to the advancement of the mind."[150] Yet Channing also claimed, again on behalf of popular education, that "a manufactory could not be carried on by a set of slave-operatives. Simply on account of their ignorance, they would be disqualified for such a trust. There are many mechanic arts which, for their proper execution, require intelligent, well-educated minds."[151]

It seems hardly likely, in the light of his other remarks, that Channing would have included factory labor among those mechanic arts that "require intelligent, well-educated minds." Whereas Channing appears to have gone no further than to have opened himself up to contradiction in his discussions of the "manufactory," Horace Mann made some discernible effort to resolve this contradiction. Mann conceded that "the slave States of this Union may buy cotton machinery made by the intelligent mechanics of the free States, and they may train their slaves to work it with more or less skill." But because slave operatives must be denied the opportunity to develop their mental faculties, their skill would be restricted to the inferior talent of "aping" or copying educated free operatives; thus the performance of slave factory workers would forever lag behind that of free operatives:

> The copyist operates blindly, and not on principle; and therefore he is constantly exposed to failure. . . .
>   . . . even supposing the aping community to be able, after long delays and toils, to equal the originating one, still, before the period shall have elapsed which the pupil will require for studying or copying out the old lesson, his master will have studied out some new one; will have discovered some new improvement, diffusive of new utility, and radiant with new beauty: so that the distance will be kept as great as ever between him and the learner.[152]

Mann offered up to a point a convincing explanation of how the "more educated community" would likely maintain a competitive advantage over the "aping community": it would invariably be quicker to devise "more ingeniously-wrought machinery" to meet the ever-changing "wants and refinements generated by the progress of the age."[153] But what Mann failed to explicitly confront was the possibility that such machinery might in fact lower the intellectual and skill requirements of manual labor, thereby trivializing it, and might in this way ultimately damage the inventive capabilities of at least the laboring segment of the "more educated community." There were in fact precious few factory operatives, at Lowell or in other "educated communities," who had demonstrated their superior "inventiveness" by taking out patents for improved tools and machines.

The remarks of Channing and Mann reflected the countervailing pressures from two countermodels of labor, those of Southern slavery and industrial wage labor. The desire to represent Southern slavery as barbaric and anachronistic and incapable of successfully expanding into factory labor pushed Mann and Channing, along with most other antislavery writers, in the direction of exaggerating the mental content of developing industrial employments for free manual labor. Yet their familiarity with Smith's theme, together with their acceptance of the popular image of industrial workers in the Old World as intellectually deprived and otherwise debased led Mann in particular to acknowledge that the mental demands of such labor might be in fact minimal and within the capabilities of slave operatives. "Free" uneducated child operatives of ten years or younger had for decades been compliantly and with acceptable results executing many factory tasks; and more recently, New England factory proprietors had been hiring uneducated and supposedly "docile" adult male Irish immigrants to replace educated "Yankee-born" girls in the factories of Lowell and other mill towns.[154] These circumstances, which could not have been completely lost on writers like Mann, certainly suggested that factory work need be neither so mentally demanding as to preclude its efficient execution by slaves nor so mentally stimulating as to undermine the ignorance and docility from which slavery supposedly drew much of its strength.

Mann's whole argument—one closely identified with his tenure as secretary of the Massachusetts Board of Education—was that intellectually cultivated and educated operatives, adult or child, could execute such factory tasks more efficiently and productively than uneducated ones, be they free or slave.[155] Although the validity of this argument remains a matter of debate among scholars, its power in antislavery literature is beyond question. Even antislavery writers who adhered to the notion that industrial labor, like some of the traditional mechanical arts, offered significant intrinsic mental stimulus, could simultaneously identify the dignity of free manual laborers with the general opportunities they enjoyed for intellectual development outside the workplace, in considerable part because these writers valued any and all such opportunities as fundamentally hostile to the condition of slavery. The *National Anti-Slavery Standard* explained the necessity of laws banning the teaching of reading and writing to slaves: "No truth is more capable of demonstration, and none needs it less, than that an intelligent people cannot be held as slaves. Slavery can only exist in connection with the grossest ignorance. . . . There is no need to adduce proofs of the ignorance, of the moral and intellectual debasement of the slave."[156]

And here the pressures from the two primary countermodels of dignified free labor coincided rather than conflicted. "It is the first duty of those who think Slavery wrong," Frederick Law Olmsted wrote, "to remove to the utmost all such excuse for it as is to be found in the occasional hardships and frequent debasement and ignorance of the laboring class in free communities."[157] The North could help end slavery, Olmsted added on another occasion, by "making the best possible use of free labor, by demonstrating that the condition of the laborer is *not* necessarily a servile one; that the occupation of the laborer does *not* necessarily prevent a high intellectual and moral development, does not necessarily separate a man from great material comfort."[158]

The notion that manual labor was incompatible with these improvements, that it was above all, perhaps, "enervating to the mind," Olmsted remarked, was an argument that proslavery ideology had borrowed from "the aristocratic party of Europe" and was applied in the South as in the Old World to keep the laboring population in permanent subjugation.[159] Among high-tariff members of the Republican party particularly, the desire to attack and isolate Southern slavery dovetailed with the desire to underscore the debasement of low-paid industrial and other wage labor in Europe, above all Britain.[160] Their ignorance and supposed inefficiency notwithstanding, both the Southern and the European countermodels of labor appeared to pose serious economic threats to the more exalted condition of labor in the Northern states.[161] In those states, the Republican Carl Schurz maintained, "every laborer thinks, and is required to think . . . in order to be what he ought to be—an intelligent laborer."[162] The general ideological tendency to highlight the sharp yet fragile contrast between Northern labor, on the one hand, and both Southern slavery and European "pauper labor," on the other, provided considerable impetus for the idea that dignified, truly free manual labor was distinguished less by its intrinsic mental content than by the qualities of mind the laborer was permitted and motivated to develop outside the workplace and bring to his tasks.

4

Drudge Work: Menial Services, Dirty Work, the Death Trades, and the Case of the British Climbing Boys

Although factory labor still encompassed only a few trades in this period, the contemporary sense of it as a harbinger of economic change lent it disproportionate significance in the discussions of free labor. Indeed, factory work even left its imprint on antislavery comparisons between free and slave labor. For intellectuals to whom Adam Smith's warning about the division of labor in manufacturing had continuing relevance, mechanized factory labor represented a peculiarly new and insidious kind of drudge work; the repetitive, constricting, and relentless character of that labor, as it existed within the context of the factory system, rendered it not merely tedious and intellectually unsatisfying, but actually destructive of the intellectual faculties of workers. To radical labor reformers particularly, individuals who were intent on promoting, through the example of American labor, the emancipation of manual labor everywhere from the centuries-old stigmas that tied it to dependence, debasement, and ignorance, factory work represented the most modern threat yet to their hopes. And the visibility and symbolic significance of factory labor manifested themselves as well in the discussions of other writers, including many of the proponents of the antislavery cause, who took the contrary position that factory work in fact posed little or no impediment whatever to the intellectual development and dignity of free manual labor.

Because it appeared to represent the shape of things to come, factory labor was, perhaps, bound to arouse controversy in any case. But sharp disagreement regarding the effects of factory work on the intellectual faculties of operatives was assured by the varied, complex, and continually changing nature of the machinery and technical processes with which factory work was linked in different trades. Disagreements also grew out of the difficulty of distinguishing the intrinsic effects of factory labor from those effects more derivative of the long hours, close surveillance, and other working conditions that were frequently imposed on operatives by capitalist "factory masters."

Most forms of drudge work were the objects of considerably less controversy and disagreement. First, many drudge workers were only tangentially related to the emerging economic order and thus seemed of limited potential significance. As the Bible attested, lowly bond laborers and "hewers of wood and drawers of water" had existed since time immemorial, but one more sign, in the view of many, of labor's general character as a divinely inflicted punishment. Second, most types of drudgery involved no complicated and changing machinery or technical processes that might muddy the waters of interpretation. And finally, in large measure because the individuals who engaged in such drudge work were often, if by no means always, self-employed "casual laborers" or pliers of various "street trades," there was no highly visible set of powerful vested capitalist or other authoritarian interests to compete with the nature of the work itself as the most likely source of the laborer's degradation.[1] With respect to at least the independently employed drudge workers, in contrast to factory operatives or, for that matter, workers in the sweated trades, there was a certain surface plausibility to the notion that such workers exploited themselves.[2]

Yet if most drudge work proved less controversial than factory labor in terms of its intrinsic effects, the very absence of grounds for disagreement should itself have been unsettling to those middle-class writers and intellectuals who sought to uphold the inherent dignity of all "free" manual labor. If William Ellery Channing's own criticisms of the mentally deadening effect of factory work weakened his general argument that manual labor might be rendered more intellectually satisfying though the worker's intellectual development, then how much more clearly did the various "last resort" employments belie such versions of the work ethic that stressed the intellectual potential in all labor? There was, and continues to be, perhaps, a certain ineluctable repugnance in many of these employments, a quality duly noted by Oscar Wilde: "To sweep a slushy crossing for eight hours on a day when the east wind is blowing is a disgusting occupation. To sweep it with mental, moral, or physical dignity seems to me to be impossible. To sweep it with joy would be appalling."[3]

One need not refer to a late nineteenth-century "non-authoritarian" socialist sensibility such as Wilde's for the opinion that some kinds of work, whatever their legal status, could not be dignified or redeemed.[4] The "miserable business" of bone gathering and rag picking, but two of the many forms of "dirty work" by which the more desperate elements of the working classes in major European and American cities lived off the scraps of metropolitan economies, was at midcentury the object of nearly universal middle-class astonishment, disgust, and occasionally even alarm.[5] In his *The Sanitary Condition of the Labouring Population of Great Britain*, one of the principal authors of the New Poor Law, Edwin Chadwick, provided the following description by an unnamed "eye-witness" of the bone-gathering population in British workhouses:

> The bone-pickers are the dirtiest of all the inmates of our workhouse; I have seen them take a bone from a dung-heap, and gnaw it while reeking hot with the fermentation of decay. . . . I have not observed that these creatures were savage, but they were thoroughly debased. Often hardly human in appearance, they had neither human tastes nor sympathies, nor even human sensations, for they revelled in the filth which is grateful to dogs, and other lower animals, and which to our apprehension is redolent only of nausea and abomination.[6]

Contemporary descriptions of the urban underclasses may have been hopelessly compromised by middle-class values; this was, perhaps, especially true of someone like Chadwick, to whom the impoverished, economically dependent segment of the laboring and "dangerous classes" posed so worrisome a threat to both social order and public health. But our concern is not how such descriptions reflected a lack of empathy and failure to connect with their subjects, but how middle-class impressions of the legally free drudge worker and his employment, accepted on their own terms, left their mark on middle-class attitudes toward the intrinsic character of manual labor generally. Some groups and individuals regarded all drudge work, as it was presently distributed within existing societies, as indeed a "problem," irreconcilable with a condition of dignified, truly free manual labor; and they invested their hopes in a variety of economic solutions. Other unreconstructed "elitist" interests offered not solutions so much as justifications for the existence of a class of socially necessary drudge laborers, within which they frequently envisioned a sizeable component of slave factory operatives. The irreducible class of laborers to whom drudge work fell was as necessary as the fact that the work itself must lack dignity for anyone qualified by native attributes or social circumstances for more civilized activities. Some but by no means all of these elitist writers concluded that employment in manual labor generally was incompatible with the development of the intellectual and moral faculties, and that it was contemptible for this reason. Still other individuals also accepted the present distribution of manual labor and unskilled drudgery, industrial or otherwise, in existing societies, but with a view that was more muted in its elitism. Although they did not necessarily disagree that such work lacked desirability and dignity for individuals qualified for more intellectually demanding and civilized pursuits, they emphasized the redemptive value such work might have for those upon whom it did fall. These writers frequently acknowledged and deplored the degraded condition of the classes of drudge laborers; but they also insisted that the intrinsic nature of the work itself, particularly if it provided regular and secure employment, was not necessarily an affirmation of this condition—it might even provide an antidote to debasement; drudge labor need not be degraded labor. Before taking up the various responses to drudge work, we need a better sense of what middle-class writers meant by and included in it.

Writing for *De Bow's Review* in 1860, S. D. Moore of Virginia contended that slavery already existed in all the states of the Union; for "he who performs menial services, no matter what his color, is a slave." No one would black boots or be a body servant, Moore explained, "except as a matter of necessity, and this is slavery or servitude."[7] Moore was offering what had become a standard denigration of conditions in "free societies" for the purpose of defending Southern black chattel slavery. But Moore's emphasis upon certain kinds of "menial services" as especially disagreeable and degrading, performed only by legal slaves or the most desperate "slaves" of economic necessity, was shared by some individuals completely out of sympathy with Moore's proslavery views. Frederick Douglass and Gerrit Smith, among other abolitionists, believed that part of the antislavery cause must be directed to breaking down black stereotypes in the free states and that this entailed diluting the concentration of Northern urban blacks in the "menial and debasing employments" engaged in by bootblacks, waiters, coachmen, and the like.[8] Douglass, in particular, hoped along with many other black leaders that free blacks might learn a trade, and he took some comfort from the fact that the effect of the racial discrimination which had for long consigned blacks to "servile employments" was now being undermined by the tendency of poor Irish immigrants to displace blacks in those employments. Douglass urged free blacks to convert apparent misfortune into opportunity: "We must not only be able to *black* boots, but to *make* them."[9]

Support for Douglass's objectives did not require the argument that menial service employments were intrinsically degrading, or at least any more so than any other "needful labor."[10] Efforts to break the association between low-grade service jobs and the black population could well be inspired by the belief that it was the unjustified stigma attaching to the group that initially imposed the stigma on the labor, even if the stigmas became at some point mutually reinforcing. An address issued by free blacks at their Cleveland National Convention of 1848 maintained that "such employments have been so long and universally filled by colored men, as to become a badge of degradation, in that it [*sic*] has established the conviction that colored men are only fit for such employments."[11] Yet as in the case of other forms of drudge work, critics of "menial service" labor nevertheless often suggested that there was a quality intrinsic to such work that blighted the character of those who undertook it. Porters and barbers, Douglass argued, were led into improvidence and vice by their attempts to ape the rich whom they served.[12]

In America especially, moreover, an egalitarian premium upon occupational ambition and advancement clashed with the traditional Old World view that the ideal society was one of fixed ranks and orders. As suggested earlier, these egalitarian expectations might be fueled either by republican exaltation of a condition of economic independence, a liberal capitalist attraction to more unlimited occupational and material success, or by an amalgam of these values. Which one of these values dominated the egalitarian outlook of a particular commentator is often less clear than the fact that, in either case, that outlook carried pronounced disdain for both the traditional Old World ideal of a fixed social hierarchy and one of the principal corollaries of that ideal: that individuals who passed their lives serving others well were above reproach.[13] An unsigned article in the *American Review,* quite likely penned by Horace Greeley, echoed Greeley's denigration of "permanent" hod-carriers and street sweepers quoted earlier:

> We talk much in this country of the "dignity of labor," and this is well within certain limits; but the dignity of working till death as some other man's hireling, is not evident. "Labor is honorable in all;" and it is far better to clean boots for a consideration than to saunter in idleness; but he who sits down to clean boots for life, can hardly be said to indicate in his person the true dignity of manhood. He who does well in any sphere, is naturally fitting himself thereby for a higher sphere, or for more decided usefulness in that which he fills. . . . He is not the best workman in any department who is content to remain there evermore. To be a useful dependent is rightfully but an apprenticeship for useful independence.[14]

Skilled mechanics, of course, might also fail to achieve the independence of self-employment; and lawyers and other professionals were as well, in a sense, permanent hirelings who rented out their services.[15] But the "menial" service employments were singled out as the most blatant and grating reminder that American culture had not entirely forsaken the hierarchical traditions and servile economic dependence characteristic of aristocratic societies. As the labor reformer William Heighton wrote to George Henry Evans, he hoped for a day "when SERVICE occupations shall be known no more forever, when no man or woman shall any more be a cook, waiter, shoeblack, or coachman for another man or another woman."[16]

If American egalitarian values strengthened the stigma on menial service employments as intrinsically degrading and confirmed their place within the category of disagreeable drudge work, prejudices of a possibly even more deep-seated and long-standing nature secured a similar place for "dirty work." Michael Walzer has written that "in principle, there is no such thing as intrinsically degrading work; degradation is a cultural phenomenon. It is probably true in practice, however, that a set of activities having to do with dirt, waste, and garbage has been the object of disdain and avoidance in just about every human society."[17] The example of the bone gatherers has already been provided, and as in the case of menial service employments, similar illustrations of abhorrence with "dirty work" appear in a variety of contexts. The *New York Express,* a Northern Democratic newspaper opposed to the antislavery movement, sought to discredit the *Stafford House Address,* an antislavery appeal from upper-class women in Britain directed to the wives of slaveholders in the South. The philanthropic pretensions of the *Address,* the *Express* claimed, were belied by the thousand instances of economic suffering and injustice perpetrated within Britain itself and ignored by the *Address*'s authors. Among these injustices was the desperate poverty that forced women in Liverpool to work at "gathering horse manure in their ragged aprons, saving themselves by this degrading toil from the still deeper degradation of British charity."[18]

In its series of articles in the mid-1840s on "Labor in New-York," the *New-York Tribune* noted that "although there are of course many exceptions to its application, yet it is a general truth that the nature of an employment exerts a very strong influence over the manners and habits and even the appearance of those engaged in it."[19] Dirty work, particularly in its most unskilled and extreme forms, appeared to present the most perverse application of this principle, as the "hardly human" characteristics of the British bone gatherers attested. Yet as in the case of other drudge labor, the middle-class abhorrence of dirty work, the sense that it was inherently debasing quite apart from the subsistence recompense that reinforced the debasement, clashed with, and was tempered by, a number of considerations. There was, first, the acknowledgment that dirty work was often of some social value; the ragpickers, for example, purportedly filled a vacuum created by the absence of adequate municipal sanitary operations.[20] More fundamentally, respect for the operations of a free market economy included a certain moralistic assurance that even the worst employments represented a correct match of worker and work, that laborers engaged in even these occupations must somehow be receiving their just desserts.[21] Radical labor reformers and English Romantics alike derisively characterized this competitive capitalist ethic of the early nineteenth century as "Every man for himself and the devil take the hindmost."[22] With the possible exception of prostitution, there was indeed no form of legally free drudge work, dirty or otherwise, that was deemed so innately repugnant by the American and British middle classes that it failed to enjoy at least minimal sanctioning as an outcome of competitive market activity.[23] Pro-slavery elitist ideology, which deplored the hardships experienced by workers in "free labor" societies, made a permanent class of drudge laborers a philosophical necessity. But the free market egalitarian attack on institutionalized hierarchy could in its own way accommodate permanent drudge labor since this attack rarely extended to an advocacy of equality of outcomes or conditions. Legally free individuals who were drawn to and remained in drudge work were choosing their condition; and permanent drudge work, like lifelong poverty, accordingly became a reflection of the laborer's character failings rather than an expression of the injustices of the economic order. A rigid, almost mechanical adherence to the mythology of American exceptionalism operated, in many instances, to encourage the moralistic disdain for the class of drudge laborers. The shibboleth of equal opportunity in America often encompassed the view that the alleged vices of urban drudge and day laborers themselves constituted the root evil, the proper targets of reproach, rather than the complex of circumstances— onerous and repugnant work, inadequate recompense, seasonal unemployment—under which they labored.[24] Salmon P. Chase commended his country in 1832 for, among other things, its lack of a law of primogeniture, in consequence of which "nearly all the individuals of each successive generation, start in the race of life from about the same point; and they are the most successful in that race, who are the most intelligent and the most industrious."[25] Some years later, just such an assumption led the *New-York Herald* to denounce anti-rent agitation, Fourierism, and other "agrarian and insurrectionary principles" and to express the common view that "the poverty and sufferings of certain classes" arise from their own "vice, or crime, or sloth" rather than "the present organization" of American society.[26]

Middle-class competitive morality could, quite naturally, most easily sanction those forms of drudge work that were most obviously socially productive and valuable. Writing in 1852 during the great wave of Irish immigration, the Massachusetts Unitarian clergyman and author, Edward Everett Hale, justified the relegation of canal digging and "our simplest drudgery of factory work and farm work" to the newly arrived Irish on the ground that their lack of skills eminently suited them for this onerous but necessary labor. A certain line of thought, common to both nineteenth-century discussions and academic literature, has held that successive arrivals of different immigrant groups, "each entering at the bottom of the job pyramid," have acted to constantly exert a "downward drag" on the status of American labor.[27] But with regard to the Irish immigrants, Hale's reasoning in *Letters on Irish Emigration* was quite different. In comprising the base of American society's "pyramid," the Irish, Hale first of all maintained, pushed native-born Americans up toward the "apex" of the pyramid, freeing the latter for "other and more agreeable walks of duty," including more skilled and elevated types of manual labor. Hale insisted of the Irish: "It must be, that when they come in among us, they come to lift us up. As sure as water and oil each finds its level they will find theirs." Through its immeasureable contribution to the expansion of the American economy, Hale proceeded, Irish-dominated, productive drudge labor actually increased the demand for native-born "head-workers": the "foremen of factories, superintendents of farms, railway agents, machinists, inventors, teachers, artists, &c." Finally, Hale warned, these higher employments would prove the more dispensable and perishable ones were the Irish turned back from American shores:

> The soil is to be tilled and the roads built and repaired. . . .
> . . . Exclude your foreign population, and your whole fabric sinks. You find you have still men at hard and loathsome labor. They are now your own sons. You have lost what you had; the highest results of your civilization. For every grade descended when you moved the lowest grade away.[28]

Notwithstanding their superior qualifications and situations, many native-born Americans, Hale insisted, would be obliged in the absence of the Irish to undertake the repugnant labor at the base of the pyramid. The "coarsest" and most "painful" kinds of work must remain, at least for the indefinite future, the most basic and "absolutely necessary" employments of all, given the nature of economic growth and the dearth of technology that could supersede them. Were the Irish excluded from America, one might infer from Hale's analysis, native-born Americans could at best expect only a somewhat higher recompense for performing the same drudgery, a circumstance largely owing to the smaller size of the resulting labor force. Their present gravitation to the higher, more "civilized" employments would in any case have been thwarted.

Hale's assumptions about the nature of common labor in America differed fundamentally from those of many of his nativist contemporaries. Antebellum antagonism to Irish immigrants drew strongly on the premise that they constituted a major economic threat to American-born laborers, that they were competing for work within the same labor market. Hale minimized this competitive threat: his emphasis on the ways in which more elevated employments depended upon and were linked with common labor was attended by an insistence on how higher and lower employments were nonetheless essentially different from one another. Somewhat anticipating modern "dual labor market" theory, Hale and like-minded writers such as Horace Greeley argued, contrary to the nativists, that the incoming Irish could not significantly depress the wages of native American laborers because the employments to which the Irish were drawn by their work inclinations and level of skill existed in a virtually separate labor market altogether from the occupations on which native-born Americans were increasingly dependent.[29] And whereas, too, opposing nativist perspectives often assumed that culturally if not innately inferior Irish Catholic immigrants actually degraded factory work, domestic service, and other of the unskilled employments which they filled, rendering this work increasingly undesirable to native-born members of the working classes, Hale responded not only that such employments existed in their own distinct economic sector, but that they were intrinsically disagreeable, if not degrading, to begin with.[30] Native American workers should be relieved that this drudgery was being done by others, that they were not compelled, by the absence of the Irish, to rely upon it for their livelihoods.

With its emphasis upon the economic and social dislocation and conflict generated by antebellum immigration, modern scholarship has hardly confirmed the accuracy of Hale's model—the clear-cut occupational demarcations and skill differentials it presumed and the facility and speed with which it implied that the Irish would help propel native-born workers "of superior ability" into more elevated kinds of work. Recent scholars have instead tended to support the nativist position that, in the short term at the very least, the Irish and other immigrants did in fact compete with native-born workers within the same labor market and contribute in general to depressing antebellum American wage levels.[31] The Irish did this in part by directly competing with native-born workers for existing skilled positions, but since only a small proportion of their number had craft expertise, the primary way in which they undermined the competitive position of skilled native-born artisans was by greatly adding to the unskilled, cheap labor pool from which the factories, sweatshops and other growing, "dishonorable" sections of the manufacturing trades drew.[32] Of course, many unskilled native-born white laborers experienced either a decline in wages or the loss of a job as a result of Irish competition; although a good case can be made that, nativist preoccupations notwithstanding, the unskilled free blacks of the urban North suffered most severely of all from such direct economic competition with Irish immigrant labor.

Yet despite the accuracy of many economic nativist perceptions, Hale's arguments were not without validity and merit, this aside from the fact that he was employing these arguments in the defense of a liberal cause: the right of impoverished Irish Catholic and other emigrants to find homes and improve their situation in America. Hale reminded those who offered nativist objections to this right on economic or religious grounds that the foreign-born were making a fundamental contribution to the common good, that they were, quite literally, "building America" by taking many kinds of necessary "rude" jobs, particularly in the hinterlands, which native Americans did indeed scorn and avoid whenever possible. And as Hale suggested, the low-status, undesirable nature of this heavy labor was, if not necessarily primordial and inevitable, certainly antecedent to the coming of the Famine and even earlier generations of Irish; the stigmas attaching to this labor owed at best only a portion of their strength to its monopolization in America by this desperately poor and "vulgar" ethnic group.[33]

Ironically, it was service to a liberal cause that occasioned Hale's embrace, by way of his "pyramid" metaphor, of arguments that were common to aristocratic and elitist defenses of superior and subordinate social functions. But there was at least one significant difference: unlike most such aristocratic and elitist defenses of "dirty work" and social inequality, Hale's affirmation of the productive value of Irish immigrant drudge labor did not appear to foreclose the possibility of significant, even unlimited advancement for the Irish who presently formed the base of the American occupational pyramid. Hale was, it is true, somewhat ambiguous on this point. He referred to the "inferiority" of the Celtic "race," its lack of "any element of intellectual ability"—remarks which hardly reflected confidence in that people's prospects for upward mobility in America. But he also suggested that it was only "at first" that the competence of the Irish would be confined "to the simplest hand-work."[34] Even more clearly in other writings than in *Letters on Irish Emigration,* Hale indicated that in a competitively open society like America, the class of drudge laborers would be continually changing its membership and that many of the Irish immigrants, or at least their children, could in time hope to leave the base of the pyramid, replaced by newer arrivals to America.[35] Hale's implication was that the drudge labor of which he was speaking was justifiable not merely because it was socially valuable, but because it did not, by its intrinsic character, intellectually and morally debilitate, and thereby prevent, the advancement of those engaged in it.[36] The existence of this "meanest work," while in Hale's view clearly disagreeable because of its physically onerous and mentally unstimulating character, did not by itself subvert the values of equal opportunity and upward social mobility.[37]

Hale's defense of the present suitability of the Irish for American drudge labor revealed in one further sense his commitment to the ideal of social fluidity based on competitive, free market processes. His defense, that is to say, was notable for what it did not include: the explicit argument that the Irish possessed innate propensities that made their drudgery less *naturally* disagreeable for them than the same labor might be for native-born Americans. In Hale's writing, to be sure, there is certainly the strong suggestion that because most native-born Americans are qualified by way of skill and education for higher callings, their employment in drudge labor would be a more painful experience for them than for the Irish. But this suggestion is quite different from the argument of natural attraction, of an innate fit between an individual and a particular type of work. Hale's failure to express this idea distinguished him from both more radical and more elitist thinkers than himself. It distinguished him, on the one hand, from the Fourierists, whose principle of "passionate attraction" formed the cornerstone of their utopian alternative to division of labor arrived at through competitive capitalist, free market processes; it also distinguished him, on the other hand, from proslavery writers who defended enforced division of labor for black bondsmen partially on the racist grounds that the black man was innately suited for and thrived under heavy drudge labor performed in "tropical" climates.[38] Hale's defense of the existing division of labor in America, or at least in the free states, simply did not require the claim, even had he believed it, that the drudgery to which unskilled Irish immigrants were presently confined was uniquely and naturally palatable to them.[39] His principal means of defense rested on the conviction that social conditions remained sufficiently fluid in the North—particularly so long as access to educational and other beneficent institutions continued to be widened—that the Irish could in time escape such drudgery and achieve higher occupational positions commensurate with their talent, enterprise, and acquired experience and skills.

The burden of recent evidence indicates, at least with respect to the first generation of Famine emigrants, that Hale's more hopeful and optimistic remarks reflected wishful, if not self-deceiving, thinking; if the unskilled, "hardest," and often dangerous labor of these Irish was not by itself debilitating, great numbers of them nonetheless failed to rise above it for reasons of poverty, disease, or intemperance. One of the most recent and comprehensive scholarly assessments has in fact given some support to a contemporary claim that the typical Famine emigrant died within six years of his arrival in America.[40] But Hale's optimism, as suggested, had never been unrestrained. Apart from his seeming beliefs regarding the inferior ability of the Celtic race, he always maintained that the elevation of the existing corps of Irish immigrant day laborers and their children up the social pyramid required more than the arrival of newer, unspecified groups; it also called for some considerable "Christian" intervention in the free market, through the establishment of schools, labor exchanges, and the like.[41] Yet even could Hale have known or foreseen that such intervening agencies would prove ineffective or insufficient in effecting immigrant social improvement, it is an interesting question whether he would have been any the less restrained in his enthusiasm for immigrant drudge labor. He might well have argued that the Irish were still better off in America than in their homeland, that their drudgery itself was not the cause of their debilitation and immobility, and that, perhaps most important of all, their productive contributions remained in any case the basis of the more "civilized" attainments of native-born Americans. Of course, to the extent that he relied on this last argument alone, Hale would have come perilously close to the candidly elitist, Southern defenses of black slavery and social stratification that were also being made in the name of civilization— defenses that were despised by Hale and other proponents of Northern "free labor ideology." That Hale recognized and resisted this hateful philosophical affinity partially explains why his affirmation of the valuable drudgery of immigrants existed in tandem with the belief, the hope, which he indulged: that their drudgery would not eventuate in a people's sacrifice on the altar of civilization, that it would, on the contrary, prove compatible with the Northern free labor ideal of universal social fluidity and improvement.

More pronouncedly than in the case of the productive, "coarse" physical labor monopolized by the Irish immigrant, American middle-class competitive morality remained ambivalent about dirty and other forms of drudge work; this was so not only because these were of less obvious social utility, but because their debasing and debilitating effects may have seemed more clearly implicit in the labor. In early nineteenth-century Britain middle-class competitive morality was hardly more instrumental than upper-class evangelical paternalism and humanitarianism in abolishing or regulating brutalizing forms of human labor, slave and free. But in America particularly, the evangelically inspired reform impulse had a pronounced humanizing impact upon middle-class competitive morality itself and existed in a continuous state of tension with the mythology of American exceptionalism that operated to harden that morality.[42] One should not, accordingly, exaggerate the tendency of competitive morality to acquiesce in drudge work, to overwhelm the middle-class disgust and disapprobation of it. The emergence of American urban missionary organizations was a sign of middle-class evangelical perceptions that the degrading nature of dirty and other drudge work simultaneously impeded "the upward tendencies of man" and disadvantaged those who performed this drudge work for the competitive struggle, regardless of any character failings which might have drawn such individuals to that work in the first place. These and other uplift organizations and reform movements recognized, moreover, that the juvenile ragpickers and other drudge laborers of the large commercial cities, like child factory operatives in the mill towns, hardly "chose" their means of employment, but were often forced into them by the "greed and need" of working-class parents.[43]

That category of drudge work which posed the greatest hazards to the free laborer's health conflicted most obviously with an insistence on the inherent dignity of all free manual labor. For if the quality that bound most if not all drudge work together, that distinguished it from less tedious and more skilled manual labor, was an especially pronounced inhospitality to the laborer's development of his "upward tendencies" or "higher nature," then how much more glaring was this quality in drudge work that resulted in the premature termination of life itself? Not all exceptionally dangerous manual labor, of course, was unskilled drudgery. Even more than in the case of cotton textile mills, mid-nineteenth-century coal mines, for example, operated on the basis of a hierarchical division of labor; and some of the tasks performed by adult male colliers demanded considerable expertise, although even here the dangerous and unhealthy, as well as arduous and dirty, nature of the work stigmatized and rendered it repellant to many workers outside the trade.[44] Just as clearly, occupational hazards were in many instances susceptible to reduction if not complete elimination, as the fencing of factory machinery attested. But in Britain especially, where the harshness of the new economic order was most apparent, the period of early industrial capitalism provided numerous examples of unskilled and semi-skilled labor notorious for its intrinsically dangerous if not ultimately lethal character. It was common knowledge that the Sheffield metal grinders and the Staffordshire iron puddlers, even more than was true of coal miners or operatives in textile mills, inhaled particles or fumes from their materials that doomed them to an early death. "No occupation in this kingdom," Dr. George Calvert Holland reported, "is so destructive to human life as fork-grinding," one of the branches within the grinding trade.[45] A Parliamentary commission reported that the grinders themselves resisted the introduction of techniques to somewhat decrease the hazard; the grinders believed that any corresponding reduction in the stigma attached to their work would attract more laborers into it and thereby lower its high level of "death wages."[46] But Dr. Holland found the primary explanation for the high mortality rate among the grinders to be more complex. The "destructive tendency" of grinding, Holland pointed out, was greatest in those "dry-grinding" branches where the remuneration was in fact the lowest, where the competition for work was already intense. In these branches, the artisan grinders lacked the education and foresight of artisans in the more advantaged branches of the trade, and labor combinations and cooperation among these artisans were ineffective or nonexistent. When times were prosperous, Holland claimed, artisans in the dry-grinding branches blindly sought to capitalize on the temporarily increased demand for their products by expanding without limit the number of cheap juvenile apprentices. The inevitable consequence was a permanent oversupply of dry-grinders, prevented from withdrawing from the trade by their poverty and ignorance of all other work. No less characteristic of these grinders, artisan and apprentice alike, was a desperate and reckless disregard for the conditions that endangered them. The intellectual and moral education and enlightenment that might have sensitized the grinders to their hazards, that might have opened their minds to existing technology that could in fact reduce these hazards, was itself dependent upon a level of remuneration and standard of living that the persistent labor surplus altogether precluded. Holland looked to Parliament to force upon the majority of economically desperate and uninformed artisan grinders what only "a few of the more intelligent" in their trade had introduced already: new technology and labor processes that would reduce the grinders' lethal inhalation of metallic particles.[47]

Holland's analysis of working conditions in one of the most notorious of the "death trades" serves as a reminder of how self-perpetuating and intractable the causes of such conditions may have been when they so largely lay in the impulses and habits of the workers themselves. Yet worker habits and impulses hardly bore so significant a responsibility for the failure to contain health hazards in other highly dangerous trades, in those where nonworking capitalists rather than independently employed artisans determined working conditions. In the United States, where the so-called death trades were also not without examples, the *Chronotype* claimed that a white lead factory in Roxbury, Massachusetts, took the lives of a dozen, mostly Irish, wage laborers per year. The paper suggested that in this particular case, capitalist negligence consisted of the refusal to close up shop completely. Cotton and woolen factories were unhealthy work environments in considerable measure because of the overwork laborers experienced in these enterprises; but the Roxbury lead factory was one of a number of irredeemably "death-dealing businesses."[48]

Even in those highly dangerous trades where capitalist power was clearly demarcated, there were always tendencies to employ Holland's argument, to attribute illness and accidents to the habits and behavior of the workers themselves. Anthony F. C. Wallace has suggested how the theme of the "careless miner" in the mid-nineteenth-century Pennsylvania coal trade developed as an inevitable outgrowth of the desire of colliery owners and operators to minimize not only their legal liability, but their sense of guilt as well, for the suffering and death experienced by miners and their families. Yet Wallace has demonstrated that the circumstances which substantially added to coal mining's intrinsically hazardous character were overwhelmingly the outcome of capitalist decisions. Those decisions reflected the largely illusory assumption that the cheaper, defective technology and safety precautions utilized in the region's anthracite mines would prove cost effective. Although mining catastrophes might be as financially ruinous for the owners as they were destructive of the miners' life and limb, the owners assumed—perhaps for the most part unconsciously—that the increased risk of catastrophe imposed by deficient technology and safety precautions was justified by the day-to-day savings.[49]

In part because it combined the attributes of "death work" and "dirty work," in part because it was a form of child labor where the worker's responsibility for the circumstances of his employment was unmistakably negligible, perhaps no form of nonslave drudge work more forcefully challenged the notion of manual labor's intrinsic dignity than that of the British climbing boys, or chimney sweep apprentices. If British society, even more clearly than American, attached an importance to intellectual activity and cultural development that imposed upper limits on the status of even the most highly skilled manual laborers, then the case of the climbing boys demonstrated that there were no limits on how low the status of nonslave manual labor could descend. In an essay published in 1824, Samuel Roberts made a compelling case for the argument that "the poor little British-born Children, employed by Chimney Sweepers in climbing and cleansing chimneys," suffered a degree of injustice, suffering, and debasement which in fact surpassed that experienced by black chattel slaves:

> The poor African negro is kidnapped and sold, but it is by strangers, or by foes. These children are kidnapped and sold, and that by their own countrymen, and by their own parents. The negroes are selected for their strength and consequent power of bearing hardship; these poor children are chosen for their youth, small stature, and consequent inability to sustain labour. The labour of the negroes, however severe, rarely impairs their health, deforms their frames, or distorts their limbs; that of these weak little children almost invariably produces some, if not all, of these lamentable effects; it moreover subjects them to peculiar diseases of the most shocking and painful kinds, which rarely fail, if not stopped in an early stage, to terminate in a premature death. . . . They are scantily clothed, poorly fed, ill lodged, and exposed to the unrestrained capricious cruelty of one of the most ignorant, violent, and depraved classes of human beings in this or perhaps any other civilised kingdom.[50]

The plight of the British climbing boys was commonly invoked by writers whose overriding motive was the protection of British West Indian or American black slavery; the hypocrisy of British antislavery philanthropists who ignored this home-grown injustice thereby stood exposed for all to see.[51] But motivation does not necessarily invalidate argument; chimney sweeping indeed contained possibly unparalleled evils, whatever the dominant objectives of some of the writers who publicized these evils. What proslavery writers and other critics of abolitionist reform priorities conveniently passed over, however, was the fact that some prominent antislavery figures, such as Lord Shaftesbury, did in fact practice "charity at home" and fight just as vigorously for the extirpation of the "slavery of sweepdom."[52] Success in achieving the abolition of slavery in the British West Indies may have indeed inspired Shaftesbury and others to press their efforts to outlaw the use of climbing boys, a seemingly less daunting task given the relative weakness of the vested interests opposed to such efforts.[53] The proslavery case for the horrors of chimney sweep apprenticeship, one might add, was itself based on documentation in Parliamentary debates and commission reports whose very existence was owing to individuals like Shaftesbury, although criticisms of various kinds of child labor similar to those made by Shaftesbury did extend back to the 1780s.

The plight of the climbing boys held the most obvious parallels not with black chattel slavery but with the exploitation of other child apprentice labor, also drawn from parish workhouses or working-class families, in the early British cotton mills. Long after this form of factory labor had all but disappeared, the notorious travails of the "infant slave" factory apprentices, like those of the climbing boys, continued to be publicized by proslavery interests, as well as by organized labor and upper-class paternalist movements genuinely seeking reform of factory conditions.[54] But the occupation of climbing boy contained significant differences from child factory apprenticeship. Its growth, first of all, was, like many other forms of drudge work, at most indirectly related to the Industrial Revolution. The trade originated before the seventeenth century, and it primarily owed its expansion at the end of the seventeenth century to coal's displacement of wood as the major fuel in British homes.[55] By 1792 London contained, according to one estimate, two hundred master sweepers with two hundred journeymen and five hundred climbing boys, only the last of whom actually performed the work of entering the flues and removing the highly flammable coal soot.[56] By 1841, the year before a Parliamentary act outlawing the use of boys in climbing flues went into effect, the dimensions of the trade had hardly changed, although interim regulatory legislation and the introduction of sweeping machines had dramatically shifted the balance within it; according to Henry Mayhew, there were by then in London only sixty-two climbing boys, as against approximately three hundred and fifty master sweepers and four hundred journeymen.[57]

More fundamental to our purpose of illuminating contemporary perceptions of drudge work, the occupation of climbing boys was, to a greater and more explicit degree than child factory labor, perceived as irredeemably hazardous and evil. Although critics of the factory system regarded its use of children as particularly "unnatural" and "unwholesome," even most of these critics believed that child factory labor's worst effects might be ameliorated through legislation that would effectively shorten the hours or fence the machinery.[58] But a basic theme of the chimney sweep reform movement in the early nineteenth century was that nothing less was needed than the complete abolition of the use of climbing boys. Dr. Stephen Lushington, a member of Parliament and a charter member of the committee of the Society for Superseding the Necessity of Climbing Boys, referred in a speech of 1818 to the singular "calamities which are absolutely inherent in the nature of the trade; no care, nor caution, nor humanity, on the part of the master chimney-sweepers, can by possibility protect the boys from those sufferings. . . . This is the grand and unanswerable argument against the practice; it cannot be mended."[59]

Small and delicate children, as young as five years old, fetched the highest prices from master sweeps, and they almost invariably experienced some deformity as a consequence of ascending and descending narrow flues when their bones were still "in a soft growing state."[60] The training process for these young apprentices was itself necessarily brutal; their initial forays into the flues produced open sores and bruises, upon which master sweeps rubbed brine to hasten the formation of callouses.[61]

Scattered throughout Dr. Lushington's testimony, together with that of others who preceded and followed him in the chimney sweep reform movement, were the horror stories of seemingly inevitable deaths from suffocation and burning that rendered this employment a form of "infanticide."[62] Adding to the primary occupational hazards were consumption and, most peculiar to the trade of all, one obliquely noted by Samuel Roberts above, a cancer of the scrotum, commonly referred to as "sooty cancer" or "the chimney sweep cancer." Dr. Lushington estimated that no more than one-third of the chimney sweep apprentices escaped death or disablement from these assorted occupational hazards during their seven or more years of "training."[63]

Dr. Lushington and his colleagues acknowledged that some of these hazards were theoretically reducible; but they also insisted, in an argument similar to that made by Dr. Holland regarding the dry-grinders, that the living and working conditions which prevailed among sweeps generated a level of moral and intellectual debasement that must in practice frustrate all such attempts to reduce these hazards. The climbing boys could diminish their risk of contracting "sooty cancer," for example, by washing themselves with regularity; but in the course of their employment they reportedly acquired an intense aversion to cleanliness, and they took pride in their propensity to "sleep black."[64] The idleness and vice in which apprentices and journeymen of the trade indulged during their leisure hours, the complete neglect of their moral and religious education, were extensions of the brutalizing physical exploitation to which climbing boys were exposed from an early age, and so long as that exploitation existed, any efforts to cultivate their blunted moral and intellectual faculties must remain largely unavailing.[65] As Lord Shaftesbury observed in Parliament in 1854, "There was a great deal of professed zeal for the inculcation of religion and the education of the [climbing boys] people; but this system was as destructive to the soul as to the body."[66]

Notwithstanding the reformers' best efforts, and the advent of sweeping machines in the early nineteenth century that made the employment of climbing boys as increasingly "unnecessary" as it was "disgusting," that employment demonstrated a quite remarkable resiliency; there were cases of climbing boy deaths in England as late as the 1870s.[67] Observers have distributed the blame for that resiliency among all the parties most closely involved, apart from the boys themselves: the parents and workhouse overseers who relieved themselves of these children for a few pounds; the master sweeps who kidnapped other boys for the trade; the sweeps and householders who rejected, for various reasons, the new machines; the magistrates who refused to enforce the legislation that increasingly restricted the use of climbing boys.[68] But the persistence of the British climbing boys employment was also attributable to an underlying apathy and acquiescence on the part of the middle and upper classes which itself had various sources. The worst employments, including the death trades, could, first of all, appear justifiable, or at least rationalized, through recourse to a Benthamite logic stressing "the greatest good of the greatest number." The Congregationalist clergyman from Connecticut, Samuel Nott, argued that Southern slavery, like British coal mining, deserved support because it benefited the entire society even while "dooming a few"; the same argument, as Dr. Lushington noted, was used to defend the use of climbing boys.[69] The physically repugnant character of the climbing boys' "dirty work," including the very appearance of the sweeps, also served to acclimate and harden public consciousness to the employment's painful and dangerous nature. J. C. Hudson, another of the prominent figures in the chimney sweep reform movement, wrote of the British climbing boy: "He partakes in some degree of the fate of the negro: we lose, in his sooty complexion, all sympathy with him, as a fellow-creature; forgetting that he was ever one of ourselves, or that a single plunge into a bath would restore the relationship. . . . I really believe that to his filthy disguise is to be attributed all the indifference which is manifested towards the miserable condition of infant chimney-sweepers."[70]

Hudson's letter suggests at least a partial explanation of why the employment of climbing boys in early nineteenth-century America, a subject on which much less information has been extracted by historians, provoked even less public debate and decisive action than did the plight of English climbing boys in Britain.[71] There is, of course, the possibility that for one reason or another objective conditions were simply much better for the American climbing boys than for their English counterparts. But a more plausible reason for the relative lack of concern lay in the fact that since colonial times, virtually all American climbing boys, as well as many of their masters, appear to have been black—in the case of sweeps in ante-bellum Northern cities, free blacks "apprenticed" to the trade. The few individuals who did express sympathy for the plight of these American sweeps may have done so out of a sense that consigning those with black skins to this "blackest" of work represented a particularly cruel irony, if not an outright injustice. As one New York "philanthropist" wrote of his city's climbing boys, "We treat them forever, when in our houses, like thieves, as if it were not a hard enough fate to be both a negro and a chimney sweep."[72] To others, however, the irony of children with black skins monopolizing a dirty and degrading trade may have seemed natural and fitting, neither unjust nor even a subject for sympathy or notice. In the case of the black sweep, to borrow Hudson's imagery and to follow his logic, the soot from the chimneys did not "disguise" a different skin color at all, and a bath would not have truly "cleansed" him, would not have rendered him a more likely object of sympathy in the public eye. In her proslavery book, *Tit for Tat,* Marion Southwood professed outrage at the plight of the British climbing boys, underscoring the anomaly of white children who were exploited worse than the "natural" slaves of black "blood" and who had acquired, in the bargain, a superficial resemblance to the latter. If, as one historian has noted, Southwood was guilty of "shutting her eyes to the fact that hundreds of colored slave boys were sweeping our flues," she may have been little different from many other Americans, North or South.[73] The apathetic American public served as witness not to the British spectre of poor white children performing hard and "sooty" work, but to what must instead have seemed a more consistent and appropriate arrangement, one where the most disagreeable, deforming, and low status of employments was consigned to members of a race whose color and presumed inferiority suited them unmistakably for it.

Returning to the subject of J. C. Hudson's comments, we note that even apart from the repugnant coat of blackness that served to weaken the British climbing boy's claims upon humanity, Hudson recognized that mere force of "habit"—the public's long familiarity with "the morning cry of the chimney-sweeper"—had also played its part: it has "reconciled to us" his "disgusting and painful profession . . . a practice abhorrent under any disguise."[74] Here Hudson touched on what was possibly a yet deeper and more long-standing source of the public acquiescence. If racial prejudice and stereotyping helped legitimate the plight of America's black climbing boys, class stereotyping may have been quite sufficient by itself to acclimate the British public to the condition of its own sweeps. According to some scholars, the ancient Greek essayist and historian, Xenophon, credited Socrates with the opinion that the mechanical arts were justifiably disdained, "For these arts damage the bodies of those who work at them" and through physical degeneration they lead to the "deterioration of the soul."[75] For the participants in the chimney sweep reform movement, the moral and intellectual debasement of the climbing boys constituted all the more compelling justification for the prohibition of their employment. But an indeterminate part of the British middle- and upper-class majority that was unmoved by the plight of the climbing boys may have assimilated Socrates' way of thinking and regarded that intellectual and moral debasement as ratification of a long-standing occupation, as confirmation of the climbing boys' suitability for their work. The stigma attaching to the worst physical labor and the stigma falling on the low caste segment of the population which was obliged to perform that labor reinforced each other. As John Rule has written, with regard to eighteenth-century British attitudes toward the climbing boys: "The meanness of their occupation confirmed the lowness of their being. Their crippled bodies marked and dehumanised them."[76] The apathy reinforced by traditional elitist disdain for the lowest echelons of labor and laborers was also strengthened by the harshest strain of the more modern competitive market morality, which suggested that such laborers were dispensable by virtue of both their high numbers and their low character, and that parents and workhouses, in any case, might dispose of their charges as they pleased. In this competitive morality, there was no place for the notion that climbing boys and others who performed the useful drudge work of society—work that was recognized as physically abhorrent and often highly hazardous—should be compensated at a level above that determined by the "natural" rate of wages.[77] The labor of the lowest drudge workers, like that of more fortunate members of the working classes, was a commodity with no value beyond what the market assigned it.

5

The Technological and Fourierist Solutions to Drudge Work

During the Parliamentary debates of 1819, additional legislation to curb the use of British climbing boys was resisted on a number of grounds, among them being that public opinion would by itself correct the evil once householders became aware of the boys' travails and once, above all, the journeyman-tended sweeping machines proved their efficiency. To these arguments William Wilberforce replied, in making the case for further legislation: "The argument of interest did not always furnish an incentive to action. . . . In a long course of years machines might get the better, but, what numbers of poor wretched boys would suffer in the meantime! Besides, the anti-machinists would, from the shame of admitting that they had been in error, continue to employ climbing boys."[1]

Wilberforce's remarks, which cast doubt on at least the immediate effect of available technology in eliminating one particular form of drudge work, raise questions regarding attitudes toward the general relationship between technology and drudge labor in the first part of the nineteenth century. To a wide range of individuals in this period, those who challenged the harshest implications of competitive morality, legally free drudge work in any or all of its various forms was intrinsically undesirable, if not absolutely incompatible with a condition of dignified, truly free manual labor. In the most extreme cases, particularly, such work could not be made significantly more satisfying or palatable through efforts to improve working conditions. Nor was there any class of persons, however low their caste, for whom such work was truly suited and who could escape further intellectual and moral debasement as a consequence of shouldering its burden. Regardless of the social utility some forms indisputably possessed, drudge work was worthier of immediate elimination than less tedious and degrading, more highly skilled employments in manual labor. One can find considerable support in the early and mid-nineteenth century for Oscar Wilde's sentiments that "all unintellectual labour, all monotonous, dull labour, all labour that deals with dreadful things, and involves unpleasant conditions, must be done by machinery."[2]

But individuals who regarded drudge work as a social problem differed among themselves on two primary matters. The actual efficacy of labor-saving machinery as a solution to human drudge work was one point of contention, as Wilberforce's remarks suggest. The other point of dispute—one which, in fact, only a few writers like Timothy Walker treated in a manner free of ambiguity—was the extent to which the technological solution should be applied not merely to the extirpation of the most repugnant and undesirable employments, but ideally to the eventual elimination of all other manual labor as well.

We have already seen how a group of profactory polemicists acclaimed factory technology, especially "self-acting" machines, for dispensing with much of the drudgery that remained in factories and workshops where the division of labor and performance of specialized tasks were as yet unmechanized. British writers like Andrew Ure and Edward Baines, Jr., together with their followers in America, maintained that the steam engine had obviated the necessity of hard and continuous labor by children and other operatives in cotton mills. Baines supplied extensive testimony for his position from Edward C. Tufnell, a British factory commissioner. Taking particular note of the many "idle" moments enjoyed by child piecers in British mule-spinning departments, Tufnell reported that contrary to the "common prejudice," the steam engines were the drudges of the workmen, rather than the workmen being the slaves of relentless machines. The labor of sewing girls in workshops and homes was far more irksome, continuous, and unhealthy than that of factory operatives in part because no machinery was involved.[3] Charles Knight, author of the widely reviewed *The Results of Machinery,* insisted in 1831 that machinery was increasingly performing the lowest of drudgery in manufacturing enterprises while also increasing employment opportunities in higher forms of labor.[4] The Reverend Joseph B. Bittinger similarly claimed in 1860 that invention had released operatives from the "poisonous atmosphere" of workshops.[5] The contemporary profactory perspective on drudge work has received general reinforcement from the "optimistic" school of historians regarding the effects of the Industrial Revolution on British workers. By virtue of its superior technology, factory production, according to this school, put out of business a good part of the tedious and poorly paid detail labor that children and females had been performing as part of the older network of domestic industries.[6]

Any form of human labor deemed especially menial and unsatisfying, nonmanufacturing as well as manufacturing, might be represented as a viable and likely target of elimination through technology. Bittinger suggested that invention would end the "sad monotony" that marked the history of the world's "hewers of wood and drawers of water," by whom he seemed to mean the unskilled echelons of the laboring population generally.[7] Frederick Law Olmsted extended the application of technology to farming specifically: he claimed that "modern progressive farming" was much different from mindless drudgery and that the informed farmer in America could buy and invent machinery to dispense with half of the most disagreeable labor.[8] Greeley's *New-York Tribune* added that the use of machinery to perform brute labor in England's agricultural districts did not at all displace the regular and permanent farm laborer, but "merely removes the necessity for the irregular and vagrant workman, whose labor is universally admitted to be a curse alike to him who gives and him who receives."[9] And finally, in the period's most visionary manifesto of technological progress, John A. Etzler contemplated man's mechanical channeling of the wondrous forces of wind, tide, and sunshine to create a "paradise" free of the "monotonous drudgery" of common labor in agriculture, manufactories, and workshops.[10]

These paeans to labor-saving machinery were made at different times in different contexts, and many of their authors may have shared only a professed dislike for drudge work, as well, perhaps, as a corresponding impatience with what they took to be an undiscriminating "Luddite" hostility to all labor-saving technology. The particular arguments of Baines, Knight, and other proponents of the factory system were part of their total response to that system's critics; they sought to counter both the actual physical threat of further Luddism and the verbal assaults of skilled laborers and radical labor reformers who characterized technological unemployment and labor-saving machinery as "Europe's curse and America's dread."[11] The effect, if not invariably the intent, of the arguments in behalf of the factory system was to confound the blessings of technological progress with the impact of industrial capitalism, to suggest that the two were necessarily part of one total force. The machinery that, according to Hepworth Dixon, stimulated and disciplined the operative's mental faculties in Manchester's cotton mills was the same machinery that would, by virtue of its productive powers, extend its material benefits to the masses outside the factories. The luxury goods of three centuries ago, enjoyed then only by society's upper classes, were destined to become standard fixtures among the working classes. Next to the beneficent and revolutionary implications of machinery's productive capacity, the technological unemployment that "may injure some temporarily" paled in comparison.[12] Dixon wrote that "the great problem of society" was that the worker "must be physically enfranchised. He must be set free from the thraldom of the bodily wants; and from the harassing dread of those wants." To this problem—"the inadequate store of food and clothing"—machinery represented the fundamental solution; it was "an obedient slave . . . stronger than a thousand Sampsons [*sic*]," yet one, Dixon marvelled, that "obeys the controlling hand of a child."[13]

Labor-saving machinery was a blessing, Dixon and other defenders of factory enterprises noted, not only because it assumed "the drudgery of life for man," but because it foretold an end to the condition of poverty and limited resources which had forced human laborers to undertake that drudgery in the first place. This theme was shared by other proponents of technological progress who did not so inextricably link the future of technology with that of industrial capitalism. Etzler's machine paradise was a series of "utopias of abundance," distinguished alike by the absence of want and by the absence of human menial labor.[14] Marx himself reserved some of his greatest praise for the technological advances that had been achieved in response to the profit motive and that now needed only to be liberated from the grip of the industrial capitalist property structure for their fruits to be truly shared by the masses.[15] As Marx's critique indicated, social values— which in large part meant, for the time being, capitalist preferences— played a critical role in shaping the uses and direction of technology, both how evenly its fruits were distributed and what kinds of human labor it in fact superseded.[16] Articulators of the mythology of American exceptionalism implicitly recognized the directing role played by social values when they insisted that in the United States, at least, technology would indeed be harnessed to raise the condition of manual laborers. Before the Cincinnati Lyceum and elsewhere, Salmon P. Chase maintained that the introduction of machinery and technological unemployment only appeared to be a primary cause of the distress experienced by England's laboring population. In fact, the "more deep-lying causes" lay elsewhere, in England's "vicious political institutions," in her "unequal laws," and in her "grinding taxation." The natural effect of machinery, to lighten "the burthen of labor," would reveal itself more clearly in the United States. Chase reasoned that

> Machinery is naturally, and in well-regulated communities always will be, a source of great good. The evils necessarily incident to its

introduction are slight, partial and transient. They reach only the surface of society, affect but small portions of the community, and speedily pass away. . . .

This question [of mechanization] may be more advantageously discussed in our country, than in any other. . . . The natural course of industry is not obstructed here, in any great degree, by unwise legislation. The profits of labor are secured to the laborer, the burthens of taxation are light.[17]

Egalitarian social values and institutions, Chase argued, insured that in America, above all, labor-saving machinery would have "a fairer trial" and produce its "appropriate effects."[18] A critic of Thomas Carlyle's proslavery views, probably the abolitionist and Fourierist sympathizer Elizur Wright, Jr., promoted labor-saving technology in a somewhat more tentative manner, one that suggested the tension that could arise between commitment to the rising cause of Northern nationalism and the continued wish for a yet more egalitarian Northern social structure. The writer noted that in "fire, wind, water and the forked lightning" the "free North" had "slaves that never rebel nor run away," and he confidently predicted that in time "the emancipation of muscles by machinery" would bring an end to poverty there, proslavery taunts of Northern "wage-slavery" notwithstanding. But the abolition of poverty in the free states required, the writer added, that there occur "a just distribution of the gains" from "the new sources of wealth and power," and this was a development that in turn depended upon, among other things, an end to land monopoly.[19]

Contemporaries of Chase who took a less favorable view than he of American social values and institutions and who had not yet, at least, developed like this second Northern writer the tendency to soften in the face of Southern proslavery attacks a critical perspective on Northern institutions and values, were that much less sanguine about the applications of technology in the United States.[20] Owenite socialists of the 1820s and the 1830s had argued, contrary to Charles Knight, that the pressures of competitive capitalism, which were hardly weaker in American than in British society, favored the invention of technology to supersede the more expensive and more satisfying skilled forms of human labor. True drudgery, the cheaper and more tedious forms of human labor, would remain because capitalists lacked the economic incentive to mechanize it.[21] The historian, Daniel T. Rodgers, has supported the Owenite analysis, observing that in nineteenth-century America, "the economics of manufacturing focused invention not on the dullest or even the most machinelike jobs in a factory, but on the most intricate and most expensive. The complex motions of a shoe peggar or a seamstress fell early to mechanization, but there were rarely comparable profits to be made in turning over to machines the far simpler, far more repetitious, but far cheaper tasks that intervened between the mechanized processes."[22]

Only in its major urban centers did mid-nineteenth-century America begin to approach Britain in the size of its reservoirs of cheap, unskilled, and casual labor. But one can provide numerous instances where, even in the United States, the presence of such inexpensive labor pools left factory proprietors and other capitalists with little economic incentive to introduce costly machinery and "capital intensive" techniques to supersede human drudge labor. Frequently, countervailing economic pressures together with growing community sentiment led capitalists to replace this labor only slowly and inconsistently. Just as British chimney sweep masters resisted using sweeping machines for decades, so Rhode Island cotton factory proprietors delayed until the late 1830s their investment in power looms and other machinery; the cheapness and availability of child and other unskilled labor made the introduction of such labor-saving machinery inexpedient.[23] And in the case of many other forms of drudge labor, such as the menial service employments and the self-employed dirty work of the cities, capitalism generated virtually no economic incentive whatever to alleviate and supersede such work with labor-saving technology.

In its problematic relationship with technology, legally free human drudge labor bore illuminating parallels with American chattel slavery. The most avid enthusiasts of labor-saving machinery, writers like Etzler and Thomas Ewbank, confidently predicted that slavery could not withstand the course of technological progress. Notwithstanding the social attitudes, the political and legal framework, even the black man's biological inferiority that at present sustained it, black slavery, according to Ewbank, must inevitably be "rendered commercially impossible by the superior economy and efficiency of inanimate forces"—"inorganic" motors run by steam, electricity, and coal-generated heat. Next to these forces, the "moral power" of the antislavery movement was as feeble as it was unnecessary.[24] Writing on the eve of the Civil War in an effort to avert violent "national strife," Ewbank wished to demonstrate to both sections of the Union that his projection of slavery's demise was "nature's plan, and therefore effectual, without being violent; mild, progressive, and conservative, injurious to no class, but advantageous to all interests."[25] The land reformer Thomas A. Devyr also maintained at about this time that technological progress was the ideal solution to slavery, that it would, if given the opportunity, peaceably supplant slave labor just as it had superseded England's handloom weavers. As with Ewbank, Devyr's enthusiasm for technology carried a corresponding hostility to the antislavery movement: "If a tenth of the toil, and cost, and ingenuity which have been thrown away upon slavery agitation had been given to encouraging inventive genius, the great question with the South would be: What will be done with these slaves? How will we get rid of them?"[26]

But a more convincing case could be made that the institution of slavery, no less than legally free drudge work, would be strengthened, or at least left untouched, by technology, if social values and economic interests so determined. Just as Wilberforce, in calling for Parliamentary legislation, questioned the adequacy of labor-saving machinery in ending the use of climbing boys, so Abraham Lincoln noted that technology might be used, not to extirpate slavery, but to indeed *remove* the so-called natural limits of climate and soil to slavery's geographic expansion. Contrary to that creation of Illinois Senator Stephen A. Douglas, the morally neutral Kansas-Nebraska Act, what was required, Lincoln insisted, was a legislative ban on slavery's expansion, together with the moral force such a ban signified. Only this legislation could prevent a reoccurrence of "Brooks cotton gin basis," by which the dim economic prospects the Founding Fathers had envisioned for slavery had been completely overturned and revolutionized by Whitney's cotton gin:

> [Representative Preston S.] Brooks of South Carolina once declared that when this Constitution was framed, its framers did not look to the institution [of slavery] existing until this day. When he said this, I think he stated a fact that is fully borne out by the history of the times. But he also said they were better and wiser men than the men of these days; yet the men of these days had experience which they had not, and by the invention of the cotton gin it became a necessity in this country that slavery should be perpetual. I now say that . . . Judge Douglas has been the most prominent instrument in changing the position of the institution of slavery which the fathers of the government expected to come to an end ere this—*and putting it upon Brooks' cotton gin basis.*[27]

Social attitudes—approbation, opposition, or indifference—would determine how human invention was brought to bear upon both chattel slavery and legally free manual labor; technology was not an independent variable. The introduction of the Davy lamp permitted British coal miners to work at deeper levels and extract more coal. This circumstance served the productive needs of British society and the economic interests of the coal mine proprietors, and in some ways undeniably advanced the economic interests of miners themselves, But all this occurred at the expense of exposing the miners to still greater hazard to life and limb.[28] The implication of this particular application of technology, the social assumption it reflected, was that miners were at some point expendable, that the promise of increased productivity justified the increased risk of catastrophic accident. Quite apart, however, from the social values and economic interests that determined and sanctioned the applications of technology, it might be added that those applications frequently had unforeseen effects which, also contrary to the most zealous proponents of labor-saving machinery, resulted in no real abridgement or alleviation of labor. The introduction of the sewing machine in the 1850s only shifted the strain experienced by the seamstress, who had previously sown entirely by hand, from the arms to the lower torso.[29] A series of technological innovations introduced into the home beginning in the early nineteenth century, such as the conversion from hearth to stove, appear to have increased rather than reduced the burden of household tasks for women in ways that could not possibly have been anticipated, even though the fact that cooking and other household tasks had always been "stereotypically allocated to women" was itself hardly accidental.[30]

Technology itself, then, imposed some limits on the degree to which it superseded the most tedious kinds of work, although social preferences set the most critical limits. One might speculate on the basis of those preferences. Did they primarily reflect, apart from the economic interests of employers, mere public indifference or ignorance of the plight of those who performed the worst drudgery? Did they, instead, arise for the most part from the belief, sometimes left unspoken and implicit, other times directly articulated, that drudge labor and drudge laborers made an appropriate match? Or did the social values that protected human drudge labor and resist its displacement by machinery draw most of their strength from the conviction that the time absorbed and the money earned in such work made it manifestly preferable to the only alternative existence that was usually contemplated for these workers—a life of idleness and complete dependence on the pauper relief rolls? Even the worst employments might, after all, continue to be regarded as better than none. The arguments by mid-nineteenth-century Americans justifying the existing distribution of human drudge work on the basis of its social value and moral content are considered in chapter 7. But we should note now that the very existence of such beliefs suggests something of the complexity and range of American attitudes toward manual labor: affirmation by some individuals of the benefits of even the most menial and tedious human labor coexisted with the sharply contrasting premise, shared by some of the most avid enthusiasts of labor-saving technology, that even the most skilled and satisfying manual labor was worthy of elimination. D. H. Lawrence wrote that "You *can't* idealize hard work. Which is why America invents so many machines and contrivances of all sort: so they need do no physical work."[31] Like the creed of upward mobility out of poverty and manual labor, the articulated enthusiasm for labor-saving technology reflected a basic ambivalence, if not actual dislike and disdain, toward all physical labor. Although Etzler appeared to single out chattel slavery and legally free drudge labor as most worthy of elimination, his projected paradise promised "super-abundance" for all men without labor; it would contain, Etzler wrote ambiguously, "no more slaves to labor."[32] The *North American and United States Gazette* repudiated a group of Philadelphia bakers who objected to the competition threatened by a new mechanized bakery. Among the many benefits of labor-saving machinery, the newspaper noted, not the least was that it "leaves time for more elevated pursuits than merely filling the mouth and barely covering the body."[33] And in its exultation of the promise of labor-saving machinery, the *American Quarterly Review* approached Timothy Walker in frankly equating all manual labor with drudgery and suggesting that dignified manual labor was a contradiction in terms:

> It [machinery] does all the drudgery, all that requires mere brute force, leaving to man the higher task of exerting chiefly his mind, and by that exertion surrounding himself with the sources of ease and refinement. How grand would be the spectacle of a nation whose inhabitants were all abundantly supplied with every article of comfort, luxury, and taste, by machinery alone, and whose whole time should be occupied in the pursuit and enjoyment of that happiness which springs from the exercise and improvement of the mind, the enjoyment of the social and domestic affections, and the refined pleasures of taste! Such a state of society is indeed impossible, but the nearer we can approach to it the better: the direct tendency of every improvement in machinery is to bring us nearer to it than before, and by producing abundantly with little labour, to require from man the exertion of his mind which ennobles him, rather than the corporeal drudgery which degrades him.[34]

We have, again, returned to the theme that "mental work and mental enjoyments" enjoyed the highest regard in American culture because "they constitute civilization."[35] Vehement proponents of a mechanized factory system were foremost in denying the critics' arguments that capitalist technology had immediate and obvious effects of an intellectually deleterious nature, that it was either draining skilled craft labor of its mental and creative content or generating a market for new forms of intellectually deadening work. But whatever its present tendencies, capitalist technology was also justified by proponents of the factory system for its long-range intellectual benefits for the working classes. The *American Quarterly Review* maintained that the attacks on the current applications of labor-saving machinery, both in Europe and America, were shortsighted, because they failed to foresee that such applications would in time so abridge all physical labor and produce such material abundance that the laboring population would invariably approach those classes above them in their opportunities to enjoy the intellectual fruits of civilization.[36]

The most telling critics of this view denied that technology, as long as it remained in the service of industrial capitalism, would have long-term intellectual consequences for the working classes that were any more beneficial than its present ones. But some of these critics, notably Charles Fourier, Robert Owen, their followers in Europe and America, and Marx and Engels, also challenged the assumption that the greater part of the nonmanual laboring portion of society itself truly experienced the intellectual fruits of civilization. The extreme division of labor and occupational specialization that characterized existing social arrangements victimized even those who secured their livelihood through "mental labor," denying them the genuine intellectual stimulation and development that was only more visibly absent from the lives of manual laborers. Adam Smith's pin-maker represented division of labor reduced to its barest, quintessential form; but the unusually intense repugnance to specialization that linked the various radical critics also signalled an awareness of other social developments, not the least of these being the tendency of the professions in the mid-nineteenth century to become both more specialized and more demanding of their practitioners. Fourierism and other contemporary socialist movements, as suggested earlier, represented only particularly intense and radical manifestations of a more widespread Western distaste and uneasiness regarding the demands of specialization, a malaise that even many defenders of the status quo could share up to a point. And although the most seminal, and in some cases, profound contributions to the definition of this malaise emanated from European thinkers—Adam Ferguson, Adam Smith, on up through Fourier and Marx—various of its most conspicuous expressions surfaced almost simultaneously in America and Europe among less original, more "middle-level" intellectuals and writers, as the Euro-American Fourierist movement attested.[37]

Marx and Engels, of course, placed their aversion to specialization within a uniquely anticapitalist theoretical framework, and they shed few tears for the professional whose common dilemma with the industrial worker did not obviate the fact that he, like the capitalist who directly owned the tools of production, was still at or far nearer the top of the social hierarchy. Engels observed in *Anti-Dühring* that

> in the division of labour, man is also divided. All other physical and mental faculties are sacrificed to the development of one single activity. . . . And not only the [industrial] labourers, but also the classes directly or indirectly exploiting the labourers are made subject, through the division of labour, to the tool of their

function; the empty-minded bourgeois to his own capital and his own thirst for profits; the lawyer to his fossilised legal conceptions, which dominate him as a power independent of him; the "educated classes" in general to their manifold local limitations and one-sidedness, to their own physical and mental short-sightedness, to their stunted specialised education and the fact that they are chained for life to this specialised activity itself—even when this specialised activity is merely to do nothing.[38]

The Fourierists and other utopian socialists, to whom Engels here credited the discovery of the evils of occupational specialization, described the bourgeois victims of the process with a good deal less harshness, befitting their objective of restoring "harmony" among social classes and winning the support of the wealthy and privileged for their community experiments.[39] A good number of the utopian socialists, some more clearly than others, favored agricultural and handicraft enterprise as the economic basis of their communities and shared the common bias against factory and other industrial work as unnatural and unwholesome.[40] But the Fourierists in particular argued that it was not specific kinds of work that generated intellectual stultification, but rather the prolonged and repeated performance of any kind of work. Intellectual drudgery was a consequence of the occupational specialization that entrapped members of all classes equally. One of the French disciples of Fourier, Madame Gatti de Gamond, maintained that

> in civilization almost all labors are repugnant. If we consult the laborers in all professions, with a few exceptions, each will complain of fatigue and disgust. From the manufacturer, the agriculturist, the workman, languishing in the monotony of never-ending labor which deadens all the thinking faculties, to the tradesman behind his counter, the soldier who obeys, the officer who commands, the pedagogue in his chair, the artist who labors for a living; from the lowest officers of state, up to the minister, the greatest number are annoyed in mind, and bodily fatigued by the insipid labors, which daily recommence with an eternal and insufferable monotony.[41]

In maintaining that an underlying "monotony" linked nonmanual to manual employments and was a primary source of their common "repugnant" character, Fourierists were driving at a fundamental point about the division of labor: that even tasks which pose significant initial intellectual challenges for the novice may become tedious and deadening as a consequence of their mastery through repetition. As "W. H. C." wrote in the

American Fourierist organ, the *Harbinger*, "the most dearly loved employment grows distasteful from its monotony" without rest and alternation of occupations.[42] The intellectual "drudgery" experienced by professional and commercial men was sufficiently apparent that it was invoked not only by the Fourierists, who truly wished to alter existing social arrangements. As we have seen, other individuals who were considerably more protective of those arrangements also invoked intellectual drudgery to discredit the claims of organized labor that the lot of manual workers was a particularly intolerable one.[43]

Quite apart from the monotony to which it gave rise, occupational specialization upset the healthy and natural balance between the mental and physical faculties of the individual, thereby obstructing his complete development. Professional and commercial men, who lived exclusively off their mental labor, were as vulnerable to one-sided development as the manual laborers who failed to develop their intellectual faculties; and in this respect, too, the former's plight was invoked by both radical critics of the prevailing social division of labor and other writers who defended or acquiesced in its development. Among the latter group, the French classical economist Jean-Baptiste Say noted that the "sub-division of the various occupations of industry," despite its tremendous economic advantages for society, was "inseparably" attended by certain "inconveniences":

> A man, whose whole life is devoted to the execution of a single operation, will most assuredly acquire the faculty of executing it better and quicker than others; but he will, at the same time, be rendered less fit for every other occupation, corporeal or intellectual; his other faculties will be gradually blunted or extinguished; and the man, as an individual, will degenerate in consequence. To have never done any thing but make the eighteenth part of a pin, is a sorry account for a human being to give of his existence. Nor is it to be imagined that this degeneracy from the dignity of human nature is confined to the labourer, that plies all his life at the file or the hammer; men, whose professional duties call into play the finest faculties of the mind, are subject to similar degradation.[44]

As an example of the "degradation" effected by the intellectual specialization of professional men, Say cited their ignorance of all practical matters, such as how "to mend the simplest article of their furniture," or how "to save a drowning friend."[45] Taking off like Say from Smith's pinmaker example, Fourierists and others who strongly sympathized with their cause offered a virtually identical description of division of labor's one-sided development of individuals engaged in mental as well as manual labor employments. James Freeman Clarke noted that "the mind and soul" of "a man who is occupied all his life in making the thirtieth part of a pin . . . are narrowed and cramped. His work does not enlarge and ennoble him as it should." Clarke then proceeded to write that

> this is the most obvious evil of division of labor, and it applies to all pursuits. He who works only with his mind, he who spends his life in writing reviews or essays, is narrowed by that exclusive labor almost as much as the pin-maker by his. We all need a wide and varied experience, a diversified culture. We need to educate, by work, our head, heart and hands. But as society now is, only one part or faculty of our nature is educated. That becomes preternaturally active, and is monstrously developed, like the left leg of a fencing-master, while our other powers wither away.[46]

In their more uncompromising attacks on the social division of labor, Fourier's followers often refused to concede even its economic benefits, displaying a fuller appreciation than Say of the symbiotic character of the relationship between man's faculties. Occupational specialization, Parke Godwin argued, did not produce the best possible job, because "a man whose faculties are developed in perfect equilibrium, is more intelligent and more adroit than he who develops only a single one, to the disease and atrophy of the rest."[47]

But Fourierist and other radical labor reform criticism of occupational specialization distinguished itself still further from more mainstream criticism by the extent to which it emphasized the oppression of manual laborers specifically. In their effort to demonstrate the relevance of their doctrines for all classes, Fourierists might speak of the intellectual drudgery and undeveloped physical faculties of those who lived off their mental labor; but the "repugnant, monotonous, and disgusting" character of manual labor was, in their view, particularly evident and offered the most compelling proof of the need to abolish the "false organization" of society.[48] Marx specifically argued that despite the one-sided development and other evils of capitalism to which they, too, were subject, members of "the possessing class," unlike those of the working class, were at least "satisfied" in their condition of "self-alienation"; recognizing "this self-alienation as *its own* power," the capitalist class did not, in contrast to the "proletarian," feel "crushed" by it.[49] Although the Fourierists were hardly so biting in their castigation of capitalist exploitation, they, too, imposed limits on the degree to which the plight of those in nonmanual occupations and those in manual labor employments could be regarded as comparable. Albert Brisbane, the leading proponent of the effort to bring Fourierism to America under the guise of Associationism, suggested that whatever their drawbacks, commercial and professional occupations in existing society retained obvious advantages and understandable appeal relative to manual labor employments:

> Capital controls—often exercises an absolute tyranny over Labor. Capital is held by a small minority, while the laboring multitude, deprived of its possession, are, for the most part, the dependent hirelings, the menial subjects of capitalists. This unnatural relation must be remedied. . . .
>
> . . . we must, in the first place, render Industry ATTRAC-TIVE—make its pursuits avenues to fortune, rank and honor in society, as the military life or career, politics, banking, commerce and some of the professions now are.[50]

Parke Godwin similarly suggested that Fourierism was, above all, addressed to the centuries-old stigmas and suffering with which manual labor specifically was associated:

> The most inspiring and consolatory word that was ever spoken to them, has been spoken to the trodden and worn millions of the laboring classes, who in all ages and nations, and more in civilized nations than in others, have cried to Man in vain for relief in the agonies of their distress. After centuries of hopeless degradation, of remedialess [sic] wrongs and sufferings, they have at last received the assurance that their destiny is not for ever to a debasing, monotonous, repugnant, ill-paid, painful, and disease-producing Toil.[51]

For Brisbane, Godwin, and other Fourierists, the subsistence recompense, poor working conditions, and subordination to capital which, in conjunction with its intellectually stunting effect, characterized manual labor in developing industrial capitalist society, constituted occupational drudgery in a far more definitive sense than the monotony and tedium that marked commercial and professional employments. It was, in fact, as a solution to the ills of manual labor, particularly its most menial and undesirable kinds, that Fourierism made its most distinctive contribution and lasting impression.[52] The Fourierists, both European and American, were hardly alone among radical social reformers of the time in incorporating in their utopian vision diversified activity and job rotation as a primary solution to drudge labor; such schemes figured prominently as well in the proposals or actual community experiments of contemporary radicals like Oneida's John Humphrey Noyes and the British Owenite socialist William Thompson.[53] But among these and other radicals, Fourier and his disciples offered a theory of human motivation—the principle of "passionate attraction"—that constituted the most systematic philosophical explanation of why diversified and freely chosen labor in a planned community would prove a viable alternative to the prevailing division of labor, a division that unjustly consigned drudge work to the lowest rungs of society.[54] We need, however, to give only limited space to a consideration of the Fourierist philosophy and proposals bearing on drudge labor, since these have already received extensive attention from other scholars.

As Alasdair Clayre has noted, the questions "Can work involve play? Can it be intrinsically enjoyable? . . . haunt nineteenth century philosophy."[55] Fourier and his followers went well beyond even most other radical thinkers of their time in providing affirmative answers to these questions, in arguing that truly free, dignified labor must be genuinely pleasurable. Marx took fundamental issue with Adam Smith for suggesting, along with later classical economists, that man is naturally indolent and that true work is, accordingly, naturally irksome. But although Marx maintained with the Fourierists that man derives natural fulfillment and enjoyment from productive activity, he also insisted that Fourier went too far in claiming that "labour can be made merely a joke, or amusement. . . . Really free labour . . . is at the same time damned serious and demands the greatest effort."[56]

Marx's suggestion was that he had staked out a middle position between the classical economists and Fourier. But in some of his most mature writing, as a number of scholars have noted, Marx moved closer to the perspective that an irreducible portion of work even in socialist society would be dictated by economic necessity and that this portion must remain painful, unfulfilling, and in effect unfree; man's self-realization and emancipation lay in an expanded sphere of leisure activity outside the workplace altogether.[57] Contrary to this later perspective, that man's true freedom lay in the curtailment of the working day, Marx and Engels had earlier, at a well-known point in the *German Ideology,* actually come quite close to the Fourierists' own utopian vision of "Work-Play," or "Attractive Industry." "In the communist society," Marx and Engels suggested, man will pass his day in diversified pursuits that possess the character of both productive labor and pleasurable leisure activity. In this, the most advanced stage of society, "nobody has one exclusive sphere of activity but each can become accomplished in any branch he wishes, society regulates the general production and thus makes it possible for me to do one thing today and another tomorrow, to hunt in the morning, fish in the afternoon, rear cattle in the evening, criticise after dinner, just as I have a mind, without ever becoming hunter, fisherman, shepherd or critic."[58]

In the vision that dominates Marx's earlier writings particularly, manual labor wins its freedom, and becomes fulfilling and enjoyable for its own sake, in the absence of a division of labor that had forced individuals into employments of varying desirability. The division of labor was overturned when the conditions of economic inequality and necessity that determined its shape were rendered archaic by a classless system of production and distribution, a system that fulfills, for the first time in history, the egalitarian potential of technologically produced material abundance.[59]

In the Fourierist vision, the forced division of labor becomes unnecessary, and a similar utopia of diversified activity takes its place, but through a different explanatory mechanism. Individuals are distinguished by their different innate tastes and talents—their "passionate attraction" for different kinds of work—and these tastes and talents are sufficiently varied so that in a well-organized society all socially necessary work, even seemingly repugnant and undesirable work, will be freely, enthusiastically, and productively undertaken by some set of individuals. Indeed, one of the prime objectives of Fourier's utopian community, the phalanstery or Harmony, was to satisfy the varied tastes and preferences of its members, which remained unfulfilled and frustrated in the "false organization" of society where forced and unnatural division of labor and an "anarchy" of conditions prevailed. "As affairs are now managed," "W. H. C." wrote of this "false organization," "labor is unattractive, because chance more than taste or natural qualification, determines men's pursuits, making life, to a vast majority, a true hell of tantalizing situations."[60] To the principle that informed Harmony's efforts to reward the hidden and varied work instincts of individuals, George Bernard Shaw later gave expression perhaps as well as Fourier or any of his followers: "Some people have such very queer tastes that it is almost impossible to mention an occupation that you will not find somebody with a craze for. . . . The saying that God never made a job but he made a man or woman to do it is true up to a certain point."[61] Fourier added the argument that where working conditions were rendered greatly more attractive, as under Harmony, the enjoyment virtually all individuals derived from consuming the products of labor would itself come into play to increase their taste for participating in the production and preparation of these products.[62]

In the notion of the "Little Hordes," Fourier provided his most famous example of the manner in which the individual's "natural instincts" or "passional attractions" offered a superior basis for matching work and worker. Brisbane observed that

> one of the greatest apparent difficulties of Association is to procure the performance of repugnant and dirty labor which in civilization degrades those on whom its burthen falls. This obstacle is constantly brought forward by persons who are opposed to the idea of Association.
>
> If every body is well off, they ask, how are all those dirty and filthy branches of work to be executed, which excite so much

repugnance, and which in civilization are undertaken from want and poverty? Among those branches are the cleaning of sinks, sewers and privies, the performance of the lowest kinds of work in the kitchens and stables; the blacking of boots, and all other menial services, which are now performed by a class composed of the dregs of society.

Fourier has solved the difficulty in the most original, and at the same time, in a most natural manner.[63]

Fourier's solution was to exploit "the inclination for dirt, which we find predominant in children," and to organize the younger members of the phalanstery into "a corporation of the little hordes" whose specific function was the performance of this dirty work. The gratification of their peculiar "passion" was itself the primary incentive and compensation of the "Little Hordes" in executing this socially necessary labor. But Fourier would insure that the children's instinctive inclination for dirt, "*but a rude germ,*" was properly channeled and "refined" by the promise of several additional compensations holding natural appeal for children, such as the awarding of first place in all parades. Thus would some of the most "repugnant occupations" in the larger society "become for children the sports" of an attractive industry within the phalanstery.[64]

The "Little Hordes" dramatized the role played by the individual's natural attraction to a specific kind of work. But Fourier and his followers also claimed that "nothing is as natural as a taste for variety"; all individuals possessed the "butterfly passion" to move from one activity to another, just as the butterfly flies from one flower to the next.[65] The proposed division of labor within the phalanstery, accordingly, not only corresponded with the natural and varied preferences of its members, but was itself, just as naturally, limited by job rotation. Members were trained in the execution of several kinds of work of their choice and were organized into "groups" and "series" given over to the execution of each task. Like Marx's complete and fulfilled individual in communist society, individuals in the phalanstery would ideally develop all of their natural faculties. Varying their activity among as many as eight different daily tasks and spending no more than two hours at a time on each, they would move back and forth between the workshop and mental culture, "from manual work to intellectual labor."[66] Because members of the phalanstery were able to change from one kind of labor to another "as often as they please," John Allen noted, "every part of the body is exercised, health is promoted, and labor becomes agreeable and attractive."[67] Systematized job rotation, which Fourier himself claimed would enable each member of Harmony to "successively exercise all the parts of his body and mind," was Fourierism's answer to the highest and most idealized expression of the mechanic arts, in which physical labor itself embodied a significant stimulus of the individual's creative and intellectual faculties.[68]

Just as American Fourierists recalled proponents of the manual labor school movement in justifying diversified activity in terms of the principle of balanced faculties, so the advocates of Association also expressed a like conviction that the distribution of the most servile tasks among intellectuals represented a necessary egalitarian assault on "the barriers of caste."[69] Individuals who had thus far avoided physical labor would, upon joining such a community, rediscover their kinship with the working classes, and the stigma of repugnance that socially necessary labor had acquired through its historical association with the poor and uneducated would also disappear. Charles A. Dana thus boasted that Brook Farm had "as one of its first impulses," prior even to its application of Fourier's elaborate system, the abolition of "domestic servitude": "At Brookfarm they were and are all servants of each other—no man is master. We do freely from the love of it, with joy and thankfulness those duties which are usually discharged by domestics. There we have no mean and degrading labor. There is in practical Association as it already exists there, no degrading labor."[70]

Dana, among other Associationists, exhibited nothing less than a determination to reverse prevailing social values and market conditions, and to reward unskilled physical labor with a degree of honor and recompense commensurate with its socially necessary character. Proponents of Fourierism were, in this sense at least, more radical than writers and trade union leaders of the late 1820s and 1830s who had articulated the labor theory of value primarily in behalf of skilled labor.[71] Dana claimed that in Association

> those very duties which are repulsive, which in civilization are shunned and avoided, except by those who, from necessity, are compelled to do them, and in doing them are for ever disgraced— these fundamental labors are the honorable occupations in Association. The man who discharges one of these duties—he who digs a ditch or discharges any other repulsive duty, is not at the foot of the social scale—he is at the head of it. These are honorable duties, though duties which society scorns.[72]

The insistence that the most necessary menial labor should be honored rather than stigmatized ran through many strains of socialist thought, utopian and scientific, secular and religious; George W. Taylor referred to the dignity even kitchen labor possessed at Skaneateles, the Owenite community organized in upstate New York by the abolitionist John A. Collins.[73] Indeed, the proponents of utopian experiments who did not embrace

Fourier's distinctive contribution to radical thought—that the most disagreeable labor was naturally attractive to some—had in a sense a stronger case for arguing that unskilled physical labor deserved the highest accolades; for their case was built not only on the socially valuable character of such labor but also, unlike Fourier's, on its universal and inevitable disagreeableness and on the consequent sacrifice made by those who undertook it. Dana went on to suggest that, for no other reasons, members of the pre-Fourierist Brook Farm community shared the most "repulsive" tasks out of a "religious" sense of duty and an egalitarian distaste for aristocratic "idleness and uselessness."[74] John Allen argued that similar unselfish and democratic impulses would operate in the "true social order" of the phalanstery in the event that Fourier's special mechanism broke down—in the event, for example, that the "Little Hordes" somehow lost their love of dirt and their corresponding willingness to carry on with the dirty work of the community.[75]

Despite, then, the argument which most distinguished Fourierism from other radical creeds, that virtually no form of labor was intrinsically repugnant given the diversity of human instinctual preferences, Allen and other Fourierists did appear to recognize that such preferences might not by themselves insure adequate participation in the performance of the most menial yet necessary work. Elizabeth Palmer Peabody, it may be recalled, defended the principle of remunerating physical labor at a rate equal to that of intellectual labor on the grounds that those who undertook it were sacrificing the "higher pleasures" of intellectual activity. Fourier himself acknowledged a similar need in his complex calculus for remunerating labor. That portion of the phalanstery's net income that went to manual labor in the form of dividends was to be distributed to each series in direct proportion to the unpleasantness and unattractiveness of the labor it performed, as well as in proportion both to the usefulness and necessity of the labor in sustaining the phalanx. As a general rule, the more appealing the work among Harmony's members, the smaller was to be its pecuniary reward.[76] Fourier furthermore indicated that if some of the most disagreeable but necessary labor failed to attract a special group of individuals such as the Little Hordes, then its very distribution among the phalanstery's members might itself render that labor more naturally attractive; work on a manure pile or garbage collection might appeal to some individuals if they only had to perform it two hours a week. "Because no one in Harmony would ever be transformed into a function," because no one there would be obliged as he was under Civilization's forced division of labor to perform a given kind of work full-time, almost no work would remain so repugnant as to lack "empassioned devotees."[77] The fact, moreover, that such work in Harmony was not only rotated but performed within the uplifting and collegial context of a group also removed that particular dimension of repugnance deriving from the customary performance of this labor in demoralizing "isolation."[78]

Other aspects of Fourierist doctrine, such as the payment of dividends to "capital" and "special talent" as well as to manual labor within the phalanstery, are of little relevance here. This is not to deny the prominent part these principles played in the disputes American Fourierists conducted with contemporaries who were in some cases more, in other cases less, radical than themselves—above all the controversial Fourierist insistence that the phalanstery could retain private property and yet still end anarchic and brutalizing competition among classes and individuals by harmonizing and even unifying capital and labor.[79] Nor is our concern here either the significant degree to which the phalanxes established in the United States failed to implement or sustain many of the principles laid down by Fourier or even his primary American interpreters or the reasons why such phalanxes disappeared after relatively short lives.[80] Of more immediate relevance are certain inconsistencies or disagreements regarding manual labor that the various American writings in defense of Fourierist doctrine themselves displayed; such inconsistencies throw further light on this unique response by intellectuals to the existence of drudge labor.

As already suggested, the proponents of Fourierist doctrine could not seem to agree whether drudge labor represented an entirely subjective concept or not. The example of the "Little Hordes" indicated that the dirtiest and heretofore most despised work, when honored and adequately recompensed, when matched with the right group of workers, and when performed under the right circumstances, shed its repugnant, drudge-like character. In their suggestion that no work was intrinsically and inevitably degrading, but became so only when the individuals who undertook it failed to regard it as pleasurable, Fourierists held a certain ironic affinity with the most conservative proponents of a moral work ethic. These latter proponents also insisted that the worker's attitude toward his labor was all-important; although they took far different positions on whether dignified labor need be or, indeed, could or even should be pleasurable, and on whether existing social arrangements could be significantly improved upon.

But Fourierists also suggested on occasion that some kinds of drudge labor might be objectively or "inherently repugnant." John Allen noted as much when he acknowledged the possibility that the "Little Hordes" might not prove a viable solution to the problem of dirty work.[81] Fourier himself observed that individuals were not naturally attracted to manufacturing labor other than perhaps small-scale arts and crafts production. The fact that, in his view, factory work and mining were in large part also economically dispensable insured their limited role in his phalanstery, which was distinguished by a "pre-industrial" reliance on agriculture, horticulture, and handicrafts.[82] And although Parke Godwin affirmed the objective of the phalanstery "to transform all the occupations of men into pleasures," he similarly conceded that, "as to some works of such a nature, . . . it will never be possible to draw men to them by a direct attraction. These are few in number, and association, aided by the progress of mechanical invention, will reduce them still further, and render the execution of them less disagreeable."[83] Recognizing limits in the power of natural tastes and "passional attraction" to render all labor pleasurable, Godwin and other Fourierists accordingly assigned at least a limited role to labor-saving technology, just as they did to the principle of a higher rate of recompense for the most unattractive labor. To the extent that they so valued technology, they held an affinity with many of their radical contemporaries, including Marx and the Owenite socialists. Although the Owenites also looked to job rotation in their community experiments as a way of alleviating the monotony of menial labor, they left no doubt that such human drudgery remained worthy of complete elimination, if only because it exacted the greatest intellectual sacrifices from those who assumed its burden. Thus they noted of various kinds of manual labor, notably the tedious household tasks that consumed the time of wives and servants:

> But now behold the effects of machinery in a co-operative community. They might have their cooking done by steam apparatus or machinery; washing might be done by machinery; house cleaning might be done by machinery; sawing, grinding, thrashing, ploughing, weaving, spinning, lighting, watering, and endless labours might be performed by machinery; *and the more machinery they might invent the more time they would have to spend in amusements, or to devote to literary and scientific acquirements.*[84]

Whatever potential value they, with the Owenites, assigned to labor-saving machinery, the determination of some Fourierists to recognize unskilled and socially valuable physical labor as the most honorable labor could not be completely shared by other of Fourierism's proponents and sympathizers. Horace Greeley maintained that the "common property" community experiments of the Owenites, like the "Communistic basis" of much of socialism generally, provided a labor incentive system that was fatally destructive to individual liberty and enterprise alike; they failed to recognize that "an ingenious, efficient mechanic, whose services are worth $5 per-day" on the free market, should receive more than "an ignorant ditcher, who can at best earn but $2 per day."[85] Yet although Greeley applauded Fourierist doctrine for not abolishing private property and thereby going so far in disregarding market values, there remained that impetus within Fourierist doctrine and practice to remove the stigma on useful drudge labor by rewarding and honoring it more than Greeley and other proponents or sympathizers might have wished.[86] When Frederick Law Olmsted visited the North American Phalanx in New Jersey, he noted its achievement: "One great point they have succeeded in perfectly: in making labor honorable. Mere physical labor they have too much elevated I think, but at any rate the *lowest* and most menial and disagreeable duties of a civilized community are made really reputable and honorable, as well as generally easy and agreeable." Olmsted proceeded to write that "an *Associationist* I very decidedly am, more than I was before I went to the Phalanx." But the North American Phalanx, he added, was in great need of an "*Educational Series*"; not only did the phalanx excessively devalue the more highly skilled, thoughtful forms of manual labor, but it paid insufficient attention to the importance of sheer intellectual activity.[87] Nathaniel Hawthorne put the same thought more colorfully, grumbling that the early Brook Farm's retreat from the materialism and one-sided development of the larger society had resulted in an overly zealous exaltation of simple manual labor. The classical stigma attached to such work, Hawthorne suggested, had a certain validity, after all: "A man's soul may be buried and perish under a dung-heap or in a furrow of the field, just as well as under a pile of money."[88]

6

Elitist Responses to Drudge Work

In their effort to challenge the scale of social values that invested intellectual activity and non-manual labor employments with a recompense and status far above that of useful physical labor, Fourierists and other radical labor reformers differed greatly from other contemporary writers who did not regard the general social division of labor in capitalist societies as a fundamental "problem" in need of a solution. These latter writers were by no means themselves of one mind. Although they stopped well short of calling for new social arrangements and an overturning of the prevailing division of labor in society, mainstream moralists like William Ellery Channing and Freeman Hunt, for example, might actually join active labor reformers and radicals in deploring developments like the overcrowding of the professions and the depopulation of northeastern farm districts as symptoms or consequences of an unjustified stigma on hard physical and other manual labor. Although such moralists were opposed to obstructing or otherwise challenging free market processes, and also differed from labor radicals by defending the legitimacy and the superior material rewards of exclusively mental labor employments, they nonetheless agreed that the status and appeal of manual labor needed to be upgraded.[1] Above all, perhaps, they shared the labor reform premise that farming and other employments heavily dependent on physical labor could and should engage individuals of marked intellectual abilities and interests. There were, however, still other American writers of a more pronouncedly and forthrightly elitist persuasion who departed from this premise at least implicitly. If these last writers shared any of the unease over agricultural depopulation and other social developments that signalled a decline in the appeal of manual labor employments, they were nonetheless the most inclined of all to accept such developments as proof of the deservedly and inevitably greater attractiveness that jobs dependent upon mental labor held for the ambitious, the talented, and all those other individuals desiring to identify themselves with the higher reaches of civilized society.

In recent times *elitist* has become a commonplace word of choice for discrediting a policy or institution by impugning its commitment to "equality" and democratic values. In acquiring this pejorative, not to say stigmatizing, connotation, "elitism" has departed significantly from its precise and neutral early meaning and application: originally the term denoted merely the process of selecting or separating out from a larger group an "elect" smaller number, without specific reference to the criteria employed in making this selection.[2] Possibly because "elitism" was in the nineteenth century still largely tied to this earlier and narrow meaning, Americans seldom if ever used the term itself in their discussions of social and other inequalities. But in those discussions nineteenth-century Americans did align themselves along a spectrum, from the most egalitarian of utopian socialists and democrats to the most hierarchically minded of conservatives. Without employing the word *elitism*, antebellum American discussions of inequality may therefore be said to have reflected attitudes of elitism in many of its modern shadings and degrees. Applied with care and discrimination, the term *elitism* can be a useful descriptive device for distinguishing antebellum Americans along the spectrum of views regarding various kinds of inequality,

In perhaps its most diluted sense, one entirely compatible with at least a limited egalitarianism, mid-nineteenth-century American elitism accepted the notion that natural or innate differences in talent and enterprise among individuals carried some significance and that in an open, competitive society occupational diversity and significant social inequalities must still develop as the legitimate reflection of those individual differences. Even in his early labor reform period, prior to his shift to a conservatism grounded in Catholicism, Orestes Brownson was enough of an elitist in this general sense to raise a standard objection to radical schemes for a leveling of property, such as that proposed by Thomas Skidmore: "The agrarian scheme would accomplish nothing, even were it just; because were property made equal today, with the existing inequality in men's powers and capacities, it would soon become as unequal again as ever."[3] The Massachusetts political leader, Marcus Morton, who characterized himself as a "*radical* Democrat" uncompromisingly opposed to monopolies and unequal privileges, similarly noted in a gubernatorial address the existence of such natural inequalities.[4] He furthermore suggested that it was just as well that they did exist; for the need for a division of labor, calling upon diverse talents and tastes, was engrained in the fabric of even the best societies: "Perfect equality, moral, social or pecuniary, is not attainable. God created men with unequal physical and intellectual powers," a circumstance which made them "better adapted . . . to the ever varying duties and employments of life" and was "doubtless the best calculated to promote the general happiness."[5]

Brownson's claim that innate differences among individuals were considerable and Morton's observation that such differences had actual functional value by making more palatable to such individuals the social inequality and occupational diversity inevitable in every civilized society, illustrate how elitist beliefs penetrated even egalitarian circles in mid-nineteenth-century America.[6] Perhaps, indeed, it is somewhat misleading to characterize such beliefs as "penetrating" American egalitarianism in the sense that egalitarian doctrines had always, or at least since the Revolutionary era, accommodated the "elitist" belief that individuals varied in their native capabilities.[7] Just as the egalitarianism of the Founding Fathers had manifested itself in a hostility to legally sanctioned, ascribed hereditary status and privilege that created unjust and artificial inequalities over and above the natural ones, so the social perspectives of a Brownson or Morton, while accepting the existence and even the value of differences in native talent and taste, deserve to be characterized as "egalitarian" because they were for the most part taken up with the defense of equal economic opportunity and the manual laborer's right to equal education and the full development of his intellectual and other capabilities.

As articulated by liberal and radical Democrats like Brownson and Morton, elitist beliefs in their most diluted form enjoyed pervasive acceptance in American society and were repudiated all or in part only by some of the utopian socialists and other labor radicals like Skidmore.[8] When, however, it passed from the nature of assumption to that of systematic ideology, the theme of unequal innate talents as well as other differences in inherited condition, together with the theme of a corresponding inexorable and functional social inequality and occupational hierarchy, became the bulwark of pronouncedly more traditional and conservative forms of elitism, forms that had a far more restricted following in American society.

Conservative elitist ideology, specifically its responses to the existence of drudge labor and its manifestations in Southern antebellum proslavery

thought particularly, receives considerable attention in this and the following chapter; but it is again worth emphasizing that we are dealing with
shadings and degrees of belief rather than with absolute and discrete categories. An editorial from the *Springfield Republican* (Massachusetts) illustrates this fact even more clearly than the statements of Brownson and
Morton. As one of the principal organs of the Republican party, the
Springfield Republican joined in that party's attack on the elitist disdain
exhibited within Southern proslavery circles toward the Northern free
white laborer's capacity for self-government and intellectual and moral
refinement.[9] Yet the *Springfield Republican* expressed its own frustration
with the creeds of equal opportunity and "self-help"; such creeds were
going too far in suggesting that innate differences in intellectual capacity
and talent, differences which legitimated the existing occupational hierarchy in the free states, could be ignored without deleterious social consequences. The popular books of Samuel Smiles were particularly at fault for
encouraging the mediocre to make poor occupational choices and enter
professions for which they were unqualified; enthusiasm could not compensate for lack of talent. "Young men who would have become very good
stage-drivers, or dry goods porters, have, under the stimulus of this mischievous twaddle, undertaken to be lawyers, or physicians, or preachers."
The effect of Smiles's "self-help" doctrine was "to draw mediocrity out of
the lot it was born to, and adapted to, into a field which it can only
dishonor." The desired professions threatened to become filled with incom-
petents, and self-help became "self-destruction" when it lifted mediocrity to
high and important positions. The editorial elaborated:

> There's a will in all men to get rich, but there is not a way for more
> than a fifth to a fiftieth part of them to do so. . . . We have never
> seen a "self-made man" whom God had not made to start with.
> Never. . . . [notwithstanding] such sickening devotion to the idea
> of achieving distinction, such discontent with the allotments of
> Providence, and such efforts on the part of inferior men to be
> what God never intended them to be. . . . There is a legitimate
> sphere of ambition to every man—a sphere where his powers are
> at home. . . . Will, work, perseverance, determination . . . [cannot
> lift a man] one inch above the sphere to which his powers are
> adapted.[10]

Ultimately, the *Springfield Republican* editorial was doing no more
than expressing a wish that individuals exercise common sense in choosing
an occupation suitable to their talents. What occasioned the paper's emphasis upon differences in natural talent was not support for the existence of
rigid class distinctions, but instead impatience with the very occupational
fluidity of American society. There is no suggestion in the editorial that all

individuals should resign themselves to the social positions into which they were born, nor that educational opportunities should correspond to one's social position, nor certainly that the legal right of individuals to make occupational choices and improve their social position should be abridged. In these fundamental respects the *Springfield Republican* remained egalitarian. Yet in its last remark particularly, that regarding the subordinate "spheres" of activity to which "inferior" men were naturally consigned by "Providence," the newspaper's editorial could easily be mistaken for a traditional conservative elitist paean to universal social stratification, such as that made by eighteenth-century Anglican clergymen in defense of poverty or one of a type made by nineteenth-century proslavery writers in defense of legalized servitude.[11] With these sources of traditional conservative elitist values, the *Springfield Republican* shared a respect for division of labor and occupational hierarchy within civilized society. Even, moreover, in its unstated assumption that the role of free market forces in shaping the division of labor should remain unconstrained, despite the poor judgment shown by untalented individuals in choosing an occupation, the newspaper editorial bore important similarities with what might be categorized as a less traditional, more "liberal" free market version of elitism, one closely identified with anti-poor law sentiment and classical economic doctrine, and one which was far less disposed than traditional elitist doctrines to approve patterns of social hierarchy and stratification determined by inherited and other ascribed differences. In the *Springfield Republican* editorial, that is to say, there are traces of a tendency that assumes more pronounced form in classical economic thought: the tendency of an increased commitment to meritocracy and free market competitive egalitarianism, to a society free of legalized slavery and other institutionalized and fixed restraints, to generate its own elitist and moralistic disdain for the poor and economically unsuccessful.[12]

But it is the more traditional, conservative elitism, which expressed frequent disgust with the sanctification of the free market forces of supply and demand, that is of more immediate interest here for several reasons. The argument regarding much existing manual labor upon which it sometimes relied, that such labor did not require more equitable distribution because it matched the natural capacities of those who already performed it, offered parallels with the Fourierist stress on the need for an organization of labor in harmony with the "natural wants and aptitudes" of individuals.[13] And notwithstanding its defense of the historic division in civilized societies between intellectual activity and manual labor as natural and inevitable, traditional conservative elitism shared in the burgeoning Victorian sensibility to various outcomes of that division, such as the heavy physical work and other wage labor undertaken by poor working females, as highly unnatural and objectionable. The distinction between these two themes within conservative elitism merits exploration. Finally, although the less traditional, free market expressions of elitist ideology are of primary interest for their discussions of extrinsic labor incentives—the various forces that effectively induced the laboring populations of different societies to perform "the dirty work of the world"—traditional conservative elitism holds more interest for its inconsistent answers to the question of whether "menial" and "lowly" work should also be considered intrinsically contemptible work.[14] Long-standing aristocratic elitist values that disdained members of the laboring classes as irredeemably brutish, values which persisted into the nineteenth century among even some middle-class entrepreneurs, coexisted with, in some cases inextricably blended into, more "paternalistic," equally traditional hierarchical elitist notions which maintained that useful laborers of even the most "humble" condition possessed dignity.[15] Even those workers most blatantly incapable of intellectual and moral development, these latter strains within conservative elitist thought held, were human beings who should be treated with at least a due regard both for the services they rendered and the helplessness of their condition; social stratification and a rigidly hierarchical division of labor need not imply contempt and mistreatment for those consigned, however justifiably, to society's lowest rungs.[16]

Traditional conservative elitist ideology in mid-nineteenth-century America was distinguished by several primary arguments, although it will become apparent that its prominent advocates did not attach equal importance to all of these arguments and even in certain respects repudiated them. It held, first of all, that the functioning and order of civilized society required a general division of labor between a wealthier, more leisured class that did the thinking and governing and a poorer class that performed the manual labor, including a subgroup to which was relegated the most menial and disagreeable kinds of work. This general hierarchical division of activity into "higher" and "lower" functions was indeed so basic that it might be said to define civilization itself. The division, furthermore, was fixed and entrenched in that manual and "menial" laborers particularly could entertain little expectation of ever "rising" from their sphere. To a considerable degree, the social division of labor should be recognized and institutionalized, possibly by limiting the political power and educational opportunities of manual laborers. Conservative elitist ideology, finally— and this in particular was hardly less true of some of the less traditional, free market expressions of elitism—regarded the lowly but socially necessary position of the manual laborer as natural, rendered permanent and legitimate both by the interests of civilized society and by the fact that different spheres of activity corresponded to vital differences between individuals.[17] The precise nature of the most vital individual distinctions—whether they were, for example, differences in innate capacity or differences in inherited wealth and social station—was one of the points on which the various proponents of nineteenth-century traditional conservative elitism themselves disagreed as they sought to legitimate a division of labor in society between intellectual activity and manual labor.

As a way of approaching more detailed consideration of these arguments and the questions they raised regarding the division of labor and drudge work, it may be useful to refer to the work of one of the major predecessors of antebellum conservative elitism, the Scottish writer Adam Ferguson. Although his contribution was ultimately obscured by that of his contemporary, Adam Smith, Ferguson's works enjoyed great influence among the literate European and American public in the late eighteenth and early nineteenth centuries; and Marx credited him for giving Smith his insight into the division of labor's deleterious impact on the intellectual capabilities of workers in manufactories.[18] In his classic work, *An Essay on the History of Civil Society,* first published in 1767, Ferguson argued that in the most advanced, or "polished," stage of civilization, one distinguished by intense commercial and manufacturing activity and which Ferguson took to describe Great Britain, the degree of social subordination experienced by individuals had three basic sources: "There is one ground of subordination in the difference of natural talents and dispositions; a second in the unequal division of property; and a third, not less sensible, in the habits which are acquired by the practice of different arts."[19] Of these three sources of subordination, "the practice of different arts"—or the division of labor—was the most distinctive to "polished" societies. It decisively contributed to men's social power and social rank by building upon their innate differences in intellectual capacity: "If many parts in the practice of every art, and in the detail of every department, require no abilities, or actually tend to contract and limit the views of the mind, there are others which lead to general reflections, and to enlargement of thought."[20] In a later major work, *Principles of Moral and Political Science,* Ferguson observed that

> In the several departments into which the business of trade is distributed, it may be observed, that variety of talents being required, the faculties of mind are unequally cultivated. While invention employs the superior genius, and while the direction of a work requires the enlargement of knowledge; the execution of a single part consisting, perhaps, in a mere movement of the hand or the foot, supersedes every act of thought or exercise of ingenuity: Insomuch, that the human faculties seem to be as much suppressed in the one case, as they are raised and invigorated in the other.[21]

In certain parts of his writing, Ferguson left little doubt that he, like Smith, regarded the differential intellectual impact of occupational specialization as a worrisome and pernicious basis of social subordination, as a troubling new kind of social inequality. Somewhat more fully, perhaps, than Smith, Ferguson feared that the division of labor, acting in conjunction with economic inequalities, posed particularly grave threats to the organic bonds holding "polished" societies together. And although he believed that all classes in these societies were vulnerable to developing a deficient sense of community, Ferguson again singled out the laboring classes as special victims of this estrangement.[22] The implications for social cohesion and stability were most serious of all in those progressive commercial societies that strove to practice at least a limited "democracy," where all political power was not concentrated in the hands of a despotic monarchy. Of the "lowest orders of men" in these societies, Ferguson wrote:

> Ignorance is the least of their failings. An admiration of wealth unpossessed, becoming a principle of envy, or of servility; . . . the crimes to which they are allured, in order to feed their debauch, or to gratify their avarice, are examples, not of ignorance, but of corruption and baseness. If the savage has not received our instructions, he is likewise unacquainted with our vices. He knows no superior, and cannot be servile; he knows no distinctions of fortune, and cannot be envious. . . .
>
> Whether in great or in small states, democracy is preserved with difficulty, under the disparities of condition, and the unequal cultivation of the mind, which attend the variety of pursuits, and applications, that separate mankind in the advanced state of commercial arts. . . .
>
> Under the *distinction* of callings, by which the members of polished society are separated from each other, . . . society is made to consist of parts, of which none is animated with the spirit of society itself.[23]

But despite the social atomism and the atrophy of the manual laborer's mental faculties encouraged by specialization, Ferguson remained committed both to the division of labor and the structure of entrenched social distinctions to which it contributed. He insisted that "a people can make no great progress in cultivating the arts of life, until they have separated, and committed to different persons, the several tasks, which require a peculiar skill and attention."[24] As to social hierarchy, Ferguson noted that "It has pleased Providence for wise purposes, to place men in different stations, and to bestow upon them different degrees of wealth. Without this circumstance there could be no subordination, no government, no order, no industry. Every person does good, and promotes the happiness of society, by living agreeable to the rank in which Providence has placed him."[25] And in a separate writing Ferguson added: "They ['mankind'] have indeed by nature equal rights to their preservation, and to the use of their talents; but they are fitted for different stations. . . . It is obvious, that some mode of subordination is as necessary to men as society itself; and this, not only to attain the ends of government, but to comply with an order established by nature."[26]

David Kettler, the author of one of the most definitive studies of Ferguson's thought, has convincingly argued that in his desire to vindicate commercial society and the status quo, Ferguson ultimately, and perhaps unconsciously, retreated from the intellectual dilemma raised by the division of labor: "He withdrew, in most respects, from the attempt to overcome the narrowing of human capabilities attendant on the division of labor because he was convinced that this could not be achieved without destroying society; . . . he urged the lower classes to accept the human indifference, the debasing drudgery, and the grinding poverty which falls to their lot as inescapable consequences of their situation."[27] Ferguson's fundamental insight into the constricting and degrading effects of the division of labor carried the implication that the tasks performed by individuals in "polished" societies bore a highly imperfect and unjust relationship to their innate capabilities, to, that is, the distribution of natural talents. To the extent that the lower orders were naturally inferior in terms of intellectual capacity and enterprise, this inferiority was limited in magnitude.[28] Notwithstanding this insight, Ferguson was "compelled simply to sacrifice the poor upon the altar of social necessity," largely because he valued the division of labor, because he regarded it as inevitable, and because he believed, finally, that "it cannot be substantially altered" for the reason that "by its very effects, it disqualifies men for the performance of tasks other than those to which they are assigned."[29] Ferguson accordingly tended to subordinate his critical view of the division of labor to an alternative, conservative elitist one in which natural differences among individuals, their inequalities in wealth, and the tasks they performed under the division of labor represented consistent and legitimate links in one chain. "Wherever property is established, it comes of course to be unequally distributed . . . this inequality may be traced to its origin in the unequal dispositions of men to industry and frugality, as well as more casual advantages."[30] The condition of economic inequality that in some measure reflected natural differences was also justified by its decisive role in shaping the necessary distribution of activities. Without such economic inequality, there would be no division between intellectual activity and manual labor, for

> If all men were equally rich, every one might be willing to pay the hire of labour, while no one would be willing to labour for hire: But, as labour is necessary to supply the consumptions of life;

on the supposition of equal riches, every one would be reduced to labour for himself; and thus a supposed equality would reduce the fortune of every person to the fruit merely of his own labour, and, in fact, would be to render every person alike and equally poor.

The ancient republics, amongst whom it was proposed, in some instances, to equalize the fortunes of citizens, had recourse to the labour of slaves, and the object, without this provision, would have been altogether chimerical and wild.

Nature seems to have ordered, that, in proportion as men shall depart from their original poverty, they shall depart also from that original state of equality, in which it was necessary for every individual to labour for himself.[31]

As Orestes Brownson expressed the same idea some eighty years later, long after he had left his days as a labor reformer behind him: "There must always be a laboring class in every country. And such class as a class must always be poor, for if rich they would not labor, and if all classes were alike rich all would be alike poor, and every man would have to perform his own labor . . . black his own boots."[32]

Ferguson's works went through numerous editions in early nineteenth-century America, and there is a strong likelihood that Brownson, along with many of the other American proponents of conservative elitism, either read them or were at least affected by them indirectly.[33] But apart from his probable influence, Ferguson has also received space here because his attempts to confront the issue of intellectually deadening labor, to ultimately legitimate both its existing distribution and the structure of economic inequality in which it existed, foreshadowed and illuminated the later responses of American conservative elitists to drudge work in their society. In 1856 a writer of a proslavery essay in the *Southern Literary Messenger* noted "the tendency of modern progress," specifically the application of mechanical invention, to reduce "the inequality of physical powers" among individuals; such application "tends to reduce the importance of superiority in muscle and sinew, and consequently to equalize the condition of men in that respect." But at the same time, the writer observed, in a manner similar to Ferguson,

> It is equally manifest that the general tendency of modern civilization is to increase the mental disparity between different individuals and classes in society. One of the necessary consequences of modern invention is a minute division of labour. . . . While . . . those who have only capacity enough to perform the menial offices or minute details of the supposed operation, or whose necessities are such as to compel them to accept such employment, are continually cramping their faculties with new fetters,

those whose mental abilities enable them to take charge of higher departments—receive more wages—have more leisure, and are constantly widening the difference between themselves and their inferiors.[34]

The writer took the differential impact of the division of labor upon individuals as the most compelling modern evidence of the divinely intended "irredeemable inequality of men." The poverty and physical suffering of the "mentally weak" in modern civilization—a category coincident with at least the lower ranks of the laboring poor—could and should be mitigated by "a judicious liberality." The most inhumane consequences of exploitation were a product of "free competition," or unrestrained free market capitalism, and this, the *Southern Literary Messenger* contributor made clear in the manner of George Fitzhugh, was not inevitable. In contrast, neither "the natural effects" of the division of labor nor the initial or innate inequality in intellectual capacities among individuals upon which specialization built could be substantially removed.[35] The writer would likely have agreed with the assessment by Jesse Foot, in an earlier defense of slavery in the British West Indies, that "if various ranks and orders of men *be necessary . . . the only duty is to make all occupations and all conditions of men as comfortable as the nature of their stations will admit.*"[36]

This discussion in the *Southern Literary Messenger* of "the tendencies of modern civilization" culminated, as so many did in Southern proslavery literature, in an affirmation of the peculiar institution over "socialism" as the more viable means of alleviating the physical misery and mental anxiety induced by free market capitalism in the laboring population. Slavery and other institutionalized forms of paternalism and subordination, such as relationships within the family, minimized suffering because they derived from, and constructively built upon, the intellectual weakness of those it sought to assist; but socialism was doomed to failure because its efforts to alleviate social evils through a redistribution of property ignored these fundamental intellectual disparities.[37] That the "judicious liberality" to be extended to the white laboring poor of Europe and the free states should actually take the form of legalized enslavement, as it did for the great majority of Southern blacks, was a conclusion that the author of this particular essay did not explicitly draw, but one toward which he certainly seemed to lean.

Adam Ferguson's own case had illustrated that traditional conservative elitist principles need not incorporate a vindication of slavery on the grounds of either class or race. Unlike inequality of property and the division of labor, any attempt to establish property in man, to treat him as a thing under the law, Ferguson argued, represented a violation of the natural rights doctrine to which he gave his support.[38] Writers like Jesse

Foot who shared Ferguson's understanding of the value of social subordination to civilization, who were similarly protective of social order and the status quo, determined that the natural rights doctrine could also accommodate chattel slavery, or that it was invalid and dispensable if it could not. The recent Denmark Vesey slave insurrection in Charleston, Virginia, as well as the lingering specter of the French Revolution, may have inspired the remarks of another of a long line of British and American proslavery writers in this tradition, Edward Brown. Perfect equality, even were it possible, Brown noted in 1826, encouraged insubordination and anarchy, because it precluded the mutual dependence and attendant restraints on behavior that were generated by a diversity of social ranks and conditions. The division of mankind into grades, together with the consequent mutual dependence, Brown noted, was the "very soul of civilization." The more numerous the grades, the more highly civilized the country. Slavery, Brown made clear, was but one of these grades, and one that was legitimate and in fact highly necessary to those civilized nations suffering from a deficiency of free labor.[39]

Recent historians have debated the extent to which the application of traditional conservative and hierarchical arguments to the defense of slavery, such as that exemplified by Brown, contributed to proslavery ideology in the later antebellum years.[40] The emerging consensus appears to be that writers such as Fitzhugh and George Frederick Holmes, who similarly justified slavery in terms of a universal and inexorable social subordination, were atypical of proslavery Southerners.[41] More characteristic was the "Herrenvolk democracy" defense of slavery, which insisted upon the essential equality and access to equal opportunity of all individuals not belonging to prominent stigmatized racial minorities, and which indeed insisted that this generalized equality was actually dependent upon the guaranteed subordination of these minorities.[42] What seems to be the developing historical consensus frequently notes that Fitzhugh himself retreated from his suggestion that formal slavery might be the best condition for the mass of whites as well as blacks in modern societies; he withdrew, that is to say, from his argument that class rather than race constituted the natural basis of slavery.[43] To the extent that late antebellum Southern proslavery ideology was indeed more racist and white egalitarian than it was traditional conservative elitist in character, it was more in keeping with what other historians have found to be the dominant middle-class ideology in the free states.[44] That ideology had long renounced a condition of entrenched social ranks and rigid class distinctions as a vision of the best society possible, in favor of an alternative ideal of unlimited social mobility opportunities and an equal, virtually atomistic economic competition among individuals.[45] Like the prevalent Southern proslavery ideology also, the dominant ideology in the

North could readily accommodate notions of racial and ethnic inferiority, albeit in less extreme, institutionalized form.[46]

But the issue of whether Southern vindications of slavery more typically relied on the notion of black racial inferiority than they did on the principle of pervasive social subordination and class inequality creates something of a false dichotomy, for the most characteristic slavery defenses incorporated both principles. This would, at least, seem to be true if the issue is considered in terms of proslavery responses to the division of labor and particularly to the distribution of drudge labor in civilized societies. We might recall the observation of the *Southern Literary Messenger* contributor above that members of the laboring population who perform the most mentally undemanding tasks under the division of labor are either "those who have only capacity enough" for this menial work to begin with, or those "whose necessities are such as to compel them to accept such employment."[47] In principle these represented two distinct groups of individuals even if Ferguson, in his defense of drudge work and social subordination, had in fact ultimately made at least a tenuous connection between the two and suggested that the economically impoverished and desperate were in considerable measure those who were of naturally inferior talent and the ones most suited, therefore, to undertake society's drudgery. The distinction between the racist, white egalitarian and the class-conservative elitist defenses of slavery appears to narrow considerably when one considers that both defenses argued that Southern society was well situated precisely because social subordination among its white population was minimal, and that this circumstance was above all attributable to the fact that Southern society contained a sufficiently large racial minority of low intellectual capacity upon which it could effectively impose through slavery virtually all of the necessary drudge work.[48] It served the ideological purposes of defenders of the Old South to attach even more exclusive significance than Ferguson had to the tasks which individuals performed under the division of labor as a basis of social subordination in civilized societies. Defenders of Southern slave society could not easily deny that significant inequalities in property existed among Southern whites; but they could and did argue, with somewhat more plausibility, that in the South above all, economic necessity did not drive the white laboring poor into many forms of debasing work which in other societies were commonly taken as confirmation of intellectual and social inferiority. A major achievement of Southern civilization, so the argument ran, was its demonstration that the presence of a distinctive group whose manifest lack of intellectual capacity made it perfectly suited for the exclusive drudgery created by the division of labor might obviate a major basis of social subordination among all other members of the community. On this fundamental point, the "class" and "racial" proslavery arguments came close to fusing into a single defense of the peculiar institution. We can perhaps best illustrate this confluence through consideration of one of its best-known and consummate expressions, the so-called mud-sill speech delivered in Congress by South Carolina Senator James Henry Hammond in March, 1858.[49] Amidst the heated confrontation between proslavery and antislavery forces, both within and outside Congress, over the ratification of the proslavery Lecompton Constitution in Kansas, Hammond offered these comments:

> In all social systems there must be class to do the mean duties, to perform the drudgery of life. That is, a class requiring but a low order of intellect and but little skill. Its requisites are vigor, docility, fidelity. Such a class you must have, or you would not have that other class which leads progress, refinement, and civilization. It constitutes the very mud-sills of society. . . . Fortunately for the South, she found a race adapted to that purpose to her hand. A race inferior to herself, but eminently qualified in temper, in vigor, in docility, in capacity to stand the climate, to answer all her purposes. We use them for the purpose, and call them slaves. . . . I will not characterize that class at the North with that term; but you have it; it is there; it is everywhere; it is eternal.
>
> The Senator from New York [William Seward] said yesterday that the whole world had abolished slavery. Ay, the name, but not the thing; and all the powers of the earth cannot abolish it. God only can do it when he repeals the *fiat,* "The poor ye always have with you;" for the man who lives by daily labor, and scarcely lives at that; and who has to put out his labor in the market and take the best he can get for it; in short, your whole class of manual laborers and operatives, as you call them, are slaves. The difference between us is, that our slaves are hired for life and well compensated; there is no starvation, no begging, no want of employment among our people. . . . Yours are hired by the day, not cared for, and scantily compensated, which may be proved in the most deplorable manner, at any hour, in any street in any of your large towns. Why, sir, you meet more beggars in one day, in any single street of the city of New York, than you would meet in a lifetime in the whole South. Our slaves are black, of another, inferior race. The *status* in which we have placed them is an elevation. . . . They are happy, content, unaspiring. . . .
>
> Your slaves are white, of your own race; you are brothers of one blood. They are your equals in natural endowment of intellect, and they feel galled by their degradation.[50]

Some thirteen years before delivering this speech, Hammond had written the British abolitionist, Thomas Clarkson, that "I am no more in favor of slavery in the abstract, than I am of poverty, disease, deformity, idiocy or any other inequality in the condition of the human family."[51] On the basis of his 1858 speech, Hammond was being partially disingenuous in his comments to Clarkson; for if he did not vindicate slavery here on completely "abstract" grounds, he did of course idealize or romanticize its impact upon its victims.[52] With respect to his attitude toward poverty, however, Hammond was more accurate in his remarks to Clarkson. Through the centuries and into modern times, proponents of traditional conservative elitism had characteristically expressed a religious appreciation of gross inequalities—poverty was a "blessing" both for the Christian virtues with which that humble condition favored the poor and for the opportunity it afforded the wealthy to practice charity and stewardship.[53] Almost as characteristic was the aesthetic appreciation of a diversity of ranks and conditions—the "beauty in variety" exemplified by social hier- archy, in contrast to the "monotony" of equal conditions proposed by various leveling schemes.[54] But Hammond's own brand of traditional conservative elitism offered a quite different response to poverty and social inequality; for if he also saw God's work behind these, he did not, nonethe- less, justify them by romanticizing them.[55] The value of poverty, like that of slavery, was primarily utilitarian; economic necessity and legalized enslave- ment represented alternative forces for getting the world's necessary dirty work done. By confining such work to those who could be exploited, slavery and poverty alike freed other members of civilized society for division of labor's more elevated and rewarding tasks. But if exploitation was the way of the world, chattel slavery, at least as it existed in the Old South, represented a far more humane form of exploitation than the "wage slavery" generated by poverty. This was so for two basic reasons. First, the condition of chattel slavery offered adequate protection and compensation to its victims, whereas wage slavery did neither. The latter condition was, furthermore, an inevitable consequence of the tendency of population to overrun the means of subsistence and reduce even prosperous and inde- pendent, truly "free" labor to a subsistent and servile state. The Southern proslavery use of Malthus to challenge the mythology of American excep- tionalism regarding Northern free labor, to lend reinforcement to the Biblical decree of poverty's inexorable and growing presence even in the most favored societies, is a subject unto itself and requires treatment in a separate study. But it might be noted here that proslavery Malthusianism demonstrated the willingness of slavery's defenders to adopt classical eco- nomic principles when it suited their purposes, even as they declared their disgust with classical economy—with less traditional, free market elitism— for its indifference to the plight of market economy's wage slaves.[56]

But apart from the subsistence it assured its victims, chattel slavery in the South was in Hammond's view a more humane form of exploitation than wage slavery for the basic reason that the dirty work it imposed on its victims was not below their intellectual capacities. As another proslavery writer claimed in the *Southern Quarterly Review,* the African blacks brought over for slavery were "essentially a base class . . . it would be wrong to call them degraded, as the term implies a previous better condition."[57] Indeed, some proslavery writers, such as William Gilmore Simms, Henry Hughes, and above all John H. Van Evrie, went so far as to suggest that as a description of the condition of black bondsmen in the South, the term *slavery* was a misnomer, since a true slave was one who was *"forced into a position in society below the claims of his intellect."*[58] But although dirty work, under the coercion of legal enslavement, in fact rescued an intellectually inferior race from idleness and barbarism, the same labor, imposed by the coercion of poverty and the fear of starvation in "free societies," degraded and effectively enslaved a body of white workers whose innate intellectual capacities demanded more from their employment. Thus William J. Grayson took issue with Fitzhugh's suggestion that "the white race is the very best slave race." Fitzhugh was correct, Grayson claimed, in the sense that a person of "distinguished genius and intelligence," such as Henry Clay, "would have made the most accomplished body-servant in the world, yet we also hold that he would have made the very worst," because he was capable of so much more.[59]

Apart from his own observation of the starving "beggars" of the northeastern cities, where, in fact, unemployment and want had reached unprecedented levels during the depression winter of 1857–58, Hammond's "mud-sill" speech represented the distillation of a variety of intellectual traditions, many of which were more evident in longer proslavery defenses by Fitzhugh and others.[60] In addition to the Bible and Malthus's contribution to political economy, Hammond's remarks drew on Aristotle's notion of higher and lower social functions and their assignment to different individuals as a necessary basis of civilized society. The theme of the "utility of poverty" as a labor incentive dated at least to the cynical early eighteenth-century work by Bernard Mandeville, *The Fable of the Bees,* and ran through much mercantilist and anti-poor law thought.[61] Hammond's distaste for the brutalizing mechanism of poverty even as he recognized its efficacy as a spur to labor borrowed from socialist and trade union perspectives, while his related disgust for the impersonal "cash nexus" principle that governed capital–wage labor relations in market economies was likely also inspired by the body of Tory-Romantic criticism.[62] The vital principle that the nature of the labor itself, quite apart from economic inequality, constituted an independent source of social subordination and social distinctions to the extent that it demeaned and constricted the natural capabilities of those who undertook it, derived from the tradition of Ferguson and Smith. And finally, the argument that restricting low-grade labor to those of naturally inferior intellect served to considerably diminish subservience and distinctions in the larger society, even if poverty and economic inequalities maintained their inexorable presence there—the sense in which Hammond's proslavery defense was sensitive to divisions of both race and class—was itself the culmination of a series of "mud-sill" type vindications of Southern slave society initiated nearly forty years earlier during the Congressional debates over the Missouri Compromise.[63]

In relatively few words, Hammond managed to touch base with all of these traditions. Masterful as it was, however, his speech offered less enlightenment on a most germane question than had many of his proslavery forerunners or, for that matter, than did many of the Southern Congressmen who flew to his defense in the months after his controversial presentation. What exactly, that is to say, was the nature of the "mud-sill" or drudge work from which the laboring whites of Southern society were in unique degree freed owing to the presence of black slaves?

That labor consisted, above all, of the range of "menial services" described in chapter 4. S. D. Moore's suggestion that such services were an intrinsically contemptible form of employment that confirmed the essential slavery of the individuals who performed them, regardless of their true legal status, typified the Southern proslavery tendency to focus its scorn on low-grade service employments.[64] Wage laborers occupied, by definition, a subordinate economic position; but the subordination of workers, free or slave, who performed this low-grade service work was adjudged uniquely servile and contemptible. There remained, however, a certain ambiguity and inconsistency in Southern proslavery pronouncements on "menial services": did the principal degradation of these tasks reside in their intrinsically menial character, or rather in the degree to which they were indeed performed as either wage or slave "service" labor for another? A majority of white Southerners, it should be recalled, did not own slaves; they performed their own domestic chores and were their own "hewers of wood and drawers of water."[65] Proslavery tracts and political speeches were conceivably exhibiting some sensitivity to this fact to the significant extent that they did emphasize how menial tasks were above all loathsome and stigmatized work, fit only for an inferior race, when they became service work performed for an employer or master. On the other hand, proslavery ideology unmistakably suggested on occasion that domestic and other menial tasks were by their very nature contemptible, and on those occasions it conveyed at least an implicit disdain for all individuals, including non-slaveholding white Southerners, whose circumstances obliged them to perform these tasks for themselves. In 1844 the abolitionist newspaper, the *Emancipator,* cited the comments reportedly made by Henry Clay in Committee of the Whole during the debates over the Missouri Compromise Bill in 1819: "If gentlemen will not allow us to have *black* slaves, they must let us have *white* ones; for we cannot cut our firewood, and black our shoes, AND HAVE OUR WIVES AND DAUGHTERS WORK IN THE KITCHEN."[66]

There is a related issue to be raised. In reporting Clay's alleged remarks, the *Emancipator* commented that "there are two points on which you can easily test the real extent of a man's sympathies with labor—his sense of justice with regard to the wages of labor, and his sentiments with regard to the intrinsic dignity of labor itself." The *Emancipator* left no doubt that it found Clay's sentiments wanting on the second score, and in this the *Emancipator* was typical of abolitionist and later Republican opinion. Despite, that is to say, the tendency of proslavery pronouncements to focus their explicit scorn on domestic and other menial tasks, whether these tasks were performed as "service" for others or not, standard antislavery opinion insisted that proslavery values in the South generated and carried an elitist disdain for *all* forms of manual labor. To the limited degree, furthermore, that it acknowledged the existence within the free states of some comparable disdain for manual labor employments, antislavery sentiment characteristically blamed that contempt upon the corrupting influence of the South's "peculiar institution."[67]

As already noted, in antebellum America generally, middle-class attitudes encompassed some definite disdain for manual labor employments for reasons that had little or nothing to do with the institution of Southern slavery. Whether, however, that institution gave some additional or special impetus to a contempt, not merely for menial service employments, but for manual labor generally, would certainly seem plausible—the criticisms of a Frederick Law Olmsted can hardly be completely discounted. Yet the real significance or magnitude of slavery as a discrete source for such contempt remains a question without a single or unequivocal answer; for in the South as elsewhere, the social practices and economic realities to which one might appeal for that answer were complex and many-sided, and social values gave out different signals. Consider, for example, the following remarks of Mississippi Senator Albert Gallatin Brown, one of the many who anticipated Hammond's "mud-sill" remarks. Brown informed his Northern colleagues in 1854 that

> the line that separates menial from honorable labor with you is not marked by a caste or distinct color, as it is with us. In the South, as in the North, all the mechanic arts are treated as honorable, and they are not the less so because sometimes practiced by blacks. . . .
>
> But there are certain menial employments which belong exclusively to the negro—. . . it would take you longer to find a

white man, in my State, who would hire himself out as a boot-black, or a white woman who would go out to service as a chambermaid, than it took Captain Cook to sail around the world. . . .

I do not say that it is disreputable for white men and white women to go out to service and to perform even these lower grades of labor. But I say that with you, as with us, they lose their position in the social scale when they do it. With you it must be done by whites, and therefore the whites lose position; with us this menial labor is performed by negroes, and the equality among the whites is preserved.[68]

In denying, if only implicitly, that the more highly skilled forms of manual labor—"the mechanic arts"—were *deserving* of contempt, Brown was typical of all but the most elitist defenders of slavery. He was no less typical in rebutting antislavery charges that these forms were in fact shunned or demeaned in the Southern states, and in this rebuttal he has enjoyed the rather able support of some historians.[69] In drawing, however, a characteristic proslavery dichotomy between the reputable standing of skilled manual labor employments in the South and the low status of various menial ones there, Brown's remarks contained nuances that signalled some of the tensions and crosscutting pressures within antebellum Southern society. Brown, first of all, only explicitly characterized those "lower grades of labor" that were performed in the service of others as stigmatizing in the South, so here there were signs of that sensitivity to the circumstances of nonslaveholding Southern whites referred to earlier. More than this, Brown exhibited some hesitation at categorizing even menial service work as *intrinsically* "disreputable"; there is a suggestion that the low esteem from which such work suffered was rather a function of prevailing social values, North and South. Brown's particular version of the racist, white egalitarian defense of slavery might be said to bear the earmarks of a proslavery Southern politician who in other respects too, as in his populist support for homestead legislation to aid the landless white poor, deviated quite markedly from full-blown proslavery elitist, antidemocratic sentiments.[70]

Yet it remained more generally true for racist, white egalitarian defenses of slavery such as Brown's to include a more unequivocal disdain for menial services. Proslavery commentators could not generally, perhaps, resist making full ideological capital out of the circumstance that in the South above all, members of a superior race did not perform these services. Not a few commentators, indeed, went further than Brown; they extracted from the general confinement of menial services to blacks in the South the conclusion that those other, "free labor" employments monopolized by whites in fact enjoyed a higher standing in the South than anywhere else, including the Northern states. North Carolina Senator David S. Reid thus argued that

> where slavery exists, free labor, so far from being degraded, is elevated. The kind of labor which is imposed on white men in the free states is imposed upon slaves in the South. . . .
>
> . . . When there are low, menial services, *that white men never were intended to perform in a free country* [italics mine], they are performed by the slave race. . . .
>
> . . . therefore in the slave States free labor, instead of being degraded, is in fact elevated.[71]

The proslavery focus upon menial service employments as intrinsically lowly and base work, suitable only for a race of inferior intellect, raises a number of interesting points beyond those already considered. A far greater number of Southern slaves were of course engaged not as these stigmatized "hewers of wood and drawers of water" at all, but in agricultural field labor. One might suppose that such slave work could have been equally disdained by slavery's defenders as "unintelligent physical labor" from which whites should be exempt.[72] However, in part because many Southern whites who owned few or no slaves also manifestly engaged in agricultural hand labor, and also because proslavery ideology sought to rebut the antislavery argument that merely performing the same kind of work as slaves, often alongside them, was itself degrading to whites, slavery's defenders did not consistently include the very kind of work in which the majority of slaves engaged as intrinsically contemptible. One historical opinion holds that the relative lightness of their work, together with the proximity they enjoyed with their owners, put house servants, coachmen, and other "menial service" slaves among the more highly favored, higher status bondsmen, part of the "aristocracy of slave society," at least as defined by whites.[73] But if this was the case, it also remained true that it was these very menial service positions, and not the ruder and rougher agricultural field work performed by lower status bondsmen, that suffered the brunt of proslavery's ideological disdain.

Historians have also amply documented a circumstance at which Senator Brown hinted: the persistence in the South of a considerable body of slaves, as well as free blacks, in the non-"menial" mechanic arts.[74] Not a few proslavery writers and politicians wished to minimize or altogether eliminate this slave presence.[75] That desire could reflect some very practical aims: to mollify the complaints of free white mechanics regarding unfair and degrading competition, and to otherwise ease and avert class tensions in the South.[76] Some proslavery writers may have also been moved by a more abstractly philosophical wish to free their ideological distinction between black slave/menial and free white/mechanical arts employments from existing empirical contradiction. Yet if Southern blacks remained employed in skilled work for which abstract argument often held them to be intellectually unqualified, native-born whites in the slave states, however impoverished their economic condition, did not to a corresponding degree cross over into those "menial" service employments deemed fit only for an inferior race. In this latter respect, existing research and census data does lend support to the prevailing proslavery argument.[77]

It is also true, however, that until the mid 1840s the "hewers of wood and drawers of water" of the Northern states, particularly those in the larger cities, consisted overwhelmingly of blacks also. One of the more obvious consequences of the large influx of Irish immigrants after this time was "Paddy's" displacement of blacks in urban low-grade service employments. Just as it was common knowledge that blacks and Irish immigrants competed for these and other of the most disagreeable and "degrading" employments, the ones that nobody else wanted, so it was widely recognized that the Irish generally won the competition.[78] Defenders of Southern society commonly disdained the immigrant Irish as a disruptive and raffish population and heralded its *relative* absence from the South as a measure of slave society's superiority.[79] But they were not above exploiting the employment and demographic patterns in the free states. Although proslavery Southerners had claimed for decades that degrading work like valet service or bootblacking was imposed on members of the superior white race in the free states, the increasing employment of the immigrant Irish in this and other "mud-sill" work likely encouraged slavery's defenders to employ the argument with increasing frequency. The concentration of impoverished immigrants in work they themselves saw as unprecedented economic opportunity served a quite different function in proslavery ideology. Louisiana Congressman Miles Taylor observed in the wake of Hammond's speech, "In Europe, where all the people are nominally free, the great and broad distinction which obtains, is distinction between those who have capital and those who have none; . . . No matter what may be a man's worth; no matter what may be his moral qualities; if his poverty compels him to discharge menial offices, that man stands there in an inferior position. And now, let me ask my northern brethren if this feature of European society is not displaying itself among them."[80]

Taylor, it might be added, was, in this speech rather more all-inclusive than some of his proslavery colleagues regarding the nature of "menial offices." Although at some points he restricted it to intrinsically contemptible service work, fit only for a "different and inferior race," he elsewhere appeared to equate it with all intellectually undemanding but "honest" physical toil—that labor performed by those "whose only capital is their "bone and muscle." In these places, he followed Albert Gallatin Brown in suggesting that pernicious values in the free states, in the fashion of Europe, had unjustly stigmatized such work along with the poverty that induced white laborers to perform it. Open to criticism were both the mere employment of immigrant and other whites in the low-grade service jobs, and the tendency in the free states to disdain the poorest whites for their employment in *all* physical labor that less impoverished groups were able to avoid.[81] Taylor's polemical objective was clearly to expose both free market economic forces and the "cash nexus" capitalist ethic as related agents of exploitation in free societies. Free market forces entrapped the white poor in intrinsically demeaning work, the "cash nexus" ethic stigmatized much if not all of the white working class for its poverty, regardless of the specific nature of the work performed by that class. The consequence was that there prevailed among white workers outside the slave South a degree of social subordination and sense of social inferiority over and above that arising from the mere existence of poverty and economic inequality.

The dichotomy drawn between menial and manual labor as justifiably grounded in racial rather than class differences represented one part of the effort of slavery's defenders to interpret social change in the free states to their advantage. The inability to consistently confine intrinsically contemptible menial service work to blacks in the free states was seized upon as perhaps the primary reason why free white labor in the North was less rather than more elevated than free white labor in the South. Only in a slave state, Virginia Congressman Thomas H. Bayly noted in 1848, would whites refuse to drive coaches or black boots and only here, accordingly, where "the distinctions in society do not grow out of the difference of pursuits, but of condition and color."[82] A particular thread of proslavery thought, however, looked beyond the menial service employments as the only work fit exclusively for blacks and sought to ideologically exploit, as well, other social changes in the free states. The reference here is to the theme that black slaves would make the ideal factory operatives, and that the division of labor in free societies degraded white workers not only by forcing them into the age-old tasks performed by "hewers of wood and drawers of water," but also by imposing on them the newer industrial forms of "mudsill" work. It was the argument that saw Southern slaves as perfectly suited for factory drudgery by virtue of their very lack of intellectual capacity which the opposing antislavery claims earlier described were largely intent on refuting. The appropriation by slavery's defenders of the criticisms made by Adam Smith and other European thinkers of manufacturing division of labor, together with those defenders' use of the imagery of Britain's ignorant and "degraded" factory workers, dramatically exemplified the intersection on the attitudinal level of industrial changes in the Western World with the indigenous sectional conflict over slavery.

As early as 1810, Kentucky Congressman Matthew Lyon indicated how the negative perceptions of industrial labor might provide an additional justification for black Southern slavery: negro chattels would make ideal factory hands since "no country can boast of a more abject, degraded set of people . . . nor a class more fitted to do all the drudgery of manufactures than our blacks."[83] Dr. Thomas P. Jones filled in many of the details of this argument in an address before Philadelphia's Franklin Institute in 1827. An Englishman who had lived in the South for some years, and who had observed the use of slaves in both agriculture and some of the early Southern industries, Jones declared himself convinced that blacks were "peculiarly suited" to be employed in manufactories. If blacks were indeed the intellectual inferiors of whites, the extreme division of labor would turn such inferiority to its advantage, because "only a small degree of intelligence is necessary to the acquisition of the utmost skill in the performance of an individual operation, however delicate it may be. In all extensive manufactories, we meet with the veriest dolts, who become, as it were, a part of the operative machinery; performing, from habit, the business allotted to them, with a degree of dexterity and precision which appears almost miraculous."[84] Jones went on to observe that, apart from their presumed intellectual inferiority, blacks possessed other qualities that would make them superior operatives, including an imitative propensity and an actual capacity to derive satisfaction from being confined to one simple and repetitive operation.[85]

Jones, it should be noted, contended that his was an argument not in defense of black slavery, but rather one on behalf of Southern economic development. The employment of slaves in factories, he argued, would in fact prepare them for freedom by training them in habits of industry. Factory employment should also be extended to poor whites in the South as a means of improving their condition as well.[86] Notwithstanding these additional remarks by the Englishman, the argument of a natural fit between blacks and factory work joined the body of thought designed to vindicate and strengthen Southern slavery. To some of slavery's defenders it appeared as a particularly powerful argument, because at the same time that it put free societies in an unfavorable light for their exploitation of white factory operatives, it tied slavery to the future of Southern economic development and furthered the cause of Southern economic diversity and independence. Jones's address, which was printed in the *American Farmer,* was preceded and followed by a flurry of enthusiastic correspondence in that journal of a more unequivocally proslavery nature. One such writer noted that slaves were the most profitable of all operatives in the manufacture of coarse fabrics. They were cheaper, more docile, and their lack of "inventive genius" was an advantage, enabling them to endure the "monotonous occupation of attending a spindle or a loom." That black slaves could easily master such work was evident from the fact that "the very *children* of the *white slaves* of Europe" learned within a month to use these simple machines for drawing out a thread with a mule or joining it with a spindle.[87] Nathaniel A. Ware, a Southern planter who favored industrialization in his region, similarly suggested some seventeen years later that it was fortunate that the South possessed black slaves in such numbers, given their "highly imitative" quality. Their suitability for manufacturing and factory work would enable the South to exempt its "free people, and particularly [its] delicate [white] females and children, from factory drudgery and labor." Slaves can do the "worst, most unhealthy and degrading sort of duties and labor."[88] A writer in the *Augusta Constitutionalist* was more explicit in extrapolating from the black slave's unique propensity for agricultural gang labor in oppressive tropical climates, as well as from their limited use in existing Southern factories: African slaves were "peculiarly qualified" as operatives, since "they are more manageable, more pliable, and can best endure the heated atmosphere of a confined room—to which hundreds of the whites are daily falling victims."[89] Well into the 1850s, the argument that blacks made ideal factory workers retained its appeal, invoked most notably perhaps, by those who wished to reopen the African slave trade and recruit fresh supplies of slaves for new fields of Southern enterprise. Leonidas W. Spratt claimed that "the negro, in his common absence from reflection, is perhaps the best manupalatist [i.e., manipulator of machinery] in the world."[90]

The notion that black slaves were singularly suited for factory work was also utilized by Southern proslavery men who were less interested in the industrialization of slave labor than in its geographic expansion into new agricultural regions. Although Thomas H. Bayly claimed that menial service work represented the most suitable work for blacks, he nonetheless agreed that slaves "are fully equal" to the minimal skill demands of factory work. This fact had serious implications for those "indigent whites" of the South whose present or future livelihood depended on their employment in Southern industry and who stood far more to lose than the large planters did from the confinement of slave labor to existing areas. "If there is no outlet" for the slaves, Bayly insisted, "in a short time it will be difficult to employ them profitably in agriculture." Their growing supply in relation to the demands of agriculture would reach the point where they must spill over into non-agricultural enterprise; they would invariably supplant white laborers in the factories and even in the skilled "handicraft and mechanical employments" of the South.[91]

Proslavery use of the theme that black slaves made perfect industrial "mud-sills" must be viewed in the perspective of differing concerns and opposing arguments that existed at the time. As the case of Thomas P. Jones indicated, the theme was not the exclusive province of Southerners intent upon strengthening slavery. To the labor reformer, Robert Dale Owen, the match between slaves and industrial drudgery stood above all as a threat to the economic security of free laborers everywhere, much in the nature of labor-saving machinery or increasing population density. "The operations now performed by factory workers are chiefly of a simple and mechanical kind, demanding no special exertion of intellect," Owen warned. Thus "a Southern slave of ordinary intelligence can readily be taught to perform them."[92] The economic well-being of white factory workers in the North was the particular concern of the Democratic newspaper, the *Pennsylva-nian,* which described the dreaded development that would come to pass if the "Black Republicans" successfully blocked slave labor's expansion into new agricultural regions in the territories. The *Pennsylvanian* offered a variation on Bayly's thesis, suggesting that free soilism together with the slaves' adaptability to industrial labor would destroy the livelihood of Northern workers by taking away the markets for their products:

> As soon as the negroes increase to over supply the demands for their usual out-door pursuits, their owners will of necessity find employment for them indoors; first in the ruder mechanic and manufacturing arts, and then the more refined, until they will absorb them all. . . . Instead of being as they now are, the great consumers of the products of the mechanics and manufacturers of the North, they will become their rivals, and then supersede them in the markets of the world. . . . Inferior, as the negroes are, they are nevertheless well qualified for operatives in manufactories.[93]

A radical labor perspective, one that perceived the factory system as an unmitigated curse rather than as a valuable source of employment for whites, took a still different view of the issue of slave labor in factories. George Henry Evans sadly noted in 1845 that "even southern planters have caught the Factory contagion, and are preparing to sink their slaves one degree lower in the scale of misery: the poor blacks are to exchange the healthful field for the consumptive factory atmosphere. . . . They will die prematurely as they do in the Eastern Factories."[94]

Contrary to Evans's observation, it is quite possible that never more than a small minority of Southern planters and other defenders of slavery either recognized the natural fit between black slaves and factory work, or for other reasons favored the increased employment of slaves in industry. Some concurred with predominant antislavery opinion that the intellectual demands of even factory work were inconsistent with the condition of slavery, if not with the capabilities of black men, and that extensive attempts to employ slaves in this capacity would subvert and undermine the peculiar institution.[95] Other of slavery's proponents, as it has been well docu-mented, preferred for a variety of reasons the employment of poor South-ern whites in factories, while still others, of course, opposed significant industrialization of any kind in the South as incompatible with the values and quality of life of an agricultural slave society.[96]

We are not concerned here with any of these opposing viewpoints, nor with the economic and technical reasons why actual industrialization in the antebellum South, based on either black slave or free white labor, proved of such limited magnitude. Certainly the argument that factory and other industrial work was a natural and desirable form of employment for black slaves was a far more controversial one among defenders of slavery than the argument regarding menial services. In a sense, too, the intellectual appeal that the factory argument did enjoy carried less significance than the one step further which Bayly and some others moved, that black slaves were capable of displacing whites altogether in the most skilled forms of manual labor. For the admission that the intellectual capabilities of blacks were not so limited after all revealed the strictly utilitarian character that the "nigger work" argument possessed for many of its proslavery proponents. Blacks alone should perform certain kinds of work not because they were incapable of more demanding and attractive labor, but because such work was by its very nature demeaning. Its relegation to blacks freed Southern whites from much of the dirty work of the world. The conviction that menial work, particularly when performed as service for others, was disagreeable and degrading work, was not in itself a particularly or distinctively elitist conviction; for that belief was, to some degree, also reflected in the claims of upholders of egalitarian values in the free states that the existence of a class to do household servant's work, hardly less than slavery itself, was incompatible with republican society, and that domestic tasks would be freed of much of their stigma if undertaken more consistently by the members of affluent families themselves.[97] What was most distinctively elitist about the proslavery argument was the explicit claim that certain groups of individuals must, in contrast to other groups, be for all time "too good" for this work; and, even more than this, that this difference among groups deserved institutionalized recognition and support in the form of legalized slavery. Horace Greeley, among some other antislavery Northerners, acknowledged that such reprehensible elitist principles might be hardly less woven into the fabric of employer–domestic servant relations in the North than they were embedded in the slaveholder's dominion over his slave: "Every household constructed on the basis of a superior and an inferior caste—on the assumption that some of us are born to wait and serve, others *to be* served and waited on—that some must work to live, while others may justly live without working—the former being the less and the latter the more honorable class—*that* household, I say, is built on a foundation of un-Christian slavery and unmanly falsehood."[98]

At the same time, defenders of slavery who singled out menial service and certain other work as intrinsically contemptible and who just as typ-

ically insisted that such contemptibleness supported rather than contradicted their belief in the dignity of all other forms of manual labor in the
slave states, revealed something else about the nature of proslavery ideology: the extent to which liberal and egalitarian pressures in America constrained that ideology's aristocratic and elitist impulses and encouraged its
proponents to join in at least the common rhetorical defense of manual
labor's dignity. Many of Southern slavery's most avid proponents, perhaps
most of all those in the political arena who had laboring constituencies with
which to contend, were not, in this sense, one with ancient Greek philosophers or defenders of the Old Regime who more frankly disdained all
manual labor.[99]

Efforts to demonstrate the compatibility of principles bearing contrasting democratic and elitist implications could be made to rather comic
effect. A case in point was Matthew Estes's *A Defence of Negro Slavery*.
Consistent with the title of his work, and with some of the other efforts we
have already examined, the Mississippi writer earmarked the physical activity best left to a grossly inferior, enslaved people: "intense agricultural
toil in a southern climate, and in new settlements in all climates—the
rougher portion of mechanical toil, rough labor on public works, and a
thousand menial offices in society, are totally incompatible with any high
degree of mental culture."[100] But Estes was also trying to tread a line;
invoking that tried and true example, Elihu Burritt, the proslavery author
could also write as if he were establishing his credentials for membership in
a Manual Labor Society: "a certain degree of labor is essential to high
mental effort; it imparts to the body the degree of health and vigor which is
essential to high mental effort. A sound mind and a sound body, are much
more closely connected than philosophers belonging to the old school ever
dreamed of." Some kinds of "labor," then—though not too much of it,
Estes hastened to add—was actually "promotive" of "high mental culture":
"mechanical and professional labor, for instance, and agricultural labor,
when not too severe."[101] That Estes threw in "professional" labor here as
one of the symbiotic opposites of elevated *mental* activity only further
muddied—and muddled—his line of division between "good" and "bad"
physical activity for true nonslaves.

There were, of course, defenders of slavery who did not mince words
like Estes, authors like George S. Sawyer who appeared to go further than
Estes and did not distinguish among forms of physical labor when they
categorized it as a degrading curse.[102] An anonymous writer in Charleston,
Virginia, suggested in 1835 that inherited wealth and privilege were vital to
civilized society precisely because they exempted their beneficiaries from
manual labor. The notion of a symbiotic relationship between an individual's mental and physical faculties, insofar as it insisted upon the value of
manual labor for every member of society, was absurd; for even limited

manual labor could be an "agony" so burdensome to thought that it could "exhaust the very source of . . . perception," destroy the intellect, and render one "a mere animal . . . brutalized and besotted—a slave—a tool—an instrument in the hands of a master."[103] Finding its way into Southern proslavery literature was a remark by the French writer and statesman, Chateaubriand, itself derivative of Aristotle, similarly attesting to the incompatibility between manual labor and substantive intellectual activity: "It is certain that you cannot exercise all the faculties of the mind, except when you are relieved from the material cares of life."[104] Assenting to the truth of this statement, the Virginia politician Abel P. Upshur noted that in thereby freeing a segment of society from the mentally debilitating effects produced by manual labor, Southern slave society represented modern civilization's best opportunity to produce a leisured class of wise and "great" men: "The great man is not formed by book alone. He must have leisure to *think* as well as leisure to study; his mind must be free from the distractions and perplexities which attend the necessity of daily labor for daily bread; his feelings must be at ease, and his ideas unconfined, and free to range where they will. Such is the condition of the slave owner." Upshur proceeded to add that this class of individuals, by whom he appeared to mean the largest and wealthiest of the plantation slaveholders, might, in the tradition of the leaders of the ancient slave republics, use their leisure not only to make important intellectual contributions, but also to reflect upon, and thereby more truly appreciate and sustain, the republican freedoms they were privileged to enjoy. Although small in numbers, this group of leisured and truly cultivated Southern slaveholders would become the most zealous guardians of their nation's republican heritage.[105]

To a certain extent, Upshur's remarks carried disdain not merely for manual labor, but for all active modes of livelihood; the pressures experienced by professional and commercial men presumably impeded them, as well, from attaining that degree of virtue, wisdom, and reflection that only a truly leisured existence—the condition of some of the wealthier slaveholders—encouraged.[106] Yet clearly and most explicitly, Upshur disdained daily manual labor as singularly inhospitable to, if not absolutely incompatible with, meaningful intellectual activity.

Antislavery Northerners, it should be noted, did not necessarily dissent from such proslavery elitist sentiments in all essential respects; they recognized the obvious truth that all members of society could not develop all of their faculties equally, that innate individual tastes and talents, together with the occupational division of labor, imposed inevitable limits and variations on such development. In addressing himself to young scholars in the North, Horace Greeley conceded that "there is, there must be, a pre-eminently Educated Class among us." The acquisition of the knowledge which is "now confined to this class . . . exacts a devotion of time and of means, to say nothing of tastes and habits, which can only be given by the comparatively few."[107] Yet in Greeley's view the complete development of the individual remained an ideal, and "the divorce of Learning from Manual Labor—the absolute dependence of the Educated on the Uneducated class for the means of supplying its physical wants"—produced a class of scholarly weaklings whose achievements were limited rather than maximized by their freedom from physical work. Proslavery elitism's disregard of this fact was, in Greeley's view, no more objectionable than its disdain for that other part of the axiom of balanced faculties, the part which affirmed the manual laborer's need for a greater share of the knowledge now monopolized by the Educated Class. If the majority of manual laborers must remain, in a comparative sense, ignorant, they might still so advance themselves through education as to throw off their abject dependence on the Educated Class for their thinking.[108]

As the most prominent torchbearer for the principles of the manual labor school movement in the late antebellum period, Greeley was more explicit and pronounced than most antislavery Northerners in invoking the ideal of full and harmonious development as a standard for condemning such proslavery elitist arguments as Upshur's.[109] That ideal did, to be sure, manifest itself in a variety of standard antislavery responses, not the least of these being the debunking of Upshur's vision of the elite planter as republican intellectual. Rather than fostering the optimum environment for high intellectual achievement by a leisured few, antislavery voices typically claimed, compulsory servitude extended its mentally blighting and atrophying effects to the wealthy slaveholders themselves: the very circumstances that established their freedom from the necessity of work encouraged their laziness and lack of application in other spheres of activity too. "In consequence of their indolent habits and sportive methods of life," Charles Elliott observed, "intellectual culture is low even among" the "rich planters" and their sons, and the latter, "brought up in luxury and idleness, will rarely undergo the labor necessary to a liberal education. They have a stronger propensity for pleasure and amusement, and even vices, than for the acquirement of knowledge."[110] All of this existed on top of slavery's victimization of both the bondsmen and poor nonslaveholding whites of the South.

In so characterizing the antebellum planter elite as more typically a home-grown version of intellectually inert and decadent Old World landed aristocrats than a new generation of Thomas Jeffersons, standard antislavery formulations were incorporating a somewhat diluted version of the principle of symbiotic faculties articulated by Greeley.[111] Those formulations, that is to say, linked the presumed intellectual lassitude of elite planters and their sons not to their lack of engagement in healthy and productive physical labor per se, but rather to their supposed divorce from any form of active "work." One can see why this kind of antislavery response, concerned as it was with accentuating the distinctions between North and South rather than with addressing the deficiencies of Northern scholars, would have departed from the ideal articulated by Greeley. If only unconsciously, that response accommodated itself to the fact that in the free states as well as the slave, manual labor was hardly an attribute of positions of wealth and influence. After deploring the divorce in existing civilized societies of "the work of the limbs" from "that of the head"—a divorce that rendered both activities unnaturally "repulsive"—Harriet Martineau proceeded to celebrate the fact that professional men in the North could always return to manual labor if they had to.[112] A healthy and vigorous intellectual climate, in antislavery eyes, manifestly precluded the presence of an exploitative, parasitic, and debilitating system of compulsory servitude; but vindication of the Northern social order would hardly have been served by going further than this and arguing what most antislavery writers did not in any case believe: that a vibrant "intellectual culture" also precluded the existence of a division of labor between manual and nonmanual labor employments. If the abundant public schools, libraries, and other signs of Northern intellectual vigor did not exactly disprove one of the more frequent proslavery claims that the merchant princes and others who inhabited the topmost ranks of the Northern occupational structure were money-grubbing intellectual yahoos—those institutions did, in antislavery opinion, unmistakably document something else: the intellectual uplift that was available to the masses—the so-called mud-sills—in an open, "free labor" system.[113]

In explicitly and repeatedly extolling the value of universal engagement in physical labor, Greeley's position, as suggested, was more extremely "egalitarian" than the typical antislavery response to proslavery apologists like Upshur. Yet that position retained certain ambiguities and likely qualifications, reflections of Greeley's own awareness that he was invoking an unattainable ideal. Was, for example, the "constant participation in Manual labor," and not merely exercise, which Greeley deemed "indispensable" to invigorating the mental faculties really to apply to mature members of the Northern educated class as well as to students, and if so, had he not already signified his agreement that the realities of occupational division of labor, the demands of scholarly life, must effectively overrule such participation?[114] And with respect to manual laborers themselves, did Greeley believe, any more fully than proslavery elitists themselves, that intellectual refinement was compatible with the most unskilled and physically "rude" of these laborers' employments—with, for example, the Northern hod carrying and street sweeping for which Greeley admitted disdain when these became occupations that were no longer confined to one's youth?

These quite possible limitations in Greeley's differences with even the most elitist proslavery doctrines were obscured by developments which highlighted the differences. Proslavery literature, together with such actual incidents as a Southern Congressman's fatal shooting of an Irish restaurant waiter for his alleged insolence, provided more than enough fuel for escalating antislavery claims that slavery's defenders viewed all manual laborers as irredeemably contemptible and inferior, irrespective of their color and their type of work, and that these defenders indeed wished to return all free laborers to their "natural" condition of legalized slavery.[115] In its attack upon the proslavery character of the Democratic presidential bid of James Buchanan, a Republican campaign document of 1856 reiterated themes that abolitionists had been expressing for years. In the South particularly but not exclusively, newspapers and "public men" who supported Buchanan "openly avowed and defended the monstrous and shocking" doctrine that "Slavery is not to be confined to the NEGRO RACE, but must be made to include laboring WHITE MEN also."[116] In support of its charge, the Republican document included excerpts from a variety of these proslavery newspapers, including the following one from the "leading" Buchanan paper in South Carolina:

> Slavery is the natural and normal condition of the *laboring man,* whether WHITE or *black*. The great evil of Northern *free* society, is, that it is burdened with a *servile* class of MECHANICS and LABORERS, *unfit for self-government,* and yet clothed with the attributes and powers of citizens. Master and Slave is a relation in society as necessary as that of parent and child; and the Northern States will yet have to introduce it.[117]

Included as well was an excerpt from the Muscogee (Alabama) *Herald* which enjoyed particular notoriety judging from the degree to which it found its way into other antislavery literature as well:

> Free society! we sicken of the name. What is it but a conglomeration of GREASY MECHANICS, FILTHY OPERATIVES, SMALL FISTED FARMERS, and moonstruck THEORISTS? All the Northern, and especially the New England States, are devoid of society fitted for well-bred gentlemen. The prevailing class one meets with, is that of mechanics struggling to be genteel and small farmers who do their own drudgery; and yet who are hardly fit for association with a Southern gentlemen's body servant.[118]

Proslavery excerpts such as these reflected any number of possible considerations and objectives relating to the intensifying ideological warfare between North and South.[119] By claiming that dignified manual labor—at least in the free states—was a contradiction in terms, some of these writings may have even intended to undermine one of the central premises of antislavery Republicanism: that the territorial expansion of black slavery would "degrade" Northern "free white labor." For how could such a process of degradation occur, the proslavery writings implicitly questioned, if Northern manual labor was contemptible to begin with?

But these and similar proslavery excerpts were also more than a product of immediate sectional polemics. Their insistence that manual labor was demeaning, and that individuals who did "their own drudgery" were incapable of intellectual activity and refinement, also represented one of the possible outcomes of the underlying, long-standing belief in the essential propriety of the broad division of labor in civilized societies between intellectual and manual labor. The necessity of this division of labor went unchallenged even by thinkers like George Frederick Holmes who shared the criticism that American commercial and professional men commonly debased their mental labor in the pursuit of Mammon.[120] A writer in the *Southern Quarterly Review* noted that "it is the diversity of pursuits and the appropriateness of various minds to the demands of them, which stimulate and so nicely adjust the industry of men." The value to society of the "diversity of pursuits" was sufficiently self-evident to the writer that he never raised the issue of whether the pursuits themselves unjustly enlarged upon the innate differences among the "various minds," or whether the most brutish and deadening of these in fact incapacitated those entrapped in them for the "higher" pursuits of which they may have at one time been capable.[121] It was the value of the division of labor, the writer maintained, which was so foolishly ignored by the various utopian hopes for "perfect equality," hopes that had been most recently raised during the European revolutionary turmoil of the late 1840s. In such a state of perfect equality "the philosopher, whose intellectual exertions produce such wonderful ameliorations of evils, shall be forced to become his own drawer of water and hewer of wood, and the operatives of society their own speculators in the sciences, as well as their own instructors in knowledge. Do we not see that by such arrangement an interruption would occur in the entire progress of the affairs of life?"[122]

But the belief in the necessity of the division of labor and entrenched social distinctions need not generate a proslavery conservative elitism characterized by undisguised disdain for manual labor. The Reverend Rufus William Bailey of South Carolina noted that slaves and the lower classes generally should not envy the higher orders "since every man has due respect in his own class and sphere of duty."[123] Similarly, Thomas R. Dew, in one of the more influential defenses of slavery, agreed in 1836 that no "honest employment is disgraceful" although it is also true that not "all confer equal honor, if well followed even."[124] Like the racist, white egalitarian defenders of slavery who followed him, Dew was here advancing the argument that social distinctions among Southern whites, and thus the dangers of agrarianism, were minimal, because a significant population of black slaves was present to fill the least honorable employments. Yet unlike many of these defenders, Dew retained the notion that even the "menial service" work most suitable for black slaves carried a measure of dignity. To a degree this notion reflected Dew's traditional hierarchical values: all useful labor was honorable in its sphere. To some extent, too, Dew seemed to share the Fourierist sense that work which was commonly disdained as repugnant became agreeable and dignified if it truly matched the tastes and talents of the individual performing it. Thus did Dew put what was to become a prominent utopian theme to the defense of Southern slavery:

> Any one who has ever seen the negro at hard labor by the side of the white man, or who has noticed him while performing menial services along with his white associate, has marked no doubt the striking difference. The negro is all gaiety and cheerfulness—his occupation seems to ennoble him. His companion, on the contrary, whom the world calls a freeman, but really treats as a slave, is seen sullen and discontented, and feels himself degraded for the very reason that he calls himself a freeman.[125]

To an even more pronounced degree Dew's position diverged from those particular class defenses of slavery, ones that the Republican press was so fond of citing, which were characterized by a disdain for the condition of manual labor generally, and not merely its most "menial" forms.

George Frederick Holmes, one of the foremost exponents of conservative principles and their application in the class defense of slavery, added a final dimension to this defense, noting that aside from any measure of respect which they deserved, manual labor employments generally were capable of generating a limited degree of fulfillment. In view of the divine decree that had assigned physical work to the greater part of mankind as punishment for Original Sin, Fourierist and other utopian doctrines remained absurd, for

> It is ridiculous to fancy that the obligation of daily labour, as the daily price required for the procurement of the daily bread, can be transmitted by any theoretical or practical alchemy of ideal politics into pure gratification: but it may be made to generate a certain satisfaction of its own, neither small in amount, nor mean in degree, and it is not incompatible with such happiness as humanity can grasp, whilst it is often favorable to the manifestation of those virtues which are of more importance to man than either happiness or pleasure.[126]

Holmes's view of the fulfillment and virtue afforded by manual labor moved him closer to those writers, considered below, who extolled the moral content of manual labor under existing social arrangements and who insisted that the Scriptural sentence for Original Sin was more a blessing than a curse. To a commensurate degree, Holmes's view established his distance, like Dew's, from those proslavery writers who regarded all manual labor and manual laborers as base and contemptible.

The proslavery principle that manual laborers occupied subordinate spheres of activity under the division of labor did not, furthermore, inexorably lead to the position that manual labor was incompatible with intellectual activity. Holmes himself suggested that the working classes be educated if only to alert them to socialist "delusions" of "imaginary equality"; and notwithstanding the excerpts quoted by the anti-Buchanan Republican campaign document, his position likely typified the tendency of even many of the more hierarchical defenses of slavery to argue not that political power be denied the working classes, but that they receive some education in order that they might exercise their power responsibly and conservatively.[127]

Yet few of the conservative defenders of black slavery could agree with the Virginian James C. Bruce and the more optimistic Northern proponents of mass education that schooling would serve as an effective antidote to the intellectually narrowing effects of the division of labor, or that it would effectively counter differences in inherited wealth and social station and provide all individuals with an "even start in the great race of life."[128] As these conservative writers were inclined to insist, "the poor ye have always with you."[129] One of their number, "P," insisted in 1849 that he was not in favor of abandoning all efforts to educate the white laboring population of South Carolina: "None can see with greater pleasure than we do every advance which the poor make in intellectual progress; none can sympathize more than we with the efforts which youthful ambition, from time to time, makes to break the fetters of ignorance which poverty has imposed upon it." "But," "P" concluded,

> from the very nature of things, such efforts must be rare examples. . . . Let the poor lad, if he will, nobly strive to elevate himself by the labors of his mind; but you can never urge him to make the efforts which are necessary to the acquisition of knowledge if he knows that, after he has opened the portals of science, he shall be compelled to return to the habits and occupations of poverty. . . . There is nothing in a refined education which unfits a man for activity, but there is unquestionably a sense of incongruousness in the position of him who, after having sipped at the fountain of Castalia, finds himself reduced to the necessity of becoming a daily laborer for his daily bread.[130]

"P" did not go so far as to suggest that white members of the laboring population were uneducable, nor even that efforts to educate them might prove dangerous by rendering them discontent with the condition of manual labor in which they would likely remain. He was rather suggesting that all but the most limited efforts to educate the white laboring population would in all likelihood prove a waste of taxpayers' money; most members of the laboring poor would not strive to advance themselves mentally because they recognized all too well the "incongruousness" between knowledge and the hard labor that was almost certainly their destiny. "P's" argument was not without Northern counterparts. In several letters to the *Morning Courier and New York Enquirer,* one "Justice" berated the efforts underway in 1847 to establish a Free Academy that would make higher education available to working-class families at public expense. The funds for such an enterprise would be far better spent elsewhere, "Justice" insisted, for it remained true that "a large portion" of mankind

> are necessarily destined to employments most useful and respectable, yet inconsistent with that devotion which science and learning require. In every organism there must be diversity of members. There will be head, and hands, and—we must venture to say it—feet, too. The sentiment may be denounced as undemocratic; yet it is the dictate of a sober practical view of things and mankind as they really are. Uneducated men of good common sense, instead of viewing themselves as insulted by it, will most cordially admit the truth of what is here set forth. When society can do without hod-carriers, or when hod-carriers, *qua* hod-carriers, can live without continued labor, then the demagogue may ask why they cannot be liberally educated as well as others. Even in the Fourier paradise, it is thought, there must be some whose passional attraction will be inconsistent with the savor of learning and letters. . . .
> . . . Free colleges cannot change the natural course of things. They cannot give capacity where nature has denied it, or time and leisure where they do not exist.[131]

The position of "P" and "Justice" was fundamentally at odds with the dominant view among middle-class Northerners, borne out of an equal desire to maintain social stability, that manual labor and intellectual refinement were compatible and harmonious, and that the justification, indeed the necessity, for mass education lay not only in increasing the worker's prospects for advancement and greater material returns from his labor, but in providing him with the self-esteem and intellectual satisfaction that his employment could not alone provide. "P" went still further in his dissent from prevailing Northern ideology, taking issue, it would seem, even with George Frederick Holmes by denying that education of the politically enfranchised masses would prove of much value to the maintenance of republican government.[132] Northern educational perspectives, and the relationships between their various justifications for popular education, will be considered at greater length in chapter 7. With regard to conservative proslavery ideology and the contrasting skepticism it expressed regarding the benefits of working-class education, of which "P's" remarks might be taken as a prime specimen, some scholars have taken this conservative ideology to be the single body of thought in mid-nineteenth-century America that was strongly reminiscent of traditional British Tory–High Church opposition to all mass education.[133] The resemblance, however, was not absolute; it was more characteristic of even the more conservative defenders of slavery to support a limited education of the white working classes in accordance with the laborer's humble circumstances in life, together with the right of the wealthy and the "privileged few" who governed to seek their advantages in more exclusive schools.[134] And in this regard, these defenders of slavery had more in common with those members of the British upper and middle classes who, from the early eighteenth century onwards, supported charity schools and other limited education of the laboring poor as a means of instilling in this population an appreciation of its subordinate social rank and proper sphere of activity.[135]

Perhaps the most characteristic proslavery discussions of mass education were distinguished, like Hammond's "mud-sill" speech, by a sensitivity to both racial and class divisions. In one of the most interesting of these discussions, a wealthy South Carolina planter, William H. Trescot, warned of the danger of attempting to educate the laboring population of Europe; that population was "identical in blood and capacity" with the Old World's "privileged and governing class," but because of both its surplus numbers and oppressive political and social institutions it was entrapped in brutalizing, unremitting toil for a bare subsistence. Even apart from the likelihood that such laborers were not educable given their circumstances, Trescot observed that "so long as hard and distasteful work is the necessary rule of his life, it is questionable how far you are really serving him when you foster and develop in the laborer capacities which he can never exert, tastes which he can never indulge. History has recorded more than one revolution which has sprung from the restlessness of large social classes, dissatisfied with the existing order of things, because they feel that their higher faculties are shut out from the natural field of exercise."[136] "Fortunately," Trescot added, such a "wild and ruinous social convulsion" was far more unlikely in South Carolina, his specific area of concern, because "the great mass of coarse and unintellectual labor which the necessities of the country require, is performed by a race not only especially fitted for its performance, but especially unfitted and disqualified for that mental improvement which is generally understood by education."[137] Extending education to all of the white working classes of the state was safer than extending it to those in Europe, because South Carolina's whites enjoyed an unparalleled measure of well-being and dignity owing to the presence of an inferior group to perform the worst labor. More than this, such education was necessary to maintaining the very distinction "between the lowest and humblest form of white labor and the highest development of black" in the South; "the white race must preserve its superiority by making its work mental as well as bodily."[138]

But Trescot also made clear his belief that all Southern whites were not equal; the class distinctions and inequalities existing among them were fixed and legitimate, and this hierarchical social order should be reflected and perpetuated in different kinds of schooling for different classes of whites. Although all the members of the adult white male population of South Carolina were, in Trescot's view, "politically equal, . . . they are distributed in various conditions of life, and destined to occupations re-quiring very different kinds of knowledge." "Higher and more abstract studies," above all university education, were appropriate for the class of whites that provided the "large slave owners, the great merchants and bankers," the "learned professional men" and the "men of science"—in short all those whose occupations consisted of demanding intellectual labor.[139] But the education of the mass of white manual laborers in South Carolina should be of a more practical and limited nature, one that would better equip them to "control and direct" the labor of slaves and thereby enable them to preserve their dignity and unquestioned superiority over black slaves. It was by so training white manual laborers in this superin-tending function that education was to impart to their work an elevating "mental" dimension. But much beyond this limited purpose, the education of the mass of South Carolina whites need not, and should not, extend.[140]

To the degree that Trescot's analysis extolled and supported a racial basis to the division of labor in Southern society, it could be said that it shared with all racist, white egalitarian defenses of slavery an interesting resemblance to the modern concept of the "dual labor market." Supporters of this kind of slavery defense argued that there was a fundamental dichot-omy within manual labor between its "menial" and honorable kinds and that Southern slavery was a success in part because it institutionalized differences in native intellectual capacity between whites and blacks and effectively channeled these different elements of the labor force into their appropriate and discrete labor sector. What antebellum Southerners attrib-uted to legal slavery, modern promoters of the dual labor market concept have attributed, albeit from an opposing critical perspective, to pervasive social prejudices and economic and environmental pressures. These forces have entrapped a disproportionate number of women and racial minorities in minimum wage, dead-end menial work in a secondary job sector, from which it is extremely difficult if not impossible to cross over into a primary job sector monopolized by white males and distinguished by better-paying, more highly skilled and career-oriented work of both a manual and professional nature. Women and minorities have been entrapped in the "menial" sector not by being formally denied access to educational opportunities that would improve their marketable skills and qualify them for work in the primary sector. Rather, they have been socialized from birth into accepting more limited educational and career aspirations appropriate to their sex or race and discouraged as well from expressing modes of behavior that advance one's career in the primary labor sector. It remains more "natural" for women than for men to balance and subordinate activities in the marketplace with a strong domestic presence; and low-grade service and other work requiring minimal training and commitment and permitting easy exit and reentry into the job market continue to appear as more appropriate and attractive choices for females, at least to many of those anticipating parental responsibilities.

In the case of young members of impoverished racial minorities, particularly black children and teenagers, the socialization process resigning them to positions within the secondary job sector is rendered still more powerful by persistent racist attitudes. This process receives dramatic reinforcement from the cultural values, pressing economic needs, and demoralizing conditions of ghetto life, all of which completely discourage commitment to education as a long-term economic investment.[141]

In consequence, the "blind" market forces of supply and demand that ostensibly lead employers to fill jobs according to the best available trained talent and ambition, irrespective of sex or race, become reflections of the deep-seated social prejudices and economic pressures which confirm that trained talent and ambition will become sex- and race-related. This process operates quite apart from the actual discrimination practiced by many employers against those qualified women and racial minorities who do compete for positions within the primary sector. The implication for the modern American job market is a stratification between menial and non-menial manual labor that is less institutionalized but hardly less real than the duality openly defended by many proslavery writers on the basis of supposed unbridgeable intellectual differences between the races.[142]

Trescot's analysis not only anticipated the "dual labor market" concept in his emphasis upon the "immense" and "impassable gulf" between white and black slave manual labor.[143] At the same time that it would reinforce that gulf by providing some educational opportunities to all whites and none at all to slaves, his educational structure would not disturb that division of labor which reflected class differences among whites. It would, in fact, reinforce and sustain the differences in inherited wealth and social station by offering different and unequal kinds of education, each of which would prepare and channel members of the different classes into the occupations appropriate to their inherited class. To a degree, the program Trescot favored was not so very different from some middle-class Northern ideas of "popular education," in which an emphasis upon "useful knowledge" carried the understanding that the sons of craftsmen and unskilled laborers should logically be exposed at some point to different bodies of knowledge than the sons of professional and business men were. Here too, education was valued not as a vehicle of upward mobility across class lines, but as a means of democratizing the existing occupational division of labor by dignifying manual labor employments. Manual laborers would become more knowledgeable in the ways of their callings than their fathers were, and in this sense they would become thinkers as well as workers, but the expectation was that they would remain manual laborers.[144] Trescot's proposals differed from such Northern ones in the explicit and pronounced degree to which he defended differential educational programs as functions of inherited social status and class privilege. His belief, furthermore, that higher education and extensive occupational mobility were virtual impossibilities for the multitude of whites, and that they should be directed into discrete, nonscholastic institutions well before college age, was also at odds with many of the Northern defenses of the common school system. In these basic respects, Trescot's analysis was grounded in traditional conservative elitist principles; and it differed perceptibly from those defenses of slavery, such as that of the Northern physician and newspaper editor, John H. Van Evrie, which combined a virulent racist elitism with an equally fierce antagonism to all differences in class power and privilege among whites, in the New World as well as the Old.[145]

As a defense of the existing distribution of menial and nonmenial manual labor in Southern society, Trescot's discussion, together with other examples of Southern proslavery ideology that we have been considering, dominated pronounced elitist thought in antebellum America. To the extent, particularly, that such discussions relied more on class rather than strictly racist elitism, they were, if not typical of Southern social thought, nonetheless less alien to the Southern ideological mainstream than were Northern defenses of rigid social hierarchy outside of that section's ideological center. Atypical as they were, it may be useful to consider one of the foremost of these Northern defenses, that offered by the Philadelphia lawyer Sidney George Fisher, both for its points of similarity and difference from Southern proslavery elitism, and for purposes of returning to one of the original thoughts of this chapter that the most pronounced defenses of traditional conservative elitist principles embodied certain values and assumptions that were also present within the antebellum ideological mainstream.

With the Southern class defenders of slavery, Fisher shared an emphatic belief in the dependence of civilized society upon superior and subordinate social ranks and spheres of activity and upon a general division of labor into intellectual and manual labor. Although Fisher placed a traditional Whig premium upon class harmony, his brand of Whiggery was far too conservative elitist to accommodate the notion of Daniel Webster and later Republican Northern nationalists like Abraham Lincoln that class harmony was attainable in America through a condition of class fluidity.[146] That condition of fluidity was hardly more viable in America than anywhere else, Fisher wrote, for here too "Cultivated people cannot do their own work. There must be hewers of wood and drawers of water; there must be a portion of mankind to supply the physical wants of another portion, . . . or there can be no class for mental work and mental enjoyment, and the whole community would sink to a common level of ignorance and coarseness. Now, mental work and mental enjoyments are by far the most valuable to society. They constitute civilization."[147]

In Fisher's case, even more clearly than in those of Dew and Holmes, affirmation of the primacy of exclusive intellectual activity was not accompanied by an explicit disdain for the position of manual, or even menial laborers. Indeed, precisely because the function of servants was to free "cultivated people" generally for their more important intellectual tasks, servants' work was itself too important to be left to individuals who were by nature incapable of executing it competently. Fisher, in this connection, did Van Evrie and the Southern racist, white egalitarian defenders of slavery one better: with his own agreement concerning the permanent inferiority of the "barbarian" black race, he coupled an insistence on the virtually equal inferiority of the "ignorant, uncouth, dirty, impudent" class of Irish who most regrettably provided the bulk of available servants in the Northern states. In contrast to that proslavery perspective which held that domestic service and other menial service employment was intrinsically base work that demeaned those members of the white race who engaged in it, Fisher suggested that such work was not inherently contemptible, but had in fact been made so in both the South and the North by the inferior blacks and Irish who respectively made up the bulk of the servant class in the two sections.[148]

Sharing "the universal complaint" among more affluent housekeepers in the North, Fisher's concern was to attract a higher quality of individuals into the servant class, specifically more refined, native-born girls.[149] This objective itself helps explain why he portrayed domestic service in a more favorable light than those defenders of slavery who touted the superiority of Southern society on the basis of its ability to exempt whites from the most "degrading" employments. Fisher's objective was shared by a variety of Northern writers and organizations which similarly argued that although domestic servants occupied a lowly and "inferior station" which made up "the meanest link in the chain" of society, there was still "no inherent degradation" in their work.[150] With the service recruitment organizations, and with, most notably, George Fitzhugh's class defense of slavery, Fisher invoked the ideals of patriarchal authority, social hierarchy, and the dignity of labor appropriate to each rank. He characterized the proper master-servant relation as one of "domestic monarchy," in which superior and subordinate were "bound by love" and reciprocal obligations, the former to govern and protect, the latter to offer "obedience, fidelity, zeal, and deferential respect." This relationship grew out of the "laws of man's nature," which established great disparities in intellectual and moral power among individuals, and which held that, in a well-ordered society, he who by nature should govern and he who by nature should obey would "find his best happiness in his appropriate sphere."[151]

In some respects, Fisher might well have regarded himself a truer guardian of traditional conservative elitist principles than either many of the Southerners who defended slavery on class grounds or those other Northerners seeking to uphold the dignity of domestic service. Fisher was as insistent as anyone else that "the negro race must be held in subjection by some system equivalent to slavery."[152] But contrary to Fitzhugh and others, he was highly critical of existing slave laws for bestowing slaveholders with virtually absolute control over their slaves while failing to require from the masters commensurate reciprocal responsibilities for their charges. By treating the slave as "mere merchandise," slave laws did not contest but in fact epitomized the pernicious and cold-blooded "cash nexus" ethic rampant in modern civilization.[153]

As for those Northern organizations that hoped to improve the quality of domestic service and dispel the "false pride" of native-born girls who spurned it for lower-paying but less stigmatized work, such organizations often sought to increase the appeal of service by arguing that the servant's position of subordination and "humility" was compatible not merely with refinement and education, but with "republicanism" itself.[154] Fisher recognized no such compatibility between the servant's position and republican values any more than did American writers on the opposite end of the ideological spectrum who appealed for an abolition of the class of servants in the name of those republican values.[155] Fisher for his part despised "high flown notions of liberty and equality," both for leading native-born girls to avoid domestic service and for encouraging insolence and insubordination among the Irish who monopolized this work. To Fisher, in fact, the "Rights of Man" doctrine of Jefferson and Paine was hardly less guilty than

Jeremy Bentham's doctrine of "money and utility as the measure of all relationships" for destroying the ties of mutual obligation and affection that had marked master-servant relationships in some golden age. These "new doctrines of political and moral philosophy"—republicanism and the cash nexus ethic—had together fostered a social climate that was contrary to true natural laws, one in which

> all men are not unequal but exactly equal and therefore not related, but isolated. There is no dependence one upon the other. No ignorance and folly and poverty, entitled to guidance and government and care; no wealth and knowledge and intellectual power, entitled to obedience and service and respect. There is no government at all, in the family or the State, only self-government. . . . There are . . . no servants, only "helps." The great principle of society say these teachers, is not mutual aid, but competition, thus making of life a struggle and battle of selfishness.[156]

The insubordinate, mercenary, and opportunistic attitude exhibited by the current class of inferior servants was, in Fisher's view, an outgrowth of "something wrong in our social system." It was a microcosm of the destruction on a larger social scale of traditional relationships of affection, dependence and authority that had occurred in the onslaught of Jeffersonian and Benthamite values. Individuals no longer had any moral claims on other members of society; "every man for himself and the devil take the hindmost."[157]

Notwithstanding his disdain for the political economic ethic that celebrated free market forces, Fisher ultimately found cause for optimism in those same market forces. The current relegation of domestic service together with "so much hard and rough work"—virtually all of "the work that requires least mind and most body"—to the members of "the Celtic invasion" represented an intermediate stage in an inexorable process of social stratification in the North. "The vast increase of private wealth, and with it, of expense and luxury, the growth of a large class doomed permanently to labor and servitude, have created orders of society as distinctly marked by disparity of education and habits as those of Europe." The Irish have up to now taken virtually all the places of drudgery "once occupied by the negroes in the North," because they too are "by nature and education" fitted for these. But with regard to domestic service at least, market forces and increasing social stratification would ultimately work further changes for the better; social realities would intrude upon "our theoretical equality" and force the more competent native-born into positions of service: "But laissez-faire and competition, if they encourage pauperism, will also produce a class of better servants in the end, and simply because they encourage pauperism. The increasing pressure for subsistence will at length overcome the prejudices which now exclude multitudes from a comfortable position and a respectable occupation. . . . The mutual attachment, the human tie" which in Fisher's view once distinguished relations between the master and his "family servant" would, he acknowledged, never be recaptured; the cash nexus ethic was here to stay. But "the demand and supply principle" would in time, at least, produce a superior, if still predominantly mercenary, brand of domestic servant now so sorely lacking in the more affluent households of the North.[158]

Fisher's writing displayed an ambivalence toward the division of labor in civilized societies that was characteristic of antebellum expressions of traditional conservative elitist principles. The broad division of activity into an amorphous category of intellectual "labor" by the privileged few and a category of manual labor by the many was represented by the proponents of these principles as natural, inevitable, and desirable, although many of them acknowledged that society might benefit by extending limited educational opportunities to at least a segment of the population of manual laborers.[159]

At the same time, these proponents recognized that the division of labor had in many specific instances resulted in a mismatch between different types of manual labor and those assigned to perform them. In some of these cases the intellectual demands of the work were adjudged to fall short of the laborer's capabilities, in other cases the physical demands of the work were held to exceed the laborer's capabilities, although as was often true, the intrinsic nature of the work was not explicitly distinguished from long hours and poor working conditions as the root evil. For Fisher, perhaps the most obvious such mismatch between work and worker was the concentration of the intellectually and culturally inferior immigrant Irish in positions of service in affluent and cultivated Northern households. In his view such work called for more refinement than other hireling labor employments of an essentially nonintellectual nature. To Southern defenders of slavery, "free societies" were rife with such mismatches between work and worker. Quite apart from the intellectually superior whites who filled the "menial offices," the most notorious of these mismatches included the "delicate" females and children who slaved for long hours at tedious and taxing labor in Northern and British factories and sweatshops, and the young girls and women who were degraded and "de-sexed" by onerous physical labor in Britain's agricultural and coal mining districts.[160] For writers intent on demonstrating the superiority of Southern slave society, such mismatches represented not a reproof of the principle of the broad division of labor between intellectual and manual labor, but rather an indictment of civilized free societies for failing to distribute their manual and menial labor more rationally and humanely. As the *Richmond Enquirer* summarized, the "experiment" in Western Europe and the Northern states to dispense with legal slavery, the "natural" condition of labor and the most venerable of institutions, had among other evils "forced women and children to do the work of men."[161]

One might, of course, point out that under Southern slavery as well, instances of females performing strenuous labor more appropriate to men were quite possibly the rule more than the exception. In allocating work, slaveowners made only limited concessions, most notably in the case of pregnant slaves, to the lesser physical strength and more "delicate" nature of the female sex.[162] Here as elsewhere social practices undermined proslavery assertions of the superiority of Southern society, although it is a difficult, possibly unanswerable question what one can consequently ascribe to the commentators who made the assertions: some deliberate deception or hypocrisy, an unconscious screening out of discordant realities, simple ignorance of those realities, among the obvious possibilities.[163] We should emphasize, in any case, that the abhorrence expressed toward the mismatches between work and worker was widespread, no more confined to those who shared the *Richmond Enquirer*'s elitist attachment to legalized slavery than to those utopian socialists who called for radically different social arrangements in all "free societies," and who agreed with John Humphrey Noyes that "labor is sport or drudgery according to the proportion between strength and the work to be done."[164] In an article for the *Democratic Review* entitled "White Slavery," John L. O'Sullivan remained true to the Jacksonian tradition by suggesting that the worst of such mismatches was the consequence not of truly open competition in a free society but of a stratified social structure whose "monopoly producing" laws and oppressive taxation weighed down a laboring population already burdened by "severe competition" among its members. Even in the United States, artificial tariff barriers were permitting "the principles of WHITE SLAVERY" to gradually take root. How else might one explain the "hapless" condition of "thousands of destitute females" at Lowell and elsewhere who "passively" toiled in the unnatural "dungeon-walls" of factories? Such forms of enterprise were all the more incongruous and criminal in America with its abundant fertile and uncultivated expanses; greedy and powerful capitalists had succeeded in "forcing" industry upon a nation which "Nature" had meant to remain agricultural for decades to come.[165]

Yet the overall condition of labor in the Northern states, O'Sullivan observed, was still relatively sound, given American republican political institutions, the healthy demand for labor in relation to its supply, and the inability of the Whig party up to that point to completely pervert free competition in the North. One needed to look to Britain instead for existing evidence that, however deplorable Southern slavery might be, its enormities were exceeded where the class of capitalists was permitted to build up "undue privileges" and pursue its interests in a totally irresponsible and selfish fashion. Like many writers who demonstrated a more unequivocal and unrestrained support for Southern black slavery, O'Sullivan drew heavily from the Parliamentary Commission investigations into British labor conditions; and like these other writers he was drawn to the particularly notorious practice of underground "hurrying" performed by female pit workers. Here "the remorseless cruelty" and the "uncontrolled will" of the coal mine proprietors had created a situation where excessive and coarse physical labor unnatural to the female sex was intimately linked with conditions of moral indecency and degradation:

> Granting that there is something very oppressive at first sight in the employment of children hurrying all day in passages under 30 inches in height, and altogether not much above the size of an ordinary drain,—how shall we find terms in which to deprecate the brutality of subjecting females to similar degradation! . . . The practice of employing females in coal-pits is flagrantly disgraceful to a Christian as well as to a civilized country. Girls, some of whom were of the age of puberty, have been seen standing stark naked down to the waist with men in a complete state of nudity, and thus assist one another to fill the corves, eighteen or twenty times a day.[166]

To the extent that writers of a pronouncedly elitist persuasion regarded different types of manual labor as appropriate to workers of a particular race, sex, ethnicity, or age, they shared a bond with O'Sullivan and other more egalitarian thinkers who did not subscribe to such benchmarks of elitism as the conviction that civilized society required an entrenched social division between superior and subordinate social functions, or the insistence that intellectual activity was the province of the wealthy and privileged. Stereotyping of work, as historians have shown, was a pervasive tendency among writers in mid-nineteenth-century American and British societies, one that played roles both in attempts to justify and perpetuate exploitative labor practices and in efforts to check various abuses. The range of arguments invoked to legitimate slavery as the most suitable condition for African blacks and their offspring represented the most extreme example of stereotyping in the service of labor exploitation; but as noted earlier, the concentration of stigmatized groups of individuals in various types of repugnant work was frequently excused, and not merely by strongly elitist writers, in terms of a natural fit between work and worker. The writer of popular literature, William H. Rideing, thus explained the indifference of the residents of Charleston, South Carolina, to the hard lot of the black children who served as chimney sweep apprentices in that city through the later decades of the nineteenth century: "Nature made him [the apprentice] black, and his occupation has deepened the shade. . . . Who would think of associating with him . . . except another of his own sort? He is an absolute outcast, and as he slouches along, beating the pavement with his brush, few pitying glances are cast upon him."[167] And as one expression of the widespread nativist prejudices and antagonisms of mid-century to which he contributed his share, the writer of sensational fiction, E. C. Z. Judson, alias Ned Buntline, expressed his hope in a series of lectures that native-born women remain above the menial kitchen tasks and other servant drudgery which were dominated by immigrants and for which the latter were especially suited by virtue of their inferiority.[168]

The rationale that there was a natural link between undesirable work and particular low status elements of society may always have been a firm part of various precapitalist and noncompetitive moralities. But that rationale was also intricately connected to a common, though by no means universal, more modern free market or competitive exploitative morality, one which often assumed that most such low-status elements, apart from legal slaves, freely chose their form of employment, voluntarily taking up the slack left by others who chose to avoid the most disagreeable labor. John L. O'Sullivan's "White Slavery" article in the *Democratic Review* exemplified the egalitarian side of the commitment to open competition: as a consequence of such competition and the elimination of unequal privileges restricting it, economic inequalities and suffering would become truly minimal compared to their existing state.[169] But when it was unattended by an emphasis on the monopolistic practices and capitalist power that limited and even perverted competition, exaltation of the competitive market assumed more markedly conservative, status quo dimensions. Free market competitive morality in such cases characteristically attributed the greater part of the suffering that attended developing occupational patterns to poor occupational choices on the part of the victims themselves, thereby minimizing employer responsibility for poor working conditions. It was easy, for example, to pass off exploitative wage levels in the Northern urban sewing trades on the stubbornness of women who chose to remain in an overcrowded field, where their labor was a glut, rather than sensibly swallowing their "false pride" and accepting more comfortable positions in lowly domestic service.[170] Free market competitive morality here as elsewhere was hardly prepared to confront the more complicated and intractable web of circumstances that led to conditions of overcrowding and underpayment and that rendered occupational choice something of a fiction—the family responsibilities, to name but one, that tied many lower class women to the home and made outwork sewing the only viable occupation open to them.[171]

Criticism of the free market exploitative morality existing in the

Northern states and Britain was a marked characteristic of strongly elitist, self-serving Southern proslavery literature; but similar criticism was also voiced by authors of a more liberal persuasion who, to no less a degree than proslavery elitists, drew support for this criticism from a presumed mismatch between types of work and the physical attributes of the worker. Denouncing the occupational segregation of women that a market economy had up to then fostered, Virginia Penny cited the need for a reorganization of labor in America: "There should be, in the different callings pursued by human beings, enough employment for women suited to their natures and capacities. . . . A strong, healthy man behind the counter of a fancy store, . . . is as much out of place, as a woman chopping wood, carrying in coal, or sweeping the streets." With regard to the latter kinds of work, Penny was insistently opposed: "Coarse labor is not proper for woman, nor heavy, out-door employment. . . . Few women are men's equals physically, and therefore the mass of women should not perform such labor as calls for an equal strength of body."[172]

The Unitarian minister and agricultural writer Henry Colman expressed still greater abhorrence at the first incongruity referred to by Penny: the "miserable effeminacy" of the crowds of young men who had fled the hard but honest work of the farms and "thrust themselves into woman's sphere" in the cities, taking jobs behind store counters or jobs measuring pins and ribbons.[173] Elsewhere Colman also underscored the low moral state to which heavy physical labor exposed the female agricultural classes of Britain. Like John L. O'Sullivan, he attributed this mismatch between work and worker in large part to a structure of undue privileges and "artificial ranks and classes." Together with the "superabundant" numbers of the laboring population, this structure gave free rein to the exploitative mentality of employers—buy cheap and sell dear—and made mockery of the notion that there was "perfectly free and equal competition" between capital and labor.[174] Colman was careful to deny that outdoor work per se was unhealthy for females—indeed, the vigor and physical well-being of many women field laborers compared favorably with "the effeminacy, debility, and early decay of those who are confined in heated and closed manufactories, or in sedentary employments within doors." But Colman, like many of his middle-class contemporaries, insisted that heavy agricultural labor, work that "unnaturally taxed" women's strength, tended strongly to have a deleterious impact upon their morals, especially when these women were ignorant and unrefined to begin with. In Britain "the natural effect of such employment . . . is to render them negligent of their persons, and squalid and dirty in their appearance; and with this neglect of person, they cease to be treated with any deference by the other sex, and lose all respect for themselves. Personal neglect and uncleanliness are followed by their almost invariable concomitants, mental and moral impurity and degradation."[175] Such a state of immorality, Colman added, was rendered all the more likely by the fact that female agricultural laborers in Britain "continually" worked "promiscuously" alongside "the lower class of men." Demoralization was assured under those particularly "despotic and severe" working conditions imposed by the agricultural public gang system, conditions which, many writers agreed, strained the lesser physical capacities of female farm laborers to the breaking point.[176]

The rhetorical stereotyping of work along sexual lines, a practice that assumed unprecedented popularity in both America and Britain in the nineteenth century, may have particularly functioned as a double-edged sword.[177] Writers like Colman and, perhaps most notably of all, Catharine E. Beecher, articulated a definition of "fit work for women" that denounced the very real exploitation of females who were engaged in taxing labor in fields, factories, and sweat shops.[178] But the same definition could be used to legitimate the exclusion of females from all but those very few fields of employment, such as domestic service, that did not threaten to "desex" women by impairing their "natural" homemaking inclinations and capabilities and their preparation for an exclusively domestic role.[179] Frequently but not exclusively for reasons of economic self-interest, working-class males and their spokesmen often lent their support to a similar exclusion of female labor from "masculine" employments.[180] Efforts to increase the status and appeal of domestic service was Victorian domestic ideology's major answer to the degradation suffered by working-class females engaged in marketplace work ostensibly more suited to men. Those efforts were part of the larger attempt by the same ideology to dignify and "professionalize" the domestic tasks and responsibilities of women of all economic classes, including the more affluent female's supervisory role over her servants.[181] In this manner did domestic ideology seek to compensate for a certain decline in status experienced by mid-nineteenth-century females when the household lost its role as the basic unit of economic production.[182] And by exalting the "nonproductive" functions that remained for women in their "true sphere," the home, domestic ideology also sought to both justify and compensate for another circumstances: the exclusion of women of all economic levels from the more prestigious nonmanual labor employments, an exclusion that appears to have become more systematic, more explicit, during this period of time.[183]

In noting all of these developments, a number of scholars, to be sure, have criticized "the cult of domesticity," or "cult of true womanhood," on rather different grounds. They have found domestic ideology chiefly wanting not for any oppressive attempts to "protect" working-class females by urging the latter's confinement to labor more appropriate to their sex. Rather, they have found domestic ideology wanting for its very insensitivity to the suffering of working-class females, as well as for the reinforcement it lent continued male domination of the most attractive employments. The authority and moral superiority supposedly enjoyed by nonworking middle-class women within the sanctuary of their "true sphere," their exemption and protection from the competitive struggle, was exalted by many proponents of domestic ideology at the cost of altogether screening out both the economic pressures that forced lower-class females out of the home into the marketplace and the exploitation they experienced there.[184] The mid-nineteenth-century American feminist, Jane Swisshelm, lent contemporary support to this view in her accusation that the arguments for "woman's sphere" were intended by males to justify the exclusion of females from the more satisfying and remunerative employments in intellectual labor even as these arguments hypocritically sanctioned or conveniently overlooked the imposition of the most disagreeable and arduous "masculine" employments on impoverished females:

> It is very well known that thousands nay, millions of women in this country are condemned to the most menial drudgery, such as men would scorn to engage in, and that for one-fourth wages; that thousands of women toil at avocations which public opinion pretends to assign to men. They plough, harrow, reap, dig, make hay, rake, bind grain, thrash, chop wood, milk, churn, do any thing that is hard work, physical labor, and who says anything against it? But let one presume to use her mental powers—let her aspire to turn editor, public speaker, doctor, lawyer—take up any profession or avocation which is deemed honorable and requires talent, and O! bring the Cologne, get a cambric kerchief and a feather fan, unloose his corsets and take off his cravat! What a fainting fit Mr. Propriety has taken! Just to think that "one of the deah creathures," the heavenly angels, should forsake the spheres—woman's sphere—to mix with the wicked strife of this wicked world![185]

Swisshelm was no doubt correct regarding the hypocritical indifference some of the proponents of domestic ideology displayed toward the exploitation of working-class females.[186] One could go somewhat further and suggest that the antebellum "public opinion" to which Swisshelm referred may have, if only on an subconscious or inchoate level, drawn on nativist and racial prejudices and rendered the middle-class cult of domesticity a still more insidious exploitative ideology in certain social contexts. The creed of domesticity, that is to say, may have acted in some measure not merely to screen out the conditions under which working class women toiled in the marketplace. There were also tendencies within it to strengthen public apathy and inertia by conveniently accepting and sanctioning such labor exploitation as the predictable, even deserved, fate of immigrant and

free black females in the Northern states who had demonstrated and confirmed their innate lack of "respectability" by "choosing" to venture forth
from woman's "natural" sphere of duties in the first place.[187] That many
prominent articulators of the cult of domesticity, in prescriptive literature
and elsewhere, not only did not expect, but may never have even *intended*
the roles they laid out to apply to these working-class females is only further
indication of how the definition of those roles was bound up in an implicit
social acceptance of inequality and hierarchy.[188] Working-class women who
were the recipients of this implied disdain or condescension may, of course,
have evidenced no little contempt of their own for the prevailing, restrictive
middle-class canons of female respectability and gentility; but this possibility, needless to say, removed neither the fact of their deprivations nor
the role played by those canons in conditioning social acquiescence in those
deprivations.[189] The "class" functions of the cult of domesticity, and of
Victorian bourgeois ideology generally, were likely even more pronounced
in Britain. Hardly all members of the middle class there shared the belief of
an observer like Henry Colman that heavy physical labor performed in
proximity with working-class males explained the "coarsening" and "licentiousness" of female laborers, or that the possible liabilities to society arising
from this work in fact outweighed its naturalness and social benefits. As one
historian has suggested, the very "health" and vigor of British working-class
women at times carried the "connotations of masculinity" and were "often
seen unsympathetically as necessary for the drudgery of hard physical
work. . . . comparisons between 'the little health of ladies' and the supposed
physical fitness of working-class women served, . . . to maintain the social
class differences between women and to justify the relatively 'useless' activities in which ladies might participate and the relatively 'useful' tasks that
working-class women might engage in."[190]

Yet, of course, not all women outside the "working class," either in
Britain or America, were "ladies" who could remain above hard, if not
exactly onerous, physical work. There were subtle and complicated, reinforcing links between the attributes and obligations assigned to middle-
class women by the cult of domesticity, the undervaluing of certain manual
tasks because they were unpaid "housework," and the stigma attaching to
those tasks because they *were* manual. Consider the following observations
of Minnie Myrtle, an American writer of popular nonfiction, regarding the
predicament of the wives of businessmen who lacked the servants to perform household work:

> How many sensible husbands do I know, who think a
> woman's toil is nothing, and deserves no reward because she is
> not engaged in coining money.

. . . the "wearying, harassing, perplexing toil," is all performed by men, and they earn all the money!

. . . [In fact] His wife has not known a moment's cessation
from toil and care and anxiety, but that is nothing, it is her duty to
be cheerful and patient, and long suffering and forbearing. She is
a woman—her labor is of no account, it brings no money.

. . . He does not believe it need take all her time to do the
work. He cannot afford to hire *"help,"* it *"is paying out money."*

He hires a man to open the shutters and sweep the office,
whilst he is sleeping and picking his teeth, but then it would not
be proper for him to perform that menial labor. Sweeping and
dusting and scrubbing,—weary days and wakeful nights—this is
woman's sphere![191]

Myrtle gives little indication of sharing Catharine E. Beecher's confidence that time-consuming domestic tasks could be made more elevating
and rewarding—less "weary" and "harassing"—through some process of
increased mastery or professionalization.[192] Nor, on the other hand, does
she—at least here—suggest that woman's dutiful "suffering" in her sphere
be relieved by her emancipation from that sphere. Myrtle may have wished
for little more than a consoling change of heart by middle-class husbands—
their abandonment of the attitude that housekeeping skills and tasks were
of "no account" (and Myrtle, incidentally, included at least the more mundane aspects of mother's nurturing in this category of under-appreciated
labor). But Myrtle herself fortifies the view that she is engaging in wishful
thinking: the contempt men of business harbor for housework resides only
partially in the fact that it is unrewarded by the market; they similarly
disdain *paid* "menial labor"—they would not stoop to perform it themselves. Their contempt, that is to say, lies deeper, and is commensurately
more resistant to change.[193]

In returning to the subject of paid work for women, we should
recognize, finally, one obvious fact: the efforts by some proponents of
domestic ideology like Catharine E. Beecher to discredit working-class
female exploitation, to define many types of arduous paid labor as "unfit
work for women," were hopelessly inadequate in the face of the economic
forces that continued to drive women into such work as an alternative to
unemployment and starvation. Female employment in American and British factories and sweatshops, and in the British public gang system, persisted for decades after the transatlantic Victorian sensibility that abhorred
it developed.[194] Even for the most notorious of all forms of female employment, underground pit work by British female colliers, the 1842 prohibitory
legislation that gave expression to this Victorian abhorrence failed to put an

end to the employment in many coal mining areas. Indeed, in those other regions where the use of underground pit women did disappear, this development appears to have been underway long before the rise of public opposition, a reflection instead of changing coal mining technology and new alternative employment opportunities for females.[195]

Yet despite the inefficacy of such domestic ideology perspectives as Catharine E. Beecher's in curbing exploitative labor conditions, and notwithstanding the truth contained in feminist criticisms of that ideology by Jane Swisshelm and others, the sex-typing of work by Victorian domestic ideology did remain the most significant instance, apart from objections to industrial child labor, in which the effort to link types of manual labor with the physical attributes of the worker was directed at criticizing lower-class exploitation rather than merely justifying it. If the concept of "women's work" was often used to impede the expansion of female economic opportunities and even to justify the inferior "pin money" recompense that existing female employment generally brought, it still remained capable in the hands of *some* proponents of domestic ideology of focusing its indignation on the physical strain and abuse female laborers frequently experienced.[196] In this one respect, at least, the concept of "woman's work" did not carry the unequivocal support for an exploitative status quo that the concepts of "nigger work" or work appropriate to Paddy did. To the extent that proslavery writers of a strongly conservative elitist persuasion criticized, for the primary purpose of vindicating the Old South, the poor fit between working-class females and their forms of employment under the division of labor in free societies, they expressed a Victorian sensibility common to the larger, more egalitarian society.

7

Moral Content in Drudge Work and Manual Labor

In their warnings regarding the intellectually stultifying impact of the division of labor in manufactories and mechanized factories, Smith, Ferguson, and their followers had suggested that all workers exposed to this process would be affected in the same way, if not necessarily to the same degree. Even if such labor were not intrinsically degrading, it still carried pronouncedly harmful implications for workers regardless of their sex, race, ethnicity, or age; people were sufficiently equal in native capabilities to ensure that all would be mentally damaged by the most tedious work.[1] Yet we have just described a quite different tendency of writers to evaluate labor in terms of the physical attributes and alleged natural capacities of the particular workers performing it. Inherently contemptible as they were, "menial" services became still more demeaning when performed by whites rather than blacks; selling items in a "fancy goods" store was degrading work for males but not for females; onerous physical labor was far more likely to debase "the weaker sex" than the stronger one.

The contemporary arguments extolling the moral rewards of all manual labor, including the most tedious drudgery, reflected both of these tendencies. On the one hand, these arguments addressed qualities that were supposedly intrinsic to work, and they were in this sense blind to the attributes of the particular workers who performed the task, as well as representing ideological abstractions completely removed from actual working conditions. On the other hand, the middle-class individuals who made these arguments were to a very large degree speaking or writing with a definite sense of those particular elements of society obliged to perform these labors, be they chattel slaves, inmates of various kinds of correctional institutions, factory operatives, or members of the laboring population generally. The notion that the moral content of all work lifted it above condemnation, and that only the attitude and deportment of workers could prove wanting, was a significant mid-nineteenth-century rationale for the existing distribution of drudge work of both an industrial and more traditional nature, and for the worker's acquiescence in his drudgery.[2] Less avowedly elitist than arguments that relied exclusively on the division of labor principle, and that legitimated the concentration of dirty work among a permanent class of "hewers of wood and drawers of water," the moral arguments could prove no less a powerful voice for the intellectual and economic status quo. In certain basic respects, indeed, the two arguments overlapped.

Before proceeding further, however, with the discussion of what represented the most conservative formulations of the mid-nineteenth-century "work ethic" or "gospel of work," we take due note of its coexistence with more liberal and even radical working-class expressions. From a common recognition of the moral content of work, these competing versions derived something altogether different than a rationale for exploitative working conditions and unpleasant forms of labor. Seeking in general to rescue or liberate manual labor from its biblical, classical, and aristocratic stigmas, the proponents of these versions insisted that the objective economic conditions that for centuries had oppressed manual labor in accordance with these stigmas should be reversed rather than accepted. Socially productive and valuable manual labor—the primary if not the sole source of society's wealth—demanded a social status and recompense, an instrumental or extrinsic value, commensurate with its inherent moral worth and dignity. There were, to be sure, prominent antebellum figures like William Ellery Channing whose writings incorporated intellectual themes from both the most conservative and more liberal versions of the work ethic. The author of the most comprehensive study of the work ethic in late nineteenth-century America, Daniel T. Rodgers, has in fact suggested that the mingling of discrete and even contradictory themes was characteristic of antebellum pronouncements on the "essential worth of labor"—so much so that it may be misleading to speak of altogether different versions of the work ethic.[3] "At the advent of the factory system," and throughout most of the nineteenth century, Rodgers writes, "few of the keepers of the Northern moral conscience did not, in some measure, believe in all" of the disparate and contradictory strands of the work ethic: work was both "a creative act and a means of self-repression"; even its humblest forms possessed intrinsic dignity and usefulness while also carrying instrumental value as a route to status, wealth, and escape from the necessity of manual labor altogether.[4] Yet as Rodgers and other scholars might readily acknowledge, antebellum writers who expressed a common appreciation of labor's worth were often sharply divided in their ideological objectives, a circumstance that led them to attach widely varying degrees of emphasis to different components of the work ethic. We need to take a closer look at mid-nineteenth-century expressions of the work ethic, with a particular view toward distinguishing those formulations that focused on the inherent moral benefits of manual labor from those expressions that placed greater stress on either its capacity to provide intellectual rewards or its value in winning material and occupational gains for the laborer. No dimension of antebellum discussions of "free labor" has in fact received more attention from historians than that which affirmed the dignity of work on the basis of its intrinsic moral character; and scholars have raised an array of issues relating to the emphasis on work's moral rewards that distinguishes much American and British Victorian middle-class literature. These issues, which will be touched on here in varying degrees, include the relationship of the work ethic to such other intellectual currents as "industrial morality," the "gospel of success," and the "capitalist ethic," and the relationship which the work ethic also bore to actual social and economic change in Victorian capitalist societies.

Many of the writers who embraced the importance of manual labor as an intellectual stimulus or "creative act" unquestionably extolled its intrinsic moral content as well. For such writers work was a primary medium through which individuals would develop both their moral and their intellectual faculties, these together defining the "higher nature" by which man distinguished himself from the beasts. For William Ellery Channing, labor "was its own reward" in the moral as well as the mental sense. Not only could the enlightened and educated worker ferret out intellectual pleasures—and thereby find contentment—in many of the most seemingly intellectually undemanding forms of labor. Arduous physical labor was also compatible with the full development of the moral faculties. Indeed, in a number of statements widely quoted by his contemporaries, Channing endorsed the notion that the hardest labor developed character and virtue through its very difficulty and painfulness. It was precisely due to the moral as well as the intellectual benefits of toil that the "elevation" of individuals who performed it did not require, and would even be prevented by, the extensive introduction of labor-saving technology. On one occasion Channing declared:

I do not expect a series of improvements, by which he [the labourer] is to be released from his daily work. Still more, I have no desire to dismiss him from his workshop and farm, to take the spade and axe from his hand, and to make his life a long holiday. I have faith in labour; and I see the goodness of God in placing us in a world where labour alone can keep us alive. I would not change, if I could, our subjection to physical laws, our exposure to hunger and cold, and the necessity of constant conflicts with the material world. . . . Easy, pleasant work does not make robust minds, does not give men a consciousness of their powers, does not train them to endurance, to perseverance, to steady force of will, that force without which all other acquisitions avail nothing. Manual labour is a school, in which men are placed to get energy of purpose and character. . . . They are placed, indeed, under hard masters, physical sufferings and wants, the power of fearful elements, and the vicissitudes of all human things; but these stern teachers do a work which no compassionate, indulgent friend could do for us; . . . I have great faith in hard work. The material world does much for the mind by its beauty and order; but it does more for our minds by the pain it inflicts, . . . Work we all must, if we mean to bring out and perfect our nature. Even if we do not work with the hands, we must undergo equivalent toil in some other direction.[5]

Channing seems to have been speaking here primarily in vindication of traditional agricultural and handicraft labor. Quite aside, for the moment, from the reservations which he himself entertained about repetitive factory work, he never appears to have addressed the question pondered by such missionaries for the urban poor as Charles Loring Brace: the question whether, apart from the dangers posed by unemployment and low wages in the city, much of the city's menial and casual drudge labor was itself without redeeming moral and intellectual value—whether this was labor that indeed merited its stigma if only because it seemed, from the viewpoint of these missionaries, to mix so naturally with the prostitution and other "depraved" activities in which members of the urban underclass took recourse to supplement their earnings.[6] One can speculate that Channing might have regarded such forms of urban drudge labor as a fraudulent challenge to his work ethic. They lacked, to be sure, the structure, the insistently full-time nature, of more conventional modes of earning a living. And in American cities, at least, some of the worst of this drudgery, such as the gathering of rags for sale to rag shops and papermakers, was monopolized by children, a circumstance which rendered criticisms of such labor no more serious a contradiction of the work ethic than the criticisms of other forms of child labor that were shared by Channing.[7] During the mid-nineteenth century, all employments for children—although some like factory labor more so than others—became increasingly subject to objections by middle-class writers that, by possibly damaging the child's "powers of development," they in fact subverted the work ethic by diminishing the child's future capacity to be an effective member of the adult labor force.[8]

But the "debasing" drudgery which so concerned Brace and other urban missionaries was also in some respects a fair test of Channing's sweeping thesis that all work carried intrinsic rewards. In European cities any and all of this drudgery indeed provided a legitimate, primary means of subsistence for adult as well as juvenile members of the laboring population.[9] And the mere circumstance that much of this drudgery was physically "unclean" and repugnant did not necessarily mean that it was in fact any more onerous, more tedious, or overall more disagreeable than the kinds of "hard" manual labor exalted by Channing.

Many of these forms of urban drudge labor existed on the fringes of Western capitalist economies; and although the demoralizing conditions that seemed virtually intrinsic to this labor may have indeed sorely tested Channing's work ethic, it is hardly surprising that he failed to take these kinds of drudgery into account in his encomiums to work. At most, his sermons and writings extended to a consideration of the related issues of poverty and pauperism.[10] But it was in still other, more essential respects that Channing occupied a truly ambiguous position in the articulation of the mid-nineteenth-century gospel of work. His insistence that hard work might develop both the intellectual and the moral potential of the manual laborers placed him squarely within the stream of Anglo-American Victorian consciousness which denied that the lower orders were a different species of being from the middle and upper classes, which insisted that they too possessed intellectual and moral faculties capable of development.[11] Undeniable was Channing's strong antipathy to traditional elitist doctrines which derived from the existence of occupational specialization a justification for a division between the activities of thinking and physical labor.[12] Channing bore, too, an affinity with those participants in the manual labor school movement, utopian socialists, and other labor reformers who wished to improve the social status of physical labor and free the working classes from the legacies of contempt and self-contempt. With these other antebellum reformers Channing shared the general insistence that the refutation of such crippling legacies lay largely in the fact that the "active life" of the true laborer enjoyed great advantages over the pampered idleness of great wealth, that it might readily be, where it was not already, "the guardian of virtue, and the greatest preservative of health, of body and mind."[13]

Yet Channing's formulation of the work ethic not only humanized and dignified the working classes and thereby stood as an egalitarian assault on traditional elitist doctrines. It also, in a number of respects, indeed made him an "unconscious spokesman of the managing classes" and the status quo.[14] His suggestion that mental labor was no less taxing and virtuous than labor done "with the hands" was a standard argument made in defense of capitalist profits and the superior living standard enjoyed by professional and commercial men and put him immediately at odds with radical labor reformers who shared his critical view of aristocratic idleness.[15] Channing's downplaying of the importance, particularly in America, of any increased material "acquisitions" achievable through manual labor was part of his general perception that "the matter of complaint is, not that the laboring class wants physical comforts,—though I wish these to be earned by fewer hours of labor,—but that they live only for their physical natures."[16] Intended quite deliberately as a rebuttal of the class exploitation doctrines of Orestes Brownson and other radical labor reformers, Channing's insistence that moral character and not material comfort was the most valuable fruit of hard labor could easily become a rationale for exploitative working conditions and subsistence wages.

Channing's support for the elevation and dignity of the laboring classes, his insistence that there was nothing in their condition to prevent them from achieving through "self-culture" full intellectual and moral equality with other elements of society, bore perhaps its closest affinity with the doctrines of Britain's Samuel Smiles, whose *Self-Help* was published in America seventeen years after Channing's death in 1842. Had he lived, Channing would have found a kindred voice in Smiles's claim that "there is no reason why the condition of the average workman should not be a useful, honorable, respectable, and happy one. . . . It is not the calling that degrades the man, but the man that degrades the calling."[17] And as in the case of Smiles and his "self-help" creed, Channing's was an injunction of individualistic character development and inner reform that placed him in an ambiguous if not unequivocally antagonistic position to the phenomenon of organized labor movements.[18] Quite aside from the premium that such movements put upon the worker's need for higher wages, Channing resisted the notion that collective efforts and a mandated reduction in working hours were a necessary or effective means to the intellectual and moral improvement of factory workers and other wage laborers in America. His support for educational legislation for child factory operatives notwithstanding, Channing held to the position that adult workingmen, at least, possessed the means within themselves and had sufficient time and opportunity already, without a mandated ten-hour day, to improve their moral and intellectual condition.[19]

Yet if he looked askance at the willingness of individuals to rely upon collective action and state assistance for their improvement, Channing granted on occasion the principal argument of ten-hour day advocates that a more rested and invigorated physical constitution was necessary for the worker's intellectual and moral improvement.[20] And following Adam Ferguson on the tendency of employments under the modern division of labor "to dwarf the intellectual powers" of the working classes, Channing also signified his general agreement with the view that limiting the exposure of factory operatives and other manual laborers to their work was increasingly desirable.[21] Indeed, Channing seemed to imply that, in consequence of the modern division of labor, formal education and self-culture would assume even greater value in the future as a means of insulating the worker from the mentally dwarfing tendency of his employment than education presently possessed as a means of increasing the laborer's capacity to derive genuine intellectual satisfaction from his work. It was primarily because of the mental effects of the modern division of labor that physical work "in excess . . . does great harm. . . . It must be joined with higher means of improvement, or it degrades instead of exalting."[22] But despite this acknowledgement, Channing also appeared to believe in a general way with the Fourierists that the division of labor, like overwork or "incessant toil," did not burden one class alone and that occupational specialization had the same narrowing effects on all members of society. The corrective mechanism lay for Channing not in the coercive methods and principles of organized labor, which in its unwarranted assault on the values of class harmony insisted on defining general social ills as class problems. The solution lay rather in that "wise philanthropy [which] would, if possible, persuade all men of all conditions to mix up a measure of this toil with their other pursuits."[23]

Given all of the various themes and qualifications that ran throughout his sermons and lectures, Channing's message to the laboring classes was sufficiently ambiguous and many-sided that it could find support among some writers more sensitive than he to capitalist economic power and existing social arrangements as a source of working-class subservience.[24] More seemingly clear-cut and less ambiguous than the nature of his support for the elevation of the laboring classes was Channing's argument that the paramount benefits of labor were intrinsic, and that these benefits were at once intellectual and moral. In fact, however, this argument of Channing's had diverse intellectual roots and passed over a distinction between the intellectual and moral faculties that assumed considerable significance in the writings of others who focused on the moral benefits of manual labor at the expense of the intellectual. The notion that the working classes had mental faculties worthy of development owed a good deal to the Enlightenment emphasis upon man's essential rationality; two of the preeminent members of the "Scottish Enlightenment," Smith and Ferguson, had acknowledged the existence of this universal intellectual capacity by warning of the damaging effect upon it of the division of labor. In various and complex ways, many of the intellectual movements and influences of the early nineteenth century—religious and secular utopian socialism, working-class consciousness, middle- and upper-class Victorian evangelical sensibility toward the poor and outcast, laissez faire political economy, and in the United States specifically, republican and democratic values and the mythology of American exceptionalism—fertilized and brought to fuller development the notion that members of the working classes had unfulfilled intellectual potential. Each of these movements reinforced this notion even if they differed sharply in other essentials from one another, and even if some of them patronized the working classes or were in fact highly moralistic and unsympathetic to their economic deprivations. The guiding principle of the most moralistic of these movements, that the solution to both the economic distress and the social turbulence of the lower orders lay in their acquisition of such middle-class character virtues as forethought and self-direction, was itself an egalitarian admission of unfulfilled working-class intellectual capacity and a departure from certain previous traditions of thought that had regarded the lower orders as virtually a different species.[25] By virtue of its egalitarian implication alone, the principle of universal access to middle-class morality not only contributed to the reform optimism of middle-class intellectuals like Channing, but also won support among those elements of the American and British working classes who consciously aspired to achieving increased "respectability."[26]

Channing's argument that manual laborers had moral, as distinct from mental, faculties that might be developed through their tasks had other, more ancient intellectual roots within the Judeo-Christian tradition. Owing to this tradition, the principle that the natural function of work was to meet human needs of a distinctively moral and ascetic, rather than intellectual or creative nature, was firmly established within mainstream Western thought, notwithstanding the arguments of Channing and, most conspicuously, the Fourierists. As suggested earlier, the Old Testament, notably the book of Genesis, presented these moral needs in a significantly, perhaps predominantly, negative light: labor became a divine punishment, if not an unmitigated curse, imposed on man for disobeying God and succumbing to temptation in his Edenic paradise. The Protestant Reformation solidified the moral content of all work, largely by moving beyond the Catholic emphasis upon "good works" and representing all earthly callings in a more positive light. Under Lutheranism, work became man's chief means of attaining salvation in the afterlife; under the Calvinist doctrine of the calling, work became man's primary way of expressing Grace and glorifying God, thereby becoming even more of a moral end in itself.[27]

But although Protestantism and the "Puritan ethic" invested work with a more positive moral content than the book of Genesis, they also drew out the full implications of that story by underscoring, as Judaism itself did, the character of idleness as a fertile source of temptation and sin; the state of nonwork was "the Devil's opportunity."[28] Such was the persisting influence of this theme in nineteenth-century America that moralists like Horace Greeley who joined in arguing that "work is not a curse to be escaped, but a blessing to be accepted and improved," also valued work for what it prevented. God's decree to fallen man, that "'in the sweat of thy face thou shall eat bread,'" Greeley noted, was "our necessary vital safeguard" against depravity, one that served "to alleviate the horrors and purify the tendencies of our fallen state!"[29]

The historian Karen Halltunen has observed that "by the nineteenth century the idea of calling had been subtly secularized; men now directed their attention less to hard work for the greater glory of God, and more to character formation as a bulwark against temptation in a dangerous world."[30] To this observation we should add a distinction, one which recognizes a basic duality regarding the moral content of labor that the Judeo-Christian tradition left the nineteenth century. Work held positive moral value as an instrument of actual character formation and reform; but by simply reducing the amount of time available for "idleness," work also held negative moral value as a check on man's opportunities to indulge his "vicious propensities."[31] The nineteenth-century insistence that work was a "blessing" more strongly invoked work's reformatory powers, though it might, as in Greeley's case, embrace work's negative moral value as well. The theme of labor as a "curse," on the other hand, bore a strong intellectual affinity with labor's negative moral value exclusively: although man might not experience any real moral improvement by fulfilling the sentence imposed on him for original sin, labor at least kept him occupied and less vulnerable to the Devil's wiles.[32]

It will become clear enough, when we turn to conservative versions of the work ethic, that there was no simple or single pattern between these religious and moral themes and perspectives on nineteenth-century labor conditions. The conviction that work was a blessing that possessed great reformatory power might, for example, just as readily lend itself to a defense of exploitative forms of labor as did the insistence that labor was a divine affliction to which men must reconcile themselves. Labor radicals and others sympathetic to labor reform also responded differently to the duality posed by labor's moral content. The *New World,* for example, struggled to come to terms with the duality, seeming to deny that its negative part weakened the claims of manual labor to greater economic rewards and to the social status that propertied leisure continued to possess. This journal sounded not unlike such leading mainstream moralists as Channing when it noted that there is "a high dignity attached to labor—it is a part of our moral discipline in this probationary state. In the sweat of thy face thou shall eat bread, is a curse with which a blessing is mingled. That toil to which we have been condemned, as the tenure of our existence below, is the training by which the body is strengthened, the intellect invigorated, the soul elevated."[33]

Other labor reformers and visionaries refused altogether to acknowledge the validity of the duality's negative part. Thomas Ewbank was even more categorical in this respect than Greeley, proclaiming that "the popular absurdity that labor was imposed as a punishment receives no sanction from the Scripture—not a particle."[34] The abolitionist, Sidney Howard Gay, who directed much effort to underscoring the uniquely iniquitous character of chattel slavery among all labor systems, nonetheless also had the economic suffering of Europe's free laboring population in mind when he attacked as "blasphemous" the idea that it was "in the creator's thought that . . . labor, that best gift, the duty, privilege and right of all should be the badge of servitude."[35] And in his efforts to promote new social arrangements based on the principle of "Attractive Industry," Albert Brisbane was clearly uncomfortable with the theme of labor as a curse: "How can we reconcile the idea of Industry being naturally and inherently repugnant, degrading and brutalizing, with the goodness of the Creator, when it is, as we see, the first want of Man, the essential condition of his Existence and Happiness?"[36] To Brisbane and other radicals, long hours of taxing work in a sweatshop or factory were manifestly incompatible with the notion of work as a blessing and instrument of moral improvement. It seemed obvious to them that their opponents could more plausibly defend such work through the notion of labor as a divine curse or punishment and through the parallel argument, which was indeed used by some defenders of the status quo, that such work had significant negative moral value by keeping laborers too busy and exhausted to engage in antisocial activities.

Did particular religious backgrounds and affiliations have a significant bearing on antebellum interpretations of the biblical portrayal of work, specifically whether work emerges in the book of Genesis and elsewhere as more divinely intended blessing than curse? This is a difficult question to answer.[37] The correlation between antebellum religious affiliations and attitudes toward Southern slave labor has, of course, been a much-explored subject of historical inquiry. But perhaps because attitudes toward "work" were generally more inchoate and did not crystallize or eventuate in anything so tangible as an antislavery crusade or actual civil war, the relationship between particular antebellum religious affiliations and conceptualizations of labor remains a relatively unexplored field. If nineteenth-century Americans of Protestant background shared, regardless of denomination, the legacy of the calling, the perception that work of some kind was a fundamental moral obligation, we have already seen limited evidence that this common heritage did not prevent them from dividing on the question of whether that obligation partook more of the character of blessing or affliction—whether it was more positive than negative in its moral value. My intuitive sense is one that is probably shared by many other scholars of this period. Members of certain Protestant denominations, notably Old School Presbyterianism and conservative Congregationalism, individuals who retained with American Catholic leaders the most acute perception of man's irremediable sinfulness, or spiritual imperfectability, were as a general rule most inclined to conceptualize and extoll work as penalty and penance, and least disposed to recognize or accentuate its morally transforming capabilities. It was, on the other hand, just these moral capabilities and potentialities of work which were most apt to be emphasized by members of various "liberal" Protestant and revivalistic Calvinist sects—including Unitarianism, New School Presbyterianism, the greater part of Congregationalism—sects that contributed disproportion-ately to the abolitionist, communitarian, and other "romantic reform" movements of the period.[38] The notion that work was—or could be—a transforming "blessing," an agency whose moral value extended far beyond its role as punishment for, and check upon, man's sinful propensities, was clearly congruent with the revivalistic and romantic faith in human spiritual perfectability and unlimited social progress. This was a faith to which the earlier named, more conservative or "orthodox" denominations, along with certain of the evangelical sects themselves, remained relatively unre-ceptive or antagonistic.[39]

Yet much research remains to be done to substantiate these broad assertions, generalizations that in any case fail to touch on the neglected question of whether specific antebellum denominations, "liberal" or "or-thodox," formulated their own, distinctive interpretations of the divine sentence. And we have already referred to one respect in which patterns were certainly not clear-cut: some of the most avid proponents of the notion that work was a blessing, an agency capable of elevating and trans-forming human character were, whatever their religious affiliation, among the most zealous defenders of labor exploitation; they invoked the reform capabilities of existing forms of work to discredit "romantic" or "agrarian" schemes that would replace these forms with alternative labor systems.[40]

One should not, finally, perhaps draw too firm a distinction between the negative and positive moral value of work or insist that many nine-teenth-century writers sharply observed it. When William Ellery Channing lamented the possibility that labor-saving technology would produce "a long holiday" for workers, he was giving expression to the venerable assumption that the opposite condition of work need be an unproductive and dangerous state of idleness rather than man's fruitful use of leisure time. Channing's general theme that hard work had a morally elevating effect implicitly embraced the notion that nonwork permitted the ascendancy of man's "lower nature." The most conservative versions of the work ethic similarly failed in many instances to draw the distinction between the negative and positive moral benefits of work. Where they instead generally distinguished themselves from Channing's formulation of the work ethic was in the degree to which they highlighted the importance of the total intrinsic moral benefits of manual labor—negative and positive—at the expense of its possible intellectual or creative content.

That this divergent emphasis might result in dramatically different formulations of the work ethic and in dramatically different standards for what constituted acceptable kinds of employment may be seen by mere reference to the examples of Thomas Carlyle and his disciple, John Ruskin. The "Calvinist joy of work" that runs through Carlyle's writing led him to extoll cotton spinning and other species of "even the meanest sorts of Labour" as spiritually fulfilling and ennobling.[41] Ruskin's opposing intellectual criterion for dignified labor, that it approximate art and medieval craftsmanship in its creative content, led him, in contrast to Carlyle, to strongly repudiate machine-tending and most other forms of manual labor that were developing in modern industrial society.[42]

The most extreme, not to say perverse, application of the conservative version of the work ethic extended Channing's insistence on the ordained, moral imperative of hard labor to where he himself refused to go: the defense of black chattel slavery.[43] A number of historians have followed antebellum antislavery sentiment and argued that slavery represented a flagrant violation of both the Puritan and the nineteenth-century work ethics. Implicit even in the former, not to speak of the more secularized ethic into which it evolved, was the principle that industrious labor, together with the practice of such virtues as sobriety and frugality, yielded legitimate earthly fruits for the worker. In this regard the Puritan and work ethics embodied another prominent biblical aphorism, "the laborer is worthy of his hire."[44] No less a part of both these ethics was the biblical converse of this aphorism, one regarding the appropriate consequences of laziness and idleness or of the individual's refusal, in Channing's words, to "engage in constant conflicts with the material world": Scripture decreed that "neither shall he work, nor shall he eat."[45]

Chattel slavery allegedly contradicted and disdained these principles in a number of ways. The overwhelming antislavery criticism was that slavery failed to adequately compensate bondsmen for hard work, although to this criticism some voices added the argument that slavery also demoralized bondsmen by providing them with a guaranteed subsistence regardless of whether they worked hard or not.[46] Slaveowners, at the same time, were freed altogether from the universal obligation of labor. To many of the antislavery proponents of the work ethic, this last evil was hardly less glaring than the others; as Wendell Phillips noted, the state of South

Carolina consisted of "one half idlers, and the other half slaves."[47] Much antislavery writing was devoted to showing that both the supposed inefficiency of slave laborers and the indolence of all classes of the Southern white population derived from a system of labor which, in its reliance upon the barbaric mechanisms of physical coercion and corporal punishment, broke the natural connection between industrious behavior and its legitimate fruits and subverted the "natural" labor incentive of universal economic necessity decreed in Scripture.

Proslavery writers did not concede that slavery contradicted the work ethic's instrumental dimension. Not only did bondsmen receive in their food, clothing, and lodging a form of "disguised" compensation for their toil that compared favorably to the wages earned by most "free" laborers.[48] Slaveholders themselves performed the same "managerial" and "supervisory" function in relation to their labor force that capitalist employers of free wage laborers did in relation to theirs; to no less a degree than capitalists, slaveholders earned their profits through their "mental toil."[49] But quite aside from these arguments, a number of proslavery writers insisted that black slavery was compatible with the work ethic in the most fundamental sense in which that creed extolled work, as a moral end in itself.

Some readers may regard the following discussion of this body of mid-nineteenth commentary as an exercise in over-analysis, not merely because it discerns and highlights various, sometimes conflicting, ideas and meanings that very conceivably lay beyond the conscious intentions of proslavery writers, but for the more fundamental reason that this commentary did in all cases so opportunistically obscure the harsh social and psychological realities of chattel servitude.[50] With regard to this last point specifically, antislavery individuals of the time would have certainly expressed impatience with all such efforts to seriously discuss, and draw distinctions among, proslavery formulations of the work ethic. The fundamental argument running through all these formulations, that blacks morally benefited from and indeed "needed" slavery because they would not respond to the free labor market incentives driving white workers, was dismissed by Frederick Douglass, for example, as a virtual smokescreen for slaveholder laziness and vested economic interests. Countering with the antislavery work ethic, Douglas observed in 1862: "But it is said that the black man is naturally indolent, and that he will not work without a master. I know that this is a part of his bad reputation; but I also know that he is indebted for this bad reputation to the most indolent and lazy of all the American people, the slaveholders—men who live in absolute idleness, and eat their daily bread in the briny sweat of other men's faces."[51]

Yet however accurately Douglass may have captured the motives of many slaveholders, it seems clear that few if any of the proslavery writers considered below were advancing arguments primarily for purposes of protecting whatever slave property they themselves may have owned; the opportunism which partially fueled this writing was of a generally less cynical, more complicated kind, most manifestly of all, perhaps, in the case of those defenders of black slavery who resided outside the South altogether. The use by these writers of Old Testament themes, in conjunction with racial stereotyping, to defend the South's system of labor exploitation may in fact have been a nearly perfect example of the process whereby ideas develop into more resolute, genuinely embraced "ideologies" or "instruments of group advantage or domination."[52] The proslavery work ethic is worthy of discussion, furthermore, not only because it was, at a certain level of consciousness at least, sincerely believed in by a body of nineteenth-century writers and an indeterminate number of their readers; the disagreements and variations in meaning, unwitting as well as deliberate, that distinguished the formulations of different proslavery writers are themselves noteworthy; they reveal something of the tensions attending any ideological effort to make a system of exploitation more palatable to oneself as well as to others. In some cases, the variations in formulation no doubt reflected mere differences in intellectual strategy among writers; in other instances those variations emanated from more substantive differences in belief.

It was not an American Southerner at all, but rather Thomas Carlyle who provided one of the consummate expressions of the argument that the enforced labor of blacks contained intrinsic moral worth for those so enslaved in his notorious essay of 1853, "Occasional Discourse on the Nigger Question." The critics of slavery, Carlyle claimed, ignored the fact that labor is "grievous" and men's lot.[53] Invoking a favorite proslavery theme, Carlyle castigated the British Emancipation Act of 1833 for engineering the relapse of West Indies blacks into indolence and barbarism:

> In the West Indies itself, if you chance to abolish Slavery to Men, and in return establish Slavery to the Devil (as we see in Demerara), what good is it? To save men's bodies, and fill them with pumpkins and rum, is a poor task for human benevolence, if you have to kill their soul, what soul there was, in the business! . . .
>
> . . . it may be laid-down as a principle . . . that no Black man who will not work according to what ability the gods have given him for working, has the smallest right to eat pumpkin, or to any fraction of land that will grow pumpkin, however plentiful such land may be; but has an indisputable and perpetual *right* to be compelled, by the real proprietors of said land, to do competent work for his living. This is the everlasting duty of all men, black or white, who are born into this world. To do competent work, to

labour honestly according to the ability given them; for that and for no other purpose was each one of us sent into this world; and woe is to every man who, by friend or by foe, is prevented from fulfilling this the end of his being. . . . Whatsoever prohibits or prevents a man from his sacred appointment to labour while he lives on earth,—that, I say, is the man's deadliest enemy. . . . If it be his own indolence that prevents and prohibits him, then his own indolence is the enemy he must be delivered from. . . .

. . . The idle Black man in the West Indies had, not long since, the right, and will again under better form, if it please Heaven, have the right (actually the first "right of man" for an indolent person) to be *compelled* to work as he was fit.[54]

Carlyle's proslavery work ethic, as expressed in an earlier (1849) version of his essay, drew the notable criticism of John Stuart Mill among others, and as a target of Mill's criticism it forms the subject of later discussion. But although Carlyle's was possibly the most well-known of such proslavery applications in the mid-nineteenth century, it was hardly the first.[55] Some years before Carlyle, in 1837, William Gilmore Simms had been notable among Southern proslavery writers in elaborating the same theme: "the morals of slavery" lay in requiring the black race to face up to man's universal moral obligation to labor. Unlike Carlyle, Simms was thinking more in terms of the long-term progress of a race than in terms of the moral elevation of individual laborers within their lifetimes. Yet Simms nonetheless anticipated Carlyle and in fact went beyond him, in his insistence that, its basis in physical coercion notwithstanding, slave labor had the same positive moral value as character builder that William Ellery Channing's formulation of the work ethic attached to free labor:

Every primitive nation, of which we have any knowledge, in the whole world's history, has been subjected to long periods of bondage. They have all been elevated and improved by its tasks and labors; . . . making them hewers of wood and drawers of water in the land of the stranger; . . . which is simply a process of preparation for an improving and improved condition, to work out their own moral deliverance. For, truly it is, that we shall not only gain our bread by the sweat of our brow, but thus subdue those barbarous appetites, and degrading brutal propensities, without the removal of which our minds could never have that due play and exercise, which can alone fit them for social dependence, and the friendly restraints of a guardian government.[56]

The superior races, Simms claimed, served God by compelling inferior ones to labor, and the fruits slavemasters received from this labor were their reward for so elevating these inferior peoples. The "lousy and lounging" white Lazzaroni of Italy, Simms claimed, would be far freer and nobler if they too were forced to labor "under the whip of a severe task master."[57] Ignoring the part played by racial discrimination in confining blacks in the Northern states to the most menial and desultory labor, Simms here put the cart before the horse; white prejudice against Northern blacks was largely a justifiable response to the fact that blacks freely *chose* the most undemanding work "in compliance with their natural dependence and unquestionable moral deficiencies": "The blacks do not labor on the same terms with the whites. In fact they will not generally labor if they can help it. They will do light work—they will job, brush boots, go on errands, sweep, tinker, and thieve; but they avoid the most manly and honorable toils, which the laboring whites boldly undertake and resolutely perform."[58] Northern blacks, Simms suggested, might be better off were they too forcibly subjected to harder, continuous labor and its full disciplinary powers.

Although "very far remote, . . . the time will come, I doubt not, when the negro slave of Carolina will be raised to a condition, which will enable him to go forth out of bondage."[59] Simms, however, did come to "doubt" such a prospect; a revised version of his essay, published fifteen years later, signalled a yet more unyielding racism, a hardening of position that was itself a reflection both of "hostile pressure" from the North and the increased influence of ethnological doctrines. By this time, in 1852, Simms was proclaiming that "I do not believe that he [the black man] will ever be other than a slave, or that he was made to be otherwise; but that he is designed as an implement in the hands of civilization always."[60] But as his essay stood in its original version, Simms's argument that enslaved African blacks in the South were little or no different from other of history's morally primitive and inferior peoples, and that they too might experience indefinite and "continuous improvement" through the labor imposed by a superior civilization, was clearly at odds with more racist defenses of slavery—including his own later position—defenses that denied the capacity of blacks for significant moral and intellectual progress.[61] For John H. Van Evrie and other such vociferous proponents of the extreme racist defense, the compulsory labor of blacks had indeed the strictly negative moral and social value of minimizing the opportunity of a hopelessly inferior race for idleness, vice, pauperism, and crime. At best compulsory labor and the master-slave relation checked the indolent and savage instincts of the black race and brought out its other natural impulse toward a cheerful subservience.[62] Simms's proslavery work ethic also conflicted in spirit if not in actual principle with those slavery defenses that viewed the peculiar institution's value as largely functional, a way of getting the world's dirty work done; although James Henry Hammond, for one, attempted to temper the harsh and exploitative thrust of his "mud-sill" argument by

incorporating the view that even the disagreeable labor forced upon Southern slaves elevated them above their previous condition of barbarism and
idleness.[63]

The disdain expressed by Simms for the menial service work to which
Northern blacks were largely confined also put him in a potentially awkward position with respect to those similar employments that engaged
Southern slaves. The racist, white egalitarian slavery defenses faced no such
difficulty in disdaining such work, for they did not seek to justify slavery in
terms of any future moral and intellectual elevation of the slaves. And
although it was consistent with these defenses to highlight the existence of
these menial service employments in the South, and to trumpet their
supposed confinement to members of the inferior race, it would hardly
seem to have served the purposes of Simms's work ethic argument to
acknowledge the existence of these employments in the South at all. For if
Northern blacks, as Simms claimed, experienced no moral benefits from
light menial service work, how could it be argued that Southern slaves
would? Of course, not even all menial service work was equal, and it may be
that Simms, if he gave the matter any thought at all, regarded the kinds that
engaged Southern slaves to be of a superior nature to the "servile," "light"
work that engaged blacks in Northern cities. It may be also true that
although Simms considered the hard agricultural labor which engaged the
majority of slaves to be, above all, morally therapeutic labor, he nonetheless
regarded even lighter menial service work, so long as it was performed
within the disciplining condition of slavery and confined to the physically
less able-bodied of the Southern blacks, to possess positive as well as
negative moral value. Finally, Simms may also have believed that although
the slaves who functioned as household servants or coachmen did not reap
the same appreciable moral benefits from their labors that their more
fortunate agricultural slave brothers did from theirs, their numbers were
too insignificant to upset the case for "the morals of slavery" which he was
making.

His homage to the work ethic notwithstanding, Simms shared up to a
point, then, the dominant proslavery disdain for menial service and other
kinds of work as intrinsically servile and contemptible. That attitude of
disdain, or at least the pronounced degree it assumed in the more racist
proslavery defenses, was an outcome of the natural tendency to seize upon
any of those distinctive features of Southern society—in this case the
supposed freedom of all white laborers from certain kinds of employment—which might appear to deflate "free society's" pretensions to superiority. But the view that certain people, whatever their race or other physical
attributes, were suited by virtue of their inferior capacities for servile and
intellectually undemanding tasks need not, as suggested earlier, lead inexorably to the view that such work was base and undignified. The contrast-

ing position that all useful, conscientiously performed labor, slave no less than free, carried dignity was more logically allied with Simms's argument that work was both a divinely ordained imperative and a morally beneficent force, even if Simms himself seemed to except the menial services performed by Northern blacks. It was the antislavery movement, and not the institution of slavery itself, which challenged the work ethic, T. W. Hoit suggested, for "labor degrades no man"; the coerced labor of the African "barbarian" was honorable because it ennobled and elevated a "barbarian" race while simultaneously adding to mankind's "welfare and happiness" through the food and clothing it helped create.[64] Mississippi Congressman William S. Barry similarly invoked the intrinsic and irrepressible moral content of all labor as a weapon against the standard freesoil argument that " 'the effect of slave labor is to cheapen, degrade, and exclude free labor'. . . I cannot think so poorly of the slave as his northern friends do. *Labor is something which man cannot degrade.*"[65]

In the traditional defense of social hierarchy offered by the Northern proslavery clergyman, Samuel Nott, the affirmation of the dignity of every individual in his appropriate sphere of activity blended into the most elemental understanding of the worth of labor as morally elevating and self-justifying. Nott did not entirely reject occupational advancement as a worthy goal. But he clearly directed his attack against the emphasis given by antislavery ideology specifically, and by Northern "success" values generally, to the instrumental dimension of the work ethic, one which attached undue and disruptive importance to the laborer's access to upward mobility channels. Yet the same criticism, as Nott may possibly have recognized, could have been equally directed against any impulse, from racist proslavery as well as antislavery quarters, which blinded itself to the moral rewards and satisfactions, and hence the dignity, of "menial" work performed in the permanent service of others. Nott insisted that

> the servile employments to which so many of them [the "free colored people"] have been accustomed, are good employments whether for white or black, whenever useful service can obtain its reward. If they be "low," it is better to continue in them than to make premature attempts to "rise." . . . Servile employments are good employments when God orders them. And whoever in them, of whatever race or color, is faithful, honest, capable, will find the best elements of well-being. . . .
>
> But this "rising" to higher employments is not the thing to be desired. In large communities there must be servile employments filled by those whom Providence directs. This is not an unrighteous state of society. There is nothing degrading in serving others. "Act well your part, there all the honor lies." There is

room, even in enforced service, for the highest excellence and honor. . . . In truth, remaining for the most part as they [servants] are, in their accustomed employments, they will find themselves the happiest and most respected. . . . In order to be qualified for much, a man must be faithful in that which is little. This maxim of divine wisdom, true for all, must be more deeply true of a race in degree unimproved and barbarous. . . . Barbers, shoeblacks, and waiters, whether black or white, cannot be raised by the talk or hands of others; but acting their part well, so long as they must act it at all, are not low, not debased, not unblessed, but happy and honorable, and in the best way to "rise" to any worthy and desirable height.[66]

The capacity of the black race for moral and intellectual progress, the possibility that, after a period of indefinite duration, it might indeed attain a degree of elevation where it would no longer "benefit" from a condition of slavery, was a matter of some dispute within antebellum proslavery circles. One part of this dispute was the conflict here described, that between proslavery notions of all useful work as dignified and morally uplifting and the parallel proslavery theme that the kinds of work for which black slaves were suited remained intrinsically contemptible work, despite its value in holding that population's barbarous and idle instincts in check. The importance of this conflict, like that of the larger dispute, should, of course, be kept in perspective: both positions represented somewhat different ways of legitimating the same exploitative labor conditions. More than this, one can exaggerate the degree to which the two positions came into actual open conflict with one another. Thomas R. Dew, it may be recalled, took the supposed cheerfulness which slaves displayed in the performance of their "menial services" as an indication not only that the work suited their capacities and tastes, but that it "ennobled" them as well.[67] Most of the racist, white egalitarian defenses of slavery rarely made so strong a claim, and even less often did they acknowledge the possibility that blacks were capable of the improvement that would make them better off outside of slavery. But with Dew, Nott, and Simms, these other defenses did share the perception that different ranks of society—above all a white and a black social division—had their appropriate activities and that members of even the lowest ranks derived contentment from their activities. And these shared perceptions frequently obscured the essential point of disagreement, the further point upon which the most zealous racist, white egalitarian slavery defenses also insisted, that, contrary to the arguments of a Samuel Nott, the lowest and most menial of these activities were inherently and irredeemably base.

The final Southern proslavery specimen considered here, one offered by Abel P. Upshur in the *Southern Literary Messenger* in 1839, demonstrated how the theme of slave work satisfaction might, indeed, become a sustaining part of the proslavery work ethic, how it might be used without reference to the notion that slave labor, like all useful labor, was actually honorable or morally elevating, and how it might even be unaccompanied by the less disputed notion within proslavery circles that slave labor carried purely negative moral value as a check upon black idleness and savagery. "The curse which condemns us to labor," Upshur noted, "is tempered with infinite mercy; for whatever be our condition in life, our true happiness must be found in the proper employment of our faculties."[68] Horace Greeley and other labor reformers similarly interpreted the divine sentence as containing a great opportunity and blessing for mankind. But where they employed this interpretation to condemn slavery, other forms of labor exploitation, and an entrenched division of labor in society, Upshur used it for precisely the opposite purpose. "The proper employment of our faculties"—the necessary consequence of the decree that we labor by the sweat of our brow—must eventuate, Upshur elaborated, in some men living upon the labor of other men. In his view, Southern slave society represented the optimum expression of this religious and natural law for at least two basic reasons. The first of these has already been mentioned—the special ability of a society based upon slave labor to create a truly leisured class, one which, freed from "the distractions and perplexities which attend the necessity of daily labor for daily bread," was capable of defending republican political institutions and making great intellectual contributions to civilization.[69]

But Southern slave society was also superior to the Northern free labor system, Upshur maintained, because it did not generate among its working classes dangerously unrealistic egalitarian and mobility aspirations. Manifold economic opportunities, Upshur acknowledged, existed for laborers in the free states and would continue to do so at least until those states became "thickly peopled." But although the Northern free laborer thus "sees before him the thousand roads of industry, perfectly open and free," there was even now, Upshur suggested, still only room enough in society's upper ranks for men of superior talents and virtues. Notwithstanding this last fact, Northern egalitarian and mobility aspirations disdained many of the employments to which most Northern workers would forever remain confined. The ideal of social fluidity had opened the way for increased, pervasive dissatisfaction and contempt for kinds of work that had been traditionally accepted as integral parts of a social hierarchy. The manual laborer in the Northern states, unlike the Southern slave, was encouraged "to look above the realities of his condition" and to blame his frequent failure to rise above that condition upon the systems and laws around them. "Can it be expected that he will charge his humbler fate to his own demerit?" Upshur inquired rhetorically; this would require a rare "candor." No such socially convulsive frustration and discontent was experienced by the laboring population of the South. With respect to the white members of that population," the white laborer derived "a high sense of his own comparative dignity and importance" from the "consoling consciousness" that "however poor, or ignorant or miserable he may be, there is a still lower condition to which he can never be reduced."[70] As to the African slaves themselves, branded by their color as "the lowest class of mankind" for all time, they were indeed a laboring population condemned to "unchangeable servitude," cut off "from all hope" of ever improving its condition. Yet the black slave also found contentment in his condition and means of employment—whether this employment was intrinsically base work or labor that was merely demeaning for a race of greater abilities, Upshur did not indicate. "The African slave is contented from necessity. He has no motive to quarrel with a lot which he knows that he cannot change, and the burthens of which are best relieved by a cheerful discharge of the duties which attend them."[71] In contrast with the success values of Northern society and the disgruntlement of free laborers produced by the conflict between these values and Northern social realities, the values of Southern society confirmed the Southern slave's intuitive sense that his "humbler fate" was perfectly in keeping with the divine decree.

Even as he correctly sensed that Northern success values might constitute their own source of disdain for manual labor employments, Upshur could hardly, in looking ahead, have foreseen the future capacity of the Northern economy to expand along with population growth and to create new kinds of occupational opportunities: from the tops of developing corporate ladders down through the "new" lower middle classes. He also exaggerated the extent to which "discontentment" with conditions of poverty and with confinement to manual labor at society's bottom would develop in the free states into mass "agrarian" sentiment against Northern institutions and laws.[72] But it is not Upshur's strictures with regards to "free labor" society in the North, but rather his contribution to the proslavery work ethic which is of greater relevance here. Although it is scarcely likely that Upshur consciously intended it as such, his emphasis upon slave "job satisfaction" represented a way of bypassing the disagreement between other proslavery applications of the scriptural decree of labor. His particular emphasis ignored the discrepancy that existed between the views of writers like Simms and Nott and those other interpretations that downplayed the Protestant doctrine of the calling and found equal support for slavery in the idea that labor, above all physical labor, was an unalloyed curse and burden, without significant powers of a morally beneficent or reformatory nature.

These latter interpretations quite likely came all the more naturally to the most virulently racist defenses of slavery, defenses which, in contrast to those favored by writers like Nott, invoked the curse of Canaan and otherwise accepted the permanently degraded condition of black slaves as a matter of course.[73] But the view that work was sheer punishment could also serve as a useful adjunct to another common proslavery argument, one which held that chattel slavery was no worse and in some respects better than the condition of "wage slavery" in "free societies." According to this argument wage slavery was no less an expression of the divine sentence that plagued man, his penalty for following the Devil and disobeying his Maker. James Gordon Bennett's *New York Herald* thus editorialized: "Is not the hireling system of our Northern labor an evil? Is not labor itself an evil, inflicted as a curse upon mankind with the expulsion from 'Paradise lost?'"[74] And to this the *Herald* added:

> We all regard labor or slavery, for they are one and the same thing, as a thing hateful, part of the primeval curse afflicted on man. We [the North] have our system of slavery, the South theirs. Theirs is a system of hereditary labor, to which a certain race not homogeneous with the white race, has gradually become subject: and to the laborer it is undoubtedly a curse. Ours is a system of hired labor, lasting for a time only instead of a whole life; recompensed with specific wages, and not with a perpetual guaranty of the wants of life; terminated at will, and not necessarily attended with any personal attachment between master and slave. This also, is a curse to the laborer. He is anti-slavery, inasmuch as he would like to live without the severe toil to which he is now driven. . . . At all events, if the various kinds of labor or slavery existing in the world are to be judged by their incidental fruits as well as by their direct characteristics, that species of slavery will meet with the strongest reprobation from enlightened men, which breeds the most vices, the most crime, the most misery, the most hardship among the laborers. In this view, we have no hesitation in declaring that our Northern slavery ought to be and must be far more hateful than the system of labor employed in the South.[75]

We should not exaggerate the degree of thoughtfulness poured into such daily newspaper editorials. Yet the *Herald*'s lamentation on Northern wage slavery nevertheless remained one variation on the centuries-old notion, embedded in a number of religious and philosophical traditions, that because man's earthly lot entailed many inevitable "slaveries," the particular form it assumed for human chattels should not be singled out for condemnation. All labor, in the end, could be no freer than the human beings who performed it, and all human beings were—in senses both fundamental and not so fundamental—slaves.[76]

At the same time, although the Old Testament theme of labor as an inescapable curse might naturally seem to encourage acquiescence in the peculiar institution, and to lend itself particularly well to the active defense of that institution, the same Old Testament theme could in fact provide a basis for repudiating Southern slavery. Again, no single link existed between moral and religious themes and attitudes toward nineteenth-century forms of labor, free or slave. A writer in the *Universalist Quarterly* for 1845 argued that the fact that some are obliged to work, and others are not, "lies at the bottom of all the false odium which rests on labor." Yet although this observation would appear to identify him with such labor reform groups as the Fourierists, he in fact took a Carlylean view of labor that rendered him completely unsympathetic to the notion of "Attractive Industry." Although the writer claimed not to object to efforts to increase the attractiveness in tasks, he noted that Fourierism wholly discarded the value of work as a vehicle of "self-control of our wayward inclinations." Contrary to Fourier, man's passions and instincts required restraint, not gratification. This was, indeed, the import of Scripture, with its decree of universal labor: mankind's passions should be "either repressed, or made to do the authoritative biddings of duty."[77]

Ideas contained in both the *Herald* editorials and the *Universalist Quarterly* essay contributed to the rather distinctive religious antislavery perspective of Abraham Lincoln. It was precisely because labor was a curse or penalty imposed for original sin, Lincoln agreed with the *Herald,* that men had no love of it and sought to escape it. But this aversion rendered all the more unjustifiable the successful efforts of slaveholders, through physical force and institutionalized means, to escape labor altogether by imposing it on society's weaker members. Like the *Universalist Quarterly* essay, Lincoln took the position that the ensuing maldistribution of labor in society added immeasurably to the odium attached to it, although Lincoln's view of labor as an ordained "curse" prevented him from regarding that odium as wholly "false": "As Labor is the common *burthen* of our race, so the effort of *some* to shift their share of the burthen on to the shoulders of *others,* is the great, durable, curse of the race. Originally a curse for transgression upon the whole race, when, as by slavery, it is concentrated on a part only, it becomes the double-refined curse of God upon his creatures."[78]

Although Lincoln's position was perfectly logical, the more characteristic impulse in antislavery literature was still to insist, like William Ellery Channing, upon the positive moral value or reformatory power of free labor, rather than on its strictly negative moral character as penalty for sin. And notwithstanding the attempt of some proslavery writers like Simms to employ this positive emphasis in behalf of their cause, antislavery "free labor" ideology effectively identified the morally elevating character of work with the laborer's legally recognized ability to rise or fall according to his efforts. The full moral benefits of labor were consistent only with "freedom of contract," with a system of voluntary labor that, in contrast to chattel slavery, neither imposed legal limitations on the extrinsic rewards of diligence nor rewarded indolence and inefficiency with a guaranteed subsistence. The British author and traveler, James Stirling, differed not at all from Samuel Nott and Sidney George Fisher in taking to task the "false views of equality" that disdained domestic service and all such positions of social subordination: "There is nothing essentially degrading in one man performing certain menial offices for another. The degradation arises only when the office is performed in a menial spirit."[79] But quite unlike Nott and Fisher, Stirling then proceeded elsewhere in his writing to attach an additional condition to the dignity of all labor, "menial" or otherwise: that such labor be freely chosen and performed in the context of a truly open and competitive society. In response to George Fitzhugh's indictment of the suffering of laboring populations within free societies, Stirling insisted that the hard moral lessons labor was capable of teaching the working classes could only be learned in a society of genuine and "strict *laissez faire*," one free of both chattel slavery and such "communistic" and "emasculating" remnants of English serfdom as poor houses and poor laws:

> Free labour as never yet had fair play. Let the labourer be really and truly a free man, and he will soon vindicate his claim to genuine independence and self-reliance. . . .
>
> . . . Freedom which, in our times, means mainly freedom of contract in matters of labour, is the appointed means of developing the powers of the human will. In this stern school, as in all schools, there must be much pain; but what of that? Man was not sent into this sweating, toiling world to be saved from pain, but by pain to be ennobled.[80]

Stirling's antislavery, free market formulation of the work ethic illustrated how different components of the work ethic might be intricately tied to one another; the laborer could only experience the intrinsic moral benefits of work if he were free to benefit from its instrumental value as a securer of material gains. Still fuller illustration of the antislavery connection between the moral and instrumental rewards of work was provided by Horace Greeley. As both a prominent member of the Whig party and a one-time apostle of American Fourierism, Greeley never shared Stirling's confidence in the ability of laissez faire economic processes, in the United States or anywhere else, to ultimately redound to the free laborer's benefit. There was too much waste and "anarchy" in the "supply and demand" process for Greeley. If the condition of the laboring population were to improve rather than deteriorate, the marketplace required the continuous intervention of government and other social organizations to match the economy's labor needs with its supply, to guarantee, above all, "the *Right* of all men to Labor" at a decent recompense.[81]

Yet despite such differences in philosophy from Stirling, Greeley articulated an antislavery formulation of the work ethic that was characterized by the same delicate dependence of the moral component of the work ethic upon its instrumental dimension. During the height of his enthusiasm for American Fourierism, Greeley had stressed with other of Fourierism's proponents the potential of manual labor employments to be truly pleasurable: under "ATTRACTIVE INDUSTRY . . . The reunion of Desire and Duty, divorced and warring since the Fall, restores Man at once to the unchanging, uncloying bliss of Eden."[82] But with an upbringing on unyielding New England farm soil, and in seeming possession of a moralistic disposition from an early age, Greeley may never have completely relinquished the idea that there need be something austere and even relentless about true work.[83] In an 1855 lecture entitled, "Slavery and Labor," and with his Fourierist days behind him, Greeley affirmed the intrinsic moral benefits of hard labor in a manner similar to Channing and Stirling: where the "least labor is required to satisfy his physical needs, there is Man's moral raggedness most flagrant and repulsive"; and he then proceeded to quote Carlyle on the nobility and duty of work. That Greeley held with Carlyle that the source of labor's dignity was largely intrinsic he made still more explicit elsewhere: "Let men but profoundly realize the dignity and true meaning of Labor—let them feel that not the fruits of it alone, but the work itself is desirable, essential to the well-being of every son and daughter of Adam."[84] Indeed, Greeley insisted, "the man whose only stimulant to exertion in any field is the hope of individual gain, can hardly have risen above the condition of a slave."[85]

In further essential respects, however, Greeley's work ethic was foreign to that found in "The Nigger Question." The manual laborer in general, above all the laborer who worked for others, looked down upon his work and failed to discern its "benignly-appointed character" precisely because he was so poorly rewarded for it, in terms of both recompense and social status. The absence of appropriate extrinsic rewards for manual labor obscured its moral benefits. Lacking both respect and self-respect, the laborer mistakenly regarded his work as a penalty rather than as a divine blessing, and worked only to provide for his eventual escape from it. As a result, the laborer's prevailing conception of happiness was a vulgar one of idleness and self-indulgence. Carlyle erred, Greeley suggested, in considering the compulsory labor of blacks a force for checking the idle and self-indulgent proclivities of the laboring population. In fact, slavery was together with these vicious proclivities of the worker a natural *consequence* of the underlying, popular disdain for manual labor. The uncompensated labor of slaves was the extreme example of manual labor's insufficiently

realized instrumental value, the most dramatic reflection of those entrenched and pervasive attitudes that overesteemed careers in business and
"the learned professions" and in numerous other ways hindered society's
"higher and truer appreciation of [manual] Labor."[86]

Despite his respect for Carlyle, Greeley, along with other anti-slavery
men, could only have dismissed as perverse and transparently self-serving
for slaveholding interests that ideological tendency within proslavery
thought which isolated the inherent moral rewards of work, which de-
tached these rewards from labor's instrumental value and sought to include
the enforced labor of blacks under the legitimating aegis of the work
ethic.[87] Although but one part of proslavery ideology, the fixation upon the
moral benefits of all labor exemplified the capacity of that ideology's proponents to extract implications from antislavery themes, to produce variations
upon them, that worked to their own advantage. The proslavery version of
the work ethic was only one such example of this capacity; there were
others. One notes, for example, a sermon by the Massachusetts-born,
Unitarian clergyman of Louisiana, Theodore Clapp, in which he responded
to the standard abolitionist argument that slavery degraded men by making
them things under the law. Clapp denied that the persons of slaves were
property under slave laws—slaveowners were entitled only to the "labor"
of bondsmen. But even if it were true that slaves had the legal status of mere
property, Clapp noted, they would still bear the inscription of God's image,
as does every other thing He has formed. "The minutest particle of dust,
every atom, every blade of grass . . . all created things" and articles of
merchandise, Clapp proclaimed, exhibit proof of the being and attributes
of the "Eternal Mind"—hence the falsity of the abolitionist principle that
whatever has the image of God cannot justifiably be bought and sold or is
degraded by such transactions.[88]

Whether such arguments possessed much credibility for even the most
zealous of slavery's defenders is questionable; Clapp's use of pantheistic
notions in his sermon may have been one example of proslavery argumentation that existed outside the body of sincerely held, if self-serving, proslavery ideology altogether, and was more in the nature of reflexive
"propaganda" issued in response to hostile criticism from the North. That
proslavery writers may have genuinely believed their argument that black
slaves shared in the moral benefits of labor did not, in any case, prevent
them from trying to have things both ways: the morally salutary effects of
hard work notwithstanding, black slavery was a uniquely beneficent institution in part because the black race, unlike free society's white "wage slaves,"
lacked the temperamental capacity to be *overworked*. As Solon Robinson,
the Connecticut-born agricultural writer from Indiana, described God's
wise design for the black man, one which protected the descendants of
Ham:

For the same power that decreed him to a life of servitude, has also planted in his bosom, a principle of protection against wanton abuse and tyrannical oppression, so that though he fall into the hands of cruel or avaricious masters, who would exact more labor from him than is just that he should render, no power can force him for any continued length of time to render it. Far different from the poor starved wretches of England's manufacturing towns, he needs no act of Parliament to protect him from *over work,* for that he will surely do himself.[89]

The proslavery fixation upon the moral benefits of compulsory labor for blacks was an opportunistic response, a bizarre mirror image, of the antislavery principle of the dignity and worth of labor. But it was also an undeniable, if selective, derivation, from the body of Judeo-Christian thought which extolled work per se as thwarting "the Devil's opportunity." One cannot, moreover, ignore the fact that some of the more conservative antebellum formulations of the work ethic, those which highlighted the moral benefits of labor at the expense of both its intellectual and instrumental rewards, were not confined to the ideological defense of Southern slavery; they had similar, if less extreme applications in bolstering and legitimating various elements of "free labor" societies. Here, too, the moral imperative of compulsory labor, labor as at the very least a means of retribution and "emancipation" from a life of idleness and vice and very possibly an instrument of true reformatory power as well, was frequently underscored in connection with particular segments of the population deemed low in the scale of civilized society. A correspondent to the New York *Journal of Commerce* in 1847 interpreted the book of Genesis in terms similar to A. P. Upshur: "Employment is essential to happiness. It was the blessing that lay concealed under the apparently austere condemnation 'In the sweat of thy face shall thou eat bread.' "[90] The correspondent, however, invoked the "religious duty to labor" not in defense of chattel slavery, but in justification of a policy of firmness toward the growing population of able-bodied paupers and vagrants in the Northern cities. Using arguments that had been circulating for over a century and a half, the writer claimed that unconditional assistance to the poor not only failed to check their demoralization but made things worse by encouraging a condition of "habitual indolence."[91] The morals of the able-bodied poor must be improved, their ambition kept alive, by giving them a chance to earn what they received. The correspondent urged that many of the city poor be sent out West, where there was a great demand for labor. But as to the ones who remained, let those who can but will not work either starve or be consigned to houses of industry. "It is pure benevolence," the writer noted, not merely to give employment, but "to exact it."[92]

For Moses G. Leonard, Commissioner of the New York City Alms House in the 1840s, the compulsory labor of able-bodied paupers carried similar value and likewise made indoor relief a preferable alternative to outdoor assistance as a means of confronting the needs of the dependent poor. Like officers in other antebellum correctional institutions, Leonard harbored the hope that the employment of almshouse inmates in various unskilled tasks would alleviate the public tax burden by reducing the expenses of the Alms House Department.[93] More fundamentally, however, toil would prove an effective if harsh schoolmaster for the indoor pauper population:

> Believing that employment, even though it may not turn to very great advantages pecuniarily from the direct result of the labor, is much better for the inmates themselves than idleness— that it serves to discipline, and have a decidedly beneficial effect upon the police regulations of the institutions, as well as to lessen the numbers of those who seek the Alms House for a Home, there to indulge their idle and vicious propensities; enjoying a comfortable provision at the public expense; and that it will teach them (perhaps many . . . for the first time in their lives) that great and most important of all lessons—to wit—*self-dependence*. Make the pauper, who has the physical strength find some suitable channel for the exercise of his capacity, and feel that he is able to earn a subsistence, and our records of harboured pauperism will not present the melancholy picture now portrayed in the astonished view of the world—he will look out for another home, and perhaps his degradation will at once cease, and the natural energies of human economy place him in a position to answer the beneficent design of his Creation.[94]

As in the case of the antislavery formulations of the work ethic considered above, Leonard's affirmation of the disciplining, morally therapeutic effects of labor retained an instrumental dimension. His moralistic condemnation of the able-bodied pauper population, like that of many of other middle-class correctional officers in America, may have derived in part from the conviction that pauperism was especially unnecessary "in our highly favored country, where labor is so much demanded and so liberally rewarded"; although it can also hardly be said that Malthus, Thomas Chalmers, and others who had led the call for a drastic tightening up of England's poor relief policies were any the less moralistic than Leonard.[95] Yet however much he may have subscribed to the mythology of American exceptionalism, the possibility of great rewards for paupers was, in Leonard's view, ultimately beside the point; and the instrumental value of work he emphasized with regard to this population remained one of relatively

modest proportions. If many indoor paupers could not realistically anticipate unlimited material and occupational gains from the development of
solid work habits, they would at least comprehend the Creator's "design"
that the hard labor of fallen man can be made to yield a definite subsistence
and independence. More to the point still, the self-esteem generated by
such "self-dependence" represented a primary moral reward of labor, one of
several intrinsic rewards that Leonard deemed of great importance:

> What indeed is man without something to engage his atten-
> tion? Most of the evils in human life have their origin in idleness.
> Crime, in all its hidden and visible deformity owes its birth to this
> prolific source of error—and a prominent means of ameliorating
> the condition of the world, of rendering man the creature of
> his design is to engraft upon his mind the importance of *work*.
> What though it be *toil*, it has its reward—it preserves the mental
> sphere of his brain from dropping into early and irremedial [*sic*]
> decay—it developes [*sic*] the *physical* capacity, ennobles the heart,
> strengthens the understanding, gathers together the valuable
> things of life, confers an eminence that can by *no other* course be
> obtained and fits him for that honor and greatness that can alone
> belong to the good man's lot.[96]

Leonard's presentation of the manifold intrinsic benefits of manual
labor, his view, for example, that it invigorated the mental and physical
faculties and achieved the natural balance between them, was hardly different from the view articulated by participants in the manual labor school
movement, advocates of the ten-hour day, or representatives of other
antebellum labor movements. But if only because of the sobering nature of
the responsibility with which he was charged—the control and reduction
of New York City's population of institutionalized poor—the emphasis in
Leonard's reports remained considerably different from either those who
trumpeted the extrinsic rewards of labor in America or those who underscored the capacity of the laboring classes for intellectual elevation. In
stressing instead the disciplinary and curative effects of even the most
tedious labor, Leonard was not so much disagreeing with these other
writers as reflecting through his emphasis a lower horizon of expectations
for his charges, which included the most impoverished, desperate, ill, and
intemperate elements of the urban laboring population.[97]

At the same time, the insistence by Leonard and other correctional
officers that the most intellectually undemanding work was morally therapeutic, appropriate punishment for the able-bodied segment of the institutionalized population could easily be construed in a different light by critics
of this policy. One of several primary objections that workingmen raised to
the policy of convict labor in New York and other states concerned the blow

to their status that this practice appeared to represent. The mechanics of New York, a state legislative report reported in 1837, do not "feel as if their honorable callings were elevated by making them a part of the punishment of convicts, as if it were disgraceful to labor." Members of the professions, the report added, would feel no differently in the event that convicts were trained to pursue professional callings as part of their punishment.[98] Journeymen cordwainers in Lynn, Massachusetts, similarly protested in 1845, claiming that the notion that convicts were "punished" with "hard labor" degraded and denied the dignity of labor.[99] Solon Robinson added his assent to this objection, proposing that "enforced idleness" replace the hard labor to which convicts in the state prisons were commonly being sentenced; "blot out from your statute books" that "cursed slander upon a great majority of the laborers of the country, that labor is punishment."[100]

Leonard, for his part at least, was far from wishing to disgrace manual labor; by including it as part of the regimen of a population which he deemed responsible for their condition of "degrading" dependence, he was expressing an appreciation of labor's intrinsic worth equal to that of the critics of convict labor. Leonard regarded compulsory labor as suitable "punishment" for the able-bodied pauper in principal measure because of the hopes he entertained regarding its morally curative powers. He furthermore expressed "satisfaction" with those inmates who took the cure, who in his view indeed derived some sense of moral fulfillment and self-esteem from their labors.[101]

One can, on the other hand, hardly ignore the fact that the day-to-day grind of attempting to maintain order and control in various correctional institutions must have worn many officers down, pushing them in the direction of primarily valuing inmate labor as a sign of mere outward compliance if they were not already predisposed in this direction. Internalized discipline and reform became incidental to more strictly custodial objectives.[102] It would also be naive to deny that the explicit attitude of contempt, disgust, and frustration with which Leonard and other middle-class correctional officers, in America not to speak of England, viewed their more recalcitrant charges also encompassed an acceptance of labor as punishment in the purely punitive, vindictive, and demeaning senses of that word. This acceptance may have in many cases remained unspoken and even unconscious; but it is also true that American and English almshouses frequently employed the tread wheel and otherwise tried to make work deliberately unpleasant in order to deter the poor from seeking indoor relief.[103] That such a policy was actually counterproductive to the morally curative objective Leonard attached to almshouse labor was incisively argued by Henry Mayhew. Criticizing the "labour test" imposed by British overseers of the poor following enactment of the New Poor Law of 1834, Mayhew observed that this test was enforced simply as a punishment for poverty, and as a means of deterring the needy from applying for relief. To make labour a punishment, however, is *not* to destroy, but really to confirm, idle habits; it is to give a deeper root to the vagrant's settled aversion to work. "Well, I always thought it was unpleasant," the vagabond will say to himself "*that* working for one's bread, and now I'm *convinced* of it!" . . .

. . . for idleness being simply an aversion to work, it is almost self-evident that it is *impossible* to remove this aversion by making labor inordinately irksome and repulsive. Until we understand the means by which work is made pleasant, and can discover other modes of employing our paupers and criminals, all our work-house and prison discipline is idle tyranny.[104]

Mayhew went on to compare England's indoor pauper labor with chattel slavery. In an argument similar to the one made by Horace Greeley regarding manual labor employments generally, Mayhew claimed that in addition to its physically "repulsive" character, the "manifestly unremunerative" nature of much indoor pauper labor, the meager instrumental value which it carried for the pauper, must destroy any possible reformatory impact. Receiving, like the chattel slave, no wages, but only food, lodging, and clothing for his efforts, the pauper likewise developed no interest in his labor, viewing it not as a transaction but as a compulsory "exaction" upon him. As in the case of chattel slavery, "the system of parish labour, which has no reward directly connected with it, must necessarily be tyrannical, and so tend to induce idleness and a hatred of work altogether."[105]

The British overseers and other correctional officers to whom Mayhew was referring may have been considerably harsher and less generous in their treatment of their charges than Leonard was in his. But drawing upon antislavery principles, Mayhew's remarks nonetheless struck at the heart of Leonard's optimism that compulsory work per se—"even toil"—must prove "its own reward" and have a morally therapeutic impact upon those "with idle and vicious propensities." And even Leonard might have acknowledged that there was only a thin line between pauper labor as repugnant in the sense that Mayhew indicted it and pauper labor as disciplinary in the sense that Leonard himself favored it.[106] For Leonard and other of the more optimistic correctional officers, work would check and reform the "vicious propensities" of the able-bodied segment of the institutionalized population. But the disagreeable and even painful nature of such induced effort for the "lazy," "vicious," and criminal elements—those features of labor that comprised its power as a disciplinary and character-building force for this population—also rendered labor a natural punitive "infliction" pure and simple.[107] Correctional labor was adjudged to have "deep reformatory power," but it also remained society's retribution on those of its members who had given in to and indulged the vicious and indolent propensities above which other members of society had been able to rise.

The workingmen who criticized convict labor scarcely addressed the issue of correctional work's moral dualism, although policies that above all heralded enforced labor for institutionalized populations as morally curative clearly had less unfavorable implications regarding the dignity of manual labor callings than did policies that prescribed physical labor merely to penalize and demean. It is possible that in the case of hardened and able-bodied adult criminals specifically, as distinct from juvenile paupers, most correctional officers and defenders of convict labor simply touted the punitive and pecuniary value of such labor more than they did its morally beneficent potentialities. But even beyond this possibility, the critics of convict labor may have been correct in ignoring the distinction between the reformatory and strictly retributive objectives of labor as punishment; the particular sense in which correctional officers like Leonard regarded labor's disagreeableness as most valuable may have indeed been ultimately irrelevant—manual labor would still be demeaned in the public mind through its imposition as punishment. But the distinction remains worth recognizing here, if only because it represented one more expression of that fundamental ambivalence regarding the moral content of work left by the Judeo-Christian tradition, a tradition that had a particular impact upon the thinking of Leonard and other moralists. In a world of harsh physical laws, in which an essential part of fallen man's disposition—that part he was obliged to combat—was one of indolence and sloth, the best labor was necessarily a matter of hard, even painful, effort. Such labor was appropriate punishment for able-bodied paupers in both the strictly punitive and the therapeutic senses, just as it was both the primeval curse or affliction and the means of moral elevation for the human race in general.

The fact that workingmen and other critics of convict labor implicitly agreed with more conservative, middle-class thinkers like Leonard and Channing concerning the intrinsic moral value of manual labor was, however, hardly attributable to the influence of the Judeo-Christian tradition alone. Quite possibly, that tradition was far less significant in shaping nineteenth-century perspectives on labor conditions than in reinforcing perspectives already formed; although the fact that mid-nineteenth-century Americans felt the need to repeatedly invoke religious themes to vindicate their positions was itself evidence of the persisting influence of these themes.

Still, economic and social conditions in the nineteenth century provided an immediate, perhaps more fundamental source of inspiration for opposing perspectives that agreed on manual labor's intrinsic moral worth. Anglo-American labor radicals and reformers found particular verification of this worth in the behavior of other social classes which to them exemplified its opposite condition: the decadent luxury and parasitic idleness of Old World landed aristocracies that had persisted into the nineteenth century and—still more troubling because it was a recent "sign of the times"—the predatory and exploitative practices of new commercial and industrial wealth. But for other writers, many of them members of the middle classes themselves who advanced some of the more conservative formulations of the work ethic, the nineteenth century offered quite different kinds of compelling proof of the moral benefits of manual labor. These writers did not entirely dismiss the idleness and parasitism denounced by labor radicals as a product of demagogic imagination; the rise of classical economy and "philosophical radicalism" in late eighteenth- and early nineteenth-century Britain was itself largely an expression of middle-class hostility to entrenched aristocratic privileges and the impediments these privileges imposed on a free market economy.[108] But for Harriet Martineau, Andrew Ure, and others who zealously popularized and dogmatized these new intellectual currents in the service of bourgeois industrial capital, the drags which aristocratic privilege and idleness imposed on a free market economy were ultimately obscured by the threats represented by both the voluntary idleness and the involuntary unemployment of the laboring population itself.[109] For the most dogmatic keepers of middle-class competitive morality, self-supporting manual labor and the solid work habits this condition signified would repulse the threats of pauperism, socialism, and various other manifestations of working-class disease and unrest. For labor radicals, on the other hand, industrious and self-supporting manual labor could only exist *in spite of* the predatory capitalist interests legitimated by this same middle-class competitive morality. Beginning in late eighteenth-century Britain, as industrial capitalism itself became part of the status quo with interests to defend, the competitive free market "liberal" ideology with which it was allied itself became, one might well argue, a species of conservatism, defining itself less in relation to the entrenched aristocratic privileges it continued to oppose than in terms of the threats from below which required turning back.[110]

However diverse and complex were the actual causes of unemployment in nineteenth-century capitalist economies, the most extreme spectacles of idleness and unemployment in this period did in fact provide some plausible evidence for the position that continuous employment of any kind, even the hardest work at low wages, represented a preferable alternative. "Any work is better than none" was not a nineteenth-century maxim restricted to the most conservative circles. Although it bore a certain similarity to the eighteenth-century conservative mercantilist insistence upon the laboring population's "duty" to work, it was advice dispensed by many middle-class moralists to workingmen, an expression of their genuine dismay at the mortality, demoralization, and vice attendant upon widespread unemployment and impoverishment.[111] For the Irish who fled their homeland during the great potato famine to find rough and unskilled jobs in Philadelphia, the morally therapeutic power of such employment was manifest to the *Public Ledger:* although the Irish were "squalid, disorderly, ferocious" when they arrived, after getting work they became "temperate, orderly, neat, sober, religious."[112]

The *Ledger,* of course, may well have exaggerated the moral transformation that finding work wrought upon the Irish, just as the therapeutic powers that Leonard and other correctional officers ascribed to the compulsory labor of convicts, institutionalized paupers and delinquents, even the inmates of insane asylums, may have been largely illusory.[113] But the *Ledger* was also making a reasonable reference to the condition of much of the Irish population during one of the greatest economic catastrophes of the nineteenth century. The distinguishing characteristic of conservative formulations of the work ethic was not so much the conclusion that even the "meanest" sort of labor might have certain morally beneficial effects when set against such desperation and poverty, for this, as suggested, was a reasonable and common enough conclusion. Distinctive instead to these conservative formulations was the degree to which fixation upon the moral state of the laboring population took precedence over the contemplation of alternative social arrangements that promoted the moral elevation of laboring men in conjunction with their intellectual independence and economic power. The conservative version of the work ethic, one finds, had possibly its most widespread application in early and mid-nineteenth-century America and Britain in the range of arguments advanced to defend factory labor and the factory system on moral grounds.

From the outset, these arguments derived much of their force from the undeniable poverty, economic insecurity, and demoralization experienced by large segments of the laboring population outside of the factory system. Historians have emphasized the degree to which England's first generation of factory masters drew their labor force from the most desperate and impoverished elements of the working classes, such as agricultural laborers displaced by the enclosure movement and juvenile and other inmates of the parish poor houses.[114] But American factory entrepreneurs filled their unskilled labor needs by taking similar advantage of that poverty and economic insecurity which existed around them, and they and other proponents of the factory system naturally embraced arguments that rationalized this situation. As early as the 1780s, manufacturer's charters and petitions to the northeastern state legislatures consistently suggested that factories would alleviate the problem of poverty, as well as bring economic independence to the new nation; legislatures in Massachusetts, Connecticut, and Pennsylvania approved partially on the basis of these arguments bounties for building new machinery, tax exemptions for factories, and lotteries to raise money for them.[115] George S. White, biographer and partisan of Samuel Slater, noted that in reducing poverty, the family system of factories struck alike at vice, poverty's frequent handmaiden: "Multitudes of women and children have been kept out of vice, simply by being employed, and instead of being destitute, provided with an abundance for a comfortable subsistence."[116] When a Pennsylvania Senate committee investigating factory conditions in the state in 1837 queried textile factory owners on their extensive use of child labor, the common response was that in employing such young and "unproductive" operatives, owners were disregarding their own best economic interests and seeking to accommodate the needs of "indigent widows" and other poor parents, desperately dependent on the wages of their children.[117] Such professions of selfless benevolence provoke a natural skepticism.[118] Yet the economic desperation of the parents of factory children was real enough, and it seems likely, as some of the Pennsylvania factory owners intimated it would, to have constrained parental participation in what antebellum efforts there were to abolish, reduce, or even ameliorate the conditions of child factory labor.[119] A Massachusetts committee report of 1836 exhibited considerable apprehensiveness regarding the spread of manufacturing establishments in the state, and in recommending legislation to secure schooling for child operatives, it too identified the indigence of families as an impediment to such efforts, as a powerful motive for maximizing child factory labor:

> The families usually collected in our large manufacturing establishments, are either those that have been unfortunate, or from some cause, unsuccessful in agriculture or other employments, and are there collected in despair of obtaining more than a comfortable support, or a bare subsistence; or they are families formed around the establishments, on the strength of the then present prospect of gaining a certain support, by those young people, who depend solely upon their daily wages and have nothing to expect but what they can obtain from day to day, or week to week.[120]

There may be need to draw a certain distinction at this point: one that recognizes the passivity and acquiescence of many poor parents not themselves employed in the mills, and yet which also acknowledges the unmistakable, if intermittent, militancy of parents who with their children did work in the mills and experience harsh conditions firsthand. Such labor militancy, preeminently in the Philadelphia mills where it was fortified by British-born operatives with a background of confrontation with capital, was in fact among those factors that induced the Pennsylvania legislature to make its 1837 investigation in the first place.[121]

Our focus here, however, is not upon factory operatives' agitation to improve working conditions; it is rather upon that strain of antebellum thought which, frequently though by no means always drawing on considerations of obvious self-interest, recognized the factory system as an imperative, accepted when it did not altogether welcome capitalist industrialization for its capacity to alleviate a bad situation. By virtue of the fact that it increased employment opportunities, and thereby reduced poverty and attendant vice and demoralization, the factory system assumed in the eyes of many the character of a morally beneficent force. With reference to economically depressed elements of the labor force outside as well as within the rural northeast, the same general profactory motif reappears, again not exclusively in the pronouncements of individuals with strong economic and ideological ties to the factory system. A trip to the South in 1849 convinced the Northern free trade Democrat and writer William Cullen Bryant that the hostility of his party to the factory system should bend to the obvious benefits that factory enterprises such as William Gregg's Graniteville must have in the South upon the poor and underemployed whites there.[122] In the case of Charles Loring Brace and his Children's Aid Society, it was the specter of the impoverished working girls of New York City and their frequent recourse to prostitution that generated enthusiasm for new factory and other manufacturing enterprises that opened their doors to women: "If this is to continue—if scores of thousands of women and young girls are to be engaged continually in the factories and workshops of the city, the condition of our poorer classes will be considerably modified . . . the prisons know almost nothing now of very young girls . . . the principal cause of this most happy improvement, is *employment*. . . . We believe that female destitution and its sad accompaniment of vices has reached its acme in New York."[123]

Similar concern, finally, for the plight of New York's female laboring population, together with his general allegiance to the Whig persuasion, prompted Horace Greeley to enter into a number of defenses of the Waltham-type factory system established in Lowell and other towns by the Boston Associates. Greeley did not disagree with labor reformers more critical than he of this system that its hours were too long or that working conditions had in some respects deteriorated during the 1840s. But Greeley's observation of the conditions under which sewing girls and domestic servants of the city labored—let alone those under which the female slaves of the South toiled—led him to lose patience with these critics: "We know very well that Women are more unhealthfully employed, confined more hours, and far worse paid in many other branches of industry" than they were in Lowell or similar New England mill towns.[124] Anticipating the position taken by some modern scholars, Greeley insisted that industrialization, or at least the form it assumed at Lowell, had "emancipated" females by securing them from poverty and economic dependence on their families.[125]

The theme that factory work would lift segments of the laboring population out of an economically depressed state, and thereby check their demoralization, was not itself conservative; but many of the arguments extolling the moral benefits of such employment of course went much further than this, underscoring the value of factory labor in extending "social control" over the working classes. To the extent that factory labor performed this function merely by reducing the "idle" time available to workers, and hence their opportunities to engage in unproductive, vicious, or socially convulsive activity, it might seem that all forms of employment which kept their workers occupied carried similar value. But factory labor excelled in this respect if only because factories could be kept running the year around, twenty-four hours a day. When in 1787 a group of spinners in Europe made the complaint that they were not permitted to leave the spinning mills during the evening, the local police expressed no sympathy for their situation: "It is a well-known life that the spinners lead which forces mill-owners to apply this restraint; because they work for a time during the day, but spend the evenings on the streets, as beggars or prostitutes, and they return to the spinning mills with scabies or venereal disease, or even pregnant. In the crowded conditions one infects another, the first seeds of the direst poverty are sown, and the poor-house suffers unnecessary inconvenience."[126]

In a spirited defense of a protective tariff and a factory system for the United States, an essay in the *American Whig Review* for 1851 elaborated what by this time was no longer a new argument: that factory employment was perhaps unsurpassed in its negative moral value. The article felt obliged to address and refute those criticisms that large manufactories were a destructive moral force overall, particularly when as in England "the laborers in such establishments are collected from the lowest walks of life, and are, therefore, the most ignorant and vicious members of society; that, being brought into contact in large bodies, their vicious propensities by union . . . acquire a power greater than the sum of their individual powers when separate; and that riots, mobs, and gross immoralities are the consequences." The essay conceded that

> there is certainly an apparent force in the objection, for it must be acknowledged that . . . vice concentrated is mightier and more mischievous than when generally diffused. But . . . the laborers that yesterday lounged in idleness along the streets, without the means of life, or strolled over the country to procure by plunder the bread of subsistence, are to-day sent to a factory where they are put to regular employment, under the superintendence of men eminent for their integrity and business capacity. Here they are paid for their services, and are at the same time *incidentally*

restrained from the thousand misdeeds of which idleness and
want are the certain progenitors. Yesterday they were without the
restraint which rational control imposes: to-day they are under its
influences: yesterday they were in want, under temptations to
falsehood, robbery and murder; to-day their wants are removed,
and they are delivered from their temptations. They cannot indulge vicious propensities during the day, because they are employed, and at night fatigue inclines them to sleep.[127]

Vicious and dangerous workers were, in short, less dangerous and vicious
within than outside factory walls. Many other American proponents of the
factory system took a different line of defense from this article, underscoring the uniquely high moral character and *self*-control which American
operatives, or at least native New England girls, *brought* to the mills. Be this
as it may, no proponent of the factory system in Britain offered a more
forthright defense than the *American Whig Review* essay of the negative
moral value of factory labor, of its facility in repressing and controlling the
"vicious propensities" of the laboring population. The same theme re-
curred frequently in the arguments of American as well as British factory
proprietors.

At the same time, we are again dealing with degrees of emphasis rather
than with discrete categories of concerns: the profactory argument that
sympathized with the material suffering of the laboring population was
hardly incompatible with the profactory theme that stressed the dangerous
implications of unemployment, idleness, and impoverishment for the rest
of society. In the hands of many writers, such as Charles Loring Brace, the
two concerns were intimately blended, and in this respect profactory arguments were but a subspecies of the whole body of middle-class writing on
the condition of the laboring poor.[128] The same observation might even be
made of those arguments which, by extolling systems of labor based on
physical coercion, were in a general sense otherwise isolated from the
mainstream of bourgeois thought. The arguments in defense of chattel
slavery could mix with equal facility an expressed humanitarian concern for
the "perishing classes" with the wish to control the vicious propensities of
the "dangerous classes." It was the total picture of social turbulence that
New York City presented during the winter of 1854–1855—widespread
unemployment, starvation, and labor discontent—which led Georgia's
Alexander H. Stephens to find added justification for slavery: "There is . . .
something in life worse than being required, or even made, to work."[129] Of
course, it is highly problematic whether even Stephens's slave society could
have more successfully absorbed the volume of immigration with which
New York had been faced in just a few years—done a better job of providing that population with adequate housing, food, work, and so on. But for

Stephens, in any case, the imposed employment and guaranteed subsistence of black chattel slavery represented the preferred means of removing both the opportunity and the temptation of the laboring population—or at least a special segment of that population—to indulge its lower nature and commit acts of vice and crime. For several generations of factory proprietors and profactory writers, the continuous and reliable employment offered by the factory system carried similar value. This remained so even in those obvious instances where neither the articulated humanitarian concern nor the expressed fears regarding the condition of the laboring population were the actual driving force behind profactory positions, but rather the embellishment to more strictly economic considerations.

A number of historians have suggested that as the more cultured native-born girls from farming families were replaced in New England mills by immigrant operatives of more certifiably lower-class backgrounds, factory labor lost a corresponding degree of "respectability."[130] This last development might in turn seem to imply that the arguments affirming the moral content of factory work, or at least those addressing factory conditions in New England specifically, fell into disuse after the mid-1840s. Yet in the sense with which we have just been concerned with factory labor, as a perceived check on idleness and vice, as a carrier of negative moral value, the moral benefits of factory labor may have become even more manifest to its middle-class proponents. It was hardly likely that when the mills filled with the kind of operatives who seemed in even greater need of social control and regimentation, manufacturing proprietors would have turned away from arguments popular for almost a century. One manufacturing firm in Uxbridge, Massachusetts, expressed its belief to a state legislative committee in 1867 that the many foreign-born children employed in its factory should receive some education; for "we believe our institutions are founded upon the intelligence of the people,—the whole people,—and do not believe we can afford to allow our children to grow up in ignorance." Yet the firm balked when asked whether it would help accommodate the factory children's need for schooling by supporting a reduction in their working hours from the present legal maximum of sixty hours a week. It maintained that the measure specifically contemplated to achieve the moral and intellectual improvement of the factory children would in fact benefit no one, neither society nor the child operatives in need of instruction, because the measure overlooked the value of long factory hours in checking the descent of the children to a still lower moral level: "When we recur to the past of our own lives, and the hours of labor that we, in common with many others, endured without injury, we must say that we think the confinement in the mill will be *less* injurious to children from twelve to fifteen years of age, than the *pernicious school of the street* to which they will almost certainly go."[131]

As suggested above, it was very conceivably the immediate interests of the firm, and the economic threat which shortened hours appeared to pose to those interests, that was the driving, if unspoken, consideration, the one that overruled the expressed acknowledgement that the moral and intellectual improvement of the labor force served the best long-term interests of society. In some of these cases, no doubt, references to the value of long hours of factory work in checking the vicious propensities of the laboring population amounted to no more than a rhetorical tool, mere window dressing, for a firm's efforts to protect and maximize profits. Yet it seems equally probable that such references, like the arguments of some proslavery ideologues, often reflected a less cynical, more complicated opportunism. Manufacturing enterprises like the Uxbridge firm may with self-serving sincerity have defined their foreign-born workers as especially "undisciplined," an act of definition that in turn made it easier for them to genuinely convince themselves of the truth of arguments attesting to factory labor's negative moral value. By this process alone, such profactory arguments generated a certain force of their own as impediments to the mid-nineteenth century efforts to reduce the hours of operatives.

There were, moreover, those other arguments which found in factory employment the same therapeutic, or positive moral benefits, that parallel arguments found in slavery or in the labor of inmates of various correctional institutions. In the more sophisticated scholarly interpretations of "social control" in the early Victorian period, "ideological hegemony" has emerged as the dominant and arguably the most effective way in which the British and American middle classes sought to impose their will on the classes below them. The threat which undisciplined, economically discontent, and volatile segments of the laboring population posed to both social order and capitalist profits was best defused by making these segments over in the image of the middle classes.[132] Evangelical Protestantism, particularly, represented a valuable means of effecting this transformation, imparting a new emphasis, and a new class dimension, to those character virtues embedded in the Puritan ethic.[133] Above all, this renewed emphasis on industry, frugality, and sobriety neatly dovetailed with the premium that new industrial forms of labor placed on the worker's capacity for discipline, compliance, and punctuality. Historians have, accordingly, commonly referred to these character virtues as "industrial morality," both because they represented what many factory proprietors consciously sought in their operatives and because they capsulated what the Protestant middle classes of the early industrial period sought in general to cultivate in the laboring population in order to render it less socially dangerous, more economically secure and productive, and, within certain limitations, upwardly mobile as well.[134]

This brief summary of bourgeois ideological hegemony and industrial morality passes over a number of important issues that we can mention only briefly here. Many of these issues involve the dimension of time. Over the course of several decades middle-class concern with the control and elevation of the laboring population invariably shifted in character as it was affected by social changes and as it interacted with a variety of contemporary intellectual currents such as the rise of radical working-class consciousness. A number of scholars have, in this regard, discerned a gradual shift in British bourgeois "liberalism," a mellowing of the repressive moralism and pessimism represented by Malthus, David Ricardo, and some of the other architects of classical political economy into a more optimistic and accommodating middle-class sensibility regarding the actual prospects of working-class economic improvement.[135] There are also those issues arising from the dimension of space. Bourgeois ideological hegemony and industrial morality must have, from the outset, carried somewhat different implications and emphases in America than they did in Britain, where a nonworking landed aristocracy was a true force in society and politics and where much of the laboring population was, by comparison with America's, genuinely impoverished, volatile, and discontent during a good deal of this period.

There are other, related complicating issues as well. Evangelical social teaching, for example, was most versatile in its applications. As a call to "self-direction" and "self-help," it could and did feed into notions of "free agency" and "freedom of contract," thereby strengthening laissez faire attitudes and policies.[136] A number of historians have suggested that the premium placed by some early nineteenth-century factory entrepreneurs and master craftsmen on evangelical "self-help" was a means of rationalizing their abandonment of the employer's traditional paternalistic responsibilities for his workmen.[137] But evangelicalism could also accommodate the principle that members of the more fortunate classes should, for reasons of both personal security and Providential duty, help remove barriers to the improvement in the moral condition of the laboring population. To this extent, evangelicalism also provided an important impetus for paternalistic government intervention in the working and living conditions of the laboring population.[138]

Evangelical social teaching also confirmed more than one position regarding the specific effects of the factory system on the moral elevation and control of the laboring population. Some middle-class adherents to evangelicalism were drawn to factory labor, or almost any kind of "free" and regular labor, as a check on vice or as a source of industrious habits and morality. Other of its proponents repudiated factory conditions—and above all long hours for children—as inhumanely and dangerously hostile to the worker's development of his moral and intellectual faculties, only marginally better in this respect than conditions of idleness and unemployment.[139] Industrial forms of labor, no less than more traditional forms of work, might thus be seen to conflict with true industrial morality. The disagreements over the specific effects of factory labor obscured the growing consensus within the American and British middle classes that the recognition and at least limited development of the laboring population's "higher nature" was essential and that constant work was not the best means of controlling and stabilizing the laboring population insofar as it prevented this recognition and development. It was this broader agreement regarding the worker's "higher nature," one that scarcely existed at all before the nineteenth century, that informed the debates among members of the middle classes regarding the proper balance of work and leisure within different types of employment, the uses workers should make of their leisure time, and, not least, the question of whether factory and other manual labor did or did not possess the capacity to provide all or most of the proper moral and intellectual stimulus needed by workers.[140] In wrestling with these and other questions, evangelical Protestantism, like the more generalized middle-class concern with the condition of labor, reflected an interaction over time with other contemporary intellectual currents, including the ideas working-class radicalism itself generated regarding the needs and rights of labor. On these issues both evangelical social teaching and bourgeois ideological hegemony spoke with more than one voice, a circumstance that further complicated the related but separate question of the actual effectiveness of bourgeois ideological hegemony in instilling the values of industrial morality among the more "undisciplined" and "improvident" members of the working classes.

The concept of industrial morality itself, moreover, retains a certain ambiguity. Although the term refers above all to the internalized discipline and self-direction extolled by evangelical reformers and other middle-class writers, it also embraces an essentially distinct set of qualities—the outward compliance, tractability, and orderliness upon which many factory proprietors and correctional officers placed so high a value. Qualities that promoted the authoritarian or economic needs of institutions and that were also valued for rendering members of the laboring population less destructive both to others and themselves were not synonymous with those qualities often associated with the complete moral elevation, or "bourgeoisification," of that population.[141] Yet it is not always apparent which quality was being extolled by middle-class writers when they referred, for example, to the importance of instilling good "habits" in workers. A defense of the factory system in the *Quarterly Christian Spectator* in 1832 could speak of the need for temperance reform among American factory workers and also lavish praise upon those many pious proprietors who for motives of "secular advantage" as well, sought to truly elevate the moral condition of their operatives. But in the next breath the article could seem to move to an exaltation of industrial morality for merely enlarging the capacity for subordination and regimentation. The value of Sabbath schools, the article observed, was that "they prepare the young for those habits of obedience, diligence, and regularity, by which they are managed with ease, and their labor rendered productive, to their employers."[142]

There may be an irreducible ambiguity and variety in what contemporaries meant by industrial morality. A German writing on Manchester factory conditions, J. G. Kohl, conceded in 1844 that for children of parents of the most "depraving example and influence," the factory system indeed held moral value: "It cannot be denied that the moral education of the children is likely to be better cared-for in the worst factories than in the worst families [where] the parents may be profligate, drunken, and criminal. . . . In the factories they can hardly learn many bad habits, the severity of discipline and ceaselessness of labour prevents *that;* and on the other hand, they acquire habits of punctuality and industry which cannot but be useful and beneficial." Kohl, however, evidently regarded even industriousness and solid work habits as falling well short of true "moral and mental discipline," the "ennobling" qualities that a decent "family education" could provide: "The factory-system . . . develops no moral germs *within* the soul," even if it did "in some measure, preserve it from contamination from *without*" by developing habits of industry.[143]

POSITIVE MORAL BENEFITS
OF FACTORY LABOR

There were, of course, writers and politicians, as well as factory proprietors and other capitalists, who went beyond Kohl's lukewarm concession that factory labor was congenial to a limited moral development. In considerable measure their greater enthusiasm reflected their failure to draw Kohl's unfavorable comparison: the development of good work habits was, in their view, a good deal more than just a poor substitute for true moral and spiritual character. In underscoring factory labor's positive moral benefits, its character as a force for social control and social stability in the full reformatory sense, these other arguments support and extend the more subtle scholarly interpretations of bourgeois ideological hegemony; for under these arguments the factory work regimen emerges not merely as the beneficiary of the work habits and discipline cultivated in schools and churches, but also as an active agency in its own right in the formation of these virtues. The theme that there was an intrinsic moral basis to factory labor's dignity was the counterpart to those arguments attesting to its intrinsic intellectual content, and it is not surprising that it found its greatest support among the same group of zealous profactory advocates. Noting that "it is, in fact, in the factory districts alone that the demoralizing agency of pauperism has been effectually resisted" in England, Andrew Ure attributed this circumstance in part to the regularity of habits instilled by regular factory labor; a moral shield had been created to "check drunkenness" and the "torpor" that pervaded the farming parishes.[144] The Whig Congressman from Vermont, George Perkins Marsh, earlier quoted along with Ure on the intellectual stimulus provided by machine tending, noted in his same speech that the factory system, under the aegis of the all-important protective tariff, provided a "certainty of constant employment," a punctuality of payment, and a form of work that "has made the laborer more regular in his habits"; it has required "the exercise of higher and more active faculties than the old routine of rural labor."[145] Although appreciative of the unprecedented "money value" the "cotton-factory" gave the labor of American women, one of the more celebrated of the Lowell mill girls, Harriet Hanson Robinson, also attributed to her factory work an inculcation of internalized discipline and moral development not unlike that which William Ellery Channing and Moses G. Leonard ascribed to labor in general: "The discipline our work brought us was of great value. . . . We were taught daily habits of regularity and of industry; it was, in fact, a sort of manual training or industrial school."[146] Elisha Bartlett, author of one of several antebellum "vindications" of conditions at Lowell that appeared in response to criticisms made by Seth Luther, Orestes Brownson, and other labor reformers, claimed that girls left the mills "with their minds quickened and their manners and morals improved." Bartlett seemed to attribute this achievement to the nature of factory labor itself as well as to the battery of "improvement circles" and institutions of close moral supervision that had for several decades made Lowell an internationally known "showcase" of how factory life might benefit the laboring population.[147]

Finally, as if in specific response to those who faulted manufacturing division of labor for failing to leave workers with a true skill and a lasting viable means of livelihood, Jesse K. McKeever of the Philadelphia House of Refuge invoked the reformatory power of factory discipline to justify a policy of hiring juvenile inmates out to contractors engaged in the production of brushes and daguerrotype-cases: "The contractors find it more profitable to systematize the labor, putting one or more boys at particular parts of the work. This division of labor prevents any one from acquiring a knowledge of the whole business. The chief object in the employment of boys is the formation of industrious habits, not the learning of business that might afford them the means of a living after they leave here."[148]

"Nature loves regularity as it abhors a vacuum."[149] The belief that regular work and routine in general promoted industrious habits and sound morals as well as good health, enjoyed a certain mainstream of middle-class support that defenders of factory labor sought clearly to tap.

Assenting to this general belief were even such writers as Henry Mayhew. Meticulous and severe criticism of the "sweating" and other relentless and exploitative labor processes that distinguished "overwork" in the "dishonourable" trades did not leave Mayhew unappreciative of the value of regular employment for the worker; and he was hardly more critical of the repetitive drudgery and labor intensity in these trades than he was of the very different kind of conditions that prevailed for "casual labor."[150] Observation of the casual laborers seeking work on the London docks convinced Mayhew that "the very conditions necessary for the formation of any habit whatsoever are, that the act or thing to which we are to become habituated should be repeated at frequent and regular intervals. It is a moral impossibility that the class of labourers who are only occasionally employed should be either generally industrious or temperate—both industry and temperance being habits produced by constancy of employment and uniformity of income."[151]

Writers for whom the claims of factory employment's intellectually stimulating character carried limited plausibility or importance might be strongly drawn to the notion that factory labor was morally disciplining and elevating by mere virtue of its continuous, even relentless character. George Frederick Holmes provided indications that he found this notion congenial, notwithstanding the anti-industrial, agricultural bias with which Southern proslavery ideology has been generally associated.[152] Invoking an argument used by Alexander Hamilton, Tench Coxe, and some of their eighteenth-century proindustrial predecessors, Holmes criticized various contemporary land reform proposals for their hostility to nonagricultural enterprise.[153] In their zeal to relocate the entire laboring population to plots of lands, these proposals ignored the fact that many segments of this population lacked either the inclination or the talent for farm labor and would remain idle or underemployed.[154] More than this, however, Holmes was troubled by the vagaries and irregular work rhythms of free and self-employed agricultural labor, as well as by the ease of gaining a bare subsistence from the soil. The lack of continuity and regularity that distinguished such labor bred idleness and indifferent work habits, of which Holmes cited the ex-slaves of the West Indies as a prime example. On much the same ground that Mayhew criticized London's casual labor as morally injurious, Holmes suggested that agricultural work lacked the moral benefits and other advantages of industrial employment: "The requirements of the farm, however negligently attended to, would create such interruptions as would prevent steady and continuous labor at any thing else. Yet, without this, the absence of the favourable influence of routine and frequent repetition would destroy the inclination for other labour, and would certainly annihilate that manual dexterity and educated skill which spring from the recurrence of uniform operations."[155]

Clearly, there was a sense that continuous, routine, and regular employment, which factory labor certainly exemplified, not only called for but in itself encouraged an internalized work discipline and industriousness that was highly valued by the early Victorian middle classes. Yet if the establishment of the factory system, in America or England, had depended upon the appeal and persuasiveness of these specific moral arguments made on its behalf, rather than upon the power and drive of the capitalist economic interests behind it, then that system would hardly have secured the prominent place it did. For although many observers, including some of those discussed above, did recognize a convergence between manufacturing capitalist interests and the moral improvement of the laboring population, it can still scarcely be said that among the middle classes generally, let alone among the working classes themselves, the notion that factory work carried positive moral, or therapeutic, value ever truly "caught on." However pervasive among the middle class was "industrial morality" and the wish to control the laboring population by elevating its moral condition, neither of these translated into more than limited enthusiasm for the notion that factory labor might be an instrument of actual moral reform. Factory labor faced certain handicaps, rooted in both objective working conditions and entrenched social attitudes, which rendered suspect even its efficacy as an instrument of negative moral value, as a mere check on the worker's opportunities for idleness and vice. Those handicaps rendered that much more suspect the idea that factory work, any more than chattel slavery or other labor systems grounded in blatant physical coercion, could be consistent with the work ethic in the full, positive moral sense of that term. One middle-class critic of the British factory system, in fact, added his support for ten-hour legislation by suggesting that the moral evils of that system lent a damning validity to the parallels between wage slavery and chattel slavery. Under present factory conditions, Dr. Joseph Henry Green testified in 1832, where the operatives "even at the tenderest age, and without respect to the distinction of sex, and without regard to decency, are crowded together under all the circumstances that contribute to disease and vice, . . . the labourers themselves are degraded into the mere negro slaves of Europe."[156]

Green's criticisms were but one specimen of the handicaps, the ideological resistance, with which mid-nineteenth-century American and British proponents of the factory system had to contend; those criticisms suggest why the majority of the profactory proponents were obliged to spend so much of their time on the defensive, denying that this new form of labor being promoted by powerful economic interests was a force of moral destruction. Green's particular formulation was broadly humanitarian, made with almost exclusive reference to the best interests of the workers themselves; and in this respect, it was not unlike other attacks on the factory system made by working-class and labor radical and reform groups. But with slight modifications and shifts in emphases, criticisms of the moral evils of the factory system could assume more conservative, social control overtones and objectives, ones with hardly less impedimental implications for the profactory cause. It was these more conservative objections to factory labor to which the essay in the *American Whig Review* quoted earlier was above all referring—objections that the factory system contributed to the "debasement" of the laboring population by encouraging both its vicious and socially insubordinate, perhaps incendiary, tendencies. It did this chiefly by congregating the two sexes in promiscuous fashion and by bringing workers together in large numbers under one roof, the most initially corrupt of whom would infect the others. Whether it was more humanitarian or more socially conservative in the particular formulations it assumed, the general theme of factory labor's morally destructive effect on the operative population occupied a hardly less prominent place in diatribes against the factory system than did Smith's theme regarding the intellectually injurious effects of factory division of labor.[157] The most fervent factory advocates on the different sides of the Atlantic had rather distinct preferred ways of meeting this broad moral criticism, although both essentially came down to arguing that factory labor's intrinsic moral benefits were generally obscured or impeded by extraneous conditions and circumstances.

One of these preferred American profactory responses, particularly popular in the earlier stages of industrialization when it retained greater plausibility, was that the factory population in the New World would never crowd together in large numbers, instead remaining safely and virtuously dispersed among a multitude of lightly populated mill villages. The factory system would provide employment opportunities where they were needed without establishing that corrupt urban presence that seemed particularly threatening and offsetting to the freehold basis of American republican virtue. Historians have described this characteristic embrace of rural-based industry as part of the "middle landscape" ideal, locating the source of its appeal both in the notorious countermodel of urban Manchester and in the influential heritage of Jeffersonian republican values which condemned densely populated cities more unequivocally than they did manufacturing enterprise per se.[158] New England would never develop a Manchester, its factory labor would indefinitely sustain rather than subvert republican virtue, the Rhode Island textile manufacturer Zachariah Allen argued in 1832, because its factory system had no need of the steam power that was responsible for building up large populations of economically dependent and depraved operatives in England:

Where steam engines are in use instead of water power, the laboring classes are collected together, to form that crowded state of population, which is always favorable, in commercial as well as in manufacturing cities, to the bold practices of vice and immorality, by screening offenders from marked ignominy. . . .

In most of the manufactories in the United States, sprinkled along the glens and meadows of solitary watercourses, the sons and daughters of respectable farmers, who live in the neighborhood of the works, find for a time a profitable employment. The character of each individual of these rural manufacturing villages, is commonly well scanned, and becomes known to the proprietor, personally; who finds it in his interest to discharge the dissolute and vicious. . . .

It may be intended as a blessing that an all-wise Providence has denied to the barren hills of New England the mines of coal, which would allow the inhabitants to congregate in manufacturing cities, by enabling them to have recourse to artificial power, instead of the natural water power so profusely furnished by the innumerable streams, . . . Whilst a cold climate and an ungrateful soil render the inhabitants from necessity industrious, thus distributed in small communities around the waterfalls, their industry is not likely to be the means of rendering them licentious.[159]

The abundance of water power in the United States notwithstanding, it was already becoming apparent at the time of Allen's writing that the expanding American factory system would indeed require steam power, and that industrialization was in any case assuming at Lowell and elsewhere an unmistakably urban dimension. One of the Boston Associates, Nathan Appleton, suggested in a memoir, however, that with their founding of the Waltham-type mill system some twenty years before Allen's writing, Appleton and Francis Cabot Lowell had in fact anticipated some of the problems that steam power and urbanization raised for the profactory position. The congregation of even large numbers of operatives in urban mills need not have a morally pernicious effect, Appleton argued, if precautions and measures beyond those mentioned by Allen were taken by factory proprietors to screen the incoming factory population and to preserve a high moral standard among it. The morally benign nature of factory labor would manifest itself by, above all, overwhelmingly confining the operative force to a single sex, the female, and to closely supervising its behavior both at work and in residential boarding houses. As Appleton noted in a well-known passage:

The operatives in the manufacturing cities of Europe, were notoriously of the lowest character, for intelligence and morals. The question therefore arose, and was deeply considered, whether this degradation was the result of the peculiar occupation, or of other and distinct causes.

. . . Here was in New England a fund of [female] labor, well educated and virtuous. . . . The most efficient guards were adopted in establishing boarding houses, at the cost of the [Waltham] Company, under the charge of respectable women, with every provision for religious worship.[160]

When the reformer Dorothea Dix cast doubt on the high moral character of the Lowell female work force and suggested that considerable numbers of the women were finding their way to the Middlesex County Prison, Appleton wrote to her in 1841 acknowledging Lowell's urban character but insisting that the structure established by the Boston Associates was largely sufficient to repel its dangers: "It is true that a city the size of Lowell will attract to it idleness and vice from other quarters in the hope of preying on the fruits of their [the operatives] industry. It is for such intruders that the police court was early introduced into that place—and which I believe is very effectual in preserving the place from contamination from without—whilst its own police and institutions are peculiarly favorable to moral purity."[161]

Circumstances, of course, continued to change, making Appleton's profactory variation on American exceptionalism as obsolete as Allen's. During the late antebellum period, the Waltham system's boardinghouses and other institutions of moral supervision were largely dismantled, as the urban factory population at Lowell and elsewhere came increasingly to be dominated by the same Irish-born work force to whose presence James Phillips Kay had attributed some of the worst degradations of the Manchester factory system itself.[162] One implication that this development had for the profactory position has already been suggested: factory proprietors and agents in the 1860s continued to make use of the old argument that mill work had negative moral value by keeping raffish foreign-born operatives occupied, well supervised, and perhaps above all, off the streets. Implicit, too, in the profactory position was a presumption that similarly drew on the supervisory powers of the factory: mills could as effectively check immorality among the young as schools, churches, or any other institutions that congregated large numbers of youths together.[163]

We should also make some reference to the specific impact that increased Europeanization of the northeastern factory system had on the mythology of high American wage levels. That mythology had always figured prominently in the defense of the Waltham, if not the "family" type, mills. In his letter to Dix, written toward the end of Lowell's "golden age," Appleton repeated decades-old arguments: the Lowell girls "earn wages

above the average in other occupations. Industry well paid has no temptation to vice."[164] As Appleton and other advocates took pains to emphasize,
it was not factory labor itself which was responsible for the moral degradation of the Old World factory population; rather, it was overpopulation and
the complex of anti-republican institutions and influences that degraded all
segments of the European laboring population equally by denying them a
decent living. In affirming the national "comfort" and "prosperity" attributable to the protective tariff of 1842, the Pennsylvania Whig Congressman,
E. J. Morris, went beyond like-minded partisans who denied that conditions for the Lowell girls had been deteriorating. He furthermore informed
one of the Democratic critics of the American factory system, Robert Dale
Owen, that

> the error of the gentleman lies in applying the condition of tax-
> oppressed and over-populated England to other countries widely
> different from it in natural resources, extent of territory, and
> institutions of government. In England wages are low from the
> superabundance of labor, while rent and breadstuffs are high
> from the heavy taxation on real estate for the support of an
> expensive throne, and from the corn laws. . . .
>
> In England, the man of humble means has no participation
> in the affairs of government. He cannot rise to posts of honor in
> the kingdom, from his inability to compete with the favored sons
> of fortune. The control of the government is vested in the weal-
> thier classes, who administer it more for their own benefit than
> that of the productive classes.[165]

It suited Morris's purposes to embrace a theme also popular among
Britain's profactory advocates: "misery and discontent" were not "the
natural results of the manufacturing system"; the deprivations experienced
by workers outside that system in fact exceeded the deprivations of those
within it. It was also consistent with Morris's American exceptionalist,
Whig perspective and purposes to accentuate more than British profactory
advocates that degree of distress and demoralization which did prevail
among England's factory population. Attributing the "famished" state and
the moral degradation of British operatives to Old World institutions and
conditions that were extrinsic to factory labor itself was one of Morris's
principal means of vindicating the American factory system and the protective tariff particularly. The uniquely high instrumental value that factory
labor at Lowell and elsewhere supposedly carried would realize that labor's
intrinsically benign moral effects. Such was the exceptional character of
American institutions and wage levels, Morris even appeared to be suggesting, that it could check the demoralizing, baleful influence of what Zachariah Allen and Appleton too had at various points acknowledged to be

highly undesirable: the urbanization and congregation of large numbers of uncultivated operatives of both sexes together.

Morris's exceptionalist faith, his tendency to defend the uplifting, republican, nature of northeastern factory labor on the basis of how well it paid, irrespective of the nationality of those earning the wages, hardly withstood the test Morris himself appeared to be making for his arguments. When by the mid-1860s Europe's oppressed "pauper" operatives had clearly established themselves as America's own operatives, the effect was to throw a damper on the use of traditional high-wage defenses of the mills. In the specific case of the Waltham system, retreat from those defenses by the manufacturing corporate interests themselves was, of course, mute ac-knowledgement of a very tangible set of developments—of the economic pressures and consequent deterioration in wage rates and other conditions which, by encouraging the exodus of native-born female operatives, had stimulated the need for immigrant replacements in the first place.[166] But above and beyond the operation of such material forces, the perceived char-acter of the immigrants was itself used by factory interests to validate their acquiescence in the erosion of the Waltham system's distinctive, republican character—their concurrence in the loss of whatever social esteem factory labor in America had managed to acquire. There had always been, to be sure, a rather severe cap on that esteem; to his battery of criticisms of the Waltham system, Seth Luther had in 1832 added an observation that also runs throughout various of the "factory girl" journals: "the *wives* and *daugh-ters* of the *rich* manufacturers would no more associate with a *'factory girl,'* than they would with a *negro slave*."[167] But after a period of time marked by rising prejudice toward the Irish as a culturally, if not racially inferior group, factory proprietors and agents at Lowell and elsewhere were hardly offering even the pretense of respect for the workers now in their employ. The high wage and other exceptionalist claims that once dominated their descriptions and justifications of working conditions had by the mid-1860s given way to a palpable disdain, at once genuine and self-serving, for the newer corps of disorderly and "unrefined" operatives—for the foreign-born adults and their children who were "mostly of the lowest class."[168]

BRITISH FACTORY ADVOCATES

A ready supply of European labor, together with pervasive nativist prejudices toward that labor, fed the complacency regarding worsening operative conditions. The acceptance in all quarters of the northeastern factory system as a fait accompli likely worked to the same effect: it further relieved the pressure on factory interests and their allies to offer arguments affirming the unique benefits, material and moral, of that system. But we might turn now to considering how the same basic criticisms of factory

labor which for the first half of the nineteenth century at least had succeeded in keeping proponents of America's factory system on the defensive
worked to similar effect in England. Saddled with the lingering notoriety
not only of urban Manchester but of the rural water-powered mills manned
by "infant slaves" from the poor houses, British factory advocates also
lavished far more effort explaining why factory conditions need not be
morally pernicious than upon how factory labor was intrinsically morally
therapeutic. Beyond this shared defensiveness, one discerns in the British
profactory arguments basic differences as well as similarities from the
American arguments. Distinctive first of all was the general context in
which the British factory debates occurred, that of a society where the
issues of labor discontent and pauperism at time assumed crisis proportions, and as a consequence of which these issues could not help but
interject themselves into the British factory debates and impart a unique
urgency to them. Apart from this distinctive context was the fact that
British proponents of the factory system were from a relatively early point
obliged to deal with Manchester as a negative reality rather than as a future
possibility. One outcome of this circumstance was that many of the British
vindicators of factory conditions, including leading Manchester liberals like
John Bright, gave much more prominence to the theme that the squalid
living conditions of British operatives in Manchester and other urban
centers, as distinct from factory conditions themselves, were responsible for
the low moral state of the operatives.[169] Yet the distinctive British emphasis
on this theme held in turn a basic similarity with the American profactory
position. Just as Allen, Appleton, and before them such factory advocates as
Tench Coxe argued that the New World would "purify" and provide a fair
test for the factory system, so did such British factory advocates as William
Cooke Taylor contend that the ongoing ruralization of English factories,
with their own institutions of moral paternalism and supervision, would at
last permit his country's factory system to be "fairly tested on its own
merits."[170] Factory labor and factory discipline were not themselves to
blame for existing moral defects in the British operative population, a fact
which would be evident enough were the system confined to more pristine
surroundings. Even as it was undergoing its transformation from mill
village to city, Lowell figured hardly less significantly in British than in
American profactory arguments as a paternalistic, morally unimpeachable
model to which both factory proprietors and operatives elsewhere should
strive to emulate.[171] Like the American factory advocates, the British
advocates played off the image of the corrupting influences wielded by the
densely populated, anonymous city.

   In the demoralized and economically depressed state of great segments
of the British agricultural laboring population, factory advocates like Taylor, Andrew Ure, and Edward Baines, Jr., also possessed a polemical

advantage that American proponents largely lacked. To the pernicious mixing of the sexes in urban cotton mills, the British advocates readily juxtaposed Parliamentary investigations that represented, in Baines's words, "the licentiousness and depravity of the cottagers as regards the sexes as exceedingly great, owing to the practice of whole families sleeping in one room."[172] As Baines observed generally in 1843, in attacking yet another Factory Bill for unfairly singling out conditions for factory children as intellectually and morally pernicious: "Far be it from me to treat the country as others have treated the town,—to cull out all the evidences of ignorance, immorality, and degradation which might be found among the rustics, and to rejoice in painting them in the blackest colours. But I am driven, in mere defence, to institute a comparison in some points; and if the result should not be favourable to them, they must thank their friends who have so grossly libelled the Manufacturing Districts."[173]

In their defenses of the intrinsically benign and beneficial effects of factory labor, American advocates like Congressman Morris themselves utilized Baines's very comparison: by virtually every yardstick, Britain's factory population was represented as more economically secure and more intellectually and morally enlightened than much of its agricultural laboring population.[174] Indeed, the comparison could be and was frequently extended to include the exploited and impoverished workers of the sweated trades or the self-employed laborers who stubbornly persisted in such declining trades as handloom weaving.[175] Driven by the logic of this comparative argument, many of the American and British factory advocates acknowledged the degradation of the Manchester factory population up to a point and no further; that degradation was limited in the relative sense, circumscribed if by no other circumstance than by the fact that Manchester operatives secured from their employment a recompense generous by comparison with that earned by most other unskilled and semiskilled segments of the British laboring population.[176]

Some of the factory system's defenders, such as James Kay-Shuttleworth, clearly showed the strains of attempting to vindicate factory conditions in Manchester from the criticisms made on moral and other grounds.[177] In a letter to the Scottish minister, Thomas Chalmers, published together with his 1832 study of the Manchester working class, Kay-Shuttleworth praised the efforts of "enlightened manufacturers of the country" to remove "the miseries of large masses of the operative body"; here and in the study itself he led the way among factory advocates in arguing that crowded and unsanitary living conditions, together with the degrading habits that the wave of Irish-born operatives had brought over with them, were largely responsible for the low moral state of the city's cotton mill work force.[178] Characteristic of the profactory position was Kay-Shuttleworth's argument that "capitalists, whose establishments are situated in the country, enjoy many opportunities of controling [*sic*] the habits and ministering to the comforts of those in their employ, which cannot exist in a large manufacturing town."[179] Typical, too, of the profactory position was Kay-Shuttleworth's insistence that the wage level, or instrumental value, of factory labor in Manchester's cotton mills was sufficient to provide "all the decent comforts of life" and to check the operatives' descent into moral degradation.[180] But more than some of the more uncritical proindustrial polemicists, Kay-Shuttleworth also felt obliged to acknowledge the substance of many of the antifactory criticisms. In this respect, indeed, he went beyond conceding that the Manchester factory system had a morally pernicious impact by crowding large numbers of workers together. In a statement that could be easily mistaken for one emanating from the most radical labor reform perspective, a perspective of uncompromising hostility to the factory system, Kay-Shuttleworth argued that the intrinsic tendency of factory labor was to encourage man's domination by his lower nature:

> Prolonged and exhausting labour . . . is not calculated to develop the intellectual or moral faculties of man. The dull routine of a ceaseless drudgery, in which the same mechanical process is incessantly repeated, resembles the torments of Sisyphus—the toil, like the rock, recoils perpetually on the wearied operative. . . . The intellect slumbers in supine inertness; but the grosser parts of our nature attain a rank development. To condemn man to such severity of toil is, in some measure, to cultivate in him the habits of an animal.[181]

Such a description of factory work was fundamentally at odds with the perspective that found in the same routine and discipline of the new form of labor a source of moral and intellectual elevation.[182] But unlike the radical critics of the factory system with whom he agreed in this respect, Kay-Shuttleworth looked neither to alternative property or social arrangements, nor even to reduced working hours as the essential antidote to the baleful moral and intellectual effects of factory labor. His preferred antidote, and indeed his general social vision, was indicated by his observation that merely reducing the hours of labor without introducing a "*general system of education*" would result only in increasing the time spent by the operative population "in sloth or dissipation." The "ignorance and immorality" of the poor, he added, endanger the "political safety of the wealthy." A direct reference to the tendency of cholera and other community-wide epidemics to spread outward from their beginnings in urban slums, this last statement also reflected the common upper- and middle-class belief that the moral debasement of British factory operatives and other workers, far from rendering them inert, increased their proclivity to engage in riots and turnouts.[183] As much as anyone, Richard Johnson has written, Kay-Shuttleworth exemplified the early Victorian middle-class "obsession" with determining "through the capture of educational means, the patterns of thought, sentiment and behaviour of the working class."[184]

As related earlier, the sense that new forms of industrial labor signally lacked intellectual or creative content, and that they were in fact mentally pernicious in their effects upon workers, gave significant impetus to the movement for extending educational opportunities to the laboring population. And insofar as mainstream middle-class writers in mid-nineteenth-century America, as well as radical labor reform groups and workingmen's parties, lent their support to this movement, this support was not without a more conservative, social control dimension. If, for example, Fanny Wright and other labor radicals of the 1830s regarded education as a means of achieving intellectual equality and independence for workers entrapped in degrading forms of labor, a significant segment of American middle-class support for popular education, as some historians have stressed, viewed the situation rather differently.[185] The education that was to develop the intellectual faculties of workers, that was to provide what manual labor itself could not—a necessary intellectual component to the "dignity" of free laborers—was intended to win or solidify the allegiance of workers to existing capitalist social arrangements and values; it was hardly intended to provide them with the increased intellectual tools or capacity to challenge and subvert these existing arrangements.[186]

The parallel and overlapping movement, in which Kay-Shuttleworth played so prominent a role, to fill though educational institutions the deficiency in manual labor's moral content, was still more predominantly middle and upper class in composition, and correspondingly even more uniformly and unambiguously conservative in its objectives. The telltale sign of this conservatism was a preoccupation with a distinctively moral and religious education, an emphasis upon developing the moral faculties of operatives and other elements of the laboring population, as distinct from their intellectual faculties. Kay-Shuttleworth, it may be recalled, was not only the author of an influential work on the condition of Manchester's factory population. He also served as Secretary to the Committee of Council of Education in Britain from 1839 to 1849, and in this capacity he was a leading advocate of industrial schools for workhouse children, who "must be trained in industry, in correct moral habits, and in religion, and must be fitted to discharge the duties of its [the workhouse's] station."[187] That Kay-Shuttleworth regarded such moral education of the institutionalized juvenile poor as a prototype, for purposes of social control, to be extended to all segments of the laboring population, may be seen by his claims that the great object to be kept in view in regulating any school for the instruction of the children of the labouring class, is the rearing of hardy and intelligent workingmen, whose character and habits shall afford the largest amount of security to the property and order of the community. . . .

The poor man will not be made a much better member of society, by being only taught to read and write. His education should comprise such branches of general knowledge, as would prove sources of rational amusement, and would thus elevate his tastes above a companionship in licentious pleasures.[188]

The year in which Kay-Shuttleworth's book on Manchester appeared also preceded by only two years the enactment of the New Poor Law, a culminating expression of years of middle- and upper-class alarm at the "demoralizing" impact that less stringent poor relief policies had presumably been exercising upon the work incentives and moral values of "industrious," self-supporting laborers.[189] Kay-Shuttleworth shared fully in this alarm. The particular educational antidote that he urged for factory labor in Manchester—that operatives degraded by their employment "be instructed in habits of forethought and economy"—can only be understood in the context of the raging debate over the best means of controlling and reducing the population of dependent and "vicious" poor, a population that posed in the minds of many so grave a threat to the stability of British capitalist society.[190]

There was another part to the context within which Kay-Shuttleworth's book on Manchester factory labor appeared, one suggested by his argument that the education of paupers, factory workers, and the general laboring population would render them less susceptible to demagoguery.[191] The harsh new poor bill that was enacted shortly thereafter initiated a new nationwide wave of bitter labor protest and unrest. Like previous waves, this one challenged the classical economic doctrine that labor combinations must prove ineffectual in permanently raising wages above the level set by the so-called natural relation between the supply of capital and the size of the labor force.[192] For Kay-Shuttleworth, a firm believer in the classical economic verities, correct working-class education would not only help dispel the "contagion" of pauperism by training the laboring poor in correct moral values and work habits. The same education would dispel as well the scourge of labor agitation and radical economic doctrines that threatened to spread through the ranks of the working classes and disrupt the balance of power in class relationships: "The ascertained truths of political science should be early taught to the labouring classes, and *correct* political information should be constantly and industriously disseminated amongst them."[193]

By seeming to suggest that one of factory labor's intrinsic effects was to so weaken the moral fiber of laborers as to render them more susceptible to pauperism and pernicious economic doctrines alike, Kay-Shuttleworth indeed broke with more uncritical defenders of the factory system. His own perspective provided a bridge with other British writers who shared his wish to contain social disorder from below but who were still more censurious than he of factory conditions. Kay-Shuttleworth's brother, Joseph Kay, another well-known author of writings on working-class education, expressed in 1846 the traditional objection to the factory system on moral grounds, that it was a nursery of vice and labor unrest. "In assembling masses of workmen," Kay warned, "there are always two special dangers; a low state of intellect, occasioning improvidence, and an absence of religious feeling, producing immorality and insubordination. . . . If Government is not prepared, . . . to give a religious education to the people, nothing can justify its having suffered our manufacturing system to grow to its present dimensions."[194] In much of his writing, Kay followed his brother in giving first priority to the development of the worker's moral faculties and in emphasizing that any development of the worker's intellectual faculties should above all be directed to rendering him immune to inflammatory economic doctrines. In fact, Kay made a special point of warning primary schools that a policy of providing "mere instruction" to the working-class child without religious and moral training was an invitation to vice, improvidence, and social turbulence:

> It awakens his intellect sufficiently to render it a powerful and dangerous auxiliary to his unbridled and to his unruly passions; whilst the religious and humanizing influences of his soul remaining dormant, . . . He is no longer dull, stupid, and totally without capabilities of reasoning, as the labourers in many of our agricultural districts, but sufficiently enlightened to indulge, not only the more sensual appetites and demands of his ill-governed body, but the restless, wild, and rebellious promptings of his scarce-awakened and unreflecting mind.[195]

Writing several years after the most radical phase of the Chartist movement, Kay left no doubt that the predominantly moral training and the narrowly intellectual education that factory laborers required as an antidote to the conditions of their employment was a matter of urgent necessity:

> When cheap literature, and that often of the most inflammatory kind, is reaching the hovels of the meanest labourer,—when communication and combination among the masses of labourers is daily increasing,—when their intellects are awakening to ac-

tion, unchecked and unguided;—let the church and state take care. There is but little time left for reformation . . .

. . . with democratic ideas of the wildest kinds, and a knowledge of the power of union daily gaining ground among them.[196]

In the writing of both Kay-Shuttleworth and Joseph Kay disgust and fear regarding the behavior of the laboring poor coexisted with recognition of the economic and institutional causes of that behavior. In Kay-Shuttleworth's case, especially, a "crude moralism" reflective of that disgust and fear appears in general to have retained the upper hand in explanations of social distress.[197] In the tradition of Malthus, Kay-Shuttleworth insisted that paupers, operatives and other segments of the working classes owed both a considerable portion of their degradations and their subordinate economic position to their own "moral errors" and weakness: "in a much worse state of society, sobriety, prudence, industry, and forethought, would produce more real comfort."[198] The laboring population might, accordingly, reduce the gross economic disparities in British society and elevate themselves into a "situation of physical comfort," through the development of the standard character virtues.[199]

There was, on the other hand, acknowledgement from Kay-Shuttleworth that existing social arrangements, of which factory labor was but one part, and over which workers had no control, were themselves a source of degradation. Upon observing that the poor's "own ignorance or moral errors"—their "insobriety, uncleanliness . . . improvidence and idleness"— were the immediate cause of the cholera and other "evils" that ravaged the poor, Kay-Shuttleworth added that these evils "may often be traced to the primary influence of the imperfect institutions of society on their character." The "errors" of the poor "are not more their fault than their misfortune."[200]

If recognition of the environmentalist causes of the plight of the laboring poor somewhat tempered the moralism in Kay-Shuttleworth's writing, Joseph Kay was a good deal more emphatic and fervent in his environmentalism and sense of social injustice. Kay's warning that "church and state" had better "take care" was as much a call for certain social reforms, above all the implementation of land allotments, as it was an appeal for working-class moral education. He devoted an entire volume to a critical assessment of the plight of the hard-working, proletarianized English peasant, observing that "no system has ever been invented so well qualified to stupefy the peasant, and to destroy all his hopes and all his virtues, as the system of landed tenures. . . . It deprives him of every worldly inducement to practise self-denial, prudence, and economy; it deprives him of every hope of rising in the world; it makes him totally careless about self-improvement, about the institutions of his country, and about the security of property."[201]

The improvidence and discontent of the poor, Kay maintained, stemmed very largely from their recognition that they "have no stake whatever in the country," that with the existence of such "frightful" class contrasts, they quite naturally "fancy they have nothing to lose and everything to gain from a revolution."[202] Kay's general argument that under existing property arrangements the virtues of the laboring poor would prove of little economic value to them, that these arrangements truly subverted the work ethic by depriving manual labor of its just instrumental rewards, was fully consistent with radical working-class and labor reform perspectives. Yet Kay's almost hysterical fear of the spread of pauperism, vice, "Chartists' risings" and other radical political movements and beliefs among the laboring population, his near obsession with the idea that these might somehow culminate in a revolution that completely transformed existing social arrangements rather than merely removed their most glaring inequities, ultimately linked him more closely to his brother's perspective than to that of labor radicals. If Kay regarded religious education as an antidote to the rise of the factory system, he suggested that even the narrowest, most conservative intellectual education for England's peasants might still be too dangerously enlightening. As long as they were legally obstructed from acquiring property and unable to improve their condition naturally, Kay claimed, such education would only enable the peasants to more clearly perceive and resent the obstacles before them: "If it be necessary or expedient that the present landed system should be continued, it would be wiser to get rid of every school in the whole country."[203] Kay's genuine support for mass education and limited social reforms was frequently overpowered by his concern that the wrong mix of these two would eventuate in violent and sweeping changes from below.

Given their admission of the structural or institutional obstacles impeding the economic improvement of the laboring poor, and the sense that these obstacles would at most be modified rather than removed entirely, Kay-Shuttleworth and Kay hardly embraced moral training and other forms of education as a means of altering the nature of class relationships within British society. To the contrary, Kay-Shuttleworth, in particular, conspicuously valued such education as a means of securing the British poor's acquiescence in existing hierarchical distinctions, even when those distinctions remained characterized by gross economic disparities. A number of historians have argued, indeed, that in a society where upward mobility and the redistribution of wealth and economic power were very largely circumscribed, the middle-class movement to instill solid work habits and character virtues in the laboring population was never intended

to do much more than palm that population off with the compensating satisfaction of achieving middle-class moral "respectability." To the extent that
it looked to some economic improvement of the laborer within his class and
explicitly repudiated indifference or acquiescence on his part to a wretched
earthly existence, the bourgeois injunction of worker "self-help" through
moral education did differ in a significant respect from the moral pieties
expressed by Hannah More and other evangelicals active around the turn of
the century.[204] But in the essential objective of insuring the social deference
and class subordination of the laboring poor by training them in habits of
industry and respectability, the mid-Victorian bourgeois gospel of worker
"self-help" differed hardly at all from these earlier evangelical efforts.[205]

Viewed in their totality, the statements of Kay-Shuttleworth, Kay, and
other British writers who expressed similar fears and concerns about the
laboring poor do not completely remove the ambiguity regarding the
precise economic gains they expected the moral education and elevation of
that population to bring to it. It does seem clear that they hoped that
effective moral education, in conjunction with the sharp restriction of
outdoor poor relief, improved living and sanitary conditions, and such
limited economic reforms as land allotments to peasant farmers, would
bring the laboring population a modest economic competence as well as
moral respectability. What remains more questionable is whether these
writers believed that without these other measures working-class moral
elevation through education could bring even this competence—Joseph
Kay, certainly, suggested that it would not—and whether they believed
that moral elevation was itself even possible in the absence of these additional measures.

At the same time, such writers did not anticipate that industrial morality, even if it secured some economic improvement for British laborers and
created a moral bond between the working and the middle classes, could
ever result in any but the most negligible social mobility from the working
into the middle classes. In fact, they often characterized such an eventuality
as highly undesirable. It might be recalled that Kay-Shuttleworth and other
proponents of mass education in Britain partially justified their cause with
the argument that if properly administered, such education would increase
rather than diminish the workingman's contentment with his station in
life.[206] Joseph Kay included in one of his books a *Report* from the Rev.
H. W. Bellairs on the "enlightened" schooling available in the western
agricultural districts: "It is often supposed that the intention of its promoters is to instruct the peasant above his situation in life, whereas in reality the
object is to fit him properly for his situation in life."[207] But if Kay-Shuttleworth and other prominent promoters of mass education in Britain hardly
shared the radical social objectives of groups that called for an expansive,

intellectual education for the working classes, they nevertheless did not regard the radical educational doctrines as the major threat to their own agenda.[208] Rather, they directed most of their criticism toward the lingering sentiment, at the other end of the ideological spectrum, which considered the laboring population as existing "only to labour and to die," and which consequently denied or minimized the value of any secular instruction for that population at all.[209] This deeply conservative, even reactionary, sentiment, in the view of Kay-Shuttleworth and his colleagues, failed to perceive that it was precisely such instruction which was so desperately needed to win the deference and allegiance of dangerously discontented workers to a society of entrenched economic distinctions.

AMERICAN PROPONENTS
OF MASS EDUCATION

The contemporary American proponents of mass education did not have an extreme conservative opposition of such magnitude with which to contend, although some such sentiment did emanate from the most strongly elitist, and predominantly Southern proslavery, quarters, particularly but not exclusively with regard to the dangers of educating a black slave laboring population.[210] More fundamentally, the rationale supplied by Horace Mann and some of the other mainstream middle-class supporters for an educated laboring population reflected the mythology of American exceptionalism and to that extent, it was distinctly alien to the social vision of Kay-Shuttleworth and his colleagues.[211] For Mann, popular education was not something to be grafted onto a society of entrenched class distinctions for the purpose of making these conditions more tolerable for the masses. Rather, "universal education" was itself a prime cause of exceptionalism in America, or at least in Northern "free labor" society. By "capitalizing" labor, rendering it more "inventive" and correspondingly productive, common school education added an immeasurable degree of wealth to the country's generous stock of natural resources.[212] Through its enlightening influence as well, it discouraged that working-class servility which tolerated the imposition of artificial class barriers, barriers that were among the crucial impediments to the diffusion of wealth.[213] "Universal education" represented a key ingredient in that vision of Northern free society, one to which Whig and Republican political spokesmen like Mann gave particularly prominent expression, in which the majority mixed capital and labor in a condition of self-employed economic independence. To the enlightening influence of their common school system, Mann claimed, the people of Massachusetts above all largely owed their "unexampled prosperity," their "general intelligence and virtue," and their freedom from the permanent hireling status and "tyranny" to "capital" that enslaved "the lower classes of Europe." Massachusetts was proof that

> if education be equably diffused, it will draw property after it by the strongest of all attractions; for such a thing never did happen, and never can happen, as that an intelligent and practical body of men should be permanently poor. Property and labor in different classes are essentially antagonistic; but property and labor in the same class are essentially fraternal. . . .
>
> Education, . . . is the great equalizer of the conditions of men.[214]

Together with his lectures on behalf of temperance and other antebellum moral reform causes, Mann's writing on education presented a picture of Northern society where class fluidity was such that the most self-disciplined and enterprising individuals who commenced life as wage laborers could, with the assistance of a common school education, in due course accumulate enough wealth to leave their hireling status behind them.[215] Indeed, they might very conceivably join the ranks of those capitalists, professionals, and party leaders who, by employing and directing the labor of hirelings or by some other legitimate means, dispensed with performing their own manual labor altogether. Addressing the condition of paupers and others who occupied the lowest rungs of the Northern free labor system, Mann insisted that habits of temperance and self-discipline would bring to them, at the very least, an honest and secure competence: "in this country, with but few exceptions, nothing but proper *exertion* is required to raise men from poverty, and to surround them with all the less expensive comforts of life."[216] To an extent that was generally undreamed of in Britain, the industrial morality and middle-class moral respectability that was to bind the manual laborer to existing social arrangements, to create, so to speak, his stake in society, was conceptualized by Mann, along with Lincoln and others, as encompassing far more than a mere economic subsistence for the Northern laborer.[217] The Public School Society of New York, in an attempt to increase the appeal of the common school program among the city's poor in 1838, advanced in one of its publications an argument that would not likely have been made in any other nation: although poor parents might be reluctant to surrender the present earning power of their children, "give them a *good schooling,* and in a few years, they will be earning *ten, twenty, fifty or a hundred* times as much as they do now."[218]

The claims Mann and others made for educated labor in Northern society raise many questions. Not the least of them is the degree to which the skill dilution generated in the job structure by antebellum industrialization and technology in fact reduced or limited the demand for "educated" manual labor in the sense that Mann used this term. If nothing else, such reduced demand—the disassociation between education and manual labor which it signalled and portended—may have contributed to an increased social distance in the antebellum period between remaining wage-earning manual laborers and various proliferating lower-middle-class white-collar groups.[219] It is not without significance, in any case, that the factory proprietors whose support Mann claimed to have in his educational crusades placed a rather different emphasis on the value of schooling for operatives than he himself did. Mann argued that expanding educational opportunities for the Massachusetts factory population, as well as enforcing existing legislation regarding the education of child operatives, would serve the interests of employers by increasing the workers' inventiveness and productivity. But the proprietors and other businessmen who responded to the questionnaire Mann sent them in 1841 hardly stressed the need for greater skill and inventiveness on the part of their workers. For them the major benefits of education lay instead in improving the capacity of workers to follow directions, to be punctual, tractable, and reliable in their habits, and to behave "reasonably" during periods of labor unrest.[220]

Mann himself by no means completely overlooked these other considerations in his writings on education. When he observed, for example, that "agrarianism is the revenge of poverty against wealth," he was offering a corollary to his argument regarding the social benefits of an enlightening education for the masses.[221] Wild and violent attacks against property, the impulse to "level down" rather than up, were generally grounded in poverty and ignorance. The common school education that protected the American working classes from poverty and a servile tolerance of class oppression would also discourage them from embracing fallacious agrarian doctrines as solutions to perceived injustice.

But Mann also believed that the very uniqueness of American conditions made the continued extension and availability of common school education all the more necessary. The temptations afforded by American abundance, together with the liberating influence of her republican political institutions, tended to increase the danger of socially destructive and incendiary behavior. "All men," Mann observed, "are born into the world with many appetites and propensities of a purely animal and selfish nature."[222] The natural effect of American conditions was to "quicken the activity and enlarge the sphere" of these "innate," organic appetites and propensities. When "bridled" by education, such propensities as the love of wealth had invaluable social benefits; left unrestrained, they would more easily in America than anywhere else degenerate, as the love of wealth easily degenerated into a pervasive cupidity and avarice.[223] Above all, Mann insisted that the particular education that must be provided dare not neglect the development of the moral faculties. For without the restraining influence exerted by an individual's developed moral sense, an education that cultivated his intellect exclusively did not bridle the individual's selfish propensities but instead increased their destructive powers by focusing and turning them loose upon society. "There is no necessary incompatibility between the upward progress of one portion of our nature, and the lower and lower debasement of another. The intellect may grow wise, while the passions grow wicked."[224]

Mann hardly warned against a defective education exclusively with regard to the danger in America of incendiary and socially destructive behavior from below. The "fraud, robbery, rapine, and all the enormities of the slave trade, the opium-trade, the rum-trades" were to Mann evidence of deficient moral development no less egregious than the condition of some of free society's poorest elements.[225] But Mann also left no doubt of his view that the working and living conditions of these poorer elements required an antidote in moral training, and that the failure to provide one would have disastrous consequences. Factory and other regular work was a virtue, Mann insisted, but it did not, he also suggested, hold sufficient moral value to meet the laborer's basic spiritual needs. Continued neglect by some parents and corporations of the education of child factory operatives, he warned in 1839, would reverberate upon society once the children grew older and left the constraining environment of the mills. With weak moral powers and strong passions, they would almost inevitably add to society's growing criminal population.[226]

Mann's example indicates that American middle-class mainstream support for mass education which so explicitly reflected the mythology of American exceptionalism was also clearly quite capable of incorporating themes and anxieties common to the British movement represented by James Kay-Shuttleworth and Joseph Kay. The commonality of concerns and impulses was still more evident in those cases where, to a much more concerted and single-minded degree than with Mann, popular education was favored as an antidote to trade unions and the "agrarian claims of labor." During the trade union movement of the early 1830s, Joseph Tinker Buckingham, the owner and editor of the *Boston Courier* and defender of what he called society's "Middling Interest," berated the insanity of those who "work to convince the mechanics of this country—the laboring and producing classes—that they suffer privations and disabilities that are not felt by all other men. . . . Individual instances of oppression or wrong," Buckingham claimed, were attributable to human passions, and for this the "one all-efficient remedy is Moral and Religious Education. . . . Let them [workingmen] be taught that their chief good is to be found in the enjoyment of subdued appetites, disciplined passions, temperate habits, moderate desires, well-informed minds."[227]

Like the factory proprietors whom Mann surveyed, Buckingham and other writers emphasized the value of working-class education both as a means of developing correct moral values and work virtues, and as a means of engendering a desirable intellectual conformity in the laboring population. Enlightened workers, the most "reasonable" ones, would reject the same agrarian and incendiary doctrines that Kay-Shuttleworth and Kay also wished to dispel. The distinctive American dimension to this theme was that educated workers in Northern "free labor" society would not only be persuaded of the inexorable character of supply and demand in establishing wage levels, they would also readily perceive that the great demand for labor and the unsurpassed openness and resources of their society made those laws work to a unique degree in their behalf.[228]

The prescriptions for working-class education made by Buckingham and others of a similar persuasion in part reflected matters of emphasis. The most radical working-class movements and labor reform doctrines, in America or Britain, did not reject the development of the moral faculties as an unworthy goal, any more than they rejected as virtues the qualities of industriousness, discipline, and sobriety with which this development was universally associated. Rather, these radical movements did not attach so exclusive an importance to the development of the moral faculties. And, more fundamentally still, at least a segment of these movements consciously rejected efforts to harness these virtues in the service of existing forms of labor and social arrangements that they deemed, even in America, to be exploitative and entrapping. To a corresponding degree, radicals—above all radicals in Britain who entertained a pronounced suspicion of middle-class support for popular education—denounced the inculcation of character virtues intended to foster intellectual conformity and discredit economic doctrines that exposed the injustice and illegitimacy of existing social arrangements.[229]

Even, however, among certain middle-class writers who did embrace the mythology of American exceptionalism, one can discern a tendency, considerably less pronounced but still somewhat in the fashion of Kay-Shuttleworth, to exalt the moral education and inculcation of industrious work habits among the lowest ranks of the urban and laboring poor while scaling down the extrinsic rewards that such inculcation would in all likelihood secure for them. The tremendous swelling of New York City's antebellum laboring population by desperately poor and "brutish" Irish immigrants fueled middle-class anxieties just as a similar infusion of Irish into Manchester a generation earlier had alarmed individuals like Kay-Shuttleworth. Along with other members of his class who closely witnessed this more recent infusion, the urban missionary Charles Loring Brace exhibited a certain restraint regarding the material gains that industrial morality would bring many of the slum children of New York City, provided of course that they could even be brought under the influence of that morality.[230] To the extent that he raised the question of limits, Brace also provides an example of how the conflict between egalitarian and upward mobility values, on the one hand, and acceptance of a measured degree of social hierarchy, on the other, may have contributed to the ambiguities in the middle-class notion of industrial morality.

Although Brace shared Henry Mayhew's general opinion of the "street trades," considering bootblacking and other irregular unskilled labor to be "idle and vagrant," morally unwholesome forms of work, he was also no defender of a work ethic that sanctified tedious manual labor of a more continuous and unlimited nature, industrial or otherwise.[231] Of hod-carriers, sewing girls and others belonging to the ranks of the urban laboring poor, Brace noted that "the whole life is work, work," and far from checking vice, the "dull, constant drudgery" of which this work consisted promoted to no lesser a degree than casual, intermittent labor an addiction to "gross dissipation" and debauchery. These laborers returned from work, in Brace's view, "tired, stupid and hungry," with a semiconscious craving for escape in low "animal" pleasures. Working conditions under these circumstances reinforced overcrowded and debasing living conditions and the city's opportunities for corruption, discouraging altogether the moral elevation and development of "higher tastes" in the laboring poor.[232]

Unlike, moreover, many factory proprietors, correctional officers, and other charity reformers, Brace subscribed to evangelical reform principles which led him to quite explicitly disdain that form of industrial morality which penetrated no deeper than an outward obedience and tractability. Brace looked to the industrial schools, workshops, and lodging houses he helped establish to do more than momentarily safeguard children from the temptations of the streets. If these institutions were to give their charges a true chance for success in life, they must develop in them a true, internalized discipline and self-direction; they must instill in them "habits of industry and self-control and neatness, and give them the rudiments of moral education. . . . A child in any degree educated and disciplined can easily make an honest living in this country."[233] Indeed, the hopes Brace above all invested in the "placing out" of urban street children to rural farm homes were strongly informed by the mythology of American exceptionalism. In the nation's countryside there was an "unlimited" demand for the labor of children, and "every child of bad habits who can secure a place in a Christian home, is in the best possible place for his improvement. . . . He feels, too, the great impelling powers which help everywhere to elevate the laboring class in America: the instinct of property . . . the consciousness of equality; the chance of great success; and, at an early period, a liberal payment for labor."[234]

At the same time, Brace provided some indications that, along with Kay-Shuttleworth, he did not regard genuine moral improvement in the condition of the laboring poor as incompatible with positions of social subordination and permanent hireling labor status. He seems, in particular, to have held lower expectations of upwardly mobile success for the population of foreign-born slum girls, whom he may have deemed less suitable for escaping the city through rural farm labor.[235] The best education of these unemployed and casually employed females, he suggested, would morally purify and raise them above the temptations of prostitution; but it would also give them the work habits and vocational skills that would confirm this resolve by qualifying them for membership in a permanent servant class. Of the Girls' Lodging-House which his Children's Aid Society formed in 1862, Brace noted that it was meant "to reform habits and character" and "to teach them [the girls] to work, to be clean, and to understand the virtues of order and punctuality; to lay the foundations of a housekeeper or servant; to bring the influences of discipline, of kindness, and religion to bear on these wild and ungoverned creatures."[236]

In these remarks Brace appeared to be including both true character reform and some of its external manifestations as the marks of a good servant. But elsewhere he expressed doubts about the moral character of girls who would in fact settle for positions as domestics, who would "be willing to sacrifice all privacy, independence, and chances of rising in the world . . . we never wonder that American young women have such a horror of domestic service." The occupation demanded and attracted "a somewhat irregular, dependent, and unambitious person"—not, one may infer, the kind of child from the slums whom Brace believed might achieve great success by developing internalized discipline and self-direction on some farm out West.[237] In the case of the immigrant girls whom he helped prepare for and direct into service, Brace may after all have been lowering his standards, settling for a morally superficial, outward compliance and deference from his charges that suited, in his view, the requirements of permanently servile work. It may also be true that Brace was tempering his faith in American exceptionalism, in the unlimited mobility and material gains that industrious habits could bring, with a realistic appraisal of what genuine moral reform could accomplish for certain classes of individuals. In Brace's view, the life of deferential and permanent household service for which immigrant slum girls improved and prepared themselves was a veritable moral and economic haven, a very significant and possibly sufficient step up for them, from the debased and "animal"-like life of the streets.[238]

Other American middle-class supporters of the education and moral elevation of the working classes placed considerably more explicit and pronounced limitations than Brace did on the instrumental value which education and moral elevation need possess. For certain prominent moralists like William Ellery Channing, consideration of the social mobility factor seems hardly to have played a part in support for mass education. The mobility prospects of individual workers, like the matters of higher wages and reduced working hours, was incidental to the larger issue, the ability of workingmen, acting in an individual capacity, to raise the condition and esteem of the laboring classes as a whole.[239] Enlightening the poorer members of society was for Channing right in itself; it would, among other things, enable them to improve themselves by increasing their "foresight," their capacity to anticipate the disastrous consequences of not providing for themselves through labor. But Channing's concluding argument that "we may expect the steadiest labor from men whose faculties have been enlarged by education" was embraced by other supporters of American mass education who put a different construction on it, one with a definite view toward limited and diminishing mobility opportunities.[240] Though in a less pronounced and pervasive degree than in England, the sense that education and respectability might compensate members of the laboring classes for their inability to rise clearly contributed something to American support for mass education, including working-class higher education. The New York Free Academy established in 1847 by the newly formed New York City Board of Education was to provide mechanics and other laboring men with advanced learning in chemistry, mechanics, and classical and modern languages. To those who entered the long-standing objection that such an institution would only serve to dissatisfy manual laborers with their present means of livelihood, the *Memorial* from the Board of Education responded that, on the contrary, the Academy education "would remove the foolish prejudice which now induces thousands to abandon the honest and healthy pursuits of their fathers, in order to establish themselves in professions and mercantile pursuits which are already crowded to excess; . . . such a change would overturn the erroneous opinion so prevalent among, and fatal to, many young men, at the present day, that some occupations are more honorable than others, and for that reason more desirable."[241]

Long popular among labor radicals, participants in the manual labor school movement, and other groups had been the theme that mixing education with manual labor was desirable if only because it raised the dignity and status of laboring employments. To this theme was added here the explicit sense that limited access to the higher levels of the social pyramid rendered working-class education all the more compelling. By providing workingmen with some of the mental rewards that were embodied in occupations into which they and members of their families could not rise, such education would increase the appeal that manual labor employments held for disgruntled workingmen. Although far more ambitious and expansive than the working-class education promoted by Kay-Shuttleworth and his colleagues, the Academy plan would perform the similar function of securing the allegiance of workers to social arrangements distinguished by limited upward mobility opportunities.

It cannot be claimed that the originators and supporters of the Academy plan embraced none of the other standard justifications for working-class education. There is some indication that New York Democratic support especially reflected the expectation that the sons of workingmen would be able to use the tuition-free education to qualify for entry into the professions, an expectation that proved to have a limited basis in fact during the 1850s.[242] Quite apart from considerations of intergenerational mobility, the broadening of higher education opportunities for working-class families, like the system of common schools, could also be justified as a good in itself, something to which the poor as well as the rich were entitled. As the Board of Education noted, "If the wealthy part of the community seek instruction to enlarge the minds of their children, why should not an opportunity be given to the sons of toil to give the *same* advantages to their children? and why should the intellectual enjoyments, which the former seek as a 'great good' for their children, be denied to those of the latter?"[243]

Then, too, support for the Academy invoked the venerable principle of "useful knowledge" and with it the characteristic assumption that such knowledge would render manual labor callings more productive as well as more dignified. In a letter to the New York *Journal of Commerce* the most instrumental figure in the Free Academy's establishment, Townsend Harris, denied the claims of critics that the Academy plan would extend impractical and inappropriate educational opportunities to the working classes. On the contrary, Harris pointed out, the plan indeed offered different instruction for students who were contemplating different occupations upon their graduation from the public schools: "To the future carpenter, instruction in the mechanical powers, architecture, and a certain amount of mathematics. To the smith's apprentice, instruction in metallurgy and something of chemistry. To the intended merchant, French, Spanish, bookkeeping, etc., etc. . . . To the small number who may desire to follow what are called the 'learned professions,' classical instruction will be given."[244]

Through such differential training, Harris proceeded to note, the Academy plan "intended to elevate those callings, and to raise the mechanic from being a mere machine to the place of a man of science, operating under laws which he has studied and understands. It appears to me that nothing but good can arise from this mental and moral elevation of the mechanical callings, to say nothing of the benefit we will derive from their additional skill and knowledge growing out of their superior education."[245]

It was no doubt sometimes the case that the conviction that manual labor employments should be made more productive, more elevated, and ultimately more appealing through the infusion of useful knowledge did not emanate primarily or even at all from a concern that more "liberal" pursuits were largely inaccessible to workingmen's sons. Yet support for the Academy's method of elevating the "mechanical callings," hardly less than conservative opposition to the plan, was characteristically tied to the assumption that even a majority of those workingmen's sons who were able to take advantage of the education would remain manual laborers. In the same document in which it noted that education was a good in itself, the Board of Education Committee over which Harris presided reported that with the establishment of the Academy "the laboring class of our fellow citizens may have the opportunity of giving to their children an education that will more effectually fit them for the various departments of labor and toil, by which they will earn their bread."[246] It must remain something of an open question whether members of the Board of Education, together with other supporters of the Academy Plan, expected workingmen's sons to remain in manual labor callings primarily out of choice or out of necessity. The Board of Education *Memorial,* which Harris co-authored, clearly stressed the factor of necessity in its reference to the "over-crowded" state of professional and mercantile occupations.[247] And Harris individually, in his letter to the *Journal of Commerce,* suggested as well that increasing the dignity and mental content of manual labor callings through the infusion of useful knowledge was a positive way of taking into account, of confronting, so to speak, the limited upward mobility prospects of workingmen's sons. The differential training that was to be provided effectively answered, Harris claimed, the "cry [that] has been raised, that in the proposed institution *every lad* was to be made a classical scholar, without reference to his prospects in life, and that thus, instead of a benefit, it would prove an injury to the community by *spoiling* a large number of youth for useful pursuits."[248]

To the extent that the originators and supporters of the Academy plan were indeed addressing the inability of manual laborers and their children to "rise" into nonlaboring occupations, it still remains problematic whether they attributed limited mobility opportunities to an actual hardening of class divisions or rather to an extreme social fluidity that had, paradoxically, permitted the most desirable occupations to become overcrowded. The thrust of much recent historical writing, above all that concentrating on the more urbanized and industrialized northeast, has been to underscore the first of these social phenomena, increased social rigidity. This body of writing has furthermore emphasized the diminishing upward mobility opportunities experienced by members of the antebellum Northern working classes in a total sense—not merely their reduced likelihood of achieving professional and commercial status and with this considerable wealth, but above all the diminishing prospects of wage laborers for achieving a secure self-employed status at the uppermost ranks of manual labor.[249] These studies have suggested, in particular, that to the degree that American formulations of the work ethic celebrated diligence and other character virtues for their capacity to bring economic independence and further upward mobility to free wage laborers, these formulations carried increasingly limited validity. Perhaps, indeed, such formulations carried little more validity than the claims that "self-help" could bring the overwhelming number of England's laboring poor much more than a meager subsistence. A number of scholars have emphasized in this regard the extent to which the work ethic was a freehold farm and "craft ethic" that economic developments rendered steadily obsolete even as many middle-class Americans continued to embrace it as an accurate description of social reality.[250] Just as American industrialization undermined that ethic by creating new forms of drudgery and work rhythms that lacked the mental and creative rewards of the skilled artisanal trades, and just as it generated a rigid, oftentimes oppressive division between work and leisure, so industrialization had by 1860 already destroyed many of the traditional career ladders and avenues to economic independence that were characteristic of an agricultural and craft economy.

This study cannot provide what only extensive quantitative analysis can—answers to the questions of how deeply and pervasively antebellum industrialization in fact eroded manual laborers' opportunities for self-employment and mobility into the middle classes, and of how it may have otherwise contributed to a more stratified social order.[251] If only because of their variety, the attitudes of mid-nineteenth-century Americans are themselves of very limited value in answering these questions. Proslavery and radical labor reform critics of the Northern social order may well have exaggerated the pace and extent of social stratification there in pursuit of their particular ideological objectives; far from being static, their conception of existing tendencies in the free states verged on the catastrophic. Other Americans—abolitionists and antislavery politicians, clergymen and other moralists who were outraged by the growth of pauperism or labor agitation—conversely pursued ideological objectives that led them, in many cases just as unwittingly, to understate or screen out discordant changes and to insist through to the end of the antebellum period that the Northern free labor system continued to possess unlimited economic and mobility opportunities for the industrious members of its lowest rungs. There were still other middle-class writers and reformers like Charles Loring Brace who were more in tune with those expanding economic realities that reflected increased social stratification—the spread of factories and sweatshops and the development of great contrasts between the wealthy and a sizeable, largely foreign-born lower class and underclass in the major urban centers. These individuals, as suggested, gave certain indications of accepting such changes by moving toward a more "industrial" work ethic, one less grounded in the mobility assumptions of a craft ethic.[252]

But whatever the actual extent of social stratification in the antebellum period, it would be inaccurate to conclude that either stratification or labor exploitation contradicted the most deeply conservative formulations of the work ethic. Those formulations were frequently offered in defense of some of the meanest forms and conditions of work, such as chattel slavery and long hours of factory drudgery, as necessary checks upon idleness and antisocial behavior. Because the *tendency* of some of these formulations was to attach paramount importance to the moral value of *any* work that was industriously and conscientiously performed, irrespective of the work's intellectual or extrinsic rewards, they possessed a timeless resiliency to changing economic conditions that a "craft ethic" patently lacked.[253]

But if the logical premises of the most conservative formulations of the work ethic were not out of sync with exploitative conditions, this hardly meant that such formulations enjoyed unlimited support. Rising working-class consciousness, together with awakening upper- and middle-class Victorian sensitivity to various forms of labor—both new and old—as brutalizing and unacceptable, imposed definite limits on the appeal of the most conservative versions of the work ethic. At the same time, these versions were undermined by another source as well, one quite distinct from increased abhorrence of exploitative conditions. The conservative values extolling the intrinsic moral content, or "duty," of manual labor clashed, as Carlyle lamented, with a pervasive free market "capitalist ethic" that demeaned such moral content by insisting that "the worth of a thing is what it will bring."[254] The seeds of this conflict were planted when Benjamin Franklin and others materialized and secularized industriousness and the other character virtues of the Puritan ethic, when they began to value these virtues less for their intrinsic religious worth than for their utility in bringing worldly gain and success.[255] By the second half of the nineteenth century, expressions of the "gospel of success" that Franklin helped originate were routinely exalting proper character formation in terms of the material fruits to be won through it.[256] As a eulogy of acquisitiveness, some of these expressions closely intersected with the capitalist ethic.

It is no small irony that the capitalist ethic undermined not only the most conservative versions of the work ethic, but its most radical working-class versions as well. For if the capitalist ethic was antagonistic to the tendency to identify and highlight an intrinsic, self-justifying moral value in even the meanest labor, it was hardly less hostile to labor reform doctrines which also claimed that hard and useful manual labor possessed an inherent moral value, one entitling it to a commensurate level of extrinsic rewards. In its insistence that manual labor was a mere commodity, with no "value" other than that established by marketplace supply and demand, the capitalist ethic highlighted the strictly calculative or instrumental dimension of work just as the most conservative formulations of the work ethic strongly subordinated that dimension.[257] In the hands of middle-class entrepreneurs and writers who resisted the efforts of organized labor and other radical groups to achieve through collective means a redistribution of economic wealth and power, the capitalist ethic became a primary rationale for rebuffing such efforts; through enterprise and self-discipline, but only on an individual basis, workers could make the capitalist ethic work in their behalf and improve themselves through the operations of the free market. Although Andrew Ure and other polemicists for industrial capitalism persisted in arguing that mechanized factory work had intrinsic moral benefits and articulated a conservative version of the work ethic along these lines, that version was not so absolute as Carlyle's conservative formulation; nor did Ure and like-minded writers mean that manual labor had moral worth in the still different fundamental sense in which the labor radicals defined it.[258] By means of regular and disciplined labor, members of the laboring population might acquire the work habits that would equip them for achieving economic self-support and possibly even greater success in a free market economy. A primary role of education was to help the laborer "see and understand the true principle of toil and competition," a principle that was consistent with, and even necessary to, man's development of his *"higher properties."*[259] But the only proper measure of labor's worth remained the "cash-nexus" standard, the returns that labor was able to command in the competitive marketplace.[260] In the opposing labor radical and populist perspectives, the most conservative, Carlylean formulations of the work ethic in fact appeared to pose a far less insidious source of economic exploitation than this competitive marketplace ethic, one which not merely denied that productive manual labor carried an inherent "just price," but which indeed, despite its talk of solid work habits, seemed in practice to most highly reward shrewdness and other qualities altogether removed from the time-honored virtues of plain hard work.[261]

8

Conclusion

It remains beyond the scope of this volume to treat in any detail the antebellum debates over the appropriate instrumental value of different occupations in a capitalist economy—the debates over the extrinsic rewards to which honest and productive manual labor, as distinct from the mental activity of professional men and employers of labor, were entitled. But although the various working-class organizations and middle-class radicals who occupied one position in these debates represented a small minority of American society, their position nonetheless signalled a distaste for the evolving occupational hierarchy and raised questions about the definition of true "work," that were hardly less fundamental than the more prominent disagreements in other societies over the legitimacy of private property itself.[1] Theophilus Fisk, the radical pamphleteer and prominent member of the labor movement of the late 1820s and early 1830s, was some twenty years later still railing against "lazy drones" and their so-called mental labor: "But the monopolists, the professional men, the men of wealth, *they* labor, it is said, as well as the farmer and the mechanic. They do labor to be sure—but *it is laboring to collect that which others have earned.* The Lawyer's 'May it please your honor' never made the pot boil."[2]

Radical fervor carried Fisk beyond the point of arguing merely that the rewards enjoyed by capitalists and professional men were disproportionate to the social value of the services they provided. The services themselves were completely valueless and fraudulent, a facsimile of "useful occupations" that was no less bogus and destructive than "paper money" systems which created wealth "out of nothing" and in so falsifying and inflating true value, feathered the nests of a banking "money power" at the expense of "honest industry."[3] Fisk was not atypical of a populist brand of radical who held an extreme literal view of labor: the product of true work was something one could see, or touch, or feel; and if Fisk manifested little or no appreciation of the various defenses of "mental labor" employments that underscored the contributions of businessmen or professionals to the total stock of wealth, he was not alone. The rhetoric of many more mainstream Jacksonian Democratic politicians oftentimes tended to similarly define productive labor in narrow terms, even as some of these politicians, at least, also acknowledged that some considerable occupational specialization, even hierarchy, would manifest itself in the best of societies.[4]

The most careful students of Owenite socialist and other Anglo-American radical doctrines have, furthermore, noted the disagreements and confusion with which these doctrines addressed the question of whether all manual labor was itself "productive" or "useful." Quite aside from the persisting problems that the role of the master craftsman raised for such doctrines, radical writers, as Gregory Claeys has observed, pressed for different hierarchies of social need that rendered suspect the usefulness and even the legitimacy of various existing wage labor employments. The body servants who attended leisured aristocrats, to take an extreme example, and one that generated much discussion among more orthodox as well as radical economists, were clearly not useful or productive in the sense that factory workers were. Perhaps it is not surprising, given the diversity of social conditions and of types and uses of employment, that radical writers, no more than orthodox ones, could fully agree on "who the laborer was," or upon a definition of true work, especially, perhaps, with regard to managing, decision making, and the clearing of legal and political paths for the effective distribution and marketing of goods and services.[5]

That mid-nineteenth-century radicals could not decisively resolve these questions any more successfully than other writers of their time hardly negates, however, the special urgency they brought to these questions. In America, one most closely associates the dissenting radical perspective with the "small producer" ideology of antebellum reform movements that saw in mercantile and industrial capitalism an assault on the social status and economic well-being of skilled manual labor above all. But estrangement over the existing distribution of status and rewards could also find expression in affirmations of the dignity of the most unskilled and disdained laborers, and not merely Fisk's farmer and mechanic. Such affirmations dramatically illustrated how subjective the matter of "the dignity of labor" could be. One "L," writing in the *Golden Rule,* declared his inability to understand why the work of New York City's rag gatherers was deemed disgusting and degrading. Quite aside from the "abstract honorableness" upon which the dignity of all labor partially rested—the fact that work is "both a law of nature, and of Christianity"—more specific criteria determined the relative true dignity of different kinds of labor. "The motive should be noble, and the labor honest and useful." By these criteria, "L" insisted, the rag gatherer was not inferior to other manual laborers. He cleared the street and contributed to the cleanliness and happiness of the community. Although his filthy appearance was repulsive on sight, that appearance followed inevitably from the nature of his important tasks and did not, as in the case of the prostitute or swindler, conceal a corrupt inner character. And perhaps above all, the ragpicker was, in "L's" judgment, a true "producer": unlike the speculator, merchant, or banker, the ragpicker added to the "common stock of wealth" by selling his collectibles to paper manufacturers for conversion into "useful" products.[6]

Affirmations of the moral benefits and dignity of the lowest forms of labor could be utilized, as we have already seen, to justify the most exploitative conditions—the entrapment of laborers in compulsory servitude or in "free labor" at long hours for low wages. But as appeared to be the case with "L," the worth of unskilled physical labor could also be invoked as corroborative support for notions of "moral economy" that asserted the worker's guaranteed right to a decent living or "just price" for his toil. The usefulness of the most unskilled "common" labor could even be invoked in support of radical versions of the labor theory of value that called for a more definitive upgrading of the recompense and status of productive manual labor commensurate with its unequalled contribution to the wealth of society.[7] In the mid-nineteenth century, two distinct impetuses, one conservative and one radical, powered the greater part of what emphasis there was upon the intrinsic moral worth, or "divinity," of manual labor; and both of these impetuses met, in the literature of the period, considerable opposition from various writers who insisted that manual labor was a "mixed bag," neither intrinsically noble nor ignoble, and who rejected the "divinity of labor" theme as largely "cant." The concluding part of this inquiry begins with an examination of the efforts to downplay the moral content of manual labor in the face of both radical and conservative pressures to affirm it.

ATTEMPTS TO MINIMIZE THE MORAL
CONTENT OF MANUAL LABOR

Such downplaying of the moral value of manual labor reflected more than simply an adherence to the capitalist ethic, to the liberal economic axiom that human labor was a commodity like any other and that the free market forces of supply and demand were alone the legitimate determinant of its value. Other intellectual currents were also frequently involved. Consider the case of one writer, Peter Walker, and his repudiation of the radical working-class claims for the intrinsic dignity of labor on what he took to be common sense grounds. In the beginning of his repudiation, which appeared in 1849 following the "Year of Revolutions," Walker appeared in fact to be allying himself with the radical position that existing social arrangements subverted the natural and intrinsic dignity of manual labor by failing to reward it in proportion to its productive value. With possibly the continuing Chartist upheavals in Britain and the national workshop movement and working-class convulsion in France most directly in mind, Walker noted that

> amid the present agitations of society the struggle of the workman to place himself in a better position is everywhere apparent. He feels the deprivations attached to his condition, but he is annoyed by a sense of his degradation not less than by his miseries. He sees no dignity in labor—the paradox is too absurd to make a convert of him. It is a strange dignity: he neither feels it himself, nor does he perceive its effect upon others. The men who talk of "the dignity of labor," and of its being "the God with us in the flesh," are those who, unless the click-clack of the tongue can be accounted labor, willingly for themselves forego all its dignities and divine incarnations.[8]

But despite this beginning, Walker's principal objective was not to discredit the conservative impetus behind the "dignity of labor" rhetoric— those clergymen and others who sought to generate working-class acquiescence in the laborer's lowly condition and his "dirty work" by extolling the "divinity" of these.[9] Walker's primary target was the stream of working-class radicalism that also affirmed manual labor's intrinsic dignity; and he proceeded to introduce a series of arguments suggesting that insofar as prevailing social arrangements did in fact fail to reward human physical labor—the alleged "bone and sinew" of society—such arrangements were not unjust.[10] First, Walker insisted, the intrinsic nobility of such labor was limited. True, a certain measure of dignity derived from the fact that while man is engaged in such manual labor, "he is employed in obedience to the purpose of his Creator. But this glory," Walker wryly observed, man "must divide with the ox and the horse, who in many respects excel him."[11]

More fundamentally, Walker lodged the rewards and status of society's different occupations in their capacity to advance "civilization," and the thrust of his essay was to underscore the limited nature of the contribution manual labor occupations made in this regard. The critical fact was that many of these occupations, however necessary they might be, did not require significant mental activity, the cornerstone of civilization, and were by virtue of this deficiency fatally limited in their productive capabilities:

> Society owes much to those who do its drudgery—to those appointed to be its beasts of burden. But still the mere laborer has done as little to promote production as the beast of burden, and is entitled to, and he knows he receives, no more honor than the horse or the engine he attends. . . .
>
> . . . the energies of nature are subjected to man, not by the strength of his muscles but by the powers of his mind. And if a man has no mind, or is too apathetic to exert it, or sinks into an occupation that precludes its use, why should he not suffer the odium attached to his position? . . . The language of nature to man is, *Choose those employments in which you can best exemplify the nobility of your nature;* if you merely employ the animal portion, you shall have an animal's reward. . . . Is it unreasonable that a man who has done nothing to advance the cause of civilization should enjoy none of its blessings? Hands and arms could do as much in the infancy of society as now, and are only entitled to what hands and arms can produce. The ameliorations of the condition of society are the products of mind—certainly not products without labor—but it is for the excellence and the value of the product, not for the quantity of the labor, that the producer is honored. The architect of the building is honored, not the hodman, the hewer of the stone, or the windlass employed in raising it. Mental labor, if unproductive, is as contemptible as bodily labor, but to its successful achievements mankind owe all their blessings; and to it, of right, they have acceded their honors. In accordance with this, degrees of respectability are awarded to the various occupations of men, not according to the labor, but in proportion to the mental effort, required in their prosecution. Is it not absurd then to talk of the dignity of labor? Could words be chosen that would run more counter to the common sense of men?[12]

We have, of course, already encountered similar sentiments. When Theodore Sedgwick and other writers declared that the proportion of mental to physical activity required by a given occupation determined its social standing, he was affirming a moral principle a well as making a statement of fact.[13] And in his celebration of labor-saving technology, Timothy Walker suggested that most if not all manual labor employments were necessarily mindless and best eliminated for this reason. Peter Walker did not go quite this far, and he may have agreed with the more explicit claims of many of his middle-class contemporaries that many forms of manual labor could be redeemed, elevated, and made more productive through an infusion of intellect. But with his earlier namesake, Peter Walker embraced the position that the existing mindlessness of much manual labor discredited the claims made for its intrinsic moral worth and dignity. Contrary to the conservative perspective that justified constant manual labor as a shield protecting both society and the laborer from the temptations and worst effects of his lower nature, Peter, like Timothy, Walker disdained much of this labor as a very expression of man's lower nature. Walker was heir to the classical disdain for manual labor, but with the important difference that he and like-minded writers democratized that disdain by suggesting that an increasingly small proportion of the members of a just, technologically progressive society need be engaged in this labor. As Edward Everett Hale noted, the higher the society's civilization, the fewer would be the number directly employed in bodily labor for production.[14]

In resisting the argument that the natural effect of manual labor was to favor the development of the worker's higher nature, Walker took issue not only with writers who defended exploitative working conditions as morally beneficial for the laborer. He also took issue with labor radicals who invoked the superior moral worth of all manual toil to denounce exploitation. If Walker agreed with these radicals that *excessive* work and underpay must limit the moral elevation of individuals engaged in manual labor, he nonetheless challenged their assumption that the natural, uncorrupted tendency of this labor was to be morally uplifting. The professional and capitalist occupations most naturally and exclusively dependent upon mental activity, many of which gave physical labor its direction and purpose, were for Walker the sine qua non of production and civilization, and merited their superior recompense and honors.

"Mankind have universally awarded their honors, not to those who labor, but to those who avert it."[15] Walker's essay amounted to a justification of this state of affairs, and in his particular justification at least, the conviction that "the worth of a thing is what it will bring" on the market played only a secondary and implicit role. The capital investment, training, and native talent upon which "mental labor" occupations called established practical barriers to the development of a labor surplus that were largely absent from manual labor employments, particularly the more unskilled ones. But the economic laws that most highly rewarded certain skills merely because they were in lesser supply were, for Walker, primarily an endorsement of the larger cultural truth that these same mental skills were also the ones that were most socially productive and valuable.

As suggested, however, some of the most prominent mid-nineteenth-century criticisms of the doctrine of manual labor's intrinsic dignity and superior moral worth were, in contrast to Walker's, primarily aimed at discrediting the conservative, not the labor radical, uses of that doctrine. For John Greenleaf Whittier, such conservative uses clearly included the tendency to invoke the moral benefits of labor in defense of the new industrial capitalist working conditions. Whittier found much to commend in the condition of the Lowell factory girls. Their wages furthered the independence and dignity of the female sex. Their yearning for intellectual enlightenment and accomplishment, as revealed in the pages of the *Lowell Offering,* offered a standing rebuke to proslavery and other elitist attitudes that disdained manual labor as incompatible with the development of the intellectual faculties. But Whittier also insisted that the achievements of the Lowell girls should in no sense provide support to the "good many foolish essays written upon the beauty and divinity of labor, by those who have never known what it really is to earn one's livelihood by the sweat of the brow—who have never, from year to year, bent over the bench or loom, shut out from the blue skies, the green grass, and sweet waters, and felt the head reel, and the heart faint, and the limbs tremble with the exhaustion of unremitted toil."[16]

By contributing to the "sentimentalism" regarding the nobility of labor, the very achievements of the Lowell girls, Whittier suggested, had played into the hands of defenders of the status quo, those who opposed the efforts to reduce working hours. The factory girls who retained sufficient energy and incentive to continue their education after work, the relative few who contributed to the *Lowell Offering* were, after all, "only an exception to the general rule, that after twelve or more hours of steady toil, mind and body are both too weary for intellectual effort"; "the trials and disadvantages" experienced by most of the Lowell girls, like that of the laboring population generally, remained considerable.[17]

Attacks on the "cant" exalting the dignity of manual labor could also, in the hands of proslavery advocates, become attacks on the "cant" exalting the dignity of "free" manual labor exclusively. In one such defense, L. Q. C. Lamar of Mississippi mocked the notion that the laborers starving in "free" societies could curb their hunger with the "glorious" thought of their labor's dignity.[18] Whittier's theme that the divinity of labor rhetoric was a cover for free labor exploitation could easily become directed to a purpose alien to his own position of antislavery. But the period's most devastating attack on the "divinity of labor" theme, that made by John Stuart Mill in 1850, was turned against proslavery ideology as well as against the use of the theme to legitimate free labor exploitation. Thomas Carlyle had been among those whom Whittier found most guilty of indulging in the sentimentalism "concerning the romance and beauty and miraculous powers of Work—in the abstract"; and Carlyle was also the principal target of Mill's essay.[19] When Mill delivered this attack, specifically a reply to Carlyle's "Occasional Discourse on the Nigger Question," (1849) he was already moving away from the doctrinaire utilitarianism and free market doctrines of his early period toward the more hospitable view of socialism that characterized his later years.[20] But Mill's essay demonstrated how utilitarianism itself need not be tied to an uncritical free market defense of exploitative working conditions, how it might instead be used to discredit those conditions.

Contrary to Carlyle's gospel of work, Mill argued, work was not intrinsically valuable, an end in itself, but beneficial only as a means of meeting the needs of oneself or others: "There is nothing laudable in work for work's sake. To work voluntarily for a worthy object is laudable; but what constitutes a worthy object?"[21] By this last statement Mill sought to fully expose the inhumanity of Carlyle's doctrine; the victimization of West Indian slaves was highlighted, rendered even more unjustifiable if possible, by the banality of the spices and other products this slave labor had been used to produce:

> The multiplication of work, for purposes not worth caring about, is one of the evils of our present condition. . . . How many of the so-called luxuries, conveniences, refinements, and ornaments of life, are *worth* the labour which must be undergone as the condition of producing them? The beautifying of existence is as worthy and useful an object as the sustaining of it; but only a vitiated taste can see any such result in those fopperies of so-called civilization, which myriads of hands are now occupied and lives wasted in providing.[22]

Quite aside from the fact that legal bondage was in itself a more primitive and degrading condition than legally free labor, Mill questioned the social values of a writer who assumed that the "fopperies" formerly produced by West Indian slaves in such abundance were more "noble" than the "pumpkins" that freed slaves now raised for their subsistence. "Is what supports life, inferior in dignity to what merely gratifies the sense of taste?"[23] Mill came close to accusing Carlyle of the very philistinism that Carlyle himself had excoriated as one of the plagues of modern civilization.

Carlyle's gospel of the divinity of labor was most immediately objectionable, Mill suggested, because it was tantamount to making the wolf the accuser: it ignored the idleness of slaveowners even as it condemned the behavior of ex-slaves as a dereliction of the universal "duty" to labor.[24] But by inflating work per se with an intrinsic dignity and importance it did not deserve, Carlyle's gospel, Mill agreed with Whittier, also idealized and thereby legitimated the oppressive conditions under which many free workers as well as slaves labored: "The exhausting, stiffening, stupefying toil of many kinds of agricultural and manufacturing labourers. To reduce very greatly the quantity of work required to carry on existence, is as needful as to distribute it more equally; and the progress of science, and the increasing ascendancy of justice and good sense, tend to this result."[25]

Mill accepted and valued work in moderation as a necessity of life, and he insisted, just as labor radicals and Carlyle himself did, that every able-bodied member of society was bound, "in justice," to perform his fair portion of it; no individual was entitled to a free ride.[26] But in Mill's impatience with conservative efforts to find intrinsic moral value in work and to use this as a basis for justifying the overwork of manual laborers exist traces of more modern views disdaining work as a repressive bourgeois concept and extolling leisure time as the true expression of man's freedom, if not now, then in the utopia of the future. Work, these modern views emphasize is enslaving in large measure because so much of it is directed toward the production of extraneous consumer items and other "false needs" that likewise dominate and trivialize the leisure time pursuits in which the working classes *are* free to engage.[27] Whittier revealed traces of this disdain toward work in his similar tendency to attribute to acquisitiveness and consumerism the excesses of the work ethic: "After all, it may well be questioned whether this gospel according to Poor Richard's Almanac, is precisely calculated for the redemption of humanity. Labor, graduated to man's simple wants, necessities, and unperverted tastes, is doubtless well; but all beyond this is weariness of flesh and spirit. Every web which falls from these restless looms [in Lowell and other factory cities] has a history more or less connected with sin and suffering beginning with slavery and ending with overwork and premature death."[28]

In his idealization of the "simple life," and in his own argument that all too much of man's activity was directed toward producing and consuming goods he did not need, Thoreau even more fully than Mill and Whittier anticipated modern attitudes toward work as enslaving. Indeed, he went beyond them, as he went beyond Marx, in his explicit insistence that the urge to be productive was not an essential part of man's nature and that productive activity was itself an unwarranted attempt by man to impose mastery over Nature.[29] Yet Thoreau's disdain for work was not specifically directed to the overwork and exploitation of manual laborers; in this respect his critique had as much in common with the preoccupation of some clergymen and writers with overwork among commercial and professional men as it had with the emphasis of Mill and Whittier.[30]

"I would . . . maintain that human beings *cannot* rise to the finer attributes of their nature compatibly with a life filled with labour."[31] Mill's statement regarding the working classes typified an increasingly prevalent point of view, if not necessarily a consensus, that had developed among members of the British and American middle classes by midcentury. Quite apart from the views of labor radicals and the working classes themselves, possibly a majority of middle-class writers embraced the position that the future contentment and control of the laboring population rested in considerable measure on their moral and intellectual elevation yet that most forms of manual labor, free or slave, lacked the intrinsic intellectual and moral rewards adequate to achieving this elevation.[32] We have already, as in the discussion of the New York Free Academy, considered some of the concerns that led to this position, and to, specifically, middle-class support for mass education. It might be useful, however, to summarize some of these themes. Many of them are contained in Andrew Preston Peabody's essay in the *North American Review,* "The Future of Labor." Aside from its remarks, earlier quoted, deploring the mentally deadening effects of manufacturing and mechanized division of labor, Peabody noted other compelling reasons why manual laborers needed intellectual compensation for their work.[33] There was, perhaps above all, the matter of class harmony and the functioning of society. Peabody made no claim that social forces which kept talented and qualified laborers from rising into nonmanual employments—either unequal laws and institutionalized restrictions such as those embodied by slavery, or a more informal process of class stratification— were either desirable or necessarily inevitable.[34] But occupational division of labor itself was both desirable and inevitable: "Labor there must always be, and it must, for the most part, be performed by professional laborers. The requisite strength and skill can be acquired for each separate department only by making it a distinct avocation. To blend manual labor with the intellectual professions is to degrade both, by making the former awkward and imperfect, the latter superficial and ignorant."[35]

The importance of occupational division of labor lent a dimension of dignity to all useful employments, and here the correct attitude of the worker became vital as well: "Every avocation that contributes to the general comfort and welfare is worthy of honor, in proportion to the diligence and faithfulness of those who fill it." Yet members of the working classes in America failed, in Peabody's view, to adopt this attitude and to accept with equanimity the positions assigned them or their children by the division of labor: "Hand-laborers of all descriptions . . . almost uniformly desert their callings, when they can," entering retail clerical and other soft work that was far less useful to society and also far less congruent with their natural talents as able-bodied workmen. "Equally unfortunate in its tendency" was "the frequent reluctance of laborers and mechanics to educate their children in their own callings."[36] That the social stigma against physical labor was both undeserved and especially troubling because it, together with low recompense, encouraged workers to abandon their occupations for nonmanual labor employments was affirmed as well by the *New-York Times* around the same time. Although it should in fact be abundantly clear, the *Times* insisted, that "brain work is no more honorable per se than handwork" and "no less toilsome and wearing," the paper acknowledged the existence of certain common "phenomenon" that gave short shrift to these facts. "Why is it," the *Times* asked, "that when a man has made himself rich by a course of honest physical industry, his children should blush to be thought laborers in the same line? Or if he has only acquired a competence, and is respected by them, why should they feel loath to confess to the necessity of the same employment?"[37]

It may be, apart from the possibility of actual disagreement, that Peabody and the *Times* editorial were simply being less forthright than writers who found considerable validity in the stigma against much existing manual labor precisely because of its deficient mental content—those like Horace Greeley who pressed for working-class education in part to remove this deficiency and who, along with Peter Walker, Theodore Sedgwick and others, signified his approval of the rule that "every useful vocation is respected in proportion to the measure of intellect it requires and rewards, and never can rise above this level."[38] Or it may be a matter of different remarks tailored to respond to a different set of concerns. Greeley and Walker were reflecting their impatience with radical claims they deemed irrational—that even the most unskilled, mentally undemanding physical labor was entitled to the same respect and recompense as all other forms of employment. Such claims, Greeley seemed to suggest, only served to undermine the cause of working-class education.[39] Had Peabody been seeking to answer these same radical claims, he may have responded in precisely the same fashion as Greeley and Walker. In emphasizing, to the contrary, the "diligence and faithfulness" with which any useful work might be executed as the proper determinants of its dignity, Peabody was reflecting the different task that he had set itself: that of exposing the false basis of the self-contempt of manual laborers, an attitude which, in Peabody's view, in fact threatened to deplete "the actual services to a community which can in nowise dispense with their aid."[40] It is, of course, highly questionable, given the economic pressures upon working-class families, whether many laborers, most of all those in the most highly stigmatized and underpaid employments, could have abandoned such necessary work even had they wished to. As Alonzo Potter suggested, the less "agreeable" modes of employment rarely suffered from a shortage of laborers, for "multitudes, from want of education, are fitted only for inferior pursuits, and, therefore, can compete for no other."[41]

WORKING-CLASS EDUCATION

Problematic as was the actual threat perceived by Peabody to society's labor needs, working-class education in fact became, in conjunction with increased leisure time and a higher level of wages, Peabody's very means of removing this threat, of alleviating the disgruntlement of manual laborers and keeping them in their necessary callings. Peabody acknowledged that the stigma against useful and industrious physical labor, however unjustified he believed it to be, was hardly confined to the minds of workingmen themselves; were manual laborers given more time and opportunity to develop their higher nature, "the artificial distinctions of society would lose their basis, and would gradually fall away. All occupations would become, in a certain sense, liberal professions. . . . All the menial offices of society would be discharged without degrading associations being attached to them; for those who performed the humblest functions, instead of being, as now, wholly merged in and identified with their callings, would have an intellectual, social, and moral existence entirely independent of them."[42]

If long hours of manual toil failed to win for the laborer adequate respect and dignity from society, and if, indeed, the actual effects of some forms of labor, whatever their social utility, was to intellectually and morally debase the laborer, then an externalized source for that dignity and respect must be provided through working-class education. Peabody's favored means of serving both social stability and social justice may have enjoyed especially prevalent support among middle-class, educated American Whigs, for whom the *North American Review* was a primary vehicle of expression. Some historians have critically observed the tendency of propertied American Whiggery, in a self-serving pursuit of "class harmony," to embrace "internal reform" and intellectual uplift through education as a virtual panacea for working-class grievances, a painless alternative to substantive social change.[43] Yet this criticism somewhat understates the subtlety of the argument for mass education that was advanced in "The Future of Labor" essay and other like-minded pieces, and it also fails to take into sufficient account the significance of the appeal working-class education held for a diversity of social groups.

In the Whig view, working-class education would not merely bring to disgruntled laborers the social status and intellectual stimulation with which their work was not providing them. Education was also expected to increase very substantially the instrumental value of the laborer's work. It would accomplish this first by rendering a good deal of that work more intelligent and productive; although the accompanying criticisms of industrial labor negated the force of this argument by implying that such repetitive labor repelled the exercise of the mental faculties. But second, education would increase workers' incentive to maximize their recompense by developing their taste outside the workplace for the more expensive, "artificial wants" that defined civilization. This argument, again particularly popular among liberal and moderate American Whigs, reflected an ethic of commercialism and consumerism that had been on the rise in Britain and America since at least the late eighteenth century, and it may also have owed something to antislavery notions that attributed the economic "stagnation" of the South to the lack of consumer power enjoyed by slaves.[44] The appeal the "artificial wants" argument exerted on behalf of working-class education may have held even greater potential importance than the increased productivity argument, perhaps because it could apply with equal force to workers employed in repetitive industrial work.

Sophisticated as some of these arguments may have been, the middle-class Whig case for working-class education may have nonetheless exaggerated the instrumental value of that education; it remained to some degree an illusory panacea for the ills of society. But the appeal of working-class education nonetheless extended beyond the confines of propertied Whigs to include a good many other elements of society, including some that were far more antagonistic than they to existing social arrangements. As already suggested, Owenite and other segments of Anglo-American labor radical groups may well have valued intellectual enlightenment and moral discipline for the working classes in part for their capacity to serve very different ends—the overhaul or overturning of these social arrangements rather than the fortifying of existing society's labor needs. And it is also possible that elements within these radical groups, like those workers who pressed for educational opportunities to increase their ability to compete in the marketplace, may have ultimately put a higher value upon the diffusion and enjoyment of material produce than upon education and cultural enlightenment as ends in themselves. Yet it remains true that labor radical and reform movements attached the same premium more conservative middle-class writers did to the worker's development of his higher nature though education.[45] This particular affinity will further manifest itself in the discussion that shortly follows on contemporary views of working-class leisure time; but noted here is the defense of Manual Labor Schools made by Orestes Brownson during his radical reform phase, one which closely paralleled much of Peabody's argument for working-class education. Manual Labor Schools, Brownson noted, have the

> tendency to elevate labor to the rank of a liberal profession. From the fact that manual labor has almost always been performed by the poor, the uncultivated, the ignorant, or the enslaved, men's associations with it are of a very unpleasant character. They are in

a majority of cases, impatient of it, anxious to flee from it, and obtain their living by some other means. . . . To make men love it, all we have to do is to make it honorable, and then the energy which is now wasted in fashionable dissipation, in branches of trade now crowded, or in devising methods to get a living without labor will be profitably and pleasantly employed in the mechanic's shop, in the garden or on the farm.[46]

This summary of some of the primary arguments advanced in behalf of working-class education only raises more underlying questions, some of which have been touched on earlier. How does one explain the mid-nineteenth-century climate of criticism of which both Peabody's essay and Brownson's remarks were a part? Why did writers during this particular period in time, in Britain as well as in America, come to reject traditional elitist assumptions that occupational division of labor, however inexorable it might be, legitimated and rendered equally inevitable a division of labor between thinking and employment in physical labor? How does one account for the emergence of an unprecedented body of literature criticizing various modes of manual labor for failing to provide the laboring population with sufficient intellectual and moral rewards and emphasizing the need of this population to find some kind of redress in their outside lives? Why, in other words, did a consensus of expressed concern develop during the first part of the nineteenth century regarding the manual laborer's "higher nature"?[47]

All of these related questions—different forms, in fact, of the same question—remain among the central ones of historical writing for this period, and some of the possible answers can only be suggested here. The industrialization and mechanization of many forms of labor since the end of the eighteenth century clearly played a major role in the developing concern with the worker's "higher nature." Reinforcing a process of division of labor that had been underway for decades in workshops, the Industrial Revolution without question served in many instances to trivialize and intensify the productive process and to deteriorate working conditions. The Puritan ethic, which had affirmed the intrinsic dignity of all earthly callings and the moral value of labor even for children, could hardly have anticipated these developments, above all the manifold possibilities for rigorous, long hours of work and exploitation created by the factory system and the Industrial Revolution generally.[48] Many of the forms of labor which with the help of artificial illumination emerged and spread during the first part of the nineteenth century, forms that included factory work, workshop slop work, and outwork, provided compelling evidence for arguments that "honest" labor need not be respectable labor; and the contemporary consciousness that long hours of manual labor impeded the development of the worker's "higher nature" was thus on one level simply an accurate and direct response to these newer kinds of labor.

It is also true, however, that the mid-nineteenth-century abhorrence of working conditions extended to such older forms of exploitation as black chattel slavery and to forms of "free" labor, like juvenile chimney sweeping and urban casual labor, which were only tangentially related to industrialization. Quite possibly, abhorrence over developing industrial conditions actually stimulated in some members of the middle and upper classes a new critical attitude toward nonindustrial employments as well, just as the tendency of some entrepreneurs and writers to isolate chattel slavery as uniquely iniquitous undeniably reflected a contrasting, possibly unconscious desire to screen out and legitimate the travails of industrial laborers.[49]

But it is also possible that the increased sensitivity to conditions of labor as inhospitable to the worker's elevation had sources quite independent of the actual deterioration in those conditions wrought by industrialization. One of the more valuable contributions of the "optimistic" school of historians regarding the effects of the Industrial Revolution on the British working classes has been its reminder that much preindustrial labor, such as the domestic system of manufacturing that employed large numbers of women and children, was hardly idyllic and that a good deal of it may have in fact been just as monotonous and time-consuming for workers as long hours of repetitive factory labor. Pursuing a line of argument advanced by Thomas Macaulay, these historians have argued with varying degrees of effectiveness that the new early Victorian consciousness that criticized hard labor for "delicate" women and children as unnatural and degrading, developed out of all proportion to any actual deterioration in working conditions that occurred during industrialization.[50] One must look to other factors to help explain this increased sensitivity, such as the fact that the exploitation of the labor of women and children simply became more conspicuous when it moved out of the home into industrial settings. Perhaps even more important, that exploitation, as has been already suggested, was commonly perceived by adult male members of the working classes, as well as by middle-class writers, to be primarily objectionable because of the threat to patriarchal authority and familial stability it appeared to represent. The labor of women and children became challenged as never before largely because it was increasingly labor controlled and recompensed by factory masters and other "outsiders" rather than work meted out and rewarded by husbands and fathers within the home. The labor of wives and mothers, specifically, became more objectionable in some measure because of its mere shift to a marketplace context; such labor was perceived as interfering with women's "natural" domestic responsibilities in a way that equally demanding home-based labor had never been.[51]

These and other factors have been emphasized by the "optimistic" school of historians, as well as by a number of scholars in the burgeoning field of women's studies, to help account for anti-industrial sentiment. Some of the other Anglo-American developments and intellectual currents have already been referred to—such as those emanating from the Enlightenment, evangelical religion, romanticism and, in the United States specifically, republican and democratic values and the mythology of American exceptionalism—which came together and contributed to a new total sensibility, a primary characteristic of which was the concern among members of the middle and upper classes for the manual laborer's "higher nature."[52] Not the least of these other developments, as Andrew Preston Peabody's essay demonstrated, was middle-class anxiety regarding the diverse manifestations of working-class discontent and consciousness—the pressures that the ascendant "claims of labor" imposed on middle-class consciousness. The various forms of working-class and radical consciousness were, to be sure, themselves largely a product of the Enlightenment and other intellectual currents, as well as a reaction to the overwhelming social fact of a developing industrial capitalist structure.[53] But it is not without significance that even employers and other members of the middle classes who continued to regard the laboring population as mere manipulable tools of production felt the need to justify and rationalize long hours of factory and other kinds of manual labor in the terms that they did, as intrinsically rewarding and beneficial for the workers themselves.[54]

Possibly only a minority within the middle classes, primarily some of the most zealous defenders of black chattel slavery, mechanized factory work, and compulsory labor for able-bodied indoor paupers and other institutionalized populations, persisted in holding that existing manual labor could by itself, without the assistance of schooling or other forms of outside moral or intellectual stimulation, achieve a significant reform or elevation of those engaged in it.[55] But it would seem questionable, to introduce yet another issue, that the matter of manual labor's intrinsic rewards was in fact ever one of overriding concern to a large proportion of the working classes themselves. The focus of this study upon perceptions of labor's inherent intellectual and moral content has rather naturally led to a concentration upon the views of middle-class writers and intellectuals who could afford the luxury of contemplating and articulating the value of work's intrinsic rewards in existing or future societies. The conviction that living for work rather than working to live should be the dominant concern of all members of society united Carlyle with such middle-class visionaries as Fourier and the early Marx, for whom work's predominantly instrumental value under existing social arrangements represented a primary indictment of those arrangements. Under a radically different social order, not only would all individuals engage in varied and stimulating productive activity; but they would be psychologically capable as never before of enjoying such activity because their basic material needs and comforts would be easily provided for, and they would at last be freed of the anxiety of confronting their productive activity as a way of securing their subsistence.[56]

It remains hazardous, and possibly presumptuous, to offer sweeping generalizations about the work attitudes of laboring people themselves. Undoubtedly, some workers over the millennia, in consequence of the dominant religious or cultural values of their particular societies, found intrinsic rewards and meaning in tasks and working conditions that we now regard as oppressive and exploitative.[57] And precisely because they were not rigidly divorced from drinking, singing, and other leisure pastimes, many preindustrial tasks "provided [their] own recreation" and fulfillment for laborers even if they were not intrinsically satisfying and elevating in the sense that a middle-class intellectual or utopian thinker may have envisioned or idealized manual work.[58] Some scholars have theorized that members of the laboring populations of Western cultures in fact only came to develop a genuine, often hostile, sense of their productive activity and means of livelihood as "work"—as something clearly distinct from leisure time and other activities—with the coming of the Industrial Revolution and the accelerating intrusion of cash crops and wage labor into subsistence village life.[59]

Yet it still seems probable that immediate economic pressures must have always encouraged a significant proportion of the laboring population, in preindustrial as well as industrial cultures, to slight the importance of intrinsically satisfying and rewarding productive activity—work as an end in itself—and instead to value that activity for its more strictly pragmatic or instrumental importance as a source of income, as a means, in many cases, of sheer subsistence and survival.[60] As suggested earlier, the skilled journeymen mechanics and their spokesmen who participated in mid-nineteenth-century American labor movements were registering at least an indirect protest of manual labor's loss of mental content and emptiness when they complained of the debasement of working standards by "cheap and nasty" competition or when they bemoaned the tendency of the division of labor to limit workers' involvement in the creation of an entire product.[61] But that work should carry deep intrinsic satisfactions appears in general to have been hardly more of an issue among workers in America, many of whom made up the ranks of this "cheap and nasty" competition and who did not share the perspective of craftsmen who perceived their skills under assault, than it has been among possibly a majority of workers throughout history. The trivialization of labor under mechanization and industrialization may at most have confirmed the traditional inclination of the laboring population to above all value work for its extrinsic rewards rather than its intrinsic content.[62] Newly arrived impoverished Irish immigrants accepted almost any work that they could find, although not a few became in time disgruntled and disillusioned, not merely with the disagreeable, often dangerous, and poorly remunerated features of many of these employments, but with the pervasive, in some cases racist, stigma that native-born Americans attached to them.[63]

Even the bulk of "respectable" and "enlightened" native-born mill girls of Lowell and other mill towns appear to have embraced their labor for its exclusively instrumental value. There were two vocal minorities among this factory population during the 1840s, one of which denounced the factory system as oppressive and exploitative, and the other of which provided support for the policies of the proprietors by defending factory labor as morally and intellectually uplifting—or at least as no less honorable than other forms of manual labor.[64] But standing apart from both these vocal minorities was a "silent majority" of mill girls which, perhaps in part because they regarded their tenure in the mills as only temporary, seem to have routinely accepted the terms of their employment. Entertaining no particular illusions about the dignity of factory work, they appear at the same time to have even opposed well-intentioned efforts to limit their hours; they were above all concerned with maximizing the amount of money they could earn during their limited period in the mills.[65]

A number of historians have generalized that certain circumstances may have rendered it even less likely that female members of the working classes in Western cultures would have looked for much intrinsic satisfaction or meaning in their work, to have valued it in appreciably other than the narrowly utilitarian sense of holding down a "job." Women's work, whether inside or outside the home, has always tended to be of a more uniformly menial character than men's, and it has also always fallen upon women to balance and if need be subordinate their role as producers to the obligations of child rearing and housekeeping. The breakup of the household unit of production during industrialization did not, whatever its other effects, alter these general circumstances. Encouraged by competing domestic social roles or—in the case of young single women—by the anticipation of such roles to devalue employments which were singularly lacking in intrinsic rewards to begin with, female members of the labor force had even more reason than their male counterparts to attach a limited, exclusively instrumental importance to their work.[66]

Instrumental attitudes toward work, on the other hand, are not all of one kind; and historians have speculated, in the absence of written records of their views left by members of the working classes, that many workers held one of two distinctly different instrumental views of their labor. Scholars have described the first of these views as particularly prevalent among laboring populations in precapitalist or preindustrial cultures: workers were interested in labor only as a means of meeting bare subsistence or the most elementary needs, and once these needs were met, they abandoned work in favor of "unproductive" leisure activity. The second view reflected a more expansive appreciation of the instrumental value of labor. The extent to which it actually implanted itself among members of the laboring population attested in part to the influence of late eighteenth- and early nineteenth-century bourgeois ideological hegemony, particularly the effectiveness with which bourgeois values touted character improvement as a means to economic improvement as well as a good in itself. The mark of the worker who had developed "foresight" and internalized discipline was that he embraced increased work and the additional income it provided as a security net against future economic bad times. The laborer valued more disciplined and less intermittent work as a means of actually improving his economic condition, of increasing his capacity to develop and indulge the "refined wants" and "gratifications" characteristic of civilized cultures. Work in this second instrumental view was also valued by the laborer as a means of achieving a more "civilized" use of leisure time compatible with his increased capacity to satisfy his "refined wants."[67]

The resistance with which the first generation of factory workers greeted middle-class efforts to inculcate it with the values of industrial morality has been a subject of much recent historical writing. To the extent that workers came to adopt the more expansive appreciation of labor's instrumental value, this development corresponded to the emphasis developed by a wide range of middle-class writers. Some of these deplored with Mill the "cant" regarding manual labor's intrinsic rewards and argued that the justification for manual labor essentially rested on whatever instrumental value it possessed for the laborer. Other writers like Andrew Ure who maintained that mechanized industrial labor was stimulating and rewarding in itself, also touted the instrumental value of steady and lucrative employment as a further argument for discrediting the resistance of free wage laborers to the factory's more regimented and continuous work rhythms.[68] And the value of hard labor in achieving for workers a share of civilized society's refined wants could also be exalted by middle-class writers with still different ideological objectives in mind. It could, for example, be paradoxically touted by writers in defense of compulsory servitude, by writers who argued that the mark of a naturally inferior people or race was its complete inability to conform to the standard rule of progress. Edmund Ruffin held no particularly high expectation that the laboring population belonging to the "superior" white race would respond to greater extrinsic rewards with increased industriousness; he retained a long-standing, traditional distrust of high wages as a stimulus to indolence.[69] But African blacks, Ruffin argued, were all the more likely to forever retain the most limited instrumental view of work; they could never be induced to labor harder or longer by the prospect of greater extrinsic rewards that would increase their share of civilized society's "artificial wants." Because their "aversion to labor" was more profound and intractable than that of less "barbarous" peoples, it could only be overcome through a system of closely supervised, involuntary servitude.[70]

Regardless of the actual extent to which members of the working classes themselves came to adopt the view of the more expansive instrumental possibilities of manual labor, the mid-nineteenth-century middle-class writers who articulated this view disagreed on certain fundamental issues, or at least approached them with different emphases. John Stuart Mill, for example, clearly agreed on the need for workers to develop greater internalized discipline, and he hardly denied that this must increase the likelihood of their enjoying a rising standard of living; a more highly developed sense of acquisitiveness on the part of the working classes would help lift them out of poverty.[71] Yet the increasing emphasis in Mill's writing was upon prevailing materialism and acquisitiveness as part of the problem rather than part of the solution. His insistence that slavery and the overwork of free wage laborers derived much of their strength from the impulse of the middle and upper classes to indulge their jaded sensibilities with the products of this exploitation was part of his increasing criticism of materialist values, of which he found the most extreme manifestation among the American middle classes. He looked forward to society's attainment of the "stationary"—or no-growth—state of the future, where economic striving would be far less pronounced and pervasive.[72]

Mill's reservations and criticisms regarding the acquisitive spirit stood in contrast to the more fully enthusiastic reception that other middle-class thinkers accorded it. In defending the degree to which Americans were in fact "a people, beyond all others, devoted to business and accumulation," the Reverend Orville Dewey insisted in terms more unequivocal than Mill's that the redemption of manual labor lay in the materialistic impulse, in the extent to which the working classes everywhere embraced acquisitive values. It was precisely because the great majority of American people were neither slaves nor in the condition of the European peasantry, and had succeeded with the aid of political freedom in bettering themselves, Dewey noted, that they were in the enviable position of having drawn the criticism of being overly materialistic.[73] This is not to characterize Dewey's perspective as one of gross or uncritical materialism; economic depressions invariably produced from Dewey and other clergymen a myriad of jeremiads attributing the ensuing suffering of all classes to a short-sighted consumerism, to acquisitiveness and accumulation for the misguided purpose of spending rather than saving. And with regard to saving and delayed gratification themselves, moreover, Dewey retained enough of the Puritan ethic to condemn even these when they had as their objective the ultimate escape from a life of work and virtuous self-denial—industriousness and accumulation for the shameful purpose of retiring to a life of ease and "luxurious and self-indulgent leisure."[74]

That both middle-class writers and members of the working classes held more than one perspective on work's instrumental value raises a related issue for consideration: attitudes regarding the nature of the leisure activity to which laborers would and should direct part of their extrinsic rewards. The traditional Puritan view that leisure's principal value was as a mere restorative for work maintained a strong measure of influence among members of the early Victorian middle classes who insisted that work was a blessing.[75] One even discerns the influence of this view in the argument advanced by labor petitions and labor movements, as well as by their middle-class sympathizers, that a reduced working day would prove to the advantage of employers by rendering their labor force fresher and more productive.[76] But the concept of leisure as a mere restorative for manual labor, as utterly subordinate in importance to it, nonetheless met increasing opposition among the middle classes in the mid-nineteenth century, just as did the notions that manual labor held adequate intrinsic rewards and that anything beyond the most limited leisure time for the working classes was necessarily ill-advised because it gave freer play to their "vicious propensities."[77]

One can identify, first of all, the dominant alternative view of working-class leisure time held by middle-class writers, that such time might serve the interests of social stability and be otherwise beneficial if it were utilized to develop the worker's "higher nature," something that long hours of manual toil seemed itself increasingly incapable of doing. This view, to be sure, incorporated recognition of the value of leisure time as a restorative for work. Quite aside from the fact that working-class education would more fully reconcile and acclimate the laboring population to the industrial and other modes of employment to which division of labor had assigned it, such education also supported society's labor needs, Andrew Preston Peabody noted, by observing the physiological truth of balanced and symbiotic faculties: "The most effectual repose is found in the change of occupation, in the diversion of thoughts to other channels, in the vigorous exercise of a new class of faculties, in the transfer of activity from the weary body to the untasked mind and unjaded affections." But there were compelling reasons beyond leisure activity's restorative power, Peabody added, why the laboring population should make the most serious and civilized use of its time outside the workplace: such uses would both dispel the traditional opposition of employers to increased leisure time for workers and also serve, through its improvement in the general condition of the working classes, the cause of social justice:

Toilsome recreation, active sports, convivial dissipation . . . wear upon the bodily powers already exhausted by the six days' labor, and leave the higher nature dormant still. And it is these latter uses or abuses of the day of rest, that make employers grudge the laborers' Sabbaths, and spurn all thought of superfluous holidays. But let it be shown that the weekly rest is time not wasted for industrial, but saved for intellectual and moral, uses, and let the laborers, by means of it, ascend continually nearer the elevated standard of character which this institution is adapted to create, then will he be able to claim, with authority, and to receive, as his manifest right, the full amount of daily leisure requisite for bodily comfort, mental culture, and moral progress.[78]

Peabody's reference to the hostility with which employers greeted "the laborers' Sabbaths" raises the complicated question of the relationship which that institution, as a special subcategory of "leisure-time" activity, bore to industrial morality and the factory system.[79] Some of the early industrial employers who saw their own best interests in reducing the leisure time of workers to the minimum and keeping their enterprises running seven days a week, were accordingly hostile to the very concept of a work-free Sabbath. As James Walvin notes, "time was money and free time meant idle machinery which was hence unprofitable."[80]

Quite apart from this immediate pecuniary consideration, there were clearly capitalists and other members of the middle classes who regarded the idle and vicious propensities of the laboring population as more or less unalterable, who continued to regard steady work as the only truly effective check upon those propensities, and who held a corresponding animus or suspicion of work-free Sundays. Whatever the degree of support it commanded, however, this last view was hardly distinctive to the period of ascendant industrialism. In the 1770s Sabbatarianism had been attacked because of the opportunities it gave the English poor for idleness and disorder, and such writers of the time as Arthur Young who distrusted high wages as a stimulus to worker indolence were quite naturally similarly disposed to the idea that the laboring population could not be trusted with an entire day off from work.[81]

More fundamentally, however, an indeterminate number of other factory proprietors may have come to share the belief of middle-class writers like Peabody that their best interests lay in directing workers toward a not inconsiderable time spent in "rational recreation," including Sabbath schools and other forms of expanded education for child workers.[82] Writers who believed that factory and other hard work might have a truly morally elevating or transforming effect upon those employed may have been, like the author of the *Quarterly Christian Spectator* essay discussed earlier, particularly enthusiastic about the capacity of Sabbath schools and Sunday religious duties generally to serve a complimentary role in fostering internalized work discipline and other productive work habits. The preference for "rational recreation," which, as we have seen, might also be shared by writers like Peabody who were strongly critical of factory labor, could combine on occasion with hostility to *all* working-class leisure activity to fuel the various Anglo-American middle-class campaigns directed at discouraging or eliminating "traditional," "preindustrial" working-class amusements.[83]

But the impact of new industrial work regimens upon attitudes toward the Sabbath extended further still than this, even if we continue to restrict ourselves, for the moment, to considering those who took a generally uncritical view of those regimens. There were many employers, either deeply religious themselves or reflecting again that traditional suspicion of the vicious propensities of the laboring population, who held to the position that members of this population were entitled to their Sundays off only if they spent them in the performance of their religious duties, and who opposed for this reason the maintenance of Sunday trains and other services that would give urban working-class families wider access to recreational activities.[84] Yet just as clearly, there were still other factory proprietors and middle-class writers who, although obviously not sanctioning debauchery, welcomed Sunday outings and other more or less frivolous and light forms of working-class amusements for the presumed recuperative effects they had upon members of the laboring population; rested workers made better workers.[85] To some degree, the emphasis upon physical rest, while reflecting the contemporary tensions generated by intensified, industrialist capitalist work regimens, could also be said to harken back to the Mosaic concept of the Sabbath, a concept that made only muted reference to the active performance of any religious duties on that day, and decreed that men were to honor the prime Creator and to observe the holiness of the Sabbath, through abstention and relaxation from labor.[86]

That factory proprietors and other proindustrial members of the middle classes could assume such a variety of positions with respect to a work-free Sabbath may be taken as another illustration of the principle of variations on a theme, referred to in chapter 1 and raised implicitly throughout this study. Individuals who shared an underlying commitment to the industrial capitalist social structure frequently disagreed on the best means of ensuring workers' ability to function compliantly and productively within that structure, and the debates over the value and content of a work-free Sabbath were in many instances one expression of these disagreements over means. It can hardy be overlooked, however, that individuals who took a more hostile or critical view of the factory system and industrial capitalism might also manifest their perspective through the Sabbath issue. In a certain sense, the factory system, and the ascendancy of "time work" over "task work" it epitomized, was fundamentally inimical to one of the original presumptions on which the meaning of the Sabbath rested: that work was marked by finite stages, and that after participating in the creation of something from beginning to end, the laborer could step back after six days of toil and conclude that what he had accomplished "was good." Although one can scarcely presume that there were no factory workers who derived a strong sense of accomplishment from their work, the fragmented yet continuous nature of factory labor nonetheless meant that one of the original meanings of the Sabbath, one that held special relevance for traditional, preindustrial task work, was obscured or lost.[87]

To critics of the factory system, the fragmented, continuous nature of factory labor, although it negated or blurred the parallels between God's Creation of the world and the work of the operative, also rendered the rationale for a work-free Sabbath all the more compelling. Peabody was perhaps typical of middle-class critics in the emphasis he placed upon the theme of fragmentation; "rational recreation" on the Sabbath, along with expanded educational activities, would check or compensate for the intellectually stultifying effects of factory labor. But in valuing Sunday as a sanctuary of rest and recreation, other critics of the factory system, including operatives themselves, were at least as likely to complain of other characteristics of factory work, notably its continuous, unremitting, and exhausting work rhythms and its capacity under artificial illumination to destroy all boundaries between day and night, work and leisure. Some of the most relentless antagonists of the factory system, notably Richard Oastler, were even inclined to turn the argument around, to maintain that the operative's effective performance of his religious duties on Sunday required a shorter, less fatiguing work regimen during the rest of the week.[88] And as we have indicated, proprietors who supported a work-free Sabbath, a reduction in hours during the other six days, or who made other concessions to workers and critics, were in many cases acknowledging the force of these criticisms of factory labor, if only with a view toward protecting their own interests.

Although it is probable that Peabody's preference for "rational recreation" over less purposeful and serious working-class leisure-time activities was typical of the middle-class critics of the factory system, it was hardly confined to these critics. The position that the laborer's time outside of the workplace, during Sundays and evenings, should be productively employed toward his moral and intellectual improvement, that social justice required that manual laborers be accorded their "right" to develop their "finer" faculties was one that labor movements themselves could fully share with writers like Peabody.[89] That attitude had, in fact, a rather venerable tradition, reflecting as it did the ethos of artisanal self-improvement that had helped give rise to Mechanics' Institutes in both Britain and America earlier in the century.[90] In making the case for the ten-hour day for New England factory operatives, Huldah J. Stone, member of the Female Labor Reform Association and the New England Workingmen's Association and one of the most militant of the mill-workers, rhetorically inquired in 1845:

> Is it really necessary that men and women should toil and labor twelve, sixteen, and even eighteen hours, to obtain the mere sustenance of their physical natures? Have they no other wants which call as loudly for satisfaction as those? Call ye this *life*—to labor, eat, drink and die, without knowing anything, comparatively speaking, of our mysterious natures—of the object of our creation and preservation and final destination? No! 'tis not *life*. It is merely existing in common with the inanimate and senseless part of creation.[91]

Johnson's arguments that excessive labor was a curse and not a blessing, that leisure time alone allowed for the worker's development of his "higher nature," and that there were indeed "higher objects to be attained in life than mere labor" were characteristic themes of the short hours movement.[92] Mill, among middle-class intellectuals, had given preeminent expression to the same themes, concluding in his attack on Carlyle that a "gospel of leisure" was desirable to confront the impulses of the middle and upper classes to overwork the laboring population in their quest for ever more products.[93] And although segments of the abolition movement contentiously rejected claims that poverty and long hours of legally free wage labor could be worse than chattel slavery, some abolitionists remained hospitable to the notion that social arrangements which encouraged the overworking of free laborers had the same debasing effects as compulsory servitude.[94] The abolitionist newspaper, the *Philanthropist,* approvingly quoted from an article in the labor press entitled "Republican Aristocracy" which suggested that the excessive influence wielded by wealthy Northern capitalists could hardly be considered apart from the effect of sixteen-hour workdays on their employees. That effect, the *Philanthropist* noted, was the confinement of the working classes "to the lower part of our nature, the *body.*" Although they could not be bought or sold, or their families broken up by their employers, "so far as the improvement of the *higher* parts of our nature—the intellectual, the *moral*—is concerned," overworked free laborers were "in as hopeless a condition as the slaves on a sugar or cotton plantation in Louisiana." In their crippled state of "qualified slavery," free laborers could hardly mount an effective resistance to the unwholesome authority of the burgeoning Northern aristocracy.[95]

This and other critiques of free labor exploitation gave much play to the notion of increased leisure time for workers as a means of enabling them to improve their "finer faculties." There was a certain symmetry in arguing, as the more radical of these critiques did in particular, that overwork "robbed" laborers of the time and opportunity to develop their higher nature and to become full and equal citizens just as the capitalist class robbed laborers of their just recompense. But there was yet another view of leisure time which, although less characteristically tied to antagonistic assaults on the exploitation of free wage laborers, in a sense even more unequivocally challenged the notion that work was the be-all and end-all of life. The prominent New England clergyman Horace Bushnell has, in this connection, drawn the attention of a number of scholars for the degree to which he turned the general order of priorities around, arguing in one of his most well-known addresses that work was but a means to an end, a broadly defined and "exalted" state of "play." Bushnell also added, however, that the "transitional" character of work increased rather than diminished work's dignity.[96] Thus he remained far from anticipating that modern disdain for work referred to earlier. Bushnell's remarks, furthermore, were no more than Thoreau's specifically critical of the consuming role that earning a living assumed in the lives of manual laborers. For the latter reason, in particular, we should not exaggerate the relevance to this study of a view of leisure activity that was undeniably unusual for its time in the degree to which it downplayed the centrality of work.[97]

The more prevalent notion that members of the working classes simply needed some increased leisure time for relaxation and "play," as distinct from purposeful self-improvement, was quite naturally advocated with particular reference to the needs of the children of the laboring poor. In a letter to the *New-York Times* Minnie Myrtle urged that playrooms be attached to the Industrial Schools of the city. Those whose lives were swallowed up in "the dull routine of labor" not only sacrificed their health but became "morose and stupid." There was a distinct danger, Myrtle wrote, that the juvenile inmates of the Industrial Schools, and the children of the working classes generally, would grow up believing that "a life of order is a life of intolerable restraint . . . they need to be convinced that there are animal pleasures which are not sinful, and which afford far more real enjoyment than any with which they are familiar."[98]

Myrtle's view of working-class leisure time shared elements with other of the views already described. Her suggestion that overwork repressed and alienated the working classes, and might thus prove dysfunctional to the smooth operation of society's laboring force, entailed the theme that recreation had restorative value for individuals engaged in manual laborer employments. Yet because Myrtle gave no credence to the view that work was entitled to be so all-consuming, she rejected the assumption that leisure's only value was restorative. Her disdainful reference to the "dull routine of labor" suggests that play and amusement were above all her answers to kinds of work that could not be made more satisfying.

The increased opportunity for play and amusement that Myrtle advocated, on the other hand, was, despite her vague defense of certain innocent "animal pleasures," hardly an invitation to the working classes to indulge the "low" and brutish appetites against which middle-class writers had characteristically moralized. To this extent her argument was, apart from the recognition of these "animal pleasures," akin to the more dominant view that stressed the value of increased leisure time for workers as an opportunity for their purposeful self-improvement.

That middle-class writers held different views regarding the ways in which members of the working class might most beneficially spend their leisure time should not obscure the essential agreement among many of these writers concerning the dangers of excessive work. One should not, moreover, overstate the dichotomy between middle-class views favoring increased leisure time for purposes of education and improvement and those views favoring that time for more unstructured relaxation and play. "Providence," Andrew Preston Peabody maintained, has "indicated for the laborer ample season for relaxation and improvement."[99] A Massachusetts government commission report of 1866 similarly valued both kinds of leisure activity, objecting to the same kind of employer opposition to a reduction in working hours for wage-earning manual laborers that was referred to by Peabody in his 1852 essay.[100] The Massachusetts report suggested that the benefits of common school education would be largely nullified if the adult members of the state's laboring population did not possess sufficient leisure time in which to continue the development of their intellectual faculties. But the report added that

> we do not expect that all will use the time saved from labor in study, or that all will make a wise use of it. . . . Each will spend his leisure as he likes, . . . some will spend it foolishly—some wickedly. But others, we believe many others, and an increasing number, would spend the time profitably, in healthy recreation or home duties, cultivating the little patch of ground, repairing or adorning the house, playing with the children, providing domestic comforts and conveniences, reading the papers, keeping informed in national affairs, so as to vote intelligently at the next election; and a few of higher reading tastes reading more substantial books of science, art, history or religion. It is manifestly unjust that those who would employ their leisure hours wisely should be denied the privilege of having leisure hours, because others would abuse them.[101]

Interestingly, the commission report's argument for shorter hours did not rest on the assumption that all, or even most, workers would consume improvement products such as books and thereby develop their "finer nature." It acknowledged that some laborers might indeed react to their release from work as many of the opponents of reduced hours had always argued they would: by spending their increased time drinking, gambling or in other "wicked" or idle ways.[102] The report's argument for shortened hours for laborers was based, instead, on the principle of equity, and if one wishes to claim that the history of consumerism and leisure-time activity among members of the American working classes has largely failed to fulfill the report's hopes that laborers would use their free time for purposeful self-improvement, one might also wish to note the mid-nineteenth-century observation made by a writer in the *Edinburgh Review:* "Few can be found in *any* class who habitually prefer intellectual gratification to the allurements of animal indulgence."[103]

It would be absurd to overstate the effect the rhetorical admonitions against the work ethic and the accompanying exaltation of leisure activity had upon economic behavior. Although the early Victorian middle- and upper-class abhorrence of some of the worst working conditions, with a push from organized labor agitation, eventuated in some tangible ameliorative legislation, it could hardly be said that the sum total of exploitation and overwork among free wage laborers abated as industrialization proceeded on its course during the first part of the nineteenth century. There were always a host of formidable values, interests, and forces that competed with the good intentions that would as a matter of principle reduce this work load—belief in the "freedom of contract," as well as in the impracticality and inefficacy of short hours legislation; competitive morality that attributed the predicament of the laboring poor to their own failings; fatalistic and complacent acceptance of the unfolding of the division of labor in society and a generalized public apathy and inertia in the face of ongoing economic change; and employers' perceptions of their own best economic interests, together with continued claims by capitalists and their supporters that the idleness rather than the overwork of laborers posed the greater danger to society.[104] In the second half of the century, moreover, notwithstanding the incremental enactment of labor legislation that shortened the working day for many members of the working classes, conservative Social Darwinist doctrines and other new ideologies would arise to strengthen racist and ethnic prejudices that had long legitimated labor exploitation among certain stigmatized groups. These ideologies and doctrines would do their part to thwart the optimistic prediction of Mill and others that technology together with "justice and good sense" must appreciably reduce the work load among much of the laboring population.[105]

Despite, then, the increasing emphasis in the realm of intellectual discourse during the first part of the century upon the manual laborer's need to develop his unfulfilled mental and moral potential, the pressures of grinding poverty and the necessity of virtually constant labor in jobs with few or no advancement possibilities, remained the realities of life for many unskilled laborers in America as well as England. More highly skilled and well-situated members of the working classes, such as those in the expanding trades, may have even given more voluntary sustenance to the work ethic, toiling as long as they could in pursuit of job advancement and increased earnings that would maximize their capacity as consumers to share in society's "refined wants." To some degree these more advantaged workers contributed to the general state of affairs bemoaned by Charles Loring Brace, in explanation of the desperate and dangerous condition of the lowest ranks of the laboring poor, those living on the margins of society: "Society hurried on selfishly for its wealth, and left this vast class in its misery and temptation. . . . The worldliness of the rich, the indifference of all classes to the poor, will always be avenged."[106]

Intellectual discourse, and even the most sincerely felt social values, are highly uncertain guides to actual human behavior and social developments. They are in fact among several kinds of abstractions with which this study has so far had to deal. As Mill and Whittier suggested, some of the most conservative versions of the work ethic, those which highlighted labor's intrinsic moral content or benefits, represented the kind of abstraction that legitimated or slighted the travails of manual laborers. By way of contrast, Adam Smith's remarks regarding the intellectually deadening effects of manufacturing division of labor developed in the hands of his followers into a powerful abstraction that may have in fact overstated, and certainly offered no empirical proof, of the pernicious mental effects of either un-mechanized or mechanized division of labor in workshops and factories. There remains the possibility touched on earlier, that in some workshops manufacturing division of labor did not erode the skill content of tasks, or at least not in the ways Smith suggested.[107] More basically perhaps, and notwithstanding the commonly self-serving nature of the profactory arguments, many workers, particularly those who came from more solitary and equally unskilled work environments, may have found a certain intellectual stimulus in the peer relationships, if not in the coordinated and mechanized work process itself, which distinguished the factory setting. As a number of scholars have observed, complaints about tediously repetitive and monotonous factory labor were in some measure a middle-class cliché which obscured the possibility that many factory workers did not in fact experience their tasks as deadening and boring, perhaps because they had developed no *need* to derive significant intellectual satisfaction and meaning from their work itself.[108]

The general emphasis of this study upon attitudes toward industrial labor itself imposes, admittedly, some distortion upon economic reality. Although that emphasis reflects my conviction that one can hardly overstate the influence of developing industrialization upon informed opinion and attitudes regarding the condition of labor, it remains true that antebellum America, and even the northeast, was still predominantly "preindustrial" in 1860. Many members of the working classes, which may well have been the most migratory segment of a geographically mobile people, continued to perform more than one kind of physical labor, gravitating between city and hinterland during different times of the year. Overspecialization and entrapment in a factory was far less characteristic of the antebellum labor force than a certain labor versatility, although it also remains highly problematic whether such versatility entailed for many laborers skills that were consistently more marketable and lucrative than those developed by factory workers.[109]

There is, finally, that other abstraction referred to earlier, one which passes over the great variety in the demands made by both nonmanual and manual labor employments. "Mental labor" occupations themselves, of course, imposed in actuality a great range of intellectual demands upon their practitioners, a range that scarcely diminished as the size and complexity of the nation's lower middle class and small entrepreneurial sector increased in tandem with expanding urban-commercial activity. Some of the most intensely mental of these mental labor occupations could include employments of a relatively low-paying, clerical status, and these, needless to say, were hardly the occupations accorded the highest prestige.[110] The most highly skilled manual labor employments may have, in their turn, called upon the intellectual and creative resources of the worker no less than some of these nonmanual occupations did upon their practitioners. Even beyond this possibility, the physical demands of manual labor employments themselves varied greatly. Horace Mann and others suggested as much when they noted that workers employed in factory and other indoor sedentary labor were in no less need of physical exercise than professional and commercial men; thus was factory labor even held wanting in developing the physical, not to speak of the intellectual or moral, part of individuals.[111] The range of physical demands made by manual labor employments was invoked by Dr. Edward Jarvis in 1865 to explain his opposition to the enactment of an eight-hour law in Massachusetts:

> The severity or lightness of labor, the violence of exertion, as in wielding the sledge-hammer, lifting stone, or, on the other hand, tailoring, shoemaking, engraving, & c., the persistence or variableness of the exertions, employments that require the exercise of one set of muscles only, as in drilling rocks with the drill-bar, or of all the muscles of the body, as farming and gardening—all

these have their influence in the expenditure and exhaustion of force, and on the continuance of the supply of strength and power to labor, and all should be considered in determining the hours that should be given to work. . . .

. . . The English census divides the people among somewhat more than 1,200 various occupations. These, with their circumstances, conditions and influences on health of the workman, and his duration of power, vary so much and so widely, that no rule of hours can be applied to them, no single system can be adopted for the good of some, without being injurious to others, if all are required to conform to it.[112]

Intended as a warning against the harmful abstraction that a single mandatory labor standard must represent, Jarvis's detailed reference to the plethora of physical demands that were actually made by manual labor employments might also serve another function: it might stand as a reminder of the danger of falsely homogenizing these employments in a study of social attitudes that seeks to set "manual labor" off against nonmanual occupations. Yet without necessarily engaging in so wholesale a homogenization, many of these social attitudes themselves suggested that a broad dichotomy between manual and mental labor retained substantial historical force and explanatory value. In addressing the issue of overworked manual laborers, the Massachusetts commission report of 1866 made the following comparison:

Men in mercantile or other pursuits, masters of their business and their time, may attend to their respective callings ten or twelve hours in the day, or more, without injury. They are on and off, can run out of office or counting room just when they wish, walk on 'change, meet friends, making business itself a recreation while the hours run smoothly on in grooves of interest, oiled by the expectation of profit corresponding to fidelity of service. Such men are apt to say, quite complacently, "I think the workmen should not complain of ten or eleven hours; I work more than that." True, but work so diversified; linking every extra hour with the hope of extra gains, is a very different thing from solid, monotonous toil for a fixed number of hours, for a fixed compensation. True, if the laborer be a *workman,* and takes a workman's pride in his work, it is relieved of much of its monotony, and becomes, in a measure, educational in itself; but only slightly so, as compared with the business of the merchant, lawyer or physician, that brings so large a class of faculties into play, and stimulates them all by increasing the compensation in proportion to the work done.[113]

The "workmen" to whom the report referred were, above all others, factory wage-earners; the report's remarks can hardly be isolated from the postbellum context of ongoing industrial proletarianization and trade union unrest in which they were made.[114] But the comparison between industrial hirelings and professional and mercantile men also reflected assumptions about the differences between mental and physical labor generally. The greater extrinsic rewards and work autonomy that professional and commercial men enjoyed, the report makes clear, were themselves a source of their work's superior intellectual stimulus. Yet there is also the underlying suggestion of physical labor's inherent lack of certain vital rewards, quite apart from its generally inferior recompense and degree of work autonomy. In some measure, the report was responding to waged factory work as an encapsulation in undistilled form of physical labor's historic and intrinsic liabilities.

"We believe in the 'dignity of labor,' but we do not believe in the dignity of drudgery."[115] The Massachusetts commission report, in defending the principle of a shorter working day, insisted that this statement could only have real meaning with reference to manual labor occupations.[116] True enough, commercial and professional men could overwork themselves; and as the earlier participants in the manual labor school movement argued, excessive mental labor could overtax the brain, lead to the atrophy of the physical faculties, and ultimately prove as unhealthy as excessive physical labor. But there remained something more inherently brutish, more drudge-like and degrading, regarding those employments that overtaxed the physical faculties at the expense of the mental ones. And this special quality of degradation that excessive manual labor bore, the Massachusetts report suggested, included but went beyond the obvious fact that, in its present guise of waged industrial labor, excessive manual labor was overwhelmingly less voluntary in character than was overwork in non-manual occupations. Typically exacted by a powerful outside authority for a pittance, rather than calibrated to a more inner-directed ambition and confidence that such added diligence would secure commensurate rewards in the marketplace, physical overwork was for these reasons also more onerous than overwork among professional and business men. But even apart from this, there was that special degradation attached to excessive manual labor, one reflecting the circumstance that manual labor less significantly stimulated the use of the mental faculties to begin with. Individuals engaged in manual labor employments were deemed particularly vulnerable from the outset to that shutting out of the "higher nature" which was associated above all else with manual labor performed in excess.

But how much manual labor was too much? The continuous reductions in the length of the working day achieved by organized labor since the middle of the nineteenth century suggest that there is no fixed or objective answer to this question, and one might argue, as some have done, that what factory operatives and other workers have above all needed is not shorter hours but more varied and more stimulating work.[117] Yet the question of "excessive" labor touches upon one of the basic ambiguities or disagreements regarding the intrinsic character of handwork that distinguished attitudes during the first part of the nineteenth century. Even apart from the most obvious example, prostitution, a few forms of "legitimate" employment, such as juvenile chimney sweeping in England, were commonly stigmatized as hopelessly degrading even when performed in only "moderate" degree; so pronounced was the physically oppressive and lethal character of such special work, that but small amounts of it rendered it drudgery. The stigma attaching to domestic service, an occupation far more significant in terms of the numbers it employed, also derived only in part from the perception that this work left the employee insufficient time for other activities. To a more obvious degree than in the case of other manual labor employments, one of the major rationales for the existence of a household servant class was its assumption of tasks that the propertied classes deemed thankless, repellant drudgery and sought to avoid as a waste of their time and abilities.[118] That household and "menial service" drudgery merited the stigma attached to it, that it was indeed intrinsically contemptible work as well as necessary labor appropriate to a subordinate social class, was something, we have seen, upon which not even all American proponents of strongly elitist and hierarchical values agreed. But more pervasive egalitarian and success values in America lent their own kinds of reinforcement to the stigma attaching to domestic service, the former through its distaste for this most obvious form of social subordination, the latter through its measured contempt for those individuals who gravitated to servant positions.[119]

There were other indications, apart from the attitudes which stigmatized certain forms of manual labor over and beyond all others, of an underlying perception of manual labor employments generally as intrinsically disagreeable and demeaning, except when performed in the most moderate of amounts. There was the hope expressed by some advocates of "labor-saving" technology that human physical labor would disappear altogether. A more implicit and subtle disdain was expressed by individuals who suggested that more equitable social arrangements would so redistribute and abridge the amount of manual labor performed by each member of society as to render it a "mere amusement," if not a minor annoyance.[120] It is, perhaps, not surprising that such notions played so small a role in the arguments of mid-nineteenth-century labor movements, for they scarcely fortified the position of these movements that the intrinsic character of manual labor was one of virtue and dignity, and that a reduction of working hours was above all needed to restore this character to it.

Although the Massachusetts commission report was hardly atypical in drawing on a broad dichotomy between manual and nonmanual labor employments, it remains true that the stigma which attached to manual labor for less significantly calling upon the use of the mental faculties extended most obviously and unambiguously to the more unskilled modes of employment. Even in the country of the "common man," where the opportunities and rewards for physical labor remained greater than perhaps anywhere else, the age-old stigmas against such labor resurfaced in a variety of manifestations, beyond those already mentioned. Horace Greeley defended the dignity of Northern free labor against Southern proslavery barbs, but he would not go so far as another antislavery man, Harmon S. Conger, who declared his "every respect and admiration" for all "humble though honest labor"—the work of the bootblack as much as that of the bootmaker.[121] For Greeley as for Peter Walker and the proslavery advocates themselves, common sense dictated that the dignity of certain kinds of labor, particularly those of a most intrinsically mentally undemanding nature, was highly suspect, whatever their legal status.

The very absence of hereditary ranks in the United States, and the consequent readiness of those in a position to do so to seize on the few existing trappings of social superiority that they could, seemed, moreover, to lend their own measure of support to the deep-seated stigmas against unskilled physical work. Some employers in Southern cities *preferred* to employ whites over blacks as maids and coachmen, just as some Northern employers, aspiring or existing members of America's "mushroom aristocracy," favored males over females as domestic servants; the added degradation that such low work entailed for members of groups that were ordinarily able to avoid it added proportionately to the prestige value servants possessed for their employers.[122]

But there were other indications that the venerable stigmas against physical labor encompassed manual labor employments per se in America, regardless of their skill content. The ascendancy of the cult of true womanhood, the prestige it bestowed upon middle-class families for the ability of its female members to lead a leisured existence, was still another sign that being a middle-class "lady" meant not having to do certain kinds of paid work, specifically work of a physical nature. It was just such a circumstance which led Caroline H. Dall to observe that women's existing manual labor employments would "never be better paid til women of rank begin to work for money, and so create a respect for woman's labor." But, Dall added, "women of rank will never do this till American men feel what all American men profess,—a proper respect for Labor."[123]

Then there was the issue of slavery, specifically the antebellum discussions over the degree to which debasing competition from black slave labor threatened the rewards and status of free white labor in the Northern states, and whether even Northern white labor might itself fall victim to enslavement by an aggressive "slaveocracy." A full examination of these discussions requires another study, one which would take into account the debates among reform groups concerning whether Southern slavery was the primary cause or rather merely a symptom of a generalized and growing "disesteem" for manual labor in America. But of relevance here is what was almost completely absent from the voluminous debates over slavery: the suggestion that nonmanual labor employments in the Northern states might themselves be ultimately jeopardized by slave competition. One of the few to introduce into these debates the idea of slave professionals, the Republican and ex-Democratic politician from Missouri, Francis P. Blair, Jr., once suggested that the exclusion of black slaves from nonmanual labor employments was above all a function of power: slaveholders did not educate their bondsmen and place them into business and the professions because the slaves would then be competing with the slaveholders themselves.[124] One might extend this argument, and note the obvious point that the Northern propertied classes themselves possessed too much political and economic power to permit, quite apart from their own actual enslavement, the intrusion of slave competition into their own fields of livelihood.

But even beyond considerations of political and economic power, certain social assumptions regarding the superior mental stimulus afforded by nonmanual labor employments explained why Blair's remarks were so unusual for their time—why the concept of a population of slave lawyers or merchants, black or white, would have seemed so implausible to contemporaries, and why the observation of another antislavery politician, that even "a physician, a lawyer, or a minister" would be degraded if he were owned, seems so unfamiliar a concept even to us now.[125] That these assumptions included the mid-nineteenth-century racist certitude that blacks were not equal to the mental demands of professional and commercial employments suggests the nature of the comparison being implicitly drawn between nonmanual and manual labor occupations and the measure of relative disdain this comparison carried for even the most highly skilled mechanic arts. Many of these discussions simply assumed—an assumption that, incidentally, was supported by a good deal of historical evidence—that any and all types of free white manual labor were vulnerable to debasing black slave competition and could indeed themselves be performed in an oppressive chattelized state and that nonmanual labor occupations were by virtue of their intrinsic nature exposed to neither of these degrading possibilities.

The many contemporary voices, then, who noted even as some deplored the extent to which "brainwork" enjoyed more appeal than handwork, were driving at something deeper than the fact that nonmanual labor employments appeared more attractive simply because they offered the prospect of greater extrinsic rewards.[126] The British traveler Charles Mackay was intent on deflating the egalitarian pretensions of American culture; but his biases do not completely remove the truth of his observation: "The native-born American, of Anglo-Saxon descent, looks upon all rough labour, except that of the farm, as somewhat derogatory from his dignity. It is for him to labour with his brains, rather than with his thews and sinews; to barter, not to dig and delve; and to set others to do the hard work rather than to do the hard work himself."[127]

The complaints emanating from the agricultural press suggest that Mackay need not have excluded even venerable freehold farm labor from what he perceived as a general American distaste and disdain for physical labor. Of the existence of this disdain, particularly as it was directed toward the more unskilled forms of manual labor, Peter Walker added his approval: "Is it not beneficial that there is so universal a feeling of contempt for some employments, to deter men from making so unworthy a choice?"[128] Walker, of course, ignored the extent to which many of those individuals employed in the most drudge-like of physical labor—that labor most lacking in head work and consequently labor of the lowest status of all—were so situated precisely because their powers of occupational choice were so limited, constrained by poverty, ignorance, and by prevailing prejudice and discrimination against the low status groups to which they very likely belonged.

There remains, however, need to at least raise and briefly explore one further ambiguity, one regarding the extent to which members of the laboring population themselves shared in the disdain for physical labor. To what degree did the attitudes and concerns that ran through the "middle ground" of discourse upon which this study has concentrated—a terrain dominated by middle-class commentators who for the most part fell short of formalizing and systematizing their ideas in a "high ground" of canonical "texts"—succeed in penetrating a yet "lower ground" of values: "the culture of everyday life"?[129] Quite possibly, the middle-class writers and intellectuals who claimed that manual laborers of all skill levels did share in the disdain for physical labor—even those middle-class writers and intellectuals who themselves denied that this disdain was justified—were engaging in a middle-class conceit, greatly exaggerating the degree to which manual workers wished to be something that they were not.

Although their evidence is hardly conclusive, a number of historical studies have indicated that immigrant and other unskilled laborers at least, workers with the lowest expectations who appeared to view success in terms of achieving a modest economic security, were among those most resistant to the American individualist, "entrepreneurial" striving for occupational advancement and material wealth, ambitions that implied a discontent, if not outright disdain, for manual labor employments.[130] In part because of the predatory working conditions to which they were exposed after their arrival in America, in part because of the disdain for their employments which both those conditions and pervasive success values reflected, antebellum Irish construction laborers and servant girls were among those workers who did develop some discernible resentment and dissatisfaction regarding their employments.[131] Such malaise, it is true, did not evolve into any significant radical working-class consciousness, if only because, as one historian has noted, class-based movements foundered on the difficulty of organizing "mobile laborers who had no trade."[132] Yet neither did this malaise, particularly in the case of the migrant generation of Irish Catholic males who did so much of the "rude" physical labor, appear to translate during the antebellum period into any great mainstreaming, or "bourgeoisification," of immigrant values.[133]

It seems clear enough, on the other hand, that native-born north-eastern farmers and their sons did manifest a pronounced preference for more "genteel," urban white-collar employments, including generally less intellectually demanding clerical work as well as the "liberal professions," and that this preference reflected not only a distaste for the more laborious work with which they were familiar, but the acknowledgement that farming carried diminishing social esteem. As much as Horace Greeley loathed the "demagoguery" of militant radicals like Theophilus Fisk, the occupational preferences expressed by farmers produced in the exasperated *New-York Tribune* editor a denunciation of the favored "mental labor" occupations that was hardly less severe than Fisk's own: "We are confronted by the low idea which everywhere prevails of the true rank of useful manual toil. . . . The farmer will not feel gratified, though he should, if assured that he can give his son no fitter, no better calling than his own; the hope of the family must be trained to the chicanery of Law or the futility of Medicine, [although he might have] no genius or taste [for such work]."[134]

In a similar wish to keep male youths down on the farm and "ploughing the fields," Freeman Hunt added in 1856 his recognition of the appeal that urban commercial pursuits held for "ambitious" young men from the country: "They offer the hope of wealth, influence, ease, and a high social standing."[135] As a leading journalist for the New York business community, Hunt sought as much as anyone to defend mercantile pursuits from criticism, to demonstrate that lasting economic success enjoyed by individuals in the field of trade reflected neither "chicanery" nor luck, but solid character formation. Yet hardly less strongly than Greeley, Hunt also insisted that the aspirations of farmers and their sons were misguided. In referring, indeed, to the artificiality of mercantile as well as professional pursuits, their slavish and debasing dependence upon the "caprice of customers and the chicane of trade," Hunt not only echoed Greeley but a myriad of voices, within and outside the agricultural press, extending at least as far back as the late eighteenth century. Hunt distinguished himself from the more extreme of these other voices in the degree of play he gave his parallel theme: that merchants, like lawyers and doctors, earned their rewards and performed valuable social functions when their numbers were moderate. But the swollen ranks of commercial middlemen, he agreed, only depleted the body of truly necessary, productive manual laborers. The influx of farm youth into commercial pursuits was resulting "in an unnecessary multiplication of those who come between the producer and the consumer, adding nothing to the value of the commodity. It is not too much to say that a quarter of those engaged in commerce, in our cities, could do the work which all do, [the remainder leading] an unproductive, if not useless life."[136]

The demographic evidence of rural-urban migration, together with the abundance of supporting contemporary testimony, suggests that Greeley and Hunt were not far off the mark regarding the occupational preferences of the more ambitious segment of the northeastern farm population, regardless of whether or not one shares these writers' objections to those preferences. It is less clear how pervasively and deeply highly skilled manufacturing workers, along with other participants in antebellum labor movements, may have also shared the disesteem for manual labor employments. Neither their articulation of a "pride in craft," nor even their resentment and denunciation of the social arrangements that rewarded nonmanual labor employments more than their own, removes the possibility that skilled workers did share some of the disesteem.[137] The ambiguity surrounding this question is amplified all the more by the fact, well known to historians, that some if not most of the spokesmen of the mid-nineteenth-century labor organizations to which skilled wage earners belonged had dubious worker credentials or backgrounds; they were often either disgruntled master craftsmen or radicals of even more undisputed middle-class status.[138]

It nonetheless remains true that the writers who feared that manual laborers generally preferred "softer," more genteel callings might have taken a certain comfort from much of the rhetoric of these labor movements, rhetoric that contained more than a hint of "anti-intellectualism" in its attacks upon the effeminate and parasitic nature of nonmanual labor employments.[139] But these attacks, it must also be recalled, frequently coexisted with an expressed yearning for the worker's intellectual development; and they were also perhaps no more fundamental to the body of labor movement rhetoric than the criticism that commercial and professional men were above all guilty of misusing their mental labor. Individuals who insistently defended the social value of commercial and professional employments could themselves display an unmistakable defensiveness regarding the "dollar worship" toward which members of the business and learned professions applied and devoted their mental labor.[140] But alongside this defensiveness was that expressed in the literature of skilled, "mechanic" labor, as well as in the organs of "semi-skilled" factory labor, regarding manual labor employments. "Cash"—the superior material rewards enjoyed by nonmanual labor occupations—was not, these labor voices insisted, "the only evidence of intellect, . . . the only token of moral worth."[141] Yet even some of these voices most insistent on the inherent dignity and superior virtue of productive manual labor, some of those which most vociferously and repeatedly attacked the prevailing social values by which "the Jack-plane is less honorable than the Lawyer's green-bag," gave a certain limited, if oftentimes unintended, support to those values.[142] Frequently underlying the invocation by spokesmen for organized labor of the theme of balanced and symbiotic faculties—the insistence that physical labor was an aid and not a hindrance to the acquisition of virtue and intelligence—was a note of defensiveness regarding the degree to which nonmanual labor employments did in fact demand "brain work" more naturally and completely than manual labor ones.[143] And that defensiveness was compounded by a general sense that the economic forces and social arrangements from which professionals, manufacturing entrepreneurs, and other capitalists profited were also depriving skilled manual labor of what mental content it did possess.

It should be clear enough by now that mid-nineteenth-century social attitudes toward manual labor employments, the dignity with which these attitudes invested physical work, were inextricably bound with social attitudes toward nonmanual labor employments. And it is equally evident that these attitudes hardly placed commercial and professional occupations above criticism, or in all cases conceded that the superior status they enjoyed must continue unabated. A preindustrial line of thought persisted, one that fed into criticism of the excessively narrow intellectual nature of the learned professions, that the old "mechanic arts" might set the natural, uncorrupted standard for virtually all forms of handwork, and that these should approach the learned professions in their intrinsic mental or creative content. In an argument with relevance for early Victorian America as well as England, the *North British Review* noted that "it would be an unspeakable boon to society if the distinction between 'liberal' and 'illiberal' professions, between 'gentleman' and 'operatives' . . . could be done away with, and new terms substituted which should rather suppose that all men were 'operatives'—the distinctions lying between such as worked with, and such as worked without thought and invention."[144]

White-collar professional work, especially as it existed at present, was no more intellectually stimulating and inventive than manual labor employments might be. In fact, the superior prestige or mystique enjoyed by the "liberal professions," the *Review* suggested, acted in Britain at least as a kind of straitjacket on those of its practitioners who might find handwork more enjoyable and stimulating, if only as an avocation: "Many a 'gentleman' would feign work hard, on some handicraft to his taste, but he is restrained by the foolish trammels of society, which would call him a 'common man,' so soon as his idle limbs should bestir themselves and do work."[145] Upper- and middle-class women, the *Review* maintained, were in this respect better off than the male members of their classes. The cult of domesticity added to the disdain for physical work by exalting the freedom that middle- and upper-class females enjoyed from its paid varieties, including servant's work. Nonetheless, domestic ideology did not, in the opinion of the *Review,* impose on British upper- and middle-class women quite the same burden of having to maintain the constant appearance of "gentility" under which their male counterparts labored:

> Few would deny that the lady of the house . . . should be able to wash her child, better than a servant can wash it, should make the best pastry, and, if requisite, do all domestic work in a superior manner to her handmaids, and show skill in dress and cap-making, that might vex her milliner,—few would respect the woman less, who should own to these accomplishments, and even give proof of having practised them successfully; yet, forsooth, the man must grow weak and languid for want of the very work he would delight in, lest his neighbours overlooking his garden or shed, should call him a "common man," because he could excel his men-servants and tradesmen in their several departments.[146]

It is unlikely that gentlemanly status in America ever required quite the distance from physical work complained of by the *North British Review.* Democratic, less class-stratified traditions, as evidenced by the great political value that men running for high office could derive from their past familiarity with manual labor and poverty, clearly imposed limits in the United States on the degree to which manual and mental labor were perceived as alien to each other. A different kind of support, moreover, for the argument that nonmanual labor employments were not always considered to enjoy unlimited natural intellectual advantages over manual labor ones comes from scholars who have noted that during the mid-nineteenth century the learned professions in America possessed nothing like the legitimacy and prestige—let alone the actual expertise—that they would subsequently acquire; and that this was a time during which many of the efforts of professionals to maintain or increase their "privileged competence" and exclusive licensing authority in America were actually rebuffed in the wave of democratic resentment and opposition to all monopolies and exclusive privileges. Paralleling the criticism of professional work as intellectually narrow and oppressive were the more populist attacks on such work as needlessly esoteric and exclusive in its knowledge, qualities that these attacks attributed to a desire on the part of professional men for undeserved material rewards and status. "It had become an article of faith" in Jacksonian America, Paul Starr has written, "that every sphere of social life—law, government, religion, science, industry—obeyed principles of natural reason that were intelligible to ordinary men of common sense."[147] The pervasive hostility regarding professional claims to undisputed authority reflected, in Starr's view, the competing claims that all of these fields of knowledge and activity—or at least those parts that were truly valuable to society—remained naturally accessible to all. Put another way, and one that is consistent with the theme emphasized several times above, the hostility to the pretensions of professionalism reflected the assumption that members of all social classes possessed intellectual faculties capable of assimilating and comprehending any useful and necessary knowledge.[148]

Yet set against the popular antebellum resistance to the status and recognition demanded by the "learned professions" was the persisting mystique they enjoyed well prior to the period in which they actually consolidated their positions in the developing occupational hierarchy.[149] A "Mechanic" writing to the *New York Journal of Commerce* well described this mystique even as he, along with Greeley and many others, deplored or resisted it. It was a mistake, "Mechanic" insisted, to "send the children of persons possessing small means to college, . . . [because] it is of this description of college educated individuals that the ranks of pettifoggers and quacks are filled. They are too proud of their superior education to work either as clerks or mechanics, or to follow any active business except what is termed professional."[150]

In lending its support to the establishment of the New York Free Academy in 1847, the Democratic *Daily Globe* claimed that just such an institution was needed to break the stranglehold that lawyers had on the "road to preferment." Of the American presidents up to that time, the paper noted, only Washington failed to come from the ranks of lawyers, and a similar pattern existed among all the higher political offices. Broadening higher education opportunities for "the class of poor boys" would enable a mechanic to become president of the United States and would in general weaken the excessive intellectual influence the "liberal professions" exercised over farmers and mechanics.[151]

It may be more true than otherwise that the weight of established tradition conferred upon the learned professions in mid-nineteenth-century England a degree and a security of status that for the most part eluded their American counterparts.[152] But American professional men did hold one particular advantage over English practitioners. Alexis de Tocqueville indicated the nature of this advantage when he observed that "in America there are neither nobles nor men of letters, and the people distrust the wealthy. Therefore the lawyers form the political upper class and the most intellectual section of society. . . . It is at the bar or the bench that the America aristocracy is found." Although lawyers, or at least barristers, enjoyed a high standing in English society, Tocqueville claimed, they were "not in the first rank" because that rank was already occupied by a leisured landed and titled aristocracy.[153] The persistence of this aristocracy together with the feudal traditions and values it embodied imposed upper limits on the prestige that any occupation, any kind of work for one's living, might enjoy in England. "The English social code," John Clarke has noted, "decreed that the nearer a man was to the actual process of production the less his claim to be a gentleman."[154] Thus capitalists and professional men, although one or more steps further removed from this process than manual laborers were, still fell short of the social pinnacle. But in America, which lacked a leisured aristocracy in any significant numbers and was a more definitively "bourgeois" society, individuals who earned their living from their mental labor could more easily occupy the privileged front rank of society, assuming the mantle and status of America's "gentlemen."[155]

In offering a concluding note in explanation of the mystique enjoyed by the antebellum professions, and the corresponding stigma attached to manual labor, we might wish to recall once more the social reality that professional occupations simply involved lighter, less disagreeable work. Here, again, lay much of the appeal that even "genteel," less "manly" and less "active," often low-paying, clerical work carried for farm boys and others from manual labor backgrounds, youths whose concentration in this work, many contemporaries cried, came at the expense of less able-bodied, lower-class females who were more "naturally" suited for it but who were presently crowded into needlework and other kinds of exploitative and physically debilitating labor.[156] Above all, however, we might wish to recall our most fundamental point: that yet another source of the mystique of the learned professions, as well as of the popular resentment of their pretensions to exclusive authority, was the overall sense that, whatever the particular disadvantages and pressures they faced, practitioners in these occupations had greater existing opportunity to develop and exercise their intellectual faculties than did members of the working classes. Woven into the fabric of mid-nineteenth-century American culture was the notion that manual laborers of all skill levels and ages might "raise" and "improve" themselves through education. There was never any comparable emphasis on the idea that professional men, however narrowly and defectively they practiced their craft and employed their skills, needed to similarly improve and "dignify" themselves through education.

Still, one can hardly ignore, apart from the radical labor reform voices, both those deeply conservative thinkers and those more mainstream thinkers like William Ellery Channing who in their own different ways and for different reasons insisted upon the intrinsic dignity of physical labor, whatever popular doubts and prejudices existed to the contrary. If this study has done nothing else, it should have revealed something of the multiplicity and complexity of viewpoints and perspectives, the many deviations from even agreed upon premises, all of which pointed away from the "dignity" of free labor as a condition of objective reality. In equal measure, all of this variety and complexity of perspectives makes any concluding generalizations about American social attitudes subject to easy qualification and contradiction; some of the very evidence contained in this study is quite capable of supporting generalizations contrary to my own. It may well be that the story told here necessarily lacks overarching truths or that such truths, if they exist at all, are of less coherence, interest, even importance than the multiple perspectives and crosscutting positions that have been detailed. It might certainly seem to some readers that in this particular story, the "whole" is not only not greater than the sum of parts, but of considerably lesser magnitude, if it exists at all.

Yet I would persist in concluding that American social attitudes did not provide a ringing affirmation of physical labor's intrinsic dignity.[157] Those attitudes hardly insisted that the poverty, ignorance, low status, and relative powerlessness of groups that concentrated in certain forms of manual labor above all others were completely responsible for the disdain directed at these employments. Those attitudes generally did not deny that these employments in particular contained inherently painful, mentally unstimulating, or otherwise disagreeable features that generated their own stigma and that drew these groups to them because more desirable employments were closed off. To only a limited extent did conditions in America, more than those in the Old World, challenge the notion that manual labor employments were overall of a more disagreeable and undesirable character than nonmanual labor occupations, and that this circumstance had much to do with the fact that manual labor employments, certainly as they existed at the time and to some extent, naturally as well, embodied a lower proportion of mental to more animalistic physical activity.

Still less did American conditions give any more currency than more traditional societies to the radical idea that manual labor employments deserved more status and respect precisely to the degree that they were disagreeable and painful and imposed a greater sacrifice on the individuals engaged in them. Nor did those conditions, and the competitive morality they fostered, prove any more hospitable to the equally utopian notion that the needs of individual members of society, rather than their contributions to the intellectual foundations of "civilization," should be the ultimate determinant of the returns on their labor.[158] To some degree, if in far more muted and inconsistent a fashion, American social attitudes generally mirrored the insistence of the racist, white egalitarian defense of slavery that some of the more menial types of manual labor were intrinsically undesirable and contemptible, deserving of little status and recompense; although whether these attitudes also insisted that such employments were irredeemably or inevitably undesirable and contemptible, without all hope of intellectual elevation or improvement, is a more open question.

In an essay published at the time of the outbreak of the Civil War, Andrew Preston Peabody declared his distaste for Southern slavery—"this foul blot on our national character"—but nonetheless signified his agreement with several generations of proslavery defenses when he observed that "the peculiar institution" had "its origin in the essential conditions of human society. So long as there is an unequal distribution of talent, advantage, opportunity, and enterprise, there must be no less wide inequalities in the distribution of property; there must be the rich and the poor,—. . . the employers and the employed, . . . the privileged classes and the proletaries"; and these, Peabody observed, existed in all civilized societies.[159] Peabody went on to indicate, something in the manner of his "The Future of Labor" essay nine years earlier, how some of this economic inequality might be compensated for, how some of it might be reduced, by bringing the "laboring classes . . . in privilege, intelligence, and virtue, ever nearer to the level of their employers."[160] But Peabody's particular remedies for the problem of gross economic disparities and the suffering and exploitation that attended them need not concern us here. Of interest instead is the manner in which he addressed the sources of economic inequality, class power, and the subordinate social position of the working classes: through the invocation of differences among individuals in innate talent, enterprise, opportunity, and advantage. Like writers and thinkers before and after Peabody's time, nineteenth-century Americans across the ideological spectrum commonly used, if sometimes less explicitly, the same approach to the same circumstances of inequality. And although Americans disagreed, on the basis of ideology, over the proper weight to assign each of these individual differences—Americans of a more elitist persuasion, for example, tending to maximize the differences in innate talent and enterprise, arguing that differences in advantage and opportunity were a legitimate offshoot of these—there was considerably less disagreement that even in the "favored" environs of the New World, the economic and social position of manual labor was indeed relatively low in the scale of society.[161]

This inquiry has, essentially, attempted to provide answers to the question of how the widespread recognition of manual labor's subordinate position reflected beliefs about the intrinsic nature or content of that labor. Those beliefs—the discussions and conceptualizations of "free labor"— were, to be sure, given a distinctive context in the antebellum period by the social, economic, political, and intellectual developments that dominated it—the deterioration of the urban craft structure, the sectional conflict over slave labor, the influx of unskilled Irish, and the crystallization of the ideology of "separate spheres," to name but a few. Yet such was the deep-seated aversion to physical labor—an aversion to which George Frederick

Holmes and other antebellum commentators explicitly referred—and so primeval was the attendant social concern for distributing, and legitimating the distribution, of necessary but unappealing work, that specific historical contexts would seem to recede in importance. In northern Colorado in the 1920s, Sarah Deutsch informs us, "Anglo" American sugar beet employers and school officials justified the employment of Chicano child laborers with the following remarks: "They're needed in the fields and the school don't do them any good anyway"; "If every child has a high school education, who will labor?"; "[N]o man can accumulate anything in this world until by some means or device he is enabled to enjoy the benefit of some other man's labor."[162] If such remarks sound familiar, it is because they indeed reflect perennial and enduring attitudes on the part of individuals who occupy positions of power and privilege (although they are sometimes shared by members of the working classes as well), attitudes that go back hundreds of years and appear in many different social milieus. And although we have seen that these were by no means the only responses provoked by the issue of how and to whom society should distribute its various employments, their persevering and familiar nature nonetheless suggests why the ultimate emphasis of a study of attitudes toward manual labor in Western societies, both precapitalist and capitalist, perhaps best belongs on the stability and persistence of attitudes, rather than upon their evolution and change. If developments that transpired in mid-nineteenth-century America explained why perceptions of "free" manual labor in 1845 no doubt deviated in some ways from perceptions in 1825, and why perceptions were again somehow unique in 1865, one is still struck with what was basic to attitudes at all those points in time and with what in fact endured into the social milieu of the Colorado beet growers: the pervasive stigmatization of manual labor, especially its most unintellectual kinds, and the efforts to confront, perhaps in most cases to justify, its corresponding relegation to socially subordinate and stigmatized groups.

Yet the "dignity" of legally free employments that were heavily dependent on manual labor was undeniably rooted in American mythology; the extent to which such a condition prevailed in the antebellum period represented one of the ways in which Americans of the time, like generations before them, held their society superior to all others. The particular affirmations of American manual labor's dignity by a range of propertied middle-class commentators—by a William Ellery Channing, a Daniel Webster, or for that matter, an Andrew Jackson—were quite possibly none the less sincere for being so heavily rhetorical.[163] In many cases, those affirmations rested in part on a conviction shared by more radical voices both within and outside the organized labor movements of the period: that agricultural and other hard and "productive" physical work constituted the most elemental and compelling medium through which human beings thwarted their natural propensity for indolence, and that the intrinsic virtue of such work might be realized most fully of all—as in much of America— where it was both economically autonomous and enjoyed adequate material rewards. Some of these middle-class commentators themselves quite genuinely held what was even more pronounced and widespread among the radical reformers and labor movements of the period: a corresponding suspicion of the "softer," less tangibly productive, urban white-collar employments that were attracting American male youth in ever increasing numbers.

But affirmation of the virtuous nature of American employments dependent on physical effort was coupled by many middle-class commentators, and to some extent by antebellum labor voices as well, with something else: a deep regard for intellectual development and activity. That development and activity were variously exalted as a component of individual enterprise, productivity, and skill; as a means to the material improvement of both individuals and societies; and, not least of all, perhaps, as a good or pleasure in itself, as a defining characteristic of civilized man. If a single question dominated the discourse with which this inquiry has dealt, it was the nature of the fit between virtuous, productive physical labor and elevating intellectual activity—the degree to which they were compatible and indeed, interdependent. Perhaps all but the most elitist of the commentators of the period, whatever their backgrounds and social status, and whether they were motivated by a desire to completely transform or merely to stabilize the existing occupational structure, insisted that both traditional and newer kinds of manual labor employments could and should retain, incorporate, or somehow be balanced with a significant share of this valued intellectual stimulation and activity, that the latter need not and ought not be monopolized or appropriated by the more glamorous or "genteel" occupations resting exclusively on "head labor."

But the insistence in a good part of this antebellum discourse on the fit between virtuous, productive physical labor and elevating intellectual activity, and on the intrinsic attractiveness of manual labor employments that centuries of poverty, oppression, and subordination had obscured in the Old World especially, was belied by major social circumstances that made mid-nineteenth-century America more rather than less like the Old World. These circumstances included the deterioration under market forces of conditions in many kinds of manual labor employments, the confinement of relatively powerless, often disdained social groups to these employments, and the continued preference exhibited by the more propertied, educated, and otherwise advantaged elements of society for occupations resting exclusively on mental labor, be these occupations entrepreneurial, professional, or even clerical in nature. The widening access to, and movement into, these latter occupations was not without irony; for although the expansion and democratization of capitalist and professional opportunities during the age of the "common man" was, on the one hand, an expression of distinctive, possibly even "exceptional" American conditions, these occupational preferences were also a ratification of what was not at all exceptional to American society. Those preferences certified, that is to say, something which had also been basic to older, more stratified societies that had expressed no commensurate belief in the "dignity" of manual labor, that had articulated no commensurate resistance to the idea that individuals who worked with their hands merited characterization as part of the "lower" orders. Occupational preferences in antebellum America, like those in older societies, certified the desire of those who were able—whether because of inherited advantages or because of expertise and resources they themselves had acquired—to "rise" from or otherwise avoid occupations grounded in physical labor.[164]

Yet it can also hardly be denied that through their general appeals to the "dignity of labor," both the long-standing mythology of American exceptionalism and, in the antebellum period specifically, the particular thrust of Northern antislavery "free labor" ideology, did register some impact, did effect some movement, in Western social attitudes regarding manual labor's subordinate position. Doctor George Calvert Holland, the authority on the grinding trades of Sheffield, England, reflected the perspective of membership in a more traditional, rigidly hierarchical and stratified society when he observed that "the many, whose fate it is to labour, will necessarily be in the rear of civilization—disfigured by vices, irregularities, and tendencies, which intelligence and the affluence of means in some degree restrain."[165] Against this fatalistic assessment one can set the opinion of Frederick Law Olmsted. Writing in specific criticism of the "drudgery" performed by poor white laborers in the South and of slavery's responsibility for the demoralized condition of that population, Olmsted first made the same observation that Peter Walker and others had made in different contexts. Olmsted noted the tendency of some writers "to attach an entirely undeserved 'honor to labor.' Mere plodding manual labor," he insisted, "is not in itself honorable. Dexterity, ingenuity in the application of labor, industry and perseverance are honorable traits in all men, but labor in itself is not honorable." But Olmsted then proceeded to add: "On the other hand, in no enlightened free community"—in the free states, that is to say—"is labor in itself practically degrading, because hireling labor is everywhere the stepping-stone from poverty and mediocrity to comfort and a position of usefulness."[166] Against the mindless, not to say demeaning, character of at least some forms of physical labor, Olmsted juxtaposed the redeeming and elevating incentives that even this labor might have in the most favored section of the most favored nation: the material rewards and advancement opportunities that encouraged some of the most unskilled workers in the Northern states to make their employments more productive and correspondingly less mindless—to at least partially remedy, so to speak, the intrinsic deficiencies and disadvantages in those employments.[167] In part because of its inherent characteristics, in part because of the influence of centuries-old attitudes attesting to those characteristics, some if not all of the most socially necessary labor in the North, as in the South and the Old World, was still commonly disdained in word just as it was avoided, whenever possible, in practice. Requiring further exploration is the question raised by Olmsted's juxtaposition: how this paradox of necessary yet stigmatized manual labor was affected by attitudes regarding the peculiar mix of extrinsic work incentives and rewards with which free manual labor in America was commonly associated.

Notes

CHAPTER I: INTRODUCTION

1. Throughout this study I use the phrase *mid-nineteenth century* to refer to the thirty or so years before the outbreak of the Civil War. Departing somewhat from conventional usage, I also frequently employ the term *antebellum* to refer to the same period of time.

2. The most fundamental historical irony of all has arisen from the tendency of cultural norms to define work as paid employment exclusively, thereby disregarding, and in a sense rendering "invisible," the housework and child rearing performed by wives and mothers under the sexual division of labor; valuable studies, some of which employ Marxist perspectives, include Jeanne Boydston, "Home and Work: The Industrialization of Housework in the Northeastern United States from the Colonial Period to the Civil War" (Ph.D. diss., Yale University, 1984); Susan Strasser, "Never Done: The Ideology and Technology of Household Work, 1850–1930" (Ph.D. diss., State University of New York at Stony Brook, 1977); Maureen M. Mackintosh, "Domestic Labour and the Household," in Sandra Burman, ed., *Fit Work for Women* (New York: St. Martin's Press, 1979), 174–75; Nancy Holstrom, "Women's Work, the Family, and Capitalism," *Science and Society* 45 (Summer 1981):191–204; Julia A. Matthaei, *An Economic History of Women in America: Women's Work, the Sexual Division of Labor, and the Development of Capitalism* (New York: Schocken Books, 1982), 104–39; Ann Oakley, *Woman's Work: The Housewife, Past and Present* (New York: Pantheon Books, 1974). R. E. Pahl, however, has recently argued that prevailing definitions of productive work have not only unjustly excluded the tasks of housewives, but have also rendered invisible a variety of self-employed and unpaid activities, performed by males as well as females, that have helped sustain family economies over the centuries; R. E. Pahl, *Divisions of Labour* (Oxford: Basil Blackwell, 1984), 19–127, 321–33.

There is also the more broadly philosophical sense in which any activity, paid or otherwise, that involves some pain or "irksomeness," or at least a degree of compulsion and abridgment of personal freedom, may be considered "work." Note the heavily subjective nature of work in this sense—one individual's household avocation or hobby (e.g., gardening) becomes the "chore" or "work" of another individual who has no taste or enthusiasm for the activity. In the distinction he drew between "work" and "play," the nineteenth-century clergyman Horace Bushnell anticipated many modern sociologists and philosophers: "Work suffers a feeling of aversion, and play excludes aversion. For the moment any play becomes wearisome or distasteful, then it is work; an activity that is kept up, not as being its own joy, but for some ulterior end, or under some kind of restraint" (Horace Bushnell, "Work and Play," an oration before the Society of the Phi Beta Kappa at the University of Cambridge, Aug. 24, 1848, in *Work and Play; or Literary Varieties* [New York: Charles Scribner, 1864], 14); good modern discussions include Yves R. Simon, *Work, Society, and Culture*, ed. Vukan Kuic (New York: Fordham University Press, 1971), 4–32, 116–19; Alasdair Clayre, *Work and Play: Ideas and Experience of Work and Leisure* (New York: Harper and Row, 1974); Cyril Barrett, "The Concept of Leisure: Idea and Ideal," in Tom Winnifrith and Cyril Barrett, ed., *The Philosophy of Leisure* (Houndmills, Eng.: Macmillan Press, 1989), 16–17; Bennett M. Berger, "The Sociology of Leisure: Some Suggestions," in Erwin O. Smigel, ed., *Work and Leisure* (New Haven: College and University Press Services, 1963), 28–29; and Joffre Dumazedier, *Toward a Society of Leisure*, trans. Stewart E. McClure (New York: Free Press, 1967), 14–20, 92–95.

Bushnell's characterization of work as directed to "some ulterior end" brings us, finally, to the question of a basic difference in connotation between the terms *labor* and *work* in the Western intellectual tradition. In the best-known statement of such a view, Hannah Arendt argued that from a very early point, "labor" and its nearest equivalent expressions in other languages were identified as productive human activity that bore close associations with "toil and trouble" and pain—hence the specific derivation of women's reproductive "labor." Undertaken to meet the individual's biological needs, labor possessed instrumental value only and was never performed for its own sake. "Work," on the other hand, was productive activity that carried a less negative connotation, according to Arendt: it could be valued for itself, for the creative and other intrinsic satisfactions it offered the individual who performed it.

Whatever the extent to which labor and work have indeed carried these different connotations in various Western cultures, nineteenth-century Americans for their part failed (as Bushnell's example testified) to observe this difference in their discussions. Fully capable of recognizing the distinction between productive activity's instrumental value and its intrinsic rewards, Americans nonetheless failed to use the terms *labor* and *work* to give expression to this distinction. My inquiry follows the antebellum practice of employing the terms *labor* and *work* interchangeably and ignoring the linguistic subtleties analyzed so brilliantly by Arendt; see Hannah Arendt, *The Human Condition* (Chicago: University of Chicago Press, 1958), 79–174; Bikhu Parekh, "Hannah Arendt's Critique of Marx," in Melvyn A. Hill, ed., *Hannah Arendt: The Recovery of the Public World* (New York: St. Martin's Press, 1979), 68–99; and in the same collection, Robert W. Major, "A Reading of Hannah Arendt's 'Unusual' Distinction between Labor and Work," 132–33. See also Raymond Williams, *Keywords: A Vocabulary of Culture and Society* (New York: Oxford University Press, 1976), 145–48, 281–84.

3. The adequacy of legal self-ownership as even a minimal definition of free labor is challenged, for example, by the various forms of compulsory or "unfree" labor—serfdom, debt peonage, convict labor, indentured servitude, and the like—which commonly arose in different Western societies as alternatives to legalized chattel bondage. If in many of these instances the laborer still "owned himself" in the strict legal sense, the legal disabilities that his status incurred compromised his

legal autonomy and rendered it less than meaningful as a definition of free labor. For the importance of the spectrum of coerced labor, lying between the poles of "free" wage labor and chattel slavery, see M. I. Finley, "Between Slavery and Freedom" *Comparative Studies in Society and History* 6 (Apr. 1964): 248–49; Sidney W. Mintz, "The So-Called World System: Local Initiative and Local Response," *Dialectical Anthropology* 2 (Nov. 1977): 257–61; Mintz, "Was the Plantation Slave a Proletarian?" *Review* (Binghamton, N.Y.) 2 (Summer 1978): 81–98; O. Nigel Bolland, "Systems of Discrimination after Slavery: The Control of Landed Labor in the British West Indies after 1838," *Comparative Studies in Society and History* 23 (Oct. 1981): 615–17; Philip Corrigan, "Feudal Relics or Capitalist Monuments? Notes on the Sociology of Unfree Labour," *Sociology* 11 (Sept. 1977): 435–63; and Robert Miles, *Capitalism and Unfree Labour: Anomaly or Necessity?* (London: Tavistock Publishers, 1987).

Consider, too, the whole category of child labor. The so-called infant slaves employed in early nineteenth-century British cotton mills, to provide one illustration from this category, lacked even the nominal legal autonomy of adult factory workers, themselves so often characterized as abject "wage slaves." These and other child laborers were not chattel slaves, but because they were minors, they became passive parties in labor contracts made for them by their parents or, in the case of orphans and parish apprentices, by the state. For the recognition, even by the most forceful opponents of factory legislation for adult operatives, that child operatives were not "free agents" and merited, at least in principle, some form of legislative protection, see Lloyd Sorenson, "Some Classical Economists, Laissez Faire and the Factory Acts," *Journal of Economic History* 12 (Summer 1952): 258–62; Kenneth O. Walker, "The Classical Economists and the Factory Acts," *Journal of Economic History* 1 (Nov. 1941): 169–77; Mark Blaug, "The Classical Economists and the Factory Acts—A Re-Examination," *Quarterly Journal of Economics* 72 (May 1958): 212, 217, 223.

Finally, studies have indicated how, although it was abridged by a series of state statutory challenges, common law in mid-nineteenth-century America imposed major qualifications on the married woman's right to self-ownership by granting their husbands full legal title to their personal property and any wages they might earn. Historians, moreover, have recently emphasized the limited and ambiguous character of the changes worked by the nineteenth-century married women's property and earnings statutes; see Norma Basch, *In the Eyes of the Law: Women, Marriage, and Property in Nineteenth-Century New York* (Ithaca: Cornell University Press, 1982), 27–30, 224–32; Amy Dru Stanley, "Conjugal Bonds and Wage Labor: Rights of Contract in the Age of Emancipation," *Journal of American History* 75 (Sept. 1988): 471–500.

4. The constellation of factors—economic, social, and political—to which proponents of American exceptionalism attributed the unique condition of free manual labor in the United States provides a reference point for this entire study. For particularly confident expressions of the view that erosion in that condition was virtually impossible, see the speeches made in defense of the Independent Treasury Bill and other Democratic economic measures by Congressman Henry Williams of Massachusetts, *Congressional Globe,* 26th Cong., 1st sess., June 4, 1840, 442–43; and Congressman John Smith of Vermont, *Congressional Globe. Appendix,* 26th Cong., 1st sess., June 4, 1840, 552. Whig and Democratic politicians alike had the difficult task of discrediting the economic policies of the rival party as injurious and even calamitous to the American laborer without at the same time seeming to suggest that their faith in his supremacy was somehow suspect. Attempting to tread this line, Congressman Edmund Burke of New Hampshire, for example, denounced

Whig banking, currency, and tariff policies in the following manner: "Here, then, the laborer cannot be degraded while our present institutions exist. But the wages of labor may be affected, to some extent, by the same causes which operate to produce the rise and fall in the prices of property" (*Congressional Globe. Appendix,* 26th Cong., 1st sess., June 13, 1840, 574).

5. Horace Greeley, *Hints toward Reforms. In Letters, Addresses, and Other Writings,* 2d ed. (New York: Fowlers and Wells, 1853), 38. See also "Lecture of Horace Greeley before the Mechanics' Institute" (of California), *New-York Daily Tribune,* Sept. 13, 1859; and Horace Greeley, "The Idea of a Social Reform," *Universalist Quarterly and General Review* 2 (Apr. 1845): 138–47. In view of his dislike for the condition of wage, or "hireling," labor and of his belief during his Associationist (American Fourierist) phase that hireling labor was as inferior to Associated labor as slave labor was to the wage condition, Greeley may well have deplored the modern union worker's acceptance of permanent wage-earning status. Still, of greater relevance here is Greeley's stress on the continuous evolution of "free labor."

6. In a companion volume, I will be treating these criteria at greater length, together with the perceived threats to truly free labor that various kinds of "unfree" labor appeared to represent.

7. The antislavery writer, George Weston, was one who expressed considerably less confidence in the survival of American "free labor" than those congressmen cited in note 4. Weston emphasized that the economic and moral superiority enjoyed by free labor was the very basis of its vulnerability and fragility. After making the traditional antislavery claim that "wages are a better stimulus to industry than the lash," Weston nonetheless went on to argue that the "superior cheapness" of slave labor made a ban on its expansion into the Northern territories of Kansas and Nebraska absolutely imperative. As Weston reasoned: "When its remuneration is lowered by successive gradations, as it must be when exposed to the competition of slave labor, the freeman ceases to be educated, or intelligent, or to have any superiority to the negro except that of race. . . . It is of no avail, therefore, that educated and intelligent free labor may be an overmatch for slave labor, because in truth, educated and intelligent free labor cannot coexist with slavery. Slave labor wins the victory, not merely by its own strength, but by weakening and deteriorating free labor" (George M. Weston, *Southern Slavery Reduces Northern Wages,* address delivered in Washington, D.C., Mar. 25, 1856 [Washington, D.C.: n.p. 1856], 5, 8). Weston's theme illustrates the close parallels that existed between beliefs in free labor's vulnerability and the tradition of political thought casting doubt on the ability of republics to indefinitely withstand assault from luxury, corruption, and stagnation. The best economic system, no less than the best political one, required at the very least constant care and vigilance for its survival.

8. The importance of perspective here is obvious; for example, the female, immigrant, and other workers who performed the "slop work" and filled the other labor pools that were described by skilled white native-born male laborers and their spokesmen as "servile" and "dishonorable" did not likely view themselves in such terms, regardless of the extent to which they indeed posed an objective economic threat to the craft sectors of the trades.

9. For an interesting attempt to extend Marxist categories of evolving modes of production so that they more fully and explicitly recognize the centrality of the mental-manual labor division throughout history and its importance to "appropriation" and "class rule," see Alfred Sohn-Rethel, *Intellectual and Manual Labour: A Critique of Epistemology,* trans. Martin Sohn-Rethel (Atlantic Highlands, N.J.: Humanities Press, 1983 [1978]), 3–6, 87. For another Marxist study that specifically links

the evolution of the professions to the dominant mode of production at any given time (feudal, capitalist, and monopoly capitalist), see Margali Sarfatti-Larson, *The Rise of Professionalism: A Sociological Analysis* (Berkeley: University of California Press, 1977).

10. Lawrence Stone, "Social Mobility in England, 1500–1700," *Past and Present*, no. 33 (Apr. 1966): 17. For a study of English society in the same period that makes no reference to this broad dichotomy between manual laborers and others and emphasizes the variety, complexity, and shifting importance of the criteria determining social rank, see Keith Wrightson, "The Social Order of Early Modern England: Three Approaches," in Lloyd Bonfield, Richard M. Smith, and Keith Wrightson, eds., *The World We Have Gained: Histories of Population and Social Structure*, (Oxford: Basil Blackwell, 1986): 177–201. As I indicate in the text, I do not wish to suggest that the importance of the mental-manual labor division necessarily obscured or rendered insignificant other kinds of social gradations, such as those stressed by Wrightson. As Patrice Higonnet has written of France before the Revolution: "Members of the professions who did not work with their hands looked down on those who did, just as the skilled despised the less skilled: goldsmiths did not think much of locksmiths. In some ways, the ancien régime was a . . . continuous chain of disdain" (Patrice Higonnet, *Sister Republics: The Origins of French and American Republicanism* [Cambridge: Harvard University Press, 1988], 57). For a discussion of the low and servile, virtually "unfree," status in which wage labor particularly was regarded in sixteenth- and seventeenth-century England, not merely by the middle and upper ranks of society but by members of the laboring population as well, see Christopher Hill, "Pottage for Freeborn Englishmen: Attitudes to Wage-Labour in the Sixteenth and Seventeenth Centuries," in C. H. Feinstein, ed., *Socialism, Capitalism and Economic Growth: Essays Presented to Maurice Dobb* (Cambridge, Eng.: Cambridge University Press, 1967), 338–50.

11. James A. Henretta, *The Evolution of American Society, 1700–1815: An Interdisciplinary Analysis* (Lexington: D. C. Heath and Company, 1973), 35. I am here inverting Henretta's two statements to reflect my own emphasis. I do not believe this distorts his meaning, although I am departing from his emphasis upon the preindustrial patterns of work and leisure enjoyed by eighteenth-century self-employed farmers; see also the recent discussion of Stuart M. Blumin regarding the deep-seated, prejudicial associations attaching to manual labor in eighteenth- and early nineteenth-century American port cities, associations upon which the Revolutionary War had negligible impact. "Work with one's hands, even in a skilled and valuable craft," Blumin concludes, "was distinctly degrading. . . . both middling and poor people" could join with elite commentators in casually identifying all who lived off manual labor—"middling" skilled artisans as well as poor day laborers— "much more closely with the bottom of society than with the top" (Blumin, *The Emergence of the Middle Class: Social Experience in the American City, 1760–1900* [Cambridge, Eng.: Cambridge University Press, 1989], 30, 33, 64–65). See also Richard D. Brown, *Knowledge Is Power: The Diffusion of Information in Early America, 1700–1865* (New York: Oxford University Press, 1989), 134.

12. Remark of the labor reform editor, L. A. Hine, in "The Rich—the Poor," in Hine's journal, *Herald of Truth; A Monthly Periodical* 1 (Feb. 1847): 110, 121. See also Stephen Simpson, *The Working Man's Manual: A New Theory of Political Economy* (Philadelphia: Thomas L. Bonsal, 1831), 70; "What Is the Reason? 'How Much Land and Property, And I Have None!'" *Democratic Review* 16 (Jan. 1845): 21–23.

13. Throughout this study I use *exploitation* in what I understand to be its most

general, least technical and quantitative sense: a process in which a weaker, more vulnerable party is taken advantage of, is obliged to relinquish to a stronger party more than he or she receives back in material or intangible benefits. Application of such a definition of exploitation obviously entails considerable value judgment on the part of the historian, but this is a judgment that he should nonetheless be willing to make; a good discussion, although one with which I do not agree on all points, is Robert E. Goodin, "Exploiting a Situation and Exploiting a Person," in Andrew Reeve, ed., *Modern Theories of Exploitation* (London: Sage Publications, 1987), 166–200.

14. For statements of the position that such a fundamental "transition" in American values had occurred by the mid-nineteenth century, if not earlier, see John M. Murrin, "Self-Interest Conquers Patriotism: Republicans, Liberals, and Indians Reshape the Nation," in Jack P. Greene, ed., *The American Revolution: Its Character and Limits* (New York: New York University Press, 1987), 224–30; Gordon S. Wood, "Ideology and the Origins of Liberal America," *William and Mary Quarterly*, 3d ser., 44 (July 1987): 634–39; James A. Henretta, "Reply" to James T. Lemon, *William and Mary Quarterly*, 3d ser., 37 (Oct. 1980): 698–99. Historians are still arguing over exactly how "backward-looking" and anticommercial seventeenth- and eighteenth-century traditional, or "classical" republican, ideals really were. Yet those ideals, as I understand them, did bear a distinct animus toward acquisitive private behavior—engagement in the marketplace—as destructive of civic virtue and the "common good." Classical republican ideals exalted landed property for the independence and the insulation from corrupting financial and market pressures, as well as for the freedom from political domination, which that property supposedly brought members of a republican polity. Liberal capitalist tenets of the late eighteenth and mid-nineteenth century tended, in contrast, to minimize the significance and the inevitability of the conflict between acquisitive private economic behavior and the common good, at least with respect to the marketplace activity of the *male* members of society. Liberal capitalist tenets tended to be similarly less hostile than classical republican ones were to economic discrepancies, including concentrations of wealth, that might result from acquisitive activity in a truly open and competitive society. We should add here, however, that Jacksonian Democrat liberal capitalist formulations, to the extent that they more than Whig pronouncements minimized the differences in innate capabilities among white males, accordingly minimized the likelihood of great economic discrepancies developing in a truly open and competitive society, one free of the "special privileges" that blocked equal opportunity. On this last point of difference between Jacksonians and Whigs I have profited from many of John Ashworth's insights without sharing his conclusion that the core of Jacksonian ideology necessarily reflected an "agrarian, pre-capitalist," rather than a liberal capitalist, sensibility; see John Ashworth, *"Agrarians" and "Aristocrats": Party Political Ideology in the United States, 1837–1846* (London: Royal Historical Society, 1983), 1–2, 24–29; see also the following note and the main text below.

L. A. Hine, it should be noted, was not himself extolling acquisitive, liberal capitalist values—that is to say, he was not *complaining* about the industrious laborer's incapacity to become wealthy. Through wider land distribution and other measures that would end capitalist speculation and exploitation of wage laborers, Hine sought above all to see the right to "physical and mental comfort" secured for all who engaged in "moderate labour." Hine's remark reflected the nineteenth-century ascendancy of liberal capitalist values in America in the more subtle sense that it suggested the extent to which great economic success had already become mythologized, had already become the dominant frame of reference within which labor reformers like Hine were offering their dissenting views; Hine, "The Rich—the Poor," 111.

15. Of Philadephia's "artisans and laborers" in the first part of the eighteenth century particularly, Gary B. Nash notes: They "were far from the day when the failure to acquire property or to accumulate a minor fortune produced guilt or aroused anger against those above them." Of course, Nash has devoted much of his work to relating how, during the Revolutionary era, Philadelphia's white laboring population developed a more acute sense of economic deprivation and injustice, a sense that was attributable to deteriorating material conditions and to their exposure to—and reactions against—the liberal capitalist, acquisitive behavior of merchants and other better situated urban groups; Nash, *Race, Class, and Politics: Essays on American Colonial and Revolutionary Society* (Urbana: University of Illinois Press, 1986), 246; Nash, *The Urban Crucible: Social Change, Political Consciousness, and the Origins of the American Revolution* (Cambridge: Harvard University Press, 1979), 340–49. See also the study by one of Nash's students, Ronald Douglas Schultz, "Thoughts among the People: Popular Thought, Radical Politics, and the Making of Philadelphia's Working Class, 1765–1828" (Ph.D. diss., University of California, Los Angeles, 1985), 4–13, 62–127.

16. By idealizing a "middle state" of comfortable independence, even the more egalitarian strains of eighteenth-century republican thought did not encourage the economic aspirations of working people to the degree that later liberal capitalist "success" values did. However, this is not to deny that those same egalitarian strains could jibe with, and fuel, a plebeian sense of economic injustice—a "producer ideology"—by virtue of their animus toward concentrated wealth as subversive of republican political freedom; see John Ashworth, "The Jeffersonians: Classical Republicans or Liberal Capitalists?" *Journal of American Studies* 18 (Dec. 1984): 430.

In drawing a contrast between eighteenth- and mid-nineteenth-century American values, in affirming the more clear-cut ascendancy of liberal capitalist values during the later period, I am speaking of differences of degree rather than kind. The content of early American republican thought continues to be a subject of much debate. But many historians have emphasized the extent to which, by the time of the Revolution, American republican discourse bore a distinctive liberal capitalist and "procommercial" stamp, one that marked its departure from European classical republican traditions. Moreover, contemporary commentary suggests that by this time mass behavior itself embodied the values of enterprise and acquisitive individualism, although some scholars stress the "liberating" impact of such events as the Revolution and the War of 1812. Conversely, republican themes that distrusted and demeaned the pursuit of great wealth as subversive of virtue and instead extolled the "middle" state of comfortable economic independence, as idealized in the figure of the virtuous yeoman farmer, continued to find expression and to serve a variety of needs in mid-nineteenth-century America. The northeastern agricultural press, increasingly defensive of the occupation for which it spoke, remained a major repository of these values, while master and journeymen mechanics who were not yet torn by conflict and who were on the whole complacent about conditions in their trades characteristically embraced as a harmonizing theme the notion that hard-working, virtuous, and comfortable economic independence was as preferable to great wealth as it was to desperate poverty. For an especially full and sensitive treatment of the ambiguities, complexities, and tensions in eighteenth- and early nineteenth-century American republican thought with respect to wealth and commercial development, see Drew R. McCoy, *The Elusive Republic: Political Economy in Jeffersonian America* (Chapel Hill: University of North Carolina Press, 1980). Of the many other recent works which explore the relative importance and the respective contributions of the classical republican and liberal paradigms to American republicanism during the same period, see especially Robert E. Shalhope, "Republicanism and Early American Historiography," *William and Mary Quarterly,* 3d ser., 39 (Apr. 1982): 334–51; Joyce Appleby, "The Social Origins of American Revolutionary Ideology," *Journal of American History* 64 (Mar. 1978): 935–58; Appleby, "Republicanism in Old and New Contexts," *William and Mary Quarterly,* 3d ser., 43 (Jan. 1986): 20–34; Lance Banning, "Jeffersonian Ideology Revisited: Liberal and Classical Ideas in the New American Republic," *William and Mary Quarterly,* 3d ser., 43 (Jan. 1986): 3–19; John T. Agresto, "Liberty, Virtue, and Republicanism: 1776–87," *Review of Politics* 39 (Oct. 1977): 473–504; Gordon S. Wood, "Interests and Disinterestedness in the Making of the Constitution," in Richard Beeman et al., eds., *Beyond Confederation: Origins of the Constitution and American National Identity* (Chapel Hill: University of North Carolina Press, 1987); Steven Watts, *The Republic Reborn: War and the Making of Liberal America, 1790–1820* (Baltimore: Johns Hopkins University Press, 1987).

17. Philip Elliott, among others, has argued that in preindustrial England the professions themselves partook less of the character of active "work" than of a "gentlemanly leisure," an appropriate reflection of the fact that a good number of the higher-ranking professional positions were filled by younger sons of the gentry. During the nineteenth century, Elliott notes, the practice of the professions in England became more specialized, time-consuming, and mentally demanding. The major thread of continuity from the preindustrial period, and the continuing basis of the "gentility" of the professions, then, was their practitioners' exemption from physical labor; Philip Elliot, *The Sociology of the Professions* (New York: Herder and Herder, 1972), 21–22, 32. For a good summary of the various problems one encounters in attempting to rigorously define *professions* and *professionals,* particularly in the context of their historical development, see Michael Hawkins, "Ambiguity and Contradiction in the 'Rise of Professionalism': The English Clergy, 1570–1730," in A. L. Beier, David Cannadine, and James M. Rosenheim, eds., *The First Modern Society: Essays in English History in Honour of Lawrence Stone* (Cambridge, Eng.: Cambridge University Press, 1989), 241–46.

My emphasis here is upon the strength of the broad *correlation* between wealth and engagement in one of the favored mental labor occupations. To the great extent that these occupations, in America as well as England, proved attractive to young men who had inherited considerable wealth and social standing, their importance as a primary *source* of those individuals' wealth may have remained limited; see Edward Pessen, *Riches, Class, and Power before the Civil War* (Lexington: D. C. Heath and Company, 1973), 52–71. Studies beyond those already cited that have particularly influenced my thinking include Carlo M. Cipolla, "The Professions: The Long View," *Journal of European Economic History* 2 (Spring 1973): 37–49; Michael Miles, "'A Haven for the Privileged': Recruitment into the Profession of Attorney in England, 1709–1792," *Social History* 11 (May 1986): 197–210; Peter Dobkin Hall, "The Social Foundations of Professional Credibility: Linking the Medical Profession to Higher Education in Connecticut and Massachusetts, 1700–1830," in Thomas L. Haskell, ed., *The Authority of Experts: Studies in History and Theory* (Bloomington: Indiana University Press, 1984), 114–19, 134–35; John M. Murrin, "The Legal Transformation: The Bench and Bar of Eighteenth-Century Massachusetts," in Stanley N. Katz and John M. Murrin, eds., *Colonial America: Essays in Politics and Social Development* (New York: Alfred A. Knopf, 1983), 540–71; Thomas M. Doerflinger, *A Vigorous Spirit of Enterprise: Merchants and Economic Development in Revolutionary Philadelphia* (Chapel Hill: University of North Carolina Press, 1986). For further discussion of the evolution of the professions in America, see Jonathan Andrew Glickstein, "Concepts of Free Labor in Antebellum America" (Ph.D. diss., Yale University, 1989), 10n.

18. Paul Starr, *The Social Transformation of American Medicine* (New York: Basic Books, 1982), 81–82; Lawrence M. Friedman, *A History of American Law* (New York: Simon and Schuster, Touchstone, 1985 [1973]), 305–7.

19. On, for example, the successful efforts in Jacksonian Massachusetts to destroy the power of the bar associations and lower the entrance requirements for the privileged, "inbred" legal profession, see Gerard W. Gawalt, "Sources of Anti-Lawyer Sentiment in Massachusetts, 1740–1840," *American Journal of Legal History* 14 (1970): 306.

20. By exaggerating the importance of any of the muddying circumstances noted above, one can, accordingly, *underestimate* the superior status and appeal that the professions enjoyed in nineteenth-century America; see, for example, Robert H. Wiebe, *The Search for Order 1877–1920* (New York: Hill and Wang, 1967), 13–14, which in the following remarks seems to me to infer too much from the lack of rigorous educational requirements that still distinguished the professions in the latter part of the nineteenth century: "The so-called professions meant little as long as anyone with a bag of pills and a bottle of syrup could pass for a doctor, a few books and a corrupt judge made a man a lawyer, and an unemployed literate qualified as a teacher." Apropos here is Gary B. Nash's analysis of the Philadelphia legal profession during the first part of the nineteenth century, an analysis whose arguments parallel many of those in Gawalt's essay on the Massachusetts legal profession ("Sources of Anti-Lawyer Sentiment"). Nash observes how democratic and populist political pressures contributed to an "erosion of respect for the bench and bar" during this period. Yet his study also indicates how those same pressures confirmed the continuing appeal of the legal profession. By effecting changes in the training requirements for lawyers, egalitarian forces succeeded in their aim of breaking the "upper-class monopoly" of the profession and opening it up to "infusions of middle-class sons"; Gary B. Nash, "The Philadelphia Bench and Bar, 1800–1861," *Comparative Studies in Society and History* 7 (Jan. 1965): 209, 218–20.

The circumstances that limited and indeed lowered the standing of the professions of law and medicine during the middle third of the nineteenth century must be set against those that continued to give a disproportionate number of professional men elite standing in their communities. That the relative importance of these sets of circumstances continues to be a matter of dispute among specialists of the professions may be seen in Ronald L. Numbers, "The Fall and Rise of the American Medical Profession," 185–88, and Barbara Gutmann Rosenkrantz, "The Search for Professional Order in Nineteenth-Century American Medicine," 220–27, both in Judith Walzer Leavitt and Ronald L. Numbers, ed., *Sickness and Health in America: Readings in the History of Medicine and Public Health,* 2d rev. ed. (Madison: University of Wisconsin Press, 1985).

The preeminent work on the importance of "professional values" in nineteenth-century America, but one which treats quite different themes from those covered in this study, is Barton J. Bledstein, *The Culture of Professionalism: The Middle Class and the Development of Higher Education in America* (New York: W. W. Norton and Company, 1970). For an interesting discussion of the rise of "professional power" in nineteenth-century Britain as a development that sustained not only the "invidious distinction" between mental and manual labor but also the division between female and male labor, see Julia Swindells, *Victorian Writing and*

Working Women: The Other Side of Silence (Minneapolis: University of Minnesota Press, 1985), 2–4, 16–30, 44.

21. Donald E. Brown, *Hierarchy, History, and Human Nature: The Social Origins of Historical Consciousness* (Tucson: University of Arizona Press, 1988), 14. That mid-nineteenth-century America lacked the formal barriers to advancement present in more closed, "hereditarily stratified" societies hardly means that it was truly nonascriptive. Birth did not generally fix social position (Southern slaves constituting the most obvious exception); but recent social historians have nonetheless shown how fully ascribed circumstances of birth—economic origins, sex, race, and ethnicity—undermined the equal opportunity to compete and achieve, unequally affected the ability of individuals to develop their talents and ambition; see Harvey J. Graff, *The Legacies of Literacy: Continuities and Contradictions in Western Culture and Society* (Bloomington: Indiana University Press, 1987), 351.

Throughout this study I refer to the strength of middle-class competitive morality in the antebellum North, but the ascriptive features referred to above suggest that there were always definite limitations to the nature and pervasiveness of that morality (quite apart from the question of the hold it exercised upon members of the working class). How genuinely committed to open competition can a society be when it excludes major groups—women, blacks, immigrants—from competing on an equal basis through educational and economic discrimination and other means? The antebellum Northern labor market was hardly one in which all workers were competitive with one another, but rather one in which sex, race, and ethnicity played major roles in relegating workers to particular tracks and delimiting their employment opportunities. An important theme of this inquiry is the capacity of competitive morality in the free states to bend to and accommodate sexual, racial, and ethnic prejudices—the facility with which "free labor" was assigned different meanings and definitions according to the physical attributes of the worker performing it.

22. For the Revolutionary period, see Gordon S. Wood, *The Creation of American Republic, 1776–1787* (Chapel Hill: University of North Carolina Press, 1969), 72, 607. Hereditarian thought in the late antebellum period was heavily ethnological and racist in nature, emphasizing not only the variations in native endowment among individuals but the extent to which these variations were racially and ethnically based. Among the many studies that point to a decline in the late antebellum period of environmentalist explanations of social inequality and a corresponding ascendancy of doctrines that interpreted inequality more in terms of innate racial and ethnic inferiority, see George M. Fredrickson, *The Black Image in the White Mind: The Debate on Afro-American Character and Destiny, 1817–1914* (Middletown: Wesleyan University Press, 1987 [1971]), 12–16, 97–164; and Dale T. Knobel, *Paddy and the Republic: Ethnicity and Nationality in Antebellum America* (Middletown: Wesleyan University Press, 1986), 56–181. Reginald Horsman, however, has suggested that it was during the Jacksonian period that "scientific theories of superior and inferior races [began to be] eagerly grasped" by American society; Horsman, *Race and Manifest Destiny: The Origins of American Racial Anglo-Saxonism* (Cambridge: Harvard University Press, 1981), 4–6, 159, 301; for parallel developments in Britain especially, see L. Perry Curtis, Jr., *Apes and Angels: The Irishman in Victorian Caricature* (Washington, D.C.: Smithsonian Institution Press, 1971). For the view that Curtis exaggerated the racist component of Victorian English prejudices toward the Irish, see Sheridan Gilley, "English Attitudes to the Irish in England, 1780–1900," in Colin Holmes, ed., *Immigrants and Minorities in British Society* (London: George Allen and Unwin, 1978), 81–110.

23. Ashworth, *"Agrarians" and "Aristocrats,"* 1, 25–34, 53, 66–68, 120. For a recent discussion of mid-nineteenth-century American white male beliefs regarding the particular capabilities of women and blacks, one which finds a good deal of ambiguity and contradiction even in these beliefs, see Rowland Berthoff, "Conventional Mentality: Free Blacks, Women, and Business Corporations as Unequal Persons, 1820–1870," *Journal of American History* 76 (Dec. 1989): 753–84. For a useful general discussion of beliefs regarding existing, potential, equal, and unequal human capabilities and the roles these beliefs have played in philosophical discourse, see Thomas Sowell, *A Conflict of Visions* (New York: William Morrow and Company, 1987), 121–40.

24. Speech of James T. Brady, delivered at Binghamton, New York, in "Breckinridge Rally at Binghamton," *New-York Times,* Oct. 22, 1860; the "Special Reporter" covering this rally for the *Times* may have been paraphrasing some of Brady's remarks; see also "Brady on Rail-Splitting," *New-York Daily Tribune,* Oct. 23, 1860. For a brief but illuminating portrait of the high educational and occupational level of members of Congress in 1850, one which would seem to bear out Brady's remarks, see Ruth E. Bordin, "Hofstadter and the Decline of the Gentleman—Fact or Fancy," *Mid-America: An Historical Review* 48 (Apr. 1966): 119–25.

25. Social differentiation, or division of labor, some anthropologists and other scholars hold, may in fact be the *consequence* of some preexisting pattern of stratification or power hierarchy, originating in sexual or other basic differences; see, for example, Maurice Godelier, "Language and History. Work and Its Representations: A Research Proposal," *History Workshop,* no. 10 (Autumn 1980): 170. For general discussions of social stratification see Melvin M. Tumin, *Social Stratification* (Englewood Cliffs: Prentice-Hall, 1967); S. N. Eisenstadt, *Social Differentiation and Stratification* (Glenview, Ill.: Scott, Foresman and Company, 1987); James Littlejohn, *Social Stratification* (New York: Humanities Press, 1972).

26. Kingsley Davis and Wilbert E. Moore, "Some Principles of Stratification," *American Sociological Review* 10 (Apr. 1945): 242–49; Wilbert E. Moore, "But Some Are More Equal Than Others," *American Sociological Review* 28 (Feb. 1963): 13–15. Kingsley Davis explicitly claimed in a follow-up piece to the first article cited that he and Moore were attempting only to explain the apparent ubiquity of social stratification, not to justify it; Kingsley Davis, "Reply," *American Sociological Review* 18 (Aug. 1953): 394–95.

A growing body of scholars has disputed the claims of the functionalist school, maintaining that from prehistory onward a number of cultures have exhibited minimal sexually based or other social stratification. I have found particularly valuable Gerda Lerner, *The Creation of Patriarchy* (New York: Oxford University Press, 1986), 29–31, and many of the essays in Stephanie Coontz and Peta Henderson, eds., *Women's Work, Men's Property: The Origins of Gender and Class* (London: Verso, 1986).

27. See, in particular, Davis and Moore, "Some Principles," 244; and Eisenstadt, *Social Differentiation,* 10–21.

28. The labor radical and land reformer L. W. Ryckman referred, for example, to the "frequently entirely useless or charlatanic" labors of the "Doctor, Lawyer, and Devine," however "agreeable" these labors might be, in a speech before the Industrial Congress meeting in New York City, in "Labor Movements," *New-York Daily Tribune,* Jan. 27, 1851. A president of the New England Workingmen's Association in the 1840s, Ryckman made a fuller defense of the radical labor theory of value and elaborated on his dichotomy between the class who depended "on their own useful labor" and the capitalists, professionals, and landlords who lived "luxuriously in

unproductive idleness," in *The Largest Liberty Defined, a Treatise on the Inherent Rights and Obligations of Man* (New York: W. Applegate, 1848), 1–6. This is not to claim that antebellum labor movement activists denounced mental labor employments *in toto;* despite the combativeness of his remarks, Ryckman himself exhibited some ambiguities on this score (see chapter 8, note 4). As a number of scholars have observed, mid-nineteenth-century definitions of "workingmen" and the "producing classes" could be extraordinarily broad, and notwithstanding the claims of conservative opponents of trade union "agitation"—those who most vociferously defended "mental labor"—prominent labor leaders frequently partook of some of this breadth of definition. If nothing else, George Henry Evans of the New York Working Men's Party was paying homage to the rather diverse constituency of his movement when he agreed in 1830 that "a Working Man" was "one who followed any *useful* occupation, mental or physical, for a livelihood." Precisely which mental labor employments were presently or potentially productive and useful to the community, exactly which ones were inevitably parasitic and fraudulent—the refuge of the idle and the aristocratically inclined—were questions with which labor activists grappled and frequently disagreed about; although it is also true that labor leaders, along with mainstream Jacksonian Democratic politicians, did consistently single out a few particular employments for condemnation, notably banking and "speculation." The mobility of "industrious mechanics" into morally suspect employments was itself a significant complicating dimension of the debates within labor circles; as several studies—including this one—note, an important part of the labor history of the period was the increasing estrangement experienced by rank-and-file journeymen in a variety of trades from master craftsmen who had turned exclusive mental laborers/entrepreneurs. Evans' remark is from Philip S. Foner, *History of the Labor Movement in the United States* (New York: International Publishers, 1947), 1: 136. For some representative discussions in the early labor press of productive/nonproductive labor categories, and where to place the plethora of such occupational types as general shipping merchants and retail dry goods dealers, see the following issues of the New York *Working Man's Advocate*: "Prospectus," Oct. 31, 1829; letters from "A Mechanic," and replies from Evans, Mar. 27 and Apr. 3, 1830; and "Exclusive Party," Sept. 4, 1830. For an important study of the ongoing, shifting definitions within eighteenth- and nineteenth-century American "public discourse" of such terms as *class* and *productive labor,* one that considers the views of reformers like Evans as well as those of more conservative political economists and thinkers, see Martin Joseph Burke, "The Conundrum of Class: Public Discourse on the Social Order in America" (Ph.D. diss., University of Michigan, 1987), 226–53.

29. Kenneth R. Minogue, "The Concept of Property and Its Contemporary Significance," in J. Roland Pennock and John W. Chapman, eds., *Nomos XXII. Property* (New York: New York University Press, 1980), 9–10.

30. Elsewhere Tumin more explicitly indicated that his condemnation extended to "unequal rewards" for "nominally unequal work" (Tumin, "On Inequality," in Tumin, ed., *Readings on Social Stratification* [Englewood Cliffs, N.J.: Prentice-Hall, 1970], 400–408).

31. Melvin M. Tumin, "Some Principles of Stratification: A Critical Analysis," *American Sociological Review* 18 (Aug. 1953): 392–93. See also Tumin, *Social Stratification,* 106–8.

32. Tumin, "Some Principles," 389–91; Tumin, *Social Stratification,* 107–8. To be more precise, Tumin primarily addresses his remarks to the training process for professional and other high-ranking positions, whereas the nineteenth-century thinkers to whom I am referring spoke only of the actual practice of such employ-

ments, the training process for these being far less extensive and arduous in the mid-nineteenth century than it subsequently became. Yet Tumin and the nineteenth-century radicals were still following essentially the same line of argument by denying that mental labor employments entailed commitments and demands that justified their superior rewards. For the numerous other arguments raised by both the functionalists and the antifunctionalists like Tumin, see Eisenstadt, *Social Differentiation,* 17–22; Joseph Lopreato and Lawrence E. Hazebrigg, *Class, Conflict, and Mobility* (San Francisco: Chandler Publishing Company, 1972), 93–112; and Leonard Reissman, *Class in American Society* (New York: Free Press, 1959), 83–93. For a convenient collection of many of the most important contributions to the functionalist controversy, see Tumin, ed., *Readings,* 368–435.

33. To be more accurate, in the case of Peabody, she applauded an equality of wages for physical and intellectual labor at Brook Farm.

34. See, for example, Friedrich A. Hayek, *Law, Legislation, and Liberty,* vol. 2, *The Mirage of Social Justice* (Chicago: University of Chicago Press, 1976), 92; Hayek, *The Constitution of Liberty* (Chicago: University of Chicago Press, 1960), 441; H. B. Acton, *The Morals of Markets: An Ethical Exploration* (London: Longman Group, 1971), 58–98.

35. The highly precise and technical manner in which trained philosophers and other academics, whether they are defending free market principles or not, analyze and dissect such terms as *equality, merit,* and *reward* can enrich one's approach to the nineteenth-century discussions of the "just" claims of labor and capital even if these analyses are of limited direct applicability in the examination of these earlier, less rigorous discussions; see, for example, Amy Gutmann, *Liberal Equality* (Cambridge, Eng.: Cambridge University Press, 1980); Joel Feinberg, "Justice and Personal Desert," in Carl J. Friedrich and John W. Chapman, eds., *Nomos VI. Justice* (New York: Atherton Press, 1963), 69–97; and many of the essays in J. Roland Pennock and John W. Chapman, eds., *Nomos IX. Equality* (New York: Atherton Press, 1967).

36. David Riesman, *Individualism Reconsidered and Other Essays* (Glencoe: Free Press, 1954), 72–73.

37. Mandeville elaborated: "The Welfare and Felicity therefore of every State and Kingdom, require that the Knowledge of the Working Poor should be confin'd within the Verge of their Occupations, and never extended (as to things visible) beyond what relates to their Calling. The more a Shepherd, a Plowman or any other Peasant knows of the World, and the things that are foreign to his Labour or Employment, the less fit he'll be to go through the Fatigues and Hardships of it with Chearfulness and Content" (Bernard Mandeville, *The Fable of the Bees: Or, Private Vices, Publick Benefits. With an Essay on Charity Schools and a Search into the Nature of Society,* with a commentary by F. B. Kaye, 6th ed. [1732] [Oxford: Clarendon Press, 1957 {1924}, 1: 288, 290). For the socially conservative educational objectives of the charity schools that Mandeville opposed, see M. G. Jones, *The Charity School Movement: A Study of Eighteenth Century Puritanism in Action* (London: Frank Cass, 1964 [1938]), 4–5. For Reformation and other mass education efforts that antedated the English charity schools, see Graff, *Legacies of Literacy,* 75–172 passim.

38. See Michael Sanderson, *Education, Economic Change and Society in England 1780–1870* (London: Macmillan Press, 1983), 17.

39. We should, at the same time, be careful not to exaggerate the numbers that were necessarily party to this agreement—members of the working classes, for example, whose lack of discernible objections to prevailing social arrangements reflected mere acquiescence rather than normative endorsement of those arrange-

ments; of value here is Nicholas Abercrombie, Stephen Hill, and Bryan S. Turner, *The Dominant Ideology Thesis* (London: George Allen and Unwin, 1980), 122.

40. Any number of broad categories of examples might, of course, be produced here: Indian caste labor, ancient Greek and Roman slave labor, medieval serfdom. I wish to make clear that I am far from making the outrageous claim that the majority of past laboring populations have not "thought" deeply. I am rather suggesting that their prevailing economic and social circumstances—e.g., crushing poverty, long hours of work, lack of access to educational opportunities—were antagonistic to their so doing, and that this social reality was recognized and, in many cases legitimated, by long-standing Western assumptions. I have found particularly valuable Michel Mollat, *The Poor in the Middle Ages: An Essay in Social History,* trans. Arthur Goldhammer (New Haven: Yale University Press, 1986 [1978]), 27–32, 69–74, 105.

I might add, incidentally, that my broad formulation in the main text would not seem incompatible with Karl Marx's own view. Needless to say, Marx did not consider precapitalist societies free of gross inequalities and exploitation, even if it was the historic role of industrial capitalism to generate new, more intense forms of class exploitation, together with a maturing and ultimately revolutionary consciousness of that exploitation on the part of the exploited.

41. Ira Steward, *A Reduction of Hours an Increase of Wages* (Boston: Boston Labor Reform Association, 1865; repr. in John R. Commons and John B. Andrews, eds., *Labor Movement, 1860–1880,* vol. 1, A Documentary History of American Industrial Society, vol. 9 (New York: Russell and Russell, 1958 [1910]), 299.

42. This is the initial and overall emphasis David Montgomery presents in his analysis of Steward's remark; *Beyond Equality: Labor and the Radical Republicans, 1862–1872* (New York: Random House, 1967), 30–31. But after stressing the American ambivalence toward manufacturing-generated *hireling* manual labor, Montgomery then appears (32) to slide into an interpretation more congenial with my own, one emphasizing the ambivalence toward, even disdain and aversion for, manual labor generally. Ira Steward, for his part, believed that his favored "eight-hour system" would be a crucial first step toward ending wage labor and establishing a cooperative commonwealth in which all men were both "capitalists" and laborers. But he also believed that the eight-hour system would do much by itself to weaken the popular prejudice against manual labor.

43. I am speaking above all in relative terms. Stuart M. Blumin, for example, notes that in Philadelphia in 1860 small artisanal shops with handworking masters formed a much smaller proportion of the city's total businesses than they had in the 1770s. And although the absolute number of such shops was indisputably much greater at the later date, Blumin adds that many of these were not producing skilled craft work; Blumin, *Emergence of the Middle Class,* 75–76.

44. "The artisans who revolutionized" crafts in Newark, New Jersey, Susan E. Hirsch has written, "also transformed their own work. The master craftsman had used both mental and manual skills; the manufacturer used only the mental, concentrating on management, finance, distribution, and new technology.... Manufacturers ceased to value their own manual skill and that of others, judging achievement in terms of profit alone" (Susan E. Hirsch, "From Artisan to Manufacturer: Industrialization and the Small Producer in Newark, 1830–60," in Stuart W. Bruchey, ed., *Small Business in American Life* [New York: Columbia University Press, 1980], 92, 94–95). The prevailing view articulated by Hirsch and other labor historians diverges from an older one, which emphasized that master craftsmen, hardly less than the journeymen and apprentices in their employ, were victimized by alien merchant

capitalists and their financial and industrial innovations. See also Blumin, *Emergence of the Middle Class,* 68–76, 121–22, 136–37; and Gary John Kornblith, "From Artisans to Businessmen: Master Mechanics in New England, 1789–1850" (Ph.D. diss., Princeton University, 1983), vi, 213–31, 530–43. Also see Rex Burns, *Success in America: The Yeoman Dream and the Industrial Revolution* (Amherst: University of Massachusetts Press, 1976), 93, for a discussion of the ascendancy within particular mechanic trades of men who devoted themselves to "technological entrepreneurship." Roughly parallel developments to those described by these and other scholars seem to have occurred in parts of Britain—see the description of the emergence of "the small manufacturer," as distinct from the "traditional artisan–small master," in various Birmingham trades, in Clive Behagg, *Politics and Production in the Early Nineteenth Century* (London: Routledge, 1990), 223–24.

We should also note, however, that despite the limited status enjoyed by manual labor employments, the notion that these employments were bereft of capital and mental dimensions during the period of industrialization remains to a certain extent an ideal type, one obscuring the complexities and shadings of economic reality. Nineteenth- and early twentieth-century America had its share of the English "penny capitalists" described by John Benson: working men and women, located largely in street trades and other non–capital-intensive service employments, who performed their own physical labor yet who also made all the decisions and engaged in the same kind of risk taking as larger capitalists—members of the working classes, in other words, who maintained complete control over their capital and labor; John Benson, *The Penny Capitalists: A Study of Nineteenth Century Working-Class Entrepreneurs* (London: Gill and Macmillan, 1983), 2–5, 128–39.

45. A further expression of the ascendancy of these values was the increasingly commercial and speculative orientation of those agricultural enterprises in the Northern states and territories that remained most economically viable; still of major importance on this subject is Richard Hofstadter, *The Age of Reform* (New York: Vintage Books, 1955), 23–59; see also Paul W. Gates, *The Farmer's Age: Agriculture, 1815–1860* (New York: Harper and Row, 1960), 403, where Gates quotes a contemporary observer writing in the *Ohio Farmer* for 1857: Many people migrated to developing farm areas "*to live by their wits,* rather than by cultivating the soil . . . many young men who have sought the West, are seeking for sudden wealth by the rise of land, or exorbitant interest, rather than by honest toil."

46. See, for example, L. W. Ryckman's remarks in note 28; see also "Give Your Boy a Trade," *Mechanic's Advocate. A Weekly Paper, Devoted to the Interests of the Mechanic, Mutual Protection, and the Elevation of Labor* (Albany), Apr. 8, 1848. For a sensitive discussion of the painting, prints, and other art of the period to probe the discrepancy between traditional pastoral ideals and growing speculative and commercial agricultural realities, see Sarah Burns, *Pastoral Inventions: Rural Life in Nineteenth-Century American Art and Culture* (Philadelphia: Temple University Press, 1989), 39–62.

47. The basic work on this subject remains Marvin Meyers, *The Jacksonian Persuasion: Politics and Belief* (Stanford: Stanford University Press, 1957), 135–36. For one particularly pointed expression of unease with the reigning American "commercial spirit," in consequence of which "We are ashamed of any thing but affluence," see the essay by the New York City Unitarian minister Henry W. Bellows, "Influence of the Trading Spirit upon the Social and Moral Life of America," *American Review* 1 (Jan. 1845): 94–98.

48. Wood, "Ideology and Origins of Liberal America," 639–40; Alexis De Tocqueville, *Democracy in America,* ed. J. P. Mayer, trans. George Lawrence, 2 vols.

in 1 (Garden City, N.Y.: Anchor Books, 1969 [1835]), 2: 550–51. See also the recent essay by Isaac Kramnick that elaborates Wood's categories: Western liberalism was a bourgeois "ideology of work" and competition; republicanism was an "ideology of leisure" and ascribed privilege, historically rooted in the circumstances of landed elites (as distinct from Jefferson's industrious, small freehold farmers). Yet the more subtle disesteem for manual work that meritocratic liberal values themselves carried is suggested by some of the very phrases Kramnick uses to describe those values— e.g., the liberal premium upon "success in the marketplace": the talented and deserving did not, presumably, finish the "race of life" working with their hands; Isaac Kramnick, *Republicanism and Bourgeois Radicalism: Political Ideology in Late Eighteenth-Century England and America* (Ithaca: Cornell University Press, 1990), 1–40, esp. 1, 2, 13, 14. Kramnick might very likely acknowledge the ambiguities in the bourgeois liberal idealization of work, but he passes over them here. For a more explicit treatment of those ambiguities, and one that questions the degree to which liberal ideology represented an advance over classical attitudes toward manual labor, see Ellen Meiksins Wood, *Peasant-Citizen and Slave: The Foundations of Athenian Democracy* (London: Verso, 1988), 141–42.

Partially because bondsmen did not work for their own profit or "pay," Tocqueville regarded Southern slave labor as the greatest existing exception to his dictum that in America all work "is regarded as positively honorable." He also, however, shared the apprehension that in the United States as elsewhere a peculiarly degraded and abject sort of legally free industrial labor might arise, partially in consequence of the intrinsically injurious effects of repetitive manufacturing division of labor, and partially because the workers engaged in this labor would be, for a variety of reasons, effectively denied a decent return by the powerful industrial "aristocracy" that employed them; *Democracy*, 2: 555–58, 583–84.

49. This ambivalence by no means went completely unrecognized by Tocqueville. After affirming the high regard in which men in a democracy held all work for profit, he went on to note—somewhat contradictorily to my mind—the "distaste" they felt for employments, such as those in agriculture, whose profit-making potential was limited and slow of fulfillment; *Democracy*, 2: 551–54. See also Marcus Cunliffe, *Chattel Slavery and Wage Slavery* (Athens: University of Georgia Press, 1979), xv–xvi; and Jean V. Matthews, *Rufus Choate: The Law and Civic Virtue* (Philadelphia: Temple University Press, 1980), 75–76.

50. Eric Foner, *Free Soil, Free Labor, Free Men: The Ideology of the Republican Party before the Civil War* (New York: Oxford University Press, 1970), 11–72. See also Richard Ellis and Aaron Wildavsky, "A Cultural Analysis of the Role of Abolitionists in the Coming of the Civil War," *Comparative Studies in Society and History* 32 (Jan. 1990): 113, which reinforces yet also somewhat extends Foner's perspective by arguing that although Northern competitive, free labor ideology may well have been naturally and latently antislavery, it required the new and threatening prominence of the Southern expansionist, hierarchical ideology of slavery as a positive good after 1850 to bring these antislavery tendencies to the surface on a mass scale— to generate truly popular support in the North for a self-conscious and explicitly antislavery, free labor ideology. Other historians have further narrowed the period of real crystallization and salience of antislavery free labor themes within the total Republican appeal to the years following the Panic of 1857, after Southern proslavery writers and politicians had stepped up their attacks on the Northern economic and social order; see the review by Brooks D. Simpson, "Two More Roads to Sumter," *Reviews in American History* 17 (June 1989): 226–28.

51. Stephen E. Maizlish, "The Meaning of Nativism and the Crisis of the

Union: The Know-Nothing Movement in the Antebellum North," in Stephen E. Maizlish and John J. Kushma, eds., *Essays on American Antebellum Politics, 1840–1860* (College Station: Texas A & M University Press, 1982), 173–74; Brian Greenberg, *Worker and Community: Response to Industrialization in a Nineteenth Century American City, Albany, New York 1850–1884* (Albany: State University of New York Press, 1985), 1–41, 161; William E. Gienapp, *The Origins of the Republican Party 1852–1856* (New York: Oxford University Press, 1987), 357; Bruce Collins, "The Ideology of the Ante-bellum Northern Democrats," *Journal of American Studies* 1 (Apr. 1977): 104–5; James Oakes, *The Ruling Race: A History of American Slaveholders* (New York: Alfred A. Knopf, 1982), x–xiii, 126–30, 226–27; James L. Huston, *The Panic of 1857 and the Coming of the Civil War* (Baton Rouge: Louisiana State University Press, 1987), 87–97. For all its looseness and vagueness, I do not find the term *antislavery* as unsatisfactory as some other scholars do. I agree here instead with the following remarks by Kenneth M. Stampp, made with specific reference to members of the Republican Party: "Although several historians have argued that Republicans were characteristically more anti-southern and anti-slaveholder than they were truly anti-slavery, this distinction may have been less clear in the minds of average Republicans. It would have required an exceedingly fine discrimination to enable a Republican to have negative feelings about the South, or about slaveholders, without having similar feelings about the institution that gave the South and its social elite their power and distinct identity" (Stampp, *The Imperiled Union: Essays on the Background of the Civil War* [New York: Oxford University Press, 1980], 122).

52. In this category of dubious free labor ideology I include the Stephen A. Douglas–northern Democratic doctrine of popular sovereignty, which professed indifference to whether slavery was "voted up or down" by local majorities in the federal territories; for a brilliant interpretation that wrestles with the old issue of whether Douglas and his doctrine, insofar as they anticipated free soil majorities in such territories as Kansas and Nebraska, were antislavery in unavowed intent, see Harry V. Jaffa, *Crisis of the House Divided: An Interpretation of the Issues in the Lincoln-Douglas Debates* (Garden City, N.Y.: Doubleday and Company, 1959), 41–62.

53. C. B. Macpherson, *The Political Theory of Possessive Individualism: Hobbes to Locke* (London: Oxford University Press, 1962); and Nicholas Abercrombie, Stephen Hill, and Bryan S. Turner, *Sovereign Individuals of Capitalism* (London: Allen and Unwin, 1986) 27–30, 92–110, 184–91. We should perhaps note, however, that John Locke's doctrinal contribution to "possessive individualism," to which Macpherson gives prominent space, has been particularly questioned by a number of scholars who have given alternative readings of Locke's views of property and labor; see for example James Tully, *A Discourse on Property: John Locke and His Adversaries* (Cambridge, Eng.: Cambridge University Press, 1980). See also J. G. A. Pocock, "The Myth of John Locke and the Obsession with Liberalism"; and Richard Ashcraft, "The *Two Treatises* and the Exclusion Crisis: The Problem of Lockean Political Theory as Bourgeois Ideology," both in Pocock and Ashcraft, *John Locke: Papers Read at a Clark Library Seminar 10 December 1977* (Los Angeles: University of California, William Andrews Clark Memorial Library, 1980). These objections, however, do not entirely dispose of the possibility that Locke's writing, whatever his conscious intentions, carried the *force* of a defense of possessive individualism, of unlimited capital accumulation by some at the expense of others; see Keith Graham, "How Do Illocutionary Descriptions Explain?" and Joseph V. Femia, "An Historical Critique of 'Revisionist' Methods for Studying the History of Ideas," both in James Tully, ed., *Meaning and Context: Quentin Skinner and His Critics* (Princeton: Princeton University Press, 1989), 153, 172–73.

326 Notes to Pages 12–13

54. David Brion Davis, *The Problem of Slavery in the Age of Revolution 1770–1823* (Ithaca: Cornell University Press, 1975), 343–468.

55. See, for example, the discussion of Captain John Smith's views in Stephen Innes, "Introduction. Fulfilling John Smith's Vision: Work and Labor in Early America," in Stephen Innes, ed., *Work and Labor in Early America* (Chapel Hill: University of North Carolina Press, 1988), 1–47.

56. Free labor ideology was implicitly sexist and patriarchal, and it shared widely held middle-class notions that the competitive marketplace was an inappropriate field for female activity. I have certainly seen few formulations of free labor ideology that gave any indication that they meant their exaltation of the formal right and the practical ability of workers to rise to great heights in the Northern marketplace to extend to female members of the Northern laboring population; see also Alice Kessler-Harris, *A Woman's Wage: Historical Meanings and Social Consequences* (Lexington: University Press of Kentucky, 1990), 36–37.

57. See the abolitionist rebuttals of the "wage-slavery" arguments advanced by some Northern land and labor reformers in Jonathan A. Glickstein, "'Poverty Is Not Slavery:' American Abolitionists and the Competitive Labor Market," in Lewis Perry and Michael Fellman, eds., *Antislavery Reconsidered: New Perspectives on the Abolitionists* (Baton Rouge: Louisiana State University Press, 1979), 207–16.

58. The protective tariff speeches made by Republican politicians in the 1850s tended particularly to play up the degraded state in which the "pauper" manufacturing laborers of Britain supposedly languished.

59. In his excellent analysis of antebellum free labor ideology, *Free Soil, Free Labor, Free Men,* Eric Foner characterizes the small producer, republican values to which I refer in the text as themselves a defining expression of the dynamic, yet still relatively egalitarian, capitalistic social order of the antebellum North. How "capitalistic" such values in fact were has become a matter of increasing controversy since Foner came out with his book (see also notes 61 and 62). But, in any case, Foner's analysis tends in my view to underrate the penetration into Republican free labor ideology of the more forthright acquisitive liberal capitalist values to which I also refer in the text. As the wealthy Massachusetts Senator and Republican party leader Henry Wilson claimed, partially with reference to his own rise from humble origins as an indentured servant and apprentice shoemaker, and in rebuttal of South Carolina Senator James Henry Hammond's demeaning references to immobile Northern "wage-slaves" and "mud-sills": Northern free labor society worked in considerable measure because the North's "mud-sills" of yesterday had not merely become its self-employed farmers and craftsmen of today, but its "merchant-princes" as well; Senator Henry Wilson, *Congressional Globe. Appendix,* 35th Cong., 1st sess., Mar. 20, 1858, 174. The polemicist for Whig principles, Calvin Colton, introduced the phrase, although hardly the idea, that America "is a country of self-made men"; [Colton], "Labor and Capital," *Junius Tracts,* no. 7 (Mar. 1844): 111. For a relevant, recent assessment of the values manifested in the abundant "success manuals" directed at young men in the antebellum period, see Leonard N. Neufeldt, *The Economist: Henry Thoreau and Enterprise* (New York: Oxford University Press, 1989), 134–55. Also of relevance here are the comments in Gienapp, *Origins of Republican Party,* 356. See also Eric Foner, *Reconstruction: America's Unfinished Revolution 1863–1877* (New York: Harper and Row, 1988), 29; Lacy Ford, "Labor and Ideology in the South Carolina Up-Country: The Transition to Free-Labor Agriculture," in Walter J. Fraser, Jr., and Winfred B. Moore, Jr., eds., *The Southern Enigma: Essays on Race, Class, and Folk Culture* (Westport: Greenwood Press, 1983), 25; and John L. Brooke, *The Heart of the Commonwealth: Society and Political Culture*

in Worcester County, Massachusetts, 1713–1861 (New York: Cambridge University Press, 1989), xiii–xviii, 375–93.

60. This particular point of view, however, might also be shared by the most racist members of the antislavery movement, those who were not at all concerned with the effects of slavery on the slaves themselves.

61. Gienapp, *Origins of Republican Party,* 356–57; Collins, "Ideology of Antebellum Northern Democrats," 104–5; Jaffa, *Crisis of House Divided,* 41–62; Oakes, *Ruling Race,* x–xiii, 126–30, 226–33. It remains possible, of course, that for all their agreement that black slavery and white economic opportunity were compatible, different social groups in the antebellum South differently conceptualized and idealized that opportunity. A growing number of studies have underscored the extent to which segments of the nonslaveholding yeomanry were resistant to capitalist commercial development and identified opportunity with the attainment and preservation of a virtuous "republican," agrarian competency or self-sufficiency. It also seems plausible that smaller slaveholding planters—individuals who were neither so isolated from the market as the yeomanry nor so "above" the market as a few of the wealthiest, quasi-seigneurial planters—held a more liberal capitalist construction of opportunity than these other groups, one that more forthrightly embraced enterprising, acquisitive activity as a route to increased wealth and position. In some ways, in other words, differences in social values among antebellum Southern whites may have mirrored and replicated the ambiguity in Republican "free labor" ideology referred to in the main text; see, in addition to Oakes's book, Harry L. Watson, "Conflict and Collaboration: Yeoman, Slaveholders, and Politics in the Antebellum South," *Social History* 10 (Oct. 1985): 288, 296–98; Steven Hahn, *The Roots of Southern Populism: Yeoman Farmers and the Transformation of the Georgia Upcountry, 1850–1890* (New York: Oxford University Press, 1983), 15–49; Lacey K. Ford, Jr., *Origins of Southern Radicalism: The South Carolina Upcountry, 1800–1860* (New York: Oxford University Press, 1988), 5–79; Ford, "Labor and Ideology, 25–27; Peter J. Parrish, *Slavery: History and Historians* (New York: Harper and Row, 1989), 27–29, 52–55.

62. Greenberg, *Worker and Community,* 1–41; Sean Wilentz, *Chants Democratic: New York City and the Rise of the American Working Class* (New York: Oxford University Press, 1984), 271–86, 302–6; John S. Gilekson, Jr., *Middle Class Providence, 1820–1940* (Princeton: Princeton University Press, 1986), 93, 95, 108. Wilentz provides a particularly good discussion of the "free labor ideology" of master craft employers and their allies in New York City in the 1830s and the 1840s. Yet as Charles Stephenson has noted, although "free labor ideology was a middle-class ideology," one that was especially congenial to Republican party leaders and Northern capitalists, it also "contained significant elements attractive to many segments of the working class." Notwithstanding free labor ideology's optimistic and complacent picture of social conditions and economic opportunity in the free states, its appeal, Stephenson suggests, may have actually fed on the economic insecurities and malaise of Northern wage earners. Faced with the problems of lay-offs and underemployment that were endemic to their status, some Northern workers may have been drawn to an ideology that exalted self-employed economic independence, a condition they interpreted and valued as offering an escape "from the arbitrariness of the capitalist employer"; Charles Stephenson, "'There's Plenty Waitin' at the Gates': Mobility, Opportunity and the American Worker," in Charles Stephenson and Robert Asher, eds., *Life and Labor: Dimensions of American Working-Class History* (Albany: State University of New York, 1986), 81, 89. Free labor ideology may in fact have proved congenial to many elements of society that regarded it less

as a description, an exaltation, of existing realities in the North than as the embodiment of valued, realizable ideals; this may be what Bruce Laurie means when he observes that "Jacksonian entrepreneurs anticipated the central features" of free labor when they sought through the abolition of "privilege" and "monopoly" the "creation of an open and dynamic economy that fostered economic independence for diligent and industrious farmers and workingmen. . . . The ideology of Republicanism originated in the 1830s." Laurie proceeds to argue for the existence of "several forms" and shades of "early free laborism," Whig and Democrat, Northern and Southern, in the 1830s, though he identifies "the ideology of mature free labor" with the later Republican Party; Bruce Laurie, *Artisans into Workers: Labor in Nineteenth-Century America* (New York: Hill and Wang, 1989), 51–56, 94. For an interesting discussion of the efforts of Republican leaders to square their doctrines with capital-labor conflict in the North, see James L. Hutson, "Facing an Angry Labor: The American Public Interprets the Shoemaker's Strike of 1860," *Civil War History* 28 (Sept. 1982): 200–206.

63. Eric Foner, "The Causes of the American Civil War: Recent Interpretations and New Directions," *Civil War History* 20 (Sept. 1974): 206. The complexity of this last set of questions is suggested by the recent debate they have provoked with respect to earlier British abolitionists who either seemed oblivious to free labor exploitation in Britain or explicitly denied its existence. For discussion and criticisms of David Brion Davis's argument that many of these British abolitionists were engaging in unconscious, social "self-deception" during certain periods of time, see Thomas L. Haskell, "Capitalism and the Origins of the Humanitarian Sensibility," pt. 1, *American Historical Review,* 90 (Apr. 1985): 339–61; Haskell, pt. 2 of same, *American Historical Review* 90 (June 1985): 547–66; see also the contributions of Haskell, David Brion Davis, and John Ashworth in "*AHR* Forum," *American Historical Review* 92 (Oct. 1987); and Davis, *Problem of Slavery in the Age of Revolution,* 343–468.

64. The emphasis on manual labor's instrumental value represented perhaps the principal thrust of Northern free labor ideology. But see chapter 3 for antislavery use of the additional argument that the intrinsic character of much manual labor is protean and that Northern free laborers, in possession of ample material, mobility, and educational opportunities, accordingly possessed something else that chattel slaves did not: the incentive and the knowledge to expand the "inventiveness" and intellectual content of their labor. Only rarely, however, was this argument explicitly extended to the most patently drudge-like kinds of common wage labor.

65. Robert William Fogel has recently drawn attention to the "'hidden' economic depression and social catastrophe" that engulfed native-born, especially skilled workers in the Northern cities from 1848 to 1855, primarily as a result of the economic competition and social problems generated by the huge influx of poor, predominantly Irish Catholic, immigrants. Many of these economically besieged native-born workers found a home first in the Know-Nothing movement and then in the Republican party, and it would appear that for perhaps most of them a credible "free labor ideology" continued throughout the 1850s to blend anti-immigrant labor themes—based on issues that struck close to home—with the more abstract Republican principle of sustaining and extending Northern economic opportunity in the face of the Slave Power's territorial pretensions. Immigration eased off after the mid-1850s; Fogel's analysis thus raises the interesting hypothetical question of what might have happened politically had these native-born workers continued to suffer the severe effects of large-scale immigration in tandem with the economic downturns of the late 1850s: would they have found Republican free labor

ideology increasingly less credible and relevant to their needs and deserted the fragile antislavery coalition for a new organization built upon more resolutely nativist principles?; Robert William Fogel, *Without Consent or Contract: The Rise and Fall of American Slavery* (New York: W. W. Norton and Company, 1989), 355–56, 385–86.

66. Foner, *Free Soil, Free Labor, Free Men,* 33–34, 297, contains suggestions of this same argument.

67. We might illustrate this point with a modern example. Menial, "dead-end" tasks that are commonly regarded as undesirable, perhaps even contemptible work for individuals of average abilities take on an entirely different complexion, and emerge as purposeful, productive, even dignified labor, when they are allocated to the mentally retarded—i.e., when they are used to give added purpose to the lives of individuals who lack the capacity for more demanding work.

68. See the discussion in chapter 6 of the stereotyping of female work.

69. Of the nineteenth-century thinkers who figure in this study, Karl Marx is perhaps the one whose writings most clearly approach the rarefied status of "canons," or classical texts. Yet as I indicate in chapter 5, Marx's early observations and concerns regarding specialization, alienation, the nature of work and its proper relationship to "leisure time," distinctly profound as many of them were, reflected a contemporary climate of opinion to which many "middle-level" American and European thinkers were also contributing and giving expression. For distinctions among kinds of intellectual history, see especially Laurence Veysey, "Intellectual History and the New Social History," and David A. Hollinger, "Historians and the Discourse of Intellectuals," both in John Higham and Paul K. Conkin, eds., *New Directions in American Intellectual History* (Baltimore: Johns Hopkins University Press, 1979); and David F. Lindenfield, "On Systems and Embodiments as Categories for Intellectual History," *History and Theory* 27 (Feb. 1988): 30–50.

70. The question of why certain ideas and not other ones propounded in the writings of intellectuals reach and appeal to a wider audience is a complex one; see, however, Maurice F. Neufeld, "Realms of Thought and Organized Labor in the Age of Jackson," *Labor History* 10 (Winter 1969): 5–43, for a fine illustration of how the doctrine of the social and economic primacy of the producing classes, originating largely in the writings of British classical economists and Ricardian socialists, entered the "public domain" of ideas in America and was put to conservative as well as radical uses there. Another doctrine of even more pervasive influence, Malthus's theory of population, similarly lent itself to diverse meanings and uses, in some measure because it was riddled with ambiguities to begin with; see Mark Blaug, *Ricardian Economics* (New Haven: Yale University Press, 1958), 119; and Kenneth Smith, *The Malthusian Controversy* (London: Routledge and Kegan Paul, 1951), 4, 235, 326–32.

71. The United States during this period lacked trained economists as we think of them today; economics was then commonly studied as a branch of the discipline of moral philosophy, and many of the authors of the most popular economic works were clerics who lacked specialized academic training in the field; see Joseph Dorfman, *The Economic Mind in American Civilization 1606–1865* (New York: Viking Press, 1946), 2: 707–8. Yet much of even these works is given over to technical discussions of the same issues—theory of value, doctrine of rent, etc.—that occupy the influential treatises of Ricardo and the other British classical economists. My interest lies not in these technical discussions or models, but in the selective use made of them by politicians, reformers, and others who engaged in more generalized discussions of free labor. I should perhaps add that as a study in the history of

ideas, this is not the sort of inquiry in which private correspondence and other unpublished manuscript collections played a very important role. More meaningful, certainly more extensive, discussions of work were with a few exceptions found in newspapers and other "public" kinds of literature, ones offering a deliberately analytical and argumentative context in which commentators addressed audiences.

72. Many examples covering a wide range of work situations and worker cultural traditions might be produced here. But see Evelyn Nakano Glenn, "The Dialectics of Wage Work: Japanese American Women and Domestic Service, 1905–1940," in Ellen Carol DuBois and Vicki L. Ruiz, eds., *Unequal Sisters: A Multicultural Reader in U.S. Women's History* (New York: Routledge, 1990). Glenn writes of these women: they acknowledged that their domestic service was "menial," yet they also took pride "in their physical strength and endurance" and in their ability to accomplish "whatever was asked" (358); see also the imaginative use made of the poetry and other writings of French working-class authors to reconstruct their complex attitudes toward their trades in Jacques Rancière, *The Nights of Labor: The Workers' Dream in Nineteenth-Century France*, trans. John Drury (Philadelphia: Temple University Press, 1989); and Rancière, "The Myth of the Artisan: Critical Reflections on a Category of Social History," trans. David H. Lake and Cynthia J. Koepp, in Steven Laurence Kaplan and Cynthia J. Koepp, eds., *Work in France: Representations, Meaning, Organization, and Practice* (Ithaca: Cornell University Press, 1986), 317–34. I am also indebted to Steven M. Stowe, among others, for the points raised in the text above.

73. Krishan Kumar, *The Rise of Modern Society: Aspects of the Social and Political Development of the West* (Oxford, Eng.: Basil Blackwell, 1988), 233, 234.

74. Peter N. Stearns, "The Middle Class: Toward a Precise Definition," *Comparative Studies in Society and History* 21 (July 1979): 377–96; and in the same issue, Lenore O. Boyle, "The Classless Society: Comment on Stearns," 397–413; John Seed, "Unitarianism, Political Economy and the Antinomies of Liberal Culture in Manchester, 1830–50," *Social History* 7 (Jan. 1982): 1–25; and Harold Perkin, *Origins of Modern English Society* (London: Ark Paperbacks, 1985 [1969]), 221–31, 252–70. I also refer readers to a collection of essays debating the location of noncapitalist "mental laborers"—what some regard as a truly separate "Professional-Managerial Class"—within the modern class structure: Pat Walker, ed., *Between Labor and Capital* (Boston: South End, 1979).

75. The editor of the *Morning Courier and New-York Enquirer,* James Watson Webb, belonged to the conservative wing of the Whig party and was a bitter antagonist of Greeley's efforts to associate Whiggery with many of the *Tribune* editor's pet reforms.

76. I am indebted to Jean-Christophe Agnew for alerting me to the need to address this issue, although I am not at all certain that the next few paragraphs would meet with his agreement.

77. Peter Walker, "The Dignity of Labor," *Nineteenth Century: A Quarterly Miscellany* 3 (1849): 288. Some two decades later a writer for the *Galaxy* similarly reported: "We read in men's speeches now and then fine passages about 'the dignity of labor.' It is a fine phrase—it seems to be nothing more. I have sought in vain to learn that any orator who has used this fine phrase has been desirous or even willing to have his son learn one of the manual trades. I can discover no man with any wealth at all who has taken steps to have his son engage in one of the working occupations" ("Is Labor a Curse?" *Galaxy. An Illustrated Magazine of Entertaining Reading* 6 [Oct. 1868]: 539).

78. It can hardly be overlooked, at the same time, that some of the notable

articulators of these same pieties, such as the Massachusetts Senator Henry Wilson, had undeniably "risen" from wage-laboring status.

79. See also the comments in Thomas Brown, *Politics and Statesmanship: Essays on the American Whig Party* (New York: Columbia University Press, 1985), 13–14.

80. Although they have somewhat different meanings, "beliefs," "perceptions," and "attitudes," as I understand them, share a connotation of being sincerely or authentically held at the conscious level, a fact that is of great relevance to my discussion here. A useful discussion is Milton Rokeach, *Beliefs, Attitudes, and Values: A Theory of Organization and Change* (San Francisco: Jossey-Bass, 1968).

81. For a particularly good example of an argument about work's intrinsic moral value that was used to rationalize economic self-interest, see the discussion in chapter 7 of the Uxbridge, Massachusetts, manufacturing firm that opposed reduced hours for its foreign-born juvenile workers. For examples of arguments that rationalized new kinds of economic activity, see chapter 3 for the various claims that factory workers were not lacking desirable intellectual stimulation, that they found such either in their immediate tasks or in their work environment. I have found especially valuable a number of essays by Rowland Berthoff that describe efforts in nineteenth-century America to defend industrial entrepreneurship and other practices as falling under the mantle of "republican" economic activity. Such efforts exemplified, among other things, the function performed by ideology of denying or minimizing the discrepancies between older ideals and new realities, and of thereby easing the tensions and anxieties resulting from those discrepancies; see Rowland Berthoff, "Peasants and Artisans, Puritans and Republicans: Personal Liberty and Communal Equality in American History," *Journal of American History* 69 (Dec. 1982): 579–98; Berthoff, "Independence and Attachment, Virtue and Interest: From Republican Citizen to Free Enterpriser, 1787–1837," in Richard L. Bushman et al., eds., *Uprooted Americans: Essays to Honor Oscar Handlin* (Boston: Little, Brown and Company, 1979), 99–124; Berthoff and John M. Murrin, "Feudalism, Communalism, and the Yeoman Freeholder: The American Revolution Considered as a Social Accident," in Stephen G. Kurtz and James H. Hutson, eds., *Essays on the American Revolution* (Chapel Hill: University of North Carolina Press, 1973), 256–88; see also Shalhope, "Republicanism and Early American Historiography," 347–50.

82. The pioneering body of work on this subject with respect to the "world view" of Southern slaveholders and proslavery writers, one which minimizes the numbers in this group who either engaged in cynical hypocrisy or were torn by feelings of self-doubt and guilt, is that of Eugene D. Genovese; see especially *The World the Slaveholders Made* (New York: Random House, 1969), 126, 143–50. See also Parrish, *Slavery*, 138–41; and Maurice Onwood, "Impulse and Honor: The Place of Slave and Master in the Ideology of Planterdom," *Plantation Society in the Americas* 1 (Feb. 1979): 31–56. In his earlier work particularly, Genovese refused to treat with equal seriousness the ideology of the Northern capitalists, politicians, and writers who defended Northern capitalist free society, seeming to dismiss their articulated beliefs as shallow and cynical expressions of vested economic interests; for a short but incisive critique of Genovese's work on this grounds, see Tom Wagstaff, "Political Economy of Slavery," *Studies on the Left,* 6 (July–Aug. 1966): 65.

83. I refer readers again to the stimulating discussions by Haskell, Davis, and Ashworth, cited in note 63 above.

84. For discussions of many of the relevant issues and debates, which I have condensed and simplified here, see David Harlan, "Intellectual History and the Return of Literature"; David A. Hollinger, "The Return of the Prodigal: The Persistence of Historical Knowing"; and Harlan, "Reply to David Hollinger," all in

American Historical Review 94 (June 1989); James T. Kloppenberg, "Objectivity and Historicism: A Century of American Historical Writing," *American Historical Review* 94 (Oct. 1989): 1011–30; many of the essays in Dominick La Capra and Steven L. Kaplan, eds., *Modern European Intellectual History: Reappraisals and New Perspectives* (Ithaca: Cornell University Press, 1982); virtually every issue of the *Intellectual History Newsletter*; a recent book-length, Marxist assault on poststructuralist applications: Bryan D. Palmer, *Descent into Discourse: The Reification of Language and the Writing of Social History* (Philadephia: Temple University Press, 1990); and for elaboration and criticism of Quentin Skinner's contextualist approach, Tully, ed., *Meaning and Context.*

85. David A. Hollinger suggests, too, that such applications of poststructuralist literary criticism as David Harlan's have up to this time primarily addressed the alleged limitations of the more rarefied, "canon"-dominated intellectual history, not those studies such as mine that are more exclusively concerned with the "middle ground" of perceptions and beliefs; Hollinger, "Return of Prodigal," 616–17.

86. I refer readers particularly to Blumin, *Emergence of the Middle Class,* which, in treating some of the same themes and reaching some of the same conclusions as my study, focuses much less on discourse, and alternatively provides an excellent, far more detailed social history of the material life—physical workspaces, living arrangements, consumption patterns, and the like—of different urban occupational groups in this period.

87. Describing the specific situations of many of the commentators on free labor is not possible for the reason that much of the discussion was conducted in newspaper articles or in the literature of social organizations where the particular writers remained anonymous. Michael O' Brien has a few thoughtful remarks on the troubling implications of evaluating commentary "untouched by the specifics of authorship, place, or circumstance" (specifically with respect to essays in antebellum Southern periodicals), in *Rethinking the South: Essays in Intellectual History* (Baltimore: Johns Hopkins University Press, 1988), 32–33.

88. I am indebted to the anonymous reader for Yale University Press for raising this along with a number of other issues.

89. See, for example, Foner, *Reconstruction,* 106–10, 154–57, 236–37, 277–79, 484; Fredrickson, *Black Image,* 178–83; Ira Berlin et al., "The Terrain of Freedom: The Struggle over the Meaning of Free Labor in the U.S. South," *History Workshop Journal,* no. 22 (Autumn 1986): 108–30; and for the growing, racist disillusionment of antislavery Northerners over the "intransigence" of the freedmen regarding their failure to throw themselves into agricultural wage labor with the discipline and enthusiasm called for by the Northerners' "free-labor faith," see especially Lawrence N. Powell, *New Masters: Northern Planters during the Civil War and Reconstruction* (New Haven: Yale University Press, 1980), 31, 73, 117–22.

90. Glickstein, "Concepts of Free Labor."

CHAPTER 2: MENTAL CONTENT IN MANUAL LABOR

1. Conversely, and in consequence of its obligatory nature, the service rendered by a hired professional gardener (to pursue an example from chapter 1, note 2), however much he may enjoy his labors, constitutes "work" in a fundamentally different sense from the gardening performed by the amateur who pursues this activity only for the satisfaction he receives from it; see Alasdair Clayre, *Work and Play: Ideas and Experience of Work and Leisure* (New York: Harper and Row, 1974), 210.

2. For Aristotle's views regarding "natural slavery" and manual labor, see *The*

Politics of Aristotle, ed. and trans. Ernest Barker (New York: Oxford University Press, 1962), 9–18, 36–37, 101–9, 165, 301, 317–23, 335–36; see also David Brion Davis, *The Problem of Slavery in Western Culture* (Ithaca: Cornell University Press, 1966), 69–72. Because of limitations of space, the characterization of the "classical Greek" position expressed in the text above simplifies and passes over a number of issues that bear on the actual absoluteness and pervasiveness of the ancient disdain for manual labor. How representative of ancient Greek and Roman writers were the views of a few prominent thinkers like Aristotle? To what extent was manual labor performed by self-employed, economically independent artisans or peasants, i.e., work that was dictated by economic necessity but that was neither wage nor slave labor, free of the contempt expressed toward manual labor? To what extent was the ancient aristocratic or elitist disdain for manual labor ameliorated by an admiration, articulated by some writers, for the expertise displayed by skilled craftsmen? And aristocratic disdain for manual labor notwithstanding, to what degree might at least the skilled artisan segment of the manual laboring population, just as craftsmen of later cultures, have possessed a pride of workmanship which repelled the tendency of ruling class values to filter down the social scale? For discussions of these issues, see Robert Schlaifer, "Greek Theories of Slavery from Homer to Aristotle," in M. I. Finley, ed., *Slavery in Classical Antiquity: Views and Controversies* (Cambridge, Eng.: W. Heffer and Sons, 1960), 165–204; M. I. Finley, *The Ancient Economy* (Berkeley: University of California Press, 1973), 41–42, 81–82; Finley, *Economy and Society in Ancient Greece,* eds. Brent D. Shaw and Richard P. Saller (London: Chatto and Windus, 1981), 97–114; Rodolfo Mondolfo, "The Greek Attitude to Manual Labour," trans. D. S. Duncan, *Past and Present,* no. 6 (Nov. 1954): 1–5; Maurice Balme, "Attitudes to Work and Leisure in Ancient Greece," *Greece and Rome* 31 (Oct. 1984): 140–52; G. E. M. De Ste. Croix, *The Class Struggle in the Ancient World from the Archaic Age to the Arab Conquests* (London: Gerald Duckworth, 1981), 274; and Ellen Meiksins Wood, *Peasant-Citizen and Slave: The Foundations of Athenian Democracy* (London: Verso, 1988), 22–28, 137–45.

3. See chapter 7. We might note here the converse but not necessarily contradictory argument, one which forms, for example, a part of feminist criticism of both women's unpaid housework and women's "volunteer" work, that labor has to be made instrumental, i.e., adequately recompensed, in order to win societal esteem and to render it attractive; see Deanne Bonnar, "Women, Work and Poverty: Exit from an Ancient Trap by the Redefinition of Work," in David Gil and Eva Gil, eds., *The Future of Work* (Cambridge, Mass.: Schenkman Books, 1987), 72, 79–81; Bettina Eileen Berch, "Industrialization and Working Women in the Nineteenth Century: England, France, and the United States" (Ph.D. diss., University of Wisconsin, Madison, 1976), 7; and Wendy Kaminer, *Women Volunteering: The Pleasure, Pain, and Politics of Unpaid Work from 1830 to the Present* (Garden City, N.Y.: Doubleday and Company, 1984), xv–xvii, 2. Greeley himself defended the antebellum New England factory system in part by arguing that "our Manufacturing Industry" will elevate the "social position of Woman" through the unprecedented economic opportunities and money value it attached to female labor (Horace Greeley to Pauline Davis, Sept. 1, 1852, Greeley Papers, Manuscript Division, Library of Congress, Washington, D.C.). Conservative complaints that female factory work in the Waltham-type New England mills in the 1830s and 1840s was *too* remunerative and would give the operatives pretensions above their "station" were sometimes countered by claims that high wages in fact served the needs of a capitalist economy by eroding the traditional prejudice against factory work.

4. A good discussion is Sean Sayers, "Work, Leisure and Human Needs," in

Tom Winnifrith and Cyril Barrett, eds., *The Philosophy of Leisure* (Houndmills, Eng.: Macmillan Press, 1989), 35–36.

5. Arno J. Mayer has commented, for example, on the tenuously mental character of the work performed by many white-collar clerks who contributed to the growth of the "lower middle class" after 1870: "The operators of keyboard machines do work that is manual, though not menial, labor. In fact, in terms of dependency, routinization, subordination, and (probably) income, the vast battalions of ordinary white-collars in sales, distribution, accounting, banking, and insurance are not unlike industrial workers" (Arno J. Mayer, "The Lower Middle Class as Historical Problem," *Journal of Modern History* 47 [Sept. 1975]: 428). Lower-middle-class working conditions in law offices and other work sites were sufficiently formed by the middle of the nineteenth century to lead Herman Melville, among others, to conclusions that anticipated Mayer's; see, for example, the discussion of "Bartleby, the Scrivener," in Robert Shulman, *Social Criticism and Nineteenth Century American Fictions* (Columbia: University of Missouri Press, 1987), 6–27.

6. The Italian Marxist Antonio Gramsci, for one, noted that the best efforts of Frederick Taylor, and of modern industrial capitalism generally, to remove all mental content from physical labor, to reduce the latter to the activity of a "'trained gorilla,'" must fall short of complete success; the human character of labor could not be eliminated: "in any physical work, even the most degraded and mechanical, there exists . . . a minimum of creative intellectual activity" (Gramsci, *Selections from the Prison Notebooks of Antonio Gramsci,* ed. and trans. Quintin Hoare and Geoffrey Nowell Smith [New York: International Publishers, 1971], 8, 302–10). For an interesting discussion which, invoking Gramsci among others, stresses a number of difficulties in categorizing various occupations and activities as either "mental" or "manual," see Robert Schaeffer and James Weinstein, "Between the Lines," in Pat Walker, ed., *Between Labor and Capital* (Boston: South End, 1979), 153–57. See also a study whose title encapsulates its argument: Ken C. Kusterer, *Know-How on the Job: The Important Working Knowledge of "Unskilled" Workers* (Boulder: Westview Press, 1978). Kusterer, however, seems to me to overextend his valuable documentation and insights by flatly concluding that "there is no such thing as unskilled work" (179).

7. For a recent study that emphasizes the physical demands of much skilled craft labor, past and present, and notes that these very demands lead some machine-tending unskilled workers to prefer their own employments as easier and "cleaner," see Shoshana Zuboff, *In the Age of the Smart Machine: The Future of Work and Power* (New York: Basic Books, 1988), 37–40, 49–50. On the nature of the late eighteenth- and early nineteenth-century "mechanic arts," see Gary John Kornblith, "From Artisans to Businessmen: Master Mechanics in New England, 1789–1850" (Ph.D. diss., Princeton University, 1983), 132–34.

We should also note that although social perceptions of the relative significance of mental and bodily talents in a given occupation have a significant bearing on the social standing of that occupation, those perceptions may vary over time and may hold at any given moment a very inexact correspondence to actual developments within that occupation. W. J. Reader has remarked that by the end of the eighteenth century in England, it was "particularly among the surgeons," rather than among "the arrogant and expensive physicians . . . that most of the advances in [medical] knowledge were being made. The surgeons were not hampered by veneration of the classics, and they cut people up to see what really went on inside." Yet in part because their work continued to be perceived as primarily bodily in nature, surgeons remained not "yet clearly distinguishable from skilled tradesmen"

(W. J. Reader, *Professional Men: The Rise of the Professional Classes in Nineteenth-Century England* [New York: Basic Books, 1966], 32, 42, 146). Only during the next century would British surgeons convert their contributions to knowledge into acquisition of much of the professional esteem already accorded physicians by the public. See also Wilfred Prest, "Introduction: The Professions and Society in Early Modern England," in Prest, ed., *The Professions in Early Modern England* (London: Croom Helm, 1987), 12–13.

8. Discussions of the status of master craftsmen proprietors include Clyde and Sally Griffen, *Natives and Newcomers: The Ordering of Opportunity in Mid-Nineteenth Century Poughkeepsie* (Cambridge: Harvard University Press, 1978), 53. I am using the term *capitalist* loosely, recognizing that in Marx's view, for one, farm proprietors and master craftsmen were not strictly members of the "capitalist class," but rather elements of the unstable "petite bourgeoisie" or intermediate classes, the great portion of which he predicted would be dissolved or forced into the industrial proletariat. For a discussion of Marx's various "transitional" classes, see Gavin Mackenzie, "Class Boundaries and the Labour Process," in Anthony Giddens and Gavin Mackenzie, eds., *Social Class and the Division of Labour: Essays in Honor of Ilya Neustadt* (Cambridge, Eng.: Cambridge University Press, 1982), 63–72. The nineteenth-century British radical Thomas Hodgskin well described the similarly dual character of the master craftsman in his own country: "Masters, it is evident, are *labourers* as well as their journeymen. In this character their interest is precisely the same as that of their men. But they are also either capitalists or the agents of the capitalists, and in this respect their interest is decidedly opposed to the interest of their workmen" (Thomas Hodgskin, *Labour Defended against the Claims of Capital or the Unproductiveness of Capital Proved with Reference to the Present Combinations amongst Journeymen* [London: Labour Publishing Company, 1922 {1825}], 90). See also Marx's similar statement quoted later in this chapter and the incisive descriptions of the stage of class consciousness that Hodsgkin's observation reflected in Gareth Stedman Jones, *Languages of Class: Studies in English Working Class History 1832–1982* (Cambridge, Eng.: Cambridge University Press, 1983), 136–37; and Jones, "Class Struggle and the Industrial Revolution," *New Left Review*, no. 90 (Mar.–Apr. 1975): 58.

9. In cities like Providence, Rhode Island, and Albany, New York, where antebellum industrialization hit more slowly and with less intensity than in, say, Newark, New Jersey, or Cincinnati, Ohio, journeymen seem to have clung more persistently to the belief that their economic interests coincided with those of their employers, that both were producers working in tandem, and that in terms of social esteem, material rewards, and advancement opportunities, they as journeymen maintained a condition of truly "free labor." Contrast the findings of John S. Gilkeson, Jr., *Middle Class Providence, 1820–1940* (Princeton: Princeton University Press, 1986), and Brian Greenberg, *Worker and Community: Response to Industrialization in a Nineteenth Century American City, Albany, New York 1850–1884* (Albany: State University of New York Press, 1985) with the earlier evidence of class conflict and trade unionism found in Susan Eleanor Hirsch Bloomberg, "Industrialization and Skilled Workers: Newark, 1826 to 1860" (Ph.D. diss., University of Michigan, 1974) and Steven J. Ross, *Workers on the Edge: Work, Leisure, and Politics in Industrializing Cincinnati, 1788–1890* (New York: Columbia University Press, 1985). See also Friedrich Lenger, "Class, Culture and Class Consciousness in Ante-Bellum Lynn: A Critique of Alan Dawley and Paul Faler," *Social History* 6 (Oct. 1981): 320–29; Jones, *Languages*, 139–44; Sean Wilentz, *Chants Democratic: New York City and the Rise of the American Working Class* (New York: Oxford University Press, 1984),

17, 149, 215, 247, 253; Kornblith, "From Artisans to Businessmen," 501–22; John Barkeley Jentz, "Artisans, Evangelicals, and the City: A Social History of Abolition and Labor Reform in Jacksonian New York" (Ph.D. diss., City University of New York, 1977), 149–50; Amy Bridges, "Becoming American: The Working Classes in the United States before the Civil War," in Ira Katznelson and Aristide R. Zolberg, eds., *Working-Class Formation: Nineteenth Century Patterns in Western Europe and the United States* (Princeton: Princeton University Press, 1986), 184–86; and Maurice Isserman, "An Exchange in the Rochester *Workingman's Advocate*: March, 1840," *Labor History* 20 (Winter 1979): 141–42.

10. Defenses of industrial capitalism in mid-nineteenth-century America employed a variety of arguments to legitimate the propertyless, economically dependent condition of industrial wage earners, including prospects for good wages and social mobility, and opportunities for education, moral refinement, and "character" development. Yet as indicated earlier also, industrial capitalism and its specific defenses were long antedated by notions of "possessive individualism" that sanctioned in a general way the condition of propertyless and mobile, legally free manual laborers.

11. Elizabeth Palmer Peabody, "Plan of the West Roxbury Community," *Dial* 2 (Jan. 1842): 362–63. See also Ann C. Rose, *Transcendentalism as a Social Movement, 1830–1850* (New Haven: Yale University Press, 1981), 134–35. For a probing recent sketch of Peabody's relationship to a variety of reform movements, focusing on her eventual representation in "the American literary canon" as an antislavery feminist, see Jean Fagan Yellin, *Women and Sisters: The Antislavery Feminists in American Culture* (New Haven: Yale University Press, 1989): 154, 153–169. Also valuable is the profile of Peabody by Bruce A. Ronda in his "Introduction" to Ronda, ed., *Letters of Elizabeth Palmer Peabody: American Renaissance Woman* (Middletown: Wesleyan University Press, 1984), 3–46. Ronda's emphasis is upon the more conservative and decorous dimensions of Peabody's social thought: her Unitarian-based "vision of a harmonious Christian society," her corresponding aversion to the class conflict doctrines of contemporary writers like Orestes Brownson, and her acceptance of "some of society's deepest cultural assumptions—the sanctity of the family, the nurturing role of women, the unique connection of woman to children's education" (32–33, 46). Yet Ronda's emphasis, as he himself might agree, should not obscure what was genuinely utopian in Peabody's thinking. The latter certainly included her endorsement of the Brook Farm manner of confronting the relative disagreeableness of "bodily labor." Through free market processes or more blatantly coercive means, societies past and present had recognized and certified this relative disagreeableness by esteeming and compensating bodily labor less than "intellectual labor." Brook Farm offered a radical departure from this conventional treatment.

12. See chapter 7; and P. D. Anthony, *The Ideology of Work* (London: Tavistock Publications, 1977), 314.

13. David Meakin, *Man and Work: Literature and Culture in Industrial Society* (New York: Holmes and Meier, 1976), 38–41; and Jonathan Beecher, *Charles Fourier: The Visionary and His World* (Berkeley: University of California Press, 1986), 220–96.

14. Bruce Laurie, "'Nothing on Compulsion:' Life Styles of Philadelphia Artisans, 1820–1850," *Labor History* 15 (Summer 1974): 341; Charles Stephenson, "'There's Plenty Waitin' at the Gates': Mobility, Opportunity and the American Worker," in Charles Stephenson and Robert Asher, eds., *Life and Labor: Dimensions of American Working-Class History,* (Albany: State University of New York, 1986), 82–86.

15. Leo Tolstoy, *Anna Karenina*, ed. Leonard J. Kent and Nina Berberova, trans. Constance Garnett (New York: Modern Library, 1965), 262–67. For a recent study that confirms the conclusion of the early Commons school of American labor historiography that until the early 1850s at least, the dominant goal behind organized labor's drive for shorter hours was increased leisure for self-improvement and relaxation, see David R. Roediger, "The Movement for a Shorter Working Day in the United States before 1866" (Ph.D. diss., Northwestern University, 1980), 43–93. After this time, the scholarly consensus holds that organized labor increasingly turned to shorter hours as a way of reducing the supply of labor and thereby driving up wages and reducing unemployment. The causes for this change in sensibility remain obscure, and they are not explored in the following chapters, in part because the evidence for such a change in the later antebellum years remains, in my opinion, somewhat scanty and inconclusive. Whatever the changes in sensibility among unionized labor, the weight of recent research suggests, in any case, that unorganized, largely immigrant workers continued throughout the second half of the nineteenth century to strongly value leisure time for nonpecuniary reasons; see David Montgomery, "Gutman's Nineteenth Century America," *Labor History* 19 (Summer 1978): 416–29; and for a good historiographic review of the literature, see Benjamin Kline Hunnicutt, *Work without End: Abandoning Shorter Hours for the Right to Work* (Philadelphia: Temple University Press, 1988), 9–15.

16. Alonzo Potter, *Political Economy: Its Objects, Uses, and Principles: Considered with Reference to the Condition of the American People* (New York: Harper and Brothers, 1840), 59, 60. Pages 51–231 of Potter's work are substantially a reprint of the first ten chapters of Scrope's *Principles of Political Economy, Deduced from the Natural Laws of Social Welfare, and Applied to the Present State of Britain* (London: Longman, 1833). (Scrope's equivalent remarks to those quoted in the text are on pp. 47, 48.) In this chapter I treat these observations and opinions regarding the physical pleasures of manual labor as Potter's own, regardless of the fact that he was borrowing so heavily from Scrope. As he indicates in the "Advertisement" to his study, and as, indeed, a comparison of the two books makes clear, Potter did not reprint indiscriminately from the British author. He was quite willing to alter Scrope's text, or even to provide qualifying footnotes, whenever he felt Scrope's statements deviated from the "truth" or were at least inappropriate to the "meridian" of America ("Advertisement," v–vi). The other portions of Potter's *Political Economy* are Potter's original work.

17. "H" [George Frederick Holmes], "Greeley on Reforms," *Southern Literary Messenger* 17 (May 1851): 277.

18. "Respectability of Labor in the South.—Free and Slave Labor," *The Plough, the Loom, and the Anvil* 7 (Sept. 1854): 134.

19. Jeremy Bentham, "The Psychology of Economic Man," in *Jeremy Bentham's Economic Writings, Critical Edition Based on His Printed Works and Unpublished Manuscripts*, ed. W. Stark (London: George Allen and Unwin, 1954), 3: 427–28; T. R. Malthus, *An Essay on the Principle of Population; or, a View of Its Past and Present Effects on Human Happiness; with an Inquiry into Our Prospects Respecting the Future Removal or Mitigation of the Evils Which It Occasions*, 5th ed. (London: John Murray, 1817), 2: 276; 3: 225, 275, 287, 303–4; John Stuart Mill, *Principles of Political Economy with Some of Their Applications to Social Philosophy*, from the 5th London ed. (New York: D. Appleton and Company, 1892), 1: 438–45; 2: 379–80; E. K. Hunt, *History of Economic Thought: A Critical Perspective* (Belmont, Calif.: Wadsworth Publishing Company, 1979), 115, 131; J. H. Poynter, *Society and Pauperism: English Ideas on Poor Relief, 1795–1834* (London: Routledge and Kegan Paul,

1969), 158; Jonathan M. Wainwright, *Inequality of Individual Wealth the Ordinance of Providence, and Essential to Civilization,* sermon before the Governor, Lieutenant-Governor, and Legislature of Massachusetts, Jan. 7, 1835 (Boston: Dutton and Wentworth, 1835), 26.

20. "British and Continental Characteristics," *North British Review* 21 (May 1854): 56. For the efforts of members of Boston's business and professional elite to escape, if only during their leisure hours, to a "simpler and quieter enjoyment of existence" in the form of "gentleman farming," and to exorcise in the process their ambivalence and guilt over their pursuit of economic success, see Tamara Plakins Thornton, *Cultivating Gentlemen: The Meaning of Country Life among the Boston Elite 1785–1860* (New Haven: Yale University Press, 1989), 143–45, 162–65. See also the discussion of anxiety generated by middle-class striving and overwork in the pursuit of monetary success and social status in Martin L. Adelman, *A Sporting Time: New York City and the Rise of Modern Athletics, 1820–1870* (Urbana: University of Illinois Press, 1986), 273–75.

21. Alexis De Tocqueville, *Democracy in America,* ed. J. P. Mayer, trans. George Lawrence, 2 vols. in 1 (Garden City, N.Y.: Anchor Books, 1969 [1835]), 2: 535–38.

22. [Henry W. Bellows], "Influence of the Trading Spirit upon the Social and Moral Life of America," *American Review* 1 (Jan. 1845): 95, 96.

23. "British and Continental Characteristics," 55, 59.

24. Bellows himself seemed to suggest something like this in a later address before Harvard's Phi Beta Kappa society; Henry W. Bellows, *The Ledger and the Lexicon: Or, Business and Literature, in Account with American Education* (Cambridge: John Bartlett, 1853), 21–22. This oration bears a number of interesting comparisons with Bellows' earlier essay in the *American Whig Review.* Bellows continued to refer to a condition of "universal comfort" in America, notwithstanding the indisputable presence by 1853 of a greatly increased body of impoverished immigrant Irish (49). At the same time, Bellows expressed in *Ledger and Lexicon* a much less critical view than he had earlier of the acquisitive ethos that attended this "universal comfort."

25. [George Frederick Holmes], "Ancient Slavery," pt. 1, *De Bow's Review* 19 (Nov. 1855): 571–72, 577; and pt. 2, *De Bow's Review* 19 (Dec. 1855): 618.

26. Potter, *Political Economy,* 266–304. This is not to imply what is not the case: that Potter accepted all or even most of the major classical economic contributions—e.g., Malthus's doctrine of overpopulation. What Potter did share with the classical economists was a bourgeois sense of the rectitude of competitive individualism, together with an allied belief in the "natural" ruling force of the "law" of supply and demand in the marketplace.

27. Elsewhere, however, particularly in his attacks on "demagogic" trade union agitation in the United States, Potter especially made use of these and other American exceptionalist notions; he was, as suggested, a rather conventional proponent of Northern free labor ideology, combining such exceptionalist notions with at least a mild antagonism toward Southern chattel slavery; see Potter, *Political Economy,* 60–63, 84–86, 197, 208, 242–302; [Alonzo Potter], "Trades' Unions," *New-York Review* 2 (Jan. 1838): 23; and Joseph Dorfman, *The Economic Mind in American Civilization 1606–1865* (New York: Viking Press, 1946) 2: 826–33.

28. For relevant discussions of Thoreau, see John Patrick Diggins, *The Lost Soul of American Politics* (New York: Basic Books, 1984) 209–14, 323; Diggins, "Thoreau, Marx, and the 'Riddle' of Alienation," *Social Research* 39 (Winter 1972): 582–95; Leo Stoller, *After Walden. Thoreau's Changing Views on Economic Man* (Stanford: Stanford University Press, 1957), 5–15, 20, 108–19. Discussions of the disaffection with

work within modern "bourgeois" society include Daniel Bell, *The Cultural Contradictions of Capitalism* (New York: Basic Books, 1976); Michael Rose, *Re-working the Work Ethic: Economic Values and Socio-Cultural Politics* (London: Batsford Academic and Educational, 1985); and Neala Schleuning, *Idle Hands and Empty Hearts: Work and Freedom in the United States* (New York: Bergin and Garvey, 1990).

29. For a sympathetic discussion, very much in the tradition of William Morris, George Bernard Shaw, and other late nineteenth–early twentieth-century socialists, of more egalitarian and equitable alternatives to the prevailing distribution by market forces of "dangerous work," "grueling work," and "dirty work," see Michael Walzer, *Spheres of Justice: A Defense of Pluralism and Equality* (New York: Basic Books, 1983), 165–83. For another modern appeal for "a democratic division of labor," as opposed to "the capitalist division of labor," one which calls for a more equitable division of the most menial work, see Philip Green, *Retrieving Democracy: In Search of Civic Equality* (Totowa, N.J.: Rowman and Allanheld, 1985), 80–87, 108–11. Green also follows the Fourierists by arguing that because individuals vary in their innate "motives and ambitions," even conditions that somehow gave every member of society truly equal educational opportunity and free occupational choice would not result in the abandonment of socially vital physical labor. There is "no reason to believe," Green observes, "that all people would want to work at the most demanding, most responsible, most intellectually or technically complex, or most prestigious kinds of work" (109–110).

30. A number of essays and reviews by J. H. Plumb have significantly influenced my thinking on this issue. Questioning the emphasis Winthrop Jordan gives to white racist attitudes as an underpinning of black slavery in the New World, Plumb observes, for example, that "a discussion of slavery without a consideration of the exploitation of other [white] laborers tends to obscure fundamental issues, . . . The basis of the problem is exploitation: the gross injustice which acquisitive society always inflicts on those who have nothing to offer but their body's labor" (J. H. Plumb, "Slavery, Race, and the Poor," *New York Review of Books* 16 [Mar. 13, 1969]: 4). Along with other of his contributions, this review has been reprinted in *American Experience: The Collected Essays of J. H. Plumb,* vol. 2 [New York: Harvester-Wheatsheaf, 1989], 133–41.

Plumb is here focusing his attention on capitalist English and American society from the seventeenth century onward. But as I suggested in the text earlier, the allocation of the most onerous and disagreeable kinds of manual labor among a society's most stigmatized and powerless elements would seem to be so basic a historical circumstance as to transcend more recent acquisitive capitalist societies. We might note, in this connection, the recent outpouring of scholarship that has both defined and limited the specific contributions made by mercantile and industrial capitalism to the distribution of tedious and unfulfilling work, domestic and otherwise, among females in particular. Apropos here is the observation of John Mack Faragher regarding the sexual division of labor in the rural American West of the mid-nineteenth century: "To be sure, farm women's ills were exacerbated by the growth of the market, for under commercial pressures gender divisions were widened, men's economic activity was further divorced from the household, and family economic unity shattered; for farm women there was, in consequence, a further devaluation of their already questionable status. But let there be no mistake, male privilege was an aspect of the cultural heritage of the land, expanded, not created, by the growth of capitalist market forces" (Faragher, *Women and Men on the Overland Trail* [New Haven: Yale University Press, 1979], 181). But a few of the many other valuable studies bearing on the sexual division of labor in history, from "primitive" times to the present, are Gerda Lerner, *The Creation of Patriarchy* (New York: Oxford University Press, 1986); Stephanie Coontz and Peta Henderson, eds., *Women's Work, Men's Property: The Origins of Gender and Class* (London: Verso, 1986); Barbara A. Hanawalt, ed., *Women and Work in Pre-Industrial Europe* (Bloomington: Indiana University Press, 1986); David Herlihy, *Opera Muliebria: Women and Work in Medieval Europe* (Philadelphia: Temple University Press, 1990); Eric Richards, "Women in the British Economy since 1700: An Interpretation," *History* 59 (Oct. 1975): 338–45; Maxine Berg, "Women's Work, Mechanisation and the Early Phases of Industrialisation in England," in Patrick Joyce, ed., *The Historical Meanings of Work* (Cambridge, Eng.: Cambridge University Press, 1987), 74–75; Sally Alexander, "Women's Work in Nineteenth-Century London: A Study of the Years 1820–1850," in Juliet Mitchell and Ann Oakley, eds., *The Rights and Wrongs of Women* (Harmondsworth, Eng.: Penguin Books, 1976), 75–111; Heidi Hartmann, "Capitalism, Patriarchy, and Job Segregation by Sex," in Martha Blaxall and Barbara Reagan, eds., *Women and the Workplace* (Chicago: University of Chicago Press, 1976): 137–69; and Harriet Bradley, *Men's Work, Women's Work: A Sociological History of the Sexual Division of Labour in Employment* (Minneapolis: University of Minnesota Press, 1989).

31. For references to workers in French factories and cities as "white negroes," see "H," "Laboring Classes in France," New York *Observer Weekly,* Aug. 19, 1848; and Jean Fourastié, *The Causes of Wealth,* ed. and trans. Theodore Caplow (Glencoe, Ill.: Free Press, 1960), 81. For a constellation of reasons—including their history of political oppression and their association in the popular mind with poverty and intemperance, as well as with "rough" work, it was the Irish who were most commonly characterized as "white negroes"; the abolitionist R. D. Webb even referred to himself as an "Irish man" or "white nigger" (R. D. Webb to Maria Weston Chapman, Dublin, Nov. 16, 1843, in Clare Taylor, ed., *British and American Abolitionists: An Episode in Transatlantic Understanding* [Edinburgh: Edinburgh University Press, 1974], 206); see also Carl Wittke, *The Irish in America* (Baton Rouge: Louisiana State University Press, 1956), 34. The influence wielded by ethnology in the 1850s added its own reinforcement to the designation of the Irish as *white negroes;* see L. Perry Curtis, Jr., *Apes and Angels: The Irishman in Victorian Caricature* (Washington, D.C.: Smithsonian Institution Press, 1971), vii. See also Dale T. Knobel, "Paddy and the Republic. Popular Images of the American Irish, 1820–1860" (Ph.D. diss., Northwestern University, 1976), 8–9, 56, 128, 152. It might also be noted that use of this term to characterize Irish menial laborers in America and elsewhere frequently derived from the same mix or variety of motives that popularized the parallel expression "wage slavery." Designating Irish immigrant canal or construction workers as "white negroes" was a common means of dramatizing their exploitative working conditions, but this dramatization might itself reflect either a sincere desire to ameliorate those conditions or, as was also commonly the case, the quite distinct objective of protecting black chattel slavery by deflecting criticism from it. For an example of the former use, although one that was also coupled with a bitter attack on the "nigger" philanthropists who allegedly ignored the exploitation of Irish immigrant labor in their zeal to abolish Southern slavery, see the remarks of P. J. Downie, a "Bricklayer," before the Industrial Congress meeting in New York, remarks made with special reference to the onerous working conditions of the city's Irish construction laborers, in "Labor Movements," *New-York Daily Tribune,* Jan. 27, 1851. As was the case with so many Northern antebellum labor reformers, the by-product, although not necessarily the

intent, of Downie's choice of terminology, was an exoneration of black slavery. For an unambiguously deliberate proslavery use of the term *white negro* to categorize not only Irish immigrants but all those white workers outside the slave states who were forced by economic necessity to perform various kinds of "servile labors" fit only for blacks, see the remarks of the Kentucky slaveholder and state senator, Robert Wickliffe, quoted in "The Working Man's Friend," written by "The Blacksmith's Son," in *Philanthropist* (New Richmond, Ohio), June 9, 1841.

32. The term *poverty* has multiple meanings and dimensions. Here I am referring to poverty in the sense of absolute need and deprivation, since it was poverty in this sense, rather than any sense that members of the laboring population had of their of relative deprivation, which drove them into the worst work. For an incisive discussion see Martin Rein, "Problems in the Definition and Measurement of Poverty," in Peter Townsend, ed., *The Concept of Poverty. Working Papers on Methods of Investigation and Life-Styles of the Poor in Different Countries* (New York: American Elsevier Publishing Company, 1970), 46–62. See also R. M. Hartwell, "The Consequences of the Industrial Revolution in England for the Poor," in Arthur Seldon, ed., *The Long Debate on Poverty* (London: Institute of Economic Affairs, 1972), 12.

33. Raphael Samuel, "The Workshop of the World: Steam Power and Hand Technology in Mid-Victorian Britain," *History Workshop* no. 3 (Spring 1977): 13. Samuel also notes some of Britain's other unusually hazardous trades.

34. Mill, *Principles,* 1: 475.

35. "S" [Sidney George Fisher], "Domestic Servants," *North American and United States Gazette* (Philadelphia), May 23, 1857. As with any other general rule, there were exceptions to the one which held that heavy physical, relatively unskilled labor employments need be crowded and low-paying compared to more highly skilled trades; on the "privileged niche" occupied for a time by the dockworkers of one French city, see William H. Sewell, Jr., "Uneven Development, the Autonomy of Politics, and the Dockworkers of Nineteenth Century Marseille," *American Historical Review* 93 (June 1988): 609, 628.

36. See, for example, Thomas Ewbank, *The World a Workshop; or, the Physical Relationship of Man to the Earth* (New York: D. Appleton and Company, 1855), quoted in "Industrial Education," *New-York Daily Tribune,* Feb. 11, 1856. See also Henry F. Durant, "Dignity of Labor," an address to the Norfolk Agricultural Society, in Charles L. Flint, ed., *Abstract of Returns of the Agricultural Societies of Massachusetts, for 1859* (Boston: William White, 1860), 60–61. Hannah Arendt has made a similar argument, interpreting the Book of Genesis to mean not that God's punishment introduced work to mankind, but rather that it made human work difficult and disagreeable, i.e., transformed it into "labor"; Arendt, *Human Condition,* 107, 107n. Such, evidently, was also Augustine's opinion; see Elaine Pagels, *Adam, Eve, and the Serpent* (New York: Random House, 1988), 134–37. Pagels' book also contains a discussion of the relationship of Original Sin to Eve's childbearing "labor." Many scholars have either elaborated or repudiated Arendt's arguments regarding the portrayal of work in the book of Genesis. My focus is not upon that portrayal—how the book of Genesis, not to speak of other portions of the Bible, in fact conceptualized work—but upon how nineteenth-century American interpreted that portrayal. In addition to Arendt, see Claus Westerman, *Genesis I–II: A Commentary,* trans. from 2d German ed. (1976) John J. Scullion S.J. (Minneapolis: Augsburg Publishing House, 1988), 208–67; Gerhard Von Rad, *Genesis: A Commentary,* 3d. rev. ed., trans. SCM Press (London: SCM Press, 1972), 80–95; Goran Agrell, *Work, Toil and Sustenance,* trans. Stephen Westerholm (Verbum, Sweden:

Hakan Ohlssons, 1976), 10–12; Alan Richardson, *The Biblical Doctrine of Work* (London: SCM Press, 1952), 25–26; William J. Dumbrell, "Creation, Covenant and Work," *Evangelical Review of Theology* 13 (Apr. 1989): 144–153.

37. Genesis 3: 19.

38. George S. Sawyer, *Southern Institutes; or, an Inquiry into the Origin and Early Prevalence of Slavery and the Slave Trade* (New York: Negro Universities Press, 1969 [1858]), 378–79.

39. Virginia Penny, *Think and Act: A Series of Articles Pertaining to Men and Women, Work and Wages* (Philadelphia: Claxton, Remsen, and Haffelfinger, 1869), 356. See also James DeBow, "American Legislation, Science, Art and Agriculture," *Commercial Review* 2 (Sept. 1846): 103–4.

40. From an early point on, however, some Christian writers made a point of insisting that the minority of men whose "work" did not involve physical labor, and who instead spent their time in such activities as thinking or writing, were not guilty of evading God's decree; see Pagels, *Adam,* 137.

41. Jacques Le Goff, *Time, Work, and Culture in the Middle Ages,* trans. Arthur Goldhammer (Chicago: University of Chicago Press, 1980), 80–81.

42. Lynn White, Jr., *Machina Ex Deo: Essays in the Dynamism of Western Culture* (Cambridge: MIT Press, 1968), 63–64. Both Le Goff and White, though, also confine the democratizing effect of the monk's example to the earlier Middle Ages. Le Goff argues that by the end of the medieval period, from the thirteenth century on, physical labor's servile, lowly, and menial associations were no longer acting to raise its social esteem; for a complex of reasons it was by this time, in contrast to mental labor, "held in greater contempt than ever" before (Le Goff, *Time,* xii, 69–70). For a more detailed study of evolving monastic attitudes toward labor, see George Ovitt, Jr., *The Restoration of Perfection: Labor and Technology in Medieval Culture* (New Brunswick: Rutgers University Press, 1987), 17–153.

43. Keith Thomas claims in this regard that because the early Benedictine monks chiefly valued manual labor as a "mortification of the flesh," or as a "remedy for idleness," even they had not really impressed upon others the nobility and "positive merit of hard work"; that achievement, Thomas claims, belonged primarily to Protestant religious teaching in the post-Reformation period; Thomas, "Work and Leisure in Pre-Industrial Society," *Past and Present,* no. 29 (Dec. 1964): 59.

44. A very helpful compilation of relevant contributions is Robert W. Green, ed., *Protestantism and Capitalism: The Weber Thesis and Its Critics* (Boston: D. C. Heath and Company, 1959). See also Robert M. Mitchell, *Calvin's and the Puritan's View of the Protestant Ethic* (Washington, D.C.: University Press of America, 1979). For a penetrating discussion of the curious relationship of Calvinist teaching regarding labor and poverty to the values of Anglican clergymen and British mercantilist writers, see Daniel A. Baugh, "Poverty, Protestantism, and Political Economy: English Attitudes toward the Poor, 1660–1800," in Stephen Baxter, ed., *England's Rise to Greatness, 1660–1763* (Berkeley: University of California Press, 1983), 63–107. See also Charles Constantin, "The Puritan Ethic and the Dignity of Labor: Hierarchy vs. Equality," *Journal of the History of Ideas* 40 (Oct.–Dec. 1979): 546–60; Richard Harvey, "Recent Research on Poverty in Tudor-Stuart England: Review and Commentary," *International Review of Social History* 24, pt. 2 (1979): 251–52; Gordon Marshall, *In Search of the Spirit of Capitalism: An Essay on Max Weber's Protestant Ethic Thesis* (New York: Columbia University Press, 1982); Adriano Tilgher, *Work. What It Has Meant to Men through the Ages,* trans. Dorothy Canfield Fisher (New York: Harcourt, Brace, and Company, 1930; repr. as *Homo Faber. Work*

through the Ages [Chicago: Henry Regnery Company, 1958]), 47–61; and Robert Slocumb Michaelson, "The American Gospel of Work and the Protestant Doctrine of Vocation" (Ph.D. diss., Yale University, 1951), 16, 56–58.

45. Richard Slotkin and James K. Folsom, "Introduction," in Slotkin and Folsom, eds., *So Dreadful a Judgement: Puritan Responses to King Phillip's War, 1676–1677* (Middletown: Wesleyan University Press, 1978), 12.

46. Still valuable is R. H. Tawney, *Religion and the Rise of Capitalism: A Historical Study* (London: John Murray, 1926), 211, 235. See also many of the more recent works of Christopher Hill, including *The Century of Revolution 1603–1715* (New York: W. W. Norton and Company, 1966 [1961], 16, 75; Wood, *Peasant-Citizen,* 141–42; Stephen Foster, *Their Solitary Way: The Puritan Social Ethic in the First Century of Settlement in New England* (New Haven: Yale University Press, 1971), 102, 127–28. As many scholars have noted, American populist rhetoric since at least the time of the Revolution and Constitutional Convention invoked the Puritan ethic and the Protestant character virtues to challenge the position of America's "aristocratic" upper middle classes—wealthy bankers, merchants, lawyers, and increasingly, industrial entrepreneurs as well—and to assert the competing claims of "hardworking" small-producer elements—the small freehold farmers and craftsmen whose livelihoods depended on both mental and physical labor and who partly because of this circumstance occupied the borderlands between the upper laboring and lower middle classes during the eighteenth and much of the nineteenth century. A relatively neglected part of the discourse of this same period consists of the counter-efforts of the upper-middle-class elements, which included their predominantly Federalist and Whig Party spokesmen, to similarly invoke the Protestant character virtues for purposes of defending their rewards and prerogatives and for insisting in the face of the populist rhetoric that their exclusively mental activities and enterprises indeed constituted true work.

47. In claiming that virtuous and responsible citizens must be free from the necessity of working with their hands, Plato and Aristotle's line of thought may have been an "aristocratic" counterreaction to the democratic "excesses" of fifth-century Athens—to the fact that large numbers of Athenian men who enjoyed political rights by this period were nonleisured craftsmen and "peasant-citizens"; such, at least, is the provocative argument made by Wood, *Peasant-Citizen;* see also the other citations in note 2 of this chapter.

48. [Holmes], "Ancient Slavery," 1: 576–77, also 575; and 2: 636. Holmes also noted (1: 576) that despite "antiquity's" generally greater honesty in acknowledging the aversion for manual labor, classical Greece did offer a limited counterpart to the modern trumpeting of manual labor's dignity.

49. Ibid., 1: 577.

50. [Timothy Walker], "Defence of Mechanical Philosophy," *North American Review* 33 (July 1831): 122–36, repr. in Michael Brewster Folsom and Steven D. Lubar, eds., *The Philosophy of Manufactures: Early Debates over Industrialization in the United States* (Cambridge: MIT Press, 1982), 298–99.

51. [Timothy Walker], "Popular Education," *North American Review* 29 (July 1829): 252, 257–58.

52. Ibid., 258.

53. Leo Marx, *The Machine in the Garden* (New York: Oxford University Press, 1964), 189.

54. [Walker], "Defence," 301; J. A. Etzler, *The Paradise within the Reach of All Men, without Labor, by Powers of Nature and Machinery. An Address to All Intelligent Men* (Pittsburgh: Etzler and Reinhold, 1833), 3, 14, 56.

55. See also, however, Lynn White, Jr.'s interesting argument that in the Middle Ages "massive technological development"—technology directed to eliminating manual labor—paradoxically grew out of the monastic respect for manual labor; Lynn White, Jr., *Medieval Religion and Technology: Collected Essays* (Berkeley: University of California Press, 1978), 22, 241–42; and Joel Mokyr, *The Lever of Riches: Technological Creativity and Economic Progress* (New York: Oxford University Press, 1990), 204–5.

56. Lawrence Frederick Kohl, *The Politics of Individualism: Parties and the American Character in the Jacksonian Era* (New York: Oxford University Press, 1989), 197–98.

57. For accounts of Walker's response to Carlyle that emphasize different themes from mine, see Marx, *Machine,* 181–90, and Howard P. Segal, *Technological Utopianism in American Culture* (Chicago: University of Chicago Press, 1985), 81–87. Along with such luminaries as Joseph Story and James Kent, Walker was an exemplar and apostle of legal scholarship and legal "high culture" during the first part of the nineteenth century; see Walker, *Introductory Lecture on the Dignity of the Law as a Profession,* delivered at the Cincinnati College, Nov. 4, 1837, repr. in Perry Miller, ed., *The Legal Mind in America* (New York: Anchor Books Doubleday Company, 1962), 240–55.

58. James T. Lemon has suggested that at least in the early history of this phrase, it was used by western Europeans to describe one specific area above all others: Pennsylvania in the late seventeenth and eighteenth centuries; Lemon, *The Best Poor Man's Country: A Geographical Study of Early Southeastern Pennsylvania* (Baltimore: Johns Hopkins University Press, 1972), xiii, 229.

59. Edward Everett, "Fourth of July at Lowell," speech delivered July 5, 1830, in Everett, *Orations and Speeches on Various Occasions,* 2d ed. (Boston: Little, Brown and Company, 1853), 2: 63. This is not to deny that individuals like Everett who adamantly upheld the exalted economic and social position of labor in America often disagreed about the relative contributions made by indigenous political and economic circumstances. In his correspondence with the manufacturing capitalist Nathan Appleton, the former Harvard Divinity School professor Andrews Norton, for example, dismissed the role Appleton gave to the vast extent of public lands in elevating the physical and moral condition of America's laboring classes. Norton looked instead to his country's republican political institutions (Professor Andrews Norton to Nathan Appleton, Cambridge, Mass., Nov. 11, 1844, Nathan Appleton Papers, Massachusetts Historical Society, Boston); see also Appleton's reply of Nov. 23, 1844 in the same collection.

60. Orestes Brownson referred to America's cheap and abundant land as the country's preeminent "accidental" advantage; see Orestes Brownson, "The Laboring Classes," *Boston Quarterly Review* 3 (Oct. 1840): 473; and "O. A. B.," "Rich and Poor," *Boston Reformer or Herald of Union and Progress,* July 21, 1837. An essay by L. A. Hine expressed as well as any other labor reform piece this common theme of "like causes, like effects": "Let it not be said that our laws provide for the more general distribution and division of property; for this can do but little to counteract the poverty that must unavoidably afflict every dense population, while the present general spirit prevails. . . . Is not the general nature of our civilisation the same as that of England? Is not the avarice of the people the same? Do we not bow as devotedly to Mammon in this country, as they do in any other under the sun?" (Hine, "The Rich—the Poor," *Herald of Truth; A Monthly Periodical* 1 [Feb. 1847]: 116–18). Of special relevance is Peter G. Roberts, "The Response of American Labor to English Industrial Experience, 1828–1848" (M.A. thesis, Columbia University, 1971).

61. Horace Greeley, "Slavery and Labor. A Lecture, Delivered at Boston and New-York, Jan. 1855," repr. in *New-York Daily Tribune,* June 27, 1855; "Social Evils and Their Remedies," *New-York Daily Tribune,* Aug. 26, 1846.

62. For the view that the demands of antislavery Northern nationalism did, in effect, render Greeley and other labor reformers "more and more uncritical" of existing social arrangements in the Northern states, see Eric Foner, "The Causes of the American Civil War: Recent Interpretations and New Directions," *Civil War History* 20 (Sept. 1974): 206.

63. Conservative Whigs devoted special emphasis to the dissolute character of the sons of the rich in articulating a "riches to rags" counterpart to the better-known "rags to riches" mythology, which they also favored. Because, Whig argued, the United States was still an open society, one without hardening class distinctions and "exclusive privileges," the idle and squandering habits of individuals who inherited wealth really did become a case of "private vice" making for "public benefits." There were, that is to say, no artificial barriers in America preventing the natural flow of this unearned wealth into the more deserving hands of the industrious poor—hence the great degree to which fortunes supposedly changed hands and membership in classes turned over in the course of two or fewer generations. For a good example of the invocation of the alleged downward mobility of the sons of "self-made" men, in conjunction with other standard Whig arguments, to deny the existence of an "hereditary aristocracy" in America and to discredit "demagogic" attacks on capitalist power and economic inequalities, see H. G. O. Colby, *The Relations of Wealth and Labor, Annual Address before the American Institute,* Oct. 20, 1842, repr. in the *American Laborer. Devoted to the Cause of Protection to Home Industry* 1 (Nov. 1842): 233–38; see also the discussion in Rush Welter, *The Mind of America 1820–1860* (New York: Columbia University Press, 1975), 119–21.

Interestingly enough, individuals on the other side of the ideological spectrum from conservative Whigs shared the rather moralistic presumption that individuals who had not "earned" their wealth through work—be these recipients affluent offspring or speculators in the stock market—had almost invariably weak and dissolute characters. These radical writers went on, however, to claim in contradistinction to the Whigs that the United States, hardly less than in the Old World, indeed contained artificial barriers that impeded the flow of wealth and the upward and downward movement between "rags" and "riches." This last radical claim was likely in closer accord with economic realities than the Whiggish presumption. Most of the recent historical scholarship indicates that economic elites consolidated rather than dissipated their wealth over the course of time and that the plebeian origins of American fortunes were distinctly limited. For an example of a radical who shared the common low regard for the character of the sons of the rich and who used this theme in support of his notorious plan for abolishing property inheritance and equalizing economic condition, see Thomas Skidmore, *The Rights of Man to Property! Being a Proposition to Make It Equal among the Adults of the Present Generation and to Provide for Its Equal Transmission to Every Individual of Each Succeeding Generation, on Arriving at the Age of Maturity* (New York: Alexander Ming, 1829), 219–20.

64. Horace Greeley, "The Discipline and Duties of the Scholar," *Nineteenth Century: A Quarterly Miscellany,* 4 (1849): 41–42.

65. Horace Greeley, "The Divorce of Learning and Labor," *Young American's Magazine of Self-Improvement* 1 (1847): 152–55; untitled editorial, *New-York Daily Tribune,* May 8, 1858; untitled editorial, *New-York Daily Tribune,* repr. in *Herald of Freedom* (Concord, N.H.), Sept. 25, 1846; for material on Greeley's difficult early life

on a poor New Hampshire farm, see Glyndon G. Van Deusen, *Horace Greeley: Nineteenth-Century Crusader* (New York: Hill and Wang, 1953), 6–9.

66. Harriet Martineau, *Society in America* (New York: AMS Press, 1966 [1837]), 2: 303–4.

67. Within the framework of its own communist agenda, the Chinese Cultural Revolution offered more recent and especially dramatic expression of Greeley's themes—that physical labor was unjustifiably disdained and that it could simultaneously humble and round out the development of privileged students and other intellectuals; see Maurice Meisner, *Marxism, Maoism, and Utopianism: Eight Essays* (Madison: University of Wisconsin Press, 1982), 122–31; and Marianne Bastid, "Economic Necessity and Political Ideals in Educational Reform during the Cultural Revolution," in Jerome Karabel and A. H. Halsey, eds., *Power and Ideology in Education* (New York: Oxford University Press, 1977), 589–607.

68. Horace Greeley, *Essays Designed to Elucidate the Science of Political Economy* (Boston: Fields, Osgood, and Company, 1870) 160. One might be tempted to attribute these moralistic reflections to the growing conservatism of Greeley's later years, but one can find similar pronouncements sprinkled throughout the period of Greeley's most active promotion of Fourierist and other visionary schemes designed to uplift the laboring classes.

69. See chapter 8 for Greeley's expressed chagrin at materialistic and snobbish farmers who encouraged their sons to leave agriculture for professional work in the cities.

70. Francis J. Grund, *The Americans, in Their Moral, Social, and Political Relations* (Boston: Marsh, Capen and Lyon, 1837), 172–73. Labor reformers and radicals took frequent note of the same disdain for poverty in America. One German-American resident of Pittsburgh noted: "The poor are held in more contempt, and no where in the world is poverty a greater crime than in America. . . . The laboring masses are treated in as shameful a manner as in Europe, with its ancient historical prejudices." The important difference, of course, was that such labor radicals, in contrast to Grund and others, typically if not always attacked as fiction the exceptionalist notion that hireling status, hard labor, and poverty were in fact easily escapable in the United States, that conditions there generally justified the disdain for economic "failure"; German-American radical quoted in John P. Sanderson, *Republican Landmarks* (Philadelphia: J. P. Lippincott and Company, 1856), 223.

71. "E. H. C.," letter of Mar. 22, 1846, "Life in Philadelphia. By a Philadelphian," *Baltimore Saturday Visitor,* repr. in *Herald of Freedom* (Concord, N.H.), Apr. 24, 1846.

72. As indicated in chapter 1, American attitudes toward social mobility, levels of remuneration, and economic autonomy, all most significant dimensions of mid-nineteenth-century free labor values, will be the subject of a sequel to this study. But we might note Eric Foner's incisive observation that because a Republican like Lincoln attached so much importance to the Northern wage laborer's ability to rise from his condition and achieve economic independence, his "anti-slavery . . . seemed to connect more directly with the artisan anti-slavery tradition" than with the emphasis of many abolitionists upon the centrality of bare legal freedom (Eric Foner, *Politics and Ideology in the Age of the Civil War* [New York: Oxford University Press, 1980], 73–74); see also Stephenson, "Mobility and Opportunity," 89–91.

73. Foner, "Causes of Civil War," 206, 213; Eric Foner, *Free Soil, Free Labor, Free Men: The Ideology of the Republican Party before the Civil War* (New York: Oxford University Press, 1970), 31–32, 316.

74. Daniel Webster, speech at Saratoga, New York, Aug. 19, 1840, in Webster,

The Writings and Speeches of Daniel Webster, national ed., vol. 3, *Speeches on Various Occasions* (New York: Little, Brown and Company, 1903), 24.

75. In his letter to Nathan Appleton, referred to in note 59 in this chapter, Andrews Norton recognized the distinction between class fluidity and a state of classlessness but denied its significance for American society: "There is with us no *permanent* class of rich and poor, which is almost the same thing in its effects on the character and condition of our community as if those classes did not exist" (Norton to Appleton, Nov. 11, 1844, Nathan Appleton Papers, Massachusetts Historical Society).

76. Maxine Berg, *The Machinery Question and the Making of Political Economy* (Cambridge, Eng.: Cambridge University Press, 1980), 272–76; Noel Thompson, *The People's Science: The Popular Political Economy of Exploitation and Crisis 1816–34* (Cambridge, Eng.: Cambridge University Press, 1984), 2. As suggested in chapter 1, from the late 1820s into the 1850s labor movements and radical political economy in America were directing their attacks no more against capitalists than against those professional members of the middle classes who also lived off their "mental labor" but who did not bear so active a relation to the means of production.

The economic value, indeed the moral legitimacy, of the capitalist's contribution as "mental laborer" in the late eighteenth and early nineteenth centuries continues to provoke controversy. For a radical denial of the economic superiority of the "capitalist division of labor," which supplanted the small producer putting-out system in early industrial England, and for an insistence on the "parasitical" nature of the capitalist's talents and role in this period, see Stephen A. Marglin, "What Do Bosses Do? The Origins and Functions of Hierarchy in Capitalist Production," pt. 1, *Review of Radical Political Economics* 6 (Summer 1974): 70–71; and Stephen A. Marglin, "Knowledge and Power," in Frank H. Stephens, ed., *Firms, Organizations and Labour: Approaches to the Economics of Work Organizations* (New York: St. Martin's Press, 1984), 146–64. Criticisms of Marglin's position include Maxine Berg, "The Power of Knowledge: Comments on Marglin's 'Knowledge and Power,'" in Stephens, ed., *Firms,* 165–73; and David S. Landes, "What Do Bosses Really Do?" *Journal of Economic History* 46 (Sept. 1986): 585–623.

77. "Agricola," "The American Farmers," *New-York Daily Tribune,* Mar. 25, 1856.

78. Massachusetts, *House Documents* for 1836, no. 49, *Report by the Committee on Education, Related to the Education of Children Employed in Manufacturing Establishments,* 8–9. J. H. W. Page of New Bedford similarly noted: "The man whose life is devoted to the operation of making the point of a pin, with the help of machinery, may, or may not, . . . do his work as well without as with intellectual culture. But the farmer cannot. Farming is an intellectual as well as physical labor. The man who is content to blunder on in ignorance and make no improvement, may stay on land and cumber the ground, but is not worthy to be called a farmer." Like many other promoters of a more "scientific" agriculture, Page was suggesting by his last remark that the natural intellectual promise of New England farming still remained largely unfulfilled; Page, "Importance of Agriculture," an address to the Plymouth Agricultural Society, in Amasa Walker, ed., *Transactions of the Agricultural Societies in the State of Massachusetts, for 1852* (Boston: White and Potter, 1853), 643–44.

79. "Tendency of Population to the Cities—Its Cause," *New-York Daily Tribune,* July 2, 1852; see also Horace Greeley, "Counsel to the Young," repr. in *New York State Mechanic, a Journal of the Manual Arts, Trades, and Manufactures* (Albany), Jan. 21, 1843.

80. Peabody, "Plan of West Roxbury Community," 367.

81. This theme, or variations on it, one which dwells on the "alienation" of well-educated, cultured old elites from the materialistic values of the "rising" middle classes, is, of course, most prominent among some interpretations of the period; see, for example, William Charvat, *The Profession of Authorship in America, 1800–1870. The Papers of William Charvat*, ed. Matthew J. Bruccoli (Columbus: Ohio State University Press, 1968), 61–66. For a much more receptive view of the calculative, "practical" uses to which American professionals and businessmen put their mental labor, see Bellows, *Ledger and Lexicon*.

82. Timothy Walker himself recognized that there was a significant discrepancy between the intellectually rarefied level at which the "science" of law might be practiced, and the mundane "chicanery" indulged in by the swarms of "pettifoggers" who betrayed the profession's innate "dignity" and "high functions" (Walker, "Introductory Lecture," 240, 241, 255). Others went a good deal further than Walker, suggesting that the very nature of the most lucrative legal "mental labor" weakened the law's claim to being a truly "learned profession." Observing that the collection of debts, management of unlitigated cases, and similar tasks provided the bulk of legal business in New York City, the *New World* maintained that legal "success here depends not so much upon mental endowment, as upon certain moral peculiarities" which are hardly virtues—"impudence, obsequiousness, cunning and hypocrisy." New York's financially successful lawyers, the newspaper concluded, were for the most part hardly those who had taken the trouble or shown the ability to master Blackstone and Kent ("Lawyers and Legal Business," *New World* 9 [Sept. 21, 1844]: 369–70).

The theme that the mental toil of professionals and businessmen was not conducive to true "learning"—the study of science and literature—was also of some importance in British campaigns to demonstrate the special affinity between learning and *manual* labor; see the appeal by one of the founders of the London Working Men's College, Frederick Denison Maurice, *Learning and Working: Six Lectures Delivered in Willis's Rooms, London, in June and July 1854* (Cambridge, Eng.: Macmillan, 1855), 46, 72–73.

83. As one advocate of "book farming" put this last argument, "The farmer will no longer be compelled to find his mental employment in themes apart from his own profession, for in the various problems connected with the phenomena of vegetable and animal growth and nutrition, that occur in the everyday experience of his own fields, he will perceive attractions of a most novel and beautiful kind, sufficient to occupy all of his powers, and exercise his highest faculties" (John P. Norton, Professor of Agricultural Chemistry, Yale College, "The Advantages of Science in Its Application to Agriculture," an address to the Hampden County Agricultural Society, in Amasa Walker, ed., *Transactions of the Agricultural Societies in the State of Massachusetts, for 1851* [Boston: Dutton and Wentworth, 1852], 578). William Ellery Channing made a similar argument with respect to all of "the commonest labors"; see chapter 3.

The rhetoric of scientific farming and agricultural reform in the antebellum South also embodied many of the same themes and concerns. "You hear him [the farmer] talk," Andrew P. Calhoun told a meeting of South Carolina planters, "of law and medicine as the two learned professions. He habitually defers to them as something superior to his own. . . . Now, cannot this be changed? Cannot the farmer and planter train his intellect . . . [?]" For a study emphasizing, nevertheless, the distinctiveness of the social, economic, and political circumstances and tensions that informed the agricultural "oration" in the Southern states, see Drew Gilpin Faust, "The Rhetoric and Ritual of Agriculture in Antebellum South Carolina,"

Journal of Southern History 45 (Nov. 1979): 541–68; Calhoun's statement, which appears in his "Address Delivered before the Pendleton Farmers' Society, Oct. 13, 1855, *Farmer and Planter* 6 (Dec. 1855), is taken from Faust's essay (553).

84. In addition to Greeley's and Peabody's remarks, see those of Edward E. Hale, *Public Amusements for Poor and Rich,* discourse before the Church of the Unity, Worcester, Mass., Dec. 16, 1855 (Boston: Phillips, Sampson and Company, 1857), 21. It remains, however, a matter of controversy among scholars just how much northeastern farm enterprises retained a nonmarket orientation in the first half of the nineteenth century; see, for example, Winifred B. Rothenberg, "The Market and Massachusetts Farmers, 1750–1850," *Journal of Economic History* 41 (June 1981): 283–314; Rona S. Weiss, "The Market and Massachusetts Farmers, 1750–1850: Comment," *Journal of Economic History* 43 (June 1983): 475–78; Christopher Clark, *The Roots of Rural Capitalism: Western Massachusetts, 1780–1860* (Ithaca: Cornell University Press, 1990); Allan Kulikoff, "The Transition to Capitalism in Rural America," *William and Mary Quarterly,* 3d ser., 46 (Jan. 1989) 120–44.

85. See, for example, A. Whitney Griswold, *Farming and Democracy* (New York: Harcourt, Brace and Company, 1948), 19–45; Chester E. Eisinger, "The Freehold Concept in Eighteenth-Century American Letters," *William and Mary Quarterly,* 3d ser., 4 (Jan.1947): 44–57; John Chester Miller, *The Wolf by the Ears: Thomas Jefferson and Slavery* (New York: The Free Press, 1977), 79–85. See also James A. Montmarquet, *The Idea of Agrarianism: From Hunter-Gatherer to Agrarian Radical in Western Culture* (Moscow: University of Idaho Press, 1989).

86. Sarah Burns, *Pastoral Inventions: Rural Life in Nineteenth-Century American Art and Culture* (Philadelphia: Temple University Press, 1989), 191.

87. A very good study of agricultural labor exploitation and insurrection in England, and their relationship to that country's so-called tripartite farm system of landlord, tenant farmer, and agricultural laborer, is E. J. Hobsbawm and George Rude, *Captain Swing* (London: Lawrence and Wishart, 1969). The "dumb-beast lives" remark was made by Frederick Law Olmsted, *Walks and Talks of an American Farmer in England,* new and rev. ed. (Columbus, Ohio: Jos. H. Riley and Company, 1859), 274. New York state's persisting structure of manorial land holdings, together with the high rate of farm tenancy and the long history of "anti-rent" labor wars generated by that structure, was America's nearest antebellum equivalent to agricultural conditions in England; see Henry Christman, *Tin Horns and Calicoes* (New York: Henry Holt and Company, 1945).

88. Richard H. Abbott, "The Agricultural Press Views the Yeoman: 1819–1859," *Agricultural History* 42 (Jan. 1968): 35–36, 47. See also Albert Lowther Demaree, *The American Agricultural Press, 1819–1860* (New York: Columbia University Press, 1941), 84–87, 232; and Clarence H. Danhof, *Change in Agriculture: The Northern United States, 1820–1870* (Cambridge: Harvard University Press, 1969), 24–26.

89. Untitled editorial, *Harper's New Monthly Magazine* 11 (June–Nov. 1855): 272; "Farming Life in New England," *Atlantic Monthly* 2 (Aug. 1858): 335. The writer of the latter article, particularly, shared with Greeley and others considerable hope in scientific, "experimental" agriculture as a means of breaking up the "traditional" and tedious "routine" of New England farming, and thereby of checking its general "deterioration" (337, 340). See Sawyer, *Southern Institutes,* 378, for specifically pro-slavery use of the theme that, regardless of their "boasted" economic independence, many if not most New England farmers were debased "clodhoppers" confined to an ill-recompensed and stultifying drudgery that left them no time or inclination for intellectual pursuits.

90. Horace Greeley, *Recollections of a Busy Life: Including Reminiscences of American Politics and Politicians, from the Opening of the Missouri Contest to the Downfall of Slavery* (New York: J. B. Ford and Company, 1869), 60.

91. Horace Greeley, "Life—the Ideal and the Actual," *Nineteenth Century: A Quarterly Miscellany* 2 (1848): 14. Although the antebellum period appears to have experienced a large movement of young people, especially young men, to cities in search of work, a more or less precise quantitative underpinning to the concerns and fears expressed by commentators like Greeley, Peabody, and the members of the agricultural press would clearly be useful: how many farm youth in fact migrated to New York and other large cities in the antebellum period, and what in fact was their distribution among the various occupations, white-collar and otherwise? Unfortunately, I know of no study that really addresses these quantitative questions. There are studies that document the economic backgrounds and career choices of college alumni, but these studies are of limited help in answering the questions I have raised if only because they miss those farm boys who, along with other youth, trained for and entered one of the professions without attending college; of some value, however, is Lewis D. Stilwell, *Migration from Vermont* (Montpelier: Vermont Historical Society, 1948); and Alan Stanley Horlick, "Countinghouse and Clerks: The Social Control of Young Men in New York" (Ph.D. diss., University of Wisconsin, Madison, 1969), subsequently published under a different title. It might also be noted that the fears expressed by Greeley and other antebellum commentators were not without precedent in America; in the late eighteenth century Jeffersonian Republicans were voicing concerns and complaints that Federalist economic policies were building up wasteful, "nonproductive" occupations, were stimulating the desire of men to leave the land and pursue easy wealth in commerce and speculation. The latter occupations, Jefferson noted in 1803, attracted those who desired "to live by their heads rather than their hands"; "there was too strong a current from the country to the towns"; Jefferson quoted in Drew R. McCoy, *The Elusive Republic: Political Economy in Jeffersonian America* (Chapel Hill: University of North Carolina Press, 1980), 195n; see also 158, 172–77. For examples of similar complaints in the northeastern agricultural press beginning in the 1820s, see Sidney Louis Jackson, *America's Struggle for Free Schools: Social Tension and Education in New England and New York, 1827–42* (Washington, D.C.: American Council on Public Affairs, [1941]), 122–23. On the "fragile links" that antebellum law and medicine, in contrast to the ministry, maintained with collegiate "liberal education," see Colin B. Burke, *American Collegiate Populations: A Test of the Traditional View* (New York: New York University Press, 1982), 101.

92. "W. W." [William West], letter to Thomas A. Devyr, published as "Land Reform and Labor Reform—Again," *New-York Daily Tribune,* June 18, 1850. West was responding to Devyr's earlier letter, published as "Land Reform and Labor Reform," in the June 7, 1850, issue of the *Tribune.*

93. Abbott, "Agricultural Press," 35–48; Percy W. Bidwell," The Agricultural Revolution in New England," *American Historical Review* 26 (July 1921): 683–701; Mary Alice Feldblum, "The Formation of the First Factory Labor Force in the New England Cotton Textile Industry, 1800–1848" (Ph.D. diss., New School for Social Research, 1977), 2–3, 133; Danhof, *Change in Agriculture,* 109, 113; Stilwell, *Migration from Vermont,* 233–37; and "Mr. Alling's Report on Land Reform," *National Reformer* (Rochester), Oct. 19, 1847.

94. Greeley, *Recollections,* 150.

95. George Fitzhugh, *Cannibals All! or, Slaves without Masters,* ed. C. Vann

Woodward (Cambridge: Belknap Press of Harvard University Press, 1960 [1857]), 231. For a discussion of proslavery motives behind the anti-agrarian, anti-"yeoman" remarks of Fitzhugh, Sawyer, and other Southern writers, see Henry Nash Smith, *Virgin Land: The American West as Symbol and Myth* (New York: Vintage Books, 1950), 162–64.

96. Clark, *Roots of Rural Capitalism,* 307.

97. "Farming Life in New England," 340–41; Joseph F. Kett, *Rites of Passage: Adolescence in America 1790 to the Present* (New York: Basic Books, 1977), 94; Danhof, *Change in Agriculture,* 25; Hal S. Barron, *Those Who Stayed Behind: Rural Society in Nineteenth-Century New England* (Cambridge, Eng.: Cambridge University Press, 1984), 31–36; in contrast to Richard H. Abbott, Barron finds little defensiveness and insecurity in the arguments of the antebellum local agricultural periodicals which he surveyed.

98. See, for example, Jeremy Atack and Fred Bateman, *To Their Own Soil: Agriculture in the Antebellum North* (Ames: Iowa State University Press, 1987), 274, for a recent emphasis upon the "successes" of northeastern agriculture; see also Paul W. Gates, *The Farmer's Age: Agriculture, 1815– 1860* (New York: Harper and Row, 1960), 269.

99. Abbott, "Agricultural Press," 36.

100. Demaree, *American Agricultural Press,* 101–6, suggests that "the so-called practical farmers" constituted the smallest of the various groups that contributed to the agricultural press in mid-nineteenth-century America. Demaree distinguishes two other groups, in addition to actual, full-time farmers and gentleman farmers: the journal editors themselves and "professional agricultural writers." The distinctions between these groups were scarcely hard and fast, and Demaree argues, for example, that many if not most of the editors were operating farmers in a truly meaningful sense (90). My remaining remarks in the text are, in any case, confined to the gentleman farmers, although in referring specifically to the Boston elite studied by Tamara Plakins Thornton (see note 102), I in no way intend to suggest that all antebellum individuals who fell into even this single category of "gentleman farmer" exalted the virtues of farming and "agricultural improvement" from the same complex of needs and tensions; a gentleman farmer out in the Mississippi Valley clearly owed his interest in agriculture to different circumstances and drives than did a member of an entrenched northeastern elite that was ever intent on its "self-characterization" (Thornton, *Cultivating Gentlemen,* 56).

101. George F. Lemmer, *Norman J. Colman and Colman's Rural World: A Study in Agricultural Leadership* (Columbia: University of Missouri, 1953), 12. See also Donald B. Marti, "In Praise of Farming: An Aspect of the Movement for Agricultural Improvement in the Northeast, 1815–1840," *New York History* 51 (July 1970): 351–75; and Danhof, *Change in Agriculture,* 58.

102. Thornton, *Cultivating Gentlemen.* Space limitations prevent me from detailing, and doing justice to, Thornton's finely grained arguments. It appears, though, that throughout the first part of the nineteenth century members of Boston's business and professional elite turned to gentleman farming and engaged in profarm rhetoric as a means of relieving anxieties and self-doubts arising from their "materialistic" livelihoods—from their instrumental role in the economic transformation of Massachusetts. Later in the antebellum period this elite also began to direct its agrarian rhetoric more specifically toward the "common" farmers of the state; the elite's legitimation and consolidation of its position became increasingly tied up with the objective of stemming the flow of rural depopulation, of keeping full-time farmers "in their place." To that purpose the elite combined the

standard "idealistic" emphasis of the gentleman farmer—emphasis upon both the capacity and the need of disgruntled full-time farmers to add intellectual, or "scientific," content to their enterprises—with more complacent formulations of the "agrarian myth." The latter argued more implausibly that common farming in the northeast already possessed enviable and ample, economic and intellectual satisfactions and advantages. See also Burns, *Pastoral Inventions,* 77, on the "appeal to escapist yearnings" which was a basic component of nineteenth-century "country-life imagery."

103. My indebtedness to Marvin Meyer's thesis of pervasive "ambivalence" toward rapid social and economic change in the Jacksonian period, which he advances in *The Jacksonian Persuasion: Politics and Belief* (Stanford: Stanford University Press, 1957), is obvious; Meyer's thesis seems clearly to have also influenced the discussions by Tamara Plakins Thornton and Sarah Burns.

104. Alexander Hamilton, "Report on Manufactures," reported to the House of Representatives, Dec. 5, 1791, quoted in David Montgomery, "The Working Classes of the Pre-Industrial American City, 1780–1830," *Labor History* 9 (Winter 1968): 3–4; Rolla Milton Tryon, *Household Manufactures in the United States, 1640–1860: A Study in Industrial History* (Chicago: University of Chicago Press, 1917), 1–2.

105. For instances of such unrest in the preindustrial workshops of one city, see Sharon V. Salinger, "Artisans, Journeymen, and the Transformation of Labor in Late Eighteenth-Century Philadelphia," *William and Mary Quarterly,* 3d ser., 40 (Jan. 1983): 62–84; and Salinger, *"To Serve Well and Faithfully": Labor and Indentured Servants in Pennsylvania, 1682–1800* (Cambridge, Eng.: Cambridge University Press, 1987). See also Gary B. Nash, *Race, Class, and Politics: Essays on American Colonial and Revolutionary Society* (Urbana: University of Illinois Press, 1986), 243–67; Ronald Douglas Schultz, "Thoughts among the People: Popular Thought, Radical Politics, and the Making of Philadelphia's Working Class, 1765–1828" (Ph.D. diss., University of California, Los Angeles, 1985), 320–53; Charles G. Steffen, *The Mechanics of Baltimore: Workers and Politics in the Age of Revolution 1763–1812* (Urbana: University of Illinois Press, 1984), 113–19; Paul A. Gilje, "Culture of Conflict: The Impact of Commercialization on New York Workingmen, 1787–1829," in William Pencak and Conrad Edick Wright, eds., *New York and the Rise of American Capitalism: Economic Development and the Social and Political History of an American State, 1780–1870* (New York: New-York Historical Society, 1989), 249–70; Sean Wilentz, "The Rise of the American Working Class, 1776–1877: A Survey," in J. Carroll Moody and Alice Kessler-Harris, eds., *Perspectives on American Labor History: The Problems of Synthesis* (DeKalb: Northern Illinois University Press, 1989), 86–87. For another discussion that warns against idealizing the conditions under which many preindustrial skilled craftsmen in America labored and that attributes this kind of idealization (as do many of the British historians who belong to the so-called optimistic school of interpretation of Britain's Industrial Revolution) to the overemphasis upon the supposed "degradation" of the factory operative, see David Grimsted, "Ante-Bellum Labor: Violence, Strike, and Communal Arbitration," *Journal of Social History* 19 (Fall 1985): 7–8. See also Billy G. Smith's rather similar conclusions regarding nineteenth-century industrialization, prompted by his investigation of the "bleakness" of the lives of a cross section of eighteenth century preindustrial workers, in *The "Lower Sort": Philadelphia's Laboring People, 1750–1800* (Ithaca: Cornell University Press, 1990), 200.

106. Particularly good at capturing this pride of workmanship and spirit of collaboration among masters, journeymen, and apprentices in early nineteenth-century New York City is Wilentz, *Chants Democratic,* 1–4. See also Bruce Laurie,

Artisans into Workers: Labor in Nineteenth-Century America (New York: Hill and Wang, 1989), 36–37; many of the essays in Ian M. G. Quimby, ed., *The Craftsman in Early America* (New York: W. W. Norton and Company, 1984); and Ian M. G. Quimby, *Apprenticeship in Colonial Philadelphia* (New York: Garland Publishing, 1985), 143–55.

107. Karl Marx, "Appendix" (trans. Rodney Livingstone) to *Capital: A Critique of Political Economy*, trans. Ben Fowkes, with an introduction by Ernest Mandel (New York: Random House, 1977) 1: 1029. Mandel notes that the discussion in which Marx made this remark was originally planned as a part of volume 1 of *Capital*, but has only now been published for the first time in English translation; Ernest Mandel, "Introduction," in Marx, *Capital*, 1: 943. See also David M. Gordon, Richard Edwards, and Michael Reich, *Segmented Work, Divided Workers: The Historical Transformation of Labor in the United States* (Cambridge, Eng.: Cambridge University Press, 1982), 247.

108. But we should emphasize again that the skilled artisanal trades were by no means wholly free of these stigmas; see Howard B. Rock, *Artisans of the New Republic: Tradesmen of New York City in the Age of Jefferson* (New York: New York University Press, 1979), 3–9; Stuart M. Blumin, *The Emergence of the Middle Class: Social Experience in the American City, 1760–1900* (Cambridge, Eng.: Cambridge University Press, 1989), 30–38. See also Jackson Turner Main, *The Social Structure of Revolutionary America* (Princeton: Princeton University Press, 1965), 199–200.

109. E. J. Hobsbawm, who introduced the term, if not the concept, of British labor aristocracy into modern historical scholarship, originally dated the emergence of this upper stratum of the working classes from the middle of the nineteenth century. However, Hobsbawm himself, together with other historians, has more recently stressed the ways in which the skilled trade unions of the mid to late nineteenth century had important preindustrial antecedents, originally as craft guilds and later as "trade societies." Of course, one who wishes to pinpoint instances of a preindustrial "labor aristocracy" in Britain encounters the same definitional difficulties confronting Hobsbawm and others who have debated the existence of such an entity for later periods. That a particular trade qualified for membership in "the labor aristocracy" depends, that is to say, very much upon the criteria to which the evaluator attaches most importance: earnings and standard of living, control over the productive process, life styles and values, and so on. For Hobsbawm's original formulation, see his "The Labour Aristocracy in Nineteenth Century Britain," in John Saville, ed., *Democracy and the Labour Movement* (London: Lawrence and Wishart, 1954), 200–222; for his more recent statements, see E. J. Hobsbawm, *Worlds of Labour: Further Studies in the History of Labour* (London: Weidenfield and Nicholson, 1984), 180–81, 216–72. See also Alan Fox, *History and Heritage: The Social Origins of the British Industrial Relations System* (London: George Allen and Unwin, 1985), 7–67; John Rule, "The Property of Skill in the Period of Manufacture," in Joyce, ed., *Historical Meanings*, 99–118; I. J. Prothero, *Artisans and Politics in Early Nineteenth-Century London: John Gast and His Times* (Folkestone, Eng.: William Dawson and Son, 1979), 5, 27, 330–38.

110. *Fall River News* editorial, repr. as "Labor," in the *Voice of Industry* (Lowell, Mass.), June 19, 1846. The concept of "manual skill," however, is a good deal more complex than may at first seem evident. For a most incisive discussion, one that examines the roles played by "knowledge," "discretion"," and "training" and emphasizes how the "skilled" execution of a given task may or may not involve responsibility for its "conception," see Charles More, *Skill and the English Working Class, 1870–1914* (London: Croom Helm, 1980), 15–26. One should also take note of

the argument, associated particularly with some versions of segmentation and dual labor market theory, that in many instances "skill" is less an objective fact than a "social construct," heavily reliant upon racial, ethnic, or sexual stereotypes. Whether a worker is labelled "skilled" or not may depend less on the actual content of his work than on such factors as his bargaining power and his capacity, through unions or otherwise, to affect the social definition of his work. The concept of skill, then, can be used by more advantaged workers to create an inflated picture of the training requirements for their jobs for purposes of excluding and maintaining their positions of economic supremacy over other workers, very often ones of a different race, ethnicity, or sex—hence, for example, the historic identification of craft skills with masculinity. At the same time, similar use of the concept of skill can also serve the interests of employers in capitalist societies by creating divisions within the work force and discouraging the formation of any kind of labor solidarity that crosses sexual, racial, or ethnic lines. Recent secondary literature is laying particular stress on the historical relationship that capitalist hierarchy has borne to male labor "patriarchy" in the definition of skill; see Elizabeth Garnsey, Jill Rubery, and Frank Wilkinson, "Labour-Market Structure and Work-Force Divisions," in Rosemary Deem and Graeme Salaman, eds., *Work, Culture and Society* (Philadelphia: Open University Press, 1985), 59–73; Susan Himmelweit, "Value Relations and Divisions within the Working Class," *Science and Society* 48 (Fall 1984): 337–38. For an application of the notion of skill as socially defined and "contrived" to explain the persistence of nineteenth-century British mule spinning as a privileged "male preserve," see Marianne Valverde, " 'Giving the Female a Domestic Turn': The Social, Legal and Moral Regulation of Women's Work in British Cotton Mills, 1820–1850," *Journal of Social History* 12 (Summer 1988): 619– 34. See also Catherine Hall, "The Home Turned Upside Down? The Working-Class Family in Cotton Textiles 1780– 1850," in Elizabeth Whitelegg et al., eds., *The Changing Experience of Women* (Oxford: Martin Robertson, 1982), 21. To the extent that some of these, as well as other, discussions contend that "skill" is generally nothing more than a social invention, one without any basis in objective fact, I do not find them persuasive, although they may be correct in such specific cases as the mule spinners. Some kinds of manual labor would seem clearly to require more in the way of judgment and expertise for their successful execution than other kinds. I find much more compelling those segmentation and dual labor market arguments which are content to rest on the claim that economically vulnerable and stigmatized groups have been prevented or otherwise discouraged from acquiring the necessary technical knowledge, training, experience, and expertise which constitute valued skills (see here on the case of mule spinning the subtle analysis by Mary Freifeld, "Technological Change and the 'Self-Acting' Mule: A Study of Skill and the Sexual Division of Labour," *Social History* 11 [Oct. 1986]: 319–43). The range of scholarly debate regarding the nature of manual "skill" is illustrated in one particularly useful collection of essays that was stimulated by the work of Harry Braverman: Stephen Wood, ed., *The Degradation of Work? Skill, Deskilling and the Labour Process* (London: Hutchinson, 1982).

111. Certain trades, as Craig Calhoun notes with specific reference to the London clockmaking and jewelry trades, were more resistant than others to skill dilution and subdivision of labor, and they remained "too difficult to learn to be flooded by any mass of new labor" (Craig Calhoun, *The Question of Class Struggle* [Chicago: University of Chicago Press, 1982], 46). For an emphasis upon the new opportunities that heavy industry in particular created for skilled workers, see Bruce Laurie, Theodore Hershberg, and George Alter, "Immigrants and Industry: The Philadelphia Experience, 1850–1880," in Richard L. Ehrlich, ed., *Immigrants in*

Industrial America, 1850–1920 (Charlottesville: University Press of Virginia, 1977), 130–35. Blumin, *Emergence of the Middle Class,* 259, notes that in Philadelphia and other northeastern cities "the 'disappearing artisan' appears to have reached a stable plateau" between 1860 and 1880.

112. On the misleading character of much occupational terminology in the census reports, given the changing content of manufacturing work, and the problems thus posed for students of "social mobility," see Laurie, Hershberg, and Alter, "Immigrants and Industry," 124–25. Of the many recent studies treating skill dilution in the urban craft trades under the impact of mercantile and industrial capitalism, together with such attendant developments as labor unrest and proletarianization, see Wilentz, *Chants Democratic;* Bloomberg, "Industrialization and the Skilled Worker"; Ross, *Workers on the Edge;* Robert Max Jackson, *The Formation of Craft Labor Markets* (Orlando: Academic Press, 1984), 83–115, 316–20; John Cumbler, "Migration, Class Formation, and Class Consciousness: The American Experience," in Michael Hannagan and Charles Stephenson, eds., *Confrontation, Class Consciousness, and the Labor Process: Studies in Proletarian Class Formation* (New York: Greenwood Press, 1986), 43–48; Amy Bridges, *A City in the Republic: Antebellum New York and the Origins of Machine Politics* (Cambridge, Eng.: Cambridge University Press, 1984), 50–58, 172; Iver Bernstein, *The New York City Draft Riots: Their Significance for American Society and Politics in the Age of the Civil War* (New York: Oxford University Press, 1990), 78–86; Laurie, *Artisans into Workers,* 38–112.

113. Josiah Wedgwood's ceramic factory in England was a model of how the division of labor, though a signal feature of Wedgwood's imposition of industrial work discipline, "did not destroy skill: it limited its field of expression to a particular task, but within those limits it increased it." Here the division of labor, Neil McKendrick adds, culminated in a finished product of *superior* quality and workmanship; McKendrick, "Josiah Wedgwood and Factory Discipline," *Historical Journal* 4, no. 1 (1961): 33. The capacity of manufacturing division of labor to create and increase skills was again illustrated in the precision machinery "American System" plants that came to form a small proportion of America's nineteenth-century factory complex; see Daniel Nelson, "The American System and the American Worker," in Otto Mayr and Robert C. Post, eds., *Yankee Enterprise: The Rise of the American System of Manufactures* (Washington, D.C.: Smithsonian Institution Press, 1981), 171–87.

114. Craig Calhoun has described with respect to some of the British trades how the breakdown of craft skills into simpler, repetitive tasks acted to infringe on traditional work autonomy and to contribute thereby to artisanal malaise and "alienation." Calhoun notes that previous to such deskilling "The fact that a craftsman [even in cases, one might add, where the craftsman was a journeyman working under the supervision of a master] had to exercise his own judgment and had to use his own skill and training to execute his productive tasks meant that he could not readily be controlled" (Calhoun, *Question of Class Struggle,* 120).

115. Historians have often stressed how the support given by early nineteenth-century skilled labor to free "equal and universal" education, including such particularly ambitious schemes as Robert Dale Owen's "state guardianship" plan, reflected the wish that members of the "producing classes" be recognized and treated as equal citizens of the Republic: "Next to life and liberty," the New York Working Men's Party resolved in December 1829, "we consider education the greatest blessing bestowed on mankind" (quoted in Alexander C. Flick, ed., *History of the State of New York* [Port Washington: Ira J. Friedman, 1962 {1934}] 6: 65). But beyond their support for so general an ideal, it is unclear what proportion of urban journeymen looked to education to somehow increase their economic versatility in

a manual labor market where increased division of labor and "labor-saving" technology were narrowing talents and rendering skills and knowledge obsolete. Undoubtedly some skilled artisans alternatively regarded education as a means of enabling them or at least their sons to escape manual labor altogether for clerical work or even one of the professions. Robert Dale Owen's slogan that "knowledge is power, and power commands riches," could have appealed for any number of reasons to workers whose skill and status were under assault; see "Our Motto," *Working Man's Advocate* (New York), Nov. 14, 1829; "R. D. O.," [Robert Dale Owen], reply to Thomas Skidmore's property equalization plan, *Working Man's Advocate,* Jan. 16, 1830; "Labour-Saving Machinery," *Mechanics' Free Press. A Journal of Practical and Useful Knowledge* (Philadelphia), Nov. 21, 1829. See also Paul Goodman, *Towards a Christian Republic: Antimasonry and the Great Transition in New England, 1826–1836* (New York: Oxford University Press, 1988), 50–51; Jentz, "Artisans, Evangelicals, and City," 144; Alexander J. Field, "Educational Reform and Manufacturing Development in Mid-Nineteenth Century Massachusetts" (Ph.D. diss., University of California, Berkeley, 1975), 229–62; Philip R. V. Curoe, *Educational Attitudes and Policies of Organized Labor in the United States* (New York: Bureau of Publications, Teachers College, Columbia University, 1926), 8–65; Edward Pessen, *Most Uncommon Jacksonians: Radical Leaders of the Early Labor Movement* (Albany: State University of New York Press, 1967), 183–89; David R. Roediger and Philip S. Foner, *Our Own Time: A History of American Labor and the Working Day* (New York: Greenwood Press, 1989), 21.

116. For a discussion of the particularly low persistence rates of members of the working classes in nineteenth-century cities, see Stephan Thernstrom and Peter R. Knights, "Men in Motion: Some Data and Speculations about Urban Population Mobility in Nineteenth-Century America," in Theodore K. Rabb and Robert I. Rotberg, eds., *Industrialization and Urbanization: Studies in Interdisciplinary History* (Princeton: Princeton University Press, 1981), 171–99.

117. Sean Wilentz suggests that the "bastardization" of craft organizations, in reducing the capital requirements of many enterprises, may have actually increased the ease with which journeymen could become self-employed—they could hire their own cheap labor and set up shop as small masters or contractors. But cutthroat competition rendered the survival of such enterprises precarious, and they were not by definition, in any case, segments of the "honorable trades," membership in which had been so fundamental a source of journeyman self-esteem; Wilentz, *Chants Democratic,* 116–17, 141.

118. This summary, like such other recent studies as Wilentz's, leaves a somber, if not altogether gloomy, impression of key economic developments, emphasizing as it does the plight of many skilled journeymen. But one could draw a quite different impression of those developments if one emphasized what they may have meant for other groups of workers. For apprentices who early in the nineteenth century still faced a lengthy period of training in the "secrets" of their chosen craft, the accelerating erosion of the craft structure, and with it the breakdown of the master's monopoly of craft knowledge, offered a new flexibility of economic maneuver. They could strike out on their own, after learning the "craft" through a reading of one of the new popular manuals, or they could extract cash wages and other new concessions from masters who faced increasing pressures from "slop shop" competition. To many apprentices, adolescents in search of the main chance, the "erosion" of preindustrial craft traditions and the decline of the "community of producers" may have represented a welcome democratization of knowledge and economic opportunity; see W. J. Rorabaugh, *The Craft Apprentice: From Franklin to the*

Machine Age in America (New York: Oxford University Press, 1986), 74, 89, 129, 158–59; and Ronald Schultz, "Printer's Devils: The Decline of Apprenticeship in America," *Reviews in American History* 15 (June 1987): 226–31. And if one focuses, alternatively, on the work experiences of poor young English and Irish immigrants who furnished much of the labor supply in the deskilled and expanding urban trades, one can also come away with a picture of economic developments in this period as something more than the valiant, unavailing struggle of manual labor against the process of industrial capitalism. For a study that underscores the sheer energy and frenzied pace of working-class life in antebellum New York, the vigor many immigrant laborers brought to their new economic opportunities and to their activities outside the workplace in this "high-energy" urban environment, see Richard Briggs Stott, "The Workers in the Metropolis: New York City 1820–1860" (Ph.D. diss., Cornell University, 1983), 242–45, 326–28. In a separate study Stott underscores, again without attaching a critical perspective to this emphasis, the exceptionally high pace of work in antebellum America generally; Stott, "British Immigrants and the American 'Work Ethic' in the Mid-Nineteenth Century," *Labor History* 26 (Winter 1985): 86–102.

CHAPTER 3: DIVISION OF LABOR AND MECHANIZATION IN FACTORIES

1. Although this theme runs throughout Ruskin's writings, a particularly concise expression is in John Ruskin, *Time and Tide* (1867), in Ruskin, *The Works of John Ruskin,* ed. E. T. Cook and Alexander Wedderburn (London: George Allen, 1905), 17: 426–27. There are two particularly insightful studies of Ruskin's thought: James Clark Sherburne, *John Ruskin or the Ambiguities of Abundance: A Study in Social and Economic Criticism* (Cambridge: Harvard University Press, 1972); and P. D. Anthony, *John Ruskin's Labour: A Study of Ruskin's Social Theory* (Cambridge, Eng.: Cambridge University Press, 1983). Anthony challenges the conventional view that Ruskin, for all his hatred of mechanized labor, wished to establish creative, craft work as the model for general imitation (156–67).

2. Charles Gayarré, "Influence of the Mechanic Arts on the Human Race," pt. 1, *De Bow's Review* 17 (Sept. 1854): 231.

3. Gayarré, "Influence of the Mechanic Arts," pt. 2, *De Bow's Review* 17 (Oct. 1854): 391–92.

4. Gertrude Himmelfarb has taken issue with scholars like Robert Heilbroner who, largely on the basis of Smith's "so-called alienation passage" in *The Wealth of Nations,* have emphasized the "deeply pessimistic" side of Smith's vision. This emphasis is distorted, Himmelfarb claims, if only because Smith devoted far more discussion in his treatise to the material and other benefits that the "division of labor" would bring modern society, including its working classes. More than this, Himmelfarb argues, it was the latter, "optimistic" scenario that "impressed itself on Smith's readers in his own time and for generations afterword" (Gertrude Himmelfarb, *The Idea of Poverty: England in the Early Industrial Age* [New York: Alfred A. Knopf, 1984], 57, 57n). Although it would be absurd to claim that Smith's "optimistic" scenario did not impress itself upon mid-nineteenth-century American opinion, and that it may indeed have been here too the "dominant image" of the division of labor principle, it should become clear from the text below that Smith's "pessimistic side" was also very much in evidence, and not merely in the writings and pronouncements of labor radicals.

5. Adam Smith, *An Inquiry into the Nature and Causes of the Wealth of Nations,* ed. Edwin Cannan (New York: Random House, 1937 [1904]), 4–5.

6. Ibid., 734. There is a sizeable literature on Smith's concept of worker "alienation," and the ways in which he did and did not anticipate Marx; see Nathan Rosenberg "Adam Smith on the Division of Labour: Two Views or One? *Economica,* n.s., 32 (May 1965): 127–39; E. G. West, "Adam Smith's Two Views on the Division of Labour," *Economica,* n.s., 31 (Feb. 1964): 23–32; E. G. West, "The Political Economy of Alienation: Karl Marx and Adam Smith," *Oxford Economic Papers,* n.s., 21 (Mar. 1969): 1–21; Robert H. Heilbroner, "The Paradox of Progress: Decline and Decay in *The Wealth of Nations*," *Journal of the History of Ideas* 34 (Apr.– June 1973): 248–61.

One of the interesting characteristics of Smith's passage is its discussion of the ill effects of the division of labor with exclusive reference to "men." Conceivably, Smith was simply following what may have been the common "patriarchal" practice in the intellectual discourse of the period by using "man" and "his" as shorthand references to members of both sexes. However, it is also possible that Smith believed that the division of labor posed no dangers for female members of the laboring population because he assumed that few, if any, would be seeking employment in manufacturing enterprises. This interpretation is given some support by Smith's remark, expressed a few passages earlier in *Wealth* (734), that the education of "women" should be tailored to their role as "the mistresses of a family." If this interpretation does correctly explain Smith's reference to "men," then it supports the view of a number of scholars that Smith did not in essential respects accurately foresee the Industrial Revolution. For further discussion, see Jonathan Andrew Glickstein, "Concepts of Free Labor in Antebellum America" (Ph.D. diss., Yale University, 1989), 76n–77n.

7. Melvyn Dubofsky, "Adam's Curse: Or the Drudgery of Work," *Reviews in American History* 6 (Dec. 1978): 432. A number of historians have been extending Dubofsky's point still further back in time, or at least raising questions about the role played by mechanical and technological innovations in the Middle Ages in exploiting and devaluing manual labor; see, for example, George Ovitt, Jr., *The Restoration of Perfection: Labor and Technology in Medieval Culture* (New Brunswick: Rutgers University Press, 1987), 14–17.

8. By 1800, for example, addresses delivered to New England mechanic audiences were making common reference to Smith's various insights into detail division of labor; for an interesting analysis, see Gary John Kornblith, "From Artisans to Businessmen: Master Mechanics in New England, 1789–1850" (Ph.D. diss., Princeton University, 1983), 145–53.

9. William Ellery Channing, *Lectures on the Elevation of the Labouring Portion of the Community* (Boston: William D. Ticknor, 1840), 8.

10. Baron Joseph-Marie de Gérando, speaking in the Chamber of Peers in March, 1840, quoted in [Henry Barnard], *Legal Provision Respecting the Education and Employment of Children in Factories, & c; with Examples of Improvements in Manufacturing Districts* (Hartford: Case, Tiffany, and Burnham, 1842), 39–40. De Gérando's "barely-concealed hostility to industrial capitalism" is noted in a recent study of industrialization and factory technology in France and their impact upon the French working-class family; see Colin Heywood, *Childhood in Nineteenth-Century France: Work, Health and Education among the "Classes Populaire"* (Cambridge, Eng.: Cambridge University Press, 1988), 183. See also Lee Shai Weissbach, *Child Labor Reform in Nineteenth-Century France: Assuring the Future Harvest* (Baton Rouge: Louisiana State University Press, 1989), 53, 69.

11. Gayarré, "Influence of Mechanic Arts," 2: 392.

12. This is not to deny that these and other workers who were employed in

nonfactory sectors of the British economy were also the subjects of extensive governmental investigations.

13. For the use of this term to describe Manchester, see Asa Briggs, *Victorian Cities* (New York: Harper and Row, 1963), 56. One historian has recently concluded that despite, or perhaps because of, the symbolic potency of the mechanization of the cotton industry, "What has long been believed to be a large-scale shift from handicraft to machine techniques, and from animate to inanimate sources of power," in fact "occurred irregularly or, most often, not at all in major areas of Anglo-American manufacturing" (Dolores Greenberg, "Reassessing the Power Patterns of the Industrial Revolution: An Anglo-American Comparison," *American Historical Review* 87 [Dec. 1982]: 1261).

14. It was a standard nineteenth-century practice to use the term *moral* with especial reference to sexual behavior—hence the so-called moral reform societies dedicated to redeeming the prostitute and removing the "moral evil" of prostitution. On the other hand, as noted in the text below, critics of the factory system could also embrace a broader concept of morality, one predicated upon certain assumptions regarding the "natural" and "proper" family responsibilities chargeable to members of the two sexes.

15. Yet the general value of Smith's argument has been upheld by some modern social psychologists who claim to have found that many modern forms of mentally undemanding and unfulfilling labor exercise a destructive impact upon the worker's "psychological functioning." Jobs that lack "substantive complexity," that restrict the "exercise of self-direction at work," Melvin L. Kohn and Carmi Schooler have argued, erode over time the worker's capacity to exercise "self-direction" in all areas of life. Intellectually undemanding work thereby comes to serve as an independent source of social subordination and social stratification, an argument Smith and his contemporary Adam Ferguson would have appreciated; Melvin L. Kohn and Carmi Schooler, *Work and Personality: An Inquiry into the Impact of Social Stratification* (Norwood, N.J.: Ablex Publishing Corporation, 1983), 6, 77.

16. C. Turner Thackrah, *The Effects of Arts, Trades, and Professions, and of Civic States and Habits of Living, on Health and Longevity: with Suggestions for the Removal of Many of the Agents, which Produce Disease, and Shorten the Duration of Life,* 2d enl. ed. (London: Longman, 1832), 144–47, 202–9. Thackrah's criticisms of factory labor are less open to charges of bias than many other similar contemporary attacks that we might cite, if only because he did not single factory work out for condemnation, but rather included it in a sweeping indictment of working conditions in a wide range of employments.

17. The term *silent suffering* was used by W. R. Greg of the mill-owning Greg family in an essay where he unfavorably compared the situation of English farm laborers with that of well-paid, materially comfortable factory operatives and urban artisans. In answering the attacks upon the "character" of the manufacturing districts made by "noble landlords and country gentlemen," among others, Greg's comparison is by no means without its strong points. Space limitations, however, prevent us from considering these; "W. R. G.," "Emigration or Manufactures?" *Westminster Review* 40 (Aug.–Dec. 1843): 102, 108. Defending nineteenth-century factory conditions by recourse to the argument that working conditions for preindustrial farm and domestic manufacturing laborers were less than ideal is a major characteristic of the "optimistic" school of interpretation of the Industrial Revolution in Britain. For one such debunking of the preindustrial "Golden Age myth" by one of the most prominent members of this school, see R. M. Hartwell, "The Rising Standard of Living in England, 1800–1850," *Economic History Review,* 2d ser.,

13 (Apr. 1961): 397–416; and Hartwell, "Interpretations of the Industrial Revolution in England," *Journal of Economic History* 19 (June 1959): 229–49. Comparisons between factory and preindustrial workers remain difficult, however, if only because, "We simply do not know with any precision how many hours were worked in Britain before the Industrial Revolution, in either agricultural or non-agricultural occupations" (Joel Mokyr, "The Industrial Revolution and the New Economic History," in Mokyr, ed., *The Economics of the Industrial Revolution* [Totowa: Rowman and Allanheld, 1985], 32). For a recent assessment of the issues dividing optimists from pessimists, see G. N. von Tunzelmann, "The Standard of Living Debate and Optimal Economic Growth," in Mokyr, ed., *Economics,* 207–26.

18. This allegation appears in P. Gaskell, *Artisans and Machinery: The Moral and Physical Condition of the Manufacturing Population Considered with Reference to Mechanical Substitutes for Human Labour* (New York: A. M. Kelley, 1968 [1836]), 103. Claims that heated factory environments encouraged sexual promiscuity were also made with regard to female operatives generally, to justify legislation limiting their employment; see Mary Lynn McDougall, "Working-Class Women during the Industrial Revolution, 1780–1914," in Renate Bridenthal and Claudia Koonz, eds., *Becoming Visible: Women in European History* (Boston: Houghton Mifflin Company, 1977), 262.

19. Objections to the mixing of the sexes, at work or elsewhere, were not exclusively Victorian, as evidenced by the customs of orthodox and other Jews, past and present.

20. For the controversial thesis that the short-time movement among adult male British operatives in the 1830s was a reaction to the destructive impact of technological change upon family-based employment in the cotton mills, see Neil J. Smelser, *Social Change in the Industrial Revolution: An Application of Theory to the British Cotton Industry* (Chicago: University of Chicago Press, 1959); and Smelser, "The Industrial Revolution and the British Working-Class Family," *Journal of Social History* 1 (Fall 1967): 25–30. As an explanation of organized labor agitation, Smelser's thesis has drawn cogent criticisms; see, for example, Michael Anderson, "Sociological History and the Working-Class Family: Smelser Re-Visited," *Social History* 3 (Oct. 1976): 317–34. Yet these criticisms have done less damage to the general argument that adult male workers were protective of their position of dominance within the family, which they identified with family morality, and that they may have regarded industrial changes as a threat to that dominance even if they did not necessarily or consistently manifest that perception through labor activism. Up to a certain point but no further can one accept John Clarke's generalization regarding the factory controversy in England: "The concern for morality, . . . is preeminently a middle-class preoccupation" (John Clarke, *The Price of Progress: Cobbett's England 1780–1835* [London: Granada Publishing, 1977], 123). See also Gary Cross, *A Quest for Time: The Reduction of Work in Britain and France, 1840–1940* (Berkeley: University of California Press, 1989), 27–30.

21. "Lowell: And Its Manufactures," *Hunt's Merchants' Magazine* 16 (Apr. 1847): 360; Benita Eisler, "Introduction," in Eisler, ed., *The Lowell Offering* (Philadelphia: J. B. Lippincott Company, 1977), 16; Susan Estabrook Kennedy, *If All We Did Was to Weep at Home: A History of White Working-Class Women in America* (Bloomington: Indiana University Press, 1979), 26–27.

22. One of the many expressions of this theme appears in [H. A. Miles], "The Cotton Manufactures," pt. 1, *North American Review* 52 (Jan. 1841): 49–50. Miles also produced a longer panegyric of conditions at Lowell in which he responded more explicitly to various criticisms and accusations, including the charge that

although mill girls were indeed leaving their jobs after only a few years, the real reason was that they were too sick and exhausted to continue; they were returning home "to die." For Miles's rejection of this dark interpretation of the short tenure of the Lowell girls, see his *Lowell, as It Was, and as It Is* (Lowell: Nathaniel L. Dayton, 1846), 124–27.

23. Samuel Batchelder, former agent of the Hamilton Company in Lowell, in his *Introduction and Early Progress of the Cotton Manufacture in the United States* (Boston: Little, Brown and Company, 1863), 89; see also [Miles], "The Cotton Maufactures," 50; and Caroline F. Ware, *The Early New England Cotton Manufacture: A Study in Industrial Beginnings* (Boston: Houghton Mifflin Company, 1931), 226.

24. For criticisms of the category of "semi-skilled" work, together with other observations regarding nineteenth-century occupational structure, see Bruce Laurie, Theodore Hershberg, and George Alter, "Immigrants and Industry: The Philadelphia Experience, 1850–1880," in Richard L. Ehrlich, ed., *Immigrants in Industrial America, 1850–1920* (Charlottesville: University Press of Virginia, 1977), 125.

25. For a mill-by-mill account of the parish apprentice child operatives, one which concludes that the notoriety surrounding their employment is not supported by the available evidence, see Stanley D. Chapman, *The Early Factory Masters: The Transition to the Factory System in the Midlands Textile Industry* (New York: Augustus M. Kelley, 1967), 168–209; for the work that was responsible for a good deal of this notoriety, and is a special target of Chapman's criticism, see *A Memoir of Robert Blincoe, an Orphan Boy,* (1832 ed. [1828]), ed. John Brown. For the British mule spinners, who were the closest equivalent to a craft elite within the factory system, see William Lazonick, "Industrial Relations and Technical Change: The Case of the Self-Acting Mule," *Cambridge Journal of Economics* 3 (Sept. 1979): 231–59; and Issac Cohen, "Workers' Control in the Cotton Industry: A Comparative Study of British and American Mule Spinning," *Labor History* 26 (Winter 1985): 53–85. One of the best studies of evolving factory technology and skill requirements in the different branches of the textile industry is David J. Jeremy, *Transatlantic Industrial Revolution: The Diffusion of Textile Technologies between Britain and America, 1790–1830s* (Cambridge: MIT Press, 1981).

26. The most detailed examination of the occupational hierarchy within the Lowell mills, and of the sexual and ethnic discrimination which partially determined movement within that hierarchy, is Thomas Louis Dublin, "Women at Work: The Transformation of Work and Community in Lowell, Massachusetts, 1826–1860" (Ph.D. diss., Columbia University, 1974), 63–67, 98. At the same time, after a few years' or even a few months' experience, operatives were still frequently able to move up to another department precisely because, in Henry A. Turner's word, there were "few marked natural divisions of skill between the various jobs in the cotton trades. It is all a question of degree, and otherwise of the experience of individual operatives" (H. A. Turner, *Trade Union Growth, Structure and Policy: A Comparative Study of the Cotton Unions* [London: George Allen and Unwin, 1962], 111). See also David Aaron Zonderman, "Aspirations and Anxieties: New England Workers and the Mechanized Factory System, 1815–1850" (Ph.D. diss., Yale University, 1986), 541–43.

27. See the remarks of the Reverend Henry Mandeville in Perry Miller, *The Life of the Mind in America from the Revolution to the Civil War* (New York: Harcourt, Brace, and World, 1965), 56; and also Parliament, "Special Report of Mr. George Wallis. Report on Manufactures," *Sessional Papers* (Commons), *1854 Reports from Commissioners. New York Industrial Exhibition,* Feb. 6, 1854, pp. 3–4. Wallis and

George Whitworth were British commissioners to the New York Crystal Palace Exhibition of 1853.

28. Mrs. [Francis] Trollope, *The Life and Adventures of Michael Armstrong, the Factory Boy* (New York: Harper and Brothers, 1840). Trollope's novel was centered on a fictitious factory town in Lancashire. In drawing material for her book from Robert Blincoe's *Memoir,* Trollope seems clearly to have been implying that the suffering and exploitation experienced by parish apprentice children in the early, isolated rural water-powered mills was characteristic of child factory labor generally in the expanding textile districts of the 1830s. For criticism of this viewpoint that stresses the efficacy of the 1833 Factory Act in "stamping out the worst abuses" in the steam-powered factories "before Mrs. Trollope took an interest in the subject," see W. H. Chaloner, "Mrs. Trollope and the Early Factory System," *Victorian Studies* 4 (Dec. 1960): 160–66. On the obsolescence of parish apprentice factory labor by a much earlier date, see Chapman, *Early Factory Masters,* 170–73, 199, 210; David S. Landes, *The Unbound Prometheus* (Cambridge, Eng.: Cambridge University Press, 1969), 116–17; Arthur Redford, *Labour Migration in England, 1800–1850,* 2d ed., ed. and rev. W. H. Chaloner (New York: Augustus M. Kelley, 1968 [1926]), 21–33.

29. Colt quoted in Henry Barnard, *Armsmear: The Home, the Arm, and the Armory of Samuel Colt. A Memorial* (New York: Alvord, 1866), 371. More details of Colt's testimony in 1854 before the House of Commons Select Committee on Small Arms, and its bearing on the system of manufactures by interchangeable parts, appear in David Hounshell, *From the American System to Mass Production: The Development of Manufacturing Technology in the United States* (Baltimore: Johns Hopkins University Press, 1984), 17–21. See also Hugo Arthur Meir, "The Technological Concept in American Social History, 1750–1860" (Ph.D. diss., University of Wisconsin, 1950), 194–95.

30. John Zerzan, "Axis Point of American Industrialism," *International Review of Social History* 31, pt. 3 (1986): 252; Merritt Roe Smith, *Harpers Ferry Armory and the New Technology: The Challenge of Change* (Ithaca: Cornell University Press, 1977), 271, 273, 334; Rowland Tappan Berthoff, *British Immigrants in Industrial America, 1790–1950* (Cambridge: Harvard University Press, 1953), 86, 96; Alan Dawley and Paul Faler, "Working-Class Culture and Politics in the Industrial Revolution: Sources of Loyalism and Rebellion," *Journal of Social History* 9 (June 1976): 466–80. As Dawley and Faler indicate, in developing their typology of labor mentality and attitudes toward industrial capitalist work regimens, workers who resisted those regimens through strikes and other forms of collective action were perhaps only infrequently the same workers who, skilled or unskilled, manifested their resistance by drinking and by otherwise clinging to more leisurely and casual "preindustrial" patterns of behavior, both on and off the job. Yet both kinds of workers represented trouble for industrial capitalists, and each was less suitable material for their enterprises than other workers who, for whatever reasons, were more receptive to industrial work discipline.

31. Michael Sanderson, "Literacy and Social Mobility in the Industrial Revolution in England," *Past and Present,* no. 56 (Aug. 1972): 95, 102. For the related argument that industrialization and the decline of the preindustrial family economy provided good cause for the workingman's motto, "The Pursuit of Knowledge under Difficulties," see David Vincent, *Bread, Knowledge and Freedom: A Study of Nineteenth-Century Working Class Autobiography* (London: Europa Publications, 1981), 120, 124. However, there are also advocates of the argument that industrialization, even in its earlier stages, placed a premium upon at least a minimal literacy among the British working classes, and that British economic growth in this period

accordingly owed something to expanding educational facilities in the industrial towns; see, for example, E. G. West, *Education and the Industrial Revolution* (New York: Harper and Row, 1975), 3–5. The relationship between literacy, job skills, and economic growth is a highly complex one; for a good review of the scholarly disagreements regarding this relationship in nineteenth-century England and America, see Harvey J. Graff, *The Literacy Myth: Literacy and Social Structure in the Nineteenth-Century City* (New York: Academic Press, 1979), 225–33. See also Hartmut Kaelble, *Industrialisation and Social Inequality in Nineteenth-Century Europe*, trans. Bruce Little (Leamington Spa, Eng.: Berg, 1986), 77–104; and Lee Soltow and Edward Stevens, *The Rise of Literacy and the Common School in the United States: A Socioeconomic Analysis to 1870* (Chicago: University of Chicago Press, 1981), 24, 127.

32. E. D. Allen quoted, with accompanying editorial remarks, in "Intellectual Improvement of the Mechanic," *New York State Mechanic*, Dec. 18, 1841.

33. John Ramsay McCulloch, quoted in "Extract of a Note on Adam Smith's *Wealth of Nations*, By McCulloch, Vol. 1, pp. 211, 212, Edinburgh Edition, 1828," repr. in "Appendix," *Congressional Globe. Appendix,* 28th Cong., 1st sess., 1844, 650.

34. Senator Rufus Choate of Massachusetts, *Congressional Globe. Appendix,* 28th Cong., 1st sess., Apr. 12 and 15, 1844, 646. Choate's ideological commitment to an urban, industrial civilization and an advanced division of labor that accommodated a diversity of individual talents and tastes is discussed in Jean V. Matthews, *Rufus Choate: The Law and Civic Virtue* (Philadelphia: Temple University Press, 1980), 77–80.

35. "W. J. S.," "Factory Labor," *The Lowell Offering; a Repository of Original Articles, Written Exclusively by Females Actively Employed in the Mills* 4 (Nov. 1843–Oct. 1844): 200. This is hardly to deny that other factory girls, for reasons of temperament, background, or inclination, responded quite differently. A three-week visit to Vermont, where one was "free to rove when and where they [*sic*] will among the green hills," seems clearly in the case of one sensitive mill girl to have set back her mental adjustment to repetitive and regimented work. Sometime after returning to her position at Lowell, she wrote to a friend: "You remember perhaps how I used to tell you I spent my hours in the mill—viz, in imagining myself rich and that the rattle of the machinery was the rumbling of my chariot wheels, but now alas; that happy fact has fled from me and my mind no longer takes such airy and visionary flights for the wings of my imagination have folded themselves to rest; in vain do I try to soar in fancy and imagination above the dull reality around me but beyond the roof of the factory I can not rise" (H. E. Back, letter of Sept. 7, 1846, repr. in Philip S. Foner, ed., *The Factory Girls* [Urbana: University of Illinois Press, 1977], 334–35). The gamut of attitudes expressed by New England mill girls to their work is presented in Zonderman, "Aspirations and Anxieties."

36. Some of these surveys have found that a complex set of variables—sex, ethnicity, race, prior social experiences—all contribute to the particular expectations factory workers bring to their job and affect their attitudes to work that is mentally undemanding. Then, too, modern factory labor is perhaps even less uniform in job content and work pace than its nineteenth-century antecedents. Surveys have found that "job satisfaction" is lowest among workers who tend the faster-paced, mass-production assembly lines, at least in part because their minds indeed cannot be "actively employed on any other subject" than their work. That such laborers are also the ones most signally lacking in work autonomy—the power to regulate their pace of work—is a related but distinct source of their work dissatisfaction and "alienation." There remains, however, considerable debate among sociologists and other scholars whether the movement of modern industries to still higher levels of

automation—as in the case of the "continuous process" industries—might actually begin to reverse the level of worker dissatisfaction. Under certain circumstances too, finally, modern assembly workers have been found to actually derive satisfaction from repetitive, "rhythmical" labor processes themselves. For discussion of these issues, see Michael Argyle, *The Social Psychology of Work* (New York: Taplinger Publishing Company, 1972), 34, 229–39, 246, 253; Charles P. Walker and Robert H. Guest, *The Man on the Assembly Line* (Cambridge: Harvard University Press, 1952), 12–15; Ely Chinoy, "Manning the Machines—The Assembly-Line Worker," in Peter Berger, ed., *The Human Shape of Work: Studies in the Sociology of Occupations* (New York: Macmillan Company, 1964), 51–81; Robert Blauner, *Alienation and Freedom: The Factory Worker and His Industry* (Chicago: University of Chicago Press, 1964), 2–33; Shoshana Zuboff, *In the Age of the Smart Machine: The Future of Work and Power* (New York: Basic Books, 1988), 53–55; Arthur N. Turner and Amelia L. Miclette, "Sources of Satisfaction in Repetitive Work," *Occupational Psychology* 36 (Oct. 1962): 215–31.

37. Hannah Arendt, *The Human Condition* (Chicago: University of Chicago Press, 1958), 46n; Sebastian de Grazia, *Of Time, Work, and Leisure* (New York: Twentieth Century Fund, 1962), 372.

38. W. Cooke Taylor, *Notes of a Tour in the Manufacturing Districts of Lancashire, in a Series of Letters to His Grace the Archbishop of Dublin* (London: Duncan and Malcolm, 1842), 110.

39. Alonzo Potter, *Political Economy: Its Objects, Uses, and Principles: Considered with Reference to the Condition of the American People* (New York: Harper and Brothers, 1840), 20, 20n.

40. Andrew Ure, *The Philosophy of Manufactures: Or, an Exposition of the Scientific, Moral, and Commercial Economy of the Factory System of Great Britain* (London: Charles Knight, 1835), 22–23.

41. Ibid., 22–23, 301.

42. William Cooke Taylor, *Factories and the Factory System; from Parliamentary Documents and Personal Examination* (London: Jeremiah How, 1844), 97.

43. Congressman G. P. Marsh of Vermont, *Congressional Globe. Appendix,* 29th Cong., 1st sess., June 30, 1846, 1013.

44. David Lowenthal, *George Perkins Marsh: Versatile Vermonter* (New York: Columbia University Press, 1958), 50–52, 83–84.

45. I have in fact encountered few profactory defenses by American or British factory proprietors—individuals with the most obvious and direct vested interest in justifying industrial capitalist enterprise—which rivalled in zealousness or extremity the arguments of an Ure or a Marsh.

46. Hepworth Dixon, "Manchester: Its Mental and Social Physiognomies Considered," *People's Journal* (London) 3 (June 26, 1847): 357–59.

47. Charles Wing, *Evils of the Factory System. Demonstrated by Parliamentary Evidence* (London: Saunders and Otley, 1837), xxvii–lxv, 4–8; for the range of arguments directed against, as well as in defense of, the British factory system, see Paul Henry Elovitz, "'Airy and Salubrious Factories' or 'Dark Satanic Mills'? Some Early Reactions to the Impact of the Industrial Revolution on the Condition of the English Working Classes" (Ph.D. diss., Rutgers University, 1969); and Ann B. Robson, *On Higher than Commercial Grounds: The Factory Controversy 1830–1853* (New York: Garland Publishing, 1985).

48. *Fall River Mechanic* editorial, repr. as "The Factory System," in *Voice of Industry,* Mar. 27, 1846; see also John O. Green, *The Factory System, in Its Hygienic Relations,* address delivered in Boston at the annual meeting of the Massachusetts

Medical Society, May 27, 1846 (Boston: Massachusetts Medical Society, 1846), 21–22; and Karl Marx, *Capital: A Critique of Political Economy,* ed. Frederick Engels, trans. Samuel Moore and Edward Aveling (New York: International Publishers, 1967), 1: 423.

49. Blauner, *Alienation,* 29; Simone Weil, "Factory Work," trans. Felix Giovanelli, in *Politics* 3 (Dec. 1946): 372. See also Gabriella Fiori, *Simone Weil: An Intellectual Biography,* trans. Joseph R. Berrigan (Athens: University of Georgia Press, 1989), 99–115. The difficulty of drawing confident generalizations about factory operative attitudes on the basis of the remarks of someone like Weil is well described by Joan Campbell: "Intellectuals who engage in manual labor are likely to suffer greater psychic strain than is experienced by born proletarians. On the other hand, intellectuals can always comfort themselves with the knowledge that they can terminate their suffering, if they so choose" (Joan Campbell, *Joy in Work, German Work: The National Debate, 1800–1945* [Princeton: Princeton University Press, 1989], 208).

50. See, for example, Alonzo Potter's refutation of Smith's claim that the division of labor tended to "deaden the faculties and circumscribe the intelligence of the operative," in his *Political Economy,* 20, 20n.

51. Jeremy, *Transatlantic Industrial Revolution,* 261.

52. For further discussion of the impact that technological innovations had upon the viability of child labor in Lowell and other Massachusetts mill towns, see Glickstein, "Concepts of Free Labor," 93n–94n.

53. There are many scholarly accounts of the "speed-ups" and "stretch-outs" of the 1840s; see, for example, Dublin, "Women at Work," 141–43; Hannah Josephson, *The Golden Threads: New England's Mill Girls and Magnates* (New York: Duell, Sloan and Pearce, 1949), 219–27; Kenneth Frank Mailloux, "The Boston Manufacturing Company of Waltham, Massachusetts, 1813–1848. The First Modern Factory in America," (Ph.D. diss., Boston University, 1957), 207–15.

54. The classic discussion of industrial "clock-time" remains E. P. Thompson, "Time, Work-Discipline, and Industrial Capitalism," *Past and Present,* no. 38 (Dec. 1967): 56–97.

55. John Ferral, remarks at the National Trades' Union Convention of 1834, quoted in John R. Commons and Helen L. Sumner, eds., *Labor Movement, 1820–1840,* vol. 2, A Documentary History of American Industrial Society, vol. 6 (New York: Russell and Russell, 1958 [1910]).

56. For some discussion of these issues, see Edward Pessen, *Most Uncommon Jacksonians: Radical Leaders of the Early Labor Movement* (Albany: State University of New York Press, 1967), 160–65. Judith Cohen clearly articulates the dilemmas certain kinds of work, by virtue of their intrinsic nature, pose for socialist visions of social justice: "One can understand only too well alienation in the capitalist world, but it is difficult to grasp how alienation can be completely overcome in an advanced industrial society, even when that society is socialist. Merely changing the relations of production cannot really alter the effect of automation. Although the society is humanised the productive techniques surely remain as impersonal and as intimidating as under capitalism. . . . Is fitting nuts and bolts in a Soviet factory any less soul destroying than in a Western factory? Surely the fact that the worker is not being exploited under socialism does not alter the other tyrannies under which he necessarily labours in any modern factory" (Judith Cohen, "Alienation under Socialism," *Marxism Today* 8 [June 1964]: 192).

57. [Andrew Preston Peabody], "The Future of Labor," *North American Review* 74 (Apr. 1852): 456.

58. The variation in *intensity* of beliefs on any given issue—not, of course, merely with regards to manufacturing division of labor—is a problem intellectual historians have not dealt with satisfactorily. Although Alonzo Potter, to cite just one example, expressed "antislavery" views in his political economic writings, he can hardly be placed in the same category as other individuals who made a more active and extensive commitment to the antislavery cause. Some individuals who refrained from active participation in a cause may have still felt intensely concerned about it— qualities of temperament along with a range of other factors may have determined why they manifested their position in a more passive manner. But it was also often the case that the ways in which individuals chose to express themselves on a given issue reflected how strongly they felt about it.

59. Two studies that are particularly useful regarding Marx's earlier writings are Robert C. Tucker, *Philosophy and Myth in Karl Marx,* 2d ed. (Cambridge, Eng.: Cambridge University Press, 1972); and Ali Rattansi, *Marx and the Division of Labour* (London: Macmillan Press, 1982).

60. [Orestes Brownson], "Conversations with a Radical. By a Conservative," *Boston Quarterly Review* 4 (Jan. 1841): 31.

61. George Ripley to Ralph Waldo Emerson, Nov. 9, 1840, quoted in Ann C. Rose, *Transcendentalism as a Social Movement, 1830–1850* (New Haven: Yale University Press, 1981), 105. See also Charles Crowe, *George Ripley: Transcendentalist and Utopian Socialist* (Athens: University of Georgia Press, 1967), 140–41. For an earlier radical's expression of the same theme, see Frances Wright, "An Address to Young Mechanics," New York, June 13, 1830, in Frances Wright D'Arusmont, *Life, Letters and Lectures* (New York: Arno Press, 1972), 199.

62. *The New Moral World* (London) 13 (1845): 388, quoted in Gregory Claeys and Prue Kerr, "Mechanical Political Economy," *Cambridge Journal of Economics* 5 (Sept. 1981): 270.

63. See "Labour-Saving Machinery," *Mechanics' Free Press,* Nov. 21, 1829; William Butler Scott, "Every Man under His Own Vine and Fig Tree: American Conceptions of Property from the Puritans to Henry George" (Ph.D. diss., University of Wisconsin, 1973), 131–34; Rex Burns, *Success in America: The Yeoman Dream and the Industrial Revolution* (Amherst: University of Massachusetts Press, 1976), 119–21; Amy Bridges, *A City in the Republic: Antebellum New York and the Origins of Machine Politics* (Cambridge, Eng.: Cambridge University Press, 1984), 113–14.

64. See, in particular, J. F. C. Harrison, *Quest for the New Moral World: Robert Owen and the Owenites in Britain and America* (New York: Charles Scribner's Sons, 1969), 54. Harrison observes that until the 1830s even reformers in Britain believed that the changes worked there by industrial capitalism could be reversed or over- hauled by a society built upon alternative principles. Gareth Stedman Jones makes the same point with reference to the Chartists, in *Languages of Class: Studies in English Working Class History 1832–1982* (Cambridge, Eng.: Cambridge University Press, 1983), 171. See also Howard Paul Segal, "Technological Utopianism and American Culture, 1830–1940" (Ph.D. diss., Princeton University, 1975), 15; Barry Gewen, "The Intellectual Foundations of the Child Labor Reform Movement" (Ph.D. diss., Harvard University, 1972), 187; John Humphrey Noyes, *History of American Socialisms* (New York: Hillary House, 1961 [1870]), iii. Noyes observed here (in 1869) that America "has been from the beginning, and especially the last forty years, a laboratory in which Socialisms of all kinds have been experimenting."

65. "The Organization of Labor. No. II," *Daily Chronotype* (Boston), Nov. 21, 1846.

66. The phrase "hewers of wood and drawers of water" originates from at least as far back as the Old Testament: Joshua 9: 21.

67. Catharine E. Beecher, *A Treatise on Domestic Economy, for the Use of Young Ladies at Home, and at School* (Boston: Marsh, Capen, Lyon, and Webb, 1841), 40.

68. "The People's College," *New-York Daily Tribune,* Sept. 21, 1853.

69. S. Flint, Jr., letter to "Friend Rogers" [editor of the newspaper], *Herald of Freedom* (Concord, N.H.), June 16, 1843.

70. See, for example, "The Organization of Labor," *Daily Chronotype* (Boston), Nov. 19, 1846 and "Organization. No. II," in the Nov. 21 issue for the proposed reorganization of the factories in Lowell and other mill towns along Fourierist lines, whereby the operatives and capitalists would be made partners and the former their own employers through their acquisition of stock shares in the mills. "The advantages of power and economy derived from the principle of combination and organization" would be thereby retained, and the "evils" of the factory system averted. More than many other labor reformers of the time, the writer of these articles was explicit and unequivocal in his support for factory labor itself: "Would we give up factories, and every woman go back to weaving her own cloth by her own fireside? Not at all" (quotations from the Nov. 19 article).

71. "Ruskin and Architecture," *North British Review* 21 (May 1854): 191.

72. Smith, *Wealth of Nations,* 735–39. See also David McNally, *Political Economy and the Rise of Capitalism: A Reinterpretation* (Berkeley: University of California Press, 1988), 253–54.

73. [Peabody], "Future of Labor," 457.

74. Alonzo Potter, *The Principles of Science Applied to the Domestic and Mechanic Arts, and to Manufacture and Agriculture: with Reflections on the Progress of the Arts and Their Influence on National Welfare* (Boston: Thomas H. Webb, 1840), 314.

75. Theodore Sedgwick, *Public and Private Economy. In Three Parts* (Clifton, N.J.: Augustus M. Kelley, 1967 [1836–1839]), 1: 226–27. For discussions of various Mechanics Institutes in the United States, see Bruce Sinclair, *Philadelphia's Philosopher Mechanics: A History of the Franklin Institute 1824–1865* (Baltimore: Johns Hopkins University Press, 1974); William G. Shade, "The 'Working Class' and Educational Reform in Early America: The Case of Providence, Rhode Island," *Historian* 39 (Nov. 1976): 1–20; Donald S. McPherson, "Mechanics' Institutes and the Pittsburgh Workingman, 1830–1840," *Western Pennsylvania Historical Magazine* 56 (Apr. 1973): 155–69; Thomas Bender, *New York Intellect* (New York: Alfred A. Knopf, 1987), 78–87. For accounts of the Mechanics' Institute movement in England, see J. F. C. Harrison, *Learning and Living 1790–1960: A Study in the History of the English Adult Education Movement* (Toronto: University of Toronto Press, 1971), 50–218; Harold Silver, *The Concept of Popular Education: A Study of Ideas and Social Movements in the Early Nineteenth Century* (London: Macgibbon and Kee, 1965), 204–30; Brian Simon, *Studies in the History of Education, 1780–1870* (London: Lawrence and Wishart, 1960), 177–266; Vincent, *Bread, Knowledge and Freedom,* 133–66. These and other studies hardly ignore the desire of leading middle-class participants in the Mechanics' Institutes movement, particularly in Britain, to disseminate "useful" and "appropriate" knowledge to the working classes as a means of checking labor alienation and thereby safeguarding existing social arrangements. That England's Mechanics' Institutes tended during the course of the nineteenth century to reinforce dominant social roles and inequalities in the larger society has, however, perhaps been emphasized most strongly of all in a recent "feminist" analysis by June Purvis. The typical curriculum of the "mixed-sex" Institutes, Purvis argues, was

both gender- and class-specific. Working-class male members had access to a wide range of "scientific/technical 'male' knowledge" geared to truly strengthening them vocationally. The more limited curriculum generally available to working-class adult women seems for most of this period to have been much less oriented toward widening or otherwise improving their marketability as independent wage-earners; in accordance with patriarchal ideals, and mirroring the orientation of the British elementary schools, the Institutes primarily offered working-class females the opportunity to develop the sewing and other "practical household" skills that would equip them to be full-time mothers and wives in working-class households. Young middle-class women who attended the Institutes were exposed to a still different, more gentile type of curriculum, one in keeping with their prospective social position as "ladies" of the house. "While for all women attending institute classes," Purvis concludes, "the curriculum could relate to paid work (as in the case of becoming a governess for middle-class women or taking up clerical and commercial work for working-class women)," that curriculum was "also strongly associated with female domestic roles" (159). These general patterns in the curricula of the various Mechanic Institutes seem not to have been substantially different in those cases where working-class males shared with middle-class men a significant voice in setting policy, although Purvis does note a number of variations and counter-tendencies; Purvis, *Hard Lessons: The Lives and Education of Working-Class Women in Nineteenth-Century England* (Cambridge, Eng.: Polity Press, 1989), 100–102, 133–45, 224–31.

76. Article from unnamed newspaper repr. as "Dignity of Labor," in *Emancipator* (New York), Oct. 15, 1840.

77. William Ellery Channing, *Self-Culture. Address Introductory to Franklin Lectures,* delivered in Boston, Sept. 1838, in Channing, *The Works of William E. Channing, D. D.,* new and complete ed. (Boston: American Unitarian Association, 1896), 32–33.

78. Josephson, *Golden Threads,* 85–91, 186; Bertha Monica Stearns, "Early Factory Magazines in New England: The Lowell Offering and Its Contemporaries," *Journal of Economic and Business History* 2 (Aug. 1930): 685–88. Efforts to deny the special incompatibility between factory labor and mental development occasionally amounted to the rather lame suggestion that factory work was simply no more disadvantageous in this regard than other forms of manual labor; see "Almora," "The Spirit of Discontent," *Lowell Offering* 2 (1841–1842): 113–14. In 1844 the British writer Charles Knight brought out a work entitled *Mind amongst the Spindles: A Selection from the Lowell Offering, a Miscellany Wholly Composed by the Factory Girls of an American City* (London: Charles Knight and Company, 1844). Knight had his own reasons for trumpeting the intellectual achievements of the Lowell girls. He had been a long-time enthusiast of both "labor-saving" machinery and the "wage fund" doctrine: the former imposed only a "temporary inconvenience" on the workers whom it displaced, the latter affirmed the futility of labor combinations that sought to raise wages above their "natural" level. Highlighting the achievements of the Lowell girls was for Knight another means of blunting the edge of organized resistance to social institutions and conditions which he considered sound. By reference to the example of the Lowell girls, Knight hoped to convince his working-class readers that the means of their improvement indeed lay within themselves, as individuals, rather than in dangerously antisocial collective activity; see [Charles Knight], *The Working-Man's Companion. The Results of Machinery, Namely, Cheap Production, and Increased Employment, Exhibited; Being an Address to the Workingmen of the United Kingdom* (Philadelphia: E. L. Carey and A.

Hart, 1831), 178, 197; see also the argument of Harriet Martineau, expressed in a letter of May 20, 1844, to Knight, that in terms of both wages and social "rank," the Lowell girls enjoyed no advantage over British operatives and that the latter might similarly use their minds to control their lot in life; letter pub. in Knight, "Introduction," *Mind amongst the Spindles*, xviii–xxii.

79. For an illustration of the sense of independence and economic well-being the experience of factory work at Lowell provided some New England farm girls, see Eisler, ed., *Lowell Offering*, 19.

80. Massachusetts, *House Documents* for 1850, no. 153, *Minority Report of the Committee Investigating the Hours of Labor and Considering the Petitions for the Ten Hour Day*, Feb. 8, 1850, repr. in John R. Commons, ed., *Labor Movement, 1840–1860*, vol. 2, A Documentary History of American Industrial Society, vol. 8 (New York: Russell and Russell, 1958 [1910]), 170–73.

81. Lucy Larcom, "American Factory Life," *Journal of Social Science* 15 (Dec. 1882), repr. in Sigmund Diamond, ed., *The Nation Transformed: The Creation of an Industrial Society* (New York: George Braziller, 1963), 157, 159. The most detailed treatment of Larcom's life, in which her brief tenure as a mill girl was followed by a long career as a "nationally known writer," is Shirley Marchalonis, *The Worlds of Lucy Larcom 1824–1893* (Athens: University of Georgia Press, 1989), 2. Notwithstanding Larcom's remarks quoted in the text above, Marchalonis claims that Larcom's "only consistent complaint" about factory labor concerned the noise of the machinery (269).

82. For a study which finds that the typical origins of first generation industrialists in late eighteenth- and early nineteenth-century Britain were "lower middle class," see François Crouzet, *The First Industrialists: The Problem of Origins* (Cambridge, Eng.: Cambridge University Press, 1985), 142–43. On the social backgrounds and ideology of the more prominent factory proprietors in the Lancashire textile firms specifically, see Anthony Howe, *The Cotton Masters 1830–1860* (Oxford: Clarendon Press, 1984). Samuel Greg, Jr., was along with his brothers a second-generation industrialist; see Mary B. Rose, *The Gregs of Quarry Bank Mill: The Rise and Decline of a Family Firm, 1750–1914* (Cambridge, Eng.: Cambridge University Press, 1986).

83. [Samuel Greg], second of *Two Letters to Leonard Horner, Esq, on the Capabilities of the Factory System*, from Bollington, Mar. 1838 (London: Taylor and Walton, 1840), 24, 25–26, repr. in *Conditions of Work and Living: The Reawakening of the English Conscience. Five Pamphlets, 1838–1844*, one of a series of vols. in Kenneth Carpenter, advisory ed., *British Labour Struggles: Contemporary Pamphlets 1727–1850* (New York: Arno Press, 1972). Greg, it might be added, took paternalism further than most British factory masters, paying, in the words of his family's biographer, "far more attention to the evolution of his ideal community at Bollington than to the profitability of his concern." One employee, evidently, looked back upon mill work at Bollington as more like school than work. The gratitude of Greg's operatives, however, had its limits, and in 1846 they launched a strike when he introduced a new machine for stretching cloth. Shortly thereafter Greg withdrew entirely from business and passed control of the mill over to his brothers, Robert and John; see Mary B. Rose, "The Role of the Family in Providing Capital and Managerial Talent in Samuel Greg and Company 1787–1840," *Business History* 19 (Jan. 1977): 49; and Rose, *Gregs*, 65–66.

84. O. A. Brownson, "Brook Farm," *The United States Magazine, and Democratic Review* 11 (Nov. 1842): 483. Another radical, L. A. Hine, offered an opinion similar to Brownson's when discussing the difficulties northern wage laborers

experienced in selling their labor for a "comfortable support": "While we argue against the Slavery of the South, let us not conceal the application of the same argument against the white servitude of the North. This class at the North suffer more than the same class at the South, because they have more mental development, and are more capable of suffering" ("Editor's Place," *Herald of Truth* 3 [Mar. 1848]: 204).

85. Brownson had already had occasion some two years before to discover that many of the mill girls at Lowell were more likely to resent than to share his radical criticisms. His controversial article, "The Laboring Classes," in which he had denounced the "enslavement" of the Lowell girls by industrial "nabobs," had provoked a stream of protest from the mill community. Brownson, wrote one "Factory Girl" in the *Lowell Offering,* had "slandered" the Lowell girls by "slandering" the occupation they had freely chosen; see Brownson, "The Laboring Classes," *Boston Quarterly Review* 3 (July 1840): 370; and "Defence of Factory Girls," repr. in Foner, ed., *Factory Girls,* 31. Interestingly enough, when Alabama Senator Jeremiah Clemens bemoaned the plight of the New England mill girls in similar terms ten years later, he produced very much the same reaction. Factory conditions were commonly acknowledged to have deteriorated over this period, and the deterioration had in fact generated both organized protest and mass departures from the factories by the native-born operatives. Yet those girls who remained in the mills in 1850 were nonetheless inclined to reject the diagnosis of "wage slavery," especially perhaps because it now issued forth from one whose undisguised purpose was the vindication of Southern slavery; see, for example, Nancy P. Healey, "Letter to J. Clemens from a Factory Operative," Stark Mills, Manchester, N.H., Feb. 12, 1850, repr. in *National Era* (Washington, D.C.), Oct. 17, 1850.

86. Such, Marx observed, was the conclusion drawn by G. Garnier, the French translator of Adam Smith's works who opposed Smith's plans to educate the masses; Garnier's position is quoted in *Capital* (International Publishers ed.), 1: 362–63. At the same time, we should note that not all thinkers who were antagonistic to education for manual laborers fit easily into a conservative or elitist mold. The English populist agitator William Cobbett expressed the belief that laboring people must be in charge of their own education. But he also seems to have subscribed to a plebeian form of anti-intellectualism that grew out of his genuine respect for manual labor (above all agricultural labor) and his corresponding hostility to "genteel" success values. The argument that reading and writing permitted manual laborers to "rise" in life by removing them "from the fields to the city" was not one which recommended itself to Cobbett, who held that manual laborers did not in fact need "book learning" at all to make their lives fulfilling and complete; they were, indeed, if anything, above such learning. Populist disdain for those who lived soft and affluent lives without "bodily labor" may have also contributed to Cobbett's embracing an additional argument against popular education: there was that tendency of "book education," Cobbett noted, of "disinclining men to labour." Because Cobbett believed there was no higher "station" than manual labor, provided that it was justly rewarded, he was poles apart from generations of conservatives who had opposed education for members of the laboring population for fear that it would raise them above that station. But at the same time, Cobbett associated himself with this conservative legacy when he objected to "book education" for the working classes on the ground that it created a distaste for manual labor. For further discussion of Cobbett's views, including the animus for oppressive taxation and the anti-Malthusianism that reinforced his hostility to emerging popular education schemes, see Glickstein, "Concepts of Free Labor," 109n; see also William Cobbett,

Weekly Political Register, Aug. 1807, in Cobbett, *Selections from William Cobbett's Political Works: Being a Complete Abridgement of the 100 Volumes which Comprise the Writings of "Porcupine" and the "Weekly Political Register,"* ed. John M. Cobbett and James P. Cobbett (London: Anne Cobbett, 1835), 2: 287–89, 301. See also Raymond Williams, *Culture and Society, 1780–1850* (Harmondsworth, Eng.: Penguin Books, 1961 [1958]), 34, 37; and Clarke, *Price of Progress,* 5.

87. C. B. Macpherson, *The Political Theory of Possessive Individualism: Hobbes to Locke* (London: Oxford University Press, 1962), 222. See also Edward Joseph Hundert, "The Conception of Work and the Worker in Early Industrial England. Studies of an Ideology in Transition" (Ph.D. diss, University of Rochester, 1969), 154–55, 249–50. Seemingly contradictory tendencies exist in every age; the prejudices toward much if not all of the European laboring population as irredeemably animalistic and irrational, prejudices described by Macpherson as "so generally prevalent in Locke's day" (and perhaps most pronounced of all in the writings of some British mercantilists), co-existed with one particular product of the Reformation that no doubt contributed to nineteenth-century American republican and democratic values: "the age-old, fervent Protestant belief in the democratization of knowledge through print" (Ronald J. Zboray, "Antebellum Reading and the Ironies of Technological Innovation," in Cathy N. Davidson, ed., *Reading in America: Literature and History* [Baltimore: Johns Hopkins University Press, 1989], 197). For emphasis upon the particular role of the American Revolution in unleashing "social aspirations that were associated with learning" and with widened access to general knowledge, see Richard D. Brown, *Knowledge Is Power: The Diffusion of Information in Early America, 1700–1865* (New York: Oxford University Press, 1989), 242.

88. Blacks, of course, together perhaps with certain immigrant groups, were generally considered intellectually inferior, although, as already suggested, arguments attesting to their innate and fixed inferiority and lack of aptitude, as distinct from arguments emphasizing the undeveloped state of their capabilities, appear to have been somewhat more characteristic of the late antebellum period and thereafter. Opinions of female intellectual capacity, such as those reflected in the various justifications for excluding women from the "learned" professions, had their own ambiguities. There are some grounds for maintaining that the cult of "separate spheres," which reached its ascendancy during the Jacksonian period, generally adjudged the female intellect innately "different" from the male's rather than flatly inferior to it, although this remains a matter of controversy. But the rising influence of Darwinist, Spencerian, and ethnological thought generally after mid-century seem clearly to have solidified notions that the female intellect, both existing and potential, was genuinely inferior to the male's, just as this body of thought hardened attitudes toward blacks and the immigrant Irish as innately inferior; see Nancy F. Cott, *The Bonds of Womanhood: "Woman's Sphere" in New England, 1780–1835* (New Haven: Yale University Press, 1977), 203; Barbara J. Harris, *Beyond Her Sphere: Women and the Professions in American History* (Westport, Conn.: Greenwood Press, 1978), 42–62; Mary Roth Walsh, *"Doctors Wanted: No Women Need Apply": Sexual Barriers in the Medical Profession, 1835–1975* (New Haven: Yale University Press, 1977), 8–9; Jean N. Burstyn, *Victorian Education and the Ideal of Womanhood* (London: Croom Helm, 1980), 70–83; Mary Beth Norton, *Liberty's Daughters: The Revolutionary Experience of American Women, 1750–1800* (Boston: Little, Brown and Company, 1980), 264, 297–99; Ann Firor Scott, *Making the Invisible Woman Visible* (Urbana: University of Illinois Press, 1984), 300–301; Linda M. Perkins, "The Education of Black Women in the Nineteenth Century," in John Mack Faragher and Florence Howe, eds., *Women and Higher Education in American History* (New York:

W. W. Norton, 1988), 64–86; Rosalind Rosenberg, *Beyond Separate Spheres: Intellectual Roots of Modern Feminism* (New Haven: Yale University Press, 1982), xv, 5–15.

89. As Marvin Meyers has suggested, leading success counselors like Freeman Hunt did retain a significant role for business acumen and shrewdness in the capitalist marketplace, but perhaps instinctively they did not overplay this role, for to do so might have undercut the importance they assigned the traditional character virtues as the keys to economic success; Marvin Meyers, *The Jacksonian Persuasion: Politics and Belief* (Stanford: Stanford University Press, 1957), 129n. See also Richard Hofstadter, *Anti-Intellectualism in American Life* (New York: Random House, 1962), 255. Valuable discussions of the success ethic in antebellum America include John G. Cawelti, *Apostles of the Self-Made Man: Changing Concepts of Success in America* (Chicago: University of Chicago Press, 1965); and Irvin G. Wyllie, *The Self-Made Man in America: The Myth of Rags to Riches* (New York: Free Press, 1954). Wyllie, *Self-Made,* 101–7, and Hofstadter, *Anti-Intellectualism,* 256–60, both discuss the tendency of successful nineteenth-century American businessmen, themselves without a college education, to disdain formal learning and especially higher education as peripheral and even detrimental to economic success.

90. Robert V. Bruce, *The Launching of Modern American Science, 1846–1876* (New York: Alfred A. Knopf, 1987), 8, 26; George H. Daniels, *Science in American Society: A Social History* (New York: Alfred A. Knopf, 1971), 155, 163–73; see also, however, Sally Gregory Kohlstedt, "Reassessing Science in Antebellum America," *American Quarterly* 29 (Fall 1977): 444–53; and the essays in George H. Daniels, ed., *Nineteenth-Century American Science: A Reappraisal* (Evanston: Northwestern University Press, 1972).

91. For these and other prejudices against the professions in antebellum America, see William G. Rothstein, *American Physicians in the Nineteenth Century: From Sects to Science* (Baltimore: Johns Hopkins University Press, 1972) 137–38, 148–51; Paul Starr, *The Social Transformation of American Medicine* (New York: Basic Books, 1982), 30–31, 56–57; Maxwell Bloomfield, *American Lawyers in a Changing Society, 1776–1876* (Cambridge: Harvard University Press, 1976), 32–58, 146–47; Anton-Hermann Chroust, *The Rise of the Legal Profession in America* (Norman: University of Oklahoma Press, 1965), 2: 16–19, 30–51, 70–73, 117, 165–72. See also Gerard W. Gawalt, "Sources of Anti-Lawyer Sentiment in Massachusetts, 1740–1840," *American Journal of Legal History* 14 (1970): 283–307, which attaches special emphasis to the relatively "inbred" and "exclusive nature" of the Massachusetts "lawyer class" in these years; popular resentment and eventual reaction set in against "a professional elite based on extended education, paternal occupation, and marriage alliances" (298, 304, 306).

92. Gerard Gawalt thus notes that the various eighteenth- and nineteenth-century reform movements that sought to simplify Massachusetts law, lower the educational requirements of lawyers, and otherwise limit or even abolish the legal profession "reflected a form of anti-intellectualism that associated learning with elitism" (Gerard W. Gawalt, *The Promise of Power: The Emergence of the Legal Profession in Massachusetts 1760–1840* [Westport, Conn.: Greenwood Press, 1979], 51). On the other hand, those same movements, as Gawalt suggests, reflected the faith that the average man could manage a simplified legal system were he to exercise his rational capabilities, and in this sense these movements reflected both an animus to esoteric knowledge and a belief that access to all truly valuable knowledge could be democratized and diffused through the general population. The whole question of the "anti-intellectualism" of such movements bears strong parallels with the persisting controversy regarding the nature of Jacksonian Democratic and "radical"

workingmen's party ideology—was the hostility which participants in these latter movements voiced to the existing distribution of capitalist power and privilege a reflection of genuinely "anti-capitalist" leanings or primarily an expression of the desire to open up and democratize capitalism? Richard Hofstadter, the architect of the "entrepreneurial" position that Jacksonians were "incipient capitalists" has also, of course, written notably on the theme of anti-intellectualism in American culture. One of his observations well describes the general leveling attitude toward knowledge that characterized the anti–legal profession movements described by Gawalt: "It seemed to be the goal of the common man in [Jacksonian] America to build a society that would show how much could be done without literature and learning— or rather, a society whose literature and learning would be largely limited to such elementary things as the common man could grasp and use." Yet in emphasizing how the "common man's" leveling attitude aimed to debase high intellectual standards, Hofstadter's insights also slight the capacity of that leveling attitude to encompass under some circumstances a yearning for genuine intellectual *uplift*. Hofstadter's general definition of anti-intellectualism, "a resentment and suspicion of the life of the mind and of those who are considered to represent it; and a disposition constantly to minimize the value of that life" (Hofstadter, *Anti-Intellectualism,* 7, 51, 154–55), accurately suggests the hostility with which workingmen's and labor reform organizations regarded the professionals or capitalists who they believed had appropriated learning for their own exclusive advantage; but that definition conveys nothing of their desire to acquire some of that knowledge for themselves. Exhortations of intellectual uplift and self-improvement were for similar reasons a basic part of the sermons and writings that leaders in free black communities directed to their downtrodden constituencies; see David E. Swift, *Black Prophets of Justice: Activist Clergy before the Civil War* (Baton Rouge: Louisiana State University Press, 1989), 17, 31–34. See also Richard Johnson's discussion of British labor during this period in "'Really Useful Knowledge': Radical Education and Working-Class Culture," in John Clarke, Chas Critcher, and Richard Johnson, eds., *Working-Class Culture: Studies in History and Theory* (London: Hutchinson, 1979), 75–102.

93. Stephen Simpson, *The Working Man's Manual: A New Theory of Political Economy* (Philadelphia: Thomas L. Bonsal, 1831), 201–15, 260. A strong advocate of the ideology of separate spheres, however, Simpson also opposed extending the benefits of a "republican," common school education to female members of the producing, or any other, classes; the female's education should be confined to the home and should conform to her naturally "passive" disposition and duties; see also New York *Working Man's Advocate*: "Prospectus," Oct. 31, 1829, and "Equal Education," Apr. 3, 1830; John Barkeley Jentz, "Artisans, Evangelicals, and the City: A Social History of Abolition and Labor Reform in Jacksonian New York" (Ph.D. diss., City University of New York, 1977), 144–60; Pessen, *Most Uncommon Jacksonians,* 183–89.

94. "The Ten Hour System," *Mechanics' Monthly Review,* repr. in the *Voice of Industry,* Apr. 10, 1846. That the theme of intellectual uplift was a bond of continuity between labor movements of the 1840s and those of the late 1820s and 1830s is also noted in Rush Welter, *Popular Education and Democratic Thought in America* (New York: Columbia University Press, 1962), 46–59; and David R. Roediger, "The Movement for a Shorter Working Day in the United States before 1866" (Ph.D. diss., Northwestern University, 1980), 43–93, 150.

95. See, for example, E. G. Squier, *Address. The Condition of the Laboring Population of America, and Their True Interests. Delivered before Mechanic Associations*

in New York City, Brooklyn, Albany (Albany: New York State Mechanic, and Cultivator, 1843), 8, 12–14. Squier's invocation of Burritt exemplifies the difficulty of classifying many antebellum thinkers into neat ideological categories. Squier used Burritt both to illustrate the consistency of manual labor with "the highest attainments in intellectual pursuits," and in support of his argument that in America "there is not an avenue to wealth or distinction which is closed." The latter position certainly, but not the former, would have infuriated his radical contemporaries.

If some defenders of existing social arrangements exploited Burritt's intellectual endeavors, the "learned blacksmith" himself seemed almost to disparage them; possibly he feared that his scholarly accomplishments might ultimately obscure the very link to manual labor which had made them so distinctive and symbolically significant in the first place. Burritt wanted, he told Longfellow, "to stand in the ranks of the working-men of New England and beg and beckon them onward and upward, if I can, into the full stature of intellectual men." But he also explained that he had "long ago resolved to make them [his studies] subservient to the more necessary and important avocations of life, and not to indulge them at the expense of valuable time or the price of labor." He accordingly "always confined" his " 'literary leisure' to those unoccupied hours of the day when no man can work" (Burritt to H. W. Longfellow, Dec. 1, 1840, quoted in Merle Curti, *The Learned Blacksmith: The Letters and Journals of Elihu Burritt* [New York: Wilson-Erickson, 1937], 10). See also Peter Tolis, "Elihu Burritt: Crusader for Brotherhood" (Ph.D. diss., Columbia University, 1965), 30–32. Although he became a prominent figure in the world peace and antislavery movements, Burritt's reputation was built upon his mastery of over a half dozen languages, including Latin, Greek, German, and Hebrew; Curti, *Learned Blacksmith*, 3–6.

96. [George Frederick Holmes], "Ancient Slavery," pt. 1, *De Bow's Review* 19 (Nov. 1855): 571, 576–77.

97. Theodore Parker, "Thoughts on Labor," repr. in *New-York Daily Tribune*, Apr. 29, 1841; "The Ten Hour System," in *Voice of Industry*, Apr. 10, 1846.

98. This writer was more antagonistic than Parker and others to existing social arrangements and embraced Associationist socialism as the only means of eradicating wage slavery; "What Is the Reason? 'How Much Land and Property, And I Have None!'" *Democratic Review* 16 (Jan. 1845): 24–29.

99. Horace Greeley, *An Address before the Literary Societies of Hamilton College*, July 23, 1847 (New York: William H. Graham, 1844), 13–16. For some of the European antecedents of the American manual movement, which might be taken to include the earliest of the British Mechanics' Institutes that were designed to provide education and intellectual uplift to members of the working classes, see Charles Alpheus Bennett, *History of Manual and Industrial Education up to 1870* (Peoria, Ill.: Chas. A. Bennett Company, 1926).

100. L. F. Anderson, "The Manual Labor School Movement," *Educational Review* 46 (Nov. 1913): 385.

101. Theodore Dwight Weld, *First Annual Report of the Society for Promoting Manual Labor in Literary Institutions, Including the Report of Their General Agent, Theodore Dwight Weld, January 28, 1833* (New York: S. W. Benedict and Company, 1833), 13. See also Robert H. Abzug, *Passionate Liberator: Theodore Dwight Weld and the Dilemma of Reform* (New York: Oxford University Press, 1980), 67.

102. John Frost, *An Oration Delivered at Middlebury, before the Associated Alumni of the College, on the Evening of Commencement*, Aug. 19, 1829 (Utica: Hastings and Tracy, 1829), 8–9. See also *Journal of Health* 1 (Oct. 28, 1829): 78–79.

103. John R. Betts, "Mind and Body in Early American Thought," *Journal of*

American History 54 (Mar. 1968): 790–803; John L. Thomas, review of Abzug's *Passionate Liberator,* in *Journal of Interdisciplinary History* 13 (Summer 1982): 154. For a rather distinctive physiological contribution to the manual labor school movement, one that emphasized the importance of achieving, through physical education, "a well-cultivated and well-balanced brain," see Charles Caldwell, *Thoughts on Physical Education and the True Mode of Improving the Condition of Man* (Edinburgh: Adam and Charles Black, 1836), 78, 80, 120.

104. Weld, *First Annual Report,* 31.

105. Ibid., 56n.

106. Ibid., 56. This is not to deny that concern with physical degeneration led other writers to emphasize the importance of outdoor exercise and sport, particularly for the sedentary urban middle classes but also for industrious manual workers in need of respite and relaxation; see Martin L. Adelman, *A Sporting Time: New York City and the Rise of Modern Athletics, 1820–1870* (Urbana: University of Illinois Press, 1986), 272–76. The exaltation of exercise, as distinct from anything so mundane as labor, also played a part in the mythology of the Southern planter-gentlemen. The latter specimen, David R. Hundley claimed in his encomium to Southern mores, owed his "fine physical development" to fox hunting and other outdoor activities; his condition was to be favorably compared to that of citizens in the free states classes, who in their foolish disregard of exercise, according to Hundley, epitomized the Northern disposition to regard as "sinful . . . every species of pastime which hinders the making of money" (D. R. Hundley, *Social Relations in Our Southern States* [New York: Henry B. Price, 1860], 35, 41).

107. Weld, *First Annual Report,* 41–42, 56–57, 63. See also the resolutions passed at the third meeting of the American Lyceum, in 1833, repr. in Herbert G. Lull, "The Manual Labor Movement in the United States," *Bulletin of Washington University Studies,* no. 8 (1914): 381.

108. Anderson, "Manual Labor School Movement," 386.

109. Seth Luther, *An Address on the Origin and Progress of Avarice, and Its Deleterious Effects on Human Happiness, with a Proposed Remedy for the Countless Evils Resulting from an Inordinate Desire for Wealth,* delivered before the Union Association of Working Men, Charleston, Mass., Jan. 30, 1834 (Boston: Seth Luther, 1834), 35.

110. Thomas Hodgskin, *Labour Defended against the Claims of Capital or the Unproductiveness of Capital Proved with Reference to the Present Combinations amongst Journeymen* (London: Labour Publishing Company, 1922 [1825]), 101.

111. Johann-Jakob Wehrli, whose teachers' college in Switzerland attracted international attention, voiced many of Weld's themes when he remarked that obliging the "children of the rich" to labor teaches them "to get rid of all those notions which riches are too apt to stimulate; to understand the feelings of the poor better; to treat them better, and to associate with them better; it [labor] thus diminishes the artificial distance between classes, and, with the distinction of this artificial distance, it diminishes also the jealous feelings, which false mannerism on the part of the rich too often engenders" (Vehrli quoted in Joseph Kay, *The Social Condition and Education of the People in England and Europe,* vol. 2, *The Education of the People* (Shannon, Ireland: Irish University Press, 1971 [1850]), 365.

112. See chapter 6. For an example of the principle's use in the defense of New England "book farming," see John P. Norton, Professor of Agicultural Chemistry, Yale College, "The Advantages of Science in Its Application to Agriculture," an address to the Hampden County Agricultural Society, in Amasa Walker, ed., *Transactions of the Agricultural Societies in the State of Massachusetts, for 1851* (Boston: Dutton and Wentworth, 1852), 579.

113. "The Philosophy of Labor. No. IX," *Daily Chronotype*, Aug. 20, 1846. See also "Labor," *Mechanic's Advocate* (Albany), Feb. 4, 1847 for similar remarks by a paper that supported Ten Hour legislation and the land reform movement.

114. "What Is the Reason," 25.

115. This last argument, in the view of labor radicals, applied with even greater force to landlords and other elements of the idle rich, above all Europe's titled aristocracy—individuals whose failure to pursue *any* active employment, entrepreneurial capitalist or otherwise, actually discouraged the healthy and productive use of their mental faculties. In underscoring how Attractive Industry under Association would meet the needs of all social classes, Albert Brisbane referred to the "debility and disease" that currently afflicted individuals who, "living on the labor of others, . . . pass their time in idle ease." Their "Faculties and Passions, being left comparatively inactive and having no field for development in the noble sphere of Industry," they found "pernicious" and self-destructive "outlets" for their energies in "drinking, gambling, and other kinds of debauchery and dissipation" (Albert Brisbane, *A Concise Exposition of the Doctrine of Association, or Plan for a Reorganization of Society, Which Will Secure to the Human Race, Individually and Collectively, Their Happiness and Elevation [Based on Fourier's Theory of Domestic and Industrial Association]*, 8th ed. [New York: J. S. Redfield, 1844], 41). Labor radicals like Brisbane thus shared with their principal antagonists, David Ricardo and other political economic defenders of competitive capitalist market arrangements, a view of landed wealth as uniquely idle and parasitical.

116. For amusing descriptions of George Ripley and his wife engaged in manual labor at Brook Farm, see Annie M. Salisbury, *Brook Farm* (Marlboro, Mass.: F. B. Estabrook, 1898), repr. in Joel Myerson, ed., *The Brook Farm Book: A Selection of First-Hand Accounts of the Community* (New York: Garland Publishing, 1987), 249. "Though all worked," Salisbury recalls here, "it was the workers who did the work, there as elsewhere; while the theorizers theorized beautifully and gave a charm to the common life." A recent valuable account of the early Brook Farm may be found in Edward K. Spann, *Brotherly Tomorrows: Movements for a Cooperative Society in America 1820–1920* (New York: Columbia University Press, 1989), 50–66.

117. [George William Curtis], "Editor's Easy Chair," *Harper's New Monthly Magazine* 38 (Jan. 1869); 268–71, repr. in Myerson, ed., *Brook Farm Book*, 99. For a very similar statement, see "What Is the Reason," 24.

118. Senator Benjamin F. Wade of Ohio, *Congressional Globe*, 35th Cong., 1st sess., Mar. 13, 1858, pt. 2: 1113.

119. Thomas, review of Abzug's *Passionate Liberator*, 154.

120. Alonzo Potter, *The School: Its Objects, Relations, and Uses*, pt. 1 of Alonzo Potter and George B. Emerson, *The School and the Schoolmaster. A Manual for the Use of Teachers, Employers, Trustees, Inspectors & c, & c of Common Schools* (New York: Harper and Brothers, 1842), 145.

121. Potter, *Principles of Science*, 265–66; Potter, *Political Economy*, 20n.

122. Potter, *School*, 102–45; Anthony F. Wallace, *Rockdale: The Growth of an American Village in the Early Industrial Revolution* (New York: Alfred A. Knopf, 1978), 335–37.

123. Even in Britain, however, conservatives who had been most sympathetic to this elitist argument were during the late eighteenth and early nineteenth centuries coming around to the view that social hierarchy was best served by dispensing certain kinds of knowledge to the laboring population; see R. A. Soloway's study of the Anglican clergy, *Prelates and People: Ecclesiastical Social Thought in England, 1785–1852* (London: Routledge and Kegan Paul, 1969), 350–89.

124. As Chalmers, the Malthusian Scottish minister, succinctly put it, "We are not aware of a likelier instrument, than a judicious course of economic doctrine, for tranquilizing the popular mind" (Thomas Chalmers, *The Christian and Civic Economy of Large Towns* [Glasgow: Chalmers and Collins, 1821], 3: 386). See also Harriet Martineau, *Poor Laws and Paupers Illustrated,* vol. 10, *The Tendency of Strikes and Sticks to Produce Low Wages, and of Union between Masters and Men to Ensure Good Wages* (London: Charles Fox, 1833).

125. Michael B. Katz, *The Irony of Early School Reform: Educational Innovation in Mid-Nineteenth Century Massachusetts* (Boston: Beacon Press, 1970), 88, 112; Samuel Bowles and Herbert Gintis, *Schooling in Capitalist America: Educational Reform and the Contradictions of Economic Life* (New York: Basic Books, 1976), 27–29, 164–73, 240. Bowles and Gintis push even harder than Katz the theme that long before the advent of formal tracking procedures and trade schools, American mass education was systematically reproducing the social inequalities necessary to maintain the capitalist mode of production.

126. See also Theodore Clapp, *Autobiographical Sketches and Recollections, During a Thirty-Five Years' Residence in New Orleans* (Boston: Phillips, Sampson and Company, 1858), 359–60.

127. Correctional institutions sometimes defended the work regimens they imposed on their "bold" and "bad" charges by arguing that labor itself, as distinct from classroom education, was an effective means of stimulating good habits and discipline; see the rebuttal by the Managers of the New York House of Refuge to criticisms made by J. R. Hale that school time at the Refuge was far too short compared to labor time and that the moral and intellectual development of the juvenile inmates was consequently being neglected by the Refuge; "The House of Refuge. Reply of the Managers to Mr. Hale," *New-York Daily Tribune,* Dec. 10, 1955; Hale's criticisms appeared in the issues of Nov. 20 and Nov. 22.

128. Leading Massachusetts manufacturers queried by Horace Mann in 1841 appear to have valued common school education less for any capacity on its part to develop intellectual initiative or "inventiveness" in their employees, than for its ability to socialize them for a disciplined work regimen; the manufacturers prized schooling, in Harvey Graff's words, for developing deference and other "noncognitive personality characteristics" in the workers. Yet this is not to say that these particular employers, at least, valued mass education for turning out compliant and efficient automatons; their view of the socialization process was not so stark. The manufacturers seem instead to have assumed that schooling did serve a particular cognitive function, that of encouraging employees to embrace and internalize the same "reasonable" view of the workings of society and of the relations between capital and labor that they themselves had. Insofar as literacy maximized employees' ability to follow written and other instructions, it was consistent with the same central ends sought by the manufacturers: increased harmony, orderliness, and efficiency in the workplace; see Massachusetts, Board of Education, Horace Mann, *Annual Reports on Education. Fifth Report* (1842), in Mann, *Life and Works of Horace Mann,* enl. ed., ed. Mary Mann and George C. Mann (Boston: Lee and Shepard, 1891), 3: 101–9; Graff, *Literacy Myth,* 203–7; and Maris A. Vinovskis, "Horace Mann on the Economic Productivity of Education," *New England Quarterly* 43 (Dec. 1970): 551–68.

129. The retail and wholesale sector of the antebellum economy, and even the professions, provided some openings for members of working-class families who might wish more from their education than continued employment in manual labor. Yet these openings were limited in number and were certainly perceived as such—

hence the frequent claims by writers that business and professional opportunities in the northeastern cities were insufficient to accommodate even all of the children from middle-class backgrounds. In the 1850s, too, the enormous expansion of the white-collar clerical and service sector—in particular the emergence of a "new middle class" of salaried office workers capable of absorbing significant numbers from working-class families—was still a development of the future, although commercial and manufacturing clerical positions in New York and other antebellum cities were undeniably growing in number. For valuable studies of the "old middle class," which included mid-nineteenth-century retail and wholesale storekeepers and other nonmanual proprietors and workers of various kinds, see Stuart M. Blumin, "The Hypothesis of Middle-Class Formation in Nineteenth-Century America: A Critique and Some Proposals," *American Historical Review* 90 (Apr. 1985): 299–337; and Blumin, "Black Coats to White Workers," in Stuart W. Bruchey, ed., *Small Business in American Life* (New York: Columbia University Press, 1980), 100–121.

130. "Ruskin and Architecture," 193.

131. John Greenleaf Whittier, "Justice and Expediency: or, Slavery Considered with a View to Its Rightful and Effectual Remedy, Abolition" (1833), repr. in Louis Ruchames, ed., *The Abolitionists: A Collection of Their Writings* (New York: Capricorn Books, 1963), 53.

132. Frederick Law Olmsted, *A Journey in the Back Country* (New York: Schocken Books, 1970 [1860]), 81. In their controversial work, *Time on the Cross: The Economics of American Negro Slavery* (Boston: Little, Brown and Company, 1974), 1: 208–9, Robert William Fogel and Stanley L. Engerman took this statement of Olmsted's as proof of his "pre-industrial peasant mentality," of his repugnance for labor which, in their view, had much the same work rhythms and efficiency as the "modern assembly line." Fogel and Engerman are correct in their assertion if we accept their definition of "industrial mentality" as the only one: an appreciation of labor processes that depend for their productiveness on the regimented, repetitive, docile, and even mindless actions of their human participants. But many mid-nineteenth-century Americans, particularly those like Olmsted who belonged to the Protestant middle classes, in fact embraced "industrial mentality" or morality in a quite different sense. This outlook scorned inefficient and unproductive "pre-industrial" work habits and in so doing, put a new premium on time-honored character virtues and on the individual workingman's right and capacity to exercise "self-direction" and self-restraint in all aspects of his life. In an important sense, in other words, Olmsted's repugnance for slavery and slave labor epitomized, rather than represented a repudiation of, "industrial mentality" or morality. For further discussion of the distinction between types of industrial morality, see chapter 7.

133. "Manufacturing at the South," *Springfield* (Mass.) *Daily Republican*, Jan. 29, 1859.

134. "Manufactures at the South," *National Anti-Slavery Standard*, Aug. 5, 1847; Dixon, "Manchester," 357–59. I have somewhat altered the order of the *Standard*'s remarks. See also Jonathan A. Glickstein, "'Poverty Is Not Slavery': American Abolitionists and the Competitive Labor Market," in Lewis Perry and Michael Fellman, eds., *Antislavery Reconsidered: New Perspectives on the Abolitionists* (Baton Rouge: Louisiana State University Press, 1979), 207–9.

135. Benjamin Franklin, *Canadian Pamphlet* (1740), quoted in Alexander James Field, "Educational Reform and Manufacturing Development in Mid-Nineteenth Century Massachusetts" (Ph.D. diss., University of California, Berkeley, 1975), 189; Drew R. McCoy, *The Elusive Republic: Political Economy in Jeffersonian America* (Chapel Hill: University of North Carolina Press, 1980), 51–66, 107–12; Sidney

Pollard, *The Genesis of Modern Management* (Cambridge: Harvard University Press, 1965), 161–65; E. P. Thompson, *The Making of the English Working Class* (Harmondsworth, Eng.: Penguin Books, 1968), 338; and Christopher Hill, "Pottage for Freeborn Englishmen: Attitudes to Wage-Labour in the Sixteenth and Seventeenth Centuries," in C. H. Feinstein, ed., *Socialism, Capitalism and Economic Growth: Essays Presented to Maurice Dobb* (Cambridge, Eng.: Cambridge University Press, 1967), 348–50.

136. "Letter from Henry C. Carey," Aug. 8, 1853, Burlington, N.J., in *Putnam's Monthly; A Magazine of American Literature, Science, and Art* 2 (Sept. 1853): 344.

137. James Henry Hammond, "Progress of Southern Industry. Governor Hammond's Address before the South Carolina Institute, 1850," *De Bow's Review* 8 (June 1850): 518; John E. Cairnes, *The Slave Power. Its Character, Career & Probable Designs Being An Attempt to Explain the Real Issues Involved in the American Contest*, 2d enl. ed.(New York: Augustus M. Kelley, 1968 [1863]), 112, 112n.

138. Fogel and Engerman, *Time*, 1: 179–81, is among the studies that have emphasized Olmsted's racial prejudices—his partial attribution of the unintelligent, inefficient nature of Southern slave labor to the fact that it was also black labor.

139. Mann, *Twelfth Annual Report* (1849), in *Life and Works*, 4: 265.

140. "H. W. P.," letter to the *New-York Daily Times*, Apr. 7, 1853. The writer professed a great familiarity with slavery in eastern Virginia.

141. Mann, *Fifth Annual Report* (1842), in *Life and Works*, 3: 118.

142. Channing, *Slavery* (1835), in *Works of William E. Channing*, 711. Channing, along with others who made this argument, strongly implied that educated slaves would naturally rise in revolution and that slaveholders for this reason did well to shroud them in ignorance of their "inalienable and outraged rights." Of course, such rebellions, if on a much smaller scale than that possibly envisioned by Channing, had already occurred in the American South with disastrous consequences for the slaves involved.

143. Channing, *Self-Culture*, in *Works of William E. Channing*, 32.

144. It was precisely to such a general test that the editor of the *New-York Daily Times*, Henry J. Raymond, urged William L. Yancey and other Southerners to put these antislavery arguments. Like other Northerners of more moderate or even nonexistent antislavery sympathies, Raymond shared certain of the principal axioms of the antislavery movement: he agreed, for example, that labor becomes more "valuable" as it acquires both greater intelligence and the increased hope of being fairly rewarded. But at this juncture Raymond deviated fundamentally from standard antislavery and, above all, abolitionist opinion, arguing that slave labor constituted no necessary exception to this axiom. Were slaves as a matter of general policy educated and made more "intelligent," and were they given increased material and other incentives to labor, including the guarantee that one or more of their children would be freed, then their devotion to their masters, Raymond predicted, would increase rather than diminish. Reform of slavery along these lines, the journalist appealed to Yancey, would disarm legitimate criticisms of slavery, render the South more prosperous and secure, and avert disunion in the process. At some points in his series of letters to Yancey, Raymond suggested that "free" debate in the South over the merits of slavery would indeed lead to its eventual abolition, while at other points he argued that implementation of the reforms he urged would permit slavery to continue indefinitely; Henry J. Raymond, *Disunion and Slavery. A Series of Letters to Hon. W. L. Yancey, of Alabama* (n.p. ca. 1861), 30–36.

145. Eric Foner, *Free Soil, Free Labor, Free Men: The Ideology of the Republican Party before the Civil War* (New York: Oxford University Press, 1970), 45–46.

146. Studies illustrating the versatility and viability of slave labor in a wide range of manufacturing enterprises in the South include Robert S. Starobin, *Industrial Slavery in the Old South* (New York: Oxford University Press, 1970); and Fred Bateman and Thomas Weiss, *A Deplorable Scarcity: The Failure of Industrialization in the Slave Economy* (Chapel Hill: University of North Carolina Press, 1981), 30–33, 81–85.

147. See, for example, Richard Hildreth, *Despotism in America: An Inquiry into the Nature, Results, and Legal Basis of the Slave-Holding System in the United States* (New York: Negro Universities Press, 1968 [1854]), 112–13, 132–39, 159–60; for Smith's argument that it was in the slave's interest to do as little work as possible, see *Wealth of Nations*, 365–69.

148. "Liberty," *Herald of Freedom*," Aug. 16, 1844.

149. "The Courier—Ourself [*sic*] and Reform," *Voice of Industry*, Mar. 6, 1846.

150. Remarks from Channing to a committee of the Massachusetts legislature [n.d.], and (as possibly paraphrased by a newspaper) Channing, Address at Convention for Establishing a County Association for the Improvement of Common Schools at Taunton, Massachusetts, 1837, both in *Memoir of William Ellery Channing, with Extracts from His Correspondences and Manuscripts,* with a Preface by "W. H. C." [William Henry Channing] (Boston: W. Crosby and H. P. Nichols, 1848), 3: 71, 92–93.

151. Channing, Address at Convention, in ibid., 91. Channing's understanding here of the mentally demanding character of the "mechanic arts" may have been widely shared among employers in the North, or at least used by them as a rationale for excluding free blacks from their enterprises. Blacks were even shut out of patently unskilled or semiskilled jobs in the expanding factory system, for these jobs often went to Irish immigrants instead. For discussions of this widespread job discrimination in one Northern city, see Theodore Hershberg, "Free Blacks in Philadelphia: A Study of Ex-Slaves, Freeborn, and Socioeconomic Decline," *Journal of Social History* 5 (Winter 1971–72): 191–92; and Gary B. Nash, *Forging Freedom: The Formation of Philadelphia's Black Community, 1720–1840* (Cambridge: Harvard University Press, 1988), 217.

152. Mann, *Twelfth Annual Report* (1849), in *Life and Works,* 4: 264–65.

153. Ibid., 265.

154. For a recent study of the "family system" mills and their reliance upon child labor, see Barbara M. Tucker, *Samuel Slater and the Origins of the American Textile Industry, 1790–1860* (Ithaca: Cornell University Press, 1984). See also Pennsylvania, *Journal of the Senate of the Commonwealth of Pennsylvania,* 2 vols., sess. 1837–38, for the *Report of the Committee of the Senate, Appointed to Investigate the Subject of the Employment of Children in Manufactories,* which includes testimony on the extensive child factory labor in the state. For the influx of Irish factory labor into the mills of Lowell during the 1840s and 1850s, see Dublin, "Women at Work," 174–93; and Howard M. Gitelman, "The Waltham System and the Coming of the Irish," *Labor History* 8 (Fall 1967): 227–53.

155. Mann remarked: "There is scarcely any kind of labor, however simple or automatic, which can be so well performed without knowledge in the workman as with it" (Mann, *Fifth Annual Report* [1842], in *Life and Works,* 3: 118).

156. "Manufactures at the South."

157. Frederick Law Olmsted, *A Journey in the Seaboard Slave States in the Years 1853–1854. With Remarks on Their Economy* (New York: G. P. Putnam's Sons, 1904 [1856]), 2: 58.

158. "Yeoman" [Frederick Law Olmsted], "The South. Letters on the Production, Industry and Resources of the Southern States. Number Forty-Eight—The Last. The Economical, Moral, and Political Relations of Slavery," *New-York Daily Times,* Feb. 13, 1854. With this letter Olmsted completed the first of two series of letters for the *Times* that he had begun in the Feb. 16, 1853, issue of the paper as a "Special Correspondent." With some revisions and the addition of other material, this first series of letters came to comprise *Seaboard Slave States,* the first of Olmsted's famous published volumes on the South.

159. Ibid.; Frederick Law Olmsted, *Walks and Talks of an American Farmer in England,* new and rev. ed. (Columbus, Ohio: Jos. H. Riley and Company, 1859), 278–79. Paralleling Olmsted's rejection here of the elitist, "aristocratic" division of labor theme, one that insisted upon a broad, natural incompatibility and division between manual labor and significant mental activity, was Olmsted's borrowing elsewhere of Adam Smith's emphasis upon the benefits of complex social division of labor. The second theme, like the first, partially reflected the high value Olmsted placed on skilled, intelligent manual labor. It was Olmsted's thesis that in frontier western communities, just as in the slave South, there occurred a "decivilizing process" whereby occupational differentiation broke down and was retarded. In such communities there was a relative absence of demand for the refined "wants" that distinguished the more complex and heterogeneous social environments of European and northeastern urban centers. Olmsted was particularly intrigued by, and critical of, the adjustment that skilled European emigrants to these frontier communities were gradually forced to make: "They unlearn, not only their special skill, but their demand for special skill, and acquire the distinguishing habit of the established pioneer to 'make shift,'—to 'get along' with rude substitutes for the results of civilized skill, and instead of doing anything well, do all things poorly." "Decivilizing" circumstances, that is to say, undermined complex social division of labor by minimizing the demand for the specialized expertise and mental content of skilled manual labor. Olmsted's most sustained thoughts on decivilization are in notes and drafts comprising his "Outline for the History of Civilization in the Last Fifty Years" (written between 1860 and 1870), in the Frederick Law Olmsted Papers, Manuscript Division, Library of Congress, Washington, D.C. This writing has been recently published in Victoria Post Ranney, ed., *The Papers of Frederick Law Olmsted,* vol. 5, *The California Frontier, 1863–1865* (Baltimore: Johns Hopkins University Press, 1990); see p. 694 for the above remarks. Olmsted's published antebellum writing on the South contains somewhat less fully developed thinking on the decivilizing process; see also chapter 6, note 113.

160. See, for example, Congressman Francis W. Kellogg of Michigan, *Congressional Globe. Appendix,* 36th Cong., 1st sess., June 12, 1860, 420–24; and Congressman James K. Moorhead of Pennsylvania, *Congressional Globe,* 36th Cong., 1st sess., Mar. 7, 1860, pt. 2: 1043–44. See also James Huston, *The Panic of 1857 and the Coming of the Civil War* (Baton Rouge: Louisiana State University Press, 1987), 230–75; and Huston, "A Political Response to Industrialism: The Republican Embrace of Protectionist Labor Doctrines," *Journal of American History* 70 (June 1983): 35–55.

161. See the antislavery remarks of George M. Weston, *Southern Slavery Reduces Northern Wages,* address delivered in Washington, D.C., Mar. 25, 1856 (Washington, D.C.: n.p. 1856), 5, 8, some of which are quoted in note 7 of chapter 1.

162. Carl Schurz, speech delivered in St. Louis, Aug. 1, 1860, repr. in *New-York Daily Tribune,* Aug. 29, 1860.

CHAPTER 4: DRUDGE WORK

1. Men who were the victims of impressment and who were forced to perform menial duties aboard British vessels were perhaps the most notable of those drudge laborers who lacked even the appearance of freedom from external authority.

2. Marx made this argument with reference to "independent peasants" and handicraftsmen under capitalism. The owners of their own means of production, they employed themselves as wage laborers and paid themselves, "in the surplus-value, the tribute that labour owes to capital" (Marx, *Theories of Surplus-Value,* ed. S. Ryazanskaya, trans. Emile Burns [Moscow: Progress Publishers, 1963], 1: 408). Marx's observation regarding self-exploitation may be extended and applied in partial explanation of the public acquiescence that often greeted the plight of independently employed drudge laborers of various types; see also Gareth Stedman Jones, *Outcast London: A Study in the Relationship between Classes in Victorian Society* (Oxford: Clarendon Press, 1971), 264–65.

3. Oscar Wilde, *The Soul of Man under Socialism,* in *The Complete Works of Oscar Wilde,* general ed. J. B. Foreman (London: Collins, 1948 [1891]), 1088–89.

4. Ibid., 1080.

5. For references to the international character of the ragpickers, or "chiffoniers," whose "ignorance, debased morals and recklessness with their wretched vocation, . . . aptly fit them for turbulence and riot," see New York City, *Journal and Documents of the Board of Assistants of the City of New York for 1843,* vol. 21, no. 59: John Griscom, *Communication from the City Inspector, with the Annual Report of Interments for 1842,* Jan. 30, 1843, pp. 177–78. Not the most insignificant element of the disgust felt for these and other segments of the urban underclass was the perception of widespread miscegenation among them; see New York State, *Assembly Documents for 1857,* vol. 3, no. 205: *Report of the Select Committee Appointed to Examine into the Condition of Tenant Houses in New-York and Brooklyn,* Jan. 1857, pp. 22n, 20–22.

6. Edwin Chadwick, *The Sanitary Condition of the Labouring Population of Great Britain* (London: W. Clowes and Sons, 1842), 95.

7. S. D. Moore, "The Irrepressible Conflict and Impending Crisis," *De Bow's Review* 28 (May 1860): 531–32.

8. Gerrit Smith to Rev. T. S. Wright, Peterboro, Nov. 14, 1846, in Gerrit Smith Miller Collection, George Arents Research Library, Syracuse University, Syracuse, N.Y..

9. Frederick Douglass to Harriet Beecher Stowe, Mar. 8, 1853, repr. in *North Star* or *Frederick Douglass' Paper* (Rochester), Dec. 2, 1853; see also in the same paper, "Learn Trades or Starve!" issue of Mar. 4, 1853; and "A Few Words More about Learning Trades," issue of Mar. 11, 1853. For a recent study that makes much of Douglass's "bourgeois and assimilationist outlook," his commitment to "basic American ideas about success and respectability," see Waldo E. Martin, Jr., *The Mind of Frederick Douglass* (Chapel Hill: University of North Carolina Press, 1984), 129–33, 254–63, 281–83. Douglass's recognition that the influx of unskilled Irish was rendering Northern blacks increasingly dispensable as servants and menial laborers was shared by others with very different, white racist attitudes and objectives. In contrast to Douglass, the Cincinnati physician and cultural leader, Daniel Drake, insisted upon the incapacity of Northern blacks—members of a race of "intrinsic servility" and "natural inferiority"—to perform anything other than the "menial employments" from which they were being displaced. In rendering the country's despised and impoverished free black population all the more useless and "parasitic," Irish immigration became for Drake one more reason—and he provided

plenty—why the various states should turn to Negro removal, via colonization in Africa, as the best means of solving the nation's race problem. Like other mid-western whites, Drake's perspective was dominated by fear and disgust at the prospect of emancipated slaves from nearby slave states pouring into his region to make their homes there; Dr. Daniel Drake, *Letters on Slavery to John C. Warren of Boston, Reprinted from the National Intelligencer, April 3, 5, 7, 1851* (New York: Schuman's, 1940), 31–32, 37, 39, 53–54. See also George M. Fredrickson, *The Black Image in the White Mind: The Debate on Afro-American Character and Destiny, 1817–1914* (Middletown: Wesleyan University Press, 1987 [1971]), 134–35.

10. William Pease and Jane Pease, *They Who Would Be Free: Blacks' Search for Freedom, 1830–1861* (New York: Atheneum, 1974), 129.

11. *Address* of the Cleveland National Convention of the Free People of Color, 1848, quoted in Ibid., 129–30.

12. "Make Your Sons Mechanics and Farmers," *Frederick Douglass' Paper*, Mar. 18, 1853.

13. This is not to deny that this Old World view had itself, for a multitude of reasons, been undergoing challenge and transformation since the second half of the eighteenth century and that European thinkers of varying ideological persuasions were increasingly conceptualizing and discussing social inequality in terms of the horizontal, more dynamic and combative divisions of "class" rather than in terms of the older vertical divisions of ascribed "ranks" or "orders." The starting point for discussions of this change in Britain is Asa Briggs, "The Language of 'Class' in Early Nineteenth-Century England," in Asa Briggs and John Saville, eds., *Essays in Labour History* (London: Macmillan, 1960), 43–73. See also Steven Wallech, "'Class Versus Rank': The Transformation of Eighteenth-Century English Social Terms and Theories of Production," *Journal of the History of Ideas* 47 (July–Sept. 1986): 409–31; P. J. Corfield, "Class by Name and Number in Eighteenth-Century Britain," *History* 72 (Feb. 1987): 38–61.

14. "Land Reform," *American Review* 15 (June 1852): 551, 547. In this particular case, the expressed disdain for satisfied "dependents" more explicitly reflected traditional agrarian republicanism than it did a liberal capitalist trumpeting of "rags to riches" mobility in America; the author devoted most of his essay to advocating land reform measures to relieve labor competition in the cities and facilitate individual escape from positions of dependence into the ranks of the "independent yeomanry."

15. In one expression of the theme that there are "many slaveries," Senator Robert Hunter of Alabama professed to find no significant difference between the Southern slave whose services were held as property by another for life, and "the domestics, or mechanics, or lawyers, or doctors" everywhere whose services were held as property by another "for months, weeks, days, and hours" (Excerpt of a speech delivered by Hunter in Albany, repr. as "Senator Hunter's Appeal to the North," *De Bow's Review* 21 [Nov. 1856]: 531). The radical labor reform sheet, the *Boston Social Reformer,* offered a similar assessment: "The Lawyer is a hired tool, with no more freedom than the veriest slave" ("Hired Labor," *Boston Social Reformer,* repr. in the *Phalanx: Or, Journal of Social Science. Devoted to the Cause of Association, or a Social Reform, and the Elevation of the Human Race* [New York], [December 9, 1844]: 306–7). Once again, as in the use of the term *white negroes* discussed earlier, the same parallels and metaphors were being used by individuals or groups having very different objectives. Hunter sought the vindication of Southern chattel slavery; the *Reformer* sought the abolition of a "hired system of labor" which robbed and enslaved hireling manual laborers most of all, but whose tentacles of oppression even extended into the professional classes.

16. William Heighton to George Henry Evans, Oct. 20, 1845, repr. as "True and Sham Reformers," New York *Working Man's Advocate,* Nov. 8, 1845.

17. Michael Walzer, *Spheres of Justice: A Defense of Pluralism and Equality* (New York: Basic Books, 1983), 174.

18. "Stoweism and Blackswanism," *New York Express,* repr. in *National Anti-Slavery Standard,* July 9, 1853.

19. "Labor in New-York, No. V," *New-York Daily Tribune,* Aug. 25, 1845.

20. "L," "The Rag Pickers," *Gazette of the Union, Golden Rule, and Odd-Fellows' Family Companion* 9 (Aug. 19, 1848): 131.

21. For a modern and more sophisticated defense of the level of rewards accruing to drudge labor under free market conditions, see Friedrich A. Hayek, *Law, Legislation, and Liberty,* vol. 2, *The Mirage of Social Justice* (Chicago: University of Chicago Press, 1976), 92; Hayek, *The Constitution of Liberty* (Chicago: University of Chicago Press, 1960), 441.

22. George Frederick Holmes considered the expression an old English adage, one which had been given new life by the premium upon free competition placed by Smithian political economy. [Holmes], "Failure of Free Societies," *Southern Literary Messenger* 21 (Mar. 1855): 135. The classic study of competitive market morality in Britain, and its culminating expression in the Poor Law Amendment Act of 1834, is Karl Polanyi, *The Great Transformation* (Boston: Beacon Press, 1957 [1944]).

23. And even prostitution was not entirely outside this protective wrapping. Timothy J. Gilfoyle, in fact, has recently argued that beginning after 1820 and "by the decade of the Civil War, prostitution [in New York City] enjoyed its greatest period of openness and social tolerance," a circumstance which reflected physical intimacy's new status as a market relationship. In theaters, saloons, hotels, as well as in brothels, sex assumed its place along with other goods and services as "an advertised commodity in the commercial marketplace," to be bought and sold "for the right price" (Timothy J. Gilfoyle, Jr., "City of Eros: New York City, Prostitution, and the Commercialization of Sex, 1790–1920" [Ph.D. diss., Columbia University, 1987], 253, 559). This is not to overlook the other developments that lent commercialized sexual exploitation a quasi legitimacy—viz., the emergence of doctrines at midcentury that minimized the physical destructiveness of prostitution for the prostitute and that also characterized prostitution as an inevitable and even useful social evil, one that provided an outlet for male sexual passions; see Judith R. Walkowitz, *Prostitution and Victorian Society: Women, Class, and the State* (Cambridge, Eng.: Cambridge University Press, 1980), 43, 46.

24. Insistence upon the facility with which American women might earn decent wages led the New York *Journal of Commerce* to rebuke not only those female laborers who resorted to strikes, but also those who turned to prostitution: "Very few indeed among the multitudes of abandoned women in the U. States can plead poverty in its direct pressure as an excuse or a motive for their wickedness" (*Journal of Commerce* quoted in "Female Labor," *Working Man's Advocate,* June 27, 1835).

25. [Salmon P. Chase], "Effects of Machinery," *North American Review* 34 (Jan. 1832): 237. A slightly different version of Chase's essay appears under the title, "Lecture on the Influence of Machinery before the Cincinnati Lyceum" [n.d.], Salmon P. Chase Papers, Historical Society of Pennsylvania, Philadelphia.

26. "The Anti-Rent Sympathizers," *New York Herald,* Jan. 5, 1845.

27. Caroline F. Ware, "Introduction," in Milton Cantor and Bruce Laurie, eds., *Class, Sex, and the Woman Worker* (Westport, Conn.: Greenwood Press, 1977), 8; Douglas T. Miller, "Immigration and Social Stratification in Pre–Civil War New York," *New York History* 49 (Apr. 1968): 157–68.

28. Edward E. Hale, *Letters on Irish Emigration* (Boston: Phillips, Sampson, and Company, 1852), 54–56.

29. In thus claiming that nativist "political economy" exaggerated the competitive threat posed by immigrant workers to American-born laborers, Greeley wrote: "Immigrant Laborers . . . are generally handy with the spade, while very few Americans either can or will use that implement day after day. Nearly all the earthwork on our Canals and Railroads has been done by Immigrants, because Americans would not do it at any price . . . they [the immigrants] are in good part employed in rude, repulsive avocations which Americans shrink from and could hardly be induced to undertake, yet which, when finished, make employment for a higher grade of workers" ("Know-Nothing Political Economy," *New-York Daily Tribune,* Jan. 13, 1855). My understanding of dual labor market theory is drawn from a number of studies in a rapidly growing field, including Peter B. Doeringer and Michael J. Piore, "Unemployment and the Dual Labor Market," *Public Interest,* no. 38 (Winter 1975): 68–73; various of the essays in Richard C. Edwards, Michael Reich, and David M. Gordon, eds., *Labor Market Segmentation* (Lexington, Mass.: D. C. Heath and Company, 1975; Gordon, *Theories of Poverty and Underemployment: Orthodox, Radical, and Dual Labor Market Perspectives* (Lexington, Mass.: D. C. Heath and Company, 1972), 43–50; Michael Piore, *Birds of Passage: Migrant Labor and Industrial Societies* (Cambridge, Eng.: Cambridge University Press, 1979). For a useful discussion summarizing the major criticisms of dual labor market theory, see Veronica Beechey and Tessa Perkins, *A Matter of Hours: Women, Part-Time Work and the Labour Market* (Cambridge, Eng.: Polity Press, 1987), 133–42. See also Michael Evans Gold, *A Dialogue on Comparable Worth* (Ithaca: ILR Press, New York State School of Industrial and Labor Relations, Cornell University, 1983); Michael Hechter, "Ethnicity and Industrialization: On the Proliferation of the Cultural Division of Labor," *Ethnicity* 3 (Sept. 1976): 214–23.

30. For the sentiments of one anti-Irish newspaper that conducted an extended campaign to free the American laboring classes "from the blighting effects of imported cheap labor," see "Introductory," *Champion of American Labor. A Weekly Newspaper, Devoted to the Moral, Intellectual and Social Improvement of the Laboring Classes. Published by an Association of Mechanics* (New York), Apr. 3, 1847. See also Stephen E. Maizlish, "The Meaning of Nativism and the Crisis of the Union: The Know-Nothing Movement in the Antebellum North," in Stephen E. Maizlish and John J. Kushma, eds., *Essays on American Antebellum Politics, 1840–1860* (College Station: Texas A&M University Press, 1982), 172; Miller, "Immigration and Social Stratification"; Robert Ernst, "Economic Nativism in New York City during the 1840s," *New York History* 29 (Apr. 1948): 174–84; Robert Ernst, *Immigrant Life in New York City 1825–1863* (New York: King's Crown Press, 1949), 102–3; Jean Gould Hale, "Co-Laborers in the Cause: Women in the Ante-Bellum Nativist Movement," *Civil War History* 25 (June 1979): 123–24.

31. See, for example, Robert William Fogel, *Without Consent or Contract: The Rise and Fall of American Slavery* (New York: W. W. Norton and Company, 1989), 309–12, 356–60, 470; Miller, "Immigration and Social Stratification"; Michael F. Holt, "The Politics of Impatience: The Origins of Know Nothingism" (personal copy), 18–22, 38, 41; Clyde Griffen, "The 'Old' Immigration and Industrialization: A Case Study," in Richard L. Ehrlich, ed., *Immigrants in Industrial America, 1850–1920* (Charlottesville: University Press of Virginia, 1977), 176–77.

32. As Amy Bridges has well put this point: "Nativist-labor complaints about immigrant 'competition' need to be understood" not as "the competition of those who will do one's own job, but [as] the competition of a labor force whose presence

allowed a reorganization of work" (Amy Bridges, *A City in the Republic: Antebellum New York and the Origins of Machine Politics* [Cambridge, Eng.: Cambridge University Press, 1984], 96).

33. On the monopolization of canal building in America since the beginning of the century by pre-Famine Irish, see Catherine Tobin, "The Lonely Muscular Digger: Irish Canal Workers in Nineteenth Century America" (Ph.D. diss., University of Notre Dame, 1987); and Dennis Clark, "The Irish in the American Economy," in P. J. Drudy, ed., *The Irish in America: Emigration, Assimilation and Impact* (Cambridge, Eng.: Cambridge University Press, 1985), 234. With particular respect to domestic service, Mary Christine Stansell has noted that by the 1820s and 1830s American-born women "of the poorer classes" already considered it degrading, although it is likely that this attitude of disdain was indeed strengthened, if not created, by recognition that servant's work, like heavy unskilled labor, was even by this time attracting a disproportionate number of newly arrived Irish; Mary Christine Stansell, "Women of the Laboring Poor in New York City, 1820–1860" (Ph.D. diss., Yale University, 1979), 140.

34. Hale, *Letters,* 53–55. Dale T. Knobel, for one, has inferred from Hale's remarks—again, not without some justification—a belief in the innate inferiority of the Irish; Knobel, *Paddy and the Republic: Ethnicity and Nationality in Antebellum America* (Middletown, Conn.: Wesleyan University Press, 1986), 78–79.

35. Hale, *Letters,* 55–56; Hale, *Christian Duty to Emigrants,* a sermon delivered before the Boston Society for the Prevention of Pauperism, at the Old South Church in Boston, May 9, 1852 (Boston: John Wilson and Son, 1852), 9, 12, 14, 18.

36. There were some, however, who, drawing a sharper distinction than Hale did between unskilled physical "coarse work" and factory labor, argued that the former did in fact debilitate. The political economist Francis Bowen maintained, with regard to the foreign-born and above all, immigrant Irish of Massachusetts, that the "daily brutish toil . . . the rude labor, to which they alone have been accustomed, has so incapacitated them for higher tasks, that it is now an established principle in our large manufactories, we are told, that the machines cannot profitably be worked if more than one third of the operatives be foreigners. It is . . . more economical to pay the higher wages required by native workmen." This handicap and the additional expense that afflicted New England's "infant manufactures," Bowen suggested, provided all the more justification for protective tariff legislation to insulate these manufactures from cheap European competition ([Francis Bowen], "[Willard] Phillips on Protection and Free Trade," *North American Review* 72 [Apr. 1851]: 402–3, 415, 427–28). For an even stronger, and more clearly humanitarian, statement of the debilitating effects upon Irish immigrants of rough labor, which required "mere physical exertion" and no "intellectual power," see the *New-York Freeman's Journal and Catholic Register,* Feb. 6, 1841, quoted in Tobin, "Lonely Muscular Digger," 226.

37. Hale, *Letters,* 55–56.

38. According to proslavery writers, of course, the good fortune enjoyed by blacks under conditions of American slavery, and the contrasting unhappy lot of blacks who remained in Africa, extended beyond the kinds of work in which the American slaves were engaged. Nor was the racist belief that blacks were naturally drawn to warmer regions and flourished best there limited in the antebellum period to the defenders of their enslavement; see, for example, Fredrickson, *Black Image,* 52, 142–54.

39. Hale's anti-Southern, antislavery views are revealed most particularly in his *Kanzas and Nebraska* (Boston: Phillips, Sampson, and Company, 1854).

40. Kerby A. Miller, *Emigrants and Exiles: Ireland and the Irish Exodus to North America* (New York: Oxford University Press, 1985), 313–22, esp. 319. Miller's study is based on letters and similar nonquantitative materials, although he notes (313–14) that his conclusions are corroborated by quantitative social mobility data gathered by other scholars.

41. Hale specifically observed that upward mobility for the Irish emigrants could not be entirely left to the operation of a free market, unless the "let-alone policy" was also taken to mean that "in a Christian land there will be, of course, Christian men and women to go between the employer and the laborer. . . . The Christian effort," Hale elaborated, "is to see that no class of the social order shall be filled beyond its proportion." Educational opportunities, Labor Exchanges, and other "avenues of promotion" would be expanded to achieve the desired turnover in social classes. These avenues would prevent the formation of "an [overcrowded and permanent] caste of slaves bound to the hardest labor," consisting at present of the Irish and others who faced the greatest danger of oversupply and descent into pauperism because they were without skill or trade, "of use only from their strength of body." Similar "avenues of promotion" would prevent the formation of "a yet lower [permanent] caste of lazzaroni and of paupers," those unfortunates already below the rank of Irish and other unskilled laborers who could not or would not even get a living from their bodies (Hale, *Christian Duty,* 9, 11–12, 14, 18–20).

42. For a challenging study that finds in nineteenth-century American literature evidence of the ascendancy of the middle-class entrepreneurial ideology "of manhood as competitive individualism," see David Leverenz, *Manhood and the American Renaissance* (Ithaca: Cornell University Press, 1989), 3, 76–80. I take exception to some of the conclusions Leverenz attaches to this ideological ascendancy, including his sweeping claim that "the fundamental class struggle in the Northeast from 1825 to 1850 came not from conflicts between workers and bosses but from the challenge of a capitalist middle class to an entrenched mercantilist and landholder elite" (77). I suspect, among other things, that Leverenz understates the commonality of values existing between "the old mercantile and landowning elite" and "the new middle class." Leverenz is, of course, hardly unaware of this kind of objection to his analysis.

43. Carroll Smith Rosenberg, *Religion and the Rise of the American City: The New York City Mission Movement, 1812–1870* (Ithaca: Cornell University Press, 1971), 212–43; Miriam Z. Langsom, *Children West: A History of the Placing-Out System of the New York Children's Aid Society 1853–1890* (Madison: State Historical Society of Wisconsin, 1964), 11–54; Christine Stansell, "Women, Children, and the Uses of the Streets: Class and Gender Conflict in New York City, 1850–1860," *Feminist Studies* 8 (Summer 1982): 309–27; Alba M. Edwards, "The Labor Legislation of Connecticut," *Publications of the American Economic Association,* 3d ser., 7 (1907): 7.

44. Anthony F. C. Wallace, *St. Clair: A Nineteenth-Century Coal Town's Experience with a Disaster-Prone Industry* (New York: Alfred A. Knopf, 1987), 20–23; Robert Colls, *The Pitmen of the Northern Coalfields* (Manchester: Manchester University Press, 1987), 11–13, 112–14; Michael Flinn, *1700–1830: The Industrial Revolution,* vol. 2 of *The History of the British Coal Industry* (Oxford: Clarendon Press, 1984), 329–34, 339–53, 434–35; Roy Church, *1830–1913: Victorian Pre-Eminence,* vol. 3 of *The History of the British Coal Industry* (Oxford: Clarendon Press, 1986), 194–96, 204–9, 226; Royden Harrison, "Introduction," in Harrison, ed., *Independent Collier: The Coal Miner as Archetypal Proletarian Reconsidered* (Sussex, Eng.: Harvester Press, 1978), 4–5; Arthur Redford, *Labour Migration in England, 1800–1850,* 2d ed., ed. and rev. W. H. Chaloner (New York: Augustus M. Kelley, 1968 [1926]), 58–59.

45. Raphael Samuel, "The Workshop of the World: Steam Power and Hand Technology in Mid-Victorian Britain," *History Workshop* no. 3 (Spring 1977): 13; George Calvert Holland, *The Mortality, Sufferings, and Diseases of Grinders* (London: John Ollivier, 1841), 8.

46. Parliamentary Papers, House of Commons, *Children's Employment Commission. Second Report* (1843), 105, quoted in "Juvenile and Female Labor," *Edinburgh Review* 79 (Jan. 1844): 142.

47. Holland, *Mortality,* 17–20, 23–26; George Calvert Holland, *Diseases of the Lungs from Mechanical Causes; and Inquiries into the Condition of the Artisans Exposed to the Inhalation of Dust* (London: Charles Churchill, 1842), 2–3, 30–32, 52–55, 60–63, 79, 85, 100.

48. "The Organization of Labor," *Daily Chronotype* (Boston), Nov. 19, 1846.

49. Wallace, *St. Clair,* 53, 270–73, 450–55.

50. "S. R." [Samuel Roberts], "On the Employment of Climbing Boys," in James Montgomery, ed., *The Chimney-Sweeper's Friend, and Climbing-Boys' Album* (London: Longman, 1824), 11–13.

51. See, for example, [Marion Southwood], *Tit for Tat. A Novel. By a Lady of New Orleans* (New York: Garrett Company, 1856), 348–56.

52. See chapter 2, note 31 on the distinction between individuals who were genuinely proslavery in objective and various labor reformers, in many cases equally hostile to the abolitionists, who ended up painting a positive picture of black chattel slavery as a by-product of their zeal to dramatize and relieve the exploitation and suffering of white "wage slaves."

53. The masters who employed the climbing boys were themselves hardly out of the working classes and possessed none of the wealth or political and social connections of the larger West Indies slaveowners; see Henry Mayhew, *London Labour and the London Poor* (New York: Dover Publications, 1968 [1861–1862]), 2: 347.

54. For a discussion of the various parallels between black chattel slavery and British "infant" factory slavery described in antifactory literature, including those themes that drew special inspiration from the early parish apprentice operative, see R. M. Hartwell, *The Industrial Revolution and Economic Growth* (London: Methuen and Company, 1971), 390–408.

55. Mayhew, *London Labour,* 2: 338–44; Ronald Pearsall, *Night's Black Angels: The Forms and Faces of Victorian Cruelty* (New York: David McKay Company, 1975), 144; George Lewis Phillips, *American Chimney Sweeps: An Historical Account of a Once Important Trade* (Trenton, N.J.: Past Times Press, 1957), 48–50. Conceivably, the chimney sweep trade and its expansion were like other developments more closely tied to industrial processes that preceded the early, eighteenth-century phases of the Industrial Revolution, a possibility that would prove congenial to the scholarly perspective that denies the significance, even the occurrence, of *an* Industrial Revolution; see Jordan Goodman and Katrina Honeyman, *Gainful Pursuits: The Making of Industrial Europe 1600–1914* (London: Edward Arnold, 1988), 203–10.

56. George Lewis Phillips, *England's Climbing Boys: A History of the Long Struggle to Abolish Child Labor in Chimney Sweeping* (Boston: Kress Library of Business and Economics, 1949), 2–3. Slightly different estimates of the size of the chimney sweep trade for the period 1797–1817 are given in J. L. Hammond and Barbara Hammond, *The Town Labourer, 1760–1832: The New Civilisation* (New York: Augustus M. Kelley, 1967 [1917]), 178.

57. Mayhew, *London Labour,* 2: 346.

58. This is not to overlook those writers like C. Turner Thakrah who did

maintain that child labor of any kind was wrong, particularly in the manufacturing districts; C. Turner Thackrah, *The Effects of Arts, Trades, and Professions, and of Civic States and Habits of Living, on Health and Longevity: with Suggestions for the Removal of Many of the Agents, which Produce Disease, and Shorten the Duration of Life,* 2d enl. ed. (London: Longman, 1832), 80–81.

59. Steven Lushington, testimony before the Committee in the House of Lords considering the chimney-sweepers' regulation bill, Mar. 13, 1818, repr. in *Chimney-Sweeper's Friend,* 133, 145n. See also "S. R." [Samuel Roberts], "On the Employment," 14.

60. Lushington, testimony, 124–33; see also "Extracts from the Report from the Committee on Employment of Boys in Sweeping of Chimneys; Together with the Minutes of the Evidence Taken before the Committee: and an Appendix," House of Commons, June 23, 1817, repr. in *Chimney-Sweeper's Friend,* 169–70, 182, 186; and "Address from the Committee of the Society for Superseding the Necessity of Climbing Boys . . . with the Report of the Committee of the House of Lords on the Chimney-sweepers' Regulation Bill," 1818, p. 22, repr. in *Improving the Lot of the Chimney Sweeps,* one of a series of vols. in Kenneth Carpenter, advisory ed., *British Labour Struggles: Contemporary Pamphlets 1727–1850* (New York: Arno Press, 1972).

61. Pearsall, *Night's Black Angels,* 145.

62. Samuel Roberts, *An Address to British Females of Every Rank and Station, on the Employment of Climbing Boys in Sweeping Chimnies* [sic] (Sheffield: A. Whitaker and Company, 1834), 13–14, repr. in *Improving Lot of Chimney Sweeps.*

63. Pearsall, *Night's Black Angels,* 146; "Extracts from the Report from the Committee on Employment of Boys," 188–19, 202–3; Lushington's testimony, 143n.

64. Pearsall, *Night's Black Angels,* 145–46; Mayhew, *London Labour,* 2: 367.

65. Whatever the other tribulations of their work, the climbing boys did not, by the standards of many other child laborers, toil unusually long hours; although beginning very early in the morning, they were customarily through with their labors after "the middle of the day." As suggested, the unsupervised leisure time chimney sweeping afforded the climbing boys, distinguished as they supposedly were with undeveloped or debased tastes, hardly reduced the trade's evils in the eyes of men like Lushington and Shaftesbury. Lushington, testimony, 142.

66. Earl of Shaftesbury, quoted from his speech before the House of Lords introducing the Chimney Sweepers' Amendment Bill in the Parliamentary Session of 1854, in Southwood, *Tit for Tat,* 356.

67. Phillips, *England's Climbing Boys,* 32–36, 54–55; J. C. Hudson, extracts from a letter "To the Mistresses of Families," in *Chimney-Sweeper's Friend,* 82–83. The continuing use of climbing boys in England inspired the Christian Socialist, Charles Kingsley, to write his famous children's book, *The Water-Babies,* in 1862; see Brenda Colloms, *Charles Kingsley: The Lion of Eversley* (London: Constable, 1975), 254–59.

68. Mayhew, *London Labour,* 2: 348, 356; "Extracts from the Report from the Committee on Employment of Boys," 182–83; "S. R." [Samuel Roberts], "On the Employment," 11–23; Pearsall, *Night's Black Angels,* 144–145; Hammonds, *Town Labourer,* 178, 186, 192; Phillips, *American Chimney Sweeps,* 69.

69. Samuel Nott, "Reply and Appeal to European Advisers," preface of Nott, *Slavery and the Remedy; or, Principle and Suggestions for a Remedial Cure,* 6th ed. (New York: Negro Universities Press, 1969 [1859]), xvii; Lushington, testimony 122–23. Nott was not quite so hard-hearted as the passing reference above suggests. He believed that the lot of British miners, for example, could and should be ameliorated through safety lamps, Parliamentary legislation, and the like. But his principal point, as with southern slavery, was "the impossibility of annihilating great social

facts": British mining "cannot be instantly and absolutely abolished, without greater evils even to the miners themselves [by destroying their means of livelihood], without damage to the whole well-being of the race, without dooming the world to a ruin worse than all the toils, exposures, sufferings, and even abuses of the mines." God had ordained that existing conditions could be improved only gradually, and "you cannot abolish the miner's lot, unless you can abolish God's ordinance when he built the earth and hid in its depths the treasures of iron and coal, and silver and gold, for the use of countless millions of men" (Nott, *Slavery,* xvi–xxii).

70. Hudson, "To the Mistresses," 76–77.

71. The occupation of American climbing boys deserves more comprehensive and updated treatment than it has received in the one existing monograph on the subject, Phillips, *American Chimney Sweeps.*

72. "Sweeps: By a Philanthropist," *Knickerbocker* 6 (July 1835): 78.

73. Southwood quoted with Phillip's comments in Phillips, *American Chimney Sweeps,* 66–67. See also the remarks of William H. Rideing in chapter 6, and the path-breaking discussion of the history of Western attitudes toward the "blackness" of the Negro's complexion in Winthrop D. Jordan, *White over Black: American Attitudes toward the Negro, 1550–1812* (Chapel Hill: University of North Carolina Press, 1968), 4–20, 252–59. One of William Blake's two chimney sweeper songs is the occasion of a brief but interesting discussion of the parallels and differences between the blackness of the slaves and that of the English climbing boys in Martin K. Nurmi, "Fact and Symbol in 'The Chimney Sweeper' of Blake's *Songs of Innocence,*" in Northrop Frye, ed., *Blake: A Collection of Critical Essays* (Englewood Cliffs: Prentice-Hall, 1966), 15–22.

74. Hudson, "To the Mistresses," 76–77.

75. Xenophon quoted in John Rule, *The Experience of Labour in Eighteenth-Century Industry* (London: Croom Helm, 1981), 74. I am using Rule's interpretation of Xenophon's remarks and Socrates' opinion to make a point about more modern British attitudes. However, I should note that some scholars, notably Alfred Zimmern and H. D. F. Kitto, have attached a very different construction to Xenophon's passage, and denied that it signifies that Socrates, any more than other ancient Greek thinkers, disdained manual work in any real sense. What Socrates was condemning as physically degenerative and soul-destroying, according to these scholars, was not manual labor *per se,* but rather those "mechanical arts" "which involved sitting for long periods in cramped and unhealthy postures, especially in a hot and vitiated atmosphere" (Zimmern, *The Greek Commonwealth: Politics and Economics in Fifth-Century Athens,* 5th ed. rev. [Oxford: The Clarendon Press, 1931], 272); H. D. F. Kitto, *The Greeks* (Harmondsworth, Eng.: Penguin Books, 1978 [1951]) 239–241. I continue to find more persuasive that tradition of scholarship, exemplified by M. I. Finley, which finds a good deal more ambivalence, not to say disdain, in ancient Greek attitudes toward manual labor.

76. Rule, *Experience of Labour,* 89.

77. Ibid., 87–89.

CHAPTER 5: THE TECHNOLOGICAL AND FOURIERIST
SOLUTIONS TO DRUDGE WORK

1. William Wilberforce, speech in the House of Commons, Feb. 17, 1819, *Parliamentary Debates,* vol. 39 (1819), cols. 452–53.

2. Oscar Wilde, *The Soul of Man under Socialism,* in *The Complete Works of Oscar Wilde,* general ed. J. B. Foreman (London: Collins, 1948 [1891]), 1088–89. For

similar remarks by one of Wilde's contemporaries, see William Morris, *Useful Work versus Useless Toil* (London: T. Cantwell, 1892), 37.

3. *Report by Mr. Tufnell; Supplementary Report from the Factory Commissioners* (1833), pt. 1, p. 205, excerpted in Edward Baines, Jr., *History of the Cotton Manufactures in Great Britain*, 2d ed. (New York: Augustus M. Kelley, 1966 [1835]), 458–59.

4. [Charles Knight], *The Working-Man's Companion. The Results of Machinery, Namely, Cheap Production, and Increased Employment, Exhibited; Being an Address to the Workingmen of the United Kingdom* (Philadelphia: E. L. Carey and A. Hart, 1831), 147.

5. J. B. Bittinger, *An Address Delivered before the Alumnia of "Pennsylvania College" at Their Annual Meeting*, Sept. 19, 1860 (Gettysburg: H. C. Neinstedt, 1860), 12–13.

6. See, for example, Ivy Pinchbeck, *Women Workers and the Industrial Revolution, 1750–1850* (London: George Routledge and Sons, 1930), 4: 232–33, 307–11; Ivy Pinchbeck and Margaret Hewitt, *Children in English Society* (London: Routledge and Kegan Paul, 1969), 1: 256–57, 310–11; 2: 394–99. Yet the more tenable position would seem to be that, under the control of capitalists and subcontractors, tedious nonfactory manufacturing labor, mechanized and nonmechanized, overall experienced a great expansion during the nineteenth century, and that these various forms of "outwork and slop-work" were part and parcel of the same Industrial Revolution that gave birth to the mechanized factory. The "optimistic" school of interpretation, as E. J. Hobsbawm has noted, tends on occasion to overlook this fact, equating economic growth with the factory system and drawing a false dichotomy between industrialization and nonmechanized manufacturing enterprises particularly; see E. J. Hobsbawm and R. M. Hartwell, "The Standard of Living during the Industrial Revolution: A Discussion," *Economic History Review*, 2d ser. 16 (Aug. 1963): 127–28. Marx devoted much discussion to the flourishing condition of "the so-called domestic industry . . . in which capital conducts its exploitation in the background of modern mechanical industry," although he, too, anticipated the day when the imperatives of capitalist efficiency and economy had almost completely effected a "rapid conversion of the scattered domestic industries and also of manufactures into [mechanized] factory industries" (Karl Marx, *Capital: A Critique of Political Economy*, ed. Frederick Engels, trans. Samuel Moore and Edward Aveling [New York: International Publishers, 1967], 1: 466, 470, 461–69). In fact, Marx also appears, from such remarks as this last one, to have underestimated the staying power of nonfactory manufacturing enterprises. See also Duncan Bythell, *The Sweated Trades: Outwork in Nineteenth-Century Britain* (New York: St. Martin's Press, 1978), 142–45; James A. Schmiechen, *Sweated Industries and Sweated Labor: The London Clothing Trades 1860–1914* (Urbana: University of Illinois Press, 1984), 185–87; Krishan Kumar, *The Rise of Modern Society: Aspects of the Social and Political Development of the West* (Oxford, Eng.: Basil Blackwell, 1988), 211, 262; and Shelley Pennington and Belinda Westover, *A Hidden Workforce: Homeworkers in England, 1850–1985* (Houndsmills, Eng.: Macmillan Education, 1989), 30–50.

7. Bittinger, *Address*, 8.

8. Olmsted to John Hull Olmsted, June 22 and June 23, 1845, quoted in Charles Eliot Beveridge, "Frederick Law Olmsted: The Formative Years 1822–1865" (Ph.D. diss., University of Wisconsin, 1966), 37–38.

9. "The British Labor Market," *New-York Daily Tribune*, Oct. 3, 1855.

10. J. A. Etzler, *The Paradise within the Reach of All Men, without Labor, by Powers of Nature and Machinery: An Address to All Intelligent Men* (Pittsburgh: Etzler and Reinhold, 1833), 55–56.

11. A toast made by Philadelphia workingmen, "Workingman's Celebration," *New-York Sentinel, and Working Man's Advocate,* July 14, 1830.

12. Review of Charles Knight's book, in "Results of Machinery," *American Quarterly Review* 12 (Dec. 1832): 306–13; and "Improvement," *Mechanics' Journal: A Weekly Paper for Mechanics, Manufacturers and Artists* (Albany), July 17, 1847. The latter article, however, while minimizing the dislocation caused by technological unemployment, coupled this claim with the argument that technology should be used to reduce the hours of overworked factory operatives; as long as small children and "delicate" females continued to work thirteen to fourteen hours a day, improvements had not gone far enough.

13. Hepworth Dixon, "Manchester; Considered in Its Relation to the Age and to the Progress of Civilization," *Peoples' Journal* 3 (May 1, 1847): 245–46.

14. Etzler, *Paradise Within,* 13–56.

15. See, for example, Marx and Engels, *Birth of the Communist Manifesto,* ed. Dirk J. Struik (New York: International Publishers Company, 1971), 92–99.

16. For an interesting discussion of the relationship between technology and society, see George H. Daniels, "Questions in the History of American Technology," *Technology and Culture* 11 (Jan. 1970): 3–21

17. Salmon P. Chase, "Lecture on the Influence of Machinery before the Cincinnati Lyceum" [n.d.], 5–6, Salmon P. Chase Papers, Historical Society of Pennsylvania, Philadelphia; Chase, "Effects of Machinery," *North American Review* 34 (Jan. 1832): 224. In the first part of this quotation, Chase is merely purporting to describe the point of view expressed by the advocates of machinery, but by the end of his presentation Chase has made it clear that he shares this point of view.

18. Chase, "Lecture," 5–6, 15–24; Chase, "Effects," 224–46.

19. Elizur Wright, ed., *Perforations in the "Latter-Day Pamphlets," by One of the "Eighteen Millions of Bores,"* no. 1 (Boston: Phillips, Sampson, and Company, 1850), 47–48. See also the discussion of abolitionist attitudes toward technology in Ronald G. Walters, *The Antislavery Appeal: American Abolitionism after 1830* (Baltimore: Johns Hopkins University Press, 1976), 114–16.

20. See, for example, the rather pessimistic overview in Robert Dale Owen, "Labor: Its History and Prospects," address delivered before the Young Men's Mercantile Library Association of Cincinnati, Feb. 1, 1848, repr. in *Herald of Truth* 3 (Mar. 1848): 192–201. Owen claimed that the American laborer would remain vulnerable to technological unemployment, and to exploitation generally, precisely because he was, as in Britain, a "commodity, bid for in the market, as wheat or cotton is" (199). Yet despite such critical views, Owen's biographer claims that he had stopped being a socialist, or much of any kind of a reformer, after the early 1830s; Richard William Leopold, *Robert Dale Owen: A Biography* (Cambridge: Harvard University Press, 1940), 102, 120, 190. Possibly the zeal Owen developed for Manifest Destiny during this period was in part attributable to his belief that in the continuing "safety valve" of the public lands—its defusion of population pressures upon the means of subsistence—lay the American laborer's best hope of protecting himself in the face of the reigning commodity ethic.

21. Maxine Berg, *The Machinery Question and the Making of Political Economy* (Cambridge, Eng.: Cambridge University Press, 1980), 282. See also Gregory Claeys and Prue Kerr, "Mechanical Political Economy," *Cambridge Journal of Economics* 5 (Sept. 1981): 263–70.

22. Daniel T. Rodgers, *The Work Ethic in Industrial America 1850–1920* (Chicago: University of Chicago Press, 1978), 66. For a recent discussion emphasizing how the visionary technological manifestos of Etzler and other writers in America

and England obscured the extent to which human drudge labor was persisting and even expanding in the mid-nineteenth century, see Dolores Greenberg, "Energy, Power, and Perceptions of Social Change in the Early Nineteenth Century," *American Historical Review* 95 (June 1990): 692–714.

23. Editha Hadcock, " Labor Problems in Rhode Island Cotton Mills" (Ph.D. diss., Brown University, 1946), 2: 517–18.

24. Thomas Ewbank, *Inorganic Forces Ordained to Supersede Human Slavery* (New York: William Everdell and Sons, 1860), 29, 32. See also George M. Fredrickson, *The Black Image in the White Mind: The Debate on Afro-American Character and Destiny, 1817–1914* (Middletown: Wesleyan University Press, 1987 [1971]), 143.

25. Ewbank, *Inorganic Forces,* 26.

26. "Letter of Thomas A. Devyr to Horace Greeley: Dedicated to the Reformers of New York State," Oct. 29, 1860, Greeley Papers, Manuscript Division, New York Public Library.

27. Abraham Lincoln, Seventh and Last Debate with Senator Stephen A. Douglas at Alton, Illinois, Oct. 15, 1858, in Lincoln, *The Collected Works of Abraham Lincoln,* ed. Roy P. Basler (New Brunswick: Rutgers University Press, 1953), 3: 316. See also the brilliant discussion in Harry V. Jaffa, *Crisis of the House Divided: An Interpretation of the Issues in the Lincoln-Douglas Debates* (Garden City: Doubleday and Company, 1959), 387–99.

28. Michael Flinn, *1700–1830: The Industrial Revolution,* vol. 2 of *The History of the British Coal Industry* (Oxford: Clarendon Press, 1984), 144–45.

29. Mary Christine Stansell, "Women of the Laboring Poor in New York City, 1820–1860" (Ph.D. diss., Yale University, 1979), 75.

30. Ruth Schwartz Cowan, *More Work for Mother: The Ironies of Household Technology from the Open Hearth to the Microwave* (New York: Basic Books, 1983), 12, 62.

31. D. H. Lawrence, *Studies in Classic American Literature* (Garden City, N.Y.: Doubleday and Company, 1953 [1923]), 115.

32. Etzler, *Paradise Within,* 3, 11.

33. "Cheap Bread," *North American and United States Gazette,* Jan.11, 1858.

34. "Results of Machinery," 310.

35. "S" [Sidney George Fisher], "Domestic Servants," *North American and United States Gazette,* May 23, 1857.

36. "Results of Machinery," 306–13.

37. To American middle-class intellectuals, Marx remained the least familiar of these European thinkers during the antebellum period. Yet by the end of the period Marx's writing—although not primarily those portions treating the evils of specialization and alienation under capitalism—had achieved a definite impact, largely through the activities of Joseph Weydemeyer and the German-American trade union movement.

38. Friedrich Engels, *Anti-Dühring,* trans. Emile Burns, ed. C. P. Dutt (New York: International Publishers, 1939), 318–19.

39. See, for example, Charles A. Dana's claims that reorganizing the Lowell factories along Fourierist lines would benefit the capitalist class as well as the operatives, demonstrating the "conservatism" and lack of class hostility that distinguished the Fourierist cause: Dana, in his review of works by Scoresby, Miles, and others on factory conditions at Lowell, *Harbinger, Devoted to Social and Political Progress* 1 (Aug. 30, 1845): 185–88.

40. Arthur Bestor, Jr., "American Phalanxes: A Study of Fourierist Socialism in the United States (with Special Reference to the Movement in Western New York)" (Ph.D. diss., Yale University, 1938), 11; Jonathan Beecher, *Charles Fourier:*

The Visionary and His World (Berkeley: University of California Press, 1986), 288–90; J. F. C. Harrison, *Quest for the New Moral World: Robert Owen and the Owenites in Britain and America* (New York: Charles Scribner's Sons, 1969), 24–25, 56.

41. Trans. of Madame Gatti de Gamond, "Attractive Industry," *Phalanx: Or, Journal of Social Science. Devoted to the Cause of Association, or a Social Reform, and the Elevation of the Human Race* (New York), 1 (Sept. 7, 1844): 269–70.

42. "W. H. C.," "Objections to Association—No. III," *Harbinger* 3 (Aug. 1, 1846): 124–25. "W. H. C." was almost certainly William Henry Channing, the nephew of William Ellery Channing and an activist in the Associationist and other social reform movements of the period.

43. The arguments of both Alonzo Potter and George Frederick Holmes, discussed in chapter 2, fall into this category. However, as suggested in the case of the conservative, proslavery Holmes, at least, the defense of exclusively mental labor employments as truly taxing, and the significant extent to which this defense constituted a legitimation of the *status quo* in civilized societies, did not preclude some severe criticism of the suffering and divisiveness that attended the social division of labor in competitive "free labor" societies.

44. Jean-Baptiste Say, *A Treatise on Political Economy; or the Production, Distribution and Consumption of Wealth,* trans. (from 4th ed. of French) C. R. Prinsep (New York: Augustus M. Kelley, 1964 [1880]), 98–99.

45. Ibid.

46. "J. F. C." [James Freeman Clarke], "Fourierism," *Christian Examiner. And Religious Miscellany,* 4th ser. 2 (July 1844): 66–67; Clarke's essay was also published as part of "The *Christian Examiner* on the Doctrine of Fourier," *Phalanx* 1 (Aug. 24, 1844): 246–49. Although Clarke fully embraced the Fourierist analysis of the division of labor, he also criticized Fourierism for neglecting, in its zeal to effect social reorganization, what he took to be the root cause of social evil: individual sin. For a Fourierist response to Clarke, see the same article, *Phalanx* 1 (Aug. 24, 1844): 249–52.

47. Parke Godwin, *A Popular View of the Doctrines of Charles Fourier,* 2d ed. (New York: J. S. Redfield, 1844), 55.

48. John Allen, concluding part of a lecture entitled "The American Idea of the Commonwealth," repr. as "Organization of Labor upon the Principle of Attraction," in *Pittsburgh Daily Morning Post,* Jan. 29, 1848.

49. Karl Marx, *Selected Writings in Sociology and Social Philosophy,* ed. T. B. Bottomore and Maximilien Rubel, trans. T. B. Bottomore (London: C. A. Watts and Company, 1956), 231.

50. Albert Brisbane, *A Concise Exposition of the Doctrine of Association, or Plan for a Reorganization of Society, Which Will Secure to the Human Race, Individually and Collectively, Their Happiness and Elevation (Based on Fourier's Theory of Domestic and Industrial Association),* 8th ed. (New York: J. S. Redfield, 1844), 36.

51. Godwin, *Popular View,* 27–28.

52. I cannot fully subscribe to Edward K. Spann's claim that "Despite its professed concern for 'the masses,' . . . Associationism was essentially designed for the broad middling class of ambitious small enterprisers and skilled craftsmen exposed to the ebbs and flows of a modernizing society." It seems to me that American industrialization and attendant skill dilution reinforced within Associationism what had distinguished Fourier's system as well: an overriding concern with the philosophical and empirical problem of unskilled, common labor. Spann does, however, provide a valuable detailed account of both the theory and application of American Fourierism, as well as of other prominent nineteenth-century

utopian movements, and he usefully draws attention to such stimulating influences as the "collapse of the economic boon of 1837," which undoubtedly did attract frustrated skilled workers, small enterprisers, and farmers to the Fourierist cause: Edward K. Spann, *Brotherly Tomorrows: Movements for a Cooperative Society in America 1820–1920* (New York: Columbia University Press, 1989), 141. I should also refer here to perhaps the single most distinguished study exclusively devoted to Associationism: Carl Joseph Guarneri, "Utopian Socialism and American Ideas: The Origins and Doctrine of American Fourierism, 1832–1848" (Ph.D. diss., Johns Hopkins University, 1979). "For all its European-style radicalism," Guarneri concludes, Associationism "was an emphatically American and surprisingly conservative creed. American Fourierists drew upon native forms of discontent for their ideas, and they argued that far from repudiating American pieties, utopian socialism was merely a more effective way of realizing the ideals of democracy, Christianity, and missionary nationalism . . . . Association was indeed socialism, but one so close to American ideas that it was not so much an alternative *to* American ways of thinking as an alternative, socialist version *of* them, a community-minded version of the American creed" (Dissertation Abstract, iii; diss., 319). I cannot quarrel with many of Guarneri's arguments, and as I suggest in the main text, Associationist work distribution schemes themselves expressed a more generalized American malaise regarding ongoing specialization. Yet it is precisely the intensity of their concern with the proper distribution and remuneration of labor, the intensity of their revulsion toward the free market's treatment of necessary, but "repugnant" unskilled work, which establishes, rather than belies, the radicalism of Associationist thinkers. Perhaps it is all a matter of emphasis. In contrast to Guarneri's, my discussion focuses upon the most genuinely radical dimension of American Fourierism. In a number of places Guarneri qualifies his overall conclusion and notes that "the Associationist perspective on the American scene remained an indisputably radical one, opposed to the entire contemporary American socio-economic polity" (200); see also pp. 270–319 for Guarneri's litany of reasons for his ultimate reference to "the basic duality of Association's 'conservative radicalism'" (271).

53. For Noyes and Oneida, see Mulford Q. Sibley, "Oneida's Challenge to American Culture," in Joseph J. Kwiat and Mary C. Turpie, eds., *Studies in American Culture* (Minneapolis: University of Minnesota Press, 1960), 47; Ira L. Mandelker, *Religion, Society, and Utopia in Nineteenth-Century America* (Amherst: University of Massachusetts Press, 1984), 151. For Thompson's rotation of labor scheme, which was directed particularly toward eliminating the sexual division of labor that oppressed women, see William Thompson, *An Inquiry into the Principles of the Distribution of Wealth Most Conducive to Human Happiness* (London: William S. Orr and Company, 1850), 260–367 passim. On the commitment British Owenite socialists articulated in their literature to the alleviation of "domestic drudgery" by rotating it among the various members of their communities, see Barbara Taylor, *Eve and the New Jerusalem: Socialism and Feminism in the Nineteenth Century* (New York: Pantheon Books, 1983), 37, 50–53. Taylor also notes, however, the considerable discrepancy existing between Owenite ideals and community realities; the rotation, or "collectivization," of household tasks seems almost never to have extended in fact to the male members of Britain's Owenite communities (246–51). There is now a full-length study elaborating with greater emphasis the similar failure of Owenite communities in America to break away from the "patriarchal" labor practices and values of the larger society: Carol A. Kolmerten, *Women in Utopia: The Ideology of Gender in the American Utopian Owenite Communities* (Bloomington: Indiana University Press, 1990).

54. If Fourier's philosophical rationale for a utopian division of labor was more systematic and elaborate than that of Owen and his followers, the explanation, as a number of scholars have noted, had much to do with their fundamentally different assumptions about human psychology. Heir to the Enlightenment view of the human mind as a blank slate, Owen appears to have regarded man as a perfectly plastic organism who could be completely molded by his environment. Fourier, on the other hand, believed that individuals were equipped with a set of basic instinctual propensities, or "passions," that could not be permanently altered or suppressed and that imposed severe limits on human malleability. It was these "given" innate drives, which in their precise proportion and intensity differed for each individual, that to a very large extent determined the elaborate character of the system erected by Fourier; see Beecher, *Charles Fourier,* 220; and Sidney Hook, "The Philosophical Basis of Marxism in the United States," in Donald Drew Egbert and Stow Persons, eds., *Socialism and American Life* (Princeton: Princeton University Press, 1952), 1: 431.

55. Alasdair Clayre, *Work and Play: Ideas and Experience of Work and Leisure* (New York: Harper and Row, 1974), 22.

56. Marx, *The Grundrisse,* ed. and trans. David McLellan (New York: Harper and Row, 1970), 118, 123–25.

57. Among the many discussions of Marx's apparently shifting views regarding the centrality of work, see Beecher, *Charles Fourier,* 294–95; Clayre, *Work and Play,* 54–56; John Plamenatz, *Karl Marx's Philosophy of Man* (Oxford: Clarendon Press, 1975), 170–72, 273, 376–78; Krishan Kumar, *Utopia and Anti-Utopia in Modern Times* (London: Basil Blackwell, 1987), 56–59; Graeme Duncan, *Marx and Mill: Two Views of Social Conflict and Social Harmony* (Cambridge, Eng.: Cambridge University Press, 1973), 187, 351; and for a highly original explanation of Marx's shifting views, one that stresses the rising influence of the "new physics" of thermodynamics, see Anson Rabinbach, *The Human Motor: Energy, Fatigue, and the Origins of Modernity* (New York: Basic Books, 1990), 72–83.

58. Karl Marx and Friedrich Engels, *The German Ideology,* ed. C. J. Arthur (New York: International Publishers, 1970), 53. The sense in which the vision of productive and diversified activity drawn here by Marx and Engels may or may not be distinct from a genuine merger of "work and play" poses interesting definitional questions; see Stephen Eric Bronner, "Between Art and Utopia: Reconsidering the Aesthetic Theory of Herbert Marcuse," in Robert Pippin et al, eds., *Marcuse: Critical Theory and the Promise of Utopia* (South Hadley, Mass.: Bergin and Garvey, 1988), 134–35. For a critical look at some of the assumptions about human proclivities in which Marx and Engels grounded their utopian vision, see Jon Elster, *Making Sense of Marx* (Cambridge, Eng.: Cambridge University Press, 1985), 85–92.

59. Robert C. Tucker, *The Marxian Revolutionary Idea* (New York: W. W. Norton and Company, 1969), 19, 28, 217; Tucker, *Philosophy and Myth in Karl Marx,* 2d ed. (Cambridge, Eng.: Cambridge University Press, 1972), 195–238; Ali Rattansi, *Marx and the Division of Labour* (London: Macmillan Press, 1982), 174–75; David McLellan, "Marx and the Whole Man," in Bhikhu Parekh, ed., *The Concept of Socialism* (New York: Holmes and Meier Publishers, 1975), 68–69. To extend a point raised in the text and which remains an issue of debate among Marxist scholars, it is less clear that the mature Marx believed it was either possible or necessary for the division of labor to be fully abolished: technological advances and an egalitarian system of distribution under socialism might instead enable people to work for only a fraction of the time they worked under capitalism, and thus they would not be

intellectually impoverished even if they performed the same work during these few hours.

60. "W. H. C.," "Objections to Association," 124.

61. George Bernard Shaw, *The Intelligent Woman's Guide to Socialism, Capitalism, Sovietism, and Fascism* (1937), quoted in Michael Walzer, *Spheres of Justice: A Defense of Pluralism and Equality* (New York: Basic Books, 1983), 183.

62. Beecher, *Charles Fourier,* 111.

63. Albert Brisbane, *The Social Destiny of Man: Or Association and Reorganization of Industry* (Philadelphia: C. F. Stollmeyer, 1840), 442.

64. Excerpt from Fourier's writings, in Ibid., 446–47.

65. Gamond, "Attractive Industry," 270; Beecher, *Charles Fourier,* 228, 280; Bestor, "American Phalanxes," 209.

66. "Organization of Industry. By Members of the [Albany Fourier] Association," *New York State Mechanic* 2 (Apr. 8, 1843): 157; Beecher, *Charles Fourier,* 278–82; Jonathan Beecher and Richard Bienvenu, "Introduction," *The Utopian Vision of Charles Fourier: Selected Texts on Work, Love, and Passionate Attraction,* ed. and trans. Beecher and Bienvenu (Boston: Beacon Press, 1971), 46–48.

67. John Allen, lecture, paraphrased by the *Fall River Mechanic,* Nov. 9, 1844.

68. Fourier quoted in Beecher and Bienvenu, "Introduction," *Utopian Vision,* 48.

69. "W. H. C.," "Letters to Associationists: Number Two," *Spirit of the Age* 1 (Oct. 20, 1849): 248.

70. Charles Dana, "Address" to Convention of American Associationists, *Phalanx* 1 (Apr. 20, 1844): 113–14; similar egalitarian opposition to the keeping of servants is expressed in "W. H. C.," "Letters to Associationists: Number Two." Brook Farm was reorganized as a phalanx in March 1845.

71. For a recent study noting the particular irrelevance of the "humanitarian and social reforms" of the early workingmen's party platforms to the immediate needs and condition of unskilled, largely Irish immigrant labor in Philadelphia, see Cynthia S. Shelton, *The Mills of Manayunk: Industrialization and Social Conflict in the Philadelphia Region, 1787–1837* (Baltimore: Johns Hopkins University Press, 1986), 126.

72. Dana, "Address," 113–14.

73. George W. Taylor, "Address at Proceedings of the New England Social Reform Convention, held in Boston, May 28-June 1, 1844," *The Social Pioneer, and Herald of Progress* (Boston: J. P. Mendum, 1844), 10. The New England Social Reform Society was founded as an auxiliary of the Skaneateles Community.

74. Dana, "Address," 114.

75. Allen, "Organization of Labor." Years later John Ruskin similarly noted that truly "servile" work, "if undertaken in a certain spirit, . . . might be the holiest of all," and he accordingly proposed—not, perhaps, without some degree of facetiousness—that this work no longer be left wholly to the poor but instead be gladly undertaken by the clergy and other religious persons: "You cannot possibly preach your faith so forcibly to the world by any quantity of the finest words, as by a few such simple and painful acts" (John Ruskin, *Time and Tide* (1867), in Ruskin, *The Works of John Ruskin,* ed. E. T. Cook and Alexander Wedderburn [London: George Allen, 1905], 17: 407–8).

76. Nicholas V. Riasanovsky, *The Teaching of Charles Fourier* (Berkeley: University of California Press, 1969), 61–62; Beecher, *Charles Fourier,* 279–80. For Brisbane's deviations from Fourier's specific ratios of rewards for "labor," "capital,"

and "talent" in the phalanx, see Bestor, "American Phalanxes," 199–202; Brisbane, *Social Destiny,* 125; Brisbane, *Concise Exposition,* 58–62.

77. Beecher and Bienvenu, "Introduction," *Utopian Vision,* 45

78. Beecher, *Charles Fourier,* 277–80. The performance of domestic tasks particularly—"the occupations of the kitchen and needle"—within groups and series rather than in the prevailing context of "separate" and "isolated" households would do much to render this work more "attractive" (Brisbane, *Social Destiny,* 5). Under the system of "Associated Households," according to Madame Gatti De Gamond, "women are no longer the mere slaves of solitary household duty; they are organized in corporations of industrial, artistic and religious unity, and have a morally collective, a truly social existence, in addition to their individual position in the private family" (Gamond, "Condition of Women in Harmony," *Phalanx* 1 [Aug. 10, 1844]: 236).

79. Beecher, *Charles Fourier,* 246–48; "Property—Distinction between Association and Communism," *Harbinger* 5 (July 17, 1847): 93–95; resolutions of John S. Dwight at "Meeting of Associationists in Boston," *Harbinger* 7 (June 10, 1848): 44–45; Dwight, "The Associative Theory of Property," *Harbinger* 7 (Sept. 30, 1848): 172; "Capital in Association," *Harbinger* 8 (Nov. 18, 1848): 20; "Capital in Association," *Harbinger* 8 (Nov. 25, 1848): 27. For one of the Owenite "no property" or "Communist" criticisms that provoked these Fourierist defenses, see "The *Harbinger,*" an editorial in the organ of the Skaneateles community, *Communitist* (Mottville, N.Y.) 2 (Dec. 4, 1845): 70.

80. For the ways in which various of the American phalansteries diverged in practice even from Brisbane's revised version of Fourier's blueprint, see Bestor, "American Phalanxes," 202–11; see also "Socialism," *New-York Daily Tribune,* July 27, 1855. Horace Greeley was in this editorial marking the demise of the North American Phalanstery in New Jersey, whose life span of thirteen years far exceeded that of most of the fifteen or so phalanxes Greeley estimated had been established in the United States after 1840. For an explanation of the failure of virtually all the Associationist communities to survive into the 1850s, one which finds the ultimate reason for the movement's wane in the very "Americanness" that had accounted for Associationism's popularity in the first place, see Guarneri, "Utopian Socialism," 319–27. Guarneri concludes that the return of prosperity to American "competitive capitalism" in the 1850s, together with the escalation of antislavery, Northern sectionalist sentiment, determined that "nationalistic, capitalistic socialism was too easily coopted," both "as a practical phalanx plan and as a system of ideas." Once their "critique of competition lost hold (i.e., lost favor)," Fourierists saw in Republican free labor ideology "the same promise of a harmonious, classless and progressive society their socialism had voiced" (327). This explanation for the demise of Associationism is not completely satisfactory, if only because Guarneri overstates, in view of the repeated and prolonged depressions of the late antebellum period, the "booming" character of the Northern economy in these years; thus he overstates the strictly objective basis upon which competitive capitalism in the North reestablished its superiority to alternative social arrangements as a route to prosperity and opportunity, particularly for those on the lower rungs of the social scale. As I have suggested in earlier chapters, a number of important social and economic developments in the northeastern states particularly—continuing rural malaise and out-migration, artisan skill dilution and proletarianization, competition between native-born and immigrant labor, large-scale urban unemployment and misery—did more to belie than to confirm Republican exaltations of the North as the good society.

81. Allen, "Organization of Labor."

82. Riasanovsky, *Teaching*, 69–70; Bestor, "American Phalanxes," 11; Beecher, *Charles Fourier*, 288–90; Charles Gide, "Introduction" to Charles Fourier, *Design for Utopia: Selected Writings of Charles Fourier*, trans. Julia Franklin (New York: Schocken Books, 1971 [1901]), 27–28.

83. Godwin, *Popular View*, 56, 66.

84. *New Moral World* 4, no. 195 (July 21, 1838), quoted in Berg, *Machinery Question*, 279. For a more extended consideration of the views of Robert Owen and British Owenites toward specialization and the division of labor, see Gregory Claeys, *Citizens and Saints: Politics and Anti-Politics in Early British Socialism* (Cambridge, Eng.: Cambridge University Press, 1989), 54–58, 80–82.

85. Horace Greeley, *Recollections of a Busy Life: Including Reminiscences of American Politics and Politicians, from the Opening of the Missouri Contest to the Downfall of Slavery* (New York: J. B. Ford and Company, 1869), 154–55. It was largely because Greeley was enough of a believer in "man's natural love of ease and enjoyment" that he opposed, just as Malthus and other classical economists had done before him, the Owenite and other "agrarian" schemes that would eliminate private property in their pursuit of equality of condition. Only private property, Greeley insisted, kept man's natural indolence in check: "Take away the inducements to industry and thrift afforded by the law which secures to each the ownership and enjoyment of his rightful gains and, through universal poverty and ignorance, even Christendom would rapidly relapse into utter barbarism" (Greeley, *Essays Designed to Elucidate the Science of Political Economy* [Boston: Fields, Osgood, and Company, 1870], 15); see also the following note.

86. Citing the contributions to production made by the intellectual labors of engineers and inventors, Greeley observed in 1867 that "for the narrow vision which recognizes workers only in those who live by muscular effort, I have a pity which is allied to contempt" (Horace Greeley, "Counsel to Boys. No. IV—Choosing a Vocation," *Little Corporal. An Original Magazine for Boys and Girls, and for Older People Who Have Young Hearts* 5 [July, 1867]: 24). For quite a few years, Greeley had been demonstrating his affinity with more conservative members of the Whig and Republican parties, taking issue with notions that individuals engaged in exclusively mental employments, capitalists included, were not and could not be, true "workers" and that they deprived manual laborers of the just fruits of their toil. The most vehement critics of such radical deductions from the labor theory of value insisted that capitalists and other mental laborers were completely deserving of the greater rewards society bestowed upon them. Presumably, Greeley, at least during his Associationist phase, did not go this far, since one of the points of the community experiments he was endorsing was to bring the compensation and status of arduous and "repugnant" physical labor more into line with the rewards accruing to capital and skilled labor. In part, of course, Fourierism would accomplish this by converting "rude" laborers themselves into proprietors. However, it remains true that although Greeley and some other Fourierist sympathizers believed that Fourierism needed to be restrained from going too far in rewarding unskilled, menial labor, some radical contemporaries of the Fourierists believed that Fourierist doctrines and experiments did not go far enough in this direction. These rival utopians, who embraced either absolute equality of distribution, distribution according to need, or some other communitarian doctrine, recognized in the Fourierist principle of "joint-stock" private property a fatal compromise of Fourierism's professed desire to single out for recognition the productive contributions of impoverished, unskilled labor. To radicals like Stephen Pearl Andrews, who promoted a distinctive

"labor note"—"Equity" scheme designed to insure, among other things, that street cleaners were better paid than merchants, the special rewards earmarked by Fourierism for the contributions of "capital" and "talent" seemed too much like prevailing market arrangements, whereby superior skill and capital inexorably secured more property and esteem than the most "repugnant" and "painful" menial labor. Fourierists for their part made no effort to conceal their belief that by so destroying or transforming the existing institution of private property, the schemes of Andrews, the "common property Communists," and other labor radicals would remove the incentive of the more talented members of society to work and achieve. Fourierists at most conceded that society might do without private property if and when its members underwent a complete spiritual regeneration at some distant future time. But until that time arrived, a Fourierist writer in the *Tribune* (probably George Ripley) maintained, the various anti-Fourierist radicals would remain guilty of ignoring the fact that "Genius and skill are no less indispensable elements of production than muscular force, . . . no scientific reason, as far as we know, has ever been alleged, why the latter should receive remuneration, and not the former. Shall the brute force which is devoted to labor be entitled to the product, while the skill which directs and utilizes that force is deprived of its share? . . . The Communists say that the products of labor shall be distributed, not according to the amount of labor, but equally, irrespective of labor, or at least, if a difference is made, it shall be according to the wants of the individual, not according to his industry. Very well. This may be benevolent, but it is not scientific. It proceeds from the law of friendship, not that of distributive justice" (*New-York Daily Tribune,* quoted in "Appendix" of Stephen Pearl Andrews, *The Science of Society* [Boston: Sarah E. Holmes, 1895 (ca. 1855)], 159). Some of the more interesting material that bears on Fourierist doctrine includes a letter from Robert Owen to the *Phalanx,* from New Harmony, Ind., Oct. 25, 1844, and comments by that journal, in *Phalanx* 1 (Dec. 9, 1844): 296–98; see also Andrews, *Science of Society,* 52–53, 67, 109, and "Appendix," 158–65, for more of the exchange between Andrews and the *Tribune* writer on the relative social justice embodied in Fourierist and rival radical schemes; and for an especially clear statement of a radical's suspicion of American Fourierism's breakdown of rewards within its communities, see "H. R. S.," letter from Mongoquinong, Ind., in "Correspondence," *Harbinger* 7 (Oct. 28, 1848): 203. See also the attack on Associationism made in 1846 by Herman Kriege, a German immigrant and former member of Marx's Communist League, in John R. Commons, ed., *Labor Movement, 1840–1860,* vol. 1, A Documentary History of American Industrial Society, vol. 7 (New York: Russell and Russell, 1958 [1910]), 229–30. For studies noting that Greeley's capitalist and industrialist biases inclined him to highlight different features of Associationism from those stressed by more radical advocates of the cause, see Guarneri, "Utopian Socialism," 38–54; Daniel Walker Howe, *The Political Culture of the American Whigs* (Chicago: University of Chicago Press, 1979), 193–94; Iver Bernstein, *The New York City Draft Riots: Their Significance for American Society and Politics in the Age of the Civil War* (New York: Oxford University Press, 1990), 170–71. See also untitled editorial, *New-York Daily Tribune,* Nov. 11, 1857.

    87. "An American Farmer" [Olmsted], "Association. The Phalanstery and the Phalansterians. By an Outsider," *New-York Daily Tribune,* July 29, 1852; for a draft of this article for the *Tribune,* see Olmsted to Charles Loring Brace, July 26, 1852, Frederick Law Olmsted Papers, Manuscript Division, Library of Congress.

    88. Nathaniel Hawthorne to his wife, June 1841, quoted in Beecher and Bienvenu, "Introduction," *Utopian Vision,* 49.

CHAPTER 6: ELITIST RESPONSES TO DRUDGE WORK

1. For Channing's view that mental labor employments were proving too much of a good thing in America, and that an occupational imbalance was developing as men overcrowded urban commerce and the "liberal professions" in the hopes of "escaping the primeval sentence of living by the sweat of the brow," see William Ellery Channing, *Lectures on the Elevation of the Labouring Portion of the Community* (Boston: William D. Ticknor, 1840), 9. For similar complaints by one strongly sympathetic to Fourierist principles, see "J. F. C." [James Freeman Clarke], "Fourierism," *Christian Examiner. And Religious Miscellany,* 4th ser., 2 (July 1844): 69–70.

2. *Compact Edition of the Oxford English Dictionary* (Oxford: Oxford University Press, 1971), 1: 845.

3. O. A. Brownson, "Brook Farm," *United States Magazine, and Democratic Review* 11 (Nov. 1842): 487, also 486.

4. Marcus Morton to F. A. Hildreth, May 11, 1849, quoted in Arthur Schlesinger, Jr., *The Age of Jackson* (Boston: Little, Brown and Company, 1945), 71.

5. Marcus Morton, *Address to the Two Branches of the Legislature of Massachusetts,* Jan. 20, 1843, quoted in Carl Siracusa, *A Mechanical People: Perceptions of the Industrial Order in Massachusetts, 1815–1880* (Middletown: Wesleyan University Press, 1979), 125. See also Siracusa's good discussion here of the ideology of Massachusetts Democratic leaders.

6. The emphasis in the text is upon how individuals like Morton shared certain assumptions with others of still more strongly elitist convictions. But one could also refer to other statements of Morton and like-minded Democrats—statements that were in many cases clearly directed at more populist audiences—to illustrate the considerable ideological distance they maintained from more conservative men. This John Ashworth has done in a recent book. Ashworth does not make what would seem to be a clearly untenable claim: that Morton and other Democrats denied the existence of any innate differences in talent and intellectual capacity among individuals. But he does argue convincingly that, *in comparison* to moderate and conservative Whigs, liberal Democrats minimized the importance of natural disparities as an explanation for existing inequalities of economic condition. Far more instrumental, in their view, were unequal privileges and inequalities of opportunity and were these to be eliminated, they maintained, economic inequalities in American society would be eventually reduced to a fraction of their existing size.

If one grants Ashworth's argument that liberal Democrats like Morton and Robert Rantoul, Jr., genuinely sought a society in which "inequalities both of property and of power" were "comparatively trifling" (Robert Rantoul, Jr., *Oration Delivered before the Democratic Citizens of the County of Worcester,* July 4, 1837, quoted in Ashworth, *"Agrarians" and "Aristocrats": Party Political Ideology in the United States, 1837–1846* [London: Royal Historical Society, 1983], 26), did they also believe that such a society must be free of complex occupational differentiation or division of labor? Ashworth holds that the "Democratic levelling theory," in contrast to Whig doctrines, "implied an agrarian, pre-capitalist society," one that sanctioned only "slight social differentiation" (Ashworth, *"Agrarians" and "Aristocrats,"* 1, 29). Yet it remains significant that mainstream Democrats, for all their exaltation of the independent yeoman, did not characteristically argue that American society could actually do without its merchants or lawyers, let alone its domestic servants or day laborers. (Robert Rantoul, Jr.'s vision of the good society certainly emerges as less "agrarian," less antagonistic to "capitalist progress," in Marvin Meyers's discussion than in Ashworth's discussion, although here, clearly, the targeted audience of a political leader's remarks does loom as an important consideration: Meyers's discussion, as he himself notes, centers on an address that Rantoul pitched to a more "genteel" and more economically ambitious group than the common Jacksonian audience of "plain hard-working folk of farm and shop" (Meyers, *The Jacksonian Persuasion: Politics and Belief* [Stanford: Stanford University Press, 1957], 207–33). Quite possibly liberal Democrats accepted the need for significant occupational differentiation but engaged in the wishful notion, one that has also occupied the thoughts of some modern sociologists, that such differentiation need not be inevitably attended by social *stratification*. This issue has already received some discussion in chapter 1. I do not wish to deny the undeniable: that the rhetoric of Jacksonian political leaders was more consistently and strongly proagrarian than that of their Whig counterparts and that through such rhetoric the former spoke more than the latter to the ambivalence and hostility that social change generated among large groups of Americans. Yet it also seems to me that the logic of their own positions—as politicians, lawyers, men of business, and in some cases, large slaveholders—inexorably led Jacksonian as well as Whig spokesmen to the perception that even the most just of civilized societies would, by virtue of differences in talent, enterprise, and taste, necessarily encompass a good deal more than yeoman farmers of varying degrees of wealth. See here, in addition to Morton's remarks, *Memoirs, Speeches and Writings of Robert Rantoul, Jr.,* ed. Luther Hamilton (Boston: John P. Jewett and Company, 1854) 137–38, 219–32. See also Ashworth, *"Agrarians" and "Aristocrats,"* 25–34, 53, 66–68, 127. For more recent, general reinforcement of Ashworth's position, see Lawrence Frederick Kohl, *The Politics of Individualism: Parties and the American Character in the Jacksonian Era* (New York: Oxford University Press, 1989), 61, 118.

7. Gordon S. Wood, *The Creation of American Republic, 1776–1787* (Chapel Hill: University of North Carolina Press, 1969), 72.

8. For Skidmore's belief that individuals were roughly equal in the "riches of the mind" and that this circumstance, together with their equal education and their enjoyment of equal property at an early age, would result in a continued social and economic equality throughout their lifetimes, see Thomas Skidmore, *The Rights of Man to Property! Being a Proposition to Make It Equal among the Adults of the Present Generation and to Provide for Its Equal Transmission to Every Individual of Each Succeeding Generation, on Arriving at the Age of Maturity* (New York: Alexander Ming, 1829), 153–54, 368.

9. See, for example, "The Washington Homicide," *Springfield Daily Republican* (Massachusetts), May 21, 1856.

10. "Self-Help," *Springfield Daily Republican*, Apr. 7, 1860. For a similar defense of economic disparities and the social division of labor as part of the "indispensable law of life," see Francis Lieber, *Essays on Property and Labour as Connected with Natural Law and the Constitution of Society* (New York: Harper and Brothers, 1841), 173, 199–201. Lieber, the Prussian-born professor of political economy and history at South Carolina College, here insisted that "more men in this world must needs be engaged in working than in contemplating." It would have been a tragedy, Lieber continued, had Isaac Newton been shut up in a trade, "but it would be far worse if ever it should come to pass that the majority of farmers or mechanics should think they did not fulfill their destiny if they did not strive to become Newtons." Of course, attaining the heights of Newton required something more in the way of intellect and talent than succeeding in business or in one of the "learned professions," but the point here is that Lieber, like the author of the "Self-Help" editorial, was among those who defended the notion that divisions between mental labor and

manual labor employments in civilized societies reflected significant differences in native endowment as well as being functionally necessary.

11. R. A. Soloway, *Prelates and People: Ecclesiastical Social Thought in England, 1783–1852* (London: Routledge and Kegan Paul, 1969), 64–76; Robert Malcolmson, *Life and Labour in England, 1700–1780* (New York: St. Martin's Press, 1981), 11–17.

12. In enunciating his position on poor relief, Thomas Malthus acknowledged that in the case of some members of Britain's pauper population, the practice of "industry, prudence and virtue" had failed to bring "their just reward." But he held to the general position that many, if not a majority, of the dependent poor were "idle and improvident" and were "deservedly at the bottom in the scale of society." And although he also noted that "all cannot be" in the "middle parts of society," and that society in fact needed "superior and inferior parts" in order to function, Malthus seemed clearly to believe that members of the middle classes were generally more "virtuous and industrious" than members of the "lower classes," that the former were distinguished by a greater ability and willingness to meet the demands of a competitive society. Implicit to some degree in such moralistic arguments was the egalitarian assumption that the poorest members of society have the native capability to free themselves from "slavery" to absolute want by developing and exercising "prudential restraint" and other virtues. The emphasis of the *Springfield Republican,* in the anti-Smiles editorial discussed above at least, was on the differences, not the similarities, in native endowment among individuals, but it can hardly be doubted that Malthus and other of the classical economists also accepted such differences and that they used these, along with the variations in developed capabilities and virtues, to justify economic distinctions that arose in competitive market societies; see T. R. Malthus, *An Essay on the Principle of Population; or, a View of Its Past and Present Effects on Human Happiness; with an Inquiry into Our Prospects Respecting the Future Removal or Mitigation of the Evils Which It Occasions,* 5th ed. (London: John Murray, 1817), 3: 224–25, 275, 287, 303–5. See also Richard B. Simons, "T. R. Malthus on British Society," *Journal of the History of Ideas* 16 (Jan. 1955): 60–75; D. L. Lemahieu, "Malthus and the Theology of Scarcity," *Journal of the History of Ideas* 40 (July–Sept. 1979): 472–73; and Edmund N. Santurri, "Theodicy and Social Policy in Malthus' Thought," *Journal of the History of Ideas* 43 (Apr.–June 1982): 324–27.

13. "The True Social State," *Weekly Chronotype* (Boston), Dec. 22, 1949.

14. For the argument that "cotton spinners" and "ministers of the gospel" in the free states were no different from "cotton planters" and other "Southern people" in claiming that the world's "dirty work" must be relegated to a portion of the laboring classes, see the letter from "Rover," Mar. 11, 1847, Savannah, Georgia, in *Daily Chronotype,* Mar. 18, 1847. For a valuable discussion of the Reverend Joseph Townsend, whose *Dissertation on the Poor Laws* signalled the emergence of the newer, free market version of elitism that broke with the more traditional, paternalist kind, see Reinhard Bendix, *Work and Authority in Industry* (Berkeley: University of California Press, 1956), 73–76. See also J. H. Poynter, *Society and Pauperism: English Ideas on Poor Relief, 1795–1834* (London: Routledge and Kegan Paul, 1969), xvi–xvii, 40–43. Townsend was something of a transitional figure. Like some of the earlier mercantilist writers, he appeared to regard the laboring poor as virtually a different, permanently degraded species of mankind, one which knew "little of the motives which stimulate the higher ranks to action—pride, honour, and ambition," and who would work only when they were forced to by hunger. But if Townsend accordingly shared with Bernard Mandeville and the mercantilists an appreciation of the "utility of poverty," he nonetheless went beyond them, as Bendix has noted,

in the vehemence of his demands that nothing should be done to mitigate their hunger. He thus anticipated classical economists like Malthus in recognizing the value of the "utility of poverty" theme as an ideological weapon to be used against existing poor laws and other paternalistic restraints upon a competitive labor market. As suggested in the previous note, classical economists also gave at least rhetorical credence to the idea that the laboring poor might be imbued with market-oriented rationality—that they had the potential capacity to respond to the same kinds of labor incentives that motivated society's "higher ranks." But that the "brutish" poor might possess this capacity was for Townsend, in contrast, not only unimaginable but also undesirable, for only those who were responsive exclusively to hunger—the most elemental of labor incentives—could in Townsend's opinion be induced to ably "fulfil the most servile, the most sordid, and the most ignoble offices in the community" (Joseph Townsend, *Dissertation on the Poor Laws. By a Well-Wisher to Mankind* [1786]; repr. in John Ramsay McCulloch, ed., *A Select Collection of Scarce and Valuable Economical Tracts* [London: n.p. 1859], 403–4, 415). For the popularity of the "utility of poverty" theme among eighteenth-century mercantilist writers, see Edgar S. Furniss, *The Position of the Laborer in a System of Nationalism: A Study in the Labor Theories of the Later English Mercantilists* (New York: Kelley and Millman, 1957), 117–56.

15. Of relevance to this broad distinction between elitist values is Marc Bloch's description of the change that French aristocrat attitudes toward the serf underwent during the twelfth and thirteenth centuries: "The French serf, the 'homme de corps,' was from now on thought of much less as his lord's 'man' than as the member of a despised class. . . . Servitude was less and less thought of as a personal bond and more and more as a mark of inferior social position" (Marc Bloch, *Land and Work in Medieval Europe: Selected Papers,* trans. J. E. Anderson [Berkeley: University of California Press, 1967], 65, 104).

Middle-class French industrialists of the mid-nineteenth century, Peter Stearns has found, subscribed to "a traditionalism [that] called for charity to relieve misery," but as part of that same traditionalism, they clung to the assumption that the masses were "naturally wretched" and they "certainly did not regard workers as potentially equal human beings" (Peter Stearns, *Paths to Authority: The Middle Class and the Industrial Labor Force in France 1820–48* [Urbana: University of Illinois Press, 1978], 115–16, 118, 119–39). For a variety of reasons, French manufacturing capitalists, unlike their more "liberal" counterparts in mid-Victorian England, rarely even paid lip service to the notion that members of the working class could acquire the virtues needed to rise out of their class.

16. Although it is not a historical study and does not treat "paternalism" in the context of traditional attitudes towards the laboring classes and their place within a rigid status hierarchy, a useful discussion is John Kleinig, *Paternalism* (Totowa, N.J.: Rowman and Allanheld, 1983).

17. I am thinking again primarily of Joseph Townsend's views as an example of free market elitism that viewed the members of the laboring classes as fixed by their natural endowments in positions of social inferiority and subordination.

18. David Kettler, *The Social and Political Thought of Adam Ferguson* (Columbus: Ohio State University Press, 1965), 3–4, 10; Karl Marx, *The Poverty of Philosophy* (New York: International Publishers, 1963), 129–30; Karl Marx, *Capital: A Critique of Political Economy,* ed. Frederick Engels, trans. Samuel Moore and Edward Aveling [New York: International Publishers, 1967], 1: 123n, 362n.

19. Adam Ferguson, *An Essay on the History of Civil Society,* ed. Duncan Forbes (Edinburgh: Edinburgh University Press, 1966), 184.

20. Ibid., 183.

21. Adam Ferguson, *Principles of Moral and Political Science. Being Chiefly a Retrospect of Lectures Delivered in the College of Edinburgh* (London: A. Strahan and T. Cadell, 1792), 1: 251. See also Ferguson, *Essay,* 182–83.

22. It also seems likely that Ferguson, to a somewhat greater degree than Smith, perceived manufacturing division of labor as only an *example* of the entrapment of the laboring population in intellectually deadening and socially debasing employments. Although Charles Lamb has argued that Smith, too, believed that the various forms or aspects of what Marx termed "alienation"—self-estrangement, isolation, powerlessness—extended to "all the inferior ranks of people" (Adam Smith, *An Inquiry into the Nature and Causes of the Wealth of Nations,* ed. Edwin Cannan [New York: Random House, 1937 {1904}], 308), this belief seems to occupy a still more prominent part of Ferguson's writings (Robert Lamb, "Adam Smith's Concept of Alienation," *Oxford Economic Papers,* n.s., 25 [July 1973]: 275–85).

23. Ferguson, *Essay,* 186–87, 218.

24. Ferguson, *Essay,* 180.

25. Adam Ferguson, *The Morality of Stage Plays Seriously Considered* (Edinburgh: n.p. 1757), 24.

26. Ferguson, *Essay,* 63.

27. Kettler, *Ferguson,* 284. For a less critical view of Ferguson's thought, see John D. Brewer, "The Scottish Enlightenment," in Andrew Reeve, ed., *Modern Theories of Exploitation* (London: Sage Publications, 1987), 12–26.

28. In one of his better-known remarks, Adam Smith was even more explicit on this point than Ferguson: "The difference of natural talents in different men is, in reality, much less than we are aware of; and the very different genius which appears to distinguish men of different professions, when grown up to maturity, is not upon many occasions so much the cause, as the effect of the division of labour. The difference between the most dissimilar characters, between a philosopher and a common street porter, for example, seems to arise not so much from nature, as from habit, custom, and education" (Smith, *Wealth,* 15).

29. Kettler, *Ferguson,* 279, 285–86.

30. Ferguson, *Principles,* 2: 371.

31. Ibid., 2: 422. That Ferguson disliked chattel slavery was more evident elsewhere (2: 462): whatever the extent they arrested inequalities among their "citizens," societies that introduced slave labor "trespassed most egregiously on the equality of mankind."

32. O. A. Brownson, "The Labor Question," [ca. 1870], in Microfilm Edition of the Orestes Augustus Brownson Papers, reel 16, "Unplaced Drafts," University of Notre Dame Archives.

33. The Scottish School of commonsense realism, above all, perhaps, the works of Dugald Stewart, exercised a powerful hold within antebellum intellectual circles, and Ferguson's contributions, along with those of Adam Smith, almost certainly owed some of their continuing impact to their reinterpretation at the hands of the influential Stewart; see Theodore Dwight Bozeman, *Protestants in an Age of Science: The Baconian Ideal and Antebellum American Religious Thought* (Chapel Hill: University of North Carolina Press, 1977), xii, 4–8, 21–23; and Dugald Stewart, *Lectures on Political Economy,* ed. William Hamilton (Edinburgh: T. C. Clark, 1877), 1: 317–31. Yet Ferguson also exercised his influence directly in certain highly educated circles. He was, for example, a favorite author of William Ellery Channing, a circumstance that very likely explains why Channing expressed such similar views regarding the intellectually stultifying effect of manufacturing division of labor; see David P.

Edgell, *William Ellery Channing: An Intellectual Portrait* (Boston: Beacon Press, 1955), 12, 156; and Daniel Walker Howe, *The Unitarian Conscience: Harvard Moral Philosophy, 1805–1861* (Middletown: Wesleyan University Press, 1988), 123, 186, 247.

34. "Some Thoughts on Social Philosophy, *Southern Literary Messenger* 22 (Apr. 1856): 314, 315.

35. Ibid., 313–16.

36. Jesse Foot, *A Defence of the Planters in the West-Indies; Comprised in Four Arguments* (London: J. Debrett, 1792), 27 (italics in original).

37. "Some Thoughts on Social Philosophy," 313–16.

38. Ferguson, *Principles*, 1: 243, 2: 472–73; Kettler, *Ferguson*, 314.

39. Edward Brown, *Notes on the Origin and Necessity of Slavery* (Charleston: A. E. Miller, 1826), 18–25, 33. See also Reverend H. E. [Henry Evans] Holder, *A Short Essay on the Subject of Negro Slavery, with a Particular Reference to the Island of Barbadoes* (London: Charles Dilly, 1788), 7, 11.

40. A particularly forceful statement of the view that a conservative—and national—"system of values" was at the core of Southern proslavery ideology is Larry Tise, "Proslavery Ideology: A Social and Intellectual History of the Defense of Slavery in America, 1790–1840," (Ph.D. diss., University of North Carolina at Chapel Hill, 1975), xviii, 6–7, 668, subsequently revised and published as *Proslavery: A History of the Defense of Slavery in America, 1701–1840* (Athens: University of Georgia Press, 1987), and I should like to give Tise's study some attention here. Although it does not formally cover the late antebellum period, Tise makes clear his belief that even during this time, if not so consistently, "anti-abolitionist and latter-day Federalist perspectives," rather than racist, sectionalist, or other kinds of arguments, continued to dominate Southern proslavery writing.

In maintaining that the Federalist vision of a society of harmonious, distinctly separated ranks and orders formed the core of a "national" proslavery ideology, Tise appears to have rejected—perhaps more decisively than any other recent historian—the presumption that such a Federalist vision came to be supplanted by a competitive, individualist ethos in the mid-nineteenth-century North especially. Tise, to be sure, does not explicitly mention attitudes toward competition and economic individualism in his invocation of a pervasive "conservative republican" proslavery ideology. But it seems fairly safe to infer that the "'conservative majority'" of the American body politic conceptualized by Tise, a majority that allegedly gave its support to a stable society "of ranks and orders" (*Proslavery*, 358), would have been commensurately hostile to the values of self-seeking economic individualism and competition.

There are a number of weaknesses in this provocative interpretation of proslavery thought. Tise may have extrapolated too much from the remarks of the proslavery clergymen and writers who are the focus of his study—individuals with views similar to those of the cleric Samuel Nott whom I discuss in chapter 7. The Southern slaveholders examined in James Oakes, *The Ruling Race: A History of American Slaveholders* (New York: Alfred A. Knopf, 1982) quite clearly, in contrast, evidenced and articulated individualist, competitive market values. In seeming to deny or discount the premium that antebellum American rhetoric placed upon competition and its salutary features, Tise would appear to have neglected a fundamental dimension of the American mentality. It may be that this dimension can be worked into Tise's proslavery model. Certainly Thomas Malthus and other of the classical economists believed that free market competitive processes generated their own kind of hierarchy, stratification, and order. It is not, however, without significance that most of these writers, far from being "proslavery," were discernibly antagonistic to the peculiar institution. Tise exaggerates the ideological support that chattel slavery actively drew upon in antebellum America in part because he ignores the ascendancy of doctrines and values that extolled open competition and repudiated drags on the operation of the free market. See also the text later in this chapter.

Of course, the classic argument that Southern proslavery ideology was conservative and hierarchical in nature *and,* to this extent as well, a defining feature of a distinctive Southern sectionalist "world view," was made by Eugene D. Genovese; see especially *The World the Slaveholders Made* (New York: Random House, 1969). Genovese argues for the representativeness of George Fitzhugh's ideas and values among Southern slaveholders and intellectuals.

41. Fitzhugh's defense of slavery on the basis of class rather than race, and his position that slavery represented the only means of placing "labor and capital in harmonious or friendly relations," achieved its most sustained expression in *Cannibals All! or, Slaves without Masters,* ed. C. Vann Woodward (Cambridge: Belknap Press of Harvard University Press, 1960 [1857]), 31, and *Sociology for the South, or the Failure of Free Society* (Richmond, Va.: A. Morris, 1854), 302–6. Yet in these works and perhaps still more explicitly in his various essays in the 1850s, Fitzhugh indicated that it was above all the white laboring poor in the more densely populated portions of Europe whom he believed would benefit from formal enslavement. Fitzhugh was, at least at times, a good deal more sanguine about the future status of white laborers in the Northern states, in fact making about as forceful a case as one can find for the persistence of American exceptionalism (but see note 43 in this chapter). In the same article in which he claimed that "we must defend the principle of slavery as part of the constitution of man's nature," rather than as part of a narrow, racial distinction, Fitzhugh expressed doubt that the white laboring population in the free states would ever need to be enslaved: "The North is now doing well. Her poor are not the slaves of capital, and never will be whilst there are vacant lands in the North. . . . Very large countries, such as America, are not likely to be overstocked with inhabitants." Competition was, Fitzhugh noted, if anything even "fiercer" in the North than in Europe given the absence from the former of landed, titled, and clerical orders that resisted the "money-getting" spirit and were the "natural friends of the poor." But notwithstanding this deficiency, the ability of Northern laborers to escape to the West and avoid overrunning the means of subsistence would, in Fitzhugh's view, indefinitely insulate them from the worst effects of "free competition" (George Fitzhugh, "Southern Thought," *De Bow's Review* 23 [Oct. 1857]: 345–48). On this last argument of Fitzhugh's, see also Louis Hartz, *The Liberal Tradition in America* (New York: Harcourt, Brace and World, 1955), 195–96. Important discussions of Fitzhugh's thought, aside from that of Hartz and Genovese, *World,* include C. Vann Woodward, *American Counterpoint: Slavery and Racism in the North-South Dialogue* (Boston: Little, Brown and Company, 1964), 107–39; Harvey Wish, *George Fitzhugh, Propagandist of the Old South* (Baton Rouge: Louisiana State University Press, 1943). For George Frederick Holmes's views on slavery, which can be found in many of his contributions to the major antebellum Southern journals, see particularly his "Slavery and Freedom," *Southern Quarterly Review* 29 (Apr. 1856): 62–95; and "Observations on a Passage in the Politics of Aristotle Relative to Slavery," *Southern Literary Messenger* 16 (Apr. 1850): 193–205. A good study of Holmes's views is Neal C. Gillespie, *The Collapse of Orthodoxy: The Intellectual Ordeal of George Frederick Holmes* (Charlottesville: University of Virginia Press, 1972), 178–97.

42. Studies which, while differing in some matters of interpretation and emphasis, generally agree that egalitarian white racist impulses in the South played a

more critical part in the defense of Southern slavery than did conservative and hierarchical values, include George M. Fredrickson, *The Black Image in the White Mind: The Debate on Afro-American Character and Destiny, 1817–1914* (Middletown: Wesleyan University Press, 1987 [1971]), 60–69; Oakes, *The Ruling Race*, 134–38, 192–97, 208–17; Woodward, *American Counterpoint*, 110–11; Carl N. Degler, *Place over Time: The Continuity of Southern Distinctiveness* (Baton Rouge: Louisiana State University Press, 1977), 70–95; William Barney, *The Road to Secession: A New Perspective on the Old South* (New York: Praeger, 1972), xiii, 41, 64–71; Lacey K. Ford, Jr., *Origins of Southern Radicalism: The South Carolina Upcountry, 1800–1860* (New York: Oxford University Press, 1988), 352–64. See also George M. Fredrickson, *The Arrogance of Race: Historical Perspectives on Slavery, Racism, and Social Inequality* (Middletown: Wesleyan University Press, 1988), 135–41.

43. Particularly notable is Fitzhugh's "The Black and White Races of Men," *De Bow's Review* 30 (Apr. 1861): 446–56, where Fitzhugh gives a glowing review to one of the period's supreme expressions of the "Herrenvolk democracy" defense of Southern slavery, Dr. John Van Evrie's *"Negroes and Negro Slavery": The First an Inferior Race; The Latter Its Normal Condition* (New York: Van Evrie, Horton, and Company, 1861). As George M. Fredrickson has noted, Fitzhugh's conversion to the racist defense of chattel slavery is conspicuous in this essay: "No one," Fitzhugh remarked, "would reduce white men to the condition of negro slavery, for the fact that such social condition is fitted for negroes, is abundant evidence that it is unfitted for whites" (454). Yet even here one can overstate the change in Fitzhugh's position. Just as he had never before been hostile to the notion that blacks were among the most suitable candidates for slavery, so he also retained elements of his hierarchical class defense of chattel servitude. He claimed that Van Evrie was wrong to hold that members of the white race were exactly equal, and he maintained, as he had always done, that white wives, children, apprentices, and other elements of society justifiably occupied positions of subordination that were in fact "slavery," of "different forms and degrees" (455). And Fitzhugh continued to harp on the failure of the "experiment" of "free society," as evidenced by the suffering of its poor and the intensity of its class conflict and to suggest that *some* form of institutionalized subordination might be the most natural and humane fate for those white laborers most ravaged by the effects of free competition and capitalist exploitation. If anything, Fitzhugh seemed even more disposed than he had once been to make something of the argument that, because they lacked the stewardship of a landed aristocracy and established clergy, white laborers in the North were now in even greater need of "protection" from the competitive struggle than their counterparts in Europe; no mention here is made of the redemptive effects of the Western "safety valve"; Fredrickson, *Black Image*, 59–60, 69–70.

44. Eric Foner, "The Causes of the American Civil War: Recent Interpretations and New Directions," *Civil War History* 20 (Sept. 1974): 204–5. Major party ideologies accepted, often extolled, economic competition in broadly distinctive fashions. Democratic party spokesmen, particularly during the Jacksonian period, generally stressed how economic competition was insufficiently open and equitable even in America; they were more disposed to regard class conflict, or at least conflict between the privileged and the disadvantaged, as a basic, possibly inevitable attendant of economic competition. Whig and later Republican spokesmen, especially those within the party mainstream, relied more on the mythology of American, and increasingly Northern, exceptionalism; they emphasized the degree to which competition and economic striving in the free states generated tremendous economic growth and expansion of opportunity, how the competitive process there remained

uniquely free of genuine class conflict and unequal chances, how it worked for the mutual benefit and harmony of all industrious and deserving parties involved, including capitalists and laborers.

45. Theodore Dwight Bozeman has suggested something of the impact that the atomistic implications of Newtonian physics had within antebellum religious and intellectual circles, many members of which were simultaneously drawn to the materialist and empiricist approach of the "Baconian method" to all forms of knowledge. George Frederick Holmes, for example, was among those who embraced the Baconian faith in matter and the "laws" of nature as the basis of knowledge, and he in fact demonstrated the influence of these doctrines when he offered what was very close to a standard Northern Whig rationale for the deprivations experienced by members of the working classes: "The son of the pauper often becomes the millionaire. . . . On the other hand, the beggar whom we meet to-day in the streets, . . . may be the son or grandson of some haughty aristocrat or wealthy sybarite, . . . An incessant stream of ascending and descending atoms links together the extremes of human fortune, and in some degree apportions to idleness and industry its just penalty or reward. Thus, even should it happen—which is very far from being uniformly the case—that the labouring classes are hopelessly in want, and irretrievably miserable, there is such a continuous change of the constituent atoms, as to entail neither hereditary iniquity on the lot, nor hereditary misery on the members who form those classes" ([Holmes], "The History of the Working Classes," *Southern Literary Messenger* 21 [Apr. 1855]: 195).

But Holmes's case, one must add, also illustrates the dangers of oversimplifying the ways in which Newtonian atomism and Baconian induction may have manifested themselves in the social thought of the period. One of the period's foremost critics of the creeds of individualism and laissez faire, Holmes could hardly be said to have held a view of the good society as one of competing and colliding individuals, free of the hierarchical restraints and organic ties provided by established institutions. Society's atoms were not, in his view, equally free and capable of autonomy; Bozeman, *Protestants,* 88–91; Gillespie, *Collapse,* 49–50, 163–66.

46. Sidney George Fisher, as we shall see later in this chapter, was a proclaimed opponent of competitive ideology insofar as it promoted individual selfishness and the "cash-nexus" connection between individuals. But he was typical of many Northerners in invoking notions of racial inferiority to explain why the socially subordinate position of Northern blacks confirmed rather than denied the openness of the competitive struggle in the free states. Economic opportunities existed in the North for the black man, Fisher maintained, but they were "beyond his talents" (Sidney George Fisher, *The Laws of Race, as Connected with Slavery* [Philadelphia: Willis P. Hazard, 1860], 22). Rather than acknowledging that the economic discrimination and educational and legal disabilities suffered by Northern blacks compromised the purity or integrity of the competitive struggle, Fisher and like-minded individuals suggested that the existence of such disabilities merely certified the innate inferiority of the black man and that their removal would in no significant measure alter the outcome of the competitive struggle, which included not merely the inferior and subordinate social position of blacks in the free states, but very conceivably their ultimate extinction in this region as well. Blacks would lose out in the competition wherever climate was not so tropical as to prevent the white man from obtaining a "footing as a laborer" (Fisher, *Laws,* 25, 38, 46). For a discussion of Fisher's views which places them in the context of the racist tendencies of mid-nineteenth-century Northern thought, see Fredrickson, *Black Image,* 142–47, 154–59, 182. For other discussions of competitive ideology in the antebellum free states

which emphasize its capacity to accommodate race and ethnic prejudices, see Ronald T. Takaki, *Iron Cages: Race and Culture in Nineteenth-Century America* (New York: Alfred A. Knopf, 1979), 110–17, 126–27; Phyllis F. Field, *The Politics of Race in New York: The Struggle for Black Suffrage in the Civil War Era* (Ithaca: Cornell University Press, 1982), 31; Douglas T. Miller, "Immigration and Social Stratification in Pre-Civil War New York," *New York History* 49 (Apr. 1968): 157–68; Robert H. Wiebe, *The Opening of American Society: From the Adoption of the Constitution to the Eve of Disunion* (New York: Alfred A. Knopf, 1984), 321–52; George M. Fredrickson, *White Supremacy: A Comparative Study in American and South African History* (Oxford: Oxford University Press, 1981), 151–62; and Fredrickson, *Arrogance*, 201–5.

47. "Some Thoughts on Social Philosophy," 314–15.

48. See here Peter Kolchin, *Unfree Labor: American Slavery and Russian Serfdom* (Cambridge: Belknap Press of Harvard University Press, 1987), 172–73, 185.

49. See also Fredrickson, *Arrogance*, 23–24.

50. Senator James Henry Hammond of South Carolina, *Congressional Globe*, 35th Cong., 1st sess., Mar. 4, 1858, 962. There is an interesting sidelight to Hammond's remarks, one that throws into relief the multidimensional character of antebellum "free labor" concepts. A few days after delivering his "mud-sill" speech, and under attack from Republican Senator Hannibal Hamlin of Maine for maligning the character of the North's manual laborers, Hammond expressed his wish to slightly amend his remarks; with the insertion of the term *hireling*, one of his statements would now stand as "Your whole class of hireling manual laborers and 'operatives,' as you call them, are essentially slaves" (exchange between Senators Hamlin and Hammond, *Congressional Globe*, 35th Cong., 1st sess., Mar. 9, 1858, 1005–1006). Hammond did not go into his reasons for desiring this addition, and Senator Hamlin, for one, remained unappeased, discounting the significance of this "modification." And, after all, Hamlin was correct in his judgment insofar as there were precious few Northern "operatives" who were not "hirelings" and who would, in consequence of Hammond's qualification, now enjoy exclusion from his disparaging characterization. Yet there remains some significance in the fact that Hammond took pains to correct his original remarks. He chose to soften his criticisms of Northern labor by tapping into a common sentiment, one that was shared even by some of the radical labor reformers of his day and that owed a good deal to traditional republican notions that extolled economic independence as the seat of personal liberty and virtue. Poverty and hard physical work were not themselves necessarily degrading and servile, Hammond was now suggesting, but rather chiefly became so when part of a specific wage or "hireling" economic status, one in which the laborer lacked work autonomy and was slavishly dependent upon the will of another who owned and controlled the means of production. For a recent study that emphasizes the Jeffersonian republican antecedents of Hammond's "mud-sill" doctrine but largely ignores the other intellectual influences which shaped it (see the text below for these), see Ford, *Origins of Southern Radicalism*, 351–64.

51. James Henry Hammond to Thomas Clarkson, Jan. 28, 1845, in *Selections from the Letters and Speeches of the Hon. James H. Hammond, of South Carolina* (New York: John F. Trow and Company, 1866), 120.

52. Although professing, moreover, no desire to defend the international slave trade, and acknowledging up to a certain point such "barbarities" as its substantial basis in the kidnapping of African blacks, Hammond nonetheless informed Clarkson that the efforts to end the traffic were both futile and in a fundamental sense, misdirected. For whatever the circumstances by which African blacks crossed the

Atlantic, Hammond claimed, "though they might be perpetual bondsmen, still they would emerge from darkness to light—from barbarism into civilization—from idolatry to Christianity—in short from death to life" (Ibid., 115–18). See also David Brion Davis, *Slavery and Human Progress* (New York: Oxford University Press, 1984), 240–41.

53. Richard Harvey, "English Poverty, 1675–1725," *Historian* 41 (May 1979): 500–11; Jenifer Hart, "Religion and Social Control in the Mid-Nineteenth Century," in A. P. Donajgrodzki, ed., *Social Control in Nineteenth Century Britain* (London: Croom Helm, 1977), 113–15; John K. Alexander, "Philadelphia's 'Other Half': Attitudes toward Poverty and the Meaning of Poverty in Philadelphia, 1760–1800" (Ph.D. diss., University of Chicago, 1973), 245–50.

54. Stephen Charnocke, *A Treatise of Divine Providence* (1680), 88–89, quoted in Harvey, "English Poverty," 510; Orestes Brownson, "Liberal Studies," an oration before the Philomathian Society of Mount Saint Mary's College, Maryland, June 29, 1853, in Henry F. Brownson, ed., *The Works of Orestes A. Brownson* (New York: Ams Press, 1966 [1885]), 19: 432–38.

55. Hammond, letter to Clarkson, *Selections from Letters and Speeches*, 104.

56. A pioneering study in this area is Joseph J. Spengler, "Population Theory in the Antebellum South," *Journal of Southern History* 12 (Aug. 1936): 362–88. See also Eugene D. Genovese and Elizabeth Fox-Genovese, "Slavery, Economic Development, and the Law: The Dilemma of the Southern Political Economists, 1800–1860," *Washington and Lee Law Review* 41 (Winter 1984): 22–26.

57. "British Reviewers and the United States," *Southern Quarterly Review* 13 (Jan. 1848): 200.

58. "A South Carolinean" [William Gilmore Simms], "Miss Martineau on Slavery," *Southern Literary Messenger* 3 (Nov. 1837): 653 (italics in original). Van Evrie repeated this theme ad nauseam in the New York city newspaper he edited and eventually copublished; see, for example, " 'Slave' and 'Slavery,' " *Weekly Day Book,* Aug. 29, 1857; "What Is Slavery?" *New-York Day Book,* Aug. 3, 1858, and "What Is Negro Slavery? Or Where Is the Negro a Slave?" *New-York Day Book,* Sept. 2, 1858. See also Henry Hughes, *Treatise on Sociology: Theoretical and Practical* (Philadelphia: published for the author, 1854), 82–83. For a discussion of the word games played by these and other proslavery writers, see Kenneth S. Greenberg, *Masters and Statesmen: The Political Culture of American Slavery* (Baltimore: Johns Hopkins University Press, 1985), 100–102.

59. William J. Grayson, "Civilization in Its Relations to Property and Social Life," *De Bow's Review* 26 (Feb.1859): 161–62.

60. For a good account of the depression of the late 1850s, which had less impact on the South, and its effect upon sectional ideologies, see James L. Huston, *The Panic of 1857 and the Coming of the Civil War* (Baton Rouge: Louisiana State University Press, 1987).

61. Bernard Mandeville, *The Fable of the Bees: Or, Private Vices, Publick Benefits. With an Essay on Charity Schools and a Search into the Nature of Society,* with a commentary by F. B. Kaye, 6th ed. [1732] (Oxford: Clarendon Press, 1957 [1924]), 1: 194, 286–87, 311.

62. See, for example, Carlyle's attack on the modern ethos of "Cash Payment" as "the universal sole nexus of man to man," in his 1839 work, *Chartism,* repr. in Carlyle, *English and Other Critical Essays* (London: Dent, 1967), 2: 203. In one of his letters to Clarkson, Hammond suggested that the abolitionist slighting of the food and other nonpecuniary compensations made to Southern slaves, and the fallacious superiority abolitionists attached to the money wages earned by free laborers, was

itself an indication of their obeisance to this pervasive and corrupting "cash-nexus": "It is the prevailing vice and error of the age, and one from which the Abolitionists, with all their saintly pretensions, are far from being free, to bring everything to the standard of money. You make gold and silver the great test of happiness. The American slave must be wretched indeed, because he is not compensated for his services in cash. It is altogether praiseworthy to pay the laborer a shilling a day and let him starve on it. To supply all his wants abundantly, and at all times, yet withhold from him money, is among 'the most reprobated crimes'" (Hammond to Thomas Clarkson, Mar. 24, 1845, *Selections from Letters and Speeches*, 185). The historian James Oakes sees things rather differently. He makes the interesting argument that, notwithstanding the disdain expressed by Hammond and other proslavery ideologues for cash compensation, their very insistence that Southern slaves did enjoy substantial material rewards, or "creature comforts," most clearly revealed proslavery values; that insistence evidenced the great degree to which slavery's defenders in fact embraced, rather than dissented from, reigning consumption-oriented, liberalist capitalist values; Oakes, *Slavery and Freedom: An Interpretation of the Old South* (New York: Alfred A. Knopf, 1990), 178.

63. See the discussion of the remarks of Senator Richard M. Johnson and Congressman William Brown, both of Kentucky, in Glover Moore, *The Missouri Controversy, 1819–1821* (Lexington: University of Kentucky Press, 1953), 311–12. Two works of special importance in the Southern "mud-sill" tradition, and ones almost certainly read by Hammond, were Thomas Dew, "Review of the Debate in the Virginia Legislature of 1831 and 1832" (1832), and Chancellor William Harper, "Memoir on Slavery" (1837), both of which were reprinted, along with Hammond's own letters to Thomas Clarkson, in *The Pro-Slavery Argument* (Charleston: Walker, Richards and Company, 1852). See also Larry Robert Morrison, "The Proslavery Argument in the Early Republic, 1790–1830" (Ph.D. diss., University of Virginia, 1975), 231–35. As the case with the entire body of his writing, Richard Hofstadter's few remarks on the implications of the "mud-sill" doctrine are most provocative: "If there must always be a submerged and exploited class at the base of society, and if the Southern slaves, as such a class, were better off than Northern free workers, and if slavery was the safest and most durable base on which to found political institutions, then there seemed to be no logical reason why all workers, white or black, industrial or agrarian, should not be slave rather than free" (Richard Hofstadter, *The American Political Tradition* [New York: Alfred A. Knopf, 1948], 90). Provocative as it is, however, Hofstadter's conclusion seems to slight the fact that Hammond and many of his southern colleagues were making distinctions among types of manual labor; only certain kinds, in their view, were servile and debasing enough to be suited only for slaves, just as a worker's economic deprivation was not by itself a necessarily sufficient justification for his enslavement. Of relevance here is Hammond's qualification of his original remarks regarding the "mud-sill" class, discussed in note 50 in this chapter.

We might also note that to the extent that the "mud-sill" doctrine did imply the formal enslavement of white workers, it hardly, on the basis of its own logic, offered a full solution to their misery. Enslavement, that is to say, would at best relieve their poverty and economic insecurity, although even this seems questionable, since as some proslavery critics of Fitzhugh's arguments noted, there was no reason to suppose that the enslavement of white workers in already densely populated "free societies" would relieve the pressure of their numbers upon the means of subsistence (see "The Problem of Free Society," *Southern Literary Messenger*, 27 [July, 1858]: 12–13). But even beyond this, the enslavement of northern and European white "mud-sills" would have no effect upon the intrinsically "alienating" character of their menial work, work which they would continue to be forced to perform so long as there was an inadequate supply of inferior blacks available to do it. Eugene D. Genovese touches on this point in his discussion of Fitzhugh (Genovese, *World,* 159–160). There was, to be sure, one obvious solution here: continuing infusions of new black slaves through the re-opening of the African slave trade. Had the "Slave Power" possessed the capability, as well as the desire, to actually bring about the formal enslavement of workers in the northern states—an admittedly most implausible scenario—then the re-opening of the slave trade would hardly have proved beyond its powers.

64. S. D. Moore, "The Irrepressible Conflict and Impending Crisis," *De Bow's Review* 28 (May 1860): 531–32.

65. Among other studies that stress this point are Michael P. Johnson, *Toward a Patriarchal Republic: The Secession of Georgia* (Baton Rouge: Louisiana State University Press, 1977), 90; and Laurence Shore, *Southern Capitalists: The Ideological Leadership of an Elite, 1832–1885* (Chapel Hill: University of North Carolina Press, 1986), 21, 41, 45.

66. "Henry Clay's Sympathy with Labor," *Emancipator,* repr. in *Herald of Freedom,* Mar. 1, 1844; (italics and accentuation possibly inserted by the *Herald of Freedom*). Clay was to shortly become the Whig's Presidential candidate. Evidently believing that he represented hardly more of a bargain for Northern workingmen than whomever the Democrats might offer, the *Emancipator* article sought to demolish Clay's reputation as a slaveholding Southerner who held relatively "liberal" views on the subjects of slavery and labor. The article went to considerable pains to establish that Clay actually made these remarks; one of the leading authorities on the Missouri Compromise, Glover Moore, does not appear to contest this point; Moore, *Missouri Controversy,* 43–44. A valuable recent study explores the ideological and practical considerations that led many "political" abolitionists of the kind who issued the *Emancipator* to in fact prefer Democratic over Whig party candidates in the 1840s: Hugh Davis, *Joshua Leavitt: Evangelical Abolitionist* (Baton Rouge: Louisiana State University Press, 1990), 171–75, 218–20, 266–67. For a good discussion of the variety of positions toward slavery embraced by Clay over his long career, see Thomas Brown, *Politics and Statesmanship: Essays on the American Whig Party* (New York: Columbia University Press, 1985), 137–47.

67. Jonathan A. Glickstein, "'Poverty Is Not Slavery:' American Abolitionists and the Competitive Labor Market," in Lewis Perry and Michael Fellman, eds., *Antislavery Reconsidered: New Perspectives on the Abolitionists* (Baton Rouge: Louisiana State University Press, 1979), 211–12.

68. Senator Albert Gallatin Brown of Mississippi, *Congressional Globe. Appendix,* 33d Cong., 1st sess., Feb. 24, 1854, 230.

69. See, for example, Robert R. Russel, "The General Effects of Slavery upon Southern Economic Progress," *Journal of Southern History* 4 (Feb. 1938): 37–41. Yet in claiming here that "There was no stigma attached in the South in slavery days to the performance of manual labor, as distinguished from menial" labor, Russel appeared to depart from a view expressed in an earlier work; see Robert Royal Russel, *Economic Aspects of Southern Sectionalism 1840–1861* (New York: Russell and Russell, 1960 [1924]), 51. See also G. W. Dyer, *Democracy in the South Before the Civil War* (Nashville: Publishing House of the Methodist Episcopal Church, South, 1905), 45, 48–49.

70. James Byrne Ranck, *Albert Gallatin Brown: Radical Southern Nationalist* (New York: D. Appleton-Century Company, 1937), ix, 25, 59–60, 127, 135, 135n.

71. Senator David S. Reid of North Carolina, *Congressional Globe,* pt. 2 and *Appendix,* 35th Cong., 2d sess., Feb. 25, 1859, 1339. Without changing Reid's meaning, I have somewhat altered the order in which he made the above remarks.

72. "The species of labor which requires mere . . . physical strength, directed by the most ordinary human intelligence, is, with us, rarely performed by the white man" (Congressman Miles Taylor of Louisiana, *Congressional Globe. Appendix,* 35th Cong., 1st sess., Mar. 29, 1858, 233).

73. John W. Blassingame, among others, has reminded us that slaves may have employed rather different criteria in their allocation of status; Blassingame, "Status and Social Structure in the Slave Community: Evidence from New Sources," in Harry P. Owens, ed., *Perspectives and Irony in American Slavery* (Jackson: University Press of Mississippi, 1976), 137–51. See also Eugene D. Genovese, *Roll, Jordan, Roll: The World the Slaves Made* (New York: Pantheon Books, 1974), 327–65; C. W. Harper, "House Servants and Field Hands: Fragmentation in the Antebellum Slave Community," *North Carolina Historical Review* 55 (Jan. 1978): 42–59; Michael P. Johnson, "Work, Culture, and the Slave Community: Slave Occupations in the Cotton Belt in 1860," *Labor History* 27 (Summer 1986): 325–50.

74. Robert William Fogel and Stanley L. Engerman, *Time on the Cross: The Economics of American Negro Slavery* (Boston: Little, Brown and Company, 1974), 1: 38–43; James E. Newton and Ronald L. Lewis, eds., *The Other Slaves: Mechanics, Artisans and Craftsmen* (Boston: G. K. Hall and Company, 1978), 175–239; Genovese, *Roll,* 388–98; Larry Koger, *Black Slaveowners: Free Black Slave Masters in South Carolina, 1790–1860* (Jefferson, N.C.: McFarland and Company, 1985), 37–38, 140–57; Ira Berlin, *Slaves without Masters: The Free Negro in the Antebellum South* (New York: Random House, 1974), 218–19, 221, 236–39.

75. "The Prospects and Policy of the South, as They Appear to the Eyes of a Planter," *Southern Quarterly Review* 26 (Oct. 1854): 447; R. W. Habersham, "The Port Royal Enterprise," *De Bow's Review* 25 (Oct. 1858): 412–13; For a study which claims that such proslavery writers were getting their wish, that for a variety of reasons "slaves were systematically stripped of their crafts" in the late antebellum period, and that by 1860 they exceeded 8 percent of the skilled work force only in Charleston, South Carolina, see Ira Berlin and Herbert G. Gutman, "Natives and Immigrants, Free Men and Slaves: Urban Workingmen in the Antebellum American South," *American Historical Review* 85 (Dec. 1983): 1185, 1192. Gutman devoted much of a separate work to arguing that Fogel and Engerman greatly inflated the number of skilled slaves in the antebellum period; Herbert G. Gutman, "Time on the Cross. The Economics of American Negro Slavery: The World Two Cliometricians Made. A Review Essay of F + E = T/C," *Journal of Negro History* 60 (Jan. 1975): 111–35.

76. See Barney, *Road to Secession,* 38–48, for a discussion of this subject, including evidence of Southern fears that slaveholders who persisted in training and hiring their slaves out in competition with white mechanics were fomenting class hostility and thereby endangering the peculiar institution itself.

77. A perhaps not inconsiderable amount of crossing over, however, was engaged in by poor Irish immigrant whites, who in filling domestic service, day labor, and other "menial" positions in Southern cities, supplanted free blacks just as they had been doing to a much greater degree and more conspicuous effect in the North, where most of the immigrants settled; see Berlin and Gutman, "Natives and Immigrants," 1187; and Berlin, *Slaves without Masters,* 231–32. Berlin also observes that some of the urban "nigger work" dominated by Southern free blacks—barbering and several of the other service trades with low capital requirements—de-

manded a considerable level of expertise, and that this circumstance, and not merely the stigma attaching to such "nigger work," erected a barrier against invasion from "the lowest portion of the white work force, who might not have cared what they were called so long as they could enjoy steady employment" (Berlin, *Slaves without Masters*, 237–38). As a number of scholars have noted, too, some of the most hazardous labor on plantations, "menial" or otherwise, was also performed by Irishmen, a reflection of planters' desire to avoid risking the lives of their slave property; see Broadus Mitchell, *Frederick Law Olmsted: A Critic of the Old South*: (New York: Russell and Russell, 1968 [1924]), 150; Harriet E. Amos, *Cotton City: Urban Development in Antebellum Mobile* (Tuscaloosa: University of Alabama Press, 1985), 91–98, 177; Earl F. Niehaus, *The Irish in New Orleans 1800–1860* (Baton Rouge: Louisiana State University Press, 1965), 48–53; Fred Siegel, "Artisans and Immigrants in the Politics of Late Antebellum Georgia," *Civil War History* 27 (Sept. 1981): 221–30.

78. New York Association for Improving the Condition of the Poor, *Seventeenth Annual Report* (1860), 50–51; Samuel Halliday, *The Lost and Found; or Life among the Poor* (New York: Blakeman and Mason, 1859), 185–87; "The Free Blacks in the United States—Probable Re-enactment of the Slavery Laws in the Northern States," *New York Herald*, July 21, 1859; Leon F. Litwack, *North of Slavery: The Negro in the Free States, 1790–1860* (Chicago: University of Chicago Press, 1961), 162–66; Leonard P. Curry, *The Free Black in Urban America, 1800–1850: The Shadow of a Dream* (Chicago: University of Chicago Press, 1981), 20.

79. See, for example, the remarks of the Kentucky slaveholder and state senator, Robert Wickliffe, quoted in "The Working Man's Friend," written by "The Blacksmith's Son," in the *Philanthropist* (New Richmond, Ohio), June 9, 1841; and also "The Destinies of the South," *Southern Quarterly Review* 23 (Jan. 1853): 197–98. See also the chapter on "The Wild Irish," in Niehaus, *Irish in New Orleans*, 59–70.

80. Congressman Miles Taylor of Louisiana, *Congressional Globe. Appendix*, 35th Cong., 1st sess., Mar. 29, 1858, 232.

81. Ibid., 231–33.

82. Congressman Thomas H. Bayly of Virginia, 30th Cong., 1st sess., *Congressional Globe. Appendix* 30th Cong., 1st sess., May 16, 1848, 579. Ira Berlin's finding, referred to in note 77 in this chapter, that poor white Irish were also performing a significant amount of the domestic service and other "menial" labor in Southern cities suggests, therefore, that Bayly and others who advanced this kind of proslavery argument were either genuinely unaware of this circumstance or were conveniently ignoring it or unconsciously screening it out in their desire to draw a sharp distinction between Northern and Southern society.

83. Matthew Lyon, speech of Apr. 18, 1810, in House of Representatives, quoted in Rowland Berthoff, "Independence and Attachment, Virtue and Interest: From Republican Citizen to Free Enterpriser, 1787–1837," in Richard L. Bushman et al., eds., *Uprooted Americans: Essays to Honor Oscar Handlin* (Boston: Little, Brown and Company, 1979), 115.

84. Extracts from Thomas P. Jones, *An Address on the Progress of Manufactures and Internal Improvements in the United States, and Particularly on the Advantages to Be Derived from the Employment of Slaves in the Manufacturing of Cotton and Other Goods*, delivered at the Franklin Institute, Nov. 6, 1827, excerpted in *American Farmer* (Baltimore) 9, ser. 1 (Nov. 30, 1827): 291. See also Tise, *Proslavery*, 67–68.

85. Continuation of Jones's *Address*, in *American Farmer* 9 (Dec. 7, 1827): 298

86. Ibid., 293–98.

87. "Remark on Cotton Bagging and Cordage and the Value of Slaves as

Operatives in Cotton Factories," a letter to the editor, *American Farmer* 9 (Sept. 28, 1827): 225. See also Robert S. Starobin, *Industrial Slavery in the Old South* (New York: Oxford University Press, 1970), 193–96.

88. [Nathaniel A. Ware], *Notes on Political Economy; as Applicable to the United States. By a Southern Planter* (New York: Augustus M. Kelley, 1967 [1844]), 30–32. Like partisans of other causes, Ware was capable of embracing quite contradictory arguments in pushing for Southern industrialization. After disparaging factory work by arguing that black slaves were ideally suited for it, he noted later in his book that the example of the Lowell girls proved that manufacturing need not be a degrading employment (95–96).

89. Quoted in "Negro Population," *The Industrial Resources, etc. of the Southern and Western States* (New Orleans: Office of *De Bow's Review*, 1852), 2: 339.

90. L. W. Spratt, *Report of the Slave Trade Committee, Southern Commercial Convention, Montgomery, Alabama, May, 1858,* quoted in Starobin, *Industrial Slavery,* 225.

91. Congressman Bayly of Virginia, *Congressional Globe. Appendix* 29th Cong., 2d sess., Feb. 11, 1847, 347.

92. Robert Dale Owen, *Labor: Its History and Prospects,* address delivered before the Young Men's Mercantile Library Association of Cincinnati, Feb. 1, 1848, repr. in *Herald of Truth* 3 (Mar. 1848): 201–2.

93. "Aims and Tendencies of Black Republicanism—No. 5," *Daily Pennsylvanian* (Philadelphia), Sept. 1, 1856.

94. George Henry Evans, "To The Working Women of New York," New York *Working Man's Advocate,* Mar. 15, 1845.

95. Senator Robert Hayne of South Carolina once remarked that "slaves are too improvident, too incapable of that minute, constant, delicate attention, and that persevering industry which are essential to manufacturing establishments" (Hayne quoted by Senator George M. Dallas of Pennsylvania in the Senate, Feb. 27, 1832, and repr. in Horace Greeley, *The American Conflict* [Hartford: O. D. Case and Company, 1864], 1: 92). Interesting as Hayne's point of view was, not the least because it again illustrates the disagreement and confusion over the qualities demanded by factory work, it seems not to have been widely held in the South and was hardly foremost among the objections raised there to attempts to industrialize slave labor. More typical was the position of James Henry Hammond. Like the writers discussed in the text above, Hammond never doubted that black slaves were equal to the demands of factory labor, but from his earlier support for the employment of slaves in Southern industries, he nonetheless moved to the position that underemployed poor whites should be used instead, and that the industrialization of slave labor would prove much the greater threat to Southern institutions. Bringing together poor white laborers in cotton mills, Hammond reasoned, would not endanger slavery but strengthen it, clarifying and fortifying for those laborers their economic ties with slave-grown cotton. But employing slaves in mills would have the opposite, subversive effect, just as antislavery writers in fact so often claimed. Possibly seeking to remind his audience of the artisanal backgrounds of a disproportionate number of slave insurrectionists, Hammond noted that "whenever a slave is made a mechanic, he is more than half freed, and soon becomes, as we too well know, and all history attests, with rare exceptions, the most corrupt and turbulent of his class." Even beyond considerations of security, Hammond observed that the removal of large numbers of slaves from cotton cultivation would entail serious economic drawbacks, above all an increase in the cost of labor and of goods in the South ("Progress of Southern Industry. Governor Hammond's Address before the

South Carolina Institute, 1850," in De Bow, ed., *Industrial Resources*, 3: 34–35). Indeed, it may well have been the growing demand for field hands in the late antebellum period, together with the fact that the price of slaves was rising even faster than the price of cotton, which proved the most decisive impediment of all to the increased industrialization of slave labor; see Starobin, *Industrial Slavery*, 206–9; and Fogel and Engerman, *Time*, 1: 60–61, 89–94, 102, 105.

96. Although also recognizing the advantages of employing slaves in Southern factories, the industrialist William Gregg was perhaps the region's preeminent advocate of recruiting poor whites instead, a preference he implemented in his cotton mill at Graniteville, South Carolina; see Gregg's *Essays on Domestic Industry: Or, an Enquiry into the Expediency of Establishing Cotton Manufactures in South-Carolina* (Charleston: Burgess and James, 1845), 21–22; and Starobin, *Industrial Slavery*, 206–7. See also Eugene D. Genovese, *The Political Economy of Slavery: Studies in the Economy and Society of the Slave South* (New York: Random House, 1965), 180–239; and Barney, *Road to Secession*, 38–48. For a proslavery view that took a strong stand against industrialization and urbanization in the South, see Elwood Fisher, *Lecture on the North and the South*, delivered before the Young Men's Mercantile Library Association of Cincinnati, Jan. 16, 1849, (Charleston: A. J. Burke, 1849). See also Peter J. Parrish, *Slavery: History and Historians* (New York: Harper and Row, 1989), 101–5.

97. See, for example, William A. Alcott, *The Young Wife, or Duties of Women in the Marriage Relation* (Boston: George W. Light, 1837), 153–69, 178–88. As suggested by the title of his book, Alcott's egalitarian position that the presence of domestic servants increased social distinctions and corrupted republican simplicity and unpretentiousness in American society was tied to his commitment to the restrictive notion of woman's "true sphere." Were servants somehow done away with, Alcott argued, the wives and daughters of the middle classes would return to their proper province and take up the cooking and other household tasks of which they were at present both ignorant and undeservedly contemptuous. In some measure Alcott's brand of egalitarianism could be said to merely signify a preference for one form of social subordination over another; although some scholars have emphasized the more egalitarian, proto-feminist aspects of a separate spheres formulation such as Alcott's—the degree to which it represented an advance over the competing upper- and middle-class ideal of the privileged woman as a physically useless, morally ineffectual "ornament." Antiservant sentiments such as Alcott's may have also drawn from a contemporary anxiety that some middle-class households were being overextended financially by mounting expenses, that such households could ill afford to indulge the ambitious social tastes and the "genteel" disdain for domestic tasks exhibited by their female members; see Elizabeth Blackmar, *Manhattan for Rent, 1785–1850* (Ithaca: Cornell University Press, 1989), 143.

98. Horace Greeley, "Life—the Ideal and the Actual," *Nineteenth Century: A Quarterly Miscellany* 2 (1848): 22–23.

99. For a recent discussion of eighteenth-century French thinkers who broke—up to a point—with the traditional "aristocratic" view held by that country's educated classes, a view that regarded the laboring population and its labors as irredeemably base and mean, see Harvey Chisick, *The Limits of Reform in the Enlightenment: Attitudes toward the Education of the Lower Classes in Eighteenth-Century France* (Princeton: Princeton University Press, 1981), 72–73. Extending Chisick's argument, Cynthia J. Koepp has argued in a provocative recent essay that in its hopes of "rationalizing" the mechanic arts for the benefit of an entrepreneurial bourgeoisie, the great and representative project of the Enlightenment, the *En-*

cyclopédie, retained and recast in more subtle form a good deal of the traditional, Old Regime disdain and distaste for manual work and workers; Cynthia J. Koepp, "The Alphabetical Order: Work in Diderot's *Encyclopédie,*" in Steven Laurence Kaplan and Cynthia J. Koepp, eds., *Work in France: Representations, Meaning, Organization, and Practice* (Ithaca: Cornell University Press, 1986), 229–57. Koepp seeks to severely qualify that older interpretation of the Enlightenment which inferred from the *philosophes'* attack on aristocratic idleness and ennui a more unabashedly "optimistic," nonrepressive view of manual labor; for a very able statement of this older interpretation, see Clinio Luigi Duetti, "Work Noble and Ignoble: An Introduction to the Modern Idea of Work" (Ph.D. diss., University of Wisconsin, 1954), 63, 162–75. See also Cissie Fairchilds, *Domestic Enemies: Servants and Their Masters in Old Regime France* (Baltimore: Johns Hopkins University Press, 1984), 102–4, 144–50; William H. Sewell, Jr., *Work and Revolution in France: The Language of Labor from the Old Regime to 1848* (Cambridge, Eng.: Cambridge University Press, 1980), 22–25.

100. Matthew Estes, *A Defence of Negro Slavery, as It Exists in the United States* (Montgomery: Press of the *Alabama Journal,* 1846), 170–71.

101. Ibid., 169, 170.

102. George S. Sawyer, *Southern Institutes; or, an Inquiry into the Origin and Early Prevalence of Slavery and the Slave Trade* (New York: Negro Universities Press, 1969 [1858]), 378–79.

103. *An Appeal to the Good Sense of a Great People* (Charleston, S.C.: Dan J. Dowling, 1835), 10. This pamphlet may have been written by the Reverend Henry Wilford Smith. William H. Pease and Jane H. Pease similarly quote from it as illustrative of the stigma attaching to manual labor in antebellum Charleston; see their *The Web of Progress: Private Values and Public Styles in Boston and Charleston, 1828–1843* (New York: Oxford University Press, 1985), 115–16.

104. Vicomte François René Chateaubriand, quoted in A. P. Upshur, "Domestic Slavery," *Southern Literary Messenger* 5 (Oct. 1839): 681.

105. Ibid., 679–81.

106. Jan Lewis suggests, however, that while many members of the Virginia gentry of the early nineteenth century did indeed disparage the active pursuit of wealth through commerce and business, they regarded the learned professions of law and medicine as hardly less virtuous and dignified than full-time planting; Jan Lewis, *The Pursuit of Happiness: Family and Values in Jefferson's Virginia* (Cambridge, Eng.: Cambridge University Press, 1983), 114. For a short but provocative discussion of how the Southern planter gentry of the eighteenth century may have in fact more fully realized than Northern merchants and lawyers did the classical republican ideal that Upshur was invoking—an ideal that extolled independence from the marketplace and a corresponding "disinterested gentlemanly leadership," see Gordon S. Wood, "Interests and Disinterestedness in the Making of the Constitution," in Richard Beeman et al, eds., *Beyond Confederation: Origins of the Constitution and American National Identity* (Chapel Hill: University of North Carolina Press, 1987), 87–90. Yet as Lewis has noted of pre-Revolutionary Virginia, "the great southern fortunes were built not by tobacco planting alone, but by commerce, land speculation, and money lending as well. The most successful planters in the eighteenth century were entrepreneurs and merchants in addition." Despite such activities, Lewis suggests, these planters indeed cherished classical republican, Old World gentlemanly ideals, and sought to leave their offspring with the landed estates that would secure their independence from the market; Lewis, *Pursuit of Happiness,* 112–13.

107. Horace Greeley, "The Discipline and Duties of the Scholar," *Nineteenth Century: A Quarterly Miscellany,* 4 (1849): 26.

108. Ibid., 31. And the increased education and intellectual independence of white male members of the laboring population, Greeley unshakedly assumed, would mean fewer votes for the Democrats. Like other Whigs and later Republicans, Greeley periodically expressed the belief that it was ignorance and a consequent susceptibility to the demagoguery of Democratic political leaders which explained why poor whites of the South, like those in New York City, repeatedly turned on election day to the party of oppression, vice, and destructive economic policies.

109. The Muscular Christianity movement, which was brought to America from England in the late 1850s, also had strong affinities with the earlier manual labor school movement; see the brief discussion in Martin L. Adelman, *A Sporting Time: New York City and the Rise of Modern Athletics, 1820–1870* (Urbana: University of Illinois Press, 1986), 279–80.

110. Rev. Charles Elliott, D. D., *Sinfulness of American Slavery,* ed. Rev. B. F. Tefft, D. D. (New York: Negro Universities Press, 1968 [1850]), 2: 120.

111. Elliott, for one, did make some limited concessions to Upshur's position; Ibid., 120–21. Mid-nineteenth-century American conceptualizations of a landed "gentry" reflected a variety of ideological needs and accordingly exhibited many variations and subtleties that space limitations prevent us from exploring further here. One of the key studies in this area remains William R. Taylor, *Cavalier and Yankee: The Old South and American National Character* (New York: Harper and Row, 1957), although an important recent contribution, one which treats the generally positive concepts of the gentry held by Boston's business and professional elite, is Tamara Plakins Thornton, *Cultivating Gentlemen: The Meaning of Country Life among the Boston Elite 1785–1860* (New Haven: Yale University Press, 1989).

112. Harriet Martineau, *Society in America* (New York: AMS Press, 1966 [1837]), 2: 300–304. At her most utopian in these pages, Martineau regarded Northern free society, in the various ways it dignified manual labor, as most closely approximating that truly ideal "organisation of society," one whose employments universally combined significant proportions of handwork and headwork.

113. See, for example, the speech of Massachusetts Senator Henry Wilson, *Congressional Globe. Appendix,* 35th Cong., 1st sess., Mar. 20, 1858, 171–72. It was Frederick Law Olmsted who perhaps entered into the most extensive comparisons of the intellectual and moral character—the "breeding" or lack thereof—of different social classes in the North and the South; his most distinctive contribution to the attack on Upshur's position was the thesis that a slavery-induced, prolonged "frontier condition" in the South—its pervasive intellectual and material primitiveness—had produced a class of wealthy, leisured planters distinguished not only by their indolence and lack of accomplishment, but by the very vulgarity and ostentatiousness that "our satirists and dramatists" were fond of ascribing to the parvenus of the North; Olmsted, *The Cotton Kingdom. A Traveller's Observations on Cotton and Slavery in the American Slave States,* two volumes in one, ed. Arthur M. Schlesinger (New York: Alfred A. Knopf, 1970 [1861]), 553–63. see also Robert Lewis, "Frontier and Civilization in the Thought of Frederick Law Olmsted," *American Quarterly* 20 (Fall 1977): 389–91. For a scholar's restatement of the educational and other pervasive intellectual deficiencies of the antebellum South, see Drew Gilpin Faust, *A Sacred Circle: The Dilemma of the Intellectual in the Old South, 1840–1860* (Baltimore: John Hopkins University Press, 1977), 7–10. Southern men of letters—"intellectuals" who themselves in many cases were neither large planters nor men of considerable wealth in any form—frequently echoed Upshur and defended slavery for the degree of *learned leisure* (Nathaniel Beverley Tucker's term)

it permitted a slaveholding elite. Yet Tucker, George Frederick Holmes, and other such individuals nonetheless remained all too aware, Faust indicates, of how far short Southern culture fell of classical Greece; they were deeply troubled by the extent to which the South's intellectual deficiencies signalled an indifference to the life of the mind, to mental activity engaged in *for its own sake,* as distinct from its more superficial application in the pursuit of wealth. Needless to say, contemporary Northern intellectuals might easily share a similar sense of "alienation" from the culture of their own region (see, for example, William Charvat, *The Profession of Authorship in America, 1800–1870. The Papers of William Charvat,* ed. Matthew J. Bruccoli [Columbus: Ohio State University Press, 1968] 61–66); the obvious difference was that the latters' alienation did not generally lead them to unite "the cause of the intellect with the proslavery movement" (Faust, *Sacred,* 7, 115, 122). For an attempt to rehabilitate the intellectual reputation of the antebellum South, see Michael O'Brien, *Rethinking the South: Essays in Intellectual History* (Baltimore: Johns Hopkins University Press, 1988), 33–37.

114. Greeley, "Discipline and Duties of Scholar," 29.

115. In May 1856, Democratic Congressman Philemon T. Herbert, a native of Alabama although a resident and Representative from California, fatally shot an Irish-born waiter in a Washington hotel. Herbert's acquittal in July was taken in antislavery quarters as yet another proof of the strength of the Slave Power in America, just as the shooting itself was interpreted as evidence of the Power's elitism and arrogance; see untitled editorial in *New-York Daily Tribune,* July 29, 1856. See also William E. Gienapp, "The Republican Party and the Slave Power," in Robert H. Abzug and Stephen E. Maizlish, eds., *New Perspectives on Race and Slavery in America: Essays in Honor of Kenneth M. Stampp* (Lexington: University Press of Kentucky, 1986), 51–78.

116. *The New "Democratic" Doctrine. Slavery Not to be Confined to the Negro Race, But to be Made the Universal Condition of the Laboring Classes of Society* (n.p. 1856), 1, 2.

117. Ibid., 1.

118. Ibid., 2.

119. Possibly, too, such writings expressed more strictly internal considerations. It is interesting to speculate how Alabama's own nonslaveholding farmers and mechanics might have reacted to the elitist sentiments expressed in the Muscogee *Herald* editorial quoted above. Alabama was distinguished by a particularly strong Jacksonian populist tradition that often put the planter "aristocracy" on the defensive. Conceivably, then, the editorial was at least in part a reflection of that defensiveness, rather than something triggered exclusively by the challenge from outside the South emanating from Northern free society; see J. Mills Thornton III, *Politics and Power in a Slave Society. Alabama, 1800–1860* (Baton Rouge: Louisiana State University Press, 1978), xix–xx, 206–8, 444–47.

120. See, in particular, "H" [George Frederick Holmes], "Greeley on Reforms," *Southern Literary Messenger* 17 (May 1851): 266–67, 273, 278–79.

121. "British Reviewers and the United States," *Southern Quarterly Review* 13 (Jan. 1848): 202.

122. Ibid.

123. Rufus William Bailey, *The Family Preacher; or, Domestic Duties Illustrated and Enforced, in Eight Discourses* (New York: J. S. Taylor, 1837), 154. Bailey, moreover, argued that even the lowly sphere occupied by Southern slaves might accommodate their "moral and intellectual elevation," and he would eventually see blacks all over the world, under the tutelage of slavery or otherwise, "placed on a footing with other enlightened and industrious poor." Not among slavery's most zealous

defenders, Bailey would have countenanced least of all those racist defenses of slavery that categorized blacks as a separate species from the ruling race and insisted that slavery should exist as long as there were blacks. Yet as a fervent opponent of immediate abolition and the disruptive tactics of Northern abolitionists, Bailey subscribed to the notion that the enslavement of African blacks by rulers in their native land was in itself conclusive proof that they were not ready for freedom: "Do you suppose it would be possible to make slaves of any portion of our American Anglo-Saxon race? No. And why? Because *the race* is elevated above it, and know how to assert and estimate their liberty" (Rufus William Bailey, *The Issue, Presented in a Series of Letters on Slavery* [New York: John S. Taylor, 1837], 8, 106, 107 [italics in original]).

124. Thomas R. Dew, "An Address on the Influence of the Federative Republican System of Government upon Literature and the Development of Character," *Southern Literary Messenger* 2 (Mar. 1836): 277–78.

125. Ibid., 278n.

126. [Holmes], "History of Working Classes," 194–95.

127. [Holmes], "Greeley on Reforms," 277–78; [Holmes], "History of Working Classes,' 194, 200–202. See also Carl F. Kaestle, "Elite Attitudes toward Mass Schooling," in Lawrence Stone, ed., *Schooling and Society: Studies in the History of Education* (Baltimore: Johns Hopkins University Press, 1976), 186; Carl F. Kaestle, *Pillars of the Republic: Common Schools and American Society, 1780–1860* (New York: Hill and Wang, 1983), 206–7.

128. James C. Bruce, *Popular Knowledge the Necessity of Popular Government*, an address delivered before the Denville, Virginia Lyceum, Mar. 18, 1853, in *Southern Literary Messenger* 19 (May 1853): 296–300.

129. [Holmes], "History of Working Classes," 194; William J. Grayson, "The Hireling and the Slave," *De Bow's Review* 19 (July 1855): 213; Biblical adage from Mark 14: 7.

130. "P," "The Free School System in South-Carolina," *Southern Quarterly Review* 16 (Oct. 1849): 35–36. The sentiments expressed by "P" would seem clearly to exemplify that tradition of thought, particularly pronounced in the South, which broke with the American exceptionalist themes briefly discussed in chapter 1 and lend support to conclusions such as that made by Michael P. Johnson: "Elements of free labor [i.e., upward mobility] ideology were not completely absent in the South. But as a rule, poor white men in the South were less frequently encouraged to strive upward than to look downward and to be thankful they were not black" (Johnson, "Wealth and Class in Charleston in 1860," in Walter J. Fraser, Jr., and Winfred B. Moore, Jr., eds., *From the Old South to the New: Essays on the Transitional South* [Westport: Greenwood Press, 1981], 70).

131. "Justice," letter to the *Morning Courier and New York Enquirer,* Mar. 22, 1847, quoted in Mario Emilio Cosenza, *The Establishment of the College of the City of New York as the Free Academy in 1847* (New York: Associate Alumni of the College of the City of New York, 1925), 85–87; see also 61–66, 72–79. Cosenza believes that "Justice" was a Trustee or an officer, or at the very least, a devoted alumnus of New York University, and that however genuine his conservative sentiments may have been, his opposition to the establishment of the Free Academy was in part engendered by a sense of institutional rivalry; Cosenza, *Establishment,* 60; see note 10 and the accompanying text in this chapter for similar views regarding the social division of labor, although "Justice" quite likely surpassed the commentators noted there in the elitism of his position with respect to educational opportunity.

132. "P," "Free School System," 32–33.

133. Kaestle, "Elite Attitudes," 186; Kaestle, *Pillars,* 205–7, 214–16; Rush Welter, *Popular Education and Democratic Thought in America* (New York: Columbia University Press, 1962), 131–35.

134. "Instruction in Schools and Colleges," *Southern Quarterly Review* 22 (Oct. 1852): 466–68.

135. "The [British] charity schools came into being chiefly, although by no means exclusively, . . . to condition the children [of the poor] for their primary duty in life as hewers of wood and drawers of water" (M. G. Jones, *The Charity School Movement: A Study of Eighteenth Century Puritanism in Action* [London: Frank Cass and Company, 1964 {1938}], 4–5). Apart even from conservative Southern support for the limited education of white laborers, Southern advocacy of greater religious instruction for slaves offered its own strong parallels with the aims of the British charity school movement, as described by Jones. One proslavery writer maintained that "the proper inculcation of the duties made obligatory upon the slave by the New Testament enforced by the solemn sanctions of religion, will prove a better safe-guard to the South against the machinations of the abolitionists, than walls of granite and arsenals crowded with military stores." In support of his argument for the religious instruction of slaves, the writer quoted arguments made by the noted English Baptist minister, Robert Hall, in behalf of the education of the British laboring poor; "Slavery as a Moral Relation," *Southern Literary Messenger* 17 (July 1851): 404).

136. William H. Trescot, "The States' Duties in Regard to Popular Education," *De Bow's Review* 20 (Feb. 1856): 147. Orestes Brownson had made a similar argument, as discussed in chapter 3, in suggesting that educating individuals who were entrapped in factory work was doing them a disservice. But the conclusion Brownson drew was a very different one from Trescot's: the need for a radical change in existing social arrangements and material conditions that would somehow establish a universal "moral and physical equality," thereby placing all those who were educated in a position to develop and use their talents and capabilities to the fullest (Brownson, "Brook Farm," 486).

137. Trescot, "States' Duties," 147.

138. Ibid., 150.

139. Ibid., 148–49.

140. Ibid., 148–50.

141. Presently controversial among sociologists and economists, however, is the question of whether the more intractable problem facing urban ghetto residents is not their lack of "middle-class aspirations," but rather their objective inability to realize such aspirations.

142. See note 29, chapter 4, for citations of some contemporary discussion of dual labor market processes. As David Gordon has observed, dual labor market theory developed largely out of a sense of dissatisfaction with the ways in which older economic models explained present-day poverty and job instability, particularly as they affected working-class women and minority groups; dual labor market theory "has never been intended to explain very much about labor market behavior in other historic periods" (David M. Gordon, *Theories of Poverty and Underemployment: Orthodox, Radical, and Dual Labor Market Perspectives* [Lexington, Mass.: D. C. Heath and Company, 1972], 38–39, 43). Yet women's wage work in mid-nineteenth-century America, if not before this period as well, intimately reflected the segmentation of economic life that confined women to the worst-paying trades, and the subject of antebellum "woman's work," like that of "nigger work" and "work for Paddy," would seem to be a fruitful one for the

application of dual labor market theory. That antebellum labor market segmentation in the Northern states was based at least as much on policies of outright educational and economic discrimination against women and blacks as upon more subtle socialization processes, is not itself of especial relevance to the applicability of dual labor market theory. Of more decisive significance is the fact that the kinds of jobs in which women and various ethnic and minority groups clustered—manufacturing outwork, low-grade service work and day labor—would seem to have met all of the criteria for what are now defined as dual labor market jobs, including what is possibly the single most important criterion of all: a lack of connection to avenues of advancement of any sort. As Gordon has defined this feature, with reference to work in the modern urban ghetto, "No matter how long an employee worked at these jobs or how clearly he demonstrated his diligence or skill, there seemed to be no fixed channels through which he could rise above his original job" (Gordon, *Theories,* 45). At the same time, the barriers dividing antebellum primary from secondary labor markets, such as these barriers existed, were in some respects clearly not impregnable. As chapter 2, together with a growing number of labor histories, indicates, skilled craft labor had much less success than business employments and the "learned professions" in averting "degrading" competition from low-status workers. Much to the dismay of many skilled artisans in established trades, mercantile and industrial capitalism gave freer rein to the competitive ethos in the antebellum North by virtue of its tendency to erode and homogenize skill requirements in the manufacturing sector of the economy—to break down barriers that protected and insulated skilled artisans from the competitive threat posed by untrained immigrants, females, and children. One useful exploratory essay on the application of dual labor market theory to labor markets of the past is Alice Kessler-Harris, "Women's Wage Work as Myth and History," *Labor History* 19 (Spring 1978): 287–307.

143. Trescot, "States' Duties," 150.

144. This certainly seemed to be Timothy Walker's expectation; see chapter 2. This is not to insist that expectations or hopes of upward mobility for the sons of manual laborers played no part whatever in efforts to broaden their educational opportunities; see the discussion in chapter 7 of the campaign to establish the New York Free Academy.

145. "Among the thousands of deformed and brutalized women in the mines of Cornwall," Van Evrie wrote, "there is not a single one who, had she been exchanged with the Duchess of Sutherland while in her cradle, but would exhibit all the personal graces and mental capacities, if not the 'philanthropy,' of that interesting person" (Van Evrie, *"Negroes and Negro Slavery,"* 25). For Van Evrie, all class differences among members of the white race were "artificial"; the only natural, and therefore legitimate, divisions were racial ones; see also "Antislaveryism Is Monarchism," *Weekly Day Book,* Feb. 9, 1861.

146. For two of Lincoln's variations on this theme, see his *Annual Message to Congress,* Dec. 3, 1861, in Lincoln, *The Collected Works of Abraham Lincoln,* ed. Roy P. Basler (New Brunswick: Rutgers University Press, 1953), 5: 52–53; and "Fragment on Free Labor," [Sept. 17, 1859?], *Works,* 3: 462–63; and for observations on the compatibility between manual labor and intellectual refinement which are directly at variance with views expressed by Fisher in the text below, see Lincoln, *Address before the Wisconsin State Agricultural Society,* Milwaukee, Wisconsin, Sept. 30, 1859, *Works,* 3: 479–80.

147. "S" [Sidney George Fisher], "Domestic Servants," *North American and United States Gazette* (Philadelphia), May 23, 1857.

148. Ibid.; [Sidney George Fisher], "Uncle Tom's Cabin: The Possible Amelioration of Slavery," *North American Review* 77 (Oct. 1853): 480; Fisher, *Laws of Race,* 10, 37, 46, 59, 67–68; Blaine Edward McKinley, "'Stranger in the Gates': Employer Reactions toward Domestic Servants in America 1825–1875" (Ph.D. diss., Michigan State University, 1969), 148, 160–62, 282–83.

149. [Fisher], "Domestic Servants." See also "'The Hearthstone Club,' A Move in the Right Direction," *Hearthstone, a Magazine of Domestic Economy, etc* 1 (Jan. 1859): 25; Mrs. E. F. Ellet, "To the Lady President of the 'The Hearthstone Club,'" *Hearthstone* 1 (June 1859): 121–22, 127; Daniel E. Sutherland, "Americans and Their Servants, 1800–1920; Being an Inquiry into the Origins and Progress of the American Servant Problems" (Ph.D. diss., Wayne State University, 1976), 99; McKinley, "'Stranger,'" 148, 282–83. Fisher's preferences were not, however, universally shared by writers taken up with "the servant problem." A belief that Irish immigrant girls, if not downright intellectually inferior, nonetheless possessed a less demanding and less "independent" nature than native-born girls, led others to prefer them as servants. Two decades after Fisher expressed his opinion, Virginia Townsend was writing, "Could you put just the same sort of drudgery . . . on your countrywoman's shoulders? In short, give precisely the same orders to, and make the same demands on her that you do on your Irish girls?" (Virginia Townsend, "Our Irish Girls" [1875], quoted in McKinley, "'Stranger,'" 176, 177). Then, too, as McKinley remarks in these pages, because menial housework was often considered the only legitimate means of livelihood for which Irish girls were fit, there was some concern that they would turn increasingly to crime and vice if American girls with their "more acute perceptions" supplanted them in domestic service.

150. Society for the Encouragement of Faithful Domestic Servants in New York, *First Annual Report* (1826), 15; Ellet ,"To the Lady President," 121–22; Sutherland, "Americans and Their Servants," 776; McKinley, "'Stranger,'" 117–18.

151. [Fisher], "Domestic Servants."

152. Fisher, *Laws of Race,* 37.

153. [Fisher], "Domestic Servants"; [Fisher], "Uncle Tom's Cabin," 473–92.

154. Society for the Encouragement of Faithful Domestic Servants in New York, *First Annual Report,* 15.

155. William Heighton to George Henry Evans, Oct. 20, 1845, repr. as "True and Sham Reformers," New York *Working Man's Advocate,* Nov. 8, 1845; Alcott, *Young Wife,* 37, 153–169, 182.

156. [Fisher], "Domestic Servants."

157. Ibid.

158. Ibid.

159. The category of "intellectual labor" was an amorphous one because it could embrace, as it did for Fisher, for some of the Southern proslavery writers, and for other upholders of an aristocratic ethos, individuals who possessed the wealth and social position to give all of their time, if they were so inclined, to matters of intellectual and cultural refinement. Yet for American and British articulators of bourgeois competitive values, many of whom were acutely hostile to the pretensions of a leisured aristocracy of any kind, the category of intellectual labor preeminently consisted of those professional men and entrepreneurs who actively pursued a "productive" occupation (see, for example, Harold Perkin, *Origins of Modern English Society* [London: Ark Paperbacks, 1985 {1969}], 214–28]). We might add that in spite of all their criticism of the economically exploitative practices of capitalists in "free societies," Southern proslavery writers who upheld the aristocratic ethos did not, unlike many of the radical labor reformers, at bottom deny the role of capitalist

"mental labor" as a legitimate social function—hence their periodic appeals to Northern capitalists to join Southern planters in a conservative alliance that would preserve existing social arrangements against any threat of disruption, whether that disruption originated among elements of the laboring population itself, or whether it was instead the product of abolitionism or of one of the other radical, "anti-property" "isms" that afflicted the North; see Hofstadter's discussion of John C. Calhoun, in *American Political Tradition*, 82–84.

160. Testimony and related material appearing in the various Parliamentary "blue books," which investigated these and other laboring conditions and employments, are conveniently reprinted in E. Royston Pike, ed., *Hard Times: Human Documents of the Industrial Revolution* (New York: Frederick A. Praeger, 1966).

161. *Richmond Enquirer*, quoted in "Extension of Slavery over the North," *North American and United States Gazette*, Sept. 22, 1856. For an earlier statement by a Southerner, though one that was not made in defense of chattel slavery, that "Men, in a civilised country, never expose their wives and children to labour above their force or sex, as long as their own labour can protect them from it," see Thomas Jefferson, "Notes of a Tour into the Southern Parts of France, & c." (Mar. 3, 1787), in Julian P. Boyd, ed., *The Papers of Thomas Jefferson* (Princeton: Princeton University Press, 1955), 11: 415.

162. Jacqueline Jones, *Labor of Love, Labor of Sorrow: Black Women, Work, and the Family from Slavery to the Present* (New York: Basic Books, 1985), 13–21; Deborah Gray White, *Ar'n't I a Woman? Female Slaves in the Plantation South* (New York: W. W. Norton and Company, 1985), 69, 121; Elizabeth Fox-Genovese, *Within the Plantation Household: Black and White Women of the Old South* (Chapel Hill: University of North Carolina Press, 1988), 193, 296, 316; Carole Shammas, "Black Women's Work and the Evolution of Plantation Society in Virginia," *Labor History* 26 (Winter 1985): 5–22.

163. Although I do not recall ever having encountered such a situation in the literature, it is also quite possible that proslavery critics of "free societies," had they been specifically confronted with the use of female slaves in heavy labor as reproof of their criticisms, would have retorted that black females, by virtue of their racial characteristics, were simply exempt from the norms that defined proper and humane employment for the more "delicate" sex. For suggestive comments on how the "profound racism" of Southern slaveholders helped in general to legitimate their economic self-interest and exploitative practices, see Michael Tadman, *Speculators and Slaves: Masters, Traders, and Slaves in the Old South* (Madison: University of Wisconsin Press, 1989), 179–80.

164. John Humphrey Noyes, *History of American Socialisms* (New York: Hillary House, 1961 [1870]), 635.

165. [John L. O'Sullivan] "White Slavery," *Democratic Review* 11 (Sept. 1842): 260–72. O'Sullivan was the current editor of the *Democratic Review*. In attributing this unsigned essay to him, I am following Thomas R. Hietala, *Manifest Design: Anxious Aggrandizement in Late Jacksonian America* (Ithaca: Cornell University Press, 1985), 98–99.

166. Ibid., 268, 270.

167. William H. Rideing, writing for the journal *St. Nicholas* in 1875 and quoted in George Lewis Phillips, *American Chimney Sweeps: An Historical Account of a Once Important Trade* (Trenton, N.J.: Past Times Press, 1957), 62.

168. Jay Monaghan, *The Great Rascal: The Life and Adventures of Ned Buntline* (Boston: Little, Brown, and Company, 1952), 164–65. Monaghan's source for Judson's remarks is a pamphlet written by Thomas V. Paterson, *The Extraordinary*

Public Proceedings of E. C. Z. Judson (1849), which I have been unable to locate. Judson's anti-British and anti-Irish nativist activities included a leading role in New York's Astor Place riots and participation in various nativist political organization; he is in fact credited with introducing the term *Know-Nothing* into the American political lexicon; Monaghan, *Great Rascal*, 162, 171–81, 208–9. Insofar as Monaghan accurately reported Judson's remarks, they were in a sense atypical of nativist literature. The dominant economic theme of that literature hardly disparaged Irish and other immigrants by pointing out that they were suited only for the worst, most traditionally unskilled and menial kinds of work. Far more dominant, as many historians have documented, was fear and resentment, especially on the part of American-born skilled workers themselves, that immigrants contributed to the breakdown of the apprenticeship system, provided capital with its labor supply for the "debased" sections of the trades, and otherwise intruded upon and demeaned the occupations and living standards of *skilled* labor. And as our discussion of Sidney George Fisher's views of domestic service illustrated, middle-class as well as working-class individuals no less nativist than Judson believed that the Irish were degrading the traditionally unskilled as well as the skilled occupations and that the more unskilled employments, too, should be filled by native-born Americans, both to improve the quality of goods and services these employments provided and to reduce unemployment among the native-born poor. See the brief discussion of nativism in chapter 4, including the citations in note 30 especially; see also, however, the subtle, revisionist interpretation of economic nativism among American workers in David Montgomery, "The Shuttle and the Cross: Weavers and Artisans in the Kensington Riots of 1844," *Journal of Social History* 5 (Summer 1972): 411–39.

169. As discussed in note 6 in this chapter, John Ashworth gives much attention to this dimension of Democratic thought in his study, *"Agrarians" and "Aristocrats,"* 1, 25–34, 53, 66–68, 120.

170. The "false pride" of females who resisted going into service and who "chose" to remain in more precarious and poorly recompensed trades was a significant theme in mid-nineteenth-century literature. In adding to the criticism of this attitude of "false pride," Frederick Law Olmsted implicitly slighted the historical, genuinely ancient, roots of the stigma attaching to domestic "hewers of wood and drawers of water"; he maintained that the stubbornness of "some badly-educated American women who choose to die as seamstresses, rather than to live as cooks or chamber-maids," was attributable to the influence of contemporary writers who had managed to unjustifiably stigmatize domestic service by creating a "false parallel" between it and Southern slavery (Frederick Law Olmsted, *A Journey in the Seaboard Slave States. In the Years 1853–1854. With Remarks on Their Economy* [New York: G. P. Putnam's Sons, 1904 {1856}], 1: 224–25). That the aversion to domestic service had more deep-seated causes, ones which lay both in the legacy of disdain attaching to it and in the contemporary terms of employment under which servants were actually required to labor, is suggested both by recent scholarly studies and by contemporary transatlantic evidence; some fifteen years after Olmsted's writing, in the second edition of his book on prostitution, William Acton lamented the "foolish pride" of poor girls who chose to starve as London milliners rather than learn household work and enter service; William Acton, *Prostitution, Considered in Its Moral, Social, and Sanitary Aspects: In London and Other Large Cities and Garrison Towns, with Proposals for the Control and Prevention of Its Attendant Evils,* 2d ed. (London: John Churchill, 1870), 295. See also Sutherland, "Americans and Their Servants," 2–13. For other American criticisms of the "false pride" of native-born sewing girls, see "Something about the Economy of Living—Household Words,"

North American and United States Gazette, Oct. 28, 1846; the remarks of the *New-York Express,* quoted first in an untitled editorial, *New-York Daily Tribune,* Dec. 26, 1846, and again later in "Women's Rights and Duties—False Pride and Household Service," *New-York Daily Tribune,* Oct. 28, 1851; and finally the criticisms made by the New York *Commercial Advertiser* and quoted in an untitled editorial, *New-York Daily Tribune,* Apr. 9, 1857. On these occasions Greeley's *Tribune* came to the defense of the occupational preferences of native-born working-class girls to the extent that it maintained that their aversion to domestic service, with all its current "indignities and trials" (Apr. 9, 1857, editorial), was indeed entirely justified. Greeley veered between agreeing at times with other labor reformers that service for others was by definition repulsive and servile work (Dec. 26, 1846, editorial), and arguing at other times that native-born girls legitimately objected not to service work itself "but only to the brand of inferiority—of degradation—which accompanies it" (Oct. 28, 1851, editorial). The latter position, at least, carried the implication that public and employer attitudes which sanctioned onerous and degrading working conditions for domestic servants might be appreciably modified.

171. The criticisms of the "false pride" of seamstresses cited in the previous note were not so simplistic that they entirely ignored the fact that many of the urban seamstresses were elderly widows, wives of disabled husbands, or mothers of young or sick children for whom domestic service was manifestly not a viable option. Such criticisms ordinarily directed their attack against young, single women who, they assumed, must clearly have had more latitude in abandoning sewing and other of the worst-paid work for the more lucrative domain of domestic service. One wonders how much the middle-class critics could really have known of the constraints and pressures under which even single sewing girls, immigrant as well as native-born, may have operated—the circumstances that may have further reduced their occupational options from an already limited number and that may have induced them to reject domestic service for reasons other than "false pride." Some scholars, moreover, have questioned whether the urban demand for domestic servants was as great as many contemporaries apparently believed it to be; see Carol Groneman Pernicone, "The 'Bloody Ould Sixth': A Social Analysis of a New-York City Working-Class Community in the Mid-Nineteenth Century" (Ph.D. diss., University of Rochester, 1973), 145. And in the absence of complete and reliable census data, other scholars have even questioned whether young single women *ever* constituted a significant proportion of the overcrowded ranks of American urban seamstresses during this period. To the extent that their representation was indeed always limited, their departure from the field would not have gone very far in meeting the problem of exploitation and overwork in the sewing trades; see Ava Baron and Susan E. Klepp." 'If I Didn't Have My Sewing Machine . . .': Women and Sewing Machine Technology," in Joan M. Jensen and Sue Davidson, eds., *A Needle, a Bobbin, a Strike* (Philadelphia: Temple University Press, 1984), 23. For the view that during the first half of the nineteenth century, sewing and other forms of outwork in New York City did come to draw increasingly upon the growing pool of single women, see Christine Stansell, *City of Women: Sex and Class in New York, 1789–1860* (New York: Alfred A. Knopf, 1986), 115, 263. See also Mary Christine Stansell, "Women of the Laboring Poor in New York City, 1820–1860" (Ph.D. diss., Yale University, 1979), 68–82. For testimony on the domestic circumstances of some of Boston's needlewomen, see *Report for the First Anniversary of the Needle Woman's Friend Society* (Boston: Eastburn's Press, 1848), 3–7; *Report for the Sixth Anniversary* (1853), 4–5; *Report for the Tenth Anniversary* (1857), 4.

172. Virginia Penny, *Think and Act: A Series of Articles Pertaining to Men and*

Women, Work and Wages (Philadelphia: Claxton, Remsen, and Haffelfinger, 1869), 25, 296.

173. Henry Colman, *Address* before the Agricultural and Mechanic Institute of New London and Windham Counties, Connecticut, Oct. 8, 1840 (Boston: Dutton and Wentworth, 1840), 32. Colman was one of the elite "gentleman farmers" of Massachusetts profiled in Thornton, *Cultivating Gentlemen,* 131–32, 192–94. For a more detailed discussion of his investigation of agricultural conditions and enterprise in both Massachusetts and Europe, see Donald B. Marti, "The Reverend Henry Colman's Agricultural Ministry," *Agricultural Ministry* 51 (July 1977): 524–39.

174. Henry Colman, *European Agriculture and Rural Economy,* 4th ed. (Boston: Phillips, Sampson and Company, 1851), 1: 62–65, 141–42, 344.

175. Ibid., 1: 53–54.

176. Ibid., 1: 55–57.

177. Eric Richards, for example, has observed that in "the underdeveloped, labour-intensive, agriculture-dominated economy of Britain before about 1750, . . . it was normal for women to share in the heaviest manual work," seemingly without complaint or special remark from anyone (Eric Richards, "Women in the British Economy since 1700: An Interpretation," *History* 59 [Oct. 1975]: 339). See also Harriet Bradley, *Men's Work, Women's Work: A Sociological History of the Sexual Division of Labour in Employment* (Minneapolis: University of Minnesota Press, 1989), 80.

178. See the following works by Catharine E. Beecher: *Letters to Persons Who Are Engaged in Domestic Service* (New York: Leavitt and Trow, 1842), 51, 76–77; *The Evils Suffered by American Women and American Children: The Causes and the Remedy* (New York: Harper and Brothers, 1847), 6–9; *The True Remedy for the Wrongs of Woman; with a History of an Enterprise Having That for Its Object* (Boston: Phillips, Sampson and Company, 1851), 34–40; *A Treatise on Domestic Economy, for the Use of Young Ladies at Home, and at School* (Boston: Marsh, Capen, Lyon, and Webb, 1841), 49–68, 163–66. See also Kathryn Kisk Sklar, *Catharine Beecher: A Study in American Domesticity* (New Haven: Yale University Press, 1973), 212; Joan N. Burstyn, "Catharine Beecher and the Education of American Women," in Esther Katz and Anita Rapone, eds., *Women's Experience in America: An Historical Anthology* (New Brunswick: Transaction Books), 219–34; Nancy F. Cott, *The Bonds of Womanhood: "Woman's Sphere" in New England, 1780–1835* (New Haven: Yale University Press, 1977), 68.

179. In a provocative article, Jennie Kitteringham has maintained, for example, that the British agricultural "gang" system created controversy because it was above all an affront to "bourgeois respectability." Victorian middle-class objections to the system—precisely the objections that Henry Colman registered—were, that is to say, not primarily directed at the possibility that heavy physical labor might injure or cripple the young women employed. Rather, those objections centered upon the "coarsening" effects of gang labor, its alleged tendency to both "de-sex" women and render them lascivious and promiscuous. And perhaps even more than other forms of wage labor which also took females outside the environment of the home, heavy field labor was adjudged by members of the middle class to be socially dysfunctional: by so coarsening women, it made them unfit or indisposed to assume their future roles as wives and mothers, and correspondingly unsuited to properly raise and socialize the next generation of workers; Jennie Kitteringham, "Country Work Girls in Nineteenth-Century England," Raphael Samuel, ed., *Village Life and Labour* (London: Routledge and Kegan Paul, 1975), 98, 128–33. Other historians have

made the parallel argument that despite the comparably onerous and exploitative conditions which they involved, domestic service and even sweated needlework aroused less middle-class and Parliamentary concern than did female employment in factories and mines precisely because they were considered to coincide more with woman's natural sphere; see Pam Graves and Joseph White, "'An Army of Redressers': The Recent Historiography of British Working Class Women," *International Labor and Working Class History,* no. 17 (Spring 1980): 5.

At the same time, although a nineteenth-century middle-class writer like Virginia Penny also sex-typed work, her understanding of "fit work for woman" was nonetheless more of a challenge than a surrender to the restrictive notion of woman's "true sphere." She recognized that the cult of domesticity, by disparaging paid work for "respectable" women as at most a prelude to the married state, handicapped those females who had to work—single women, widows, wives of disabled or intemperate husbands—by legitimating a limitation in the number of employments in which they were permitted to compete; see Amy Gilman Srebnick, "True Womanhood and Hard Times: Women and Early New York Industrialization, 1840–1860" (Ph.D. diss., State University of New York, Stony Brook, 1979), 193–97. For the "militant" demand, similar to Penny's, by the New York Female Moral Reform Society that clerkships and other male-dominated light indoor work that was "naturally" suited to women be opened up to them, in order that overcrowding and exploitation in existing women's trades be relieved, see Carroll Smith-Rosenberg, "Beauty, the Beast, and the Militant Woman. A Case Study in Sex Roles and Social Stress in Jacksonian America," in Nancy F. Cott and Elizabeth H. Peck, eds., *A Heritage of Her Own: Toward a New Social History of American Women* (New York: Simon and Schuster, 1979), 211. See also two works by Caroline H. Dall: *Woman's Right to Labor: Or, Low Wages and Hard Work: In Three Lectures, Delivered in Boston, November, 1859* (Boston: Walker, Wise, and Company, 1860), 5–6, 58, 86; and *The College, the Market, and the Court; Or, Woman's Relation to Education, Labor, and Law* (Boston: Lee and Shepard, 1867), 178, 207–8; and Barbara J. Balliet, "'What Shall We Do with Our Daughters?': Middle-Class Women's Ideas about Work, 1840–1920" (Ph.D. diss., New York University, 1988), 59–67.

180. But a few of the more relevant studies in a very large field include Sheila Lewenhak, *Women and Trade Unions* (New York: St. Martin's Press, 1977), 37–55; Barbara Taylor, "'The Men Are As Bad As Their Masters': Socialism, Feminism, and Sexual Antagonism in the London Tailoring Trade in the Early 1830's," *Feminist Studies* 5 (Spring 1979): 26–29; Sonya O. Rose, "Gender Antagonism and Class Conflict: Exclusionary Strategies of Male Trade Unionists in Nineteenth-Century Britain," *Social History* 13 (May 1988): 191–208; Alice Kessler-Harris, *Out to Work: A History of Wage-Earning Women in the United States* (New York: Oxford University Press, 1982), 68–70; Heidi I. Hartmann, "The Unhappy Marriage of Marxism and Feminism: Towards a More Progressive Union," *Capital and Class,* no. 8 (Spring 1979): 10–16; Jane Humphries, "Protective Legislation, the Capitalist State, and Working Class Men: The Case of the 1842 Mines Regulation Act," *Feminist Review* 7 (1981): 1–31. The "patriarchal" values and interests that induced male workers to support restrictions upon female employment opportunities are being defined increasingly broadly and variously by scholars. Beyond the motive of simple economic self-interest—the male worker's belief that female market participation undercut his earnings and threatened his job—these patriarchal values included the fear that such female participation, when it involved the male worker's own wife or daughter, both reduced the quality of family life by interfering with the female's domestic responsibilities and undermined the male's authority within the home by

granting female members a measure of economic independence. Finally, those patriarchal values might also be said to have encompassed the desire of an indeterminate number of British and American male workers to emulate middle-class male maxims of power and respectability by keeping their wives at home and unemployed, in observance of the "family wage" ideal. Which, however, among these considerations were the more important among male workers, and the extent to which any or all of them coincided with the objectives and interests of employers, remain matters of debate, and as Jane Humphries's discussion of the British male colliers in 1842 furthermore shows, whatever patriarchal values male workers held by no means always provide an obvious explanation of why they did support "sex-specific" protective legislation for female workers. For, however, some cogent criticisms of Humphries's use of the concept of patriarchy in this instance, see Jane Mark-Lawson and Anne Witz, "From 'Family Labour' to 'Family Wage'? The Case of Women's Labour in Nineteenth-Century Coalmining," *Social History* 13 (May 1988): 151–74. For one scholar's dislike of the term *patriarchy,* at least as a description of male dominance in industrial societies, see Bradley, *Men's Work, Women's Work,* 55, 50–63. For further discussion of patriarchy, and for references to and interpretations of the "family wage" ideal, which appears to have been out of reach for virtually all British male workers apart from the most highly skilled and well-recompensed ones, see Wally Seccombe, "Patriarchy Stabilized: The Construction of the Male Breadwinner Wage Norm in Nineteenth-Century Britain," *Social History* 11 (Jan. 1986): 53–76; Sally Alexander, Anna Davin, and Eve Hostettler, "Labouring Women: A Reply to Eric Hobsbawm," *History Workshop,* no. 8 (Autumn 1979): 178–80; Judy Lown, *Women and Industrialization: Gender at Work in Nineteenth-Century England* (Cambridge, Eng.: Polity Press, 1990), 210–19; Theresa M. McBride, "The Long Road Home: Women's Work and Industrialization," in Renate Bridenthal and Claudia Koonz, eds., *Becoming Visible: Women in European History* (Boston: Houghton Mifflin Company, 1977), 284, 289; Julia A. Matthaei, *An Economic History of Women in America: Women's Work, the Sexual Division of Labor, and the Development of Capitalism* (New York: Schocken Books, 1982), 121.

181. Beecher, *True Remedy,* 28–30; Beecher, *Treatise on Domestic Economy,* 28; Catharine E. Beecher, *Letters to the People on Health and Happiness* (New York: Harper and Brothers, 1855), 186; Faye E. Dudden, *Serving Women: Household Service in Nineteenth-Century America* (Middletown: Wesleyan University Press, 1983), 173–74; Jeanne Boydston, Mary Kelley, and Anne Margolis, *The Limits of Sisterhood: The Beecher Sisters on Women's Rights and Separate Spheres* (Chapel Hill: University of North Carolina Press, 1988), 119–21, 142.

182. Sklar, *Catharine Beecher,* 193. One can, however, easily overstate this loss of female status, if only for the reason that it may never have been very high to begin with. Although a decline in the northeastern preindustrial household economy during the early nineteenth century is hardly a matter of debate, it remains much less evident that women who had performed important productive functions within that economy had ever derived significant social status from those activities. Occupying the role of economic producer is hardly a guarantee of status, as the case of the chattel slave most obviously attests. For a study that persuasively challenges the idea of a preindustrial "Golden Age" of high social esteem for seventeenth- and eighteenth-century American women, despite their economically "productive" role, see Mary Beth Norton, *Liberty's Daughters: The Revolutionary Experience of American Women, 1750–1800* (Boston: Little, Brown and Company, 1980), xiv; see also Norton, "The Evolution of White Women's Experience in Early America," *American Historical Review* 89 (June 1984): 284–310; and Joan Hoff Wilson, "The Illusion

of Change: Women and the American Revolution," in Alfred Young, ed., *The American Revolution: Explorations in the History of American Radicalism* (DeKalb: Northern Illinois University Press, 1976), 393–413, 426–29; and for seventeenth-century American Puritan women specifically, see Lyle Koehler, *A Search for Power: The "Weaker Sex" in Seventeenth-Century New England* (Urbana: University of Illinois Press, 1980), 28–67, 108–29.

It may still have been true, as the historian Elisabeth Anthony Dexter argued, that eighteenth-century American women were freer than their nineteenth-century counterparts to conduct certain types of business enterprises, and there were certainly females in this period who belonged to the wealthiest ranks of American society by virtue of their inheritance of large estates through the death of relatives or husbands. But one looks in vain for the presence of women, married or single, among the active preindustrial commercial and professional elites described by scholars like Frederic Cople Jaher and E. Digby Baltzell. Largely new to the nineteenth century was not the inability of women to enter America's highest occupational ranks, but an ideology that so insistently explained and justified female exclusion from them. In this as in other respects there did occur, as Barbara Leslie Epstein and others have noted, some "hardening" of notions of domesticity, although even here, as Joan Hoff Wilson and Lyle Koehler especially stress, there were firm seventeenth- and eighteenth-century ideological foreshadowings of the nineteenth-century labor sex-typing that worked to the female's disadvantage. We might add that in her later study especially, Dexter is not incautious and unbalanced in her assessment of the occupational losses experienced by women during the first part of the nineteenth century, noting, for example, that the decline of the colonial "she-merchant" and midwife was partially offset by the rise of the female professional "scribbler"; see Frederic Cople Jaher, *The Urban Establishment: Upper Strata in Boston, New York, Charleston, Chicago, and Los Angeles* (Urbana: University of Illinois Press, 1982); E. Digby Baltzell, *Puritan Boston and Quaker Philadelphia: Two Protestant Ethics and the Spirit of Class Authority and Leadership* (New York: The Free Press, 1979); Elisabeth Anthony Dexter, *Colonial Women of Affairs. A Study of Women in Business and the Professions in America before 1776* (Boston: Houghton Mifflin Company, 1924), 18–34, 98–108, 190–92; Dexter, *Career Women of America, 1776–1840* (Clifton, N.J.: Augustus M. Kelley, 1972 [1950]), 139–40, 219–26; Barbara Leslie Epstein, *The Politics of Domesticity: Women, Evangelism, and Temperance in Nineteenth-Century America* (Middletown: Wesleyan University Press, 1981), 158; Barbara Welter, *Dimity Convictions: The American Woman in the Nineteenth Century* (Athens: Ohio University Press, 1976), 71–77; Ann D. Gordon, Mari Jo Buhle, and Nancy E. Schrom, "Women in American Society: An Historical Contribution," *Radical America* 5 (July–Aug. 1971): 22–38.

183. For a particularly forthright use of domestic ideology to oppose as a gross violation of woman's natural limits and propensities her entry into the intellectually rigorous professions, see the essay by the British manufacturer, W. R. Greg, "Why Are Women Redundant?" *National Review* 14 (1862), 434–60, portions of which are excerpted in Elizabeth K. Helsinger, Robin Lauterbach Sheets, and William Veeder, *The Woman Question: Society and Literature in Britain and America, 1837–1883* (Chicago: University of Chicago Press, 1983), 2: 136–39. Quite unlike Catharine E. Beecher, however, and consistent with his own position as manufacturer, Greg regarded industrial employment as singularly appropriate work for needy females, not at all inconsistent with their more "delicate . . . brain and frame": "Women and girls are less costly operatives than men. . . . It is clearly a waste of strength, a superfluous extravagance, an economic blunder, to employ a powerful and costly

machine to do work which can be as well done by a feebler and a cheaper one" (137). Interestingly, under many such formulations of the cult of domesticity as Greg's, the heaviest physical drudgery and the most demanding mental labor were characterized by the same regrettable tendency to "masculinize" the women who engaged in them.

In contrast to the more prestigious and orthodox learned professions, some of the unlicensed medical sects, notably botanic Thomsonianism, did not exclude women; see Joseph Kett, *The Formation of the American Medical Profession: The Role of Institutions 1780–1860* (New Haven: Yale University Press, 1968), 119.

184. Gerda Lerner, "The Lady and the Mill Girl: Change in the Status of Women in the Age of Jackson," *Midcontinent American Studies Journal* 10 (Spring 1969): 11–12; Dorothy Thompson, "Women and Nineteenth-Century Radical Politics: A Lost Dimension," in Juliet Mitchell and Ann Oakley, eds., *The Rights and Wrongs of Women* (Harmondsworth, Eng.: Penguin Books, 1976), 112.

185. Jane Swisshelm, *Letters to Country Girls* (1853), quoted in Gerda Lerner, ed., *The Female Experience: An American Documentary* (Indianapolis: Bobbs-Merrill Educational Publishing, 1977), 118; on the drudgery of farm wives, see also John Mack Faragher, *Women and Men on the Overland Trail* (New Haven: Yale University Press, 1979), 59–61. Swisshelm might well have regarded W. R. Greg's remarks, cited in note 183, as an example of such hypocrisy, although it was precisely one of Greg's arguments that the factory work he touted for needy, single females was light, untaxing physical labor.

186. The feminist Paulina Wright Davis leveled an indictment quite similar to Swisshelm's in her journal, the *Una*. I include this part of Davis's editorial here because of the difficulty interested readers might experience in acquiring a copy of the *Una*: "Conservators of female purity and decorum, make no objection to her [woman's] employment in the menial occupations of the household, the exhausting toil of the needle, and the ill paid labor of the cotton factory. This sort of labor is permitted and tenderness for the sex does not prevent a heavy discount upon its wages; but when clerkships, officeholding and professions; which pay well both in money and influence, are demanded they are refused; aye, not only refused, but the demand is treated with obloquy, and the advocates are charged with unwomanly departure from their proper sphere" ("Pecuniary Independence of Woman," *Una. A Paper Devoted to the Elevation of Women* 2 [Jan. 1854]: 200).

187. For suggestions of this latter interpretation, see Kessler-Harris, *Out to Work*, 53; Alice Kessler-Harris, *Women Have Always Worked* (Old Westbury, New York: The Feminist Press, 1981), 63; Anne D. Gordon and Mari Jo Buhle, "Sex and Class in Colonial and Nineteenth-Century America," in Berenice A. Carroll, ed., *Liberating Woman's History: Theoretical and Critical Essays* (Urbana: University of Illinois Press, 1976), 290–91; Gordon, Buhle, and Schrom, "Women," 36; and Andrew Sinclair, *The Better Half: The Emancipation of the American Woman* (New York: Harper and Row, 1965), 169–72. Without explicitly arguing that the marketplace exploitation of immigrant and black females was more natural than, or otherwise preferable to, that of white, native-born American women, Catherine E. Beecher herself provides some indications in her writings that it is the working conditions of this latter group—in the mills of Lowell, for example—which primarily disturbed her.

Carl N. Degler has questioned the significance of the cult of domesticity as a labor exploitative ideology in America by arguing, in effect, that the very pervasiveness of the cult's appeal insured that the marketplace exploitation of working-class females was a temporary phenomenon: "The women who were working, whether they were middle class or poor, were not married women—except for a very small number of free Negro women. The female workers who operated the machines, sold the goods, and performed the services in mid-19th-century America were overwhelmingly single women, waiting, and usually planning to be married. And generally when they did marry they, too, followed the cult of domesticity, that is, confined themselves to the task of child-rearing and housekeeping" (Carl N. Degler, *At Odds: Women and the Family in America from the Revolution to the Present* [New York: Oxford University Press, 1980], 375). Degler's own formulation merits qualification. Although antebellum New York City and Philadelphia were not America, any number of contemporary investigations of working conditions in those cities revealed what has been alluded to in a previous note: the large number of poor, "nonsingle" females who were obliged by a variety of circumstances—notably widowhood and the economic incapacity of husbands—to undertake sweated or other kinds of subsistence waged work, either inside or outside the home. The census data, upon which Degler possibly bases his observations, are hardly adequate to uncovering these circumstances—to revealing the extent to which these and other women were obliged, whatever their preferences may have been, to deviate after marriage from the cult of domesticity (see here Stansell, *City of Women*, 263). Degler himself is hardly unaware of the phenomenon of urban sweating—he gives some attention to it in his doctoral dissertation, "Labor in the Economy and Politics of New York City, 1850–1860: A Study of the Impact of Early Industrialism" (Ph.D. diss., Columbia University, 1952), 109–26. Possibly, he discounts its significance in the total national picture, or, alternatively, regards that considerable portion of sweated work that was performed within the working-class household—and that might be euphemistically categorized as industrial "homework"—as actually falling under the umbrella of the cult of domesticity. But that domestic ideology could legitimate or screen out such work as an extension of women's natural role might itself be taken as evidence of that ideology's capacity to buttress exploitative market conditions. Among studies that note the outwork of the wives and daughters of many urban journeymen are Bruce Laurie, *Artisans into Workers: Labor in Nineteenth-Century America* (New York: Hill and Wang, 1989), 60. For one examination of a still more neglected component of the female labor force, those working-class females who were dependent on waged employment because they never married at all, see Carol Lasser, "'The World's Dread Laugh': Singlehood and Service in Nineteenth-Century Boston," in Herbert G. Gutman and Donald H. Bell, eds., *The New England Working Class and the New Labor History* (Urbana: University of Illinois Press, 1987), 72–88. See also the essays in Eileen Boris and Cynthia R. Daniels, eds., *Homework: Historical and Contemporary Perspectives on Paid Labor at Home* (Urbana: University of Illinois Press, 1989).

188. On the intended audience for the literature of domesticity, see Mary Beth Norton, "The Paradox of 'Women's Sphere,'" in Carol Ruth Berkin and Mary Beth Norton, eds., *Women of America: A History* (Boston: Houghton Mifflin Company, 1979), 141.

189. On the construction by single lower-class girls in New York of their own "special feminine demeanor"—"gregarious, rowdy, bawdy"—that was increasingly removed from "decorous" Victorian "middle-class femininity," see Stansell, "Women of Laboring Poor," 204.

190. June Purvis, *Hard Lessons: The Lives and Education of Working-class Women in Nineteenth-century England* (Cambridge, Eng.: Polity Press, 1989), 66. Purvis's

critique of the self-serving and exploitative nature of Victorian bourgeois ideology might, then, be compared with the different, if hardly less critical, emphasis of Jennie Kitteringham, described in note 179 in this chapter.

191. Minnie Myrtle, *The Myrtle Wreath, Or Stray Leaves Recalled* (New York: Charles Scribner, 1854), 272–76. I have somewhat changed the order in which these sentences appear in the text. Minnie Myrtle was the pen name commonly used by Anna Cummings Johnson.

192. Myrtle's rather low regard for much, if not all, the activity that defined "women's sphere" is confirmed by her advice to those "ladies" who could, through the benefit of servants, escape the direct performance of this activity. Housekeepers who complained of the domestic shortcomings of their predominantly Irish "help" should, Myrtle counseled, develop greater patience and sympathy for these young women, because it is now they who must bear "the constantly recurring trials of the kitchen and nursery. They are doomed to the kitchen all day, and the garret all night,—weary, with nothing to cheer the present or brighten the future" (Ibid., 173, 175).

193. In a probing discussion, Judith A. McGaw identifies a variety of ways in which changes in work and work patterns during early nineteenth-century industrialization—e.g., simply the fact that males of all classes labored longer hours away from the home—gave men increasingly less reason "to understand and appreciate" women's household skills; McGaw, "No Passive Victims, No Separate Spheres: A Feminist Perspective on Technology's History," in Stephen H. Cutliffe and Robert C. Post, eds., *In Context: History and the History of Technology* (Bethlehem: Lehigh University Press, 1989), 181.

194. On the gang system see Ivy Pinchbeck, *Women Workers and the Industrial Revolution, 1750–1850* (London: George Routledge and Sons, 1930), 89–90.

195. Angela John, *By the Sweat of Their Brow: Women Workers at Victorian Coal Mines* (London: Croom Helm, 1980), 23–25; Richards, "Women in British Economy," 342.

196. For the notion of "pin money" and the "social definition" of woman's work as low-paid, see Sheila Rowbotham, *Women, Resistance and Revolution* (New York: Random House, 1972), 113; Rosalyn Baxandall, Linda Gordon, and Susan Reverby, "Introduction," to Baxandall et al., eds., *America's Working Women* (New York: Random House, 1976), xv; and Alice Kessler-Harris, "Women, Work, and the Social Order," in Carroll, ed., *Liberating Woman's History,* 334–35. In her essay, Kessler-Harris observes a number of different ways in which the ideology of "separate spheres" served the interests of American employers. While other scholars have focused on how domestic ideology invoked both the nature of women's "true" talents and the demands of her "natural" social role to justify her protection from the competitive struggle, Kessler-Harris has been foremost in placing needed stress on the specifically exploitative dimension of domestic ideology: the manner in which that ideology, as an argument for women's lesser capacity for success in the marketplace, legitimated the relegation of some of the most menial, mentally undemanding, and low-paying work to working-class females.

CHAPTER 7: MORAL CONTENT IN DRUDGE WORK AND MANUAL LABOR

1. We might compare this view with that of Friedrich A. Hayek, who argues that the least talented and skilled individuals, unable to fill other employments, are fortunate to get such tedious and repugnant work. Were they to be paid more to perform it, Hayek appears to be suggesting, in defense of free market over distribu-

tive justice principles, then they might be supplanted in these positions by more capable individuals, drawn to them by the increased remuneration. In that event, to pursue Hayek's line of reasoning, the least talented individuals would be left with nothing, since they would be as unable as before to fill the more skilled, vacated employments; Friedrich A. Hayek, *Law, Legislation, and Liberty,* vol. 2, *The Mirage of Social Justice* (Chicago: University of Chicago Press, 1976), 92; Hayek, *The Constitution of Liberty* (Chicago: University of Chicago Press, 1960), 441. Of course, neither Smith nor Ferguson, despite their beliefs about the injurious effects of some kinds of labor, gave any indication that they were any more receptive than Hayek to "social engineering" notions that favored compensating workers above the "natural rate of wages" for undertaking the worst labor.

2. The conservative ideological objectives that prompted many of the moralistic exaltations of drudge labor in the nineteenth century and before are not in themselves proof that these exaltations had no basis whatever in reality. A modern scholar has argued that "the most routinised and paced paid labour requires some worker's knowledge to be applied if the task is to be done in the optimum way, and thus virtually all jobs provide the raw material for workers to regard themselves as 'skilled.' Pride can be obtained from doing any job, even the most menial, well, in the eyes of bosses or other workers" (H. F. Moorhouse, "The 'Work' Ethic and 'Leisure' Activity: The Hot Rod in Post-War America," in Patrick Joyce, ed., *The Historical Meanings of Work* (Cambridge, Eng.: Cambridge University Press, 1987), 241–42. There would seem to be little way of providing authoritative historical documentation for this argument—of confirming, or for that matter, disproving the possibility that many of the laboring poor of past centuries, workers confined to the most menial modes of livelihood, took pride in their labors. It nevertheless seems more reasonable to assume that the greater of their numbers valued work above and beyond all else for the meager instrumental rewards it brought them; see also chapter 8 and the comments in Peter N. Stearns, *Lives of Labor: Work in a Maturing Industrial Society* (New York: Holmes and Meier, 1975), 350–51.

3. Daniel Tracy Rodgers, "The Work Ethic in Industrial America, 1865–1917" (Ph.D. diss., Yale University, 1973), 20. On antebellum labor movements' invocation of the work ethic, see, in particular, Jama Lazerow, "A Good Time Coming: Religion and the Emergence of Labor Activism in Antebellum New England" (Ph.D. diss., Brandeis University, 1982), 279–80.

4. Daniel T. Rodgers, *The Work Ethic in Industrial America 1850–1920* (Chicago: University of Chicago Press, 1978), 13–14.

5. William Ellery Channing, *Lectures on the Elevation of the Labouring Portion of the Community* (Boston: William D. Ticknor, 1840), 5–7. Jack Mendelsohn has suggested a psychological basis to Channing's exaltation of hard manual labor: always physically frail, he may have glorified such activity in part because he could do so little of it himself; Mendelsohn, *Channing: The Reluctant Radical* (Boston: Little, Brown and Company, 1971), 6–7, 216.

6. Although Brace pondered this question, he does not, however, seem to have given it an unequivocal and definitive answer. Of the child ragpickers and bone gatherers of one New York City ward, he said, "God help them! Ripened and diseased in vice before they are scarce old enough to know good from evil," and he proceeded to suggest the natural course from these employments to juvenile prostitution. Yet Brace was nonetheless hardly so quick as many of his middle-class contemporaries were (see chapter 4) to condemn these employments out of hand: "To all this petty and dirty work done by children and foreigners in our city, none has the right to utter a word of objection. It is immeasurably better than begging"

and the almshouse, and "at least," Brace added, it is "*honest work*" (Brace, "Walks among the New-York Poor. The Rag and Bone-Pickers," *New-York Daily Times,* Jan. 22, 1853); also relevant are other of Brace's articles in this series, especially the article subtitled "The Eleventh Ward," in the Mar. 4, 1853, edition of the *Times*. Some urban missionaries clearly shared the view of other middle-class Americans at this time that many of the more conventional unskilled and overcrowded forms of labor in the city—needlework, day labor, and the like—were objectionable not because of their inherent qualities, but because the workers employed in them could save nothing from their pay, and because the long periods of seasonal and cyclical unemployment to which these occupations were subject correspondingly exposed desperately poor workers and their families to the temptations of crime, vice and vagrancy; see "What Shall Be Done for the Poor?" New York *Monthly Record of the Five Points House of Industry* 1 (Nov. 1857): 169–77; and Carroll S. Rosenberg, "Protestants and Five Pointers: The Five Points House of Industry, 1850–1870," *New-York Historical Society Quarterly* 48 (Oct. 1964): 327–47.

As a number of historians have pointed out, members of the laboring poor who involved themselves in prostitution, the liquor traffic, or acts of petty crime probably put an entirely different construction on their behavior than did Brace and other predominantly middle-class, Protestant, witnesses who so deplored these activities of "degradation" and "depravity"; see Mary Christine Stansell, "Women of the Laboring Poor in New York City, 1820–1860" (Ph.D. diss., Yale University, 1979), 170–95, 203–7. Such witnesses may have even grossly exaggerated the scale of these activities, still more so in the case of more serious crimes like slum murder; commentators may have drawn erroneous inferences of demoralization, criminality, and vice on the basis of the squalid and crowded living arrangements that unquestionably did prevail among the Irish immigrant and other urban poor; see Carol Groneman Pernicone, "The 'Bloody Ould Sixth': A Social Analysis of a New-York City Working-Class Community in the Mid-Nineteenth Century" (Ph.D. diss., University of Rochester, 1973), xvi–xxi, 207–13. One must clearly strike a balance between accepting the horrified testimony and point of view of middle-class missionaries and other commentators as gospel truth and rejecting these as hopelessly prejudiced and without foundation. The latter course leads to the opposite danger of unduly romanticizing the lives of poverty and desperation that many members of the urban laboring population undoubtedly did lead.

7. Brace, "Walks among the New-York Poor. Rag and Bone-Pickers"; "The Rag Pickers of New York," *New York Herald,* Oct. 5, 1853.

8. For a particularly strong statement that eleven hours of daily factory labor for children was contrary to their "healthy physical development" and would so enfeeble them and shorten their life as to do great damage to the "pecuniary interest" of the state, see Massachusetts, *House Documents* for 1866, no. 98, *Report of Special Commission on Hours of Labor,* 11–12; for similar, earlier warnings by a British physician that from the standpoint of their proper physical, as well as moral, development, "children were not designed for labour," and that sharp limitations must be placed upon their employment in factories particularly, see the "synopsis of the evidence" given by Joseph Henry Green before the Select Committee of the House of Commons, Aug. 4, 1832, in *The Ten Hours' Factory Question. A Report Addressed to the Short Time Committees of the West Riding of Yorkshire* (London: John Ollivier, 1842), 10n–11n, repr. in *The Battle for the Ten Hour Day Continues,* one of a series of vols. in Kenneth Carpenter, advisory ed., *British Labour Struggles: Contemporary Pamphlets 1727–1850* (New York: Arno Press, 1972). See also Carl N. Degler, *At Odds: Women and the Family in America from the Revolution to the Present* (New

York: Oxford University Press, 1980), 68–71. For the argument that despite growing objections such as these to the employment of children in factories, older traditions endorsing the moral and other benefits of any kind of child labor remained the more powerful in antebellum America and contributed decisively to public apathy regarding factory legislation, see Barry Gewen, "The Intellectual Foundations of the Child Labor Reform Movement" (Ph.D. diss., Harvard University, 1972), 3–11, 42–43.

9. For an account of London's "Bone-Grubbers and Rag-Gatherers," that contains a briefer description of Paris's "chiffoniers," see Henry Mayhew, *London Labour and the London Poor* (New York: Dover Publications, 1968 [1861–1862], 1: 138–42.

10. See, for example, Channing, "Ministry for the Poor," discourse before the Benevolent Fraternity of Churches, Boston, Apr. 9, 1835, in *The Works of William E. Channing, D. D.*, new and complete ed. (Boston: American Unitarian Association, 1896), 73–86.

11. For this argument I am indebted in part to Steven Marcus, *The Other Victorians: A Study of Sexuality and Pornography in Mid-Nineteenth Century England* (New York: Basic Books, 1964), 139.

12. Channing, *Elevation*, 40–54.

13. "Industry a Blessing," *Fall River Mechanic*, May 18, 1844.

14. Gewen, "Intellectual Foundations," 32–33; for a more extreme attack on Channing's views along these lines, see Arthur Schlesinger, Jr., *The Age of Jackson* (Boston: Little, Brown and Company, 1945), 273.

15. In contrast, too, to some of the labor radicals of the period, Channing's criticisms of the idleness made possible by wealth were more in the nature of a moral lament than an attack on existing social arrangements. Channing's suggestion that aristocratic idlers hurt themselves worst of all was not so very different from the argument of someone like Albert Brisbane, who appealed to class harmony and sought to win the support of all social elements to his Associationist cause. But unlike Brisbane, Channing permitted his bemoaning of the "intolerable *ennui*" and pointless frivolity of leisured daughters and sons of the rich—"a misery unknown to the poor"—to actually turn into something of a defense of the status quo, an apologia for the economic deprivations of the laboring poor; see his *Ministry for the Poor*, 73–74. For Channing's other apologia for working-class deprivation, in which he emphasized the "struggles" and anxieties suffered by hard-working "professional and mercantile men," see Channing's letter to Elizabeth Palmer Peabody, Sept. 1840, in Peabody, *Reminiscences of Rev. Wm. Ellery Channing, D.D.* (Boston: Roberts Brothers, 1880), 415. Although Channing defended the legitimacy and rewards of mental labor employments against radical attack, he also, as noted earlier, shared the apprehension that young men were being drawn to these employments in inordinate numbers; Channing, *Elevation*, 9.

16. Channing to Peabody, in Peabody, *Reminiscences*, 415. With respect to Europe's laboring population, Channing's perception and consequent emphasis were quite different, as he took a characteristic American exceptionalist view of "the social evils which deform the old world." In part because the workmen there were indeed "half famished," as well as "ignorant," Channing remarked, they "will toil for any wages" and "never think of redeeming an hour for personal improvement." Yet Channing also warned that in ongoing commercialization, industrialization, and urbanization, the same "strong tendencies" existed in America as in Europe "to the intellectual and moral depression of a large portion of the community" (Channing, *Elevation*, 77–78).

17. See, in fact, Channing's very similar statement in *Self-Culture*, in *Works*, 32–

33, also quoted in chapter 3; Samuel Smiles, *Self-Help; with Illustrations of Character, Conduct, and Perseverance,* rev. ed. (Chicago: Belford, Clarke and Company, 1881 [1859], 295, 325. For a study that underscores the parallels between the thought of Channing and Smiles and notes Smiles's acknowledged intellectual indebtedness to the Unitarian clergyman, see Timothy Hugh Eaton Travers, "Samuel Smiles and the Victorian Work Ethic: The Rise and Decline of the Ideal of Self-Help, 1830–1890" (Ph.D. diss., Yale University, 1970), 74–80. There is, to be sure, a significant instrumentalist dimension to Smiles's self-help creed that Channing consciously downplayed in his own formulation. With American Whig politicians and writers like Calvin Colton, Smiles indicated in some of his writings (e.g., *Industrial Biography: Iron Workers and Tool-Makers* [Boston: Ticknor and Fields, 1864], 381) how the manual laborer's character development would not only render him rich in spirit; it might also make him much the richer materially and very conceivably lead him out of the working class altogether. This dimension of Smiles' self-help creed has drawn charges of being essentially a rationale for individual selfishness. Yet aside from the instrumentalist dimension, Smiles's theme of individual character development as a good in itself—as a means, if nothing else, of effecting the moral elevation of the worker and of the working class as a whole—was itself open to different interpretation and uses, regardless of Smiles's own particular intentions. Might the self-help creed have genuinely benefited workingmen by increasing their self-esteem and sense of individual capability or did it primarily serve the cause of capitalist exploitation by throwing workingmen the bone of moral respectability and spiritual wealth? In this basic ambiguity Smiles's message retained strong parallels with Channing's and has generated the same kind of differing interpretations among scholars; compare, for example, the sympathetic treatment of Smiles in Reinhard Bendix, *Work and Authority in Industry* (Berkeley: University of California Press, 1956), 109–16, and Asa Briggs, *Victorian People: Some Reassessment of People, Institutions, Ideas and Events 1851–1867* (London: Odham Press, 1954), 126–45, with P. D. Anthony, *The Ideology of Work* (London: Tavistock Publications, 1977), 78–79, and J. F. C. Harrison, "The Victorian Gospel of Success," *Victorian Studies* 1 (Dec. 1957): 156–63, both of which stress more than the first two works how the doctrine of individual self-help, by virtue of its contribution to middle-class capitalist ideological hegemony, set back more than it advanced the interests of workingmen.

18. Channing was repelled by Brownson's use of the term *masses*: "An odious word! as if spiritual beings could be lumped together like heaps of matter" (Channing to Peabody, in Peabody, *Reminiscences,* 415); Mendelsohn, *Channing,* 218–20; Schlesinger, *Age of Jackson,* 272–73. For Smiles's increasing intolerance of Chartism and of all militant and aggressive labor organization, as distinct from such collective expressions of self-help as workingmen's savings banks, see Travers, "Smiles," 157; Harrison, "Victorian Gospel of Success," 163; and Samuel Smiles, *Workmen's Earnings, Strikes, and Savings,* repr. from the *Quarterly Review,* new ed. (London: John Murray, 1862).

19. *Memoir of William Ellery Channing, with Extracts from His Correspondences and Manuscripts,* with a Preface by "W. H. C." [William Henry Channing] (Boston: W. Crosby and H. P. Nichols, 1848), 3: 56–57, 69–73, 124; Channing, *Self-Culture,* in *Works,* 33; Channing, *Elevation,* 54–66; Madeleine Hook Rice, *Federal Street Pastor: The Life of William Ellery Channing* (New York: Bookman Associates, 1961), 180–81.

20. Channing, "Address on Intemperance," delivered in Boston, Feb. 28, 1837, in *Works,* 103.

21. Channing, *Elevation,* 8.

22. Ibid.

23. Ibid., 9.

24. See, for example, [John L. O'Sullivan], "White Slavery," *Democratic Review* 11 (Sept. 1842): 261–62.

25. Of relevance here is the contrast Reinhard Bendix has drawn between employers and other members of the middle classes in late eighteenth- and early nineteenth-century Britain and employers in Tsarist Russia in the decades prior to the Russian Revolution. The "moralizing approach" of the British middle classes, Bendix notes, reflected the assumption that members of the laboring population were capable of internalizing an effective ethic of work performance. Russia's propertied classes held no such assumption and demanded a form of submission from their workers that depended far more on naked fear and coercion than on appeals to their employees' self-esteem; Bendix, *Work and Authority,* 205–6n. Accurate as Bendix's contrast may generally be, he may still understate the degree to which some British, as well as American, industrial capitalists, sought only docility and tractability from their workers, rather than a truly "internalized" work ethic; see the discussion in this chapter below regarding the ambiguous nature of "industrial morality." And as Bendix would also acknowledge, the propertied classes in Britain were not above resorting to the state apparatus of armed suppression and legal disciplinary measures when during the earlier part of the nineteenth century particularly, "ideological hegemony" from above proved less than effective in defusing Luddite and other forms of labor unrest.

26. Beyond the province of this study are basic questions now being debated in both British and American labor historiography. First, the question previously posed: whether middle-class capitalist interests or working-class interests were most greatly served by the workingmen's cultivation of moral respectability and the standard character virtues. Second, the related questions of whether the theme of worker respectability had genuine roots within nineteenth-century working-class traditions, militant and radical or otherwise, and whether, regardless of its roots, the influence the theme gained among segments of the working classes signified and eventuated in the virtually complete victimization of those segments to ideological "embourgeoisement." A few of the more recent and important studies in this field, all of which owe much to E. P. Thompson's *The Making of the English Working Class,* even when they disagree with that study's arguments, include Alan Dawley and Paul Faler, "Working-Class Culture and Politics in the Industrial Revolution: Sources of Loyalism and Rebellion," *Journal of Social History* 9 (June 1976): 466–80; Jill Siegel Dodd, "The Working Classes and the Temperance Movement in Antebellum Boston," *Labor History* 19 (Fall 1978): 510–31; Anthony F. Wallace, *Rockdale: The Growth of an American Village in the Early Industrial Revolution* (New York: Alfred A. Knopf, 1978), 48–51, 211–13, 326–410; Thomas Laqueur, *Religion and Respectability: Sunday Schools and Working Class Culture 1780–1850* (New Haven: Yale University Press, 1976), xii–xiii, 187–95, 215–18, 231–46; Neville Kirk, *The Growth of Working Class Reformism in Mid-Victorian England* (London: Croom Helm, 1985), 142–239; Brian Harrison, "Teetotal Chartism," *History* 58 (June 1973): 193–215; Trygve Tholfsen, *Working Class Radicalism in Mid-Victorian England* (London: Croom Helm, 1976), 16–19, 216–49; Tholfsen, "The Intellectual Origins of Mid-Victorian Stability," *Political Science Quarterly* 86 (Mar. 1971): 57–91.

27. Distinctions between Lutheran and Calvinist teaching regarding the value of work are discussed in various of the studies excerpted in Robert W. Green, ed., *Protestantism and Capitalism: The Weber Thesis and Its Critics* (Boston: D. C. Heath and Company, 1959).

28. We can only note here those criticisms of Weber's "Protestant ethic" thesis,

made by Werner Sombart and others, which insist upon the great degree to which Judaic and even medieval Catholic teaching anticipated Lutheran and Calvinist attitudes toward idleness, work, and economic rationality and acquisitiveness; see Ibid.; and Gordon Marshall, *In Search of the Spirit of Capitalism: An Essay on Max Weber's Protestant Ethic Thesis* (New York: Columbia University Press, 1982), 34–39. For discussions of the relationship between the Protestant idea of calling and American ideals of republican virtue in the Revolutionary era and the stigma which both attached to idleness, see Edmund S. Morgan, "The Puritan Ethic and the American Revolution," *William and Mary Quarterly*, 3d ser., 24 (Jan. 1967): 3–43; Isaac Kramnick, "The 'Great National Discussion': The Discourse of Politics in 1787," *William and Mary Quarterly*, 3d ser., 45 (Jan. 1988): 18–20.

29. Horace Greeley, "Slavery and Labor. A Lecture, Delivered at Boston and New-York, Jan. 1855," repr. in *New-York Daily Tribune*, June 27, 1855; Greeley, *An Address before the Literary Societies of Hamilton College*, July 23, 1847 (New York: William H. Graham, 1844), 11.

30. Karen Halltunen, *Confidence Men and Painted Women: A Study of Middle Class Culture in America, 1830–1870* (New Haven: Yale University Press, 1982), 202. Rowland Berthoff goes so far as to argue that under the original Puritan ethic and idea of calling "neither hard work nor frugal saving had any of the inherent value that the nineteenth century was to see in it," see Rowland Berthoff, "Peasants and Artisans, Puritans and Republicans: Personal Liberty and Communal Equality in American History," *Journal of American History* 69 (Dec. 1982): 581.

31. For an application of this distinction to the defense of slavery in the New World, see Sidney W. Mintz: "The Dignity of Honest Toil," *Comparative Studies in Society and History* 21 (Oct. 1979): 565–66.

32. At the same time, it was precisely because labor was not merely a "curse," but a "degrading curse," that the Louisiana lawyer, George S. Sawyer, for one, mocked labor's touted capacity to check idleness and promote virtue in even this limited, negative sense. In yet another example of a crosscutting position, Sawyer combined Timothy Walker's disdain for manual labor—Walker's view that the "progress of civilization" was synonymous with manual labor's abridgement and confinement to an ever smaller number—with the characteristic proslavery elitist position that African blacks constituted Aristotle's perfect "natural slaves," suited most of all for base physical work. To whatever extent Sawyer may have assented to the argument, one much emphasized in other proslavery defenses, that the work imposed on Southern black bondsmen did somehow check their indolent and savage propensities, and benefit them in this way, his own emphasis was clearly upon black slavery's strictly utilitarian function of freeing members of a superior race for more morally elevating and intellectually fulfilling pursuits than manual labor; George S. Sawyer, *Southern Institutes; or, an Inquiry into the Origin and Early Prevalence of Slavery and the Slave Trade* (New York: Negro Universities Press, 1969 [1858]), 378–79.

33. "Labor and Laborers in England," *New World* 9 (Sept. 28, 1844): 401–2.

34. Ewbank, *World a Workshop*, quoted in "Industrial Education," *New-York Daily Tribune*, Feb. 11, 1856.

35. Sidney Howard Gay, "Progress Is the Law of Humanity" [undated ms], p. 27, Sidney Howard Gay Papers, Rare Book and Manuscript Division, Columbia University, New York.

36. Albert Brisbane, *A Concise Exposition of the Doctrine of Association, or Plan for a Reorganization of Society, Which Will Secure to the Human Race, Individually and*

Collectively, Their Happiness and Elevation (Based on Fourier's Theory of Domestic and Industrial Association), 8th ed. (New York: J. S. Redfield, 1844), 42.

37. I am indebted to the anonymous reader of Yale University Press for emphasizing the desirability of my raising this question, and also to Jon Butler for confirming my sense of the difficulty of answering it.

George Frederick Holmes, for one, attached in one of his early essays virtually as much importance to God's curse on Cain as to His earlier curse on Adam. Whereas the labor to which man had been sentenced for Original Sin had laid the basis for a mere, subsistent "pastoral" existence, Holmes wrote, it was God's curse and condemnation of the original fratricide that rendered human labor truly ambitious and "progressive," a force responsible for cities, the arts, trade and manufacture—in short, true "civilization." I have not encountered Holmes's argument elsewhere, but I suspect that it is indicative of the varied interpretations and emphases that individuals of disparate philosophies and religious faiths extracted from their reading of both the Old and the New Testaments; George Frederick Holmes, "Schlegel's Philosophy of History," *Southern Quarterly Review* 3 (Apr. 1843): 263–317; repr. in Michael O'Brien, ed., *All Clever Men, Who Make Their Way: Critical Discourse in the Old South* (Fayetteville: University of Arkansas Press, 1982), 198–200.

38. See, in particular, Timothy L. Smith, *Revivalism and Social Reform: American Protestantism on the Eve of the Civil War* (New York: Harper and Row, 1965 [1957]); and John L. Thomas, "Romantic Reform in America, 1815–1865," *American Quarterly* 17 (Winter 1965): 656–81.

39. See, for example, many of the issues of a major organ of Old School Presbyterianism, the *New York Observer Weekly*—e.g., "Our Paper," Jan. 3, 1856: "We believe that Socialism, Owenism, Fourierism, Abolitionism, and all the various *isms* and schemes for the reform of the great evils of society on other than Bible principles, will prove not only a miserable failure, but an awful curse to the communities which cherish them. The projectors of these schemes ignore the fall of man and its consequences. . . . they propose to reform the world not by beginning with individuals, and advancing step by step till all are formed, but by reforming whole communities first and individuals afterward." In making this last point, we should note, the *Observer* erred in lumping together the various movements for romantic reform. Some of the evangelical abolitionists, for example, not only disagreed with American Fourierists as to the nature of the good society, arguing that society might indeed incorporate free market, competitive principles. They also differed precisely on the question of process, taking the very position of the *Observer* that the inner moral reform of individuals—starting with the immediate conversion of slaveholders—must indeed precede any viable and lasting social "reorganization," the position of the Fourierists and other communitarian socialists to the contrary. One of the crucial points of distinction between evangelical, immediate abolitionism and the Old School Presbyterianism of the *Observer* remained the former's much stronger faith in the real possibility of human moral regeneration, of the individual sinner's spiritual perfectability. For divisions *between* evangelical sects on the issues of human moral perfectability and man's ability to redeem society, see Curtis D. Johnson, *Islands of Holiness: Rural Religion in Upstate New York, 1790–1860* (Ithaca: Cornell University Press, 1989), 8, 67–71, 172–73; and George B. Marsden, *The Evangelical Mind and the New School Presbyterian Experience: A Case Study of Thought and Theology in Nineteenth-Century America* (New Haven: Yale University Press, 1970), 81, 122, 236–39.

40. See, for example, William Gilmore Simms's defense of Southern slavery in chapter 7.

41. Thomas Carlyle, *Past and Present* (London: Oxford University Press, 1909 [1843]), 158, 202–6; Herbert Sussman, *Victorians and the Machine: The Literary Response to Technology* (Cambridge: Harvard University Press, 1968), 25–41, 61, 113; David Meakin, *Man and Work: Literature and Culture in Industrial Society* (New York: Holmes and Meier, 1976), 42–44; Eloise M. Behnken, *Thomas Carlyle: "Calvinist without Theology"* (Columbia: University of Missouri Press, 1978), 14–19, 34–35.

42. Sussman, *Victorians,* 36, 76–113; Meakin, *Man and Work,* 44–45; James Clark Sherburne, *John Ruskin or the Ambiguities of Abundance: A Study in Social and Economic Criticism* (Cambridge: Harvard University Press, 1972) 49, 75–81, 239, 264–71, 283–84. For, however, a discussion that brings Ruskin's views somewhat closer to those of Carlyle, see P. D. Anthony, *John Ruskin's Labour: A Study of Ruskin's Social Theory* (Cambridge, Eng.: Cambridge University Press, 1983), 153–70.

43. For Channing's antislavery views, see his *Slavery,* in *Works,* 688–730, together with other of his writings and discourses collected here.

44. Morgan, "Puritan Ethic," 4–5, 22–25; Edmund S. Morgan, *American Slavery, American Freedom: The Ordeal of Colonial Virginia* (New York: W. W. Norton and Company, 1975), 295–96; Rodgers, *Work Ethic,* 31; Eric Foner, *Free Soil, Free Labor, Free Men: The Ideology of the Republican Party before the Civil War* (New York: Oxford University Press, 1970), 46.

45. Antebellum use of these and other scriptural phrases was hardly confined to strictly antislavery objectives. "Neither shall he work, nor shall he eat" (2 Thess. 3: 10) was, for example, a staple of antipauperism literature, whereas "the labor is worthy of his hire" (Luke 10: 7) was similarly basic to trade union and labor reform manifestos.

46. See, for example, Channing, *Slavery,* in *Works,* 710–20; and Henry Ward Beecher, "Northern and Southern Theories of Man and Society," a lecture before the New York Anti-Slavery Society, in *National Anti-Slavery Standard,* Jan. 27, 1855.

47. Wendell Phillips, "Disunion," lecture in Boston, Jan. 20, 1861, in Phillips, *Speeches, Lectures, and Letters,* first series (Boston: Lothrop, Lee and Shepard Company, 1891), 367.

48. James Henry Hammond to Thomas Clarkson, Mar. 24, 1845, in *Selections from the Letters and Speeches of the Hon. James H. Hammond, of South Carolina* (New York: John F. Trow and Company, 1866), 185. Proslavery writers also trumpeted the support and care that slavery extended to the young, elderly, sick, and disabled members of the slave population; see again, Hammond to Clarkson, Jan. 28, 1845, *Selections from Letters and Speeches,* 139–40. Fogel and Engerman indicate that this support was frequently not given without something exacted in return: they note the relatively high "labor-force participation rate" of the Southern slave population and attribute it partly to the use of slave women and children and partly "to institutional arrangements which permitted plantations to find methods of employing those who would, to a large extent, be unemployable in free societies, particularly in free urban societies—the mentally retarded, the crippled, the aged" (Robert William Fogel and Stanley L. Engerman, *Time on the Cross: The Economics of American Negro Slavery* [Boston: Little, Brown and Company, 1974], 1: 207). Actually, as Henry Mayhew's work attests, it was in many instances not a matter of such elements within the laboring classes failing to secure any employment at all in free market societies, but rather a matter of these groups failing to win a decent,

guaranteed subsistence for such work. Notwithstanding the existence of outdoor relief, almshouses, and like institutions, death from malnourishment and outright starvation was likely a far more common occurrence among the most disadvantaged elements of free market societies during this period than it has since become; the modern American "safety net," such as it is, was that much less developed in mid-nineteenth-century capitalist societies.

49. See for example, the speech of the New York lawyer Charles O'Conor, *Negro Slavery Not Unjust,* delivered at the Union Meeting in New York City, Dec. 19, 1859, rev. ed. (New York: Van Evrie, Horton, and Company, 1860), 12–13. O'Conor's use of this argument to defend slavery was noted by Marx, who cited its similarity to the "supervisory" arguments that were often used to rationalize the capitalist's "appropriation of the unpaid labour" of free wage laborers; Marx, *Capital: A Critique of Political Economy,* ed. Frederick Engels, trans. Samuel Moore and Edward Aveling (New York: International Publishers, 1967), 3: 385–86. For material on O'Conor's background and role in New York Democratic politics, see Florence E. Gibson, *The Attitudes of the New-York Irish Toward State and National Affairs, 1848–1892* (New York: Columbia University Press, 1951), 91–113. The proslavery "supervisory" argument, one might note, would seem to theoretically conflict with the other favorite argument that slavery's great virtue lay in its singular capacity to free a group of men for refinement, reflection, and learning—to free them from any kind of "labor" whatever. In practice, of course, even many of the wealthier and more "cultivated" slaveholders did assume an active "supervisory" role in the operation of their plantation regimes.

50. A number of historians, furthermore, have discounted the significance that the proslavery work ethic could have played either in the rhetorical defense of slavery or in its popular acceptance. On the first score, C. Vann Woodward has argued that so implausible was the idea of Southern slave labor as an expression of the Protestant ethic—as an expression of "the glory of God or many of the finer aspirations of man"—that few proslavery sermons directed at bondsmen even made the attempt to play up this labor as a moral good in itself; Woodward, *American Counterpoint: Slavery and Racism in the North-South Dialogue* (Boston: Little, Brown and Company, 1964), 34–35. On the second score, Bruce Collins had argued that "it is unlikely that most Southerners came to rationalize their acceptance of slavery by invoking complicated divine purposes. Straightforward and aggressive racism doubtless loomed larger in popular thought" (Bruce Collins, *White Society in the Antebellum South* [London: Longman, 1985], 52). Yet for a number of reasons noted in the text, the proslavery work ethic still merits discussion. For a discussion that does find evidence of this ethic in sermons directed at slaves, see Blake Touchstone, "Planters and Slave Religion in the Deep South," in John B. Boles, ed., *Masters and Slaves in the House of the Lord: Race and Religion in the American South, 1740–1870* (Lexington: University Press of Kentucky, 1988), 121–22. For a more general discussion of the theological basis of the Southern support for slavery, see two essays by Eugene D. Genovese and Elizabeth Fox-Genovese: "The Religious Ideals of Southern Slave Society," *Georgia Historical Quarterly* 70 (Spring 1986): 1–16; and "The Divine Sanction of Social Order: Religious Foundations of the Southern Slaveholders' World View," *Journal of the American Academy of Religion* 55 (Summer 1987): 211–33.

51. Frederick Douglass, "The Future of the Negro People of the Slave States," *Douglass' Monthly* (Mar. 1862), address to the Emancipation League in Boston, quoted in Thomas R. Frazier, ed., *Afro-American History: Primary Sources* (Chicago: Dorsey Press, 1988), 125.

52. George M. Fredrickson, "Introduction to the Wesleyan Edition," in Fred-

rickson, *The Black Image in the White Mind: The Debate on Afro-American Character and Destiny, 1817–1914* (Middletown: Wesleyan University Press, 1987 [1971], ix.

53. Thomas Carlyle, "Occasional Discourse on the Nigger Question," repr. in Carlyle, *English and Other Critical Essays* (London: J. M. Dent and Sons, 1915), 312; see also *Fraser's Magazine* 40 (Dec. 1849): 670–79, for the original shorter version entitled "Occasional Discourse on the Negro Question." Carlyle came out with the expanded essay in 1853 in response to critics like John Stuart Mill.

54. Carlyle, "Nigger Question," 313, 309, 311.

55. Gerald M. Straka has noted that in some respects Carlyle's enthusiasm for black chattel slavery in the South was less wholehearted than that of other writers who defended the institution at the time; Straka, "The Spirit of Carlyle in the Old South," *Historian* 20 (Nov. 1957): 54–57; and also Carlyle, "Nigger Question," 321–24, 329–30, where Carlyle asks "How to abolish the abuses of slavery, and save the precious thing in it," and proposes a vague alternative whereby the majority of blacks would be "hired for life" by members of the white race. See also note 87 in this chapter.

56. "A South Carolinean" [William Gilmore Simms], "Miss Martineau on Slavery," *Southern Literary Messenger* 3 (Nov. 1837): 654.

57. Ibid.

58. Ibid., 645n.

59. Ibid., 656.

60. W. Gilmore Simms, "The Morals of Slavery," in *The Pro-Slavery Argument* (Charleston: Walker, Richards and Company, 1852), 179, 270.

61. For a Northern voice that defended the "coerced servitude" of African blacks in terms somewhat similar to those in Simm's original essay, see *The Negro Labor Question. By a New York Merchant* (New York: John A. Gray, 1858).

62. [Simms], "Miss Martineau on Slavery," 654–57. For a few of Van Evrie's columns that play up these themes, see the following editorials in the New York *Weekly Day Book*: "Fun and Lazy Sambo," Sept. 15, 1860; "Bastard Philanthropy," May 9, 1857; and "The Ruin of the North," Dec. 5, 1983. For Van Evrie's prediction, made by some other Northerners as well, that vice, pauperism, and economic competition would render "those social monstrosities, the free Negroes of the North," extinct in the "not distant" future, see his column, "Death on Either Side," *Weekly Day Book,* Oct. 17, 1863; for a discussion of these various themes, see Fredrickson, *Black Image,* 92–93, 102–11, 154–59. As Fredrickson makes clear, neither the stereotype of the black as cheerful, docile, and childlike, nor the notion that Northern blacks were destined for extinction, was restricted to proslavery writers.

63. Senator James Henry Hammond of South Carolina, *Congressional Globe,* 35th Cong., 1st sess., Mar. 4, 1858, 962.

64. T. W. Hoit, *The Right of American Slavery* (St. Louis: L. Bushnell, 1860), 22.

65. Congressman William S. Barry of Mississippi, *Congressional Globe. Appendix,* 33d Cong., 1st sess., Apr. 27, 1854, 616. See also, "A Southern Clergyman," *A Defence of Southern Slavery against the Attacks of Henry Clay and Alex'r Campbell* (New York: Negro Universities Press, 1969 [1851]), 23–24.

66. Samuel Nott, *Slavery and the Remedy; or, Principle and Suggestions for a Remedial Cure,* 6th ed. (New York: Negro Universities Press, 1969 [1859]), 111–12.

67. Thomas R. Dew, "An Address on the Influence of the Federative Republican System of Government upon Literature and the Development of Character," *Southern Literary Messenger* 2 (Mar. 1836): 278n.

68. A. P. Upshur, "Domestic Slavery," *Southern Literary Messenger* 5 (Oct. 1839): 686.

69. Ibid., 680–81, 685–86. See also Thornton Stringfellow, "The Bible Argument: Or, Slavery in the Light of Divine Revelation," in E. N. Elliott, ed., *Cotton Is King, and Pro-Slavery Arguments* (Augusta: Pritchard, Abbott and Loomis, 1860), 500.

70. Upshur, "Domestic Slavery," 678, 684–85; see also William A. Smith, *Lectures on the Philosophy and Practice of Slavery, as Exhibited in the Institution of Domestic Slavery in the United States: With the Duties of Masters to Slaves,* ed. Thomas O. Summers (Nashville: Stevenson and Evans, 1856), 220–25.

71. Upshur, "Domestic Slavery," 686.

72. Ibid., 684–85. Upshur's strictures might be said to represent a proslavery variation on Tocqueville's theme of the dangers posed by rising expectations in democratic societies. In a sense, too, they point to the opposite danger from that emphasized in Michael Young, *The Rise of the Meritocracy, 1870–2033: An Essay on Educational Equality* (Baltimore: Penguin Books, 1961), 105–8. Young warned of the demoralization, the loss in self-esteem and "inner vitality," that those at the bottom of society might very conceivably suffer with a radical equalization of economic and educational opportunity: they would logically find it increasingly impossible to rationalize their position as a consequence of social injustice. Upshur was suggesting, in contrast, that most human beings remain temperamentally incapable of blaming themselves for their failures, regardless of the equality of opportunity that prevails in their society. The danger for the conservative Upshur was not that "free laborers" and others at the bottom would become passively demoralized but rather, as suggested in the text, that they would become "factious" and lash out at society in a series of "agrarian" assaults.

73. Larry E. Tise, *Proslavery: A History of the Defense of Slavery in America, 1701–1840* (Athens: University of Georgia Press, 1987), 118, 189.

74. "The Nebraska Question—Southern and Northern Slavery—the Constitution," *New York Herald,* Feb. 9, 1854.

75. "The Nebraska Question and the City Press," *New York Herald,* Feb. 3, 1854.

76. For a recent study of James Gordon Bennett's social attitudes and characteristics as a newspaper publisher and editorialist, see James L. Crouthamel, *Bennett's New York Herald and the Rise of the Popular Press* (New York: Syracuse University Press, 1989), 56–91.

David Brion Davis has noted that the Stoic belief that the most prevalent and pernicious kind of slavery was internal or spiritual, bondage to one's own vices, passions, and prejudices, "constantly reappears in Western culture" (David Brion Davis, *The Problem of Slavery in Western Culture* [Ithaca: Cornell University Press, 1966], 79n, 74–79). That belief received considerable support from the Christian doctrine of original sin: all men struggled against the slavery imposed by their fallen condition. In mid-nineteenth-century America, as suggested earlier, the sense of man's imperfect spiritual nature encouraged, notably among Catholic, Old School Presbyterian, and other nonevangelical Protestant clergymen, the fatalistic conviction that society itself must remain similarly imperfect, notions of romantic reform notwithstanding. Thus the proslavery Irish immigrant, John Mitchel, offered the reasoning of one Father Kenyon in attacking the antislavery movement, reasoning that would likely have struck a sympathetic chord with Bennett: "We are all slaves, in a thousand senses of the word; slaves to time, to place, to circumstance; to the habits of our great grandfathers on either side, and to the whims of our maternal ancestors in their nonsensical generations; to fire, air, earth and weather, throughout all their analyses; to tailors—a most galling yoke; snuff, washerwomen, quacks, policemen, umbrellas, London merchants, native millers, and royal engineers. If to all these slaveries there be superadded one other—namely, Slavery to slaveholders, I cannot see that our position will be very essentially deteriorated" (Kenyon quoted in a public letter entitled "Slavery," written by Mitchel to Henry Ward Beecher and published in "Mitchel's newspaper the *Citizen* [New York], Jan. 28, 1854). See also "John Mitchel's Reply to the Rev. H. W. Beecher," *National Anti-Slavery Standard* (New York), Feb. 4, 1854; G. E. M. de Ste. Croix, "Slavery and Other Forms of Unfree Labour," in Léonie J. Archer, ed., *Slavery and Other Forms of Unfree Labour* (London: Routledge, 1988), 19–32.

77. "H. B. 2d," "Fourierism, and Similar Schemes," *Universalist Quarterly. And General Review* 2 (Jan. 1845): 65–72.

78. Lincoln, "Fragment on Free Labor," in *The Collected Works of Abraham Lincoln*, ed. Roy P. Basler (New Brunswick: Rutgers University Press, 1953), 3: 462. See also John Patrick Diggins, *The Lost Soul of American Politics* (New York: Basic Books, 1984), 324–25.

79. James Stirling, *Letters from the Slave States* (New York: Kraus Reprint Company, 1969 [1857]), 33.

80. Ibid., 114–17. Stirling later carried the same themes into his attacks on the position, newly embraced by John Stuart Mill, that trade unions could protect the worker from the "competition of the market"—i.e., raise wages above "the self-adjusting mechanism of natural forces." To his continuing insistence upon the "moral power" of competition and its disciplinary benefits for the laborer, Stirling added in these attacks an emphasis upon the under-appreciated, strictly economic benefits of competition for the laborer. Stirling insisted that the "hidden" competition *between* capitalists for the worker's hire, which acted to drive up the worker's wages, was hardly less powerful and prevalent in British society than the competition among laborers for work. In Stirling's view, there seems to have been virtually no way in which unhampered free market forces did not or would not act to toughen, strengthen, and altogether benefit the "poor man" in his individual struggle with the capitalist. Each of these ways accordingly spoke out in his view against the "coercive" and "oppressive" practices of British trade unions; see James Stirling, "Mr. Mill on Trade Unions—A Criticism" [1869], in Sir Alexander Grant, ed., *Recess Studies* (Edinburgh: Edmonston and Douglas, 1870), 310, 311, 317, 309–32; and James Stirling, *Trade Unionism: With Remarks on the Report of the Commissioners on Trade' Unions*, repr. from 2d ed. [1869] (Glasgow: James Maclehose and Sons, 1889), 6–55.

81. *New-York Daily Tribune*, articles no. 5, 11, and 15 especially in H. Greeley and H. J. Raymond, *Association Discussed; or, the Socialism of "The Tribune" Examined; Being a Controversy Between the "New-York Tribune" and the "Courier and Enquirer"* (New York: Harper and Brothers, 1847), copy in Horace Greeley Papers, Manuscript Division, Library of Congress, Washington, D.C.

82. Greeley, "Life—The Ideal and the Actual," *Nineteenth Century: A Quarterly Miscellany,* 2 (1848): 23.

83. Glyndon G. Van Deusen, *Horace Greeley: Nineteenth-Century Crusader* (New York: Hill and Wang, 1964 [1953]), 6–9.

84. Greeley, "Slavery and Labor"; Horace Greeley, "Means and Chances of Success in Life," *Nineteenth Century* 2 (1848): 644.

85. Greeley, *Address before Literary Societies,* 11. See also Daniel Walker Howe, *The Political Culture of the American Whigs,* (Chicago: University of Chicago Press, 1979), 186–92.

86. Greeley, "Slavery and Labor." Greeley, together with other antebellum land and labor reformers, differed here with those abolitionists who insisted that

Southern slavery was the primary source, rather than the mere consequence, of the contempt for manual labor in America.

87. As much as Southern defenders of black slavery, Carlyle emphasized in some of his writing different, or additional, standards for the dignity of white workers. His insistence upon the intrinsic moral worth of any labor was accompanied in *Past and Present,* for example, by denunciations of the insufficient instrumental value attaching to much of this labor in Britain (209–13). In the economic exploitation of such groups as the Manchester factory workers (Ibid., 14–23), Carlyle found corroborative evidence of the hateful dominance exercised in British society by the selfish and greedy, socially corrosive principle of "Mammonism," or "Cash-nexus." Carlyle is a particularly good example of a commentator who over time and in different contexts, formulated rather different concepts of "truly free" labor; and in his case at least, these concepts sometimes rested on rather contradictory arguments. As John Stuart Mill pointed out in his criticism of "The Nigger Question," Carlyle's defense in that essay of the morality of enforced labor for West Indies blacks included assertions about the importance of this labor to the creation of certain luxury items that rather severely compromised Carlyle's famed repudiation of British materialism and greed. At the same time, Carlyle's intense belief in the necessity and divinity of labor overruled in some respects his racism and his establishment of different standards for white and black workers. In the bitter fact of their idleness and underemployment, the situation—indeed, the plight—of the West Indies blacks, Carlyle argued, was similar to that of London's "Distressed Needlewomen" ("Nigger Question," 318–21). Not unlike George Fitzhugh, Carlyle maintained that the *involuntary* idleness and economic distress of the British white sewing women could be traced to the same root cause as the permitted, voluntary idleness, or indolence, of the ex-slaves: the rule of cash-nexus, laissez faire principles. Starving, unemployed white laborers and indolent ex-slaves would both benefit from no longer being left alone by society; the former, just as the latter, Carlyle seems to be suggesting in "The Nigger Question," would be better off in a contractual condition of lifetime service to a master, a condition whereby both their subsistence and their labor were guaranteed. See also Emery Neff, *Carlyle and Mill: An Introduction to Victorian Thought* (New York: Columbia University Press, 1926), 40–43.

88. Theodore Clapp, *Slavery: A Sermon,* delivered in the First Congregational Church in New Orleans, Apr. 15, 1838 (New Orleans: John Gibson, 1838), 37–39.

89. [Solon Robinson], "Negro Slavery at the South," Sept. and Nov. 1849, in Robinson, *Solon Robinson: Pioneer and Agriculturist. Selected Writings,* ed. Herbert Anthony Kellar (Indianapolis: Indiana Historical Bureau, 1936), 2: 265, 276. Not all proslavery writers, of course, included in their defenses the argument that black slaves could not be overworked; see Smith, *Lectures on Philosophy and Practice of Slavery,* 284–87.

90. "A Citizen," "Employment of the Indigent," *Journal of Commerce,* Nov. 20, 1847.

91. For the earlier history of the ideas upon which "A Citizen" was drawing, see Dorothy Marshall, *The English Poor in the Eighteenth Century* (London: Routledge and Kegan Paul, 1969 [1926]), 27.

92. "A Citizen," "Employment of Indigent."

93. Moses G. Leonard, *Report on General Conditions of Institutions,* May 25, 1846, p. 26, quoted in Stephen A. Klips, "Institutionalizing the Poor: The New York City Almshouse, 1825–1860" (Ph.D. diss., City University of New York, 1980), 309.

94. Leonard, *Report on General Conditions,* 26, quoted in Ibid.

95. Moses G. Leonard, New York City Almshouse, *Annual Report for 1847,* 6, quoted in Klips, "Institutionalizing," 7.

96. Moses G. Leonard, *Communication on Convict and Pauper Labor* (1847), 263–65, quoted in Klips, "Institutionalizing," 320.

97. Steven J. Ross has recently described some early eighteenth-century American precedents for views such as Leonard's; Ross, "'Objects of Charity': Poor Relief, Poverty, and the Rise of the Almshouse in Early Eighteenth-Century New York City," in William Pencak and Conrad Edick Wright, eds., *Authority and Resistance in Early New York* (New York: New-York Historical Society, 1988), 138–61. For later antecedents of Leonard's views, see Raymond A. Mohl, *Poverty in New York, 1783–1825* (New York: Oxford University Press, 1971), 222–25.

98. New York State, *Assembly Documents* for 1837, vol. 3, no. 169, *Report of the Minority of the Committee on State Prisons,* Feb. 17, 1837, p. 2.

99. "State Prison 'Hard Labor,'" *Awl* (Lynn, Mass.), Jan. 4, 1845.

100. Solon Robinson, "The Penitentiary System in the United States," Mar. 1842, *Selected Writings,* 1: 314. Like many of the other issues with which this study deals, the nature of the complaint against convict labor registered here by Robinson and various mechanic groups has modern manifestations and parallels. When Mayor Edward I. Koch of New York City proposed that a public health official be punished for certain misdemeanors by being assigned to work as an orderly in a hospital ward, the president of a local hospital workers union issued the following objection: "Our members are on the bottom of the health-care hierarchy. They have had to struggle for respect from people who look down on those whose duties include emptying bedpans, scrubbing floors and doing laundry. For the Mayor to equate their honest labor with punishment demonstrates a shocking insensitivity. This form of 'punishment' insults those who do the work every day for a living, and it also undermines efforts to sustain good morale" (James Butler, President, Local 420, American Federation of State, County and Municipal Employees, N.Y.C. Municipal Hospital Workers, letter of June 13, 1986, to *New York Times,* in June 20, 1986, edition).

101. Moses G. Leonard, New York City Almshouse, *Annual Report for 1846,* 373–74, quoted in Klips, "Institutionalizing," 314.

102. David J. Rothman, *The Discovery of the Asylum: Social Order and Disorder in the New Republic* (Boston: Little, Brown and Company, 1971), 237–60.

103. Priscilla Clement, "The Response to Need: Welfare and Poverty in Philadelphia, 1800 to 1850" (Ph.D. diss. University of Pennsylvania, 1977), 172–73; M. A. Crowther, *The Workhouse System 1834–1929: The History of an English Social Institution* (Athens: University of Georgia Press, 1981), 33–34, 40–44, 122–34, 209; Michael B. Katz, *In the Shadow of the Poorhouse: A Social History of Welfare in America* (New York: Basic Books, 1986), 25–31. For a brief history of the treadmill and similar instruments of punishment at hard labor in British prisons and houses of correction, see J. Thorsten Sellin, *Slavery and the Penal System* (New York: Elsevier, 1976), 106–11.

104. Mayhew, *London Labour,* 2: 243, 243n. For Mayhew's descriptions and similar criticisms of the tread wheel and other punitive and "*useless* hard labor" in British prisons, see Henry Mayhew and John Binny, *The Criminal Prisons of London and Scenes of Prison Life* (London: Frank Cass and Company, 1968 [1862]), 110–11, 301–9, 514–15. Mayhew's disdain for almshouse and prison policies that deliberately made labor a punishment rather than a pleasure for those with "an inordinate aversion to work" is placed in the context of penal theories of the period by Ursula

Henriques, "The Rise and Decline of the Separate System of Prison Discipline," *Past and Present*, no. 54 (Feb.1972): 61–93. For some of the larger, related issues raised by the evolution of prison labor during the rise of industrial capitalism, see Robert P. Weiss, "Humanitarianism, Labour Exploitation, or Social Control? A Critical Survey of Theory and Research on the Origin and Development of Prisons," *Social History* 12 (Oct.1987): 331–50.

Although Mayhew joined with American antebellum workingmen's organizations in criticizing the punitive uses to which manual labor was put in correctional institutions, their sympathies, and quite possibly their assumptions, were very different. Mayhew had the interests of prisoners and almshouse inmates in mind and assumed that human nature was sufficiently universal that even those institutionalized elements of society that bore an unusually intense aversion to labor could be made to find work pleasant provided the right incentives and purposeful qualities were attached to it. Members of the workingmen's organizations, on the other hand, were concerned with the dignity of their callings, not with the reformability of the institutionalized elements of society. Their insistence that the use of manual labor as an instrument of punishment served to demean labor's intrinsic nobility may even have taken some of its strength from a belief that segments of these institutionalized populations possessed an innate, contemptible disposition, one easily capable of transforming labor into something contemptible. It was the use of convicts and other institutionalized populations in types of manual labor that approximated and competed with their own employments to which the workingmen's organizations were above all objecting in their various petitions to state legislatures. There is little evidence that they shared Mayhew's objections to the imposition upon such groups of the tread wheel and other types of labor that least approximated and least competed with their own callings yet that most obviously, as Mayhew argued, fit the description of manual labor as an instrument of punishment. For a particularly bitter and unsympathetic attack in the labor press on the "vagrants and *offals* of society" who inhabited Philadelphia's House of Refuge, and whose "gratuitous labour" was to be used to enrich the directors of that institution at the same time that it degraded and underbid the labor of "*honest*" and "*virtuous*" mechanics, see "Simon," "House of Refuge," *Mechanics' Free Press. A Journal of Practical and Useful Knowledge* (Philadelphia), Oct. 18, 1828.

105. Mayhew, *London Labour*, 2: 244–45. Of interest here is Mayhew's declaration that the food, lodging, and clothing given the pauper or slave could not constitute an adequate "reward" for the truly free laborer. But suppose that the amount of these provisions was truly generous, as proslavery writers in fact often claimed with reference to Southern slaves. Possibly Mayhew was simply assuming the contrary, that under the slave and almshouse systems, food, lodging, and clothing would only be doled out in the most meager amounts, and that for this reason alone they could not constitute adequate compensation for free labor. Quite conceivably, however, Mayhew believed something quite different: that the *nature* of compensation, and not merely its level, was a necessary determinant of the laborer's dignity; the truly free, well-motivated laborer required cash wages for his services—the power to make choices in the marketplace. To the extent that he did believe this, Mayhew may have been reflecting the values of an increasingly consumer-oriented society. In chapter 8, other manifestations of these values receive comment, notably the argument made by some middle-class writers that the best means of motivating and elevating the working classes lay in developing their taste for many of the comforts already enjoyed by more affluent elements of society.

106. This last point is also raised in Rothman, *Discovery,* 260.

107. For a similar interpretation see William James Forsythe, *The Reform of Prisoners, 1830–1900* (London: Croom Helm, 1987), 10, 21–23, 75–78.

108. Harold Perkin has followed many other historians in noting "the hostility of a large part of the [British] middle-class towards the landowners" and its "denial of the economic necessity of the landowning class. Brought up on the gospel of work and the horror of waste common to the Evangelical and the Benthamite," the middle class, Perkin observes, "could not separate unearned luxury from the idea of sin." Ricardo and other classical economists provided a more theoretical basis to this sense that "capitalists worked, landlords did not" (Harold Perkin, *The Structured Crowd: Essays in English Social History* [Sussex: Harvester Press, 1981], 104–5). See also Perkin, *Origins of Modern English Society* (London: Ark Paperbacks, 1985 [1969]), 214–16, 226–28; and Elie Halévy, *The Growth of Philosophic Radicalism,* trans. Mary Morris (London: Faber and Faber, 1934), 316–17, 337. See in addition, however, Joseph Hamburger's dissent from Halévy's view, in which Hamburger argues that although leading Philosophic Radicals were indeed antiaristocratic in their orientation, their overriding concern was with constitutional and political rather than with economic questions; more than this, in Hamburger's opinion, the Philosophic Radicals were middle-class *intellectuals* who did not speak for any class in Britain, including the "middle class and its interest." Hamburger's arguments are interesting but less than completely convincing; Joseph Hamburger, *Intellectuals in Politics: John Stuart Mill and the Philosophic Radicals* (New Haven: Yale University Press, 1965), 46–52, 64, 72.

Historians are attempting to reconcile the undeniable middle-class hostility to parasitic, aristocratic landlordism with the no less evident aspiration of British industrial entrepreneurs, commercial, and financial men to gain enough wealth to enable their families to one day become part of the leisured, landed upper class. For the argument that notwithstanding the "gospel of work," manufacture and trade lacked ultimate respectability even for those who practiced them, and that Britain's true "ideological hegemony" was, even during the height of the Industrial Revolution, one of upper-class leisure values rather than middle-class capitalist work values, see Martin J. Wiener, *English Culture and the Decline of the Industrial Spirit, 1850–1980* (Cambridge, Eng.: Cambridge University Press, 1981), 6–39, 127–59; and Walter J. Arnstein, "The Myth of the Triumphant Victorian Middle Class," *Historian* 37 (Feb. 1975): 205–21. For an opposing view that minimizes the "gentrification" in industrialists' behavior and attitudes, see W. D. Rubinstein, "New Men of Wealth and the Purchase of Land in Nineteenth-Century Britain," *Past and Present,* no. 92 (Aug. 1981): 125–47. For yet another perspective, see M. F. Daunton, "'Gentlemanly Capitalism' and British Industry 1820–1914," *Past and Present,* no. 122 (Feb. 1989): 119–58. F. M. L. Thompson has made perhaps the most detailed efforts to distinguish those elements of the "English bourgeoisie" that were "antiaristocratic, antilanded" from those that accepted the values of the English aristocracy and gentry and ultimately succeeded in joining the latter's ranks; see his "English Landed Society in the Nineteenth Century," in Pat Thane, Geoffrey Crossick, and Roderick Floud, eds., *The Power of the Past: Essays for Eric Hobsbawm* (Cambridge, Eng.: Cambridge University Press, 1984), 200–202; and also F. M. L. Thompson, *The Rise of Respectable Society: A Social History of Victorian Britain 1830–1900* (London: Fontana Press, 1988), 158–65.

109. For a recent study that objects to the "stereotype" of Harriet Martineau as a middle-class, laissez faire dogmatist and that in underscoring some neglected subtleties and dimensions in Martineau's thought thereby seems to me to slight

what remains the central tendency in that thought, see Betty Fladeland, *Abolitionists and Working-Class Problems in the Age of Industrialization* (Baton Rouge: Louisiana State University Press, 1984), x–xi, 74–92. On Martineau's laissez faire dogmatism, see Ann B. Robson, *On Higher Than Commerical Grounds: The Factory Controversy 1830–1853* (New York: Garland Publishing, 1985), 306, 312–13; and Deidre David, *Intellectual Women and Victorian Patriarchy: Harriet Martineau, Elizabeth Barrett Browning, George Eliot* (Ithaca: Cornell University Press, 1987), 42–45.

110. For a relevant and incisive discussion, see Rajani Kannepalli Kanth, *Political Economy and Laissez-Faire: Economics and Ideology in the Ricardian Era* (London: Rowman and Littlefield, 1986), 7,13, 43–80, 172–90.

111. Witness to the suffering caused by seasonal layoffs and cyclical unemployment in the country's largest urban center, Horace Greeley seems even in his Associationist phase to have regarded sheer want of work as the greatest of all evils facing the laboring classes. Neither the tedious and mentally unstimulating character of much manual labor, nor even the incapacity of the laborer's dependent, wage-earning status to provide him with maximum incentive to work hard and efficiently—another of Greeley's major themes—troubled Greeley so deeply; see the *Tribune,* articles 5, 11, 15, in Greeley and Raymond, *Association Discussed.* For a later statement by Greeley of the worth of any labor, including street sweeping, when compared to no work at all, see his "Counsel to Young Men," *Wood's Household Magazine* 9 (Jan. 1871), in Greeley "Articles, 1871–72," Greeley Papers, Library of Congress. For British mercantilist thought see Edgar S. Furniss, *The Position of the Laborer in a System of Nationalism: A Study in the Labor Theories of the Later English Mercantilists* (New York: Kelley and Millman, 1957), 75–116.

112. Philadelphia *Public Ledger,* Aug. 31, 1848, quoted in Philip Benedict Sheridan, Jr., "The Immigrant in Philadelphia, 1827–1860: The Contemporary Published Report" (Ph.D. diss., Georgetown University, 1957), 289.

113. For the belief of some insane asylum officials that regular physical labor and the instillation of "habits of industry" were a major part of the cure for insanity, see Rothman, *Discovery,* 144–46, 265–87; and also Gerald N. Grob, *Mental Institutions in America: Social Policy to 1875* (New York: The Free Press, 1973), 178–79. As officials in insane asylums and other corrective institutions in the late antebellum years retreated from hopes of reforming or curing their charges (an increasing proportion of whom were the Irish-born poor) and embraced mere custodianship as their major responsibility, their faith in labor's rehabilitative powers in all likelihood underwent a commensurate decline.

114. Paul Mantoux, *The Industrial Revolution in the Eighteenth Century,* rev. ed., trans. Marjorie Vernon (New York: Harcourt, Brace and Company, 1927), 409–50; E. P. Thompson, *The Making of the English Working Class* (Harmondsworth, Eng.: Penguin Books, 1968), 213–15, 237–43; Arthur Redford, *Labour Migration in England, 1800–1850,* 2d ed., ed. and rev. W. H. Chaloner (New York: Augustus M. Kelley, 1968 [1926]), 24–26; Franklin F. Mendels, "Social Mobility and Phases of Industrialization," *Journal of Interdisciplinary History* 7 (Autumn 1976): 208.

115. James Conrad, Jr., "The Evolution of Industrial Capitalism in Rhode Island, 1790–1830: Almy, the Browns, and the Slaters" (Ph.D. diss., University of Connecticut, 1973), 17–20. See also Jonathan Prude, *The Coming of Industrial Order: Town and Factory Life in Rural Massachusetts, 1810–1860* (Cambridge, Eng.: Cambridge University Press, 1983), 41–89; Drew R. McCoy, *The Elusive Republic: Political Economy in Jeffersonian America* (Chapel Hill: University of North Carolina Press, 1980), 118–19, 225.

116. George S. White, *Memoir of Samuel Slater. The Father of American Man-*

ufacturers. Connected with a History of the Rise and Progress of the Cotton Manufacture in England and America, with Remarks on the Moral Influence of Manufactories in the United States (New York: Augustus M. Kelley, 1967 [1836]), 118. For an early but still useful discussion of similar arguments in support of American industrialization made by Alexander Hamilton, Matthew Carey, and others, see Edith Abbott, "The History of Industrial Employment of Women in the United States: An Introductory Study," *Journal of Political Economy* 14 (Oct. 1906): 494–500.

117. Pennsylvania, *Journal of the Senate of the Commonwealth of Pennsylvania*, Session of 1837–1838, vol. 2, *Testimony of Witnesses, Accompanying the Report of the Committee of the Senate, Appointed to Investigate the Subject of the Employment of Children in Manufactories,* read in Senate, Feb. 7, 1838, pp. 305, 282, 324, 352, 358. Some of the proprietors also claimed that they were accommodating the wishes of less worthy, "idle and intemperate," if still indigent, parents (305).

118. For evidence that some factory proprietors in fact valued and sought out the labor of young child operatives, see William A. Sullivan, *The Industrial Worker in Pennsylvania 1800–1840* (Harrisburg: Pennsylvania Historical and Museum Commission, 1955), 43–45. Many, and perhaps most, of the youngest (under twelve), uneducated child operatives employed in these particular Pennsylvania mills may indeed, as the Senate testimony suggests, have been the children of widows and other poor parents who were not themselves employed in the mills. Yet some parents were clearly so employed; in these latter cases, presumably, proprietors could have dispensed with some of the child labor they professed to find so unprofitable and still acted to relieve the poverty of these children's families by raising the wages of the parent operatives. Sullivan reports instances of Pennsylvania proprietors who, contrary to most of the testimony, so esteemed the labor of child operatives that they threatened—and in some cases made good on their threats—to dismiss those adult operatives who sought to remove their children from the mills.

119. Pennsylvania, Senate, *Employment of Children*, 2: 301, 304. See also Alba M. Edwards, "The Labor Legislation of Connecticut," *Publications of the American Economic Association*, 3d ser., 7 (1907): 7; John Towles, "The Labor Legislation of Rhode Island," *Publications of the American Economic Association*, 3d ser., 9 (1908): 24; Peter J. Coleman, *The Transformation of Rhode Island, 1790–1860* (Providence: Brown University Press, 1963), 218, 239–40. The most detailed historical study I have seen of working-class parental attitudes toward education, one which reveals the range of those attitudes and the variety of factors that came into play, is W. B. Stephens, *Education, Literacy, and Society, 1830–70: The Geography of Diversity in Provincial England* (Manchester, Eng.: Manchester University Press, 1987), 49, 57, 61, 179.

120. Massachusetts, *House Documents* for 1836, no. 49, *Report by the Committee on Education, Related to the Education of Children Employed in Manufacturing Establishments,* 10–11. See also chapter 2, text at note 78.

121. Cynthia J. Shelton, *The Mills of Manayunk: Industrialization and Social Conflict in the Philadelphia Region, 1787–1837* (Baltimore: Johns Hopkins University Press, 1986), 60–75.

122. William Cullen Bryant, *Letters of a Traveller; Or, Notes of Things Seen in Europe and America*, 3d ed. (New York: Putnam, 1851), 345–49. Gregg established his textile factory at Graniteville, S.C., in 1845. George Winston Smith notes that Bryant (in contrast to Gregg, James Henry Hammond, and other leading Southern advocates of the factory employment of poor Southern whites) also perceived and favored such employment as a means of undermining slavery; Smith, "Ante-Bellum

Attempts of Northern Business Interests to 'Redeem' the Upper South," *Journal of Southern History* 11 (May 1945): 183–84.

123. The Children's Aid Society, *Seventh Annual Report* (1860), 5. Brace, however, was not unaware of, and unreceptive to, arguments warning of the moral dangers of factory employment (6). As his daughter wrote years later, "though there are not the same dangers for girls in the factories as for the class of street children already helped by the [Children's Aid] society, there are other risks, and Mr. Brace felt something must be done to amuse as well as instruct them in the evenings" (*The Life of Charles Loring Brace. Chiefly Told in His Own Letters*, ed. "by His Daughter" [Emma Brace], [New York: Charles Scribner's Sons, 1894], 228).

124. "Lowell—Its Aspects—Manufactures—Conditions of Labor—Reform," *New-York Daily Tribune*, May 14, 1846.

125. In addition to the above editorial, see the ones in the following issues of the *New-York Daily Tribune:* "A Voice from the Laborers of New-England—Calumny Met!" Nov. 21, 1845; "The Condition of Labor," Sept. 30, 1845; and "Labor in Lowell," Sept. 18, 1845; see also chapter 2, note 3 for Greeley's remarks in his letter to Pauline Davis. The additional employment opportunities the mills provided young single women would also give them time to postpone marriage, a circumstance not without its advantages given the high ratio of single women to single men in New England during this period; for a good discussion of the social and economic context in which the mill girls performed their work, see Nancy F. Cott, *The Bonds of Womanhood: "Woman's Sphere" in New England, 1780–1835* (New Haven: Yale University Press, 1977), 1–62. For a modern statement that the "market economy," and factory employment particularly, acted in several important ways to "emancipate" working-class women in nineteenth-century Europe—an argument that has hardly gone uncontested by other scholars—see Edward Shorter, *The Making of the Modern Family* (New York: Basic Books, 1975), 71, 259–63.

126. Quotation from Jürgen Kuczynski, *The Rise of the Working Class*, trans C. T. A. Ray (New York: McGraw Hill Book Company, 1967), 8.

127. "Nature and Effects of a Protective Tariff," *American Whig Review* 14 (July 1851): 85–86.

128. For the work that contains Brace's most extended blending of these concerns, see his *The Dangerous Classes of New York, and Twenty Years' Work among Them*, 3d ed.—"with Addenda" (Montclair: Patterson Smith, 1967 [1880]), 29–31.

129. Congressman Alexander H. Stephens of Georgia, *Congressional Globe. Appendix*, 33d Cong., 2d sess., Jan. 15, 1855, 108.

130. Gewen, "Intellectual Foundations," 52–53; Alice Kessler-Harris, *Women Have Always Worked* (Old Westbury, N.Y.: Feminist Press, 1981), 61.

131. Massachusetts, *Senate Documents* for 1868, no. 21, *Report of the Hon. Henry K. Oliver, Deputy State Constable, Specially Appointed to Enforce the Laws Regulating the Employment of Children in Manufacturing and Mechanical Establishments*, correspondence from the firm of C. A. & S. M. Wheelock, Uxbridge, Nov. 25, 1867, pp. 52–53. See also James R. Green and Hugh Carter Donahue, *Boston's Workers: A Labor History* (Boston: Trustees of the Public Library of the City of Boston, 1979), 32–33.

132. The capitalists and other members of the middle classes who sought to impose industrial morality on the laboring population were only in limited instances engaging in a double standard. The evidence suggests that they did ask much of themselves in the way of diligence, self-discipline, and sobriety, and that they sought to inculcate these qualities in their sons as well. One can, of course, hardly overlook the fact that members of the middle classes were to a much greater

degree than manual laborers compensated for their efforts by the material and intellectual rewards and the social status that their occupations brought; see Thompson, *Rise of Respectable Society,* 145; and Daniel T. Rodgers, "Socializing Middle-Class Children: Institutions, Fables, and Work Values in Nineteenth-Century America," *Journal of Social History* 13 (Spring 1980): 356–57. See also Anne M. Boylan, *Sunday School: The Formation of an American Institution, 1970–1880* (New Haven: Yale University Press, 1988), 3–5; William A. Muraskin, "The Social-Control Theory in American History: A Critique," *Journal of Social History* 9 (June 1976): 559–69.

133. A good general discussion of "ideological hegemony" is T. J. Jackson Lears, "The Concept of Cultural Hegemony: Problems and Possibilities," *American Historical Review* 90 (June 1985): 567–83. Among the more sophisticated discussions of middle-class "ideological hegemony" in mid-nineteenth-century Britain are Kirk, *Growth of Working Class Reformism,* 142–239; Tholfsen, *Working Class Radicalism,* 16–19, 216–49; and Tholfsen, "Intellectual Origins," 57–91. These and other studies, including the growing number that deal with the emergence of "labor aristocracies" in various British cities, differ on many matters of interpretation; but they appear to agree that values that were preeminently middle-class interacted with collectivist and other impulses that were more indigenous to large segments of the working classes, and that the long-term effect of these values, certainly, was to blunt the radical potential of British working-class movements; see also note 26 in this chapter.

134. For a brief discussion of the relationship of evangelically inspired "industrial morality" to the character virtues embodied in the Puritan ethic, see Dawley and Faler, "Working-Class Culture and Politics," 466–480. See also Faler, "Cultural Aspects of the Industrial Revolution: Lynn, Massachusetts, Shoemakers, and Industrial Morality," *Labor History* 15 (Summer 1974): 367–94. In his *Mechanics and Manufacturers in the Early Industrial Revolution: Lynn, Massachusetts 1780–1860* (Albany: State University of New York Press, 1981), 100–138, Faler more explicitly discounts the direct formative influence of seventeenth-century New England Puritanism on the early nineteenth century's "rigid code" of industrial morality (107). See also Daniel Walker Howe, "Victorian Culture in America," in Howe, ed., *Victorian America* (Philadelphia: University of Pennsylvania Press, 1976), 4–20. As in the case of middle-class support for mass education and labor-saving technology, middle-class efforts to diffuse industrial work values among the laboring population commonly invoked the argument that workers would share at least as much as other members of society in the national rise in living standards resulting from their increased productivity. But like these other middle-class enthusiasms, the exaltation of industrial morality bore an ambiguous relationship to "success" values that were particularly evident in America and that put a premium upon occupational advancement. Emphasis upon the capacity of the working classes to enjoy higher levels of "comforts," like the stress upon their capacity for moral and intellectual elevation, could lead to a deliberate downplaying of those other arguments that trumpeted the supposed ease with which industrious workers in America moved out of manual labor employments, including ones of a "hireling" nature. The deemphasis upon upward social mobility might seem particularly attractive to commentators who believed that there were only limited economic opportunities available, even in America, for the businessmen and others who would live entirely off their mental labor.

135. See, for example, Bendix, *Work and Authority,* 110–15; and Patrick Joyce, *Work, Society, and Politics: The Culture of the Factory in Later Victorian England* (Brighton, Eng.: Harvester Press, 1980), 136–37; Joseph A. Schumpeter, *History of*

Economic Analysis, ed. (from ms.) Elizabeth Boody Schumpeter (New York: Oxford University Press, 1954), 570–73. Malthus was hardly less moralistic in the second and subsequent editions of his work on population than he had been in his first, but his greater emphasis in these later editions upon the capacity of the laboring poor to combat population pressures through the exercise of "moral restraint" represented a considerable toning down of the gloom and doom character of the original 1798 edition. See also the discussion of the mellowing of one British entrepreneurial group's competitive attitudes in Theodore Koditschek, "The Dynamics of Class Formation in Nineteenth-Century Bradford," in A. L. Beier, David Cannadine, and James M. Rosenheim, eds., *The First Modern Society: Essays in English History in Honour of Lawrence Stone* (Cambridge, Eng.: Cambridge University Press, 1989), 511–48.

136. John Clive, *Macaulay: The Shaping of the Historian* (New York: Alfred A. Knopf, 1973), 224–25.

137. Paul E. Johnson, *A Shopkeepers' Millennium: Society and Revivals in Rochester, New York 1815–1837* (New York: Hill and Wang, 1978), 57, 136–41.

138. Even individuals, strongly evangelical or otherwise, who most firmly identified themselves with a harsh, middle-class free market morality might actively support government interventionist, "paternalist" policies that were calculated, in their judgment, to put the socially and morally disadvantaged on a more equal competitive footing. James Kay-Shuttleworth, for example, whose views are discussed at some length in the text below, was a resolute Manchester middle-class "liberal," an opponent both of outdoor poor relief policies and labor combinations that ostensibly impaired the operation of a competitive labor market. Yet he was also capable of regarding slum conditions and other "physical evils" as legitimate targets for governmental action because they impeded, in his judgment, the all-important "moral progress" or "elevation" of the working classes. In this general sentiment, if in little else, Kay-Shuttleworth shared an affinity with more traditional paternalists like Lord Shaftesbury. And to cite one of the apparent ironies to which historians have long been drawn, Edwin Chadwick was both a major architect of the New Poor Law and the promoter of sanitary and housing legislation for the laboring poor; see James Kay-Shuttleworth, "Sketch of the Progress of Manchester in Thirty Years, from 1832 to 1862" (1862), in Kay-Shuttleworth, *Four Periods of Public Education as Reviewed in 1832—1839—1846—1862* (London: Longman, 1862), 148; Richard Johnson, "Educational Policy and Social Control in Early Victorian England," *Past and Present,* no. 49 (Nov. 1970): 103. For a relevant and probing discussion of the "false antithesis" between "individualism" and "collectivism" in mid-Victorian British social thought, see Perkin, *Structured Crowd,* 57–69. See also Perkin, *Origins of Modern English Society,* 287–90, 329–31.

"Paternalism," itself, one might add, is a highly amorphous concept, one that is compatible with a wide range of values and ideological objectives. As Gregory Claeys has suggested, Robert Owen's "paternalistic" mistrust of universal suffrage and political radicalism was far more democratic than Tory–High Church and other more conventional paternalist social outlooks. Conventional paternalism extolled noblesse oblige within the context of a society of rigid social ranks and hereditary privileges. And as was the case with variations within proslavery ideology, paternalist arguments that counseled a temporary, if unspecified, period of tutelage, stewardship, and protection for the lower orders, and that assumed that the moral characters of the members of these orders would improve automatically as social conditions improved, were significantly different from more elitist and hierarchical paternalist creeds which denied or doubted that the lower orders would ever possess the capacity and resources for rational self-direction and equal rights. See Gregory Claeys, "Paternalism and Democracy in the Politics of Robert Owen," *International Review of Social History,* no. 27, pt. 2 (1982): 161–207; Boyd Hilton, *The Age of Atonement: The Influence of Evangelicalism on Social and Economic Thought, 1795–1865* (Oxford: Clarendon Press, 1988), 87; Alan Fox, *History and Heritage: The Social Origins of the British Industrial Relations System* (London: George Allen and Unwin, 1985), 2–7; John Kleinig, *Paternalism* (Totowa, N.J.: Rowman and Allanheld, 1983).

139. Thompson, *Making of English,* 393–98; Hilton, *Age of Atonement,* 15, 87–90; David Roberts, *Paternalism in Early Victorian England* (New Brunswick: Rutgers University Press, 1954), 74–75; 113–33; Ian Bradley, *The Call to Seriousness: The Evangelical Impact on the Victorians* (New York: Macmillan Publishing Company, 1976), 120–33, 151–53. The very existence of the Ten Hours Movement attests to the fact that not merely individuals who held to some form of evangelical persuasion were capable of believing that routine and excessive factory labor deprived operatives of their capacity for rationality and self-direction; see the very perceptive discussion of "the worker/slave metaphor" in the debates over British industrialization in Catherine Gallagher, *The Industrial Reformation of English Fiction: Social Discourse and Narrative Form 1832–1867* (Chicago: University of Chicago Press, 1985), 3–35.

140. It is true that the eighteenth-century charity school movement anticipated in some respects the nineteenth-century middle-class concern with developing the laboring population's "higher nature." If the primary intent of that movement, as M. G. Jones has maintained, was to so develop the moral faculties of the laboring poor to better acclimate and prepare them for their lowly stations in life, then this objective, as we shall see, was not so very different from that which governed many of the nineteenth-century middle-class efforts to increase educational opportunities for the masses, particularly in England; M. G. Jones, *The Charity School Movement: A Study of Eighteenth Century Puritanism in Action* (London: Frank Cass and Company, 1964 [1938]), 4–5; Jacob Viner, "Man's Economic Status," in James L. Clifford, ed., *Man Versus Society in Eighteenth-Century Britain* (Cambridge, Eng.: Cambridge University Press, 1968), 33–34. One can even find occasional educational schemes, some long antedating the charity school movement, that took a yet more expansive and ambitious attitude toward educating the laboring poor, schemes that anticipated the view of Thomas Jefferson and various nineteenth-century thinkers that geniuses might indeed be "raked from the rubbish" because there was no easy correspondence between native intellectual ability and social class; see A. E. Dobbs, *Education and Social Movements 1700–1850* (New York: Augustus M. Kelley, 1967 [1919]), 87n; and Lawrence Stone, "Literacy and Education in England 1640–1900," *Past and Present,* no. 42 (Feb. 1969): 73–74, 81. Yet after all these earlier enterprises and schemes have been acknowledged, it remains the case that middle-class (and British upper-class) concern for developing the "finer faculties" of the laboring population approached a scale and intensity in the first part of the nineteenth century that it had never previously attained.

141. A similar point is raised in John A. Mayer, "Notes towards a Working Definition of Social Control in Historical Analysis," in Stanley Cohen and Andrew Scull, eds., *Social Control and the State* (New York: St. Martin's Press, 1983), 19; and also, with respect to different middle-class attitudes toward child rearing in the 1850s, in Mania Kleinburd Baghdadi, "Protestants, Poverty, and Urban Growth: A Study of the Organization of Charity in Boston and New York, 1820–1865" (Ph.D. diss., Brown University, 1975), 260–66. This distinction repeatedly raises its head in discussions of the intentions and consequences of the programs pushed by middle-

class reformers. Thus K. D. M. Snell writes in regard to the New Poor Law, that contrary to the "stated priority of the Poor Law Report . . . to instill habits of 'independence' in the labour force," its effect, if not its underlying intent, was really to "increase submissiveness of labour to employers" (K. D. M. Snell, *Annals of the Labouring Poor: Social Change and Agrarian England, 1660–1900* [Cambridge, Eng.: Cambridge University Press, 1985], 120–21).

142. "Moral Influence of Manufactures," *Quarterly Christian Spectator* (New Haven) 4 (1832): 393–96.

143. J. G. Kohl, *England and Wales* (London: Frank Cass and Company, 1968 [1844]), 137.

144. Andrew Ure, *The Philosophy of Manufactures: Or, an Exposition of the Scientific, Moral, and Commercial Economy of the Factory System of Great Britain* (London: Charles Knight, 1835), 354, 355.

145. Congressman George Perkins Marsh of Vermont, *Congressional Globe. Appendix,* 29th Cong., 1st sess., June 30, 1846, 1010.

146. Harriet H. Robinson, "The Lowell Offering," separately enclosed in New York Public Library copy of *Lowell Offering* 5 (1845): 462; Harriet H. Robinson, *Loom and Spindle, or Life among the Early Mill Girls, with a Sketch of "The Lowell Offering" and Some of Its Contributors* (Kailua, Hawaii: Press Pacifica, 1976 [1898]), 26, 42. See also Claudia L. Bushman, *"A Good Poor Man's Wife." Being a Chronicle of Harriet Hanson Robinson and Her Family in Nineteenth-Century New England* (Hanover: University Press of New England, 1981), 13–31.

147. Elisha Bartlett, *A Vindication of the Character and Condition of the Females Employed in the Lowell Mills, against the Charges Contained in the "Boston Times" and the "Boston Quarterly Review"* (Lowell: Leonard Huntress, 1841), 11, 12–20.

148. Jesse K. McKeever, remarks in *Proceedings of the Second Convention of Managers and Superintendents of Houses of Refuge, Schools of Reform, and Institutions for the Prevention and Correction of Juvenile Destitution, Delinquency and Crime, in the United States of America. . . . May, 1859* (New York: n.p. 1860), 166, quoted in Baghdadi, "Protestants, Poverty, and Urban Growth," 265.

149. *First Report of the Committee on Public Hygiene of the American Medical Association* (Philadelphia: T. K. and P. G. Collins, 1849), 513–14. This report, which contains sketches of sanitary conditions in a number of antebellum cities, was here explaining why the fixed regimen of the Lowell operatives, the regular alternation of their "light, but constant" labor with their time for rest and meals, was "highly conducive to health." The report was, however, more critical of other features of the factory system at Lowell, citing poor ventilation, erratic temperature levels, and overcrowding in the work rooms; *First Report,* 514–15.

150. For Mayhew's description of subcontracting, "overwork and underpay," and other characteristics of the "dishonourable" branches of various London trades, see the collection of his letters to the London *Morning Chronicle,* 1849–1850, in Mayhew, *The Unknown Mayhew,* ed. Eileen Yeo and E. P. Thompson (New York: Random House, 1971).

151. Mayhew, *London Labour,* 3: 309.

152. For a dissection of Southern attitudes toward industrialization and urbanization that penetrates many of the stereotypes, see Theodore R. Marmor, "Anti-Industrialism and the Old South: The Agrarian Perspective of John C. Calhoun," *Comparative Studies in Society and History* 9 (Oct. 1967): 377–406.

153. Valuable discussions of eighteenth- and early nineteenth-century American attitudes toward industrialization and technology include Leo Marx, *The Machine in the Garden* (New York: Oxford University Press, 1964), 150–69; John F. Kasson,

Civilizing the Machine: Technology and Republican Values in America 1776–1900 (New York Grossman Publishers, 1976), 1–135; Hugo Arthur Meir, "The Technological Concept in American Social History, 1750–1860" (Ph.D. diss., University of Wisconsin, 1950) 2–79, 211; Drew R. McCoy, *The Elusive Republic: Political Economy in Jeffersonian America* (Chapel Hill: University of North Carolina Press, 1980), 225–26.

154. "H" [George Frederick Holmes], "Greeley on Reforms," *Southern Literary Messenger* 17 (May 1851): 273.

155. Ibid., 274.

156. Although Green, unlike some labor reformers and radicals, seemed to believe that Britain's factory system was redeemable, and that industrial enterprises owned and controlled by capitalists remained potentially beneficial for the employees, he also shared the radical (and Tory) animus toward the prevailing greedy and "oppressive" behavior of "overgrown" factory proprietors; "synopsis of the evidence" given by Green, in *Ten Hours' Factory Question*, 10n–11n.

157. P. Gaskell, *Artisans and Machinery: The Moral and Physical Condition of the Manufacturing Population Considered with Reference to Mechanical Substitutes for Human Labour* (New York: A. M. Kelley, 1968 [1836]), 93–112; *The Condition of the West India Slave Contrasted with That of the Infant Slave in Our English Factories* (London: W. Kidd, [1833]), 27–28; Thomas Guthrie, *The City: Its Sins and Sorrows. Being a Series of Sermons from Luke XIX. 41* (Glasgow: Scottish Temperance League, 1859), 78. Like other writers in this category, Guthrie did not think highly of the work supervision and surveillance provided most juvenile operatives as a moral counterweight to the pernicious effects of their congregation outside the home for employment purposes. Peer pressures within the mills, together with the measure of economic independence they gained there, Guthrie suggested, induced the grievously uneducated child operatives to "laugh at parental control, and in seeking to be their own masters, [they] become the slaves of their own master passions." Frequently accompanying this kind of criticism was the argument that when children were left at home by *mothers* who took jobs in the mills, they, again, grew up disposed to criminal and other antisocial behavior. As suggested earlier, these were the types of "moral" criticism of the factory system that male adult members of the working classes, protective of their position of authority within the home and resentful of family disruption, were most likely to share; see, for example, "The Luckless Children of the Poor," *The Factory Operatives' Guide, and Labour's Advocate: A Fortnightly Journal for the Working Classes in the Manufacturing Districts* (Royston, Eng.) 2 (June 3, 1854): 33–34. This would at least seem to be so, as Neil J. Smelser and others have argued, where and when adult males were themselves no longer exercising direct control over their children in "family unit" mill settings. One can even imagine that some of the more desperately poor adult male members of the laboring population, those who recognized their economic dependence on the factory employment of their wives or children and who took no part in the struggles to curtail the latter's hours for this reason, might still share in the uneasiness and resentment regarding the impact of the factory system upon family relationships. Of course, the entire body of radical working-class criticism of the factory system was also "moral" criticism in the sense that it presupposed that all workers—child, adult male, and adult female—who were oppressed by intense and regimented work processes and exploited by conditions of long hours at low wages, would emerge morally impaired. Yet the specific "moral evils" of the factory system that I have most in mind here were ones that above all preoccupied writers of the middle and upper classes; it would seem self-evident that operatives and other

members of the laboring population, concerned with challenging the prerogatives of the "Cotton Lords" and the capitalist class generally, did not form labor unions for the purpose of combating the alleged tendency of the factory system to encourage sexually promiscuous and socially incendiary behavior among their numbers.

158. Thomas Henry Bender, "Discovery of the City in America: The Development of Urbanism in 19th-Century Social Thought" (Ph.D. diss., University of California, Davis, 1971), 16–35; Marx, *Machine in Garden*, 116–69; Howard P. Segal, "Leo Marx's 'Middle Landscape': A Critique, a Revision, and an Appreciation," *Reviews in American History* 5 (Mar. 1977): 137–42. Segal has emphasized how the "middle landscape" ideal was not a static concept but underwent continuous redefinition and evolution during the nineteenth century to meet new social circumstances. These variations, however, need not concern us here. See also Charles L. Sanford, *The Quest for Paradise: Europe and the American Moral Imagination* (Urbana: University of Illinois Press, 1961), 155–75.

159. Zachariah Allen, *The Practical Tourist; or, Sketches of the State of the Useful Arts, and of Society, Scenery &c &c in Great Britain, France, and Holland* (1832), quoted in Michael Brewster Folsom and Steven D. Lubar, eds., *The Philosophy of Manufactures: Early Debates over Industrialization in the United States* (Cambridge: MIT Press, 1982), 341–42. See also Bender, "Discovery," 60–157.

160. Nathan Appleton, *Introduction of the Power Loom, and Origin of Lowell* (B. H. Penhall, 1858), 15–16. For details on the establishment and early history of the Waltham-type mill system, see Kenneth Frank Mailloux, "The Boston Manufacturing Company of Waltham, Massachusetts, 1813–1848. The First Modern Factory in America" (Ph.D. diss., Boston University, 1957) 27–109.

161. D. Dix to Nathan Appleton, July 28, 1841; and Appleton to Dix, Aug. 9, 1841, Nathan Appleton Papers, Massachusetts Historical Society, Boston.

162. James Phillips Kay, *The Moral and Physical Condition of the Working Classes Employed in the Cotton Manufacture in Manchester*, 2d enl. ed. (London: James Ridgway, 1832), 21–22, 27, 52–55.

163. This last presumption seems particularly evident in profactory arguments that, in characterizing the mechanized factory as a salutary learning environment, recognized parallels between it and the schoolroom; see Congressman George Perkins Marsh of Vermont, *Congressional Globe. Appendix*, 29th Cong., 1st sess., June 30, 1846, 1010–13. It was, however, the British factory proprietor R. H. Greg who perhaps made the most explicit and prominent use of the argument that factories could no more be condemned than churches or schools for bringing together young people of both sexes; see Paul Henry Elovitz, "'Airy and Salubrious Factories' or 'Dark Satanic Mills'? Some Early Reactions to the Impact of the Industrial Revolution on the Condition of the English Working Classes" (Ph.D. diss., Rutgers University, 1969), 222.

164. Appleton to Dix, Aug. 9, 1841, Appleton Papers.

165. Congressman E. J. Morris of Pennsylvania, *Congressional Globe. Appendix*, 28th Cong., 1st sess., Apr. 24, 1844, 567–68. For another example of this very common argument by advocates of an American factory system, see the *Quarterly Christian Spectator* essay discussed above, "Moral Influence of Manufactures," 380. For other examples from earlier in the century that were indicative of the increasingly favorable disposition of some Jeffersonian Republicans to large manufacturing enterprises in the United States, see McCoy, *Elusive Republic*, 245–46.

166. Deteriorating conditions, the recruitment of Irish operatives, and the departure of the Yankee girls at Lowell and elsewhere were, as Thomas Dublin remarks, "closely intertwined" factors whose relationship to one another perhaps

can never be precisely defined; Dublin, *Women and Work: The Transformation of Work and Community in Lowell, Massachusetts, 1826–1860* (New York: Columbia University Press, 1979), 140, 162–64. See also H. M. Gitelman, "The Waltham System and the Coming of the Irish," *Labor History* 8 (Fall 1967): 227–53.

167. Seth Luther, *An Address to the Working-Men of New-England, on the State of Education, and on the Condition of the Producing Classes in Europe and America* (pub. by author, 1832), 19.

168. See, for example, the remarks of agents in Massachusetts, *Senate Documents* for 1868, no. 21, *Report of the Hon. Henry K. Oliver . . . the Laws Regulating the Employment of Children in Manufacturing and Mechanical Establishments,* 23. See also Caroline F. Ware, *The Early New England Cotton Manufacture: A Study in Industrial Beginnings* (Boston: Houghton Mifflin Company, 1931), 230–34; Judith Barry Wish, "From Yeoman Farmer to Industrious Producer: The Relationship between Classic Republicanism and the Development of Manufacturing in America. From the Revolution to 1850" (Ph.D. diss., Washington University, 1976), 194–96; and Kasson, *Civilizing Machine,* 104–6. Factory interests were not, of course, the only ones to manifest this disdain for Irish-born operatives. A teacher in the mill town of Cohoes, New York, was particularly direct in 1857: "I *do* claim to be superior to the vulgar herd with which our factories are stocked, and I *do* consider them unfit to associate with me, or to move in the same society to which I belong. Such, too, is the sentiment of all 'Upper Tendom' " (reply to a series of letters from "A Factory Girl," *Cohoes Cataract,* Apr. 18, 1857, quoted in Daniel J. Walkowitz, "Working-Class Women in the Guilded Age: Factory, Community and Family Life among Cohoes, New York Cotton Workers," in Peter J. Stearns and Daniel J. Walkowitz, eds., *Workers in the Industrial Revolution: Recent Studies of Labor in the United States and Europe* [New Brunswick: Transaction Books, 1974], 259). My emphasis in the text upon the self-serving prejudices that factory interests imbibed is not intended to deny the validity of a number of points underscored by labor historians: that Irish and other immigrant operatives, particularly those who had acquired in England or Ireland the valued expertise that New England factories continued to require, often developed the capacity, techniques, and self-assertiveness needed to challenge industrial capitalist authority; that immigrant operatives and their families were able to eventually profit from their situations through limited occupational or "property" mobility; and that immigrant operatives, like other kinds of ethnic workers, possessed kinship traditions and community networks that helped fortify them against hurtful and debilitating ethnic prejudices emanating from the dominant culture; see, in addition to Walkowitz's essay, John Cumbler, "Immigration, Ethnicity, and the American Working-Class Community: Fall River, 1850–1900," in Robert Asher and Charles Stephenson, eds., *Labor Divided: Race and Ethnicity in United States Labor Struggles 1835–1960* (Albany: State University of New York Press, 1990), 151–70; and David A. Gerber, *The Making of an American Pluralism: Buffalo, New York, 1825–1860* (Urbana: University of Illinois Press, 1989), 136–41.

169. John Bright, Speech in the House of Commons, May 22, 1846, *Parliamentary Debates,* vol. 86 (1846), cols. 1051–52; William Cooke Taylor, *Factories and the Factory System: From Parliamentary Documents and Personal Examination* (London: Jeremiah How, 1844), 39–41.

170. Marx, *Machine in Garden,* 158–59; William Cooke Taylor, *Factories and the Factory System; from Parliamentary Documents and Personal Examination* (London: Jeremiah How, 1844), 39.

171. Taylor, *Factories and Factory System,* 113. Perhaps the most concerted use of Lowell in a British writing was made by the Rev. William Scoresby in his *American*

Factories and Their Female Operatives; with an Appeal on Behalf of the British Factory Population, and Suggestions for the Improvement of Their Condition (London: Longman, 1845), 78–80, 86, 97, 101, 117. Scoresby, a minister in Bradford, England, did not, in contrast to William Cooke Taylor, use the example of Lowell to defend factory labor and the factory system per se—he was, in fact, frankly critical of the long hours that Bradford's female operatives were obliged to work. His aim instead was to hold up the "self-respect" and the "superior" moral and intellectual "character" of Lowell's unmarried mill girls as an inspirational model for their British female counterparts, whom he felt were all too lax in their *"cultivation of a high tone of chaste and moral principle"* (Scoresby does not specify whether he regarded Bradford's married female operatives as similarly guilty of this laxity). Although Scoresby recognized that Bradford's female operatives labored under certain disadvantages, including lower wages and commencement of factory work without education at a younger age, he noted that the hours themselves at Lowell were "fully as long as ours." Scoresby made clear his view that to whatever extent it was within the capabilities of British female operatives to raise their condition, legitimate channels for so doing did not include combinations, strikes, or any other attempted interference with the "market price" of labor, which was fixed by the law of supply and demand. Except for his remark that the condition of the Lowell girls would be better still were their hours of labor also of a "more reasonable" length, Scoresby adopted in toto the eulogistic view of conditions in "the American Manchester" presented by such American writers as Henry Miles and Elisha Bartlett. For one who took greater cognizance than Scoresby of the complaints emanating out of Lowell of overwork and deteriorating conditions, and who used these complaints to make an even more forceful case for a legislative reduction of hours in British factories, see Lord Ashley, Speech in the House of Commons, Jan. 29, 1846, *Parliamentary Debates*, vol. 83 (1846), cols. 387–89. For a discussion of the general European tendency in this period to exaggerate the capacity of the American environment, because it was so largely rural, to absorb technology and industrialism without social costs, see Marvin Fisher, *Workshops in the Wilderness: The European Response to American Industrialization, 1830–1860* (New York: Oxford University Press, 1967), 41–43, 92–96, 122–23, 165.

172. Sir Edward Baines, *The Social, Educational, and Religious State of the Manufacturing Districts; with Statistical Returns of the Means of Education and Religious Instruction in the Manufacturing Districts of Yorkshire, Lancashire, and Cheshire, in Two Letters to the Right Hon. Sir Robert Peel*, 3d ed. (London: Simkin, Marshall, and Company, 1843), 59, repr. in *The Factory Education Bill of 1843*, one of a series of vols. in Carpenter, advisory ed., *British Labour Struggles*.

173. Ibid., 58; for a very similar comparison, see "W. R. G." [Greg], "Emigration or Manufactures?" *Westminster Review* 40 (Aug.–Dec. 1843): 101–15.

174. Congressman E. J. Morris of Pennsylvania, *Congressional Globe. Appendix*, 28th Cong., 1st sess., Apr. 24, 1844, 567.

175. Edward Baines, Jr., *History of the Cotton Manufactures in Great Britain*, 2d ed. (New York: Augustus M. Kelley, 1966 [1835]), 230, 484–96. See also the other sources cited in chapter 5, notes 3–6.

176. As Baines put this point, the only proper question was the misery of Britain's manufacturing population "compared with that of the rest of the working classes elsewhere." It was, after all, the "destiny of man to earn his bread by the sweat of his brow" and a certain, irreducible amount of poverty, "wretchedness," and attendant "dissoluteness" would follow from this fact alone (Ibid., 434).

177. Upon marrying, James Phillips Kay added the surname of his wife's family

462 Notes to Pages 239–42

to his own last name in 1842. He is hereafter referred to in the text as James Kay-Shuttleworth to more clearly distinguish him from his brother, Joseph Kay, whose writings are also treated below.

178. Kay, *Manchester*, 10–15, 21–22, 27–28, 52–55.

179. Ibid., 103–4.

180. Ibid., 43.

181. Ibid., 22.

182. Edward Baines, Jr., for one, took exception to the "highly coloured" picture of factory work presented here by Kay; Baines, *History of Cotton Manufacture*, 465. See also Robert Gray, "The Languages of Factory Reform in Britain, c. 1830–1860," in Joyce, ed., *Historical Meanings*, 160–62.

183. Kay, *Manchester*, 12, 92, 93, 107; James Kay-Shuttleworth, "Recent Measures for the Promotion of Education in England" (1839), in Kay-Shuttleworth, *Four Periods of Public Education*, 203–4.

184. Johnson, "Educational Policy and Social Control," 119. Johnson's essay is one of the best existing treatments of Kay-Shuttleworth's thought; also valuable is Trygve R. Tholfsen, "Introduction," to Tholfsen, ed., *Sir James Kay-Shuttleworth on Popular Education* (New York: Teachers College Press, 1974), 1–40.

185. See, for example, Frances Wright D'Arusmont, *Life, Letters and Lectures* (New York: Arno Press, 1972).

186. Among the most prominent of the "social control" interpretations of the mass education movement in America are Michael B. Katz, *The Irony of Early School Reform: Educational Innovation in Mid-Nineteenth Century Massachusetts* (Boston: Beacon Press, 1970), 88, 112; and Samuel Bowles and Herbert Gintis, *Schooling in Capitalist America: Educational Reform and the Contradictions of Economic Life* (New York: Basic Books, 1976), 27–29, 164–73, 240.

187. James Kay-Shuttleworth, remark in *Fourth Report of the Poor Law Commissioners, Parliamentary Papers* (1837–1838), vol. 28, p. 290, quoted in Anne Digby and Peter Searby, eds., *Children, School and Society in Nineteenth Century England* (London: Macmillan Press, 1981), 27.

188. First paragraph from James Kay-Shuttleworth, "On the Establishment of County or District Schools, for the Training of the Pauper Children Maintained in Union Workhouses," *Journal of the Royal Statistical Society* 1 (1838), quoted in Digby and Searby, eds., *Children, School and Society*, 118; second paragraph from Kay, *Manchester*, 97.

189. J. H. Poynter, *Society and Pauperism: English Ideas on Poor Relief, 1795–1834* (London: Routledge and Kegan Paul, 1969); Michael E. Rose, "The Disappearing Pauper: Victorian Attitudes to the Relief of the Poor," in Eric M. Sigsworth, ed., *In Search of Victorian Values: Aspects of Nineteenth-Century Thought and Society* (Manchester, Eng.: Manchester University Press, 1988): 56–67.

190. Kay, *Manchester*, 15–16, 44–49, 93.

191. Ibid., 94–98.

192. For examination of the various classical economic formulations of the "wage fund" doctrine, and of the different populist and labor radical criticisms of these in early Victorian England, see Edward Cannan, *A History of the Theories of Production and Distribution in English Political Economy from 1776 to 1848*, 3d ed. (London: Staples Press, 1917 [1898]), 182–319; Howard Dickman, *Industrial Democracy in America: Ideological Origins of National Labor Relations Policy* (La Salle, Ill.: Open Court, 1987), 19–147 passim; Noel W. Thompson, *The People's Science. The Popular Political Economy of Exploitation and Crisis 1816–34* (Cambridge, Eng. Cambridge University Press, 1984). For discussions of anti–Poor Law agitation and

related trade union and Chartist movements of the 1830s, see David Gadian, "Class Formation and Class Action in North-West Industrial Towns, 1830–50," in R. J. Morris, ed., *Class, Power and Social Structure in British Nineteenth-Century Towns* (Leicester, Eng.: Leicester University Press, 1986), 24–58; Edward Royle and James Walvin, *English Radicals and Reformers 1760–1848* (Sussex, Eng.: Harvester Press, 1982), 156–59; Dorothy Thompson, "Introduction," to Thompson, ed., *The Early Chartists* (Columbia: University of South Carolina Press, 1971), 8–18, 29–30; and various of the essays in James Epstein and Dorothy Thompson, eds., *The Chartist Experience: Studies in Working-Class Radicalism and Culture, 1830–60* (London: Macmillan Press, 1982).

193. Kay, *Manchester,* 97; Kay-Shuttleworth, "Recent Measures," 203–4, 229–33; James Kay-Shuttleworth, "Explanation of the Minutes of 1846" (1846), in Kay-Shuttleworth, *Four Periods of Public Education,* 453–54.

194. Joseph Kay, *The Education of the Poor in England and Europe* (London: J. Hatchard and Son, 1846), xi, xii.

195. Ibid., 163.

196. Ibid., 188, 363.

197. Johnson, "Educational Policy," 102. In Johnson's view, though, environmentalism and moralism struck a fairly even balance in Kay-Shuttleworth's thought. See also the discussion of Kay-Shuttleworth in Frank Mort, *Dangerous Sexualities: Medico-Moral Politics in England since 1830* (London: Routledge and Kegan Paul, 1987), 18–30.

198. Kay, *Manchester,* 5.

199. Kay, *Manchester,* 5, 6.

200. Ibid., 6.

201. Joseph Kay, *The Social Condition and Education of the People in England and Europe,* vol. 1, *The Peasant Proprietors* (Shannon, Ireland: Irish University Press, 1971 [1850]), 290.

202. Kay, *Education of Poor,* 363–64.

203. Kay, *Social Condition and Education of the People,* 1: 277.

204. For discussions of Methodist and other late eighteenth- and early nineteenth-century Evangelical activities directed at Britain's laboring poor, see Thompson, *Making of English,* 60–61, 385–440; Bendix, *Work and Authority,* 68–73, 110–15; J. L. Hammond and Barbara Hammond, *The Town Labourer, 1760–1832. The New Civilisation* (New York: Augustus M. Kelley, 1967 [1917]), 221–46; Jones, *Charity School Movement,* 140–62; For, however, a statement of Kay-Shuttleworth's in which he echoed the earlier evangelical emphasis on the irrelevance of "artificial distinctions" in the earthly life, see James Kay-Shuttleworth, "First Report on the Origin and Organisation of The Training College at Battersea, and the Introduction of Some of the Pupil Teachers as Students" (1841), in Kay-Shuttleworth, *Four Periods of Public Education,* 299.

205. Tholfsen, *Working Class Radicalism,* 17–18, 124–25, 210–19, 238–49; Tholfsen, "Intellectual Origins," 57–91; Harrison, "Victorian Gospel of Success," 163; J. F. C. Harrison, *The Early Victorians, 1832–51* (London: Cox and Wyman, 1851), 36; J. M. Goldstrom, *The Social Content of Education 1808–1870: A Study of the Working Class School Reader in England and Ireland* (Shannon, Ire.: Irish University Press, 1972), 72, 177–79, 190.

206. Kay-Shuttleworth, "Recent Measures," 187.

207. Rev. H. W. Bellairs, *Report on 138 Schools in the Western District,* (Feb. 1845) quoted in Kay, *Education of Poor,* 245.

208. Joseph Kay especially did himself argue at times for a more expansive

intellectual education for England's working classes—he underscored, in this regard, the superior quality of instruction available to the laboring classes in Switzerland, Germany, and other countries on the Continent; see particularly *Social Condition and Education,* vol. 2, *The Education of the People.* Unlike labor radicals, however, and as indicated above already, Kay's emphasis was also nearly always upon the dangers of developing the laborer's intellectual faculties while leaving his moral faculties unattended, an emphasis that reflected his concern with minimizing and checking vice and unrest among the laboring poor. There was, too, Kay's assumption that increasing the secular instruction of the British working classes would perform the valuable function of closing their minds to radical doctrines and solidifying their allegiance to existing class arrangements in Britain. For the contrasting importance that Owenite socialists, some of the Chartist leaders, and other British radicals attached to popular education and enlightenment as a means of challenging and overturning the status quo, see J. F. C. Harrison, *Learning and Living 1790–1960: A Study in the History of the English Adult Education Movement* (Toronto: University of Toronto Press, 1971), 90–148; Harold Silver, *The Concept of Popular Education: A Study of Ideas and Social Movements in the Early Nineteenth Century* (London: Macgibbon and Kee, 1965), 67–237; Silver, *English Education and the Radicals, 1780–1850* (London: Routledge and Kegan Paul, 1975), 41–120; Brian Simon, *Studies in the History of Education, 1780–1870* (London: Lawrence and Wishart, 1960), 177–275; and Johnson, "'Really Useful Knowledge': Radical Education and Working-Class Culture," in John Clarke, Chas Critcher, and Richard Johnson, eds., *Working-Class Culture: Studies in History and Theory* (London: Hutchinson, 1979), 75–102.

209. James Kay-Shuttleworth, "The Minutes of August and December, 1846, Considered in Their Religious and Political Aspect," in Kay-Shuttleworth, *Four Periods of Public Education,* 495–96.

210. Carl F. Kaestle, "Elite Attitudes toward Mass Schooling," in Lawrence Stone, ed., *Schooling and Society: Studies in the History of Education* (Baltimore: Johns Hopkins University Press, 1976), 184–86. White Southerners in the antebellum period appear to have divided over the question of whether the "oral" education of slaves in selected parts of the Scripture had the effect of increasing or diminishing the bondsmen's contentment and tractability. Except among some of the more fervent evangelicals, there was far more agreement—reflected in the various state prohibitions—that any rudimentary instruction of slaves which would equip them to read the Bible for themselves posed unacceptable dangers to slavery. Literate slaves would not only be exposed to the more "subversive" tenets of the Bible but would also be an easy target of Northern antislavery literature; see Carl F. Kaestle, *Pillars of the Republic: Common Schools and American Society, 1780–1860* (New York: Hill and Wang, 1983), 196–98; Anne C. Loveland, *Southern Evangelicals and the Social Order 1800–1860* (Baton Rouge: Louisiana State University Press, 1980), 206, 220–40, 253–54; Thomas L. Webber, *Deep like the Rivers: Education in the Slave Quarter Community 1831–1865* (New York: W. W. Norton and Company, 1978), 27–58.

211. See Tholfsen, "Introduction," in *Kay-Shuttleworth,* 32–35, for another comparison of the ideas of Kay-Shuttleworth and Mann that differs in some respects from the one that follows.

212. Horace Mann, *Twelfth Annual Report* (1849), in Mann, *Life and Works of Horace Mann,* enl. ed., ed. Mary Mann and George C. Mann (Boston: Lee and Shepard, 1891), 4: 252.

213. Ibid., 246–51.

214. Ibid., 251.

215. Mann presented other arguments in behalf of common school educa-tion—e.g., education as a natural right of every child—that are not discussed here because they are less germane to the subject at hand; see Jonathan Messerli, *Horace Mann: A Biography* (New York: Alfred A. Knopf, 1972), 493–94.

216. Horace Mann, "The Effects of Intemperance on the Poor and Ignorant" [n.d.], Lecture One of *Two Lectures on Intemperance* (Syracuse: Hall, Mills, and Company, 1852), 40.

217. For a probing discussion of Lincoln's views, see Richard Slotkin, *The Fatal Environment: The Myth of the Frontier in the Age of Industrialization* (New York: Atheneum, 1985), 216–19. See also G. S. Boritt, *Lincoln and the Economics of the American Dream* (Memphis: Memphis State University Press, 1978), 176–85.

218. "By a Father," *Public Schools, Public Blessings* (New York: Public School Society, 1838), quoted in Carl F. Kaestle, *The Evolution of an Urban School System: New York City, 1750–1850* (Cambridge: Harvard University Press, 1973), 101.

219. For manifestations of the social distance between antebellum wage-earn-ing manual laborers and such white-collar types as petty proprietors and counting-house and retail clerks, see, in particular, Stuart M. Blumin, *The Emergence of the Middle Class: Social Experience in the American City, 1760–1900* (Cambridge, Eng.: Cambridge University Press, 1989), 66–137.

220. Mann, *Fifth Annual Report* (1842), in *Life and Works,* 3: 101–11; see also Maris A. Vinovskis, "Horace Mann on the Economic Productivity of Education," *New England Quarterly* 43 (Dec. 1970): 551–68; Harvey J. Graff, *The Literacy Myth: Literacy and Social Structure in the Nineteenth-Century City* (New York: Academic Press, 1979), 203–7.

221. Mann, *Twelfth Annual Report* (1849), in *Life and Works,* 4: 252.

222. Horace Mann, "What God Does, and What He Leaves for Man to Do, in the Work of Education" (1840), in Mann, *Lectures, and Annual Reports, on Educa-tion,* ed. Mary Mann (Cambridge, Mass.: published for the editor, 1867), 1: 191.

223. Ibid., 192–93; Horace Mann, "The Necessity of Education in a Republi-can Government" (1838), in Mann, *Lectures, and Annual Reports,* 1: 150.

224. Horace Mann, "Means and Objects of Common-School Education" [n.d.], in Mann, *Lectures, and Annual Reports,* 1: 75.

225. Ibid., 1: 41. Like others of a similar persuasion, Mann drew an analogy here between the proslavery leadership of his own day and the conduct of those who led the French Revolution during its most violent phases: both were the consequence, not of no education at all, but rather of a "vicious or defective," i.e., insufficiently moral, education; see also Mann, "What God Does," *Lectures, and Annual Reports,* 1: 192–93.

226. Mann, *Third Annual Report* (1840), in *Life and Works,* 3: 4–9; see also Merle Curti, *The Social Ideas of American Educators* (Paterson, N.J.: Pageant Books, 1959 [1935]), 118–20.

227. Joseph T. Buckingham, *An Address Delivered before the Massachusetts Chari-table Mechanics Association. At the Celebration of Their Eighth Triennial Festival,* Oct. 7, 1830 (Boston: Dutton and Wentworth, 1830), 19; see also Anne C. Rose, *Transcen-dentalism as a Social Movement, 1830–1850* (New Haven: Yale University Press, 1981), 22–23.

228. See, for example, Alonzo Potter, *Political Economy: Its Objects, Uses, and Principles: Considered with Reference to the Condition of the American People* (New York: Harper and Brothers, 1840), 266–304; and [Alonzo Potter], "Trades' Unions," *New-York Review* 2 (Jan. 1838): 5–48. In his extended attacks on trade

unions in these pages, Alonzo Potter also argued that because competition among capitalists, as well as among laborers, was less intense in the United States, strikes and labor combinations would be more likely in America to provoke reciprocal and countervailing organized activity on the part of employers; Potter, *Political Economy,* 293–95. See also many of the writings of Calvin Colton, especially [Colton], "Labor and Capital," no. 7 (Mar. 1844) of *Junius Tracts* (New York: Greeley and McElrath, 1844): 98–111; and "Junius" [Colton], "American Jacobinism" (n.p. 1840), an attack on the radical views of Orestes Brownson.

229. For a particularly informative discussion that treats some of the radical themes cited in the text above, see Johnson, "'Really Useful Knowledge,'" 75–102.

230. For one expression of the possibility, which he then immediately discounted, that the newly arrived Irish were forming "a permanent lower class," especially in New York City, see the remarks of Brace's close friend, Frederick Law Olmsted, in *The Cotton Kingdom. A Traveller's Observations on Cotton and Slavery in the American Slave States,* 2 vols. in 1, ed. Arthur M. Schlesinger (New York: Alfred A. Knopf, 1970 [1861]), 557, 557n.

231. Charles Loring Brace, *Short Sermons to Newsboys: With a History of the Formation of the News Boys' Lodging-House* (New York: Charles Scribner and Company, 1866), 134–35.

232. "C. L. B." [Charles Loring Brace], "Parks and Chapels for the Poor," *New-York Daily Tribune,* May 3, 1855.

233. Brace, quoted in *Life of Brace,* 161. For Brace's differences with the New York House of Refuge and other juvenile correctional institutions, see Steven L. Schlossman, *Love and the American Delinquent: The Theory and Practice of "Progressive" Juvenile Justice, 1825–1920* (Chicago: University of Chicago Press, 1977), 24–49; and Baghdadi, "Protestants, Poverty, and Urban Growth," 275–86.

234. Charles Loring Brace, *The Best Method of Disposing of Our Pauper and Vagrant Children* (New York: Wynkoop, Hallenbeck and Thomas, 1859), 12–13.

235. Christine Stansell, "Women, Children, and the Uses of the Streets: Class and Gender Conflict in New York City, 1850–1860," *Feminist Studies* 8 (Summer 1982): 328–29.

236. Brace, *Dangerous Classes,* 303, 309.

237. [Charles Loring Brace], "The Servant Question," *Nation* 1 (Oct. 26, 1865): 528.

238. [Brace], "Parks and Chapels for Poor." In a somewhat later period, and in vogue with the times, Brace clearly adopted the view that poverty and criminality were, to a limited extent at least, inherited propensities, and he favored the notion that such propensities, as well as more benign characteristics, were carried by gene-like "gemmules" that distinguished individuals from one another. But such explanations for social inequality and deviance are hardly, if at all, in evidence in Brace's antebellum writings, and even his postbellum works, one must add, retain strong environmentalist leanings; he held to the belief that improved social circumstances could improve the gemmules that one generation passed on to another; see Brace, *Dangerous Classes,* 42–46.

239. Indeed, Channing, as we have already indicated, explicitly downplayed the instrumental value of manual labor in America: he resisted both the increasing consumer-orientation of American society that contributed to the rhetorical emphasis upon high wages, and he likewise rejected those success values that recognized manual labor employments as a stepping-stone to something "better"; see Channing, *Elevation,* 10, 12, 15.

240. Channing, *Address before the Association for the Education of Indigent Boys* (1817), in *Memoir,* 2: 73.

241. Townsend Harris [President of the New York City Board of Education] et al., *Memorial to the New York State Senate to Establish a Free Academy in the City of New York,* Feb.23, 1847, quoted in Mario Emilio Cosenza, *The Establishment of the College of the City of New York as the Free Academy in 1847* (New York: Associate Alumni of the College of the City of New York, 1925), 93.

242. Kaestle, *Evolution,* 106–9; Thomas Bender, *New York Intellect* (New York: Alfred A. Knopf, 1987), 105–6. There is, correspondingly, some evidence that New York's skilled and unskilled manual workers—at least those who could afford to do without the income that their sons might earn in the labor market—sent the latter to the city's public grammar schools with the expectation that they would acquire the handwriting and arithmetical skills needed for one of the countinghouse or other white-collar clerical positions that were growing in number along with the city's expanding commercial activity. Although she is less committal regarding the actual extent of such upward mobility, Selma Berrol has concluded from a study of the attendance figures of one such grammar school that "the assumed link between education and social mobility, so much a part of our social fabric today, existed in the nineteenth century as well." Of course, as Berrol herself seems to recognize, movement of the sons of *skilled* craftsmen into clerical positions, such as it occurred, is "upward" mobility of a distinctly limited nature; Selma Berrol, "Who Went to School in Mid-Nineteenth Century New York? An Essay in the New Urban History," in Irwin Yellowitz, ed., *Essays in the History of New York City: A Memorial to Sidney Pomerantz* (Port Washington, N.Y.: Kennikat Press, 1978), 58, 50–51, 57–60.

243. Townsend Harris et al., *Report* of the Committee appointed by the Board of Education, Jan. 27, 1847, quoted in Cosenza, *Establishment,* 31.

244. Townsend Harris, letter to the New York *Journal of Commerce,* June 5, 1847, quoted in Cosenza, *Establishment,* 195.

245. Ibid., 196.

246. Harris et al., *Report* of the Committee, quoted in Cosenza, *Establishment,* 30.

247. Harris et al., *Memorial,* quoted in Cosenza, *Establishment,* 93.

248. Harris, letter to *Journal of Commerce,* quoted in Cosenza, *Establishment,* 195–96.

249. More perhaps than any other scholar, Edward Pessen has directed his aim toward deflating the mythology surrounding this first kind of upward mobility— the spectacular rise of the laboring poor from "rags to riches" in the antebellum period. Among the many writings in which Pessen attempts to document the relative infrequency of such success stories, and the corresponding concentration of wealth within a relatively small number of families over several generations, particularly in the northeastern urban centers, see especially his *Riches, Class and Power before the Civil War* (Lexington, Mass.: D. C. Heath and Company, 1973); "Did Fortunes Rise and Fall Mercurially in Antebellum America? The Tale of Two Cities: Boston and New York," *Journal of Social History* 4 (Summer 1971): 340–57; and "The American Egalitarian Myth and the American Social Reality: Wealth, Mobility, and Equality in the 'Era of the Common Man,'" *American Historical Review* 76 (Oct. 1971): 989–1034. With regard to less spectacular degrees of upward mobility, many of the recent works in labor history appear to agree that industrialization and deskilling in this period destroyed or eroded job ladders in the traditional urban crafts, thereby diminishing wage earners' prospects for self-employment and economic independence in a skilled manual labor calling; see, in particular, Sean

Wilentz, *Chants Democratic: New York City and the Rise of the American Working Class* (New York: Oxford University Press, 1984), 121–42, 215.

250. Rodgers, *Work Ethic,* 20–68; Foner, *Free Soil,* 32–38; see also James B. Gilbert, *Work without Salvation: American Intellectuals and Industrial Alienation, 1880–1910* (Baltimore: Johns Hopkins University Press, 1977), ix, 3–6, 44–45, 54–57, 83–84, 98–99. Foner particularly, however, is inclined to stress the degree to which industrialization and attendant hardening class divisions were post-1860 developments for the Northern social structure as a whole; in his view there was still more truth than not to the common antebellum belief, a staple of antislavery free labor ideology, that the Northern social structure remained fluid.

251. Apart from the questionable availability of the necessary quantitative data and the choice of statistical methods to apply to its analysis, defining and distinguishing between different kinds and indices of social mobility is itself a complicated business; see the discussion in Hartmut Kaelble, *Historical Research in Social Mobility: Western Europe and the USA in the Nineteenth and Twentieth Centuries* (New York: Columbia University Press, 1981), 113–23.

252. See also Iver Bernstein, *The New York City Draft Riots: Their Significance for American Society and Politics in the Age of the Civil War* (New York: Oxford University Press, 1990), 189.

253. Of interest here is Joan Campbell's comparison of the views of Carlyle and Engels; Joan Campbell, *Joy in Work, German Work: The National Debate, 1800–1945* (Princeton: Princeton University Press, 1989), 22–23. In a valuable recent discussion of the relevance of a Carlylean work ethic in the Carolina Piedmont mills of the late nineteenth and early twentieth century, Allen Tullos explains that because "the desperate families who came to the mills," were "already accustomed to long days and years of punishing physical [farm] work for little reward," and because their own heritage of evangelical Protestantism had long acclimated them to this labor, Piedmont industrialists were the more easily able to impose onerous working conditions on them, and to justify these by reference to the same harsh work ethic (Tullos, *Habits of Industry: White Culture and the Transformation of the Carolina Piedmont* [Chapel Hill: University of North Carolina Press, 1989], 13–15, 159, 303–4).

254. See Carlyle's attack on *"Cash Payment"* in *Chartism* (1839), repr. in Carlyle, *English and Other Critical Essays* (London: Dent, 1967), 2: 203.

255. John G. Cawelti, *Apostles of the Self-Made Man: Changing Concepts of Success in America* (Chicago: University of Chicago Press, 1965), 9–24; Mary Lucy Ahearn, "The Rhetoric of Work and Vocation in Some Popular Northern Writings Before 1860" (Ph.D. diss., Brown University, 1965), 45; Marshall, *In Search of Spirit of Capitalism,* 51–54.

256. Cawelti, *Apostles,* 61; Robert Slocumb Michaelson, "The American Gospel of Work and the Protestant Doctrine of Vocation" (Ph.D. diss., Yale University, 1951), 273; Ahearn, "Rhetoric," 221; Richard Huber, *The American Idea of Success* (New York: McGraw Hill Company, 1971), 98; Richard Weiss, *The American Myth of Success: From Horatio Alger to Norman Vincent Peale* (New York: Basic Books, 1969), 32–44; Berthoff, "Peasants and Artisans," 581–82.

257. See the related argument in Anthony, *Ideology of Work,* 144–45, 304–5, that because capitalism attaches only an economic value to labor, it "is never capable of mounting the ideological exhortation to work which is embodied in communism."

258. As noted earlier, however, even Carlyle did not exhalt the duty and divinity of labor with complete disregard for actual working conditions, least of all with respect to British white laborers. Yet the primary evil for Carlyle remained

insufficiency of work—idleness that was either voluntary or imposed through unemployment; see note 87 in this chapter.

259. John Stores Smith, *Address before the Lancashire Public School Association,* 1850, quoted in Massachusetts, *Senate Documents* for 1868, no. 21, *Report of the Hon. Henry K. Oliver . . . the Laws Regulating the Employment of Children in Manufacturing and Mechanical Establishments,* 78.

260. See the discussion in Alan D. Gilbert, *Religion and Society in Industrial England: Church, Chapel and Social Change, 1740–1914* (London: Longman, 1976), 85–86.

261. Michaelson, "American Gospel of Work," 273. For the role that a commitment to frugality and simple industry played in the hostility shown by some elements of the Jacksonian Democratic party to paper money, banks, and the entrepreneurial spirit, see William Gerald Shade, *Banks or No Banks: The Money Issue in Western Politics, 1832–1865* (Detroit: Wayne State University Press, 1972), 174, 198; and James Roger Sharp, *The Jacksonians versus the Banks: Politics in the States after the Panic of 1837* (New York: Columbia University Press, 1970), 181–87, 321–25. For one discussion by an Associationist that attributed gross economic disparities and the exploitation and "debasement" of manual labor to capitalist "cunning," among other factors, see "What Is the Reason? 'How Much Land and Property, And I Have None!'" *Democratic Review* 16 (Jan. 1845): 24.

CHAPTER 8: CONCLUSION

1. The intensity and the import of these American disagreements over the definition of true work has, in my judgment, been missed by the so-called consensus studies that have focused on the historic absence in the United States of a strong socialist challenge to private property; see, in particular, Louis Hartz, *The Liberal Tradition in America* (New York: Harcourt, Brace and World, 1955).

2. Theophilus Fisk, "Capital against Labor," *Nineteenth Century: A Quarterly Miscellany* 1 (1848): 240 (italics in original).

3. Theophilus Fisk, *The Banking Bubble Burst: Or the Mammoth Corruption of the Paper Money System Relieved by Bleeding. Being a History of the Enormous Legalized Frauds Practised upon the Community by the Present American Banking System* (Charleston: n.p. 1837), 3, 7, 24. Fully committed to a specie currency, Fisk had no more tolerance for the "rotten" paper money issued by President Jackson's "pet banks" than for the "rag paper" that had been issued by Jackson's nemesis, the Bank of the United States.

4. See Lawrence Frederick Kohl, *The Politics of Individualism: Parties and the American Character in the Jacksonian Era* (New York: Oxford University Press, 1989), 191, and also note 6 and the accompanying text in chapter 6. Other radicals, although perhaps just as hostile as Fisk to nonmanual labor employments, were nonetheless less clear than he concerning how sweeping they intended their criticisms of these employments to be. L. W. Ryckman, for example, concluded a speech with the claim that "the labors of the professions were . . . frequently entirely useless and charlatanic." A few moments before, however, he had suggested that the contribution of these labors to the social good was merely overvalued: the work of "the Doctor, Lawyer and Divine" were not "of such undoubted utility as to warrant the pretenses set up of higher claims to respect and emolument" (Ryckman, remarks at Industrial Congress in New York City, "Labor Movements," *New-York Daily Tribune,* Jan. 27, 1851). For similar inconsistencies or lack of clarity in the writing or rhetoric of some of the radical leaders of the early workingmen's parties and trade

unions, see Edward Pessen, *Most Uncommon Jacksonians: Radical Leaders of the Early Labor Movement* (Albany: State University of New York Press, 1967), 181–83.

5. Gregory Claeys, *Machinery, Money, and the Millennium. From Moral Economy to Socialism 1815–60* (Cambridge, Eng.: Polity Press, 1987), 60–63, 112–15, 123, 136–39, 156. Claeys's concern is the particular definitional struggles over true work waged by Robert Owen, John Gray, and other British Owenite socialists.

6. "L," "The Rag Pickers," *Gazette of the Union, Golden Rule, and Odd-Fellows' Family Companion* 9 (Aug. 19, 1848): 131. A few observers claimed that, whatever the true productive value of their labors, some ragpickers were able to earn more than a bare subsistence from those labors, given the demand for rags by New York paper manufacturers. Possibly the repugnant features of rag picking, features that gave it such a generally poor reputation among middle-class commentators, actually helped to reduce competition in this line of work. Notwithstanding the common view that this form of drudge labor was morally debilitating work for the families engaged in it, some of the same observers noted above contended that the more industrious and frugal of the German-born ragpickers of New York actually followed a popular version of the American Dream: after four or five years in their trade, they had accumulated enough money to emigrate to the West and buy farms; see "The Rag-Pickers of New York," *New York Herald,* Oct. 5, 1853.

7. Notions that the laborer was entitled to a fair and "living wage" had roots in both scripture and the medieval doctrine of "just price" and continued to coexist in the nineteenth-century literature of labor agitation with arguments insisting that the producer was entitled to the "full product of his labor," even if the latter did represent a later stage in the evolution of that agitation. For all their inconsistencies with one another, both arguments took as their common enemy doctrines which represented labor as a mere commodity and which argued that the laboring population lacked both a "natural" claim to poor relief and the ability, in the face of irrevocable market forces, to effectively safeguard its security and well-being through combinations and other forms of collective action. For applications of the notion of "just price" to challenge Malthusian demands for harsher poor relief policies, see many of the influential writings of William Cobbett, notably "To Parson Malthus, on the Rights of the Poor; and on the Cruelty Recommended by Him to Be Exercised towards the Poor," *Political Register,* May 1819, repr. in *Selections from William Cobbett's Political Works: Being a Complete Abridgement of the 100 Volumes which Comprise the Writings of "Porcupine" and the "Weekly Political Register,"* ed. John M. Cobbett and James P. Cobbett (London: Anne Cobbett, 1835), 5: 395–405; Cobbett, series of letters to the Earl of Radnor, *Political Register,* Aug.–Oct. 1834, in *Selections,* 6: 724–60; and Cobbett, *Cobbett's Poor Man's Friend; or, a Defence of the Rights of Those Who Do the Work and Fight the Battles* (London: Anne Cobbett, 1826), 3–29, 43–49. Relevant discussions of various phases of labor radical ideology and some of the seminal radical thinkers in Britain include Claeys, *Machinery,* 1–3, 63–65, 138–39, 190–93; E. P. Thompson, "The Moral Economy of the English Crowd in the Eighteenth Century," *Past and Present,* no. 50 (Feb. 1971): 76–136; Thompson, *The Making of the English Working Class* (Harmondsworth, Eng.: Penguin Books, 1968), 212–18; Noel W. Thompson, *The People's Science. The Popular Political Economy of Exploitation and Crisis 1816–34* (Cambridge, Eng.: Cambridge University Press, 1984), 82–228; Patricia Hollis, *The Pauper Press* (New York: Oxford University Press, 1970), 204–43; William Stafford, *Socialism, Radicalism, and Nostalgia: Social Criticism in Britain, 1775–1830* (Cambridge, Eng.: Cambridge University Press, 1987); and Gareth Stedman Jones, *Languages of Class: Studies in English Working Class History 1832–1982* (Cambridge, Eng.: Cambridge University

Press, 1983), 108–73. For a discussion of how British radical versions of the labor theory of value and related emphases upon the economic primacy of the producing classes influenced the thought of American labor leaders and trade unions in the 1830s, see Maurice F. Neufeld, "Realms of Thought and Organized Labor in the Age of Jackson," *Labor History* 10 (Winter 1969): 5–43.

8. Peter Walker, "The Dignity of Labor," *Nineteenth Century: A Quarterly Miscellany* 3 (1849): 288.

9. Not only several generations of British clergymen, both within and without the Church of England, but also an American antebellum Unitarian minister on the order of William Ellery Channing could, as we have seen, be included in this category, allowing for some significant qualifications in Channing's case.

10. The phrase "bone and sinew," notably employed by Andrew Jackson to describe the "real people" of the country as distinct from the privileged moneyed interests allied with the Bank of the United States, is discussed in Marvin Meyers, *The Jacksonian Persuasion: Politics and Belief* (Stanford: Stanford University Press, 1957), 16–32.

11. Walker, "Dignity of Labor," 288.

12. Ibid., 288–89.

13. Theodore Sedgwick, *Public and Private Economy. In Three Parts* (Clifton: Augustus M. Kelley, 1967 [1836–1839]), 1: 226–27.

14. E. E. Hale, *Christian Duty to Emigrants,* a sermon delivered before the Boston Society for the Prevention of Pauperism, at the Old South Church in Boston, May 9, 1852 (Boston: John Wilson and Son, 1852), *Christian Duty to Emigrants,* 12–13.

15. Walker, "Dignity of Labor," 288.

16. [John Greenleaf Whittier], *The Stranger in Lowell* (Boston: Waite, Pierce and Company, 1845), 20–25, 118–21. For criticism similar to Whittier's, see T. Thiostle, "Factory Life in New-England," *Knickerbocker Magazine* 30 (Dec. 1847): 514–15.

17. [Whittier], *Stranger,* 22–24. Although Whittier himself favored a ten-hour day for Lowell's operatives, down from the common twelve and a half, he acknowledged the force of the monetary objectives that led some of the mill girls to oppose this measure: "The stronger and healthier portion of the operatives might themselves object to it as strenuously as the distant stockholder, who looks only to his semi-annual dividends" (117–18).

18. Congressman L. Q. C. Lamar of Mississippi, *Congressional Globe. Appendix,* 36th Cong., 1st sess., Feb. 21, 1860, 116. Despite Lamar's taunts, another proslavery man, Jeremiah S. Black, conceded the effective use that abolitionists and Republicans made of those "irresistible catchwords": "free labor" and the "dignity of labor." Black suggested that in this regard the antislavery "crusade" had the invaluable help of the strongly elitist class defenses of slavery discussed in chapter 6 above. The antislavery forces, Black noted, "managed to inspire in the minds of the northern farmer and workman, a vague apprehension, that this 'Southern Oligarchy' meant to enslave them also. It was alleged that those silly declaimers who talked about northern 'mud-sills,' interpreted the real sentiments of their class, and that free labor and the mechanic arts, were in danger of instant subversion by a barbarous despotism" (Black's Chapter 21, intended for W. H. Lamon's *The Life of Abraham Lincoln* (1872), revised copy, Jeremiah S. Black Papers, Box 74, Manuscript Division, Library of Congress, Washington, D.C.

19. [Whittier], *Stranger,* 23.

20. How and to what degree Mill's views turned socialist remain matters of dispute; for an argument minimizing Mill's departure from "the liberal-classical

tradition," see Donald L. Losman, "J. S. Mill on Alternative Economic Systems," *American Journal of Economics and Sociology* 30 (Jan. 1971): 85–104. For a more detailed and subtle interpretation of Mill's later thought, which concludes that Mill went much further in the direction of "no-property" socialist tenets than any of the other classical economists had done, but still remained "cautious and irresolute" regarding their ultimate feasibility, see Ellen Frankel Paul, *Moral Revolution and Economic Science: The Demise of Laissez-Faire in Nineteenth-Century British Political Economy* (Westport, Conn.: Greenwood Press, 1979), 171, 167–99. See also William Ebenstein, "John Stuart Mill: Political and Economic Liberty," in Carl J. Friedrich, ed., *Nomos IV. Liberty* (New York: Atherton Press, 1962), 90–107.

21. "D" [John Stuart Mill], "The Negro Question," *Fraser's Magazine* 41 (Jan. 1850): 25–51, repr. in Eugene R. August, ed., *Carlyle, The Nigger Question; Mill, The Negro Question* (New York: Appleton-Century-Croft, [1971]), 43.

22. Ibid., 44.

23. Ibid., 43.

24. Ibid., 40–42; For a contemporary anonymous attack on Carlyle's position that made explicit use of "the wolf the accuser" terminology, see "Mr. Carlyle on the Negroes," repr. in ibid., 53.

25. Ibid., 44.

26. Ibid.

27. I am thinking not only of the rather vague and general attitudes toward work held by the "counterculture" of the 1960s, but more specifically of the views of Herbert Marcuse, who ridiculed modern capitalist society's "production and consumption of waste," its social need "for stupefying work where it is no longer a real necessity; the need for modes of relaxation which soothe and prolong this stupefication" (Herbert Marcuse, *One-Dimensional Man: Studies in the Ideology of Advanced Industrial Society* [Boston: Beacon Press, 1964], 7). See also the discussion of Marcuse's thought, as well as that of Paul Lafargue, Marx's son-in-law, in David Meakin, *Man and Work: Literature and Culture in Industrial Society* (New York: Holmes and Meier, 1976), 173, 196–98. See also Alasdair Clayre, *Work and Play: Ideas and Experience of Work and Leisure* (New York: Harper and Row, 1974), 1–7; Ed Andrew, *Closing the Iron Cage: The Scientific Management of Work and Leisure* (Montreal: Black Rose Books, 1981), 10–11, 138–41; and various of the essays in Robert Pippin et al., eds., *Marcuse: Critical Theory and the Promise of Utopia* (South Hadley, Mass.: Bergin and Garvey, 1988). Of course, twentieth-century socialist societies that share Marcuse's disdain for bourgeois capitalist consumerism have, unlike Marcuse, generally moved in the direction of glorifying hard and productive physical labor—e.g., Stalinist Russia's idealization of the brawny and perspiring Stakhanovite. In fact, Marcuse for this reason apparently saw little to choose from between twentieth-century capitalism and communism: "Productivity . . . the very word came to smack of repression or its philistine glorification. . . . Efficiency and repression converge: raising the productivity of labor is the sacrosanct ideal of both capitalist and Stalinist Stakhanovism" (Herbert Marcuse, *Eros and Civilization: A Philosophical Inquiry into Freud* [Boston: Beacon Press, 1966 {1955}], 155–56).

28. Whittier, *Stranger,* 1892 ed. in Whittier, *The Prose Works of John Greenleaf Whittier* (Boston: Houghton Mifflin, 1892), 1: 352–53, quoted in Michael Brewster Folsom and Steven D. Lubar, eds., *The Philosophy of Manufactures: Early Debates over Industrialization in the United States* (Cambridge: MIT Press, 1982), 426. For a similar criticism of the too-literal adoption of "Franklin's maxims" as leading to overwork and thence to "both physical and mental deterioration," see "Farming in New England," *Atlantic Monthly* 2 (Aug. 1858): 335–36.

29. John Patrick Diggins, *The Lost Soul of American Politics* (New York: Basic Books, 1984), 209–14, 323; Diggins, "Thoreau, Marx, and the 'Riddle' of Alienation," *Social Research* 39 (Winter 1972): 582–95.

30. See, for example, the discussion of Henry Ward Beecher in Daniel T. Rodgers, *The Work Ethic in Industrial America 1850–1920* (Chicago: University of Chicago Press, 1978), 98–105. In my view Rodgers understates the degree to which mid-nineteenth-century middle-class writers recognized that wage earners and other manual laborers were overworked. But the antebellum period is only a backdrop for Rodgers's principal focus.

31. [Mill], "Negro Question," 44. Mill's equation of man's "finer attributes" with intellectual activity has led some scholars to stress his disdain—rather than his empathy and concern—for those whose lives were devoted to manual labor. For an example of such an interpretation, which I regard as incomplete if not distorted, see Sean Sayers, "Higher and Lower Pleasures," in Berel Lang, William Sacksteder, and Gary Stahl, eds., *The Philosopher in the Community: Essays in Memory of Bertram Morris* (Lanham, Md.: University Press of America, 1984), 112–29.

32. In the post–Civil War period especially, middle-class writers may have invested as much hope in working-class entertainment, including participatory and spectator sports, as they did in more refined and uplifting activities as instruments of social stability; for a brief discussion of the expansion of recreational leisure-time activities in this period, see Rodgers, *Work Ethic,* 106–8.

33. See chapter 3, text at note 57.

34. Slavery was an explicit target of Peabody's criticism in a number of writings: *Position and Duties of the North with Regard to Slavery* (Newburyport: Charles Whipple, 1847); *The Word of God Is Not Bound. A Sermon, June 4, 1854* (Portsmouth: James F. Shores, Jr., Joseph H. Foster, 1854); and "Slavery, Its Origin and Remedy," *North American Review* 92 (Apr. 1861): 505.

35. [Andrew Preston Peabody], "The Future of Labor," *North American Review* 74 (Apr. 1852): 463.

36. Ibid., 462.

37. "Who Can Explain the Phenomenon?" *New-York Daily Times,* Feb. 1, 1853.

38. Horace Greeley, *Recollections of a Busy Life: Including Reminiscences of American Politics and Politicians, from the Opening of the Missouri Contest to the Downfall of Slavery* (New York: J. B. Ford and Company, 1869), 513.

39. Ibid.

40. [Peabody], "Future of Labor," 462–63.

41. Alonzo Potter, *Political Economy: Its Objects, Uses, and Principles: Considered with Reference to the Condition of the American People* (New York: Harper and Brothers, 1840), 60n–61n. This is one instance in which Potter was enlarging upon and qualifying the remarks of George Poulett Scrope; see chapter 2, note 16.

42. [Peabody], "Future of Labor," 454.

43. Arthur Schlesinger, Jr., *The Age of Jackson* (Boston: Little, Brown and Company, 1945), 271–75; Merle Curti, *The Social Ideas of American Educators* (Paterson, N.J.: Pageant Books, 1959 [1935]), 120–25. As Schlesinger notes, and as we have seen in chapter 3, this was the substance of the criticism Orestes Brownson directed at William Ellery Channing's appeal regarding the "elevation" of the working classes.

44. [Peabody], "Future of Labor," 450, 453. Of relevance here is the brief discussion of Daniel Webster's belief in the democratizing effects of an abundance of consumer goods in Daniel Horowitz, *The Morality of Spending: Attitudes Toward the*

Consumer Society in America, 1875–1940 (Baltimore: Johns Hopkins University Press, 1985), xxix, 7–8. There is increasing interest among historians in this rising Anglo-American consumer ethic, together with the changes in actual consumption patterns that attended it. Although consumerism originated in the upper and middle classes, evidently in the second half of the eighteenth century, it clearly seems also to have affected the values of the laboring population—a possible reflection, as Neil M. McKendrick has argued with specific reference to Britain, of the tendency of the employment of women and children in long hours of factory and other industrial work to somewhat increase the discretionary income of working-class families and with this, their capacity to emulate the spending patterns of more advantaged elements of society; see Neil M. McKendrick, John Brewer, and J. H. Plumb, *The Birth of a Consumer Society: The Commercialization of Eighteenth-Century England* (London: Europa Publications, 1982), 9–31; and Neil M. McKendrick, "Home Demand and Economic Growth: A New View of the Role of Women and Children in the Industrial Revolution," in McKendrick, ed., *Historical Perspectives: Studies in English Thought and Society in Honour of J. H. Plumb* (London: Europa Publications, 1974): 152–210. For a largely alternative explanation to McKendrick's of the birth of modern consumerism, see Colin Campbell, *The Romantic Ethic and the Spirit of Consumerism* (Oxford: Basil Blackwell, 1987), 18–21, 205–9.

Historians have noted that the antislavery claim referred to in the text above was one of the bases upon which the labor reformer Ira Steward developed his later argument that an eight-hour workday would raise wages: increased leisure would stimulate new wants on the part of workers, and these wants would in turn eventuate in increased labor productivity and through this, higher wages. The notion that wage levels were, in large measure if not entirely, set by the tastes and habits of the workers themselves appears to have been one that labor radicals as well as men of Whiggish temperament like Peabody could find congenial, even if they agreed on little else; see David R. Roediger, "The Movement for a Shorter Working Day in the United States before 1866" (Ph.D. diss., Northwestern University, 1980), 227. For a fuller analysis of Steward's doctrines, see David Montgomery, *Beyond Equality: Labor and the Radical Republicans 1862–1872* (New York: Random House, 1967), 252–60.

45. Indeed, some scholars have claimed that the leaders of the workingmen's parties, no less than later, more conservative Whigs, regarded education as something of a panacea for social ills; see Frederick M. Binder, *The Age of the Common Schools, 1830–1865* (New York: John Wiley and Sons, 1974), 32–33; and Pessen, *Most Uncommon Jacksonians*, 183–84.

46. [Brownson], "Manual Labor Schools," *Boston Reformer,* July 23, 1836, clipping in Microfilm Edition of the Orestes Augustus Brownson Papers, reel 10, University of Notre Dame Archives.

47. Jenifer Hart has offered, with respect to Britain specifically, a number of cogent criticisms of the popular thesis that the early nineteenth century was a period of rising "humanitarianism." The emphasis I give here and elsewhere to an increasing concern for the "higher nature" of the laboring population and the diverse manifestations this emphasis assumed, is, I believe, somewhat less vulnerable to Hart's criticisms, in part because some of the very arguments that exalted the "higher nature" of the workers also sanctioned the frequently ruthless and exploitative competition that victimized these workers. However, Hart might still find my conclusions too impressionistic and sweeping; Jenifer Hart, "Nineteenth-Century Social Reform: A Tory Interpretation of History," in M. W. Flinn and T. C. Smout, eds., *Essays in Social History* (Oxford: Clarendon Press, 1974), 204–11; see also

Martin J. Wiener, "Introduction," symposium on mid-nineteenth-century Anglo-American social control, *Rice University Studies* 67 (Winter 1981): 4.

48. The more characteristic problem in preindustrial societies, Edmund S. Morgan has suggested in a number of studies, was not one of overwork but rather one of inducing people to perform harvesting and other work at the time it needed doing. It took a very long time to establish continuous, full-day work as the expected norm. For the complaints made by the British government regarding "lazy" English laborers, and the statutory measures it periodically enacted from the fifteenth through the seventeenth centuries to correct their idleness and desultory work habits, see Morgan, *American Slavery, American Freedom: The Ordeal of Colonial Virginia* (New York: W. W. Norton and Company, 1975), 320–24. See also Christopher Hill, *Society and Puritanism in Pre-Revolutionary England,* 2d ed. (New York: Schocken Books, 1964), 124–30; M. A. Bienefeld, *Working Hours in British Industry: An Economic History* (London: Weidenfeld and Nicolson, 1972), 30–32, 42–48, 72–81.

49. The questions raised here are manifold and complex, for they involve not only the behavior of many different individuals over several decades, but the variety and mix of conscious and unconscious motives that led a given individual to respond as he did to different conditions of labor. Something of the range of possibilities is suggested by the subtle twist given by C. Duncan Rice to the attitudes of some British labor reformers toward the abolitionist movement. Rice suggests that it was not so much a matter of moderate Chartists and activists in the Ten Hour movement being genuinely hostile and opposed to the objectives of the antislavery cause or to the attention it garnered; it was rather more a matter of it being "politically attractive for those working to improve labour conditions at home to use controversy with the abolitionists as a means for throwing their own concerns into relief" (C. Duncan Rice, "The Missionary Context of the British Anti-Slavery Movement," in James Walvin, ed., *Slavery and British Society, 1776–1846* [Baton Rouge: Louisiana State University Press, 1982], 151). The vast and complex question of how individuals in mid-nineteenth-century America and Britain came to form their reform priorities is beyond the province of this study, but see above all the citations in chapter 1, note 63.

50. Paul Henry Elovitz, "'Airy and Salubrious Factories' or 'Dark Satanic Mills'? Some Early Reactions to the Impact of the Industrial Revolution on the Condition of the English Working Classes" (Ph.D. diss., Rutgers University, 1969), 154–55, 165–68. A few samples of the large outpouring from the "optimistic" school that raise these points are Ivy Pinchbeck and Margaret Hewitt, *Children in English Society* (London: Routledge and Kegan Paul, 1969), 1: 256–57, 310–12; 2: 394–99; Pinchbeck, *Women Workers and the Industrial Revolution, 1750–1850* (London: George Routledge and Sons, 1930), 4, 232–33, 307–11; T. S. Ashton, *Industrial Revolution 1760–1830* (Oxford: Oxford University Press, 1968 [1948]); R. M. Hartwell, "The Rising Standard of Living in England, 1800–1850," *Economic History Review,* 2d ser., 13 (Apr. 1961): 397–416; and Hartwell, "Interpretations of the Industrial Revolution in England," *Journal of Economic History* 19 (June 1959): 229–49.

51. Together with Neil J. Smelser, *Social Change in the Industrial Revolution: An Application of Theory to the British Cotton Industry* (Chicago: University of Chicago Press, 1959), see particularly the discussion in chapter 6, along with the citations in notes 179 and 180 especially.

52. Although I cannot specify all of the ways in which these diverse intellectual currents may have contributed to the new sensibility of which I am speaking, I wish to note here the emergence in romantic and sentimental literature of more benign

and protective attitudes toward women and children, the latter especially being viewed as innocent beings who were closer to God and the proper subjects of Christian nurture. Recent studies have tended to emphasize these new nineteenth-century attitudes toward women and children in particular connection with rising antislavery sentiment; see Ronald G. Walters, *The Antislavery Appeal: American Abolitionism after 1830* (Baltimore: Johns Hopkins University Press, 1976), 91–110; and Karen Sanchez-Eppler, "Bodily Bonds: The Intersecting Rhetorics of Feminism and Abolition," *Representations,* no. 24 (Fall 1988): 28–59. See also Carl N. Degler, *At Odds: Women and the Family in America from the Revolution to the Present* (New York: Oxford University Press, 1980), 67–74; Bernard Wishy, *The Child and the Republic: The Dawn of Modern American Child Nurture* (Philadelphia: University of Pennsylvania Press, 1968), 17–23. Lee Shai Weissbach provides a valuable discussion of the role that more nurturing attitudes toward childhood played in first middle-class and then working-class support for child factory legislation in mid-nineteenth-century France; Weissbach, *Child Labor Reform in Nineteenth-Century France: Assuring the Future Harvest* (Baton Rouge: Louisiana State University Press, 1989), 84–86, 141–43, 153–55.

53. Although I refer to various forms of "working-class consciousness," I recognize that some scholars prefer that the term be used in a more restrictive sense, to refer only to that state of Marxist revolutionary, or "true" working-class consciousness, in which the alienation, discontent, and understanding of members of the working classes have reached a level of development where they will settle for nothing less than the overthrow of the capitalist means of production and with this, the dissolution of all classes; see R. S. Neale, *Class in English History 1680–1850* (Oxford: Basil Blackwell, 1981), 40–46, 189; John Rule, *The Labouring Classes in Early Industrial England, 1750–1850* (London: Longman, 1986), 385–89.

54. As an illustration of the indifference to the intellectual and moral improvement, and general well-being, of its operative population of which manufacturing capital was capable, many of the labor histories of the period cite the following statement, made in 1855 by one agent of a Fall River, Massachusetts, factory with regard to his largely foreign-born labor force: "I regard my work-people just as I regard my machinery. So long as they can do my work for what I choose to pay them, I keep them, getting out of them all I can. What they do, or how they fare, outside of my walls, I don't know, nor do I consider it my business to know. They must look out for themselves, as I do for myself. When my machines get old and useless, I reject them and get new, and these people are part of my machinery" (Massachusetts. *Senate Documents* for 1868, no. 21, *Report of the Hon. Henry K. Oliver, Deputy State Constable, Specially Appointed to Enforce the Laws Regulating the Employment of Children in Manufacturing and Mechanical Establishments,* 23).

Chapter 7 provided one example of an Uxbridge, Massachusetts, textile firm, from a slightly later period, which professed concern for the intellectual and moral elevation of its juvenile operatives but whose perception of its immediate economic interests contributed to its opposing legislation that would reduce the hours of labor to accommodate the operatives' education. The sentiments expressed above by a real-life Josiah Bounderby are starkly free of such conflicting impulses (or hypocrisy, if one chooses to be less charitable about the position taken by the Uxbridge firm). It is impossible to conclude with any certainty which attitude was more prevalent among American and British manufacturing capitalists and agents, or whether either was in fact more common than the paternalist attitudes and practices of a Nathan Appleton or a Samuel Greg, Jr. Despite their usual moralizing tones, the dominant concerns of factory proprietors with "work discipline" and "labor management" were of a piece with the position of the Fall River factory agent in that they carried the fundamental, implicit assumption that the laborer was indeed a factor of production who was to be made to bend and conform to the new work structures, rather than vice versa. And as Sidney Pollard and other historians have also maintained, ruthlessness and callousness—qualities that were naturally honed in the climate of intense competition in which the early industrial entrepreneurs operated—may well have been the norm among them.

Yet there remain good reasons why industrial capitalists were generally disinclined to publicly describe their workmen in so stark a fashion as the Fall River factory agent. On the most practical level, those reasons included the desire to win and retain public and governmental support for their enterprises, as well as the need to recruit and maintain harmonious relations with a labor force adequate for their purposes. Employers were most apt to regard their workers in brutal and subhuman terms, and to treat them accordingly, in situations where such considerations applied with less force, as in the isolated British parish apprentice mills where the operatives were, to an unusual degree, both powerless and socially stigmatized. More fundamentally, there is some reason to suppose that many employers actually regarded their workers in terms closer to Samuel Greg Jr.'s than to the extreme "Devil take the hindmost" terms employed by the Fall River agent. Many of them, that is to say, were genuinely drawn to the notion that long hours of work, together with the imposition of higher standards of sobriety and general "respectability" upon the labor force both outside and within the workplace, must be beneficial for the laborers as well as for their own profits. Still, there may have occurred during the first half of the nineteenth century a certain reversal in the American New England and British patterns. Historians are generally agreed that economic pressures upon the manufacturing companies in Lowell and other mill towns were already undermining paternalistic policies in the 1840s, eventuating in the exodus of all but the more desperate native-born female operatives. The subsequent complete breakdown of the Waltham "boarding-house" system and the increasing predominance of Irish and other foreign-born operatives who lacked the "refinement" and "respectability" of their predecessors may have finished the process. Employers and agents, as the quotation above suggests (although the textile mills in Fall River were never organized under the Waltham system), may have become still less inhibited about distancing themselves from their employees and assuming a purer "cash-nexus" understanding of their relationship with them. In England, however, there is considerable evidence to support the position that after the class turbulence and bitterness of the 1830s and the 1840s, factory proprietors accommodated themselves to the fact of trade unionism by developing less confrontational, more paternalistic attitudes toward their operatives, even as operatives themselves, along with other British workers, became more adapted to playing the market's "rules of the game."

Some of the studies of the ideologies of manufacturing capitalists most relevant to this discussion are Sidney Pollard, *The Genesis of Modern Management: A Study of the Industrial Revolution in Great Britain* (Cambridge: Harvard University Press, 1965), 257–58; Robert Gray, "The Languages of Factory Reform in Britain, c. 1830–1860," in Patrick Joyce, ed., *The Historical Meanings of Work* (Cambridge, Eng.: Cambridge University Press, 1987), 157–77; Anthony Howe, *The Cotton Masters 1830–1860* (Oxford: Clarendon Press, 1984); H. I. Dutton and J. E. King, "The Limits of Paternalism: The Cotton Tyrants of North Lancashire, 1836–54," *Social History* 7 (Jan. 1982): 59–74; Andrew H. Yarmie, "British Employers' Resistance to 'Grandmotherly' Government, 1850–80," *Social History* 9 (May 1984): 141–45; Patrick Joyce, *Work, Society, and Politics: The Culture of the Factory in Later*

Victorian England (Brighton, Eng.: Harvester Press, 1980), 136–54; David Roberts, *Paternalism in Early Victorian England* (New Brunswick: Rutgers University Press, 1954), 172–83; E. J. Hobsbawm, *Labouring Men: Studies in the History of Labour* (London: Weidenfield and Nicolson, 1964), 345–46; Keith Burgess, *The Challenge of Labour: Shaping British Society 1850–1930* (London: Croom Helm, 1980), 14–39; Anthony F. Wallace, *Rockdale: The Growth of an American Village in the Early Industrial Revolution* (New York: Alfred A. Knopf, 1978), 326–34; H. M. Gitelman, "The Labor Force at Waltham Watch During the Civil War Era," *Journal of Economic History* 25 (June 1965): 214–24.

55. This position may have been an increasingly minority one among British factory proprietors especially, as they relaxed their opposition to government interference in order to partially accommodate and defuse popular pressures. By 1837 R. H. Greg was conceding the desirability of legislation that gave factory children "a proper education"; if nothing else, that concession reflected Greg's clear desire to confine any future factory legislation to "narrow and intelligible limits," ones that would preclude a more sweeping and—from his point of view—damaging Ten Hours Act that curtailed the workday of adult operatives. Greg hardly softened, in any case, his overall defense of the factory system and its benefits, sarcastically referring, for example, to the "Poor Factory Children," who had been the object of previous "protective" legislation and who, having since quit the mills, had in his view only worsened in their "physical and moral condition"; [R. H. Greg], *The Factory Question, Considered in Relation to Its Effects on the Health and Morals of Those Employed in Factories and the "Ten Hours Bill," in Relation to Its Effects upon the Manufactures of England, and Those of Foreign Countries* (London: James Ridgway and Sons, 1837), 15–16, 77; repr. in *The Battle for the Ten Hour Day Continues*, one of a series of vols. in Kenneth Carpenter, advisory ed., *British Labour Struggles: Contemporary Pamphlets 1727–1850* (New York: Arno Press, 1972). For a recent study that lends support to Greg's position, one that exonerates the working conditions of British factory children by invoking the alternative prospects that faced them at home and elsewhere, see Clark Nardinelli, *Child Labor and the Industrial Revolution* (Bloomington: Indiana University Press, 1990), 7, 98, 155–57.

56. For the psychological value Fourier attached to the "social minimum" in Harmony, see Jonathan Beecher, *Charles Fourier: The Visionary and His World* (Berkeley: University of California Press, 1986), 248, 276–78.

57. Of relevance here are the comments regarding ordinary life under Pharaoh's rule in H. Frankfort, *Ancient Egyptian Religion: An Interpretation* (New York: Columbia University Press, 1948), 42–43, 49–51. See also Adriano Tilgher's inferences regarding the work beliefs of "the simple unphilosophic people" of ancient Iran in the wake of the religious prophet Zarathustra; Tilgher, *Work: What It Has Meant to Men through the Ages*, trans. Dorothy Canfield Fisher (New York: Harcourt, Brace, and Company, 1930), 19–21. For much more recent examples of laboring populations, themselves widely differing in social context, that to some degree appear to have imbibed a faith in the spiritual value of hard work, see the discussion of German working-class attitudes during the Third Reich in Joan Campbell, *Joy in Work, German Work: The National Debate, 1800–1945* (Princeton: Princeton University Press, 1989), 382; and the discussion of laboring family work values in the late nineteenth- and early twentieth-century Carolina Piedmont in Allen Tullos, *Habits of Industry: White Culture and the Transformation of the Carolina Piedmont* (Chapel Hill: University of North Carolina Press, 1989), 13–15.

58. Peter N. Stearns, *Lives of Labor: Work in a Maturing Industrial Society* (New

York: Holmes and Meier, 1975), 239; Keith Thomas, "Work and Leisure in Pre-Industrial Society," *Past and Present*, no. 29 (De. 1964): 53–55.

59. Shoshana Zuboff, "The Work Ethic and Work Organization," in Jack Barbash et al., eds., *The Work Ethic—A Critical Analysis* (Madison: University of Wisconsin, 1983), 153; and Erik Schwimmer, "The Self and the Product: Concepts of Work in Comparative Perspective," in Sandra Wallman, ed., *Social Anthropology of Work* (New York: Academic Press, 1979), 287–88; Krishan Kumar, *The Rise of Modern Society: Aspects of the Social and Political Development of the West* (Oxford: Basil Blackwell, 1985), 227–28; see also Robert M. Solow and Peter Temin, "The Inputs for Growth," in Joel Mokyr, ed., *The Economics of the Industrial Revolution* (Totowa: Rowman and Allanheld, 1985), 83. Such a hypothesis clearly owes much to E. P. Thompson's influential distinction between preindustrial "task" and industrial "time" orientations to work.

60. John Burnett, "Preface," in Burnett, ed., *Annals of Labour: Autobiographies of British Working Class People 1820–1920* (Bloomington: Indiana University Press, 1974), 15, 18; see also the discussion in Clayre, *Work and Play*, 151–68, 183–84. R. E. Pahl flatly declares: "There was no pre-industrial golden age of satisfying work" (R. E. Pahl, "Editor's Introduction: Historical Aspects of Work, Employment, Unemployment, and the Sexual Division of Labour," in R. E. Pahl, ed., *On Work: Historical, Comparative and Theoretical Approaches* [Oxford, Eng.: Basil Blackwell, 1988], 8–9).

61. For the phrase, "cheap and nasty," used to describe work in slop shops in contrast to that in the "honourable trades," see Parson Lot [Charles Kingsley], *Cheap Clothes and Nasty* (London: William Pickering, 1850).

62. Clayre, *Work and Play*, 1–7, 117, 153, 182, 209. For a study that emphasizes the instrumental work values of modern industrial workers at a variety of skill levels, see John H. Goldthorpe et al., *The Affluent Worker: Industrial Attitudes and Behaviour* (Cambridge, Eng.: Cambridge University Press, 1968), 27–33.

63. One of the Famine Irish, W. Dever, bitterly wrote in 1851 of his and others' experiences in cellar digging and other kinds of building construction and heavy day labor in America: as "Labouring men" we were "thought nothing of more than dogs . . . despised & kicked about" in the supposed land of equality (Dever quoted in Kerby A. Miller, *Emigrants and Exiles: Ireland and the Irish Exodus to North America* [New York: Oxford University Press, 1985], 318). See also Catherine Tobin, "The Lonely Muscular Digger: Irish Canal Workers in Nineteenth Century America" (Ph.D. diss., University of Notre Dame, 1987), 223–25; David A. Gerber, *The Making of an American Pluralism: Buffalo, New York, 1825–1860* (Urbana: University of Illinois Press, 1989), 126. Of domestic service in particular the British journalist and poet Charles Mackay noted: "The Irishman is seldom long in America before he, too, begins to assert the supremacy of his white blood, and to come out of what he considers the degrading ranks of 'service.' . . . The Irishwomen fall willingly at first into domestic service, but the public opinion around them soon indoctrinates them with the aristocratic idea that black men and women are the only proper servants" (Charles Mackay, *Life and Liberty in America: Or, Sketches of a Tour in the United States and Canada, in 1857–8*, 2 vols. [London: Smith, Elder and Company, 1859], 2: 46–47).

64. The first of these groups, led by Sarah Bagley, actively participated in the Female Labor Reform Association and found its main expression in the *Voice of Industry*. The second group had its most zealous spokeswomen in Harriet Farley, editor of the *Lowell Offering*, which Bagley and other militants claimed was a servile

"mouthpiece" for the factory corporate interests. For the exchanges between Bagley and Farley, see the *Lowell Advertiser,* issues of July 10, July 15, July 26, July 31, and Aug. 7, 1845; for discussions of these exchanges, see Hannah Josephson, *The Golden Threads: New England's Mill Girls and Magnates* (New York: Duell, Sloan and Pearce, 1949), 198–202; and Norman Ware, *The Industrial Worker, 1840–1860* (Chicago: Quadrangle Books, 1964 [1924]), 88–94.

65. One mill girl, Clementine Averill, thus responded to the criticism of long hours in 1846, supporting Whittier's intuition quoted in note 17 in this chapter: "We never work more than twelve and a half hours a day; the majority would not be willing to work less, if their earnings were less, as they only intend working a few years, and they wish to make all they can while here, for they have only one object in view" (Averill quoted in Alice Kessler-Harris, *Out to Work: A History of Wage-Earning Women in the United States* [New York: Oxford University Press, 1982], 61). It was just such sentiments as Averill's which provided John Kasson and other scholars with at least a partial explanation for the inefficacy of antebellum labor protest in Lowell: most of the mill girls, Kasson concludes, believed that the best means of elevation lay not in collective action to check wage cuts or to reduce hours, but in leaving the mills altogether after accumulating as much money as quickly as possible; John Kasson, "The Factory as Republican Community: The Early History of Lowell, Massachusetts" (unpub. paper read at the American Studies Convention, Oct. 19, 1973), 18–19; Kasson, *Civilizing the Machine: Technology and Republican Values in America 1776–1900* (New York Grossman Publishers, 1976), 95–98. Of course, the failure of strikes in Lowell and other New England factory towns to win their objectives is not itself incontrovertible proof of lack of operative support, and certainly not evidence that labor militancy in the Lowell mills was weaker than that prevailing in other trades in other cities. Thomas Louis Dublin, for example, has concluded that regardless of failures by disgruntled operatives to win concessions, there was "a high-level of protest" before 1850 in Lowell, a circumstance that he attributes, in contrast to Kasson's somewhat greater emphasis upon individual mobility values, to "a close-knit community among women operatives"; Thomas Louis Dublin, "Women at Work: The Transformation of Work and Community in Lowell, Massachusetts, 1826–1860" (Ph.D. diss., Columbia University, 1974), 3.

66. Joan W. Scott and Louise A. Tilly, *Women, Work, and Family* (New York: Holt, Rinehart and Winston, 1978), 76–77, 126–31; Patricia Branca, *Women in Europe since 1750* (New York: St. Martin's Press, 1978), 45–46, 218–19. Apropos of my earlier mention in chapter 3 of peer group collegiality as one of the redeeming features of "mindless" factory labor, menial wage work for women in general may have offered a compensating dimension of sociability; see Branca, *Women in Europe,* 41. Branca, however, also claims that it was partially such "a desire for a warm, human relationship at work" that led many single European women in the nineteenth century to choose domestic service over factory labor; Patricia Branca, "A New Perspective on Woman's Work: A Comparative Typology," *Journal of Social History* 9 (Winter 1975): 141. See also Judith A. McGaw, *Most Wonderful Machine: Mechanization and Social Change in Berkshire Paper Making, 1801–1885* (Princeton: Princeton University Press, 1987), 345–46; Mary H. Blewett, "Women Shoeworkers and Domestic Ideology: Rural Outwork in Early Nineteenth-Century Essex County," *New England Quarterly* 60 (Sept. 1987): 427. That female wage earners, married or single, may have tended to attach an even more circumscribed, exclusively instrumental value to their work, and brought fewer expectations to it, is like any other generalization open to exception and qualification; female wage earners were not necessarily passive recipients of exploitative labor conditions. For a recent discussion exploring the cir-

cumstances under which wage-earning women in Troy, New York, established "networks" and participated in labor organizations, see Carole Turbin, "Beyond Conventional Wisdom: Women's Wage Work, Household Economic Contribution, and Labor Activism in a Mid-Nineteenth-Century Working-Class Community," in Carol Groneman and Mary Beth Norton, eds., *"To Toil the Livelong Day": America's Women at Work, 1780–1980* (Ithaca: Cornell University Press, 1987), 47–67.

67. Peter Mathias, *The Transformation of England* (New York: Columbia University Press, 1979), 148–65; Clayre, *Work and Play*, 161, 182; Eugene D. Genovese, *Roll, Jordan, Roll: The World the Slaves Made* (New York: Pantheon Books, 1974), 298–99; Steven Dubnoff, "Gender, the Family, and the Problem of Work Motivation in a Transition to Industrial Capitalism," *Journal of Family History* 4 (Summer 1979): 128; Alan D. Gilbert, *Religion and Society in Industrial England: Church, Chapel and Social Change, 1740–1914* (London: Longman, 1976), 85–86; Milton Cantor, "Introduction," in Cantor, ed., *American Working-Class Culture: Explorations in American Labor and Social History* (Westport, Conn.: Greenwood Press, 1979), 14–15. For one middle-class moralist's expression of this second instrumental view of work, and his hope that members of the laboring classes would embrace it, see Horace Mann, "The Effects of Intemperance on the Poor and Ignorant" [n.d.], Lecture One of *Two Lectures on Intemperance* (Syracuse: Hall, Mills, and Company, 1852), 40.

68. Andrew Ure, *The Philosophy of Manufactures: Or, an Exposition of the Scientific, Moral, and Commercial Economy of the Factory System of Great Britain* (London: Charles Knight, 1835), 7–8, 279, 328–35, 355–57.

69. A. W. Coats, "Changing Attitudes to Labour in the Mid-Eighteenth Century," *Economic History Review,* 2d ser., 11 (Aug. 1958): 35–51; Richard C. Wiles, "The Theory of Wages in Later English Mercantilism," *Economic History Review,* 2d ser., 21 (Aug. 1968): 113–26. Wiles maintains that this traditional distrust of high wages and the preference for a "low-wage" economy on a number of economic grounds were already losing favor among British writers in the first part of the eighteenth century. Coats argues, in contrast, that it was not until the second half of the century that writers commonly began to embrace "high wage" doctrines, including the notion that more generous wages might develop the tastes and thereby stimulate the efforts of laborers, rather than lead to diminished efforts and "indolence" on their part.

70. Edmund Ruffin, *The Political Economy of Slavery; or the Institution Considered in Regard to Its Influence on Public Wealth and the General Welfare* ([Washington]: Lemuel Towers, 1852?), 3–4, 6, 22. For expressions of similar views among planters in the postbellum period, see Eric Foner, *Reconstruction: America's Unfinished Revolution 1863–1877* (New York: Harper and Row, 1988), 107–37; Foner, *Nothing But Freedom: Emancipation and Its Legacy* (Baton Rouge: Louisiana State University Press, 1983), 15–57; Barbara Jeanne Fields, *Slavery and Freedom on the Middle Ground: Maryland during the Nineteenth Century* (New Haven: Yale University Press, 1985), 163–66; Philip D. Morgan, "Work and Culture: The Task System and the World of Lowcountry Blacks, 1700 to 1880," *William and Mary Quarterly,* 3d. ser., 39 (Oct. 1982): 594–96. As these and other studies suggest, Southern planters who perpetuated the theme of innate black "indolence" were not negatively reacting merely—or even primarily—to the unwillingness of freedmen to work at all, but also to the latter's desire to work for themselves on their own plots of land. Planters who sought to retain the services of the freedmen as an agricultural proletariat were by this point articulating standard Victorian middle-class displeasure and impatience—particularly pronounced among earlier advocates of the

factory system—with elements of the laboring population (e.g., the British hand-loom weavers) that were conspicuously resistant to exchanging an independent subsistence for continuous, disciplined wage labor. For comparison of the "work management" situations confronting postemancipation planters and early English industrialists, see Gerald David Jaynes, *Branches without Roots: Genesis of the Black Working Class in the American South, 1862–1882* (New York: Oxford University Press, 1986), 77–78, 83.

71. John Stuart Mill, *Principles of Political Economy with Some of Their Applications to Social Philosophy,* from the 5th London ed. (New York: D. Appleton and Company, 1892), 1: 143–50, 209–12, 447; Mill, "The Claims of Labour" (1845), in John Stuart Mill, *Essays on Economics and Society,* ed. J. M. Robson, vol. 4 of *Collected Works of John Stuart Mill* (Toronto: University of Toronto Press, 1967), 366–89; Martin J. Wiener, *English Culture and the Decline of the Industrial Spirit, 1850–1980* (Cambridge, Eng.: Cambridge University Press, 1981), 33.

72. Mill, *Principles,* 2: 334–40; Wiener, *English Culture,* 31–33. One of Mill's lifelong intellectual interests lay in confronting and if possible reconciling the opposed perspectives of Utilitarianism-Liberalism and Romanticism; the first applauded "the multiplication of physical wants" which men gained from civilization, the second deplored "the slavery of so large a portion of mankind" to these "artificial wants" (John Stuart Mill, "Coleridge," in *Mill on Bentham and Coleridge,* with an Introduction by F. R. Leavis [Cambridge, Eng.: Cambridge University Press, 1950], 105). See also Raymond Williams, *Culture and Society, 1780–1850* (Harmondsworth, Eng.: Penguin Books, 1961 [1958]), 65–84.

73. Orville Dewey, *Moral Views of Commerce, Society and Politics: In Twelve Discourses* (New York: Augustus M. Kelley, 1969 [1838]), 9–10, 291–93; and Dewey, *On American Morals and Manners* (Boston: William Crosby, 1844), 12–24. In responding to charges of American vulgarity and dollar hunting, Dewey had "British accusers," such as Mill and Dickens, specifically in mind.

74. Dewey, *Moral Views,* 61, 85–86. Nor, one might add, was Dewey's commitment to materialist and commercial values so unrestrained that he abandoned that traditional ministerial impulse to romanticize poverty: "There is about as much cheerfulness among the poor as among the rich. And I suspect, about as much contentment too." Heaven's "shower," he added, falls on the poor and rich alike (Orville Dewey, "On Inequality in the Lot of Life," in Dewey, *Discourses on Human Life* [New York: David Felt and Company, 1841], 76–77).

75. R. C. Linstromberg, "The Challenge of Leisure to the Cult of Work," *Midcontinent American Studies Journal* 8 (Spring 1967): 22–27; Bennett M. Berger, "The Sociology of Leisure: Some Suggestions," in Erwin O. Smigel, ed., *Work and Leisure* (New Haven: College and University Press, 1963), 25–26; J. F. C. Harrison, *The Early Victorians, 1832–51* (London: Cox and Wyman, 1851), 36; Clayre, *Work and Play,* 42–44; Rodgers, *Work Ethic,* 6–17.

76. See, for example, Massachusetts, *House Documents* for 1842, no. 4, "Petition" to the Massachusetts General Court from the citizens of Fall River calling for the enactment of more effective factory legislation; also Massachusetts, *House Documents* for 1852, no. 185, *Minority Report* of the Special Commission considering Ten Hours legislation, 7, 11–13, 17–19; and "The Short Time Movement in Lowell," *Voice of Industry* (Lowell, Massachusetts), July 2, 1847. It remains an open question how much this argument represented a purely strategic appeal on the part of laborers and their spokesmen to the self-interest of employers, and how much of it reflected a genuine belief on the part of labor movement participants that reducing the hours of labor was consistent with the economic and moral primacy of work.

77. Suggestive here is Gunther Barth, *City People: The Rise of Modern City Culture in Nineteenth-Century America* (New York: Oxford University Press, 1980), 152–53.

78. [Peabody], "Future of Labor," 461.

79. Thomas Laqueur has noted of England that "the psychological and theological roots of sabbatarianism during this period are obscure. The desire to create a more regular rhythm of work and rest, so prominent in sixteenth- and seventeenth-century puritanism, played little, if any, part in the nineteenth century" (Thomas Laqueur, *Religion and Respectability: Sunday Schools and Working Class Culture 1780–1850* [New Haven: Yale University Press, 1976], 36); see, however, note 87 in this chapter.

80. James Walvin, *Leisure and Society, 1830–1950* (London: Longman Group, 1978), 5–9. See also J. L. Hammond and Barbara Hammond, *The Town Labourer, 1760–1832. The New Civilisation* (New York: Augustus M. Kelley, 1967 [1917]), 49. In addition, some British members of parliament who held to laissez faire notions opposed prohibitions on Sunday labor as unwarranted interference in the relations between employers and workers; see John Wigley, *The Rise and Fall of the Victorian Sunday* (Manchester, Eng.: Manchester University Press, 1980), 38, 76,

81. Wigley, *Rise and Fall*, 74, 81; Edgar S. Furniss, *The Position of the Laborer in a System of Nationalism: A Study in the Labor Theories of the Later English Mercantilists* (New York: Kelley and Millman, 1957), 118–20.

82. In the face of Sabbatarian opposition, Sir Joshua Walmsley, a radical M.P. for Leicester, favored the opening of the British Museum on Sunday afternoons in part for "the moral and religious influence which had been produced upon the minds of many who flocked to witness the glories of the late Crystal Palace. Among them were men who, sullen with suffering, were so ignorant as to confound order with oppression, and wealth with injustice; but yet those men, whose minds religious teaching had failed to soften, were subdued at the grandeur of the sights which they beheld, and for the first time they learnt to reverence genius, intellect and property" (Walmsley, speech in House of Commons, Mar. 20, 1855, quoted in Wigley, *Rise and Fall*, 105–6).

83. Hugh Cunningham, *Leisure in the Industrial Revolution c. 1780 c. 1880* (London: Croom Helm, 1980), 90–137, 178–85; Anthony Delves, "Popular Recreation and Social Conflict in Derby, 1800–1850," in Eileen Yeo and Stephen Yeo, eds., *Popular Culture and Class Conflict 1590–1914: Explorations in the History of Labour and Leisure* (Sussex, Eng.: Harvester Press, 1981), 89–116; Robert D. Storch, "The Problem of Working-Class Leisure: Some Roots of Middle-Class Moral Reform in the Industrial North: 1825–1850," in A. P. Donajgrodzki, ed., *Social Control in Nineteenth Century Britain* (London: Croom Helm, 1977), 138–56; Mark Blaug, "The Economics of Education in English Classical Political Economy: A Re-Examination," in Andrew S. Skinner and Thomas Wilson, eds., *Essays on Adam Smith* (Oxford: Clarendon Press, 1975), 593; Harold Silver, "Ideology and the Factory Child: Attitudes to Half-Time Education," in Phillip McCann, ed., *Popular Education and Socialization in the Nineteenth Century* (London: Methuen and Company, 1977), 144–47. The question of employer attitudes toward worker leisure time involves many of the same issues raised in note 54 in this chapter.

84. For an example of this point of view see "A. H. D.," letter, "Sunday-Cars in Brooklyn," *New-York Daily Tribune*, Mar. 28, 1857. In opposing a recreational Sabbath, A. H. D. raised a number of themes of special relevance to this study. Not only, the correspondent claimed, would "we see vice abounding in a fearfully increased degree" if laborers were encouraged by legislation to abandon "public

worship" for recreational activity. But manual laborers, furthermore, did not need Sunday for such activity. Unlike most men in "the higher departments of business, . . . the families of mechanics and other laborers," A. H. D. insisted, "have time for recreation in the evening." In this essential respect, "the laboring man is in general not as much overtasked as the merchant or professional man. . . . It is not so much want of time as want of right inclination that deprives our laboring population of their proper share of the enjoyments of life." See also Martin L. Adelman, *A Sporting Time: New York City and the Rise of Modern Athletics, 1820–1870* (Urbana: University of Illinois Press, 1986), 279–80.

This is not to deny that opposition to a recreational Sabbath could reflect a number of perspectives and interests quite different from A. H. D.'s. Here too there were variations upon variations of argument. It was precisely because members of the working classes *shared*, rather than deviated from, the acquisitive values and industrious habits of the middle classes which led one British writer, James Bridges, to similarly oppose a "Sabbath Railway System": "If the religious principle be once set aside, more, in the long run, will be tempted to work by the money, than will be tempted to recreate by the pleasure. People will be more ready to fall into the trap baited with gold, than into that which attracts by amusement alone." Yet, the writer also claimed, the working classes would in fact fail to advance their material interests by abandoning the "religious principle": laborers should not be tempted by the high wage, Sabbath-breaking blandishments of certain employers because the laws of supply and demand dictated that the fruits of Sunday labor—the "coveted gold" for which the worker was ready to "exchange" his soul—would actually go to those employers. For this particular British writer, in any case, the paramount dangers of a recreational Sabbath hardly lay in the encouragement it offered for "dissolute" and unproductive working-class leisure activity; in its own way, his position conformed to Fred Somkin's description of those contemporary Americans for whom "the Sabbath was a standing rebuke to greed and materialism" (Fred Somkin, *Unquiet Eagle: Memory and Desire in the Idea of American Freedom, 1815–1860* [Ithaca: Cornell University Press, 1967], 51); James Bridges, *The Sabbath Railway System Practically Discussed. A Letter to John James Hope Johnstone, Esq., of Annandale, Chairman of the Caledonian Railway Company,* 4th ed. (London: John Johnstone, 1847), 6–7, repr. in *Sunday Work. Seven Pamphlets 1794–1856,* one of a series of vols. in Carpenter, advisory ed., *British Labour Struggles*.

85. Wigley, *Rise and Fall,* 76–77, 85.

86. Lev. 23: 3; Deut. 5: 14; Robert K. Johnston, *The Christian at Play* (Grand Rapids, Mich.: William B. Eerdmans Publishing Company, 1983), 88–95; Wigley, *Rise and Fall,* 3; Samuele Bacchiocchi, *From Sabbath to Sunday: A Historical Investigation of the Rise of Sunday Observance in Early Christianity* (Rome: Pontifical Gregorian University Press, 1977), 312–17; the essays in D. A. Carson, ed., *From Sabbath to Lord's Day: A Biblical, Historical, and Theological Investigation* (Grand Rapids, Mich.: Zondervan Publishing House, 1982); and Willy Rodorf, *Sunday: The History of the Day of Rest and Worship in the Earliest Centuries of the Christian Church,* trans. A. A. K. Graham (Philadelphia: Westminster Press, 1968). The general Hebraic concept of the Sabbath as a cessation from labor encompassed some major subthemes, including: (1) the idea, which Henry David Thoreau seemed to have made part of his general philosophy, that working was controlling nature and that when men stopped working and ceased interfering with nature one day a week, he was commemorating the fact that the world was God's creation; (2) the notion that no one was master of the Jews on the Sabbath, that they, no less than their masters, were free of the servitude of work on that day; (3) the idea that once

they were delivered out of Egypt and were masters in their own land, the day of rest was to remind the Jews not to oppress their own slaves.

87. Writing of the Puritan Sabbath in the sixteenth century, Winton U. Solberg concluded that Sabbatarianism "admirably suited . . . an incipient capitalistic-industrial society" by "rationalizing time and the productive process": it "held workers to their tasks six days a week and allowed them to rest on the seventh" (Winton U. Solberg, *Redeem the Time: The Puritan Sabbath in Early America* [Cambridge: Harvard University Press, 1977], 46). To the extent that capitalists, intellectuals, workingmen, and others in the nineteenth century supported a work-free Sabbath for the restorative value it held for the other six days, their attitudes suggested a certain carryover of the considerations that prompted Solberg's observation. My point in the text above is merely that machine-tending factory labor lacked the "natural" punctuations of the traditional kinds of task work against which the day of rest was originally counterpoised; see also Hill, *Society and Puritanism*, 145–218.

88. Wigley, *Rise and Fall*, 75.

89. Roediger, "Movement for Shorter Working Day," 43–93.

90. See the citations in chapter 3, note 75.

91. Huldah J. Stone, remarks in *Voice of Industry*, Sept. 18, 1845, quoted in Philip S. Foner, *Women and the American Labor Movement* (New York: Free Press, 1979), 1: 73.

92. "Reform in the Hours of Labor," *Dover Gazette* (New Hampshire), Apr. 17, 1847.

93. [Mill], "Negro Question," 44.

94. Jonathan A. Glickstein, "'Poverty Is Not Slavery:' American Abolitionists and the Competitive Labor Market," in Lewis Perry and Michael Fellman, eds., *Antislavery Reconsidered: New Perspectives on the Abolitionists* (Baton Rouge: Louisiana State University Press, 1979), 196–97, 206.

95. "'The Working Man's Friend,'" *Philanthropist* (New Richmond, Ohio), July 22, 1836.

96. Horace Bushnell, "Work and Play," an oration before the Society of the Phi Beta Kappa at the University of Cambridge, Aug. 24, 1848, in Bushnell, *Work and Play; or Literary Varieties* (New York: Charles Scribner, 1864), 13–18.

97. See also the discussion in Adelman, *Sporting Time*, 272–76.

98. Minnie Myrtle, "Friendless Children. The Industrial or Reformatory Schools," *New-York Daily Times*, Apr. 4, 1854. See also Frederic W. Sawyer, *A Plea for Amusements* (New York: D. Appleton and Company, 1847), 91.

99. [Peabody], "Future of Labor," 454.

100. Ibid., 461.

101. Massachusetts, *House Documents* for 1866, no. 98, *Report of the Special Commission on the Hours of Labor, and the Condition and Prospects of the Industrial Classes,* Feb. 1866, 40–41. See also Carl Siracusa, *A Mechanical People: Perceptions of the Industrial Order in Massachusetts, 1815–1880* (Middletown: Wesleyan University Press, 1979), 200–201.

102. This acknowledgement was shared by many of the leading promoters of the eight-hour movement; see David R. Roediger and Philip S. Foner, *Our Own Time: A History of American Labor and the Working Day* (New York: Greenwood Press, 1989), 99.

103. "Juvenile and Female Labor," *Edinburgh Review* 79 (Jan. 1844): 155. There is a large sociological literature on the issue of whether monotonous and un-challenging work in modern capitalist societies, as distinct from such other influ-

ences as television and the power of advertising, bears major responsibility for individuals spending their leisure time in intellectually unstimulating and materialistic ways. For an extended discussion of the relationship between modern work and leisure-time activities, see Andrew, *Closing Iron Cage*. For a defense, on various grounds, of the values of the modern American worker against the emphasis attached by Herbert Marcuse and others to the narcotizing effect of consumer goods and other American bourgeois institutions, see David Halle, *America's Working Man: Work, Home, and Politics among Blue-Collar Property Owners* (Chicago: University of Chicago Press, 1984), 298–300. As suggested in the text above, there remains considerable question whether leisure-time activities pursued by most members of the middle classes, whether these individuals are members of the labor force themselves or dependent family members, are significantly more elevated in nature than those followed by working-class families.

104. A good case in point is the very Massachusetts commission report of 1866 quoted in the text. This document seems really to have been two reports. One was an eloquent defense of more leisure time for adult manual laborers, particularly those employed in factories. The other was a defense of the position that "the changes desired can be better brought about by workingmen outside the State House, than by legislators inside." The commission recognized the right and duty of government to regulate and reduce the hours of Massachusetts' child operatives, to give them "a fair chance" for "health and a good mind." But it recognized no such right and duty with respect to adult operatives: it was far better that "custom" and the "mutual agreements" reached by capitalists and operatives work out the desirable shortening of the work day, as indeed they already had been doing over time, according to the commission.

In justifying its refusal to support the demands of some Massachusetts workingmen for legislation that would reduce the common ten- and eleven-hour workdays in the state to a legal maximum of eight, the commission invoked several of the arguments noted in the text above, as well as a few others: (1) the responsibility of adult workers to make their own bargains in the marketplace; (2) the impossibility, as Dr. Edward Jarvis and others who gave testimony observed, of devising a statute that could adequately apply to a diversity of employments; (3) the mischievous encouragement that the commission would be giving, by recommending an eight-hour statute, to the fallacious "communistic" expectation of some workers that they would be entitled to earn as much for fewer hours and reduced productivity as they did at present; (4) opposition of many workers, as well as employers, to so large a reduction in hours from their very recognition that it would reduce their earnings by cutting profits; and (5) perhaps most basic of all, the tendency of legislative interference with market forces and individual freedom of enterprise to disrupt the "spontaneous sympathy" of the capitalist for the laborer and to obscure and impede the "natural" friendship and harmony of economic interests existing between them. The long struggle for the abolition of Southern slavery, the commission maintained, "consisted in nothing but the setting of the principle that it shall take two to make a bargain, and it was not til the capitalist was left as free as the laborer, that the laborer was really emancipated." This last remark might be taken as one indication of the manner, briefly alluded to in chapter 1, in which the abolition of Southern chattel slavery, together with such postemancipation developments as the treatment of the freedmen, tended to dramatize and even harden the ideological limitations of competitive "free labor" principles; Massachusetts, *House Documents* for 1866, no. 98, *Report of Special Commission on Hours of Labor,* 9, 16, 24–26, 30, 33–35, 44–48.

105. [Mill], "Negro Question," 44.

106. Children's Aid Society, *Fourth Annual Report* (1857), 6, quoted in *The Life of Charles Loring Brace. Chiefly Told in His Own Letters,* ed. "by His Daughter" [Emma Brace], (New York: Charles Scribner's Sons, 1894), 217. See also "The Little Laborers of New York City," *Harper's New Monthly Magazine* 47 (Aug. 1873): 321–31.

107. On this point, for example, see Neil McKendrick, "Josiah Wedgwood and Factory Discipline," *Historical Journal* 4, no. 1 (1961): 33–34, and chapter 2. See also David Vincent, *Literacy and Popular Culture: England 1750–1914* (Cambridge, Eng.: Cambridge University Press, 1989), 118–19.

108. Clayre, *Work and Play,* 1–7, 39, 56–58; Steven Marcus, *Engels, Manchester, and the Working Class* (New York: Random House, 1974), 215; Robert Blauner, *Alienation and Freedom: The Factory Worker and His Industry* (Chicago: University of Chicago Press, 1964), 29. Concerning modern industrial work a group of scholars has concluded: "Recent research has indicated that over quite a wide range of industrial jobs the degree of job satisfaction experienced is likely to be determined more by the culturally shaped wants and expectations which men bring to their employment than by objective aspects of the jobs themselves, so that workers with certain social and cultural characteristics may be more satisfied with simple, undemanding jobs than with more complex and challenging ones." Yet the authors also recognize the need to balance this observation against the fundamental perception of Ferguson, Smith, and Marx: "Nevertheless, . . . certain types of work in modern industry, of an extremely repetitive, fragmented, and 'meaningless' kind, are very likely a source of deprivation to those who carry them out, even if their wants and expectations from work are strictly limited" (Goldthorpe et al., *Affluent Worker,* 180n).

109. Stanley Lebergott, *Manpower in Economic Growth: The American Record Since 1800* (New York: McGraw-Hill, 1964), 116–22; Richard P. Horwitz, *Anthropology toward History: Culture and Work in a Nineteenth-Century Maine Town* (Middletown: Wesleyan University Press, 1978), 42–46; Clarence H. Danhof, *Change in Agriculture: The Northern United States, 1820–1870* (Cambridge: Harvard University Press, 1969), 77, 88–89; Richard A. McLeod, "The Philadelphia Artisan 1828–1850" (Ph.D. diss., University of Missouri, 1971), 88–91; Carville Earl and Ronald Hoffman, "The Foundation of the Modern Economy: Agriculture and the Costs of Labor in the United States and England, 1800–60," *American Historical Review* 85 (Dec. 1980): 1055–94; Stephan Thernstrom and Peter R. Knights, "Men in Motion: Some Data and Speculations about Urban Population Mobility in Nineteenth-Century America," in Theodore K. Rabb and Robert I. Rotberg, eds., *Industrialization and Urbanization: Studies in Interdisciplinary History* (Princeton: Princeton University Press, 1981), 171–99; Thernstrom, "Working-Class Social Mobility in Industrial America," in Melvin Richter, ed., *Essays in Theory and History* (Cambridge: Harvard University Press, 1970), 221–38. For discussion of the multiple occupations in which many eighteenth- and even nineteenth-century workers in Britain engaged, see Kumar, *Rise of Modern Society,* 255, 264–66.

110. The clerks who compiled, tabulated, and analyzed mortality statistics, to cite just one example, hardly enjoyed great social status, even though, as Dr. Edward Jarvis observed, "very few employments impose such a strain on mental powers, and lay such a tax on the cerebral forces as this" (Massachusetts, *House Documents* for 1866, no. 98, *Report of the Special Commission on Hours of Labor,* letter of testimony from Dr. Edward Jarvis, Dorchester, Mass., Nov. 9, 1865, p. 67).

111. Mann, *Sixth Annual Report* (1843), in Mann, *Life and Works of Horace Mann,* enl. ed., ed. Mary Mann and George C. Mann (Boston: Lee and Shepard,

1891), 3: 151–53; Peter J. Wosh, "Sound Minds and Unsound Bodies: Massachusetts Schools and Mandatory Physical Training," *New England Quarterly* 55 (Mar. 1982): 39–40. In cataloguing the physical "evils" of mechanized factory labor, anti-industrial writings had long commonly claimed that this labor's characteristic "species of exercise, . . . instead of animating the human frame, tends to give it a fixed and determined distortion" (Colonel [James] Swan, *An Address to the Senate and House of Representatives of the United States, on the Question for the Inquiry into the State of Agriculture, Manufactures and Commerce* [1817], quoted in Folsom and Lubar, eds., *Philosophy of Manufactures,* 232.

112. Massachusetts, *House Documents* for 1866, no. 98, *Report of Special Commission on Hours of Labor,* letter from Jarvis, 68–69.

113. Massachusetts, *House Documents* for 1866, no. 98, *Report of Special Commission on Hours of Labor,* 41–42.

114. Good discussions of the social and political context in which the commission issued its report include Montgomery, *Beyond Equality,* 124–25, 230–95; Charles E. Persons, "The Early History of Factory Legislation in Massachusetts: From 1825 to the Passage of the Ten-Hour Law in 1874," in *Labor Laws and Their Enforcement with Special References to Massachusetts,* ed. Susan M. Kingsbury (New York: Longmans, Green, 1911), 90–120; Siracusa, *Mechanical People,* 158–230.

115. Massachusetts, *House Documents* for 1866, no. 98, *Report of Special Commission on Hours of Labor,* 43.

116. I should perhaps again note that the commission, for a complex of reasons, did not feel that it was the role of government to bring about the desirable reduction in the hours worked by many adult laborers in the state; see note 104 in this chapter.

117. Clayre, *Work and Play,* 83–84, 174–77; Georges Friedmann, *The Anatomy of Work: Labor, Leisure, and the Implications of Automation,* trans. Wyatt Pawson (Glencoe: Free Press, 1964), 14. For a study whose focus is the twentieth century but which also provides an historical overview of the range of arguments and considerations that bore upon the incremental reductions in the work week, see Benjamin Kline Hunnicutt, *Work without End: Abandoning Shorter Hours for the Right to Work* (Philadelphia: Temple University Press, 1988), 1–8, 142–43. Although the question of how much work is too much remains a subjective one, the shorter-hours movement for organized labor, Hunnicut notes, nonetheless came to an end after the Great Depression, and his study seeks to explain the stabilization at the forty-hour week standard since that time.

118. See the interesting discussion of the association of labor, dirt, and domestic service in Leonore Davidoff, "Mastered for Life: Servant and Wife in Victorian and Edwardian England," *Journal of Social History* 7 (Summer 1974): 413 esp.

119. The stigma that white middle-class attitudes have continued to attach to domestic service is ably discussed in Phyllis Palmer, *Domesticity and Dirt: Housewives and Domestic Servants in the United States, 1920–1945* (Philadelphia: Temple University Press, 1989).

120. Senator Benjamin F. Wade of Ohio, *Congressional Globe,* pt. 2, 35th Cong., 1st sess., Mar. 13, 1858, 1113.

121. Congressman Harmon S. Conger of New York, *Congressional Globe. Appendix,* 30th Cong., 1st sess., July 25, 1848, 950. In his speech, which provided a general defense of the right of Congress to exclude slavery from the federal territories, Conger specifically deplored that circumstance over which John C. Calhoun had reportedly rejoiced: the fact that "southern [white] men were too proud to brush hats and boots, and they would not do it" (950).

122. Ira Berlin, *Slaves without Masters: The Free Negro in the Antebellum South* (New York: Random House, 1974), 231; Daniel E. Sutherland, "Americans and Their Servants, 1800–1920; Being an Inquiry into the Origins and Progress of the American Servant Problems" (Ph.D. diss., Wayne State University, 1976), 165; Francis J. Grund, *Aristocracy in America. From the Sketch-Book of a German Nobleman* (New York: Harper and Brothers, 1959 [1839]), 50, 54, 145, 163, 174–77, 217.

123. Caroline H. Dall, *The College, the Market, and the Court; Or, Woman's Relation to Education, Labor, and Law* (Boston: Lee and Shepard, 1867), 208, also 179. For the growing importance of leisured wives as status symbols for successful middle-class men in Britain and America, respectively, see Lee Holcombe, *Victorian Ladies at Work: Middle-Class Working Women in England and Wales 1850–1914* (Hamden, Conn.: Archon Books, 1973), 4; and Barbara J. Berg, *The Remembered Gate: Origins of American Feminism. The Woman and the City, 1800–1860* (New York: Oxford University Press, 1978), 61–63. Berg is particularly concerned with detailing how privileged urban women used their leisure to engage in benevolent voluntary work on behalf of the poorest, most outcast members of their sex. However, a number of historians, particularly those who have probed the dynamics of less advantaged middle-class families in Britain and America, have criticized the "stereotype" of the "idle" Victorian "lady" on other grounds, in some cases specifically finding that neither the behavior nor the attitudes of married women in these families actually entailed a "genteel" disdain toward the undertaking of paid, remunerative manual labor; Patricia Branca, *Silent Sisterhood: Middle Class Women in the Victorian Home* (London: Croom Helm, 1975), 15; Suzanne Lebsock, *The Free Women of Petersburg: Status and Culture in a Southern Town, 1784–1860* (New York: W. W. Norton, 1984), 148, 185.

Neil J. Smelser has also recently questioned whether, in America at least, the cult of true womanhood did in fact imply a disdain for work. In a provocative essay he suggests that the cults of domesticity in Britain and America derived their primary strength from quite different traditions of thought. The British case against paid work for middle-class women did indeed draw very considerably on "traditional aristocratic" values that exalted a leisured existence and deemed paid work incompatible with "respectability." But American domestic ideology, Smelser claims, drew hardly at all on this "class-related theme": it "did not denigrate work as such," but instead relied much more exclusively on "the Puritan theme" that "the sanctity and purity of women" should be protected from the "harsh reality" of the marketplace and "the profane world" (Neil J. Smelser, "Vicissitudes of Work and Love in Anglo-American Society," in Smelser and Eric H. Erickson, eds., *Themes of Work and Love in Adulthood* [Cambridge: Harvard University Press, 1980], 116). Smelser's distinction may have some basis in fact. But one need only examine antebellum servant literature for evidence that in the United States, too, the cult of "true womanhood" incorporated a marked disdain for manual labor, if not for all types then certainly for those menial household tasks that were deemed unworthy of females who occupied respectable, propertied middle-class status. See also Mary Christine Stansell, "Women of the Laboring Poor in New York City, 1820–1860" (Ph.D. diss., Yale University, 1979), 143–44. For a discussion of the particular pressures this domestic ideology placed upon "respectable" working-class women in Britain to spurn the paid work available to them, or at least to conspicuously subordinate it to domestic duties, see Judy Lown, *Women and Industrialization: Gender at Work in Nineteenth-Century England* (Cambridge, Eng.: Polity Press, 1990), 175–79. Also relevant here are those other discussions of the "family wage" ideal cited in chapter 6.

124. Congressman Francis P. Blair, Jr. of Missouri, *Congressional Globe,* pt. 1, 35th Cong., 1st sess., pt. 1, Mar. 23, 1858, 1284.

125. Senator James Dixon of Connecticut, *Congressional Globe,* pt. 2 and *Appendix,* 35th Cong, 2d sess., Feb. 25, 1859, 1339.

126. At the same time, it would be foolish to ignore the purely instrumental basis of the appeal that nonmanual labor employments exerted. Allowing even for a good deal of exaggeration, the observation expressed by the Cincinnati *Gazette* was repeated too many times with regard to mid-nineteenth-century Americans to be lightly dismissed: "Of all the multitude of young men engaged in various employments of this city, there is probably not one who does not desire, and even confidently expect, to become rich, and that at an early day" (Cincinnati *Gazette,* June 11, 1860, quoted in Eric Foner, *Free Soil, Free Labor, Free Men: The Ideology of the Republican Party before the Civil War* [New York: Oxford University Press, 1970], 14).

127. Mackay, *Life and Liberty,* 1: 177.

128. Walker, "Dignity of Labor," 289.

129. David F. Lindenfield, "On Systems and Embodiments as Categories for Intellectual History," *History and Theory* 27 (Feb. 1988): 34–35; David A. Hollinger, "The Return of the Prodigal: The Persistence of Historical Knowing" *American Historical Review* 94 (June 1989): 617. Jacques Rancière has noted, with specific reference to the values of mid-nineteenth-century French artisans, that "we look too much at worker culture and not enough at its encounters with other cultures" (Jacques Rancière, "The Myth of the Artisan: Critical Reflections on a Category of Social History," in Steven Laurence Kaplan and Cynthia J. Koepp, eds., *Work in France: Representation, Meaning, Organization, and Practice* [Ithaca: Cornell University Press, 1986], 329).

130. Howard P. Chudacoff, "Success and Security: The Meaning of Social Mobility in America," *Reviews in American History* 10 (Dec. 1982): 107; Charles Stephenson, "'There's Plenty Waitin' at the Gates': Mobility, Opportunity and the American Worker," in Charles Stephenson and Robert Asher, eds., *Life and Labor: Dimensions of American Working-Class History,* (Albany: State University of New York, 1986), 79–82; Miller, *Emigrants and Exiles,* 269, 314, 326; James Henretta, "The Study of Social Mobility: Ideological Assumptions and Conceptual Bias," *Labor History* 18 (Spring 1977): 170–77; Thomas Dublin, "Women Workers and the Study of Social Mobility," *Journal of Interdisciplinary History* 9 (Spring 1979): 650–52; Stephan Thernstrom, *Poverty and Progress: Social Mobility in a Nineteenth Century City* (Cambridge: Harvard University Press, 1964), 162–65. Rowland T. Berthoff extends this argument to claim that "as late as 1850 . . . the practical goal of ordinary people in all sections of the country, in cities as well as on the farm, remained the independence of a secure old age among their own kind" (Rowland Berthoff, "Peasants and Artisans, Puritans and Republicans: Personal Liberty and Communal Equality in American History," *Journal of American History* 69 [Dec. 1982]: 594). Such a claim is rather difficult to reconcile with the observation of the Cincinnati *Gazette,* cited in note 126 in this chapter.

131. See note 63 in this chapter. For a group of pre-Famine Irish construction laborers, see Peter Way, "Shovel and Shamrock: Irish Workers and Labor Violence in the Digging of the Chesapeake and Ohio Canal," *Labor History* 30 (Fall 1989): 489–517. See also Tobin, "Lonely Muscular Digger," 143–47, 170–99.

132. Gerber, *Making of an American Pluralism,* 162.

133. Particularly valuable is Miller, *Emigrants and Exiles,* 269–70, 319–27. See also Tobin, "Lonely Muscular Digger," 199–215, 255–56.

134. Greeley, "The Discipline and Duties of the Scholar," *Nineteenth Century* 4 (1849): 34.

135. Freeman Hunt, *Worth and Wealth: A Collection of Maxims, Morals and Miscellanies for Merchants and Men of Business* (New York: Stringer and Townsend, 1856), 36; Meyers, *Jacksonian Persuasion*, 135n–136n.

136. Hunt, *Worth and Wealth*, 387, 36. Another of the leading defenders and celebrators of business pursuits, Edwin T. Freedley, made similarly critical note of rural out-migration to the cities: "The business of clerking, or agendising, in the United States, is at the present time over-stocked by ["thousands" of] men who have no business there—by men whose proper occupation is farming." But if Freedley was concerned like Hunt with the various dangers this phenomenon posed to both the farm boys and society in general, he was nonetheless characteristically less sanctimonious, more bluntly utilitarian, in the particular maxim he thought worthy of featuring: "As a man cannot carry on extensive operations, relying on his own resources or abilities alone, he must employ agents; . . . Business men will find it greatly to their advantage to employ educated, talented assistants . . . in preference to those whose only recommendation is physical strength and stupidity" (Freedley, *How to Make Money; A Practical Treatise on Business* [London: George Routledge and Company, 1853], 154). See also Rush Welter, *The Mind of America 1820–1860* (New York: Columbia University Press, 1975), 159–61. For contemporaneous expressions by elite Boston merchants and industrialists of the same theme that "common farmers" in Massachusetts and other parts of the rural northeast should stay on their farms and not attempt to enter occupations to which this elite owed its own power and prosperity, see Tamara Plakins Thornton, *Cultivating Gentlemen: The Meaning of Country Life among the Boston Elite 1785–1860* (New Haven: Yale University Press, 1989), 186–95. As previously indicated, Thornton discusses a range of possible motives and "anxieties," over and beyond "a genuine fear of economic competition," which prompted these wealthy Bostonians to criticize migrating farm youth for their attempted "social climbing" and disinclination for physical toil.

137. That the lure of individual mobility out of manual labor, and the increased economic success with which this mobility was associated, acted to limit and undermine pride in craft, artisanal solidarity, and ultimately radical class consciousness among American skilled workers has long been a matter of dispute. Some ten years before Richard Hofstadter introduced what was to become known as the "liberal capitalist," or "entrepreneurial," interpretation of Jacksonian democracy, Herbert Harris offered a blunter version of the thesis in discounting the radicalism of the labor movements of the late 1820s and early 1830s: "In short, labor as a whole didn't want anything basically new or different; it wanted to share more fully in the advantages of existing commercial and industrial arrangements. It wanted for itself what the 'haves' possessed. It wanted its children to rise in the world. It wanted them to be farmers with a great deal of land; or even better, perhaps, it wanted them to be merchants, shipowners, lawyers, doctors, politicians, contractors, bankers, manufacturers, to wear high starched stocks, the period's equivalent of the white collar" (Herbert Harris, *American Labor* [New Haven: Yale University Press, 1938], 27). John Patrick Diggins has recently updated Harris's position in "*AHR* Forum": "Comrades and Citizens: New Mythologies in American Historiography," *American Historical Review* 93 (June 1985): 626–28, and in arguing for the hegemony of "Lockeian" liberal capitalist ideology, Diggins also confirmed the view of Eric Foner ("The Causes of the American Civil War: Recent Interpretations and New Directions," *Civil War History* 20 [Sept. 1974]: 204) and others regarding the competitive nature of the ethos that assumed unprecedented strength in the Jackso-

nian North. Diggins's particular targets of criticism were some of the newer labor histories (e.g., Sean Wilentz, *Chants Democratic: New York City and the Rise of the American Working Class* [New York: Oxford University Press, 1984]) which, in Diggins's view, have taken the "republican," community-oriented rhetoric of nineteenth-century labor movements far too seriously and mistakenly inferred that "American workers wanted a noncompetitive society, where class solidarity would protect them from the pernicious influence of [middle-class] liberalism" ("*AHR* Forum," 627). Some of the critical responses to Diggins's own criticism remain telling, and these should be noted. His dismissal of American labor movement rhetoric and ideology, as Leon Fink has observed, appears to be partially based on the premise that genuinely radical protest must conform to an orthodox Marxist model ("The New Labor History and the Powers of Historical Pessimism: Consensus, Hegemony, and the Case of the Knights of Labor," *Journal of American History* 75 [June 1988]: 123–24). But as Fink observes, this is an unrealistic standard by which to judge labor protest: Fink aptly introduces here Robert Gray's suggestion, offered in another context, that "the straw person model of a class conscious and revolutionary working class, equipped with a rigorous class ideology and theoretical understanding of the capitalist economy," is rare in any society (Gray, "The Deconstructing of the English Working Class," *Social History* 11 [Oct. 1986]: 373). And as Paul Conkin maintains, Diggins's suggestion that "high-minded" ("*AHR* Forum," 628) trade unionist language amounted to hardly more than a cynical, "strategic" cover for worker behavior—that the acquisitive and materialistic conduct of many American workers demonstrated the insincerity of their republican, anticompetitive language—would appear to oversimplify matters ("*AHR* Forum": Conkin, "Comment," *American Historical Review* 93 [June 1985]: 640–41). It seems quite understandable that economic and other pressures may have given rise to working-class behavior that, in many cases, ran contrary to labor's articulated beliefs. Such behavior no more establishes these beliefs as mere dissembling rhetoric than does Marx's partial subsidization of his work through money he took from Engels, the son of a wealthy capitalist, expose his critique of capitalism as blatant hypocrisy. Diggins's discussion has the merit of raising anew the interesting question of whether the rhetoric and ideas of nonelite groups may be just as self-serving as ruling-class ideologies; journeymen workers may have used "republican" language not merely to discredit the practices and attack the dominant position of merchant capitalists and master manufacturers but also, on a less conscious level, to exorcise their own guilt or inhibitions about pursuing market-oriented, self-interested goals. But that the behavior of workers may have in fact contradicted their rhetoric still does not disqualify the latter as at least a partial expression of their true social values—of their ideology. All that seems certain is that the contradiction signaled the tensions and competing pressures afoot in society at the time.

To a much lesser extent have either Diggins or the other scholars noted above explicitly raised the issue of whether the acquisitive motivations and behavior of American workers, such as they did exist, thereby presupposed a discontent and disesteem for manual labor callings. My own sense is that the liberal capitalist competitive ethos most recently emphasized by Diggins was powerful enough to contribute to the frustration and defensiveness that manual laborers and labor reformers sometimes expressed regarding manual labor employments, but not so powerful that it prevented a sincere and genuinely radical tradition of criticism from developing, one which, among other things, questioned claims that the more lucrative capitalist and professional nonmanual labor occupations constituted true work. For a comparative perspective that offers some support for the notion that pride in craft and artisanal solidarity, in contrast to individualistic acquisitiveness and upward mobility values, may have been particularly weak among American skilled workers, see William H. Sewell, Jr., "Social Mobility in a Nineteenth-Century European City: Some Findings and Implications," in Rabb and Rotberg, eds., *Industrialization and Urbanization*, 99. Yet Jacques Rancière has recently argued that certain artisans in mid-nineteenth-century France—working-class authors who belonged to tenuously skilled trades—harbored deep ambivalence regarding the limitations of their manual labor; Jacques Rancière, "The Myth of the Artisan: Critical Reflections on a Category of Social History," *International Labor and Working Class History*, no. 24 (Fall 1983): 4–9; Jacques Rancière, "A Reply," *International Labor and Working Class History*, no. 25 (Spring 1984): 42–44; and Rancière's difficult longer study, *The Nights of Labor: The Workers' Dream in Nineteenth-Century France*, trans. John Drury (Philadelphia: Temple University Press, 1989).

138. Pessen, *Most Uncommon Jacksonians*, 18–20, 55–99; Walter Hugins, *Jacksonian Democracy and the Working Class: A Study of the New York Workingmen's Movement 1829–1837* (Stanford: Stanford University Press, 1960), 119–28; George Rogers Taylor, "New Preface to Vols. V and VI," in John R. Commons et al., eds., *A Documentary History of American Industrial Society* (New York: Russell and Russell, 1958 [1910]), 5: vii–viii. Of course, as many labor historians have noted, even those editors and contributors to "labor literature" who may have been of undisputed working-class background marked themselves as atypical of workers the moment they took up a pen: there is, in other words, the question of the representativeness of their values and attitudes as well.

139. For one example of the tendency in labor literature to associate the inordinate status enjoyed by "genteel" professional employments in America with "the enervating fopperies of transatlantic fashion and folly," all of which were undermining republican virtue, simplicity, and manliness, see letter from "C. W. T," "The Mechanic as He Is—The Mechanic as He Should Be," in *Mechanic's Advocate. A Weekly Paper, Devoted to the Interests of the Mechanic, Mutual Protection, and the Elevation of Labor* (Albany), July 10, 1847.

140. See, for example, Dewey, *Moral Views of Commerce*, 9–116 passim.

141. "Mechanic as He Is—The Mechanic as He Should Be." See also "Industry a Blessing," *Fall River Mechanic*, May 18, 1844. The attitudes expressed by labor reform movements that enlisted genuine and substantial working-class participation—the workingmen's parties and the trade union movements of the late 1820s and the early 1830s, for example—were in many essential respects indistinguishable from the attitudes expressed by radicals of unmistakably middle-class backgrounds who were never associated with these more rank-and-file movements; see, for example, any one of a number of the articles in the "Christian Socialist"—Associationist journal, the *Spirit of the Age*, edited in 1849 and 1850 by William Henry Channing, the nephew of William Ellery Channing (e.g., "W. H. C.," "Industrial Feudalism. Number Two," *Spirit* 1 [Oct. 13, 1849]: 232–35). See also the younger Channing's insistence upon the "justly deserved dignity for [manual] labor," and his attacks on the "effeminate, unmanly contempt for honest toil" and "the miserable spirit of aristocracy" spreading in the North, in a speech delivered at the Anti-Slavery Convention in Hamilton, Ohio, in *Philanthropist*, May 19, 1841. In the latter speech Channing did distinguish himself from the perspective of antebellum labor movements in the degree to which he blamed Southern slavery for the social disesteem suffered by manual labor in America. But even this distinction disappears in his writing for the *Spirit of the Age*.

142. "The Mechanic as He Is—The Mechanic as He Should Be." The note of

defensiveness expressed by manual laborers regarding their employments was per-haps most palpable of all in various of the "factory girl" journals, of which the *Lowell Offering* was only the most famous; for one insistence upon the "moral worth, general intelligence," and overall respectability of female operatives which conveys this sense of "the lady doth protest too much," see "N. L.," "The Factory Opera-tives," *Factory Girls' Album, and Operatives' Advocate*. "Edited by an Association of Factory Operatives" (Exeter, N.H.) 1, no. 3 (Mar. 14, 1846). See also "Aristocracy vs. Labor," letter from "F. W. D.," *The Factory Girls' Garland* (Exeter, N.H.) 1, no. 2 (May 25, 1844)

143. One wonders how many skilled workers might have resented and yet simultaneously accepted as expressing an inexorable set of social circumstances Frederick Douglass's observation that they belonged to the "intermediate grada-tions" of society, gradations that well-educated blacks of a future generation might hope to leave behind them. Describing his aspirations for free blacks in the North, who were at present generally confined to the most menial employments, Douglass observed that instruction for these blacks at the high school and college level would be unnecessary for an indefinite period of time, since their occupational goals must be realistically less ambitious: "Accustomed, as we have been, to the rougher and harder modes of living, and of gaining a livelihood, we cannot, and we ought not, to hope that, in a single leap from our low condition, we can reach that of Ministers, Lawyers, Doctors, Editors, Merchants,, &c. These will, doubtless, be attained by us; but this will only be, when we have patiently and laboriously, and I may add, successfully, mastered and passed through the intermediate gradations of agricul-ture and the mechanic arts" (Douglass to Harriet Beecher Stowe, Mar. 8, 1853, repr. in the *North Star* or *Frederick Douglass' Paper* [Rochester], Dec. 2, 1853).

144. "Ruskin and Architecture," *North British Review* 21 (May 1854): 193.

145. Ibid.

146. Ibid, 193–94. On the question of how much "refined" and "gentile" English middle-class wives and mothers should actually do in the way of running an efficient household while still preserving their proper "station" and distance from domestic work, see J. A. Banks and Olive Banks, *Feminism and Family Planning in Victorian England* (New York: Schocken Books, 1964), 62–75; and Leonore Davidoff and Catherine Hall, *Family Fortunes: Men and Women of the English Middle Class, 1780–1850* (Chicago: University of Chicago Press, 1987), 391–92.

147. Paul Starr, *The Social Transformation of American Medicine* (New York: Basic Books, 1982), 56.

148. Another student of the professions has emphasized how, given the exist-ing state of medical knowledge well into the nineteenth century, popular preference for various of the medical sects, and a corresponding suspicion of the claims to superior expertise made by "orthodox" doctors (those who were usually armed with a medical degree, as well as a college diploma) remained well-founded: "The professional reputation of the regular physician was . . . based to large degree on general education and social rank rather than any obvious therapeutic advantage to the patient" (William R. Johnson, *Schooled Lawyers: A Study in the Clash of Profes-sional Cultures* [New York: New York University Press, 1978], 34, 191). See also Peter Dobkin Hall, "The social Foundations of Professional Credibility: Linking the Medical Profession to Higher Education in Connecticut and Massachusetts, 1700–1830," in Thomas L. Haskell, ed., *The Authority of Experts: Studies in History and Theory* (Bloomington: Indiana University Press, 1984), 114–19, 134–35. For a mid-nineteenth-century radical's indictment of American educational and other prac-tices, through which the nation was burdened by "onerous, expensive, tedious, and

incomprehensible systems of law and theology, encouraged, to give false occupation to individuals and bodies of men, . . . whereby aristocratical distinctions are
entailed upon the community," see Frances Wright, "Address to Young Mechanics,"
New York, June 13, 1830, in Frances Wright D'Arusmont, *Life, Letters and Lectures*
(New York: Arno Press, 1972), 200.

149. Starr notes that the American medical profession, for example, acquired
much of its present authority and prestige only toward the end of the nineteenth
century, with the growth in demand for professional medical services and the
restoration of medical licensing; Paul Starr, "Medicine, Economy and Society in
Nineteenth-Century America," in Patricia Branca, ed., *The Medicine Show: Patients,
Physicians and the Perplexities of the Health Revolution in Modern Society* (New York:
Science History Publications, 1977), 51.

150. "A Mechanic," letter to the New York *Journal of Commerce,* May 22, 1847,
quoted in Mario Emilio Cosenza, *The Establishment of the College of the City of New
York as the Free Academy in 1847* (New York: Associate Alumni of the College of the
City of New York, 1925), 146–47. The correspondent identified himself as a long-
time trustee of New York City's public schools (i.e., the Public School Society
system of schools). See Joseph Kett, *The Formation of the American Medical Profession: The Role of Institutions, 1780–1860* (New Haven: Yale University Press, 1968), 110,
for a similar statement of 1841 from an organ of the Thomsonian medical sect. In
joining in the criticism of higher education as a pipeline to the "aristocratic" and
bogus formal professions, Thomsonians sought to identify their own cause as one
embodying, rather than repudiating, a livelihood in the truly useful and productive
"laboring arts."

151. New York *Daily Globe,* June 11, 1847, quoted in Cosenza, *Establishment,*
210–11. In this connection, however, we might recall the intimation of the New York
Democrat James T. Brady that social mobility out of the laboring classes was an
axiomatic consequence of any considerable education; see excerpts from a speech of
Brady's in "Brady on Rail-Splitting" and the discussion of Brady's remarks in
chapter 1, text accompanying note 24.

152. One of the best general discussions of the professions in nineteenth-
century England is W. J. Reader, *Professional Men: The Rise of the Professional Classes
in Nineteenth-Century England* (New York: Basic Books, 1966).

153. Alexis de Tocqueville, *Democracy in America,* ed. J. P. Mayer, trans. George
Lawrence, 2 vols. in 1 (Garden City, N.Y.: Anchor Books, 1969 [1835]), 1: 268.

154. John Clarke, *The Price of Progress: Cobbett's England 1780–1835* (London:
Granada Publishing, 1977), 147.

155. Tocqueville, *Democracy in America,* 1: 266–68. At the same time, Tocqueville clearly underestimated the mistrust, resentment, and downright antipathy
toward lawyers that emanated from populist and labor radical sources. His claim in
these pages that "the people in a democracy do not distrust lawyers" is among his
most vulnerable generalizations.

156. Hunt, *Worth and Wealth,* 36; Virginia Penny, *Think and Act: A Series of
Articles Pertaining to Men and Women, Work and Wages* (Philadelphia: Claxton,
Remsen, and Haffelfinger, 1869), 25–26. It was, however, the disrepute, rather than
the inherent disagreeableness, of manual labor to which a writer in the *Galaxy*
attributed a particular phenomenon in 1868: the fact that "thousands of poor clerks"
in New York City would remain in work which paid them two dollars a day when
the going rate for masons was more than four dollars a day; "Is Labor a Curse?"
Galaxy. An Illustrated Magazine of Entertaining Reading 6 (Oct. 1868): 539–40.

157. See also the discussions in Siracusa, *Mechanical People,* 107–12; Horwitz,

Anthropology towards History, 73–74, 86–89, 127; and Stuart M. Blumin, *The Emergence of the Middle Class: Social Experience in the American City, 1760–1900* (Cambridge, Eng.: Cambridge University Press, 1989), 109, 127–32.

158. Distribution on the basis of need, rather than on the basis of ability or contribution to the social good, however the latter is defined, was a French socialist formula that Marx, of course, immortalized as the governing principle of "the higher phase of communist society"; Marx, *Critique of the Gotha Program,* in *Marx and Engels: Basic Writings on Politics and Philosophy,* ed. Lewis S. Feuer (Garden City, N.Y.: Anchor Books, 1959), 119; Robert C. Tucker, "Marx and Distributive Justice," in Carl Friedrich and John W. Chapman, eds., *Nomos VI. Justice* (New York: Atherton Press, 1963), 310, 318; Z. I. Husami, "Marx on Distributive Justice," in Bob Jessop with Charlie Malcolm-Brown, eds., *Karl Marx's Social and Political Thought: Critical Assessments,* vol. 4, *Civil Society, Ideology, Morals and Ethics* (London: Routledge, 1990), 434–35; and in the same volume, A. W. Wood, "Marx on Right and Justice: A Reply to Husami," 472. There have been many variations on this socialist formula, and the general sentiment it embodied may have been even more pervasive, if hardly dominant, in antebellum American society. As the liberal Unitarian minister James Freeman Clarke observed, in expressing support for the Fourierist alternative to free market capitalist values: "The principle of free competition is a good one for the strong, the sagacious, for those who have talent, means, energy: but it gives no choice to the weak, the poor, the friendless" ("J. F. C.," "Fourierism," *Christian Examiner. And Religious Miscellany,* 4th ser., 2 [July 1844]: 70–71). Melvin A. Tumin, the antifunctionalist sociologist discussed in chapter 1, put forth a related if somewhat different argument in support of the utopian principle of distributive justice articulated by nineteenth-century radicals like Marx. It is not only a question of the needier and less capable members of society requiring more assistance than others, whatever the size of their productive contributions. As Tumin argues, "Assuming perfect equality of opportunity, the talents required to perform . . . more important work occur as accidents of birth. For example, a special dexterity is required to become a skilled surgeon, and if only a few people are born with this talent, to argue that surgeons should receive high rewards is to argue on behalf of the accident of birth. For even if we agree that the work of the surgeon is in some ways far more important than the work of others, we could not justify extra rewards for the surgeon except on the grounds that he is lucky enough to have been born with this rare talent" (Melvin M. Tumin, *Social Stratification* [Englewood Cliffs, N.J.: Prentice-Hall, 1967], 111). Although the recognition that individuals differ in their innate capabilities is commonly used to justify inequality of condition and social stratification (see John C. Calhoun's observation in note 161), the cases of Tumin, and for that matter Marx, illustrate that this recognition need not be so used.

159. [Peabody], "Slavery, Its Origin and Its Remedy," 495–96, 505.

160. Ibid., 499, 505.

161. John C. Calhoun thus observed that a relatively free market spontaneously generated inequality for the following reason: "Now, as individuals differ greatly from each other in intelligence, sagacity, energy, perseverance, skill, habits of industry and economy, physical power, position and opportunity—the necessary effect of leaving all free to exert themselves to better their condition must be a corresponding inequality between those who may possess these qualities and advantages in a high degree and those who may be deficient in them" (John C. Calhoun, *A Disquisition on Government and Selections from the Discourse,* ed. C. Gordon Post [New York: Liberal Arts Press, 1953], 44).

162. Sarah Deutsch, *No Separate Refuge: Culture, Class, and Gender on an Anglo-Hispanic Frontier in the American Southwest, 1880–1940* (New York: Oxford University Press, 1987), 141.

163. It was perhaps with only a minimal degree of cynicism that Webster, for example, cultivated his image as a sturdy New England yeoman, although the actual agricultural labor he alternated with his political and legal activities was largely confined to the supervision of the farming operations on his fourteen-hundred-acre estate in Massachusetts; Thornton, *Cultivating Gentlemen*, 195–98, 230–31.

164. In 1868 the writer for the *Galaxy* quoted in note 156 remarked: "I find everywhere that the law and medical schools are full, and that there are many of them; and I believe it is safe to say that already there are at least four doctors for every patient and eight lawyers for every case. I find every laborer in the city [New York] is determined that his son shall study Latin and Greek at the common schools, having a vague belief that, in some ways, therein lies the secret of being able to live without work. . . . I can discover that nine men of ten are toiling and moiling, and planning and plotting to get money enough to secure their sons and daughters the ability to live without work of any kind; and at least without hand or body work. No, it is plain that no rich man educates his sons or daughters for any work, and it is plain that nearly all the poor men are planning to have their sons do brain work, not hand work; to live by their wits rather than their muscular power or dexterity." Although the writer was, obviously, a believer in "bodily work," he also saw "nothing charming about the over-worked drudge." He placed himself on the side of labor combinations and strikes for "less work and more pay"; and like earlier advocates of a shorter workday, he attributed "some portion of the hatred of work" to the fact that the laboring poor had traditionally been obliged to perform it in excess, to the detriment of both mind and body. Such, however, was the writer's regard for work and productive activity that his parting words to one trade that was striking for the "eight-hour system" were: "The bricklayers should not strike for fewer hours because they desire idleness, but rather that they may have time to develop and enjoy mind and soul"; "Is Labor a Curse?" 537, 539–40, 544, 548.

165. George Calvert Holland, *Diseases of the Lungs from Mechanical Causes; and Inquiries into the Condition of the Artisans Exposed to the Inhalation of Dust* (London: Charles Churchill, 1842), 62.

166. Frederick Law Olmsted, *A Journey in the Back Country* (New York: Schocken Books, 1970 [1860]), 301.

167. With specific reference to the Irish, those who, apart from the free blacks, took the most menial and unskilled jobs in the Northern states, Olmsted wrote in *The Cotton Kingdom* (1861): "Out of twenty Irish emigrants, landing in New York, perfectly destitute, of whose history I have been intimately cognizant, only two, both of whom were over fifty years of age, have lived out five years here without beginning to acquire wealth and becoming superior in their ambition and habits to the lowest order, which I believe to include a majority of whites in the plantation districts of the South." Olmsted qualified this statement with the observation that "in New York, especially, we seem to be taking some pains to form a permanent lower class." Such was the degraded character of the most recent wave of immigrants, and so many were their numbers, Olmsted was suggesting, that conceivably some of these would not rise above the mindless nature of their work, when they could get work at all. But Olmsted also predicted that the situation would correct itself with "the present great and apparently permanent falling off in the European emigration." As other parts of *The Cotton Kingdom* make clear, Olmsted had by this time had his fill of arguments favorably comparing the condition of Southern slaves

with that of the Irish laboring poor and other "wage slaves" in the free states, and he was prepared to make very few concessions to these arguments. Fierce and even "lawless" as it might be, the North's "competitive system" was not, in Olmsted's view, marked by widespread material suffering or the closing off of upward mobility channels. "When any real suffering does occur, it is mainly a consequence and a punishment of their [the Northern laborers] own carelessness and improvidence, and is in the nature of a remedy" (Olmsted, *The Cotton Kingdom. A Traveller's Observations on Cotton and Slavery in the American Slave States,* 2 vols. in 1, ed. Arthur M. Schlesinger [New York: Alfred A. Knopf, 1970 {1861}], 557, 557n, 489, 493).

Index